Anyone who has taught first-year Greek or learned it knows one of the challenges is often a review of English as one is learning a new, quite foreign language. Dr. Harris's first-year grammar does an excellent job of bridging the languages, much like good translation must do. The direction on everything linguistic, syntactic, and semantic is carefully and fairly set forth, as well as teaching the forms required to engage the Greek. A first-year student will be well served by this text.

> **Darrell L. Bock,** executive director for cultural engagement,
> Howard G. Hendricks Center for Christian Leadership and
> Cultural Engagement and senior research professor of
> New Testament Studies, Dallas Theological Seminary

Dana Harris has written a textbook that equips readers to appreciate the way Koine Greek works. Consequently, reading the Greek New Testament becomes more about *understanding* rather than merely *recognizing* the language. With clear discussion and examples, Harris guides readers in a way that prepares them for deeper exegetical study. Harris's conversational and practical presentations will greatly assist teachers as well as students.

> **Dennis R. Edwards,** associate professor of New Testament,
> North Park Theological Seminary

A great Greek textbook is up-to-date on Greek studies and linguistics, but functions as a simple and clear guide for (often intimidated) beginning students. It ought to be visually appealing with assignments that are challenging but not overwhelming. It should include plenty of examples and illustrations without a back-breaking page count. Impressively, Harris's introduction accomplishes all these things. Students can be relieved that this textbook will introduce Greek plainly; instructors can rest assured that the material is reliable and represents the state of biblical Greek scholarship.

> **Nijay K. Gupta,** professor of New Testament, Northern Seminary

Greek grammars in most cases all do the same thing: nouns and verbs and participles and vocabulary and exercises and parsing. In the last two decades, evangelical scholars have offered significant proposals for understanding our Greek New Testament, but the results have only occasionally trickled into a beginning grammar. With Dana Harris's new complete analysis of Greek grammar, students can become officially current. What makes this up-to-date and comprehensive grammar most beneficial is that students, once they have worked their way through this with a teacher and class, will want to return to this grammar to deepen their learning. Most grammars, once used, are put on the shelf rarely to be used again. Not this one. A real godsend for students.

> **Scot McKnight,** professor of New Testament, Northern Seminary

Written by a trained linguist and an experienced language teacher, this volume does not merely provide a first-rate textbook for beginning Greek courses. It also allows students to begin their journey in interacting with the Greek New Testament within a framework informed by the latest developments in linguistics and Greek grammar. To identify any one textbook in this crowded field as the most pedagogically effective may seem like an overstatement, but many of our Greek instructors who have used early drafts of this work can find no better way to describe it. If you are serious about learning Greek, there is no need to look elsewhere.

David W. Pao, professor of New Testament and chair of the
New Testament department, Trinity Evangelical Divinity School

Most first-year biblical Greek grammars present the outcome—what the student needs to know. This one focuses on the process—the building blocks of understanding that enable informed interpretation. In that sense it is not so much a *teacher's* grammar (though teachers will love it) as a *teaching* grammar. The focus is not merely on "what" must be learned but on the why and how that lead to textual comprehension. Enriched by the author's quarter century of Greek study and instruction in the traditional classroom as well as online, this grammar will become a standard textbook for both traditional and distance-learning settings. Written out of love for both learning and God's word, it supports student acquisition of a working knowledge of New Testament Greek in fresh, nuanced, and pedagogically effective ways.

Robert W. Yarbrough, professor of New Testament,
Covenant Theological Seminary

An excellent new introduction to biblical Greek from an experienced professor! Dana Harris helpfully positions Koine Greek within a historical context and introduces it from a linguistic and theological perspective. Based on current scholarship and using modern linguistic terminology, this well-structured grammar features clear presentations, ample student resources, and abundant examples from the New Testament. A stand-out first-year grammar.

Karen H. Jobes, Gerald F. Hawthorne Professor
Emerita of New Testament Greek and Exegesis,
Wheaton College and Graduate School

AN INTRODUCTION TO
BIBLICAL
GREEK
GRAMMAR

AN INTRODUCTION TO
BIBLICAL
GREEK
GRAMMAR

Elementary Syntax and Linguistics

Dana M. Harris

ZONDERVAN
ACADEMIC

ZONDERVAN ACADEMIC

An Introduction to Biblical Greek Grammar
Copyright © 2020 by Dana M. Harris

Requests for information should be addressed to:
Zondervan, *3900 Sparks Dr. SE, Grand Rapids, Michigan 49546*

ISBN 978-0-310-10857-3 (hardcover)

ISBN 978-0-310-10858-0 (ebook)

Biblical translations are the author's own unless otherwise noted.

Cover design: LUCAS Art & Design
Cover photos: Dogancan Ozturan / Unsplash
Interior design: Kait Lamphere

Printed in the United States of America

20 21 22 23 24 25 26 27 28 29 30 31 32 /LSC/ 15 14 13 12 11 10 9 8 7 6 5 4 3 2 1

This book is gratefully dedicated to the many students to whom I have taught Koine Greek and who have taught me a great deal and have made me a more effective teacher—thank you for your good questions and thoughtful feedback, your hard work and perseverance, your laughter and joy, and your fellowship and food! I have been richly blessed over the years!

*   *   *

To the one who sits on the throne and to the Lamb be
blessing and honor and glory and power, forever and ever!
(Revelation 5:13)

CONTENTS

EXPANDED TABLE OF CONTENTS

APPENDICES

LIST OF SUPPLEMENTAL DISCUSSIONS

ACKNOWLEDGMENTS

Writing a textbook, especially one as detailed as a Greek grammar, is never an individual effort. I am indebted to so many people! Several decades ago, I started learning Greek through the Intern Program at Peninsula Bible Church in Palo Alto, California. I am especially grateful for Lynne Fox and her passion for all things related to biblical languages. For over ten years, I taught Greek at Peninsula Bible Church and was blessed by the many students who asked such good questions, many of which I would never have otherwise considered.

For the past twenty-three years, I have been at Trinity Evangelical Divinity School, where I first started teaching first-year Greek as a masters student. I am especially grateful to supportive mentors and department chairs, including Bob Yarbrough and David Pao. Having taught first-year Greek throughout my PhD studies, including the intensive summer course for many years, I began to supervise those who were teaching first-year Greek when I became a full-time faculty member. I owe a particular debt of gratitude to these students in particular. The process of mentoring them afforded me the opportunity to articulate more clearly my understanding of certain concepts in Greek and to fine-tune the art of teaching Greek in a clear and accessible way. All of this was enormously helpful as I began to write the online course that was the foundation for this book. In the early days of this project, I am grateful for the work of several Greek fellows, especially those who did MDiv internships with me, including Madison Pierce, Heidi Ramer, Amanda Holm Rosengren, Amber Francis Jipp, Joshua Jipp, Monique Cuany, Beau Pihlaja, Christy Glick, Jeremy Otten, David Ro, Kevin Johnson, Reed Larson, John VanMaaren, Michael McKittrick, and Matthew and Bonnie Wolf—just to name a few. I am also thankful for the assistance I received from Kristen Brown and Nancy Bartell in the development of the online course. More recently, I am grateful for the Greek fellows who have taught, using my materials and who have offered valuable feedback, including Sean Christensen, Michael Porter, Jeremy Greiner, Francesco Grassi, Christopher Keheller, and especially the following individuals who gave significant feedback and assistance with converting the online materials to a written textbook: Geoff Ng, Dave Bryan,

Jennifer Guo, Pancha Yahya, and Carson Long. Finally, I want to thank one person in particular, Chi-ying Wang, who, as a Greek fellow and teaching assistant, collaborated with me in designing the online course, created many of the paradigms and several of the charts in the appendix, and devised the initial approach to the assigned vocabulary—her extensive feedback was invaluable.

I want to express my gratitude to Katya Covrett for her initial vision and support for this project, to Chris Beetham, who has been a wonderfully helpful and supportive editor, and to the entire Zondervan team who has been so helpful and great to work with. It has been a great experience!

I also want to thank the many friends and family members who have been supportive through this long project. My community group at Church of the Redeemer, Highwood, Illinois, has not tired of praying for me and this project, for which I am grateful. I am thankful for the continued, enthusiastic support of Helen Bass, Dan and Michele Becker, and Sharon Sheehan. The Lord's people are a true blessing and rich gift. Above all, I am thankful to my Lord Jesus Christ, who is my very life and joy.

June 2020

DEAR FIRST-YEAR GREEK INSTRUCTORS

Dear First-Year Greek Instructors,

Another introductory biblical Greek grammar? It's a fair question. I admit that I hadn't intended to write one, but in the process of writing an online first-year Greek course, I began to realize how much I had been supplementing existing first-year Greek grammars with my own extensive handouts and classroom discussion of key concepts, drawn from twenty-five years of teaching first-year Greek (including nearly fifteen years teaching seminary students at that time). This hybrid approach worked in a classroom, but it was cumbersome in an online course that presupposed one textbook and related audio, video, and interactive components. Eventually I realized that I would need to write the online course content. This online "textbook" was the initial basis for this textbook. The online version has been used by the Greek fellows (usually PhD students) who teach first-year Greek classes at Trinity Evangelical Divinity School, whom I supervise, for at least five years. I am very grateful for the collective input of these instructors, as well as the input from students who have used the textbook in this format.

Based on this experience and my own teaching, I have seen how important it is that students grasp basic concepts that can be expanded as their knowledge of Greek grows. In the five years that my written online material has been used, the most common comment from students is that the material is presented clearly and is easy to understand and apply. I frequently joke with my students that I simplify the universe in their beginning Greek studies, but I have tried to simplify the Greek language universe in a way that lays a foundation for subsequent expansion.

This book introduces students to basic linguistic concepts necessary for grasping Greek in an intuitive way. Although I interact with major recent advances for understanding Koine Greek (such as verbal aspect and the concept of "deponency"), I have deliberately sought to avoid technical discussions and extensive overviews of current debates that would only confuse students. Instead, I have sought to introduce students to essential concepts in clear and concise ways so that students have a linguistic foundation that enables them to internalize these concepts and apply them as they are related to more complex concepts. Initial discussion of key concepts is reiterated as it is developed in subsequent chapters. This textbook strives for conceptual clarity and rigor. For example, the present active and middle forms are discussed many chapters before the present passive forms are introduced. Although it is easier to memorize the (identical) present middle and passive forms when they are presented concurrently, this approach suggests that the middle and passive forms have the same function, which is clearly not true. Additionally, this textbook introduces verbs before nouns, since verbs are essential for understanding Greek. Students studying Greek already know (at least) one language; hence significant linguistic and conceptual categories have already been shaped and can be drawn upon to learn Koine Greek.

Several additional features contribute to the clarity of this textbook. First, the emphasis is on learning forms and identifying their functions (the form/function distinction foundational to linguistics). Key concepts are formatted to offer visual reinforcement of explanations. For example, **bolding** is used to identify morphology (e.g., suffixes, tense formatives, case endings), and *italics* to highlight syntax (e.g., prepositional phrases, dependent clauses). Second, key concepts are followed by numerous examples from the Greek New Testament. Third, students learn how to mark Greek texts (both in the textbook via four integration chapters [see below] and in the exercises in the accompanying workbook) so that they can begin to "see" the syntax in the Greek text rather than what can initially look like just a jumble of Greek words. By the end of the book, students have learned to identify the boundaries of syntactic units (such as prepositional phrases and dependent clauses) and have learned how to construct syntactic outlines as part of their preaching or teaching preparation based on "seeing" the Greek syntax. Many students state that this is one of the most helpful aspects of this approach. Fourth, four chapters (that roughly correspond to the midterms and final exams of a two-semester sequence) integrate material covered up to that point and reinforce key concepts. These chapters introduce students to exegetical and interpretive concepts and practices that they will need for their subsequent Greek studies and beyond. Fifth, additional sections entitled "Going Deeper" or "For the Curious" clearly signal supplement information that students can bypass or come back to at a later point. Finally, the sequence of how concepts are introduced and developed is designed to maximize students' ability to understand the Greek New Testament.

The textbook concludes with a series of appendices that summarize or expand concepts and information presented in the chapters. Also included is a glossary of key terms, a lexicon of all vocabulary presented in the chapters, a Scripture index, and a subject index.

In the accompanying workbook, all translations are taken from the Greek New Testament (sometimes slightly modified). Moreover, extensive syntactical and exegetical notes follow the translations in the answer key. These discussions anticipate student questions and help to reinforce key concepts.

The pronunciation used in this textbook is primarily Erasmian, although the benefits of modern pronunciation are readily acknowledged. The benefit of Erasmian pronunciation is that each letter has a unique sound; the weakness is that it does not represent how Greek was actually spoken in the first century. Instructors who prefer to use Modern Greek pronunciation will encounter no impediments for doing so in this textbook.

Key features of this textbook can be summarized as follows:

- After chapters 1 and 2, which are conceptually foundational, each chapter follows a fairly consistent pattern of presenting basic morphology (the form of words) followed by basic syntax (the function of these words as they combine with other words to form constructions).
- Key concepts are formatted to offer visual reinforcement of explanations. **Boldface** is used to identify morphology (e.g., suffixes, tense formatives, case endings), and *italics* to highlight syntax (e.g., prepositional phrases, dependent clauses).
- Four integration chapters (chapters 8, 14, 20, and 28) use a text compiled and modified from the Greek New Testament to guide students through a review and integration by offering a hands-on guided exercise identifying the forms and functions learned in previous chapters.
- Verbal aspect is presented in a simplified way that lays the foundation for fuller discussions in subsequent Greek studies.
- The middle voice is presented separate from the passive voice to facilitate conceptual clarity between these two voices. Indeed, its distinctive emphasis on agency versus verbal action is presented in comparison with the active voice. The concept of deponency is avoided in this textbook.
- Key concepts are illustrated with examples taken from the Greek New Testament. This means that examples will sometimes contain words or forms that have not yet been learned. The accompanying translation will illustrate the concept under discussion, but this preliminary exposure to

new words and forms also enables students to prepare subconsciously for subsequent material.

- Concepts are presented in logical order that somewhat corresponds to the frequency of these concepts in the Greek New Testament. The four integration chapters begin with a series of secondary, though still important, concepts or topics.

- The use of inline boxes introduces concepts that can be returned to at a later time. "Going Deeper" boxes offer explanations for apparently unusual forms, but also offer information that students do not actually need to know about required forms. "For the Curious" boxes offer interesting, but nonessential, information for curious students.

- Although μι verbs are presented in the final quarter of the book, "Heads Up!" pointers along the way encourage students to compare the forms they are currently learning with the corresponding μι verb forms (e.g., present active and middle indicative forms of λύω with present active and middle indicative forms of μι verbs). In this way, students can recognize many of these forms when they are covered in chapters 24 and 25 and thus make these chapters less intimidating. Alternatively, these "Heads Up!" pointers facilitate discussion for instructors who decide to assign μι verb forms coextensively with omega-class verbs as they are covered in chapters 3–23.

- Each chapter opens with clear objectives for that chapter and concludes with a review, a study guide, assigned vocabulary, and forms to be memorized. By the end of the book, students will have learned 610 vocabulary words from the Greek New Testament.

- Principal parts for verbs whose forms are difficult (or impossible) to derive from their lexical forms are introduced in chapter 10, using only those parts that students have learned thus far (the first and third principal parts). As students advance through the book, they are reminded to fill out the remaining principal parts for those verbs that have been previously assigned.

I have had the real joy of teaching beginning Greek for many years. Learning Greek is often intimidating for students, but it is very rewarding to watch their progress and to see their joy at being able to read and use the Greek New Testament. This textbook has truly been a labor of love for the Lord and his kingdom. I pray that it will be a blessing to current and future language instructors and the many students who will learn and benefit from it.

Getting Started!

COURSE GOALS AND STUDY STRATEGIES

Dear First-Year Greek Students,

Welcome to a great adventure! You may be feeling both excited and intimidated about learning Greek. Even if Greek is a required course in your academic program, many good reasons exist to learn Greek. Here are some motivations and goals to consider as you undertake this important endeavor.

First, there are some attitudes to cultivate:

- a deep appreciation of and humility before the Word of God
- a recognition of the centrality of prayer and the work of the Holy Spirit
- a love for the triune God through the study of God's Word
- a realization that language proficiency is a lifelong pursuit
- an appreciation of other scholars' labors, including various English translations

Next, there are some skills to acquire:

- growth in knowledge of the structure and vocabulary of New Testament Greek
- accuracy in interpreting the Word of God
- the ability to identify difficult interpretive questions (and issues)
- effectiveness in the use of Greek-based tools (grammars, lexica, concordances)
- better understanding of the underlying structure of New Testament passages

Finally, there are some responsibilities to undertake:

- development of good study habits and a system of memorization
- discipline and the "race pace" (i.e., this is a marathon, not a sprint!)

- asking questions when material is unclear
- consideration of partnering with someone for accountability and encouragement

SUGGESTED STUDY STRATEGIES

Here are some strategies that can help you persevere and finish strong in your Greek studies.

1. Work through each chapter in the order in which the material is presented. This material is augmented by exercises in the accompanying workbook that reinforce new concepts and forms. There are also additional audio-visual components for each chapter in the DVD set available from Zondervan.

2. Follow the initial chapter objectives and the concluding study guide to identify the material that you will be accountable for knowing and the forms that need to be memorized.

3. Memorizing assigned vocabulary is an essential part of learning Greek. You can either write out your own cards (you can buy blank cards from Vis-Ed or blank 3 x 5 inch cards, which you can cut into thirds) or use preprinted vocabulary cards. You should make these cards as soon as you have read each chapter. The same strategy should be applied to principal parts, once they are introduced in the book. There are also many online resources for New Testament Greek vocabulary, but you should ensure that the vocabulary glosses (or translation equivalents) that are supplied by these resources agree with the glosses that are supplied in this book. Some preprinted vocabulary cards have glosses that are seldom used in any major English translation.

4. Memorizing assigned paradigms is also essential. It works best to write these forms out on individual cards, such as 3 x 5 inch cards. Ideally, you should have one card with the entire paradigm and then smaller individual cards with each inflected form of the paradigm. You should make these cards as soon as you have read each chapter. Alternatively, there are several online resources to help memorize forms.

5. Review the new material presented in the chapter that you are currently studying. Be sure to note any questions you might have. Then try to work through any examples that are in the new chapter on your own without looking at the English translation.

6. Go over new vocabulary and paradigm cards frequently every day. Target vocabulary words that are difficult to memorize and begin to concentrate on these words.
7. Be able to *write out* paradigms from memory.
8. Review all *previous* vocabulary and paradigms *at least* once as you are working through a new chapter.
9. Do assigned exercises as if they were a closed-book quiz. You should then check your answers against the answer key. Make any corrections or adjustments in a different color. The goal for the exercises is not to have everything perfect. You are learning a new language, and you will often learn most from your mistakes. So there is a balance between trying to do the best you can after working through new material versus relying too much on the answer key. The answer key should help, not hinder, your progress!
10. Keep reviewing the content of previous chapters.
11. Keep reviewing vocabulary and paradigms as often as you can.

SYMBOLS USED IN THIS TEXTBOOK

√   This symbol indicates a verbal root, which is a linguistic abstraction that does not correspond to an actual Greek word.

stem-   A hyphen at the end of a form indicates that it is a stem, to which various other morphemes are added. Often this does not correspond to an actual Greek word.

-ending   A hyphen at the beginning of a form indicates that it is an ending that is added to a stem or other morpheme to indicate some syntactic function. An ending does not correspond to an actual Greek word.

bold   Boldface is used to present morphological features of a word.

italics   Italics are used for discussion of syntactic units, such as phrases and clauses.

!   An exclamation point is used to indicate the Greek imperative in corresponding English translations.

ABBREVIATIONS

1 pers/1st	first person
2 pers/2nd	second person
3 pers/3rd	third person
acc	accusative case
act	active voice
adj	adjective (adjectival)
adv	adverb(ial)
aor	aorist tense-form
app.	appendix
art	article
aug	augment(ed)
BIOSCS	Bulletin of the International Organization for Septuagint and Cognate Studies
ca.	circa (Latin); "approximately, about"
cf.	confer (Latin); "compare"
ch./chs.	chapter/chapters
comp	complementary
conj	conjunction
CSB	Christian Standard Bible
dat	dative case
decl	declension
dep	dependent [clause]
e.g.	exempli gratia (Latin); "for example"
ESV	English Standard Version
fem	feminine
fut	future tense-form
gen	genitive case
GNT	Greek New Testament
i.e.	id est (Latin); "that is"
impers	impersonal

impf	imperfect tense-form
impr prep	improper preposition
impv	imperative mood
ind	indicative mood
inf	infinitive
intrans	intransitive
masc	masculine
mid	middle voice
NASB	New American Standard Bible
neut	neuter
NIV	New International Version
NRSV	New Revised Standard Version
NT	New Testament
nom	nominative case
noun	noun
num	number
OT	Old Testament
pass	passive voice
pf	perfect tense-form
pl	plural
plpf	pluperfect tense-form
prep	preposition
pres	present tense-form
prin	principal [part]
pron	pronoun
prtl	particle
ptc	participle
rel	relative
RSV	Revised Standard Version
sg	singular
subj	subjunctive mood
subst	substantive (substantival)
trans	transitive
TynBul	*Tyndale Bulletin*
v./vv.	verse/verses
vb	verb (finite)
voc	vocative case

chapter ONE

IMAGE-BEARERS, LANGUAGE, LINGUISTICS, AND GREEK:
From Theological Reflections to Learning the Alphabet

OBJECTIVES AND OVERVIEW

Chapter 1 covers a lot of important, introductory information. We will draw upon the linguistic concepts and the forms that are introduced in this chapter throughout the rest of the book. Chapter 1 begins with an overview of the following:

- the theological nature of human language
- the biblical languages and the distance between them and today
- the benefits, pitfalls, and privileges of studying Greek
- a brief history of the Greek language
- the Greek of the NT and some witnesses to it
- the languages spoken in first-century Roman Judea

Chapter 1 introduces the following linguistic concepts:

- morpheme, word, construction, phrase, clause, sentence; morphology and phonology
- main/independent and subordinate/dependent clauses
- noun, pronoun, adjective, verb, adverb, preposition, conjunction
- substantive, modifier
- "slots" and "fillers"; form and function
- word order and inflection; declension and conjugation
- semantic range, lexeme, lexical form, gloss (translation)

In chapter 1, you will also learn and need to memorize the following:

- the Greek alphabet (consonants and vowels), diphthongs, iota subscripts, gamma combinations
- breathing marks
- punctuation, diacritical marks, accents
- syllabification

SOME THOUGHTS ON THE NATURE OF LANGUAGE AND STUDYING GREEK

Language is something that we use every day, yet most of us have probably never thought much about *language* and what exactly it is. For one thing, language is unique to humans. Even though animal communication can often be very sophisticated (just think of dolphins or whales!), it is significantly different from human language. For example, people can "do" things with words—just by uttering a simple request, such as, "Would you close the window, please?" one person can cause another person to perform an action.[1] Sometimes this can happen without an actual request. Consider a time when you were sitting in a stuffy room and someone said, "Wow, it's really hot in here!" Chances are that someone else got up and opened a window or a door in response. This can be described as the "performative" function of language.

With words, humans can create entire worlds (think of *The Lord of the Rings* series) or describe (often in great detail) events that have yet to happen (think of the Book of Revelation). Language is one of the primary ways that humans are linked together in community and is thus vital for human relationships. Indeed, when people do not speak the same language, we refer to this inability to communicate as a "language barrier."

We can go further. The phenomenon of human language is profoundly theological. Language is an important reflection of how we have been created in the image of God. Genesis 1 describes how God spoke the world into existence with words. It should not be surprising that the greatest revelation of God, the incarnate Son, is described as the Word in John 1. Although humans do not create in the same way that God does, humans have been entrusted with the privilege of extending God's work of creation throughout the world, and human language is

---

1. The classic work that discusses this is J. L. Austin, *How to Do Things with Words*, 2nd ed. (Cambridge: Harvard University Press, 1975).

one of the primary ways that this is accomplished. Theologian Kevin Vanhoozer writes, "In the beginning, God created language; it is his good gift, designed to be enjoyed by his creatures."[2] He adds, "Language is a God-given capacity that enables human beings to relate to God, the world, and to one another."[3] Thus, human language has the ability to create or "uncreate"—to build up or to tear down.

This theological understanding of language likely explains why some aspects of language are universal across different languages. Although the forms or mechanisms that any given language uses (the "surface structure") may look quite different from one language to another, the underlying functions (the "deep structure") are similar.[4] For example, all languages are capable of asking questions, communicating emphasis, and telling stories, but they often do so in very different ways. Some languages may use highly structured word order, whereas others may string together many prefixes and suffixes to create very long words. There is amazing diversity in the thousands of languages that have been spoken throughout history (some of which are now extinct) and that are spoken today. Yet all languages effectively communicate meaning and are used by humans to live their lives and relate to those around them.

The Biblical Languages

This general understanding of language has important implications for the languages used in the Bible. Of all the languages throughout history, God chose to reveal himself in writing through Hebrew, Aramaic, and Greek. Clearly these were not random choices! There must be some inherent properties within these languages that made them the best "guardians" of God's revelation. For example, poetic parallelism is well developed in Hebrew and is a significant element in the Psalms and much of the prophetic corpus. Greek is well suited for sustained argumentation, as is seen in many of the NT epistles, especially the Epistle to the Hebrews.[5] Attempts to define a so-called "Hebrew mind-set" or "Greek mind-set," however, often lead to unwarranted assumptions or unhelpful generalizations about Hebrew and Greek. Even so, it is important to understand that language and culture are inextricably bound together.

---

2. Kevin J. Vanhoozer, *Is There a Meaning in This Text? The Bible, the Reader, and the Morality of Literary Knowledge* (Grand Rapids: Zondervan, 1998), 31.

3. Vanhoozer, *Is There a Meaning in This Text?*, 205.

4. For a helpful introduction to linguistics, see David Alan Black, *Linguistics for Students of New Testament Greek: A Survey of Basic Concepts and Applications* (Grand Rapids: Baker, 1995).

5. Poetic parallelism in Hebrew and the ability of Greek to make sustained arguments are merely representative of some of the ways that each of these languages is suited to convey God's revelation.

It is also important to keep in mind that the original languages of the Bible are a constant reminder for us today that the worlds and times of the Bible are not the same as our world and time. Clearly, God's Word is eternal, but God has chosen to reveal that Word in the context of very specific places, cultures, and events.[6] Realizing this distance between "then" and "now" encourages humility as we seek to understand the original contexts of the biblical word and world. Thus, one goal of learning Greek is to be able to enter the first-century world and to enjoy God's Word in the original Greek, which can be quite rewarding. Yet because of the linguistic and cultural distance, the endeavor will also take a great deal of time and effort—but it will be worth it!

Some Additional Comments about Studying Greek

Studying Greek will inevitably bring you closer to the original text of the Word of God, but knowing Greek will not necessarily bring you closer to the living Word. God is committed to revealing himself through his Spirit and will do so to those who seek him . . . whether they seek him in Greek, English, or any other language. Thus, knowing Greek will not necessarily help you to be more spiritual or closer to God. It can actually be distracting or can even lessen your time with the Lord and his people. Thus, it is ultimately a matter of the heart and not the head. All knowledge is useless if it does not bring us somehow closer to the Lord. Consider 1 Corinthians 8:1: ἡ γνῶσις φυσιοῖ, ἡ δὲ ἀγάπη οἰκοδομεῖ ("knowledge causes arrogance, but love builds up").[7] So Greek will not necessarily transform your life; it may enrich it, or it may complicate it! Greek is merely a tool—and sometimes it is a tool of sanctification. You will find many answers to questions you cannot easily see in a translation (English or another language), but you may also find many more questions and interpretive issues from the Greek text than you would see in a translation. Yet the process of wrestling with these issues can bring you much closer to the Word of God and the God of the Word.

As you grow in your knowledge of Greek, be careful of using Greek in your teaching or preaching in a way that might intimidate people and make them feel removed from the biblical text. For example, suppose you were to say, "You can't see this from the English, but the Greek actually means . . ." This could easily make some people doubt whether they can really learn from the Bible unless

---

6. It can be helpful to consider a parallel between the incarnation of Jesus and the inscripturation of the Bible; just as Jesus is fully God and fully human and became flesh at a specific time (the first century) and place (Judea), so also the Bible is fully God's communication and a fully human communication and is also connected to specific authors, times, and places.

7. Unless otherwise noted, all translations are the author's.

they know Greek and Hebrew. Remember that the Holy Spirit is committed to illuminating God's Word to his people in *any* language. So we want to be careful that we do not create any barriers for God's people to receive his Word. Knowing Greek *will* help you to prepare solid, well-grounded sermons and Bible studies, but many times this preparation will not be transparent to your audience. In other words, the way that you preach or teach a passage may depend directly on the structure of the Greek passage or the meaning of some Greek words, but often your congregation will not really benefit from knowing *how* the Greek text influenced how you are preaching or teaching the text. Thus, those of us who can study Greek and Hebrew and who minister God's Word in some way are really *servants* to the body of Christ. Of course, it is always appropriate to encourage people to take Greek and Hebrew if the opportunity arises for them to do so. Perhaps you might even consider teaching the biblical languages at some point in the future to those to whom you minister!

Throughout your Greek studies, my prayer is that you will fall more deeply in love with the Lord and his Word. If you happen to become a Greek scholar, that would be great too! But I pray that you will enjoy this process of learning and that you will grow in wisdom, grace, and gratitude for the privilege of being able to study Greek and for the efforts of those who have gone before you. Sometimes it is helpful to remember—especially in the wee hours of the night when you are studying—that many brothers and sisters around the world would love to be able to study Hebrew and Greek but are not able to do so for various reasons. This helps to remind us of the privilege of being able to study and the calling the Lord has placed before us.

THE GREEK LANGUAGE

A Brief History of the Greek Language

The origins of the Greek language extend back to about 1450 BC, which makes Greek one of the world's oldest languages.[8] The earliest example of written Greek is called "Linear B," or proto-Greek, and is found on a limited number of clay tablets.[9] The subsequent development of the Greek language can be divided into five main periods.[10]

---

8. The oldest written language that is still spoken today is generally considered to be Chinese, which is about six thousand years old. (Sumerian is considered to be the oldest written language, but it is no longer spoken.) Other ancient written languages that are still used today include Tamil, Sanskrit, Hebrew, and Arabic.

9. For more information, see www.dartmouth.edu/~prehistory/aegean/?page_id=659.

10. For further reading, see Daniel B. Wallace, *Greek Grammar beyond the Basics: An Exegetical Syntax*

Early Greek—ca. 1450 BC to ca. 1000 BC. The area where Greek was initially spoken had many mountainous regions and islands. This contributed to an irregular development of the language, which resulted in many dialects. This same phenomenon can be found in other places with similar topography, such as Papua New Guinea.

Classical Greek—ca. 1000 BC to ca. 330 BC (Alexander the Great). This is sometimes called "the Age of Dialects."[11] Four major dialects gained prominence: Aeolic, Doric, Ionic (including Homer, Hesiod, Herodotus, Hippocrates), and Attic, which was the dialect spoken in Athens and is often referred to as "Classical Greek." During this time period, Athens became the political and literary center of Greece. The fifth and fourth centuries BC are often called "the Golden Age" of classical Greece, when some of the greatest Greek literature was written. Attic Greek eventually became the basis for Koine Greek.

Koine Greek—ca. 330 BC to ca. AD 330. During this period, Koine (meaning "common") Greek became the language of much of the western world, although Aramaic was the common language in the east.[12] This spread of Greek was largely due to Alexander the Great. As Alexander conquered, he planted Greek cities and colonies, which propagated Greek culture and spread Koine Greek. Greek scholar Stanley Porter writes:

> As the various propagators (soldiers, merchants, etc.) of Greek moved further from their language bases and mingled with those still using other regional dialects, the result was a standardization of Greek varieties into a "common dialect."[13]

At its height, Koine was spoken from Alexandria to Rome, and Jerusalem to Athens. Other factors, such as the Greek pantheon of deities (including Zeus and Apollo) and the Olympic Games, also contributed to the extensive reach of Koine. The implications of this widespread, common language are important for studying NT Greek and help to explain why Paul and the other epistle writers wrote in Greek.

---

of the New Testament (Grand Rapids: Zondervan, 1996), 12–30; Rodney J. Decker, *Reading Koine Greek* (Grand Rapids: Baker Academic, 2014), 1–8. Both Wallace and Decker offer extensive bibliography.

11. Wallace, *Greek Grammar beyond the Basics*, 14.

12. Stuart Creason, "Aramaic," in *The Cambridge Encyclopedia of the World's Ancient Languages*, ed. R. D. Woodward (Cambridge: Cambridge University Press, 2004), 391–426.

13. Stanley E. Porter, "Did Jesus Ever Teach in Greek?," *TynBul* 44 (1993): 206.

Byzantine Greek—330 to 1453 AD. The shift from Koine began during the time of Constantine. Eventually, when the Roman Empire and later the church split, Latin was spoken in the west, while Greek was retained in the east.

Modern Greek—1453 AD to present. Remarkably, Modern Greek is closer to Koine Greek than Koine Greek is to Attic Greek. As is true for most languages, Modern Greek simplified as it evolved from the Koine period.

The Greek of the New Testament

Noticeable differences between Attic and Koine Greek puzzled scholars for a long time, leading many to assume that Koine was an inferior form of Attic Greek. Some examples of these differences are found in the morphology and syntax of Koine. For example, Koine Greek prefers simpler, shorter sentences and often uses fewer conjunctions. Pronouns are used more frequently in Koine Greek, especially personal pronouns that are used redundantly with verbs. Whereas Attic Greek had singular, dual, and plural noun forms, the dual form dropped from Koine Greek. Similarly, the middle voice is not used as extensively in Koine Greek as it was in Attic.

Because of such differences from Attic Greek and the apparent lack of other writings that bore witness to Koine Greek, "there was a time when the scholars who dealt with the original text of the NT regarded its Greek as a special Holy Ghost language, prepared under divine direction for Scripture writers."[14] This view, however, was challenged by archaeological discoveries of papyri (documents written on material made from papyrus reeds) in Egypt, in which documents written in the same language as the NT were excavated. These included everyday documents such as personal letters, business accounts, and divorce certificates. It soon became clear that Koine was not a "supernatural" language but was rather the language of everyday people living everyday lives. These (and subsequent) discoveries shed a great deal of light on the language of the NT. Many words that were previously believed to have been unique to the NT were found instead to be common, everyday words. Consequently, it is now often possible to see how a given word was used in the much larger context of other Koine manuscripts than the more limited context in which it appears in the NT.

---

14. H. E. Dana and Julius R. Mantey, *A Manual Grammar of the Greek New Testament* (New York: Macmillan, 1957), 9.

Literary Witnesses to Koine Greek

The term *literary witnesses* refers to the various writings that contain examples of Koine Greek. The NT is one significant example of Koine Greek. The Greek translation of the Hebrew Bible, the Septuagint (more accurately referred to as Old Greek versions), is another important witness.[15] The influence of the Septuagint is seen in some NT vocabulary and syntax. Moreover, the NT evinces diverse styles of Koine Greek, ranging from simpler (Mark, John) to more literary and rhetorical (Luke, Acts, Hebrews). Additional important examples of literary Koine include works by the Jewish historian Josephus, the Jewish philosopher Philo, the Greek biographer Plutarch, and the Stoic philosopher Epictetus.

Other important witnesses also include papyri from Egypt. As noted, these include documents from everyday life, such as private letters, legal contracts, wills, court records, government documents, and records (business, technical, medical, etc.). Numerous inscriptions also have been found, which were often official announcements and decrees chiseled into marble and set in public marketplaces (the agora). Finally, there are ostraca (also called potsherds), which are pieces of broken pottery. These were often used for memos and receipts.

Here is what an ancient receipt looks like.[16]

Receipt for the delivery of two donkeys
U-M Library Digital Collections. Advanced Papyrological Information System (APIS UM).

---

15. The term *LXX* should be understood as a shorthand reference to the far more complex textual tradition of translation of the Hebrew Scripture into Greek. See, e.g., Leonard Greenspoon, "The Use and Abuse of the Term 'LXX' and Related Terminology in Recent Scholarship," *BIOSCS* 20 (1987): 21–29.

16. To learn more, visit www.lib.umich.edu/papyrology-collection/ancient-writing-materials-ostraka.

Languages Spoken in First-Century Roman Judea

Aramaic was likely the primary language of much of the eastern part of the Roman Empire, including the primarily Jewish areas in first-century Judea, although Greek was also likely common in Judea. Hebrew may have been used primarily for the study of the Torah, although evidence exists that it may have been used in other (vernacular) settings as well.

Based on the linguistic climate of first-century Roman Judea, especially areas such as Galilee, it is likely that Greek was one of the primary languages of Roman Judea during this time. Jesus may have taught primarily in Aramaic, but he most likely knew Hebrew, spoke Greek, and may have taught in Greek as well. This is supported by the linguistic and cultural character of Galilee and by the fact that the NT was transmitted in Greek from the beginning. The multilingual nature of first-century Roman Judea is also indicated by the fact that the inscription placed above the cross was written in Hebrew, Greek, and Latin (John 19:20).

Conclusion

Koine Greek was well suited as a common language for people from diverse linguistic and cultural backgrounds. It was a common language for many people, including many non-native speakers; hence Koine was ideal for the spread of the gospel. Those who wrote the NT were able to communicate the good news for all peoples in a language that would reach a large extent of the Roman Empire. This was also facilitated by the vast Roman transportation infrastructure and the "peace" effected by the *Pax Romana*. It seems likely that Paul considered all this when he wrote in Galatians 4:4: ὅτε δὲ ἦλθεν τὸ πλήρωμα τοῦ χρόνου, ἐξαπέστειλεν ὁ θεὸς τὸν υἱὸν αὐτοῦ ("but when the fullness of time came, God sent forth his Son").[17]

The fact that Koine was a "common" language is why it is important not to make Koine Greek seem "sacred" or "spiritual" and somehow create the impression that Koine Greek was for an elite group or that those who know Koine are somehow more intellectual or spiritual. Nothing could be further from the truth—Koine Greek was a common language for all types of people in all types of circumstances and places. This offers us a refreshing perspective as we minister to all types of people in all types of circumstances and places, many of whom may not ever have the opportunity to learn the biblical languages.

At the same time, however, the danger exists of minimizing the need to learn

---

17. This observation is commonly made. I remember hearing it for the first time in one of my first church-history classes in seminary. I was amazed to consider the implications of this verse.

Greek, especially with the availability of good computer tools. There are both tangible and intangible benefits to learning Greek. To begin with, there are subtleties and complexities of Greek that are not accessible from computer tools. This is especially true concerning the structure of NT passages. Knowing Greek can contribute to a more responsible handling of God's Word and may prevent interpretive mistakes and abuses. Moreover, studying Greek fosters humility, as one realizes that the NT is rooted in another culture and time. A gap stands between that world and our own that is not easily bridged. Knowing Koine Greek is one way to bridge that gap and prevents us from being limited to modern translations. Studying Koine Greek leads us into the world of the NT and one of the languages that God chose to reveal himself in writing. It is a wonderful world to enter.

INTRODUCTION TO SYNTAX AND LINGUISTICS

Why Emphasize Syntax?

One basic approach to biblical interpretation focuses on the linguistic and syntactic elements of the biblical languages with the goal of accurate interpretation. We will draw upon both linguistics and syntax in our study of Koine Greek. We will focus on **form**[18] (how a word, or unit of words, appears) and **function** (what a word or a unit of words does in a given context). Both form and function must be understood correctly before trying to determine the meaning of the passage.

It might be helpful to think about syntax as a set of rules for "playing the game" of using any given language. The words **syntax** and **grammar** are sometimes used interchangeably, and scholars debate as to what is meant by each word. Both words refer to the set of rules that are used by various languages. The following distinction is sometimes made: *syntax* refers primarily to rules that govern how words and units of words *can* function in a language, whereas *grammar* focuses on what is considered to be "proper" in a given language or how words *should* function. For example, English *syntax* does not allow a verb form such as "goes" to appear without also specifying the subject. Hence "goes" does not make sense unless a subject, such as "the train," is also supplied. Violations of syntax produce constructions that do not make sense and thus do not communicate. English *grammar*, however, is often understood to refer to such issues as when "that" or "which" *should* be used, or to avoiding split infinitives—"to go boldly" rather than "to boldly go." Violations of grammar communicate, but they are not considered to be proper language usage. Although this is a common

---

18. A fuller discussion of a **bolded** word is found in the glossary.

understanding of grammar, another (more linguistic) way of understanding this is that *grammar* refers to the overall system of a language, particularly how its words are formed (**morphology**) and the patterns of word formation (such as noun declensions and verb conjugations), whereas *syntax* concerns how words form larger constructions and what happens when words interact with other words. This is the understanding of *grammar* and *syntax* used in this book.

Basic Linguistic and Syntactic Terms

We start by considering the components used to create forms and how these forms function. **Morphemes** are the smallest language elements that have meaning.[19] They are the basic components, or building blocks, of words. Consider the following examples of morphemes from English and how they form common English words:[20]

pre-, un-, -s, -ed, -ing, -ful, -ly
premodern, **un**pack, book**s**, walk**ed**, read**ing**, grate**ful**, quick**ly**

Morphemes such as **pre-** and **un-** are called **prefixes** because they are attached to the beginning of a word stem to create a new form that has a different function than the original word stem. Morphemes such as -**ful** and -**ly** are called **suffixes** because they are attached to the end of a word stem to create a new form that has a different function than the original word stem. It is also possible to insert a morpheme into the middle of a word, which is called an **infix**. (We will see examples of this in Koine Greek later.)

It is important to note that the same form of a morpheme can sometimes have different meanings, depending on context. For example, consider the following English words: he walk**s**, two apple**s**. In the first example, the suffix -**s** is required for a singular subject, whereas in the second example, the suffix -**s** indicates a plural noun. Now consider these words: soft**er**, work**er**. In the first example, the suffix -**er** indicates a comparative, whereas in the second example the suffix -**er** denotes a member of a class of individuals (who work). Notice also that the same combinations of letters are *not always* examples of morphemes. Consider the following words in which **pre-**, **un-**, -**s**, -**ed**, -**ing**, and –**ly** do not

---

19. Eugene Van Ness Goetchius, *The Language of the New Testament* (New York: Scribner's Sons, 1965), 14. See also Gary A. Long, *Grammatical Concepts 101 for Biblical Greek* (Peabody, MA: Hendrickson, 2006), 4.

20. In this book, **bolded** text is also used to indicate morphology (or the formation of words); *italics* are used to indicate syntax (how those forms function). Some of this discussion in indebted to Goetchius, *Language of the New Testament*, 14.

function as prefixes or suffixes: **pre**y, **un**ity, **us**, **fed**, **sing**, **fly**. Thus, it is import-ant to look carefully at the context in which a group of letters appears. Not every occurrence of the same group of letters has the same function or even represents a morpheme; instead, that group of letters may be part of a word's stem. (This is true for both English and Greek.)

Words are formed by combinations of stems and morphemes. We can add various morphemes to word stems to indicate changes in function. In English, a noun or verb stem can often be used independently, although this is seldom the case in Greek (as we will see later). Consider the following examples from English:

book	noun stem
book**s**	noun stem + plural morpheme
read	verb stem
read**ing**	verb stem + participle morpheme

Constructions are combinations of words in fixed patterns. Common con-structions include **phrases**, which *do not* contain (or assume) a subject-verb com-bination and thus do not express a complete thought. There are several different types of phrases:

a ship	(*noun phrase*)
Roman merchant ships	(*adjectival phrase*)
through the Mediterranean Sea	(*prepositional phrase*)
to sail	(*infinitive phrase*)

Notice that these phrases have a *fixed* word order; "ship a" does not make sense independently, and "sail to" does not have the same meaning as "to sail." Similarly, "ships merchant Roman" and "Sea Mediterranean through the" make no sense given the "rules" of English syntax.

Another common type of construction is a **clause**, which *does* contain (or assumes) a subject-verb combination. There are many types of clauses:

It's raining!	(*independent clause*)
that I am reading	(*dependent restrictive relative clause*)
because he lives	(*dependent causal clause*)

Sentences are combinations of various constructions, such as clauses and phrases. For example:

The book [*noun phrase*] that I am reading [*restrictive relative clause*] describes how Roman merchant ships [*adjectival phrase*] used to sail [*infinitive phrase*] through the Mediterranean Sea [*prepositional phrase*].

Syntactic Structures of Sentences

A primary goal of exegesis is to understand the meaning of a given sentence in the NT by analyzing how various constructions function within that sentence. This entails identifying types of clauses (form) and what they contribute to the sentence (function). Notice that our focus is on sentences, not verses.[21] The verse divisions in the Bible were added much later than the original autographs of the OT and NT. Sometimes these verse divisions cut sentences into small units, which can make it difficult to grasp the meaning of the original sentence. For example, Colossians 1:3–8 is actually one long sentence in the original Greek.

Clauses are either **main** (or **independent**) or **subordinate** (or **dependent**).[22] Main clauses must contain a subject and a verb and communicate a complete thought. In other words, they can *stand alone* in a sentence; for example, "We love to study Greek." Subordinate clauses must also contain (or assume) a subject and a verb, but they do not communicate a complete thought, and thus they *cannot* stand alone in a sentence. In English, subordinate clauses are usually introduced by subordinating conjunctions, such as "because," "whenever," "although," and so on. For example, "because we want to understand God's Word" is not a complete thought, which is signaled by the presence of "because." So this clause is dependent on a main, or independent, clause. For example:

We love to study Greek [*main clause*], because we want to understand God's Word [*subordinate clause*].

Subordinate clauses can also be introduced by relative pronouns (e.g., "*who* is the image of God").

---

21. Keep in mind that sentences in the Bible often extend beyond a single verse.
22. The terms *main* and *independent* can be used interchangeably; similarly, the terms *subordinate* and *dependent* can be used interchangeably.

There are many types of subordinating clauses, such as *purpose* clauses (introduced by "so that" or "in order that"), *result* clauses (introduced by "that" or "with the result that"), *conditional clauses* (introduced by "if"), and *comparative* clauses (introduced by "than").[23]

Main clauses are a syntactically necessary component of a sentence. Without a main clause, there is no sentence! Subordinate clauses are not *syntactically* necessary for a sentence. Without a subordinate clause, there is still a main clause and hence a sentence. Yet subordinate clauses usually contain information that is vital for understanding the thought communicated by the sentence; for example, "We love one another, because Christ first loved us." Clearly Christ's love is a key theological affirmation. But in the above sentence, the main clause "We love one another" can syntactically stand as an independent sentence, whereas the subordinate clause "because Christ first loved us" cannot. This is an important concept to grasp.

A **sentence** is a group of words that is complete by itself. At the most basic level, a sentence contains a main clause, which has two parts: a **subject** and a **predicate**. A subject names the entity about which some comment (predication) is being made. Normally the predicate comprises a verb and often an object or adverbial modifier, such as an adverb. For example:

subject	predicate
The gospel	bears [verb] fruit [object] abundantly [adverb].

Sentences that contain only a subject and predicate (and its modifiers) are called **simple sentences**; for example, "I believe." Two or more simple sentences joined together form a **compound sentence**; for example, "I heard the gospel and I believed." Many sentences are more complicated than this, however, because they contain a main clause and several subordinate clauses. For example: "Because we want to understand God's Word, we love to study Greek, even though it takes a lot of time." Such sentences are called **complex sentences**. (In this example, the main clause is "we love to study Greek," and the subordinate clauses are "because we want to understand God's Word" and "even though it takes a lot of time".)

Most sentences contain a combination of phrases and clauses, as this example from Luke 2:1 illustrates. In this example, the main clause is not underlined,

---

23. Some dependent verbal clauses in Greek, however, are not introduced with a subordinating conjunction, but we will talk about this much more later.

the first dependent clause is dash-underlined, and the second dependent clause is single underlined.

> Now it came about [*main clause*] in those days [*prepositional phrase*] that a decree went out [*dependent clause*] from Caesar Augustus [*prepositional phrase*], that a census be taken [*dependent clause*] of all the inhabited earth [*prepositional phrase*].

Notice that phrases (e.g., the prepositional phrases in the above example) can also be embedded within clauses (e.g., the second and third prepositional phrases within the two dependent clauses in the above example).

Form (Parts of Speech) and Syntactic Function

In order to understand how a word is functioning in a phrase or clause, we must begin by identifying the word's form, or part of speech. Some basic parts of speech and their basic functions include the following:[24]

form	function	examples
noun	name of person, place, concept, or thing[1]	*Christ, gospel, truth*
pronoun	used in the place of a noun	*he, it, you, their*
adjective	modifies a noun or pronoun[2]	*glorious, faithful, good*
verb	describes an action or state of being	*think, run, exist*
adverb	modifies a verb, adjective, or adverb	*truthfully, fast, very*
preposition	shows the spatial, temporal, or logical relationship between one word and another word	*on, by, at*
conjunction	connects two or more syntactic units (such as sentences, clauses, phrases, or words)	*and, or, but*

[1] Nouns can also be classified as **proper** (e.g., Jesus, Galilee), **collective** (e.g., flock [more than one bird], crowd [more than one person]), or **abstract** (e.g., faith, hope, love).

[2] Technically an adjective can only modify a pronoun as a predicate, but we will come back to this later.

The following functional questions can help to identify a word's part of speech.

---

24. These definitions and the following questions are somewhat indebted to J. W. Wenham, *The Elements of New Testament Greek* (Cambridge: Cambridge University Press, 1965), 1–3.

question	answer
Does it name something?	noun
Does it substitute for a previously mentioned noun?	pronoun
Does it describe a noun in some way?	adjective
Does it indicate the action of a noun or pronoun? Does it indicate a state of being or command something?	verb
Does it indicate the circumstances of a verbal action or state (e.g., how or when the action occurred)?	adverb
Does it show the spatial, temporal, or logical relationship between one word and another word?	preposition
Does it show the relationship between sentences, clauses, phrases, or words?	conjunction

Multiple *forms* can have the same *function* in different contexts. For example, some forms can function like nouns, even though they are not actually nouns. To avoid confusion, we will use the term **substantive** (a functional word) to refer to any word that *functions* like a noun. The following pairs of examples present different forms (such as a pronoun or adjective) that function like nouns. In each pair, the first line is an example of the given part of speech (e.g., a pronoun). Then, to show that this form is *functioning* as a substantive, the same clause or phrase is repeated with a noun substituted (and underlined) to show that the form in the first pair that is not technically a noun performs the same syntactic *function* as the noun.[25]

form	function as a substantive
pronoun	*He [pronoun]* is Lord. Jesus [noun] is Lord.
adjective	Blessed are *the meek [adjective]*. Blessed are the disciples [noun].
participle	*Singing [participle]* is fun. The game [noun] is fun.
infinitive	*To worship [infinitive]* gives joy. The Spirit [noun] gives joy.

25. At first these concepts may be confusing, but it is important to grasp them because Greek very often uses one part of speech to perform the function of a different part of speech.

Similarly, many forms can function like an adjective, or as a **modifier** (a functional word) of a substantive. Similar to the previous examples, the first line of each pair below gives an example of a word that is not an adjective but that functions like an adjective (as a modifier). The second line of each pair then substitutes an adjective to show that the form in the first line of the pair that is not an adjective has the same syntactic function as an adjective (i.e., as a modifier of a substantive).

form	function as a substantive modifier
noun	The *office* [*noun phrase*] building is over there. The <u>big</u> [*adjective*] building is over there.
participle	a *laughing* [*participle*] child a <u>joyful</u> [*adjective*] child
prepositional phrase	The book *on the table* [*prepositional phrase*] is good. The <u>new</u> [*adjective*] book is good.
relative clause	The student *who is taking Greek* [*relative clause*] is blessed. The <u>wise</u> [*adjective*] student is blessed.

Finally, some forms can function like an adverb, or a **modifier** of a verb. Again, the first line of each pair below presents a form that is not an adverb but that is functioning to modify a verb. The second line substitutes an adverb to show that the form in the first example that is not an adverb is performing an adverbial function.

form	function as a verb modifier
noun	We will go *this year* [*noun phrase*]. We will go <u>quickly</u> [*adverb*].
prepositional phrase	They worship *with songs of praise* [*prepositional phrase*]. They worship <u>joyously</u> [*adverb*].
dependent clause	*Having been justified by faith* [*dependent clause*], we have peace with God. <u>Mercifully</u> [*adverb*], we have peace with God.

We can also consider this phenomenon of how different forms perform different functions in terms of **"slots"** and **"fillers."** Slots are associated with specific functions, such as "substantive," "substantive modifier," "verb modifier," and so on. Individual slots can only be filled by forms (parts of speech), or "fillers," that can perform these functions. The use of "slots" and "fillers" makes it easier to identify *modifiers* and words *modified* in a sentence. Correctly identifying these elements is essential for accurate translation and interpretation.

In a sentence, there are several syntactic functions for substantives, such as subject, direct object, and indirect object. Only parts of speech or phrases that are *functioning* as substantives can fill these syntactic slots. In the chart below, the parts of speech or phrases that can fill the substantive syntactic functions of subject, direct object, and indirect object are listed below those functions. For example, a pronoun could fill the slot for the syntactic function of subject, whereas an adverb could not. Similarly, only words or phrases that are *functioning* as adjectives to modify substantives can fill the slot for substantive modifier, which are listed below this slot. Finally, only verbs can fill the verb slot (phew!), but forms that are not actually adverbs can fill the slot of verb modifier, as indicated by those parts of speech listed below this slot.[26]

subject	verb	verb modifier	direct object	substantive modifier	indirect object
noun		adverb	noun	adjective	noun
pronoun		noun	pronoun	noun	pronoun
adjective		prep phrase	adjective	participle	adjective
participle		dep clause	participle	prep phrase	participle
infinitive			infinitive	rel clause	

Now let's look at some examples.

subject	verb	substantive modifier	direct object	indirect object
Worship	brings	great	joy	to us.
noun		adjective	noun	pronoun

subject	verb	substantive modifier	direct object	indirect object
To worship	brings	great	joy	to us.
infinitive		adjective	noun	pronoun

---

26. Don't get overwhelmed by this. We will come back to this multiple times. Instead, just think of how creative language can be! It would be boring if every part of speech was locked into only one function. As we go along, we'll see that parts of speech in Greek can perform even more functions than the ones indicated here—they are very flexible, which means that hopefully you will never get bored in your Greek studies.

In the first example, a noun (a substantive) fills the "subject" syntactic function slot, whereas in the second example, an infinitive that is functioning as a substantive fills the "subject" syntactic function slot. We could also substitute some other parts of speech into this "subject" function slot, such as the participle "singing"[27]: "Singing brings great joy to us." But we could not substitute a verb, such as "sings," into this "subject" function slot: "Sings brings great joy to us." Thus the concept of "slots" and "fillers" helps us to understand how creatively different parts of speech and constructions can function, but it also helps us understand which parts of speech cannot perform certain syntactic functions or fill certain slots.

Word Order and Inflection

In English, the function of substantives is often determined by the order in which they appear in a sentence. For example, consider the sentence, "God loves a cheerful giver" (2 Cor 9:7). Since "God" appears first, it is the subject of the sentence, whereas "a cheerful giver" functions as the direct object of the verb "loves." If the words are moved around, the meaning is completely changed—"a cheerful giver loves God"—or is lost completely—"cheerful God a loves giver."[28]

Now consider the same sentence in Greek:

ἱλαρὸν	δότην	ἀγαπᾷ	ὁ θεός
cheerful	giver	loves	God

Despite word order, the above Greek sentence could *not* be translated "a cheerful giver loves God." Although these five Greek words could be shifted around even more, they could only be translated as "God loves a cheerful giver." How can Greek shift words without affecting the meaning of the sentence, whereas English cannot? The answer is inflection! **Inflection** is any change in *form* to indicate a change in *function*. Inflection often involves adding morphemes to word stems.

One key difference between English and Greek is that **word order** in English is fairly *fixed*, with little flexibility as to where words can be placed in a sentence without changing the meaning of the sentence. Additionally, most English words are not inflected very much, often not at all. In Greek, however, word order is *variable*, with much greater flexibility as to where words can be

---

27. Technically, a participle functioning as a noun in English is called a *gerund*.
28. The discussion here is adapted from Goetchius, *Language of the New Testament*, 20–23.

placed in a sentence without changing the meaning of the sentence. This flexibility is possible because many Greek words are highly inflected.

It should be stressed, however, that this is a spectrum. Word order in English can sometimes be changed for effect. For example, English usually has the following sentence structure: subject-verb-object: "I love the Lord." But this can be changed for effect, often in poetry or hymns: "The Lord, I love!" It should also be noted that Greek has fixed word order in certain contexts. For example, the article always precedes the substantive it modifies (e.g., ὁ κύριος, "the Lord"); it can never follow it (e.g., κύριος ὁ, "Lord the"). We will talk more about this later.

Although English is not a highly inflected language, there are several good examples of inflection in English. For example, nouns can be inflected to indicate number (singular or plural):

cat/cats
child/children
book/books
church/churches

Nouns can also be inflected or changed to reflect natural gender (male or female):

buck, doe
actor, actress

Pronouns are perhaps the most inflected element of English. In addition to being inflected for number and gender, pronouns are also inflected to indicate their syntactic function within a sentence:

function	singular	plural
subject	I	we
	you	you (pl)
	he, she, it	they
object	me	us
	you	you (pl)
	him, her, it	them
possession	my	our
	your	your
	his, her, its	their

We also see inflection with English verbs. Consider some inflections for the verb *to bake*:

function	form
past tense	baked
singular subject	bakes
participle	baking

Declensions are patterns of inflections that occur with substantives.[29] Greek substantives are classified according to certain patterns of inflections, resulting in three declensions (first, second, and third). There is no real parallel in English, but we can begin to understand this concept if we consider English nouns and how they form their plurals.[30] Although English does not classify nouns according to declensions, we could call all nouns that form their plural by simply adding "s" "first declension nouns." Then we could call all nouns that form their plural by adding "es" "second declension nouns." Finally, we could call all nouns that form their plural by changing their stem or spelling in some other way "third declension" nouns." For example:

First declension (add "s")	Second declension (add "es")	Third declension change stem
cat/cats	church/churches	child/children
book/books	ditch/ditches	woman/women
car/cars	bus/buses	ox/oxen

Semantics, Semantic Range, Context, and Translation

We use words all the time, yet we often do not consider why certain words mean what they mean or the many ambiguities associated with some words. For example, there is no inherent reason why the mechanical piece of equipment that takes people up and down buildings should be called an *elevator* (in the United States) or a *lift* (in the United Kingdom), although both names makes sense if you know English. Looking at this piece of equipment, however, it is certainly not the

---

29. Inflection patterns with verbs are called **conjugations**.
30. This analogy to plural formation in English is noted by many grammars: Decker, *Reading Koine Greek*, 35; William D. Mounce, *Basics of Biblical Greek Grammar*, 4th ed. (Grand Rapids: Zondervan, 2018), 29–30; James W. Voelz, *Fundamental Greek Grammar*, 3rd ed. (St. Louis: Concordia, 2007), 20–21.

case that every human being would call it an "elevator" or a "lift." This helps us to see that the relationship between an object and its name is conventional; in other words, the meaning of a word is determined by the usage of that word by a particular group of language users. Additionally, the same word in a language can have different meanings depending on the context in which it is used. Consider the following usages of the English word *bank*:

> There is a *bank* with an ATM just around the corner.
> That town has a great bike path along the river *bank*.
> I *bank* at the Credit Union because of the free checking.
> Those sports cars *bank* well on curves.

Now consider the ambiguity in the following examples:

> I met them by the bank.
> He skidded around the corner and banked at the Trust Company.[31]

The first set of examples show that the word *bank* has various meanings depending on the context in which it is used. The second set of examples shows that sometimes even the immediate context is not clear enough, and more context is needed to determine the intended meaning of the word *bank*. Both sets of examples deal with **semantics**, which concerns the meanings of words and constructions in their immediate context. Both sets of examples also show that many words, such as *bank*, have a range of possible meanings, which is called a **semantic range**. The overall context usually determines which meaning from the range of possible meanings is intended by an author (although some ambiguity may remain).

Perhaps you have noticed this if you have traveled somewhere where English is not the primary language. If you were to see a sign with the words, "No Naked Flame," you would probably figure out that "open" flames were prohibited, but you would also suspect that the person who wrote the sign was not a native English speaker. Because words can have a range of possible meanings, it is nearly impossible to have a one-to-one, or "literal," correspondence between words from any two languages. We might translate the same word differently depending on the context of each occurrence, especially since the connotation of words often changes in different contexts. This is why translation software doesn't always get it right.

---

31. This discussion is indebted to and modified from Goetchius, *Language of the New Testament*, 17. The last two examples are quoted from Goetchius, *Language of the New Testament*, 17.

Consider the following examples involving the Greek word λόγος.

But going out, he began to proclaim it publicly and to spread the *news* [λόγος] around. (Mark 1:45)[32] [The context here is the leper who was healed by Jesus, and who was instructed by Jesus not to spread the λόγος about his healing.]

He was speaking the *word* [λόγος] to them. (Mark 2:2)[33] [The context here involves Jesus preaching about the kingdom of God.]

Now consider these examples involving the Greek preposition πρός:

In the beginning was the Word and the Word was *with* [πρός] God. (John 1:1)

Come *to* [πρός] me, all who are weary and burdened. (Matt 11:28)

If the Greek words λόγος and πρός were always translated with the same English words, the result would be confusing or even incorrect.

Ambiguity is not limited to words. Syntactic units, such as phrases, can have more than one meaning. For example, "the love of God" may mean that God is loved (God is the object of the verbal idea of loving) or that God loves (God is the subject of the verbal idea of loving). Consider the following:

But I know you, that you do not have *the love of God* in yourselves. (John 5:42)

Nothing . . . shall be able to separate us from *the love of God*. (Rom 8:39)

The grace of the Lord Jesus Christ and *the love of God* and the fellowship of the Holy Spirit be with you all. (2 Cor 13:14)

Without considering the surrounding context, the phrase "the love of God" is ambiguous, although the first two examples are relatively clear, with the first example most likely indicating love *for* God and the second clearly indicating love

---

32. The Greek word λόγος is translated as "news" by most major English versions, including CSB, ESV, NASB, and NIV, although the NRSV translates it as "the word."
33. The Greek word λόγος is translated as "word" by CSB, ESV, NASB, NIV, RSV.

from God. In the third example, it is possible that both understandings of "the love of God" are viable options, and perhaps both are intended.

A certain amount of ambiguity is inherent in all language. This is compounded by the gap in time and culture between the original context of the NT and the context in which we now study it. Clearly, understanding the intent of the human author, who worked under the direction of the divine author, the Holy Spirit, is essential. This is one reason why context is such a crucial factor in determining meaning. Moreover, "context" includes the immediate syntactic context of the sentence, the overall context of the passage, and the historical and cultural context of the original author and audience. Some of these contexts are more difficult to determine than others. This is why it is important to keep in mind that, together with study, humility and prayer are essential elements of biblical interpretation.

Lexical Form, More on Semantic Range, and Glosses

The preceding examples show that words can have a range of meanings and that it is not possible to have a word-for-word correspondence between Greek and English.[34] For this reason, it is helpful to introduce a final set of terms and concepts that are essential before we can begin to look at Greek texts and translate them into English.

A **lexeme** is a minimal linguistic unit that has lexical (word) meaning. Whereas most morphemes do not independently communicate meaning (e.g., "-ing" by itself is meaningless), lexemes often correspond to "words" that can be listed in a lexicon, or dictionary. Inflected forms of lexemes are not usually listed in a dictionary. For example, if you want to find out the meaning of the English word *books*, you will not find *books* as a separate entry in a dictionary. Instead you would need to look for the lexeme *book*, which is the **lexical form** for the plural word *books*.

As we saw with the English word *bank*, some lexemes have a wide range of possible meanings. The same is true of Greek. Depending on the context, λόγος can be faithfully translated into English as "word," "news," "message," "matter," "substance," "saying," "teaching," "account," with even more possible options! So clearly λόγος is *not defined* by the English word *word*. This helps us

---

34. One implication that flows from this observation is that no one single English version of the Bible can be considered the "best" or "most literal" translation. The major standard English versions all seek to be faithful in rendering the Hebrew, Aramaic, and Greek biblical texts into contemporary English, although they have different (and valid) goals for their translations. It is a good practice, therefore, to consult numerous standard versions rather than to rely on one single English version of the Bible.

to understand the difference between a "definition" and a "gloss." A **definition** is an analytical description of the meaning of a word. For example, the *definition* of the Greek verb πορεύομαι involves "linear movement." A **gloss**, however, is one possible way that a given word could be translated. This is also called a *translation equivalent*. Depending on the context, πορεύομαι could be rendered by any of the following English verbs: "go," "travel," "journey," "proceed," "live," or even "die"! So clearly if we were to say that πορεύομαι *means* "go,"[35] we would not be accurate, because this Greek verb could also *mean* any of the other options listed and even some more besides.

This brings us back to the concept of **semantic range**—the range of possible glosses that could be used to translate a particular word. Sometimes the range of options for a given word can be overwhelming. It can be tempting to go to a lexicon and simply pick a word that seems to fit the context (or perhaps to look for the Bible verse under consideration if it is listed in a lexicon and simply adopt the lexicon's translation and be done with it!). It would be overwhelming to memorize all possible glosses for each assigned Greek vocabulary word. So we will have to settle for a more limited semantic range when we translate some of our Greek texts. Thus the assigned vocabulary will often present only a subset of possible glosses for a given Greek word.[36] In other words, if you were to look up some of these assigned vocabulary words in a standard lexicon, you would find additional glosses beyond those supplied in this book. We are attempting to simplify your world at this point! But it is important to keep this in mind. As you proceed in your Greek studies, you will also be growing in your understanding of the semantic range of much of the NT vocabulary.

Some of this discussion may seem tedious or needlessly technical. Yet these are very important concepts and issues, and understanding them will help you avoid some of the more common mistakes that beginning Greek students often make. Our goal in this book is to understand Greek as clearly as possible and to grow in our sensitivity to the complexities of translation and interpretation— because the two cannot really be separated. Because these concepts are so

---

35. Technically we would want to say that πορεύομαι could be translated "I go" or "I journey," etc., because this verb's inflected form is first-person singular. We'll talk more about this in the next chapter.

36. As you proceed in the your Greek studies, it is important that you make it a habit to consult two of the standard lexica for the GNT: Walter Bauer, Frederick W. Danker, William F. Arndt, and F. Wilbur Gingrich, *Greek-English Lexicon of the New Testament and Other Early Christian Literature*, 3rd ed. (Chicago: University of Chicago Press, 2000), and Johannes P. Louw and Eugene A. Nida, eds., *Greek-English Lexicon of the New Testament: Based on Semantic Domains*, 2nd ed., 2 vols. (New York: United Bible Societies, 1989). In some cases, we also need to consult relevant historical, social, and cultural-background resources to grasp more fully what a word might mean in a given context. These resources are often introduced in second-year exegesis courses.

important, we will revisit most of them multiple times during this course. We will also present the complexities of some of these concepts after you have grown in your initial grasp of Greek.

THE GREEK ALPHABET

Introduction

If you are reading this, then you already know what an alphabet is. It is the set of symbols that a language uses for written communication. Languages around the world and throughout time have used diverse alphabets. Fortunately for our study, there are many similarities between the Greek and English alphabets, which make learning the Greek alphabet a bit easier if you already know the English one. Even so, students need to be careful because there are some Greek letters that look similar to certain English letters, but they are actually different letters. For example, you might see the Greek letter ρ and think that it makes a "p" sound, but it actually makes an "r" sound.[37]

It is essential to know the Greek alphabet well and is imperative to memorize each letter. You must know the letters in alphabetical order, but you also need to recognize each letter whenever it occurs in any Greek word or text. You can start out by memorizing the list of letters that appears in this chapter. But you should aim to be able to look at a Greek text from the NT and be able to recognize each and every letter as soon as possible.

Scholars debate how Koine Greek should be pronounced. For centuries, scholars used the "Erasmian" pronunciation, which was supposedly developed by the Dutch scholar Desiderius Erasmus (1466–1536).[38] This pronunciation system is somewhat arbitrary and is most likely not how Greek was pronounced in the first century, but it does assign a unique sound to each letter. It may also be the pronunciation that you will use in subsequent Greek courses and is used by perhaps the majority of scholars today. Some scholars, however, have begun to use modern Greek pronunciation, arguing that it is easier for students to learn and is probably closer to how Greek sounded in the first century (besides, it might be helpful when you visit Greece!).

---

37. These differences are discussed in detail in the ancillary video segment on writing the letters of the Greek alphabet (see the DVD *An Introduction to Biblical Greek Grammar* [Grand Rapids: Zondervan Academic, 2020], available for purchase).

38. It is beyond our scope to discuss this further, but it is not certain that Erasmus actually developed this system of pronunciation. See, e.g., Jody A. Barnard, "The 'Erasmian' Pronunciation of Greek," *Erasmus Studies* 37 (2017): 109–32.

For the Curious

Technically, English uses the Roman or Latin alphabet. Both the Latin and Greek alphabets originated from the alphabet devised by the Phoenicians. The Hebrew alphabet also derived from the Phoenician alphabet. Perhaps you've already noticed the similarity between Greek and Hebrew: alpha/aleph, beta/beth, gamma/gimel, delta/daleth, etc.

In this chapter, you will also learn how to transliterate Greek letters into corresponding English letters. We will not use transliterations in this book, but some reference works and commentaries do use transliterations, so it is important to learn this system as well.

In the chart on page 29, you will find the name (e.g., "delta") of each of the twenty-four letters of the Greek alphabet, the lowercase form, the uppercase form, its transliteration, and a guide for pronunciation based on the pronunciation of an English word. You should concentrate on knowing the names of the letters, recognizing their forms, and knowing the sounds that they make.[39]

For the Curious

There are two other Greek letters that were no longer used in the Koine period, but their influence is still felt in some forms. These letters are the ϝ "digamma" and the "consonantal iota"; the symbol for the latter is no longer known, but it is sometimes depicted as ι̯. We'll discuss the significance of these "phantom" letters later.

You need to know both lowercase and uppercase forms for these letters. The lowercase letters are listed first because you will encounter them more frequently. The original manuscripts of the NT, however, were written using only uppercase letters, whereas modern editions capitalize proper names and the first letter of a sentence, so you will see more lowercase letters in modern editions of the GNT and the examples and exercises for this course. Before we get started, however, here's what an early manuscript of the NT looks like.

---

39. In the DVD (see earlier note), I show you how to write these letters.

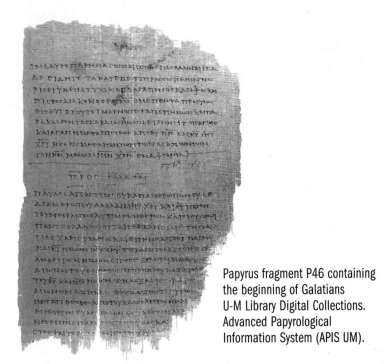

Papyrus fragment P46 containing
the beginning of Galatians
U-M Library Digital Collections.
Advanced Papyrological
Information System (APIS UM).

Some of the letters are hard to recognize because they do not closely resemble the standardized fonts that are used today. As you can see, however, these manuscripts were written with all uppercase letters and no spaces between words. This was simply the convention at that time, but it certainly makes it more challenging to read these manuscripts! For example, Galatians begins as follows: ΠΑΥΛΟΣΑ ΠΟΣΤΟΛΟΣΟΥΚΑΠΑΝΘΡΩΠΩΝ . . .

For the Curious

In some early manuscripts, an uppercase sigma also looks like the English letter "C"—if you look carefully at the title of the excerpt from Galatians, you can see this: ΠΡΟC ΓΑΛΑΤΑC. This is called a *lunate sigma*, because it looks like a crescent moon.

Names, Forms, Transliterations, and Sounds of Greek Letters

Here is the Greek alphabet. Note that there are two forms for sigma: the form σ occurs at the beginning or middle of a word, whereas the form ς occurs at the end of a word (and hence is called an "ending" or "final" sigma). The following two Greek words have each type of sigma: σεισμός ("shaking," "earthquake"), ἀπόστολος ("apostle").

name	lowercase	uppercase	transliteration	pronunciation guide[1]
alpha	α	A	a	a as in father
beta	β	B	b	b
gamma	γ	Γ	g	g as in got (not as in gene)
delta	δ	Δ	d	d
epsilon	ε	E	e	e as in bet (short)[2]
zeta	ζ	Z	z	z as in adds/daze[3]
eta	η	H	ē	e as in day (long)
theta	θ	Θ	th	th as in this
iota	ι	I	i	i as in machine[4]
kappa	κ	K	k	k
lambda	λ	Λ	l	l
mu	μ	M	m	m
nu	ν	N	n	n
xi	ξ	Ξ	x	x as in ax (not as in exact)
omicron	ο	O	o	o as in dot (short)
pi	π	Π	p	p
rho	ρ	P	r	r
sigma	σ/ς	Σ	s	s as in sing (not as in rose)
tau	τ	T	t	t
upsilon	υ	Y	u/y	u as in universe[5]
phi	φ	Φ	ph	ph as in phone
chi	χ	X	ch	ch as in loch, Bach
psi	ψ	Ψ	ps	ps as in drops
omega	ω	Ω	ō	o as in obey (long)

[1] Many letters in Greek have virtually the same sound as corresponding letters in English, in part because both languages are Indo-European. English pronunciation guides are supplied for those letters that either have multiple possible pronunciations in English or that have no real equivalent in English.

[2] There are two sets of vowels that act as "pairs": an epsilon is a short "e" sound and an eta is a long "e" sound; similarly, an omicron is a short "o" sound and an omega is a long "o" sound.

[3] This letter can be pronounced either with a "dz" sound in the middle of a word, or simply with a "z" sound at the beginning or middle of a word.

[4] Sometimes an iota can be pronounced similar to an English "y" sound. For instance, the Greek spelling of Jesus, Ἰησοῦς, should be pronounced yay-SOOS. In this word, the iota before another vowel causes the iota to be pronounced almost like a consonant. The iota can also have a short sound as in "bit."

[5] When an upsilon occurs in combination with another vowel (a diphthong; see below), it is transliterated with the English letter "u"; otherwise, the English letter "y" is used. For example, εὐλογία ("blessing") is transliterated eulogia, but συναγωγή is transliterated synagōgē.

If you already know the names of some Greek letters, you may have to adjust your pronunciation of the Greek letters in some places. For example, when we are talking about the ratio of a circle's circumference to its diameter, the word *pi* is usually pronounced "pie" as in "apple pie"; but the Greek letter π should be pronounced the way that we pronounce the English letter "p" or the vegetable, "pea."

Vowels

Of the twenty-four letters in the Greek alphabet, there are seven vowels: α, ε, η, ι, ο, υ, and ω. We can distinguish between short and long vowel sounds. Two vowels are always long, η and ω, and two vowels are always short, ε and o. The remaining three vowels, α, ι, and υ, can be either short or long, depending on where they occur in a given word. There may be a slight difference in pronunciation with these vowels, depending on whether they are long and short. As we will see, the fact that α can be either long or short is significant when we talk about iota subscripts below.

Diphthongs

Some vowels combine to form one sound, which is called a **diphthong**. (The word *diphthong* comes from the Greek word, δίφθογγος, which means "with two sounds.") Notice that diphthongs are formed with either an ι or a υ as the second vowel. These are sometimes called **proper diphthongs**, because they make a different vowel sound than either of the individual vowels do separately.

diphthong	pronunciation	Greek example
αι	as in <u>ai</u>sle	καί
ει	as in w<u>eigh</u>t	λύει[1]
οι	as in b<u>oi</u>l	οἶδα
αυ	as in <u>ow</u>l	αὐτός
ου	as in s<u>ou</u>p	οὖν
υι	as in s<u>ui</u>te, q<u>ueen</u>	υἱός
ευ, ηυ	as in f<u>eu</u>d	πιστεύω

[1] This diphthong is pronounced the same as the single vowel eta. For example, in the verb form τηρεῖν, the vowel sound is the same in both syllables, namely, tay-RAIN.

Iota Subscripts

Another combination of vowels occurs when an iota combines with a long vowel (specifically with η or ω, or a long α). In this case, the iota appears as a subscript under the long vowel and does not affect the pronunciation of the long vowel. Because there is no effect on the pronunciation (although there is often a significant change in the *meaning* of a word with the addition of the **iota subscript**), this combination is sometimes called an **improper diphthong**.[40]

ᾳ pronounced the same as α
ῃ pronounced the same as η
ῳ pronounced the same as ω

There are many words in the NT that contain an iota subscript, as we will see.

For the Curious

As noted, early NT manuscripts were written with all uppercase letters. The iota did not appear as a subscript in these manuscripts but was written next to the long vowel. So ἀγάπῃ would have been written ΑΓΑΠΗΙ. For the really curious, this is called an *iota adscript*.[41]

Gamma Combinations

Some letters have different sounds when they occur in combination with other letters. When a gamma is followed by a guttural (a consonant whose sound is made in the throat), such as γ, κ, ξ, or χ, the result is a nasal sound, as indicated below. (This is sometimes called a *gamma nasal*.)

---

40. Of course, we don't have iota subscripts in English, but we do have words that are spelled differently but are pronounced the same, such as "sea" and "see" (homophones). The difference in spelling distinguishes these words, even though it does not affect their pronunciation. In Greek, the iota subscript often indicates a different function of a word that is spelled the same except for the iota subscript. For example, ἀγάπη would be used as a subject in a sentence, whereas ἀγάπῃ would likely function as an indirect object, although both Greek words are pronounced exactly the same.

41. Goetchius, *Language of the New Testament*, 9.

combination	transliteration	pronunciation
γγ	ng	ng as in fi**ng**er
γκ	nk	nk as in thi**nk**
γξ	nx	nx as in ly**nx**
γχ	nch	nch as in thi**nk**[1]

[1] The sound here is difficult for many English speakers to pronounce. If you have ever been to Scotland, the sound is closer to *Loch*. It is a deeper guttural sound than *k*.

The most common **gamma combination** is γγ. Thus, the Greek word ἄγγελος is pronounced ANG-ge-los. This is reflected in the English word derived from this Greek word, *angel*.

Consonant Classification

Letters in an alphabet can be divided between consonants and vowels. The sounds of consonants are formed by the shape of our mouth as air exits from our lungs. Some consonant sounds are formed when there is constriction of this airflow by some part of our mouth. For example, the "p" sound is made with a little burst of air after our lips have come together to stop the airflow from our lungs. (You can test this out by saying the word "put.") Other consonant sounds (such as the "th" or "z" sound) and all vowel sounds do not involve complete constriction of the airflow from the lungs. (Notice that singers hold vowel sounds—sometimes for a very long time, but they never hold a "p" sound!) Knowing how to classify consonant sounds is helpful because changes in form (**morphology**) to indicate a different function for a Greek word are determined by the types of preferred sounds in Greek (**phonology**).[42] We will talk about phonology as it is necessary, but for now you can read the "Going Deeper" box and begin to familiarize yourself with these concepts and classifications. This information will make some later concepts much easier to understand, so we will return to these classifications. You should not memorize this information, but if inquiring minds want to know why, then these concepts can be very helpful. You can also skip this box if you are feeling overwhelmed.

---

42. Every language prefers some sounds over others. For example, in English we don't like to begin words with a "ts" sound. So, the word *tsunami* (based on a Japanese word) is pronounced by most native English speakers as if it began with the letter s ("sooNAHmee"); yet we are happy to have this same sound at the end of a word, such as *cats*.

GOING DEEPER:
Consonant Classification

It is possible to classify consonant sounds based on the way in which the sounds they make are formed. We have already noted that some consonant sounds involve temporarily stopping the airflow from the lungs. Not surprisingly, these are often called **stops**. As we have noted, an example of a stop is the Greek letter π. Stops can be further divided according to where the airflow is constricted:

- **labials** stop the air with the lips; π and β are classified as labials;
- **dentals** stop the airflow just behind the upper front teeth (at a part of the mouth called the alveolar ridge); δ and τ are dentals;
- **gutturals** stop the airflow in the throat; γ and κ are gutturals.

Additionally, stops can be further divided between those sounds that involve the vibration of the vocal cords (voiced) and those that do not (voiceless). You can feel this by placing your hand on your throat. Now say the words "pat" and "bat"—did you *feel* a difference in the initial pronunciation of these two words?

Other consonant sounds are made with minimal constriction of the airflow from the lungs; these are called **fricatives**. Fricatives that involve an "s" sound are called **sibilants**. In Greek, unsurprisingly, σ is a sibilant and so is ζ. Two **double consonants**, ξ and ψ, are also sibilants. (Specifically, χ + σ = ξ, and π + σ = ψ.) Fricatives that involve an "h" sound are called **aspirates**; in Greek, these include θ, χ, and φ. **Nasal consonants** are formed when the airflow from the lungs flows through the nasal passage; in Greek, μ and ν are nasals. Finally, two consonants are called **liquids** (which are a bit more complicated to explain!): λ and ρ. Technically nasals and liquids are different categories, but they share similar properties and can sometimes be discussed together.

It is *not* necessary to memorize these classifications. But it is helpful to know them because morphology (reflected in spelling changes) in Greek is determined by phonology (the sounds, or pronunciation, of words).

For example, in some cases Greek adds a sigma to change the form of a word to indicate a new function for that word. The addition of this sigma causes predictable spelling changes (morphology) based on the types of sounds that are possible in Greek (phonology). We will come back to these concepts later.

CONSONANT CLASSIFICATION

	Labials	Dentals	Gutturals
Stops			
voiceless	π	τ	κ
voiced	β	δ	γ
Sibilants			
voiceless	ψ	σ	ξ
voiced		ζ	
Fricatives			
voiceless	φ	θ	χ
Nasals			
voiced	μ	ν	
Liquids			
voiced		λ, ρ	

Breathing Marks

In Greek, words that begin with vowels can sometimes be pronounced with an initial "h" sound (called *aspiration*). To indicate this "h" sound, a small mark is place over the initial vowel or the second vowel of a diphthong. This is called a **rough breathing mark** (or simply *rough breathing*) and looks like a single open single quotation mark ('). Every word that begins with a rho or upsilon has rough breathing. (This explains the spelling of some English words that are of Greek origin, such as *rh*etoric, *rh*yme, or *h*yper.) Words that begin with a vowel or diphthong that are not pronounced with an "h" sound use a **smooth breathing mark** (or simply *smooth breathing*), which looks like an apostrophe ('). The addition of this smooth breathing mark does not affect the pronunciation of the word and never occurs with a rho or upsilon. As you look at the examples below, note carefully the placement of breathing marks—immediately above lowercase letters, just to the left of uppercase letters, or above the second vowel of a word that begins with a diphthong.

SMOOTH BREATHING MARKS

	lowercase	uppercase	transliteration	gloss
initial vowel	ἐν	Ἐν	en	in
initial diphthong	εἰς	Εἰς	eis	for

ROUGH BREATHING MARKS

	lowercase	uppercase	transliteration	gloss
initial vowel	ἑν	Ἑν	hen	one
initial diphthong	εἱς	Εἱς	heis	one
initial upsilon	ὕδωρ	Ὕδωρ	hydōr	water
initial rho	ῥῆμα	Ῥῆμα	rhēma	word

There is some debate about the use of breathing marks among Greek scholars. The original manuscripts of the NT did not include them, so some scholars suggest that they should not be used today. Because some words are distinguished only by their breathing mark (e.g., ἐν and ἑν), however, we will use them in this book. This practice makes it easier to distinguish words when you are first learning Greek.

Punctuation

Certain marks are used to indicate punctuation in Greek. Even though the original manuscripts of the NT did not have these marks, they have been added to modern editions of the GNT. As we progress in this book, you will see that this punctuation is unnecessary. Languages, including Greek, have many ways of signaling the start of a new sentence or a question without using punctuation, although there are some cases in the NT where the intended punctuation is unclear. We'll discuss some examples of this later. For now, these punctuation marks make it easier to learn Greek. They should be memorized.

character	English form	Greek function
θεός,	comma	comma
θεός.	period	period
θεός·	dot above line	semicolon or colon
θεός;	semicolon	question mark

Diacritical Marks

As you look at a modern edition of the GNT, you will find some other marks (more accurately called **diacritical marks**).[43] These marks are used to indicate the following:

> **elision** (') – an apostrophe that is used to indicate the omission of a final short vowel in a word, usually when the next word begins with a vowel; for example, διὰ παντός (the final α of δία remains because the next word begins with a consonant), but δι᾽ αὐτοῦ (the final α of δία is dropped because the next word begins with a vowel).[44]
>
> **diaeresis** (¨) – this symbol indicates that two vowels that would normally form a diphthong should be pronounced separately; for example, α and ι would normally form a diphthong in Greek, but in the Greek spelling of the Hebrew name Isaiah, Ἠσαΐας, they do not. Without the diaeresis, the form Ἠσαιας would have three syllables (Ἠ-σαι-ας), but with this mark, Ἠσαΐας has four syllables (Ἠ-σα-ϊ-ας).
>
> **crasis** (᾽) – this symbol indicates a contraction of two words such that some letters have been dropped; for example, in Greek the form κἀγώ actually comes from two words καί ("and") and ἐγώ ("I"). This occurs with a limited number of words.

Accents

As with the other marks that we have seen, the original manuscripts of the NT did not include accents. Modern editions, however, include them. There are three accents that you will encounter: acute (´), grave (`), and circumflex (^ or ˜ or ᷠ).[45] Note that when accents and breathing marks occur on the same vowel, they are combined as follows: ῎, ῞, ῍, ῝, ῏, or ῟.

There is some debate as to whether accents should be taught in beginning Greek. We will include them in this book for the following reasons. First, they appear in the modern editions of the GNT that you will be using as you proceed in your Greek studies. Being familiar with these accents as you learn Greek will help you in the future. Second, some words are only distinguished by the presence

---

43. Technically the iota subscript is also considered a diacritical mark. Because of its importance in identifying certain syntactic forms, however, it has been discussed separately.

44. This is somewhat similar to the formation of contractions with some English verbs (e.g., I am → I'm). English also has ways of avoiding two vowel sounds together, such as the addition of an "n" to the indefinite article before a word that begins with a vowel (e.g., a banana, but **an** apple).

45. Various font types use different forms of the circumflex accent, so these are listed here for your reference.

of an accent. For example, the Greek word εἰ indicates "if," whereas the word εἶ is a verb form indicating "you are." Third, Greek accents can help in pronunciation in that they indicate the syllable to be stressed. Unless otherwise indicated, all accents should be treated as stress accents.[46] Fourth, accents (especially the circumflex accent) can be helpful in identifying certain verb forms. We'll discuss this later.

For the Curious

The system of Greek accents was developed about 200 BC by Aristophanes of Byzantium to help non-native Greek speakers pronounce Greek correctly, especially poetry.[47] This corresponds to the spread of Greek following the time of Alexander the Great. Originally the accents indicated a rising ('), falling (`), or rising/falling pitch (ˆ). Additional information is summarized in appendix 1, "Overview of Greek Accents."

Here is the second verse of the Gospel of Mark. Notice the breathing marks, accents, iota subscripts, diaeresis, and punctuation.

καθὼς γέγραπται ἐν τῷ Ἠσαΐᾳ τῷ προφήτῃ
Just as it is written in Isaiah the prophet

Syllabification

Syllabification refers to the process of identifying how to divide words into individual syllables. In Greek, each syllable must have one vowel or diphthong. Thus, the Greek word φωνή ("voice," "sound") has two syllables, as indicated by the hyphen: φω-νή. If two vowels are together and they *do not* form a diphthong, then there should be a syllable division between the two vowels. For example, the Greek word θεός ("god") has two syllables: θε-ός.

When two consonants occur together in a word (a **consonant cluster**), if they can begin a word in Greek, then they will begin a new syllable. For example, the syllables in ἀπόστολος ("apostle") are as follows: ἀ-πό-**στο**-λος (the consonant cluster is bolded). These consonant clusters are generally easy to identify (e.g., στ, θρ, πρ, τρ, σκ, etc.), although there are some clusters in Greek that have no

---

46. Although we don't use accents in English, certain words are distinguished by the stress that is placed on certain syllables. For example, the noun "permit" places the stress on the first syllable, whereas the verb "permit" stresses the second syllable. Consider the different ways that "permit" is pronounced in the following sentence: "I per*mit* you to buy a parking *per*mit." If we were to use accents to indicate this, we would spell the noun as follows: pérmit.

47. Cf. Goetchius, *Language of the New Testament*, 317n.2.

parallel in English (e.g., βδ, γν, κτ, μν, πν, πτ, φθ). A good example of a consonant cluster that occurs in Greek but not in English is γν; for example, the Greek
word ἐπίγνωσις ("knowledge") has four syllables: ἐ-πί-γνω-σις. If two consonants
together cannot begin a Greek word, then there is a syllable division between the
two letters. For example, the syllable division in καρδία is καρ-δί-α, because ρδ
cannot begin a new word in Greek. (Of course, it will take some time to become
familiar with consonant clusters that can begin a new word in Greek!) Double consonants are divided between the two consonants (e.g., the syllables in ἐκκλησία are
ἐκ-κλη-σί-α). Syllabification does not usually pose significant problems for English
speakers. Less obvious examples of syllabification will be discussed in passing.

REVIEW OF CHAPTER 1

In this chapter we began by considering the theological nature of language and the
uniqueness of human language. We then discussed some of the reasons why we need to
study Greek, including the need to bridge the distance to a different time and culture.
We took a brief tour of the Greek language and considered some of the reasons why
the Lord might have used it for the NT. We then focused on key grammatical terms
and linguistic concepts. Be sure to review these terms as we proceed in this book by
referring to this chapter and looking up terms in the glossary. It is especially important
that you know parts of speech well. Finally, we focused on the Greek alphabet and
related marks and concepts. There is a lot of new material in this chapter—resist
feeling overwhelmed! We will cycle back over this material again and again. Some
more encouragement—this is the longest chapter in the book. Chapter 2 is also fairly
technical and long, but after that you get to jump into actual Greek phrases from the NT!

Study Guide for Chapter 1

1. Be able to identify the meaning of each of the following terms. It will
   help if you can write terms down (either on paper or electronically) as
   you work through this list. You do not need to memorize the definition
   for each term; you simply need to recognize what these terms mean
   when they appear in subsequent chapters:

form	predicate	slot
function	sentence	filler
morpheme	noun	inflection

words	pronoun	declension
clauses	adjective	semantic range
phrases	verb	gloss
constructions	adverb	diphthong
main clause	preposition	iota subscript
independent clause	conjunction	gamma combination
subordinate clause	substantive	rough breathing mark
dependent clause	substantive modifier	smooth breathing mark
subject	verb modifier	

2. Be able to identify the part of speech for a given word. For example, consider this sentence: "God <u>loves</u> a cheerful giver." What is the part of speech for the underlined word? The correct answer is "verb."
3. Be able to label clauses as either main/independent or subordinate/dependent, as indicated in the following sentence:

> We are studying Greek, because we want to know God's Word better.

> <u>We are studying Greek</u> [main clause], because we want to know God's Word better.

> We are studying Greek, <u>because we want to know God's Word better</u> [dependent clause].

Vocabulary to Memorize

Here is the vocabulary that you need to memorize for this chapter. The first column lists the Greek words, and the second column gives possible glosses (if there are more than one). The number in parentheses indicates how many times the word occurs in the GNT. Names almost always have only one translation possibility. The letters that follow some nouns (e.g., -ας after Γαλιλαία) are endings that you will learn in chapter 4, followed by the article (e.g., ἡ after Γαλιλαία, -ας), which you will learn in chapter 5. For now, you can ignore anything after the first word listed. If, however, you are writing out vocabulary cards, you should copy the word and the endings exactly as they are listed below. This will save you time later.

Ἀβραάμ, ὁ	Abraham (73)
ἀμήν	amen, truly (129)
Γαλιλαία, -ας, ἡ	Galilee (61)
Δαυίδ, ὁ	David (59)
δέκα	ten (25)
δύο	two (135)
δώδεκα	twelve (75)
ἑπτά	seven (88)
ἰδού	look! see! (200)
Ἱεροσόλυμα, τά or ἡ	Jerusalem (62)
Ἱερουσαλήμ, ἡ	Jerusalem (77)
Ἰησοῦς, -οῦ, ὁ	Jesus; Joshua (917)
Ἰουδαῖος, -α, -ον	Jewish; a Jew (195)
Ἰσραήλ, ὁ	Israel (68)
Ἰωάννης, -ου, ὁ	John (135)
Μωϋσῆς, -έως, ὁ	Moses (80)
Παῦλος, -ου, ὁ	Paul (158)
πέντε	five (38)
Πέτρος, -ου, ὁ	Peter (156)
Πιλᾶτος, -ου, ὁ	Pilate (55)
Σατανᾶς, -ᾶ, ὁ	Satan, the adversary (36)
Σίμων, -ωνος, ὁ	Simon (75)
τέσσαρες	four (41)
τρίς	three times (12)
Φαρισαῖος, -ου, ὁ	Pharisee (98)

New Forms

Below are the new forms that were presented in this chapter. These are divided between those that you need to memorize and those that you need to recognize. For the forms that need to be memorized, they need to be memorized exactly. Be sure to know each form in isolation and not just its placement on a list. The more time you spend now memorizing the alphabet and the other assigned forms the easier the next few chapters will be! To test yourself, use a Greek example in this chapter and try to identify each letter and other assigned forms.

Forms to Memorize

THE KOINE GREEK ALPHABET

name	lowercase	uppercase	transliteration
alpha	α	A	a
beta	β	B	b
gamma	γ	Γ	g
delta	δ	Δ	d
epsilon	ε	E	e
zeta	ζ	Z	z
eta	η	H	ē
theta	θ	Θ	th
iota	ι	I	i
kappa	κ	K	k
lambda	λ	Λ	l
mu	μ	M	m
nu	ν	N	n
xi	ξ	Ξ	x
omicron	o	O	o
pi	π	Π	p
rho	ρ	P	r
sigma	σ/ς	Σ	s
tau	τ	T	t
upsilon	υ	Y	u/y
phi	φ	Φ	ph
chi	χ	X	ch
psi	ψ	Ψ	ps
omega	ω	Ω	ō

DIPHTHONGS

αι, ει, οι, υι

αυ, ου, ευ, ηυ

IOTA SUBSCRIPT
ᾳ, ῃ, ῳ

GAMMA COMBINATIONS
γγ, γκ, γξ, γχ

BREATHING MARKS

Rough breathing marks

	lowercase	uppercase
initial vowel	ἐν	Ἐν
initial diphthong	εἰς	Εἰς
initial upsilon	ὕδωρ	Ὕδωρ
initial rho	ῥῆμα	Ῥῆμα

Smooth breathing marks

	lowercase	uppercase
initial vowel	ἐν	Ἐν
initial diphthong	εἰς	Εἰς

Forms to Recognize

PUNCTUATION

character	Greek function
θεός,	comma
θεός.	period
θεός·	semicolon or colon
θεός;	question mark

DIACRITICAL MARKS
elision ('), diaeresis (¨), crasis (')

ACCENTS
acute ('), grave (`), circumflex (ˆor ˜ or ^)

chapter TWO

THE GREEK VERB FROM CRUISING ALTITUDE:
Fasten Your Seatbelts, Please!

OBJECTIVES AND OVERVIEW

Like chapter 1, this chapter covers a lot of important, introductory information about verbs. We will revisit all this information in various parts of the book, and often multiple times. Chapter 2 introduces the following linguistic concepts:

- verbal root, tense stem, and tense-form
- imperfective and perfective verbal aspect
- an overview of the six tense-forms used in Koine Greek: present, imperfect, future, aorist, perfect, and pluperfect
- verbal voice: active, middle, and passive
- equative, copulative, or linking verbs; predicate nominative and predicate adjective
- transitive and intransitive verbs
- ultimate and intermediate agency
- verbal person: first, second, and third
- verbal number: singular and plural
- finite and nonfinite verbs
- verbal mood: indicative, imperative, subjunctive, optative
- nonfinite verb forms: participle and infinitive
- negation adverb
- omega and μι verbs
- a more extensive introduction to verbal aspect

AN OVERVIEW OF THE GREEK VERB

In chapter 1, we defined a **verb** as that part of speech that indicates an action or a state of being. In this chapter, we consider basic concepts necessary to understand the Greek verbal system. This is a foundational chapter. We will cover a lot of material, but don't get overwhelmed. We will refer to this information many times. So consider this chapter like a thirty-thousand-foot flyover, with extended landings for each of these concepts at later points in the book.

A verb's most basic **morpheme** is called its **root**. We can think of the **root** in two ways. *Lexically*, the root indicates the specific action or state of being in view. For example, the root √βαλ indicates a "throwing" action. (The symbol √ indicates a **root**.) *Morphologically*, the root is the basis (or source) from which all the verb's forms derive. A **tense stem** indicates the most basic form of that root in a given tense-form. For example, the present tense stem for the root √βαλ is βαλλ-. (The hyphen at the end of a form, e.g., βαλλ-, indicates a tense stem.) This present tense stem is the stem to which other morphemes (such as connecting vowels and primary personal endings) are attached. Neither √βαλ nor βαλλ- is an actual Greek word—these are linguistic abstractions that help us discuss the bigger picture.

Sometimes *root* and *stem* are used interchangeably, but they are not the same. *Root* conveys the highest level of abstraction and indicates the most basic lexical meaning; often the same root can be used to construct both verb and noun forms by using different, but related, *stems*. Related verbs and nouns that are derived from this root are called **cognates**. For example, √σταλ is a lexical *root* that has to do with "sending." The verb ἀποστέλλω ("I send") is based on the root √σταλ but uses the stem στελλ-. Similarly, the noun ἀπόστολος ("one who is sent, apostle") is based on the root √σταλ but uses the stem στολ-.

Tense-Forms

For Greek verbs, there are four main stems that derive from a verbal root: present, future, aorist, and perfect. These are called *tense stems*. These stems are used to construct all the tense-forms of the entire verbal paradigm. Greek grammars have traditionally presented six tense-forms: present, imperfect, future, aorist, perfect, and pluperfect. This can be a bit confusing because two of the four main stems are used to construct more than one tense-form. Specifically, the present *stem* is used for both the present tense-form (which occurs in all verbal forms) and the imperfect tense-form (which occurs only in the indicative mood). Similarly, the perfect *stem* is used for both the perfect tense-form (which occurs in almost all verbal forms) and the pluperfect tense-form (which occurs only in the indicative mood). The metaphor of a tree is helpful at this point. On this tree (which as no leaves!), there is one root with four stems, two of which divide further.

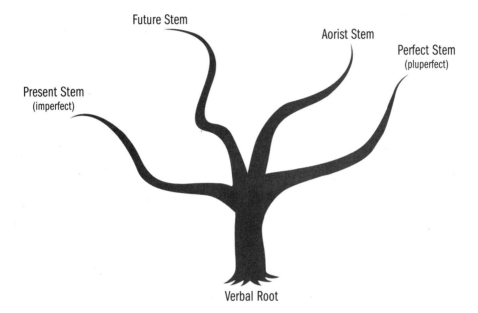

For the past several decades, there has been growing debate as to what exactly is conveyed by these tense-forms. For a long time, scholars claimed that the tense-forms in the indicative mood (which we will discuss later in this chapter) indicated time. These scholars aligned each of the tense-forms accordingly: past time (aorist, imperfect, pluperfect tense-forms), present time (present, perfect tense-forms), and future time (future tense-form). This seemed obvious because English (and many other Indo-European languages) is time based, so there was an apparently clear correlation between Greek verbs and English verbs. The problem, however, is that there are a lot of exceptions with this approach, such as the use of Greek "past tenses" to described events that are clearly future! You can read more about this at the end of this chapter, in the extended discussion of verbal aspect. For now, it is important to note that Greek tense-forms indicate *how* an action takes place (aspect) rather than *when* that action takes place (time).[1]

---

1. There are many other ways that Greek indicates *when* an action occurs, including adverbs and prepositional phrases, as well as the overall literary context. We will discuss this more fully when we talk about verbal aspect at the end of this chapter.

To illustrate this briefly, think of an important life event, perhaps your graduation. Now suppose that you have friends and family who live far away and will not be able to attend this great event in person. You can either send them a video of you walking across the stage or you can send them a photo of you receiving your diploma from the university's president. The video shows the event as it unfolds, whereas the photo shows one point in the event—though no one would think that the entire graduation lasted only for the brief second captured in the photo. So the video focuses on the duration or "ongoingness" of the event, whereas the photo offers a summary of the event as a whole. For various reasons, you may decide to send some people a video and others a photo. When considering Greek verbs, **verbal aspect** indicates how the speaker or writer wants an audience or reader to view the action—in other words, whether they are "sending" a video or a photo. We will use these concepts in our discussion of tense-forms below.

Present Tense-Form

The **present tense-form** presents an action as ongoing, continuous, or progressing. This is like a video of an event. This tense-form indicates **imperfective aspect**. It is as if we are "inside" the event, watching the action unfold. We are not really concerned about the beginning or the end of the action but rather that it is taking place as we watch it. Sometimes the present tense-form is used in narratives (which describe *past* events) to draw attention to an event or to introduce a dialogue. The present tense-form is also common *within* dialogue, or direct discourse. The present tense-form occurs in all verbal moods (indicative, imperative, subjunctive, and optative) and all verbal forms (participle and infinitive), all of which we will discuss further below. We will begin to learn the present indicative in the next chapter.

Imperfect Tense-Form

The **imperfect tense-form** is constructed by using the present stem. Hence the imperfect tense-form has the same imperfective aspect as the present tense-form (ongoing, continuous, internal), because verbal aspect is indicated by the tense stem. The imperfect tense-form also uses an **augment**. All scholars agree that the augment is a morpheme that consists of an epsilon (ε-) that is prefixed to the front of certain tense stems and that the augmented tense-forms are the imperfect, the aorist, and the pluperfect. There is much debate, however, surrounding the origin and function of the augment. Specifically, what is debated is the relation of the augment to time. We will discuss this further in future chapters. The imperfect tense-form *only* occurs in the indicative mood and can indicate an action that was attempted or habitual. It can sometimes indicate "background information" in a narrative account.[2] We will begin to learn the imperfect indicative in chapter 7.

Future Tense-Form

The **future tense-form** occurs in the indicative mood and a limited number of participles and infinitives. It indicates a sense of expectation. The verbal aspect of the future tense-form is debated, and some claim that it has no aspect at all.[3] Others suggest that this is the only indicative-mood tense-form that is time based because it indicates actual future time.[4] We will discuss this further in chapter 19.

Aorist Tense-Form

The **aorist tense-form** is the most frequent tense-form in the GNT. Like the present tense-form, the aorist tense-form occurs in all verbal moods (indicative, imperative, subjunctive, and optative) and all verbal forms (participle and infinitive). The word *aorist* indicates an "undefined" action;[5] in other words, the focus is not on the duration of an event but simply that an action occurred. This is called **perfective aspect**. This is the difference between a video (imperfective aspect; ongoing account of an event) and a photo (perfective aspect; the event captured in its entirety). Thus, the aorist portrays an action as a summary, and the action is viewed externally. We are not in the midst of an event but rather are viewing or considering it from some distance. The aorist indicative is often used in narrative, where it indicates "mainline events," or the main events that carry a narrative along.[6] We will begin to learn the aorist indicative in chapter 10.

Perfect Tense-Form

The **perfect tense-form** is not as common as the present or aorist tense-forms; hence it often reflects a deliberate choice on the part of the writer or speaker. In the NT, the perfect occurs mainly in the indicative, infrequently in the imperative and subjunctive, as well as in a limited number of participle and infinitive verbal forms. The perfect tense-form may indicate some type of

---

2. Constantine R. Campbell, *Basics of Verbal Aspect in Biblical Greek* (Grand Rapids: Zondervan, 2008), 45.

3. Stanley E. Porter, *Idioms of the Greek New Testament* (Sheffield: Sheffield Academic Press, 1999), 43.

4. Campbell, *Basics of Verbal Aspect*, 39.

5. Note that *aorist* (from the Greek ἀόριστος) is a two-syllable word that is pronounced "air-rist."

6. Campbell, *Basics of Verbal Aspect*, 38–39.

emphasis.[7] It can also indicate a summary, perhaps a past action that has ongoing results, but the focus is often on the resulting state of this past action.[8] The past action may or may not be completed.[9] Greek perfects are often translated as English perfects (e.g., "I have seen"). We will begin to learn about the perfect tense-form in chapter 16.

Pluperfect Tense-Form

The **pluperfect tense-form** is the least common tense-form in the NT, with only eighty-six occurrences, and only in the indicative mood. The pluperfect is constructed using the perfect tense-stem, so it communicates the same aspect as the perfect. In narrative, the pluperfect is used to indicate an action that began in the past and continued until some point in the past, but which ceased at some point in the past.[10] We will learn about the pluperfect indicative in chapter 16.

Verbal Voice

Verbal voice indicates how the subject is related to the action of the verb in a clause or sentence.[11] In other words, voice indicates whether a subject acts or is acted upon. In Greek, there are three voices: active, middle, and passive.

Active Voice

In the **active voice**, the subject *performs*, *produces*, or *experiences* the action of the verb. For example, "God sent the Son." The active voice may also indicate that the subject exists in a "state"; this occurs with **equative verbs** or some **intransitive verbs** (which we discuss below). For example, "we *are* Christians" or "we *are* blessed."

---

7. Campbell claims that the perfect tense-form indicates "heightened proximity"; e.g., a perspective that is "closer" to the action than a present tense-form, which indicates *proximity*, or spatial or temporal "nearness" (*Basics of Verbal Aspect*, 50). We will discuss some of this in the second part of this chapter. The aspect of the perfect tense-form is extensively debated. We will discuss this further in chapter 16.

8. This approach is presented in Buist M. Fanning, *Verbal Aspect in New Testament Greek*, Oxford Theological Monographs (Oxford: Clarendon, 1990), 119.

9. Some call the aspect of the perfect tense-form "stative" (e.g., Porter, *Idioms of the Greek New Testament*, 21–22), but this term is not clearly defined and is debated by many. Hence, we will not use this term in this book.

10. Campbell (*Basics of Verbal Aspect*, 51–52) notes the pluperfect may indicate "heightened remoteness" (e.g., a perspective further removed than the "remoteness" of the imperfect tense-form).

11. Porter et al. further specifies this in terms of causation: "Verbal voice is a formal feature of the Greek verb that is used to describe *the relation of the grammatical subject to the cause of the action of the verb*" (Stanley E. Porter, Jeffrey T. Reed, and Matthew Brook O'Donnell, *Fundamentals of New Testament Greek* [Grand Rapids: Eerdmans, 2010], 40, italics original). Causation is important and will be discussed further in a future chapter.

Middle Voice

There is no exact parallel to the Greek **middle voice** in English. In the middle voice, the subject *performs* or *experiences* the action expressed by the verb in such a way that *emphasizes the subject's participation*. Whereas the active voice stresses *the action*, the middle voice stresses *the actor*.[12] It is easy to equate the middle voice with a reflexive idea (the subject performs an action upon itself: e.g., "I wash my hands"), but this is *not* the primary function of the middle voice. The middle voice is not easy to render in English. There is no single translation equivalent that can be applied uniformly; instead, translation depends on the context and the actual verb that is used. We will discuss the middle voice more extensively in the next chapter.

Passive Voice

In the **passive voice**, *the subject is acted upon* or *receives* the action of the verb. For example, "The Son is sent by God."[13] We can distinguish between **ultimate agency** (or primary agency), which refers to the one who is ultimately responsible for an action, and **intermediate agency** (or secondary agency), which refers to the one who carries out an action for the ultimate agent. We will discuss this more in chapter 11. Finally, sometimes agency is not expressed, but is implied; this may involve the so-called "divine" or "theological" passive. For example, in Matthew 5:4, we read, "Blessed are those who mourn, for they will be comforted." The text does not state who comforts, but the context makes clear that it is God.

Transitive and Intransitive Verbs

Transitivity is a concept that is related to voice. In **transitive verbs**, the action of the verb is performed by the subject and affects the object in some way—the action is somehow "transferred" on to an object or an indirect object. For example, "The child [the subject performing the action] hugged [the action performed] the dog [the object affected by action]," or, "We [the subject performing the action] read [the action performed] the book [the object affected by the action]." Transitive verbs without an object do not express a complete thought—they leave us asking "what?" For example, "The child hugged." *What did the child hug?* Or, "We read." *What did we read?* Transitive verbs can also be made into

---

12. Wallace, *Greek Grammar beyond the Basics*, 182. Porter (*Idioms of the Greek New Testament*, 67) adds that "the Greek middle voice expressed more direct participation, specific involvement, or even some form of benefit of the subject doing the action."

13. Often a prepositional phrase will occur with the passive voice, indicating the agent who performs the verbal action; e.g., "by God."

a passive construction in which the action is performed *upon* the subject. For example, "The dog [the object acted upon] was hugged [the action performed] by the child [the subject performing the action]," or, "The book [the object acted upon] was read [the action performed] by us [the subject performing the action]."

With **intransitive verbs**, the action performed by the subject does not affect an object. In fact, intransitive verbs cannot take a direct object. Notice that we cannot say, "We go Greece," or "We arrive Bible." Moreover, intransitive verbs cannot be made into a passive; we cannot say "we are go-ed." Furthermore, intransitive verbs make sense standing alone; for example, "I go" or "I remain." Often, however, adverbs or prepositional phrases occur with intransitive verbs; for example, "I go quickly" or "I remain in Christ," but "quickly" and "in Christ" are not functioning as objects of these verbs.

Verbal Person and Number

Verbal person indicates the relationship between the subject and the verb. **First person** means that the subject is the one who is speaking or writing; for example, "*I* read the Bible." **Second person** means that the subject is being addressed; for example, "*You* read the Bible." **Third person** means that the subject is being spoken or written about; for example, "*she* reads the Bible" or "*they* read the Bible." This last example also shows that subjects and verbs can either be singular or plural. This is called **verbal number**. Subjects and verbs usually agree (**agreement**) in person and number in Greek; this is similar to English. Thus, a singular subject takes a singular verb ("he speaks"), and a plural subject takes a plural verb ("they speak"). There are a few exceptions to this in Greek that we will discuss later (e.g., some plural nouns sometimes take a singular verb). Finally, some verbs are called **impersonal verbs**, because they only occur in the third-person singular; for example, "it is necessary," or "it is lawful."

Finite verbs are verbs that are inflected to indicate person and number.[14] (Recall that an **inflection** is any change in **form** to indicate a change in **function**.) Finite verbs occur in the four Greek verbal moods, which are discussed in the next section. There are also two verbal forms (participles and infinitives) that are **nonfinite** because they are not inflected to indicate person, although participles can be either singular or plural. Recall from chapter 1 that a clause contains a subject-verb combination. In Greek, clauses often contain (or assume) finite verbs, although they can also contain a participle or infinitive. Also recall

---

14. Finite verbs are so-called because they are "limited" by person and number as opposed to nonfinite verb forms, such as an infinitive, which can discuss a verbal concept or action without associating it with a specific subject.

that clauses can be either main (or independent) or subordinate (or dependent). Sometimes beginning students associate finite verbs only with main clauses, but it is important to understand that finite verbs can appear in either main or subordinate clauses. We will stress this throughout the book.

Verbal Mood

Verbal mood has nothing to do with good, bad, happy, or sad. Instead, verbal **mood** indicates how the speaker chooses to portray the actuality or potentiality of an event.[15] This does not represent the speaker's *perception* of reality, nor does it necessarily correspond to *objective* reality. Instead mood has to do with the manner in which a statement is made and not necessarily with the truth of a statement. In Greek, there are four moods that correspond with finite verbs.

The **indicative mood** makes an assertion or statement that is presented as if it were true. This is the presentation of a certainty. Often, this statement may in fact be true. But lies are presented as if they were true and hence use the indicative mood! It is inaccurate, therefore, to think of the indicative as the mood of reality or fact. A question using the indicative mood is asking an information-seeking question, or a question that could be answered with an indicative statement. For example, if we ask, "Where is Capernaum?" then the answer would be, "Capernaum is on the northern shore of the Sea of Galilee." The indicative is the most frequent mood in the NT and is thus the "default" mood.[16]

The **imperative mood** is the mood of intention and involves volition; it is the attempt to direct someone's will or actions. A **command** is the most common use of the imperative. A **prohibition** (or negative command) forbids an action. The imperative can also be used for requests or exhortations.

The **subjunctive mood** is the mood of probability or potentiality; it indicates an action that is uncertain but probable. It can indicate a hypothetical situation. A question using the subjunctive mood is often rhetorical. For example, if we ask, "What could a person give in exchange for his or her soul?" the answer is "nothing!" The question was not asked to obtain information but rather to make a point.

The **optative mood** is the mood of possibility or (strong) contingency. It occurs in a prayer or to express a wish. The optative is the least common Greek mood in the GNT.[17]

---

15. David Alan Black, *It's Still Greek to Me* (Grand Rapids: Baker, 1998), 97.

16. Sometimes moods other than the indicative (i.e., imperative, subjunctive, and optative) are collectively referred to as **oblique moods**.

17. The subjunctive began to replace the optative, making the optative less frequent in Koine. There are about sixty-five examples of the optative in the GNT.

Nonfinite Verb Forms

Nonfinite verb forms are not inflected to indicate person and number. There are two such forms in Greek. The **infinitive** is a *verbal noun*. Like *verbs*, infinitives have tense-forms and voice, but they do not have person and mood. Like *nouns*, infinitives may function as a subject or an object.

The **participle** is a *verbal adjective*. Like *verbs*, participles have tense-forms and voice, but they do not have person and mood. Like *adjectives*, participles have case, number, and gender. Participle endings follow first, second, or third declension noun patterns.[18] Participles often function either adverbially (and are dependent on another verb form) or attributively (and modify a substantive). They may also function as a substantive. We will address attributive and substantival functions in chapter 5.

Equative Verbs

Finally, some verbs "link" a subject with some type of predication about that subject. These verbs are referred to as **equative**, **copulative**, or **linking verbs**. For example, consider the clause: "God is love." "Love" is not a direct object, because the verb "is" does not indicate that the subject is acting upon the object. Instead, this verb is making a predication, or statement, about God. In this example, "love" is a **predicate nominative** because "love" is a noun.[19] If we change the sentence to "God is faithful," then "faithful" would be called a **predicate adjective** because "faithful" is an adjective. We will discuss all these concepts in the next few chapters.

Basic Adverbs—Negation

Adverbs are words that are used to modify verbs. In English, these are often words that end in -ly, such as "quickly" or "slowly." A very basic Greek adverb, οὐ, indicates negation. For indicative verbs, οὐ is placed before a verb to negate it. For example, λύω could be translated "I release," whereas οὐ λύω would be translated "I do not release."

There are two additional forms of οὐ that are used when this adverb precedes a verbal form that begins with a vowel. (Remember that Greek tries to avoid having one word end with a vowel if the next word begins with a vowel. Changes in morphology [form] are nearly always explained by phonology [sound patterns]). The form οὐκ is used if the next word begins with a vowel that has smooth breathing.

---

18. We will learn about first and second declension noun paradigms in chapter 4. You can also review the discussion of declensions in chapter 1.

19. This is sometimes called a predicate noun or a subject complement. There are also **predicate pronouns** (e.g., "he is mine").

For example, with the verb ἀποστέλλω ("I send"), the negation would be οὐκ ἀποστέλλω ("I do not send"). Phonology also explains the morphology of the form οὐχ that is used before verbal forms that begin with rough breathing.[20] Hence the negation of the verb εὑρίσκω ("I find") would be οὐχ εὑρίσκω ("I do not find").

The negative adverb οὐ (with the related forms οὐκ and οὐχ) is almost always used with indicative verbs. There is another adverb for negation, μή, that is used with nonindicative verbs (i.e., imperative, subjunctive, and optative) and nonfinite verbal forms (i.e., infinitives and participles). We will see examples of this in future chapters.

Classes of Verbs

There are two main classes of verbs in Koine Greek. To begin with, we will focus on **omega verbs**. Not surprisingly, these verbs end with an omega in the form that is listed in a lexicon; for example, λύω. This is the most common class of verbs in the GNT. Verbs that do not have an active form (and have the ending -ομαι in a lexicon, such as ἔρχομαι, "I come") are also classified as omega verbs.

The other class of verbs is μι **verbs**. These are remnants of an older pattern of verb formation that uses different endings for some verb forms. There are fewer verbs in the GNT that belong to this class of verbs, but the verbs that do occur are very common. For example, the verb εἰμί ("I am") occurs in some form on every page of the GNT! We will begin to learn this verb in chapter 5; we will learn other common μι verbs (such as δίδωμι, "I give," and τίθημι, "I place") in chapters 24 and 25. Because the verbs are common, there will be pointers to chapters 24 and 25 before we actually cover those chapters. This will enable you to begin to recognize these verb forms even before you actually memorize them.

INTRODUCTION TO KOINE GREEK VERBS AND VERBAL ASPECT[21]

With English verbs, **tense** refers to time because English has a time-based verbal system. This means that past-tense verbs in English indicate past time, present-tense verbs in English indicate present time, and future-tense verbs in English indicate future time. English can also indicate how an action is conceived of taking place, whether it is a simple or continuous action. Consider the following examples.

---

20. If you are curious, the voiceless κ assimilates to a corresponding aspirate, χ; see the discussion of consonant classification in chapter 1.

21. We have covered a lot of information in this chapter. If you are feeling overwhelmed, you can skip this final section of the chapter and concentrate on the information presented in the first part of the chapter. You can come back and read this section later when you are feeling less overwhelmed. If you do decide to venture forth, know that we will talk about this more in future chapters. This is only an introduction to a much bigger topic.

	past tense	present tense	future tense
simple	I saw	I see	I will see
continuous	I was seeing	I am seeing	I will be seeing
perfect	I had seen	I have seen	I will have seen

For a long time, many assumed that Koine Greek verbs were also time based, particularly for indicative mood verbs. (We will talk more about nonindicative verbs and their relation to time in future chapters.) Thus, older Greek grammars claimed that the present tense-form in Greek indicated an action that occurred in the present time (present with regard to the speaker or writer); the aorist tense-form and the imperfect tense-form indicated past actions. On this view, the perfect tense-form indicated a past action with ongoing results to the present time of the speaker or writer, whereas the pluperfect indicated a past action that had ongoing results to some past point in time. Finally, the future could indicate a simple or continuous future event. There have been significant challenges to this understanding of Greek verbs, however.

In English, verbs can also indicate aspect, or the "kind of time," although English grammars do not always discuss aspect as clearly as they do tense. **Continuous aspect** indicates an action that is ongoing, whereas simple aspect does not. Consider the following two sentences.

I walked yesterday. (simple past)
I was walking yesterday. (past continuous)

The first sentence indicates an action in a summary fashion. If someone asks you what you did yesterday, you might answer, "I walked yesterday." This is an example of a *simple past* in English. There is no indication of how long you walked, just the statement that you did walk. The conversation might move on to another topic after this. Now consider the second sentence, "I was walking yesterday." This is an example of a *past continuous* in English. If you were to answer the same question about what you did yesterday this way, the person asking would probably expect you to keep on going. For example, you might answer, "I was walking yesterday when you texted me." In these examples, it is clear that English *can* indicate different ways of portraying the same action by means of **verbal aspect** and that English writers or speakers choose which aspect they want to use to describe an action depending on the larger context of what they want to communicate.

As noted, there has been a tendency to align the Greek verbal system with the understanding of aspect in English.[22] Some claim that the aorist tense-form indicates the simple past, whereas the imperfect tense-form communicates a past continuous action. Moreover, some traditional views also claim that verb tense-forms depict actions "objectively," meaning that an aorist tense-form was used because the action occurred "once-for-all," or that a perfect tense-form was used because a past action had ongoing results. At this point, we need to get a bit more technical. There are two terms that are distinct, but which are sometimes confused and discussed in unhelpful ways. **Aspect** involves how a speaker or writer chooses to portray an action; it is the *subjective* viewpoint of the speaker or writer. *Aktionsart* is a German term associated with "kind of action." *Aktionsart* involves how an action *objectively* occurs. For example, some actions can only be understood as a "point in time" kind of action, such as "to throw" or "to strike." This type of action is sometimes called *punctiliar* action. Unfortunately, *punctiliar* has often been associated with the aorist tense-form in unhelpful ways.[23] Some verbs may communicate a "point in time" idea (as noted with "to throw" or "to strike"), but this type of action is due to the actual verb itself and *not* the use of the aorist tense-form.

At this point, it is helpful to introduce the field of **lexical semantics**, which includes the study of the range of meanings that a word can have. Regarding verbs, some verbs depict actions that are inherently durative, such as "to rain" or "to breathe." Other verbs, however, indicate actions that are punctiliar—they occur at a specific point in time, such as "to hit" or "to kick." Finally, other verbs indicate a stative (or "state of being") idea, such as "to exist" or "to know." Thus, an author or speaker may choose to portray a given action by means of aspect, although that choice may be limited by the inherent type of action associated with a given verb (lexical semantics). The choice of how to portray an action may also be constrained by the larger context in view (such as a dialogue or a narrative), but we'll talk about that more later.

There has been a significant shift in understanding the Koine Greek verbal system in recent decades. This does not mean that Koine Greek has changed but rather that our understanding of Koine Greek has been expanding and is being refined. Increasingly, many scholars today do not believe that the Koine Greek verbal system is time-based. Rather, they believe that **verbal aspect** indicates a speaker's or writer's choice (sometimes subconscious) of how to portray an event. Recall the example of sending someone a video clip (imperfective aspect) of your graduation or simply a picture (perfective aspect). This is a *choice* on your part as to how to share this event with others.

---

22. Earlier, Koine Greek was often aligned with Latin or German verbal categories. This cannot be developed further here, but this also imposed certain ideas onto Greek that are unhelpful.

23. We will talk more about this later in this chapter and in the chapter on the aorist tense-form. For further discussion, see Campbell, *Basics of Verbal Aspect*, 13–16.

An aspectual approach to Greek verbs claims that aspect is a semantic feature of a verbal tense stem, which means that aspect is an essential, or uncancelable (i.e., no exceptions or counterexamples exist), feature of a tense stem. This means that the aspect of a given tense stem will be evident in any occurrence of that tense stem. For example, imperfective aspect is always evident whenever the present stem occurs as well as in any form that is built on the present stem, such as the imperfect tense-form. **Pragmatics**, on the other hand, refers to the context-specific functions of a tense stem, which may not be evident in *every occurrence* of that tense stem. Thus, the meaning (or **semantics**) of the present tense-form is not necessarily *present* time. To be more precise, the present tense-form does not indicate present time *without exception*; so present time is not an *uncancelable* feature of the present tense-form. In fact, the present tense-form can be used to indicate past action (as in narratives, especially in Mark's Gospel). Therefore, the present tense cannot *mean* (as a semantic feature) *present* time. Similarly, the aorist tense-form does not *mean* (as a semantic feature) *past* time. Instead Koine Greek verbs are aspect-based. That said, however, the present tense-form is well-suited for contexts that occur at a time present to the time of the writer or speaker, such as dialogue. This explains why dialogues have a high percentage of present tense-forms. Similarly, the aorist-tense form is well-suited to summarize, so it is unsurprising that narrative accounts of past actions contain a high percentage of aorist tense-forms. But this is not the same as to claim that present tense-forms *must* indicate present time and that aorist tense-forms *must* indicate past time. This may seem like splitting hairs, but an incorrect understanding of the verbal system will ultimately hinder interpretation.

An aspectual approach to Koine Greek verbs does not suggest that Greek speakers had no sense of time! It simply means that the verb *tense-forms* do not necessarily (semantically) align with past, present, or future time. Instead, Greek uses temporal markers, such as adverbs (e.g., "now" or "yesterday") and prepositional phrases (e.g., "on the third day"), or the overall context (e.g., a narrative that recounts a past event) to indicate time. It is also important to understand that this shift in more recent approaches to studying Koine Greek verbs was primarily based on careful observation of several phenomena in Koine Greek. One such phenomenon is that the same "tense," such as the present tense-form, can be used to describe past, present, and future events in the GNT. For example, in Mark 11:27 the present tense-form ἔρχονται ("they come") is used in a narrative account to portray an event (Jesus and the disciples arriving in Jerusalem) that clearly took place in the past from the point of view of the writer (Mark). In Matthew 8:25, however, the present tense-form ἀπολλύμεθα ("we are perishing!") is used to portray an event that is taking place in the present time from the point of view of the speakers (the disciples in the boat during a terrifying storm).[24] (Notice also that this occurs in a dialogue.) Another indicator that Koine Greek is not semantically time based is found in Synoptic Gospel accounts that use different tense-forms to portray the *same* event. For example, in the account of Jesus calling Levi, Luke 5:27 introduces Jesus's dialogue with Levi using the aorist tense-form (εἶπεν), whereas Mark 2:14 uses the present tense-form (λέγει) to describe this same event. These examples, and many others, pose significant challenges to time-based understandings of Koine Greek verbs and have pointed toward an aspectual approach.

Verbal aspect, therefore, primarily concerns how a writer or speaker chooses to portray an action. A helpful definition of verbal aspect is "the speaker's or writer's perspective on the action of a verb; aspect is expressed by the selection of a particular tense-form."[25] There are two undebated aspects in Koine Greek. The **imperfective aspect** views an action in progress; it gives an internal point of view. The action is portrayed as progressive or ongoing. The present tense-form and the imperfect tense-form indicate this aspect. The **perfective aspect** views an action as undefined or summary, with no indication of the duration of the action; it gives an external point of view. This is the aspect communicated by the aorist tense-form. Some scholars posit a third aspect, the **stative aspect**, which presents an existing state of affairs or being. The perfect tense-form and the pluperfect tense-form may indicate this aspect.[26] Others, however, challenge this view and claim that the perfect tense-form and pluperfect tense-form also communicate imperfective aspect.[27] It is quite possible that the perfect tense has more of a rhetorical function and indicates a summary or some type of emphasis. We will discuss this further in the chapter on the perfect and pluperfect tense-forms.

Several analogies are suggested to help envision verbal aspect. For example, one might think of a parade: the view from the spectators along the street is internal, or an imperfective aspect (you're there, watching the parade pass by), whereas a helicopter above the parade views the entire parade as a whole from an external or perfective aspect.[28] Or perhaps one might think of a theater stage: the set depicts the stage as a whole (perfective aspect), whereas the actors are in the midst of the scene as it unfolds (imperfective aspect); there may even be an actor delivering a monologue who is in the spotlight at

---

24. These examples are from Stanley E. Porter, *Verbal Aspect in the Greek New Testament with Reference to Tense and Mood*, Studies in Biblical Greek 1 (New York: Peter Lang, 1989), 75.

25. Porter, Reed, and O'Donnell, *Fundamentals of New Testament Greek*, 33.

26. So, e.g., Porter, Reed, and O'Donnell, *Fundamentals of New Testament Greek*, xix, 33.

27. Campbell, *Basics of Verbal Aspect*, 50–52. See also the discussion of "heightened proximity" and "heightened remoteness" in the earlier discussion in this chapter.

28. Porter, *Idioms of the Greek New Testament*, 24.

the front of the stage (the "heightened proximity" of the perfect tense-form).[29]

Despite the differing approaches to the Koine Greek verbal system, most scholars agree that the oblique moods (subjunctive, imperative, optative) and nonfinite verbal forms (infinitives and participles) are *not* time based. We will discuss this further when each of these moods and verbal forms is covered.

Finally, the goal of this discussion is not to complicate your life but to show that scholars continue to understand Koine Greek more precisely with the goal of understanding the language as first-century speakers and writers would have understood it. Thus, if the original audience of the GNT did not conceive of Greek verb tense-forms as communicating past, present, or future time, we may miss important insights into the GNT if we conceive of Greek verbs in this temporal way. Unfortunately, this discussion is further complicated because the terms used to describe the different Greek verb forms suggest that the forms *are* time based. For example, the "present tense" would seem logically to refer to the present time! This unfortunate nomenclature has a history of its own, so for now, it is not likely to change. For this reason, in the book we will always include the word "form" when discussing various tenses in Greek; e.g., "present tense-form," "aorist tense-form," etc.

One final issue that needs to be addressed is how to translate verbs from an aspect-based system (Greek) into a time-based system (English). As we've seen, a present tense-form of a verb in the GNT could be translated as past referring in one context, present referring in another context, and future referring in yet another context! While you are beginning to learn Greek, however, you will need to translate present tense-forms with either an English simple present tense or an English present continuous tense to indicate that you have correctly identified Greek present tense-*form*. So, for example, for the present tense-form βλέπω, you would need to give an inflected meaning of either "I see" (English simple present) or "I am seeing" (English continuous present). It can be difficult to know how to render a given Greek verbal form into English; for help, please refer to the "Guide for Translating Greek Finite Verbs" (app. 7).

REVIEW OF CHAPTER 2

In this chapter we have flown over a lot of ground! Because there is so much to grasp at the conceptual level, there are no new paradigms to learn for this chapter (there are limits to what the human brain can absorb!). We began by noting the difference between a verbal root and the four verbal stems, which are used to construct the six tense-forms in Greek: present, imperfect, future, aorist, perfect, and

---

29. The term "heightened proximity" is from Campbell, *Basics of Verbal Aspect*, 51–52. The theater analogy is my own.

pluperfect. We then surveyed each of these tense-forms. We also introduced the concept of verbal aspect and aligned the tense-forms with the two main aspects: imperfective and perfective. From there, we discussed the following essential concepts for understanding verbs: verbal voice (active, middle, and passive; and the related transitive and intransitive verbs); verbal person (first, second, and third) and number (singular and plural); and verbal mood, which distinguished between finite verbs (inflected for person and number and occurring in the indicative, imperative, subjunctive, and optative moods) and nonfinite verb forms (participle and infinitive). Finally, we presented the adverbs used for negation (οὐ and μή) and presented the two main classes of verbs in the GNT (omega and μι).

The second part of the chapter focused on a more technical discussion of verbal aspect, including the concepts of lexical semantics and pragmatics. This section traced developments that have led to a shift from a time-based understanding of Koine Greek verbs to an aspectual one that posits at least two main aspects: imperfective and perfective.

Study Guide for Chapter 2

1. Be able to understand each of the following concepts for the Greek verbal system:

> verbal roots and tense stems
> cognates
> tense-forms (present, imperfect, future, aorist, perfect, pluperfect)
> verbal voice (active, middle, passive)
> transitive and intransitive verbs
> verbal person and number
> verbal mood (indicative, imperative, subjunctive, optative)
> finite and nonfinite verb forms
> equative verbs
> basic negation
> imperfective aspect
> perfective aspect

Vocabulary to Memorize

Here is the vocabulary that you need to memorize for this chapter. This list is mostly verbs, plus three very common conjunctions. You will notice that there is not one single English word "assigned" to each Greek word, just as you may have observed in chapter 1. This is because Greek words often have a range of meanings. You do not have to memorize all the possible glosses, but you should avoid thinking that only one English word is the "meaning" of a given Greek word. Your knowledge of given Greek words will expand as you spend more time with the NT text, so don't despair when you see the many options for rendering a Greek word into English. For practical purposes, any option listed here would be an acceptable answer for a vocabulary quiz that your professor assigns. Each of the verbs is a present active first-person singular form, which is how verbs are listed in a Greek lexicon. In English, we usually refer to a specific verb using the infinitive (e.g., the verb "to be"), but this is not true for Greek. Instead you need to memorize the corresponding present indicative first-person singular English (e.g., a gloss for ἄγω is "I lead" not "to lead").

ἄγω	I lead, I bring, I go, I arrest (67)
αἴρω	I take, I take up, I take away, I remove (101)
ἀκούω	I hear, I listen to, I obey, I understand (428)
ἀλλά	but, yet (638)
ἀποστέλλω	I send, I send out, I send away (132)
βάλλω	I throw, I put (122)
βαπτίζω	I baptize (77)
βλέπω	I see, I look at (133)
γινώσκω	I know, I learn, I understand (222)
γράφω	I write (191)
δέ	but, now, and, on the other hand (2,792)
διδάσκω	I teach (97)
δοξάζω	I glorify, I praise, I honor (61)
ἐσθίω	I eat (158)
εὑρίσκω	I find, I discover (176)
ἔχω	I have, I hold (708)
καί	and, even, also (9,161)
κηρύσσω	I proclaim, I preach (61)
λαμβάνω	I take, I receive, I obtain (258)
λέγω	I say, I speak, I tell (2,354)
λύω	I untie, I release, I destroy (42)
πείθω	I persuade; I trust (pf) (52)[1]
πέμπω	I send (79)
πιστεύω	(+dat)[2] I believe, I have faith; with εἰς +acc[3] = I believe in (241)
σῴζω	I save, I rescue, I deliver (106)

[1] Some verbs have different meanings in different tense-forms. In the perfect tense-form, πείθω has the meaning "I trust."

[2] Some verbs have objects that are not in the accusative case, which we will learn about in ch. 4. Here "+dat" means that the verb has an object in the dative case.

[3] Some verbs have different meanings depending on the case of the noun that follows them. We will talk about this later, but "εἰς +acc" means followed by the preposition εἰς and a noun in the accusative case. We will talk about prepositions later.

chapter THREE

HOW TO BUILD A VERB:
The Present Active and Middle Indicative

OBJECTIVES AND OVERVIEW

In chapter 3, we focus on the form of the present active and middle indicative. Chapter 3 introduces the following linguistic concepts and morphemes:

- primary active and middle personal endings
- connecting vowel
- inflected form and meaning
- primary tenses
- verb paradigm
- movable nu
- indirect and direct middle-voice functions
- "deponency"
- lexical form for verbs and parsing

FIELD STUDY AND BUILDING BLOCKS

You have probably never thought about "building" a verb before, but you actually do this all the time. Recall from the discussion in chapter 1 that a **morpheme** is the smallest language element that has meaning. These are the components (or building blocks) of words. When we think about verbs in English, we might consider endings such as "-ed" or "-s." If we are talking about the verb *walk* and we want to make it past tense, we add "-ed" and get "walked."

tense stem	ending	inflected form
walk	+ ed	→ walk**ed**
walk	+ s	→ walk**s**

Greek is similar to English in that it also uses morphemes to build verbs, often by adding them to a **tense stem**. In future chapters, however, we will see that Greek can also add morphemes to the front of a tense stem or even insert them in the middle of a verb form. Unlike English verbs, Greek verbs do not need to use a separate word to indicate who or what the subject of the verb is. For example, in English we might say, "I see" or "they see." But in Greek, one would say, βλέπω or βλέπουσιν. So Greek attaches specific morphemes to indicate the subject of the verb. Thus, a single Greek word can form a complete sentence—a one-word sentence! Compare the following:

βλέπω.	I see.
βλέπουσιν.	They see.

Notice that sometimes a *single* Greek word must be translated by *two* words in English; for example, to translate βλέπω, the English pronoun "I" must be included in the translation, "I see." So we are not "adding" something to the Greek by using the English pronoun "I"; rather, we are simply giving a faithful translation of βλέπω, which requires at least two English words, namely, "I see," to communicate the same assertion.[1] This is one reason why it is not possible to have a "word-for-word" translation from any one language to another language.

Now, let's suppose that you are a linguist out in the field and that your local-language informant has supplied the following glosses for this list of Greek verbs.

ἔχεις	you (sg) have	βλέπεις	you (sg) see
λέγομεν	we speak	ἀκούουσιν	they hear
ἔχω	I have	ἔχουσιν	they have
πιστεύετε	you (pl) believe	βλέπω	I see
βλέπει	he/she/it sees	ἔχετε	you (pl) have
ἔχει	he/she/it has	ἔχομεν	we have

Now spend a few minutes looking carefully at the following list, particularly the bolded items. Can you see that these Greek words are all forms of the same verb?

---

1. It would also be acceptable to translate βλέπω as "I am seeing," which means that you would then have *three* English words corresponding to this *one* Greek word!

ἔχεις	you (sg) **have**
ἔχω	I **have**
ἔχει	he/she/it **has**
ἔχουσιν	they **have**
ἔχετε	you (pl) **have**
ἔχομεν	we **have**

Next compare the following pairs of words.

ἔχεις	**you** (sg) have
βλέπεις	**you** (sg) see
ἔχω	**I** have
βλέπω	**I** see
ἔχει	**he/she/it** has
βλέπει	**he/she/it** sees
ἔχουσιν	**they** have
ἀκούουσιν	**they** hear
ἔχετε	**you** (pl) have
πιστεύετε	**you** (pl) believe
ἔχομεν	**we** have
λέγομεν	**we** speak

Can you see how Greek uses different endings (**morphemes**) to indicate the subject of the verb? Thus, to build a verb in Greek, we start with a verb tense stem and then add an ending to indicate the person and number, which is called (not surprisingly!) a **personal ending**.

tense stem	personal ending	inflected form
εχ	+ ομεν	→ ἔχομεν

Another way to think about this is that Greek *inflects* a verb stem to indicate different functions of that verb—a change in **form** to indicate a change in **function**. For example, ἔχομεν could be translated "we have." To indicate a singular form of this verb, a different ending (-ω) would be joined with the verb stem, resulting in ἔχω, "I have." Neither the tense stem εχ- nor the personal ending -μεν is an actual word that you will find used independently; instead, these are morphemes that are used to build or construct a verb form.

Technically, there are three morphemes here. As we will see in the next section of this chapter, Greek inserts a **connecting vowel** between some tense stems and the personal ending.[2]

tense stem	connecting vowel	personal ending	inflected form
εχ	+ ο	+ μεν	→ ἔχομεν

THE PRESENT ACTIVE AND MIDDLE INDICATIVE

Now we will look at the present active indicative and the present middle indicative tense-forms in Greek. But first, let's consider Greek personal endings more carefully. Verbs can be singular or plural and can portray the action from the first-, second-, or third-person point of view. So there is a total of six personal endings that are used with **finite verbs** (verbs that indicate person and number). The personal endings for the present active indicative verb in Greek are as follows.

PRIMARY ACTIVE PERSONAL ENDINGS

1 sg	ω
2 sg	εις
3 sg	ει
1 pl	μεν
2 pl	τε
3 pl	ουσι(ν)

This is the first set of personal endings that you will learn for indicative verbs—the **primary active personal endings**. They are called primary because

---

2. It may be helpful to distinguish between **lexical morphemes**, which change the meaning of the word to which they are added, and **neutral morphemes**, which do not affect the meaning of the word to which they are added. Personal endings are clearly lexical morphemes, whereas connecting vowels are not. They are neutral morphemes because their presence does not change the meaning of the form in which they occur; they simply connect or link the personal ending to the verb stem (cf. David Alan Black, *Learn to Read New Testament Greek*, 3rd ed. [Nashville: B&H Academic, 2009], 18). These are sometimes called *stem formatives* (Goetchius, *Language of the New Testament*, 133). As we will see later on, these morphemes change to indicate verbal moods other than the indicative. But that can wait for now!

they are used with **primary tenses**, such as the present tense-form.[3] Specifically, primary active personal endings are used with active verbs with the present, future, and perfect tense-forms.

Below are the forms for the present active indicative of the verb λύω ("I untie, I release, I destroy") and possible translations for each form.[4] The personal endings have been set in boldface so that you can identify them more easily. Together, these forms are called a **paradigm**, which is a pattern of inflections that a given part of speech follows.[5]

PRESENT ACTIVE INDICATIVE

1 sg	λύ**ω**	I release
2 sg	λύ**εις**	you (sg) release
3 sg	λύ**ει**	he/she/it releases
1 pl	λύ**ομεν**	we release
2 pl	λύ**ετε**	you (pl) release
3 pl	λύ**ουσι(ν)**	they release

In the first-person and second-person plural, you can easily see the connecting vowel, which is either an epsilon or an omicron, although in some forms it is not easy to distinguish the connecting vowel and the personal ending in the present active indicative. The switch between an epsilon or an omicron for the connecting vowel is not random. If the personal ending begins with a mu or nu, then the connecting vowel is an omicron; otherwise, the connecting vowel is an epsilon.

The nu at the end of the third-person plural form is called a **movable nu**. It is in a parenthesis because it is not always used. As we have seen, Greek does not like to have two separate vowel sounds together (i.e., a combination that does not form a diphthong), so in theory the nu appears when the next word begins with a vowel. (This is somewhat similar to the indefinite article in English, "**an** animal.") This provides a buffer between the iota of the third-person personal ending and a word that begins with a vowel that follows the verb form.

---

3. These are also called *unaugmented indicative tense-forms*. Augmented verbs use secondary personal endings, which you will also learn about in a later chapter. Augmented verbs are also called *secondary tenses*.

4. Even though λύω occurs only forty-two times in the GNT, it has the advantage of being very regular and short.

5. Paradigms for verbs are called **conjugations**, whereas paradigms for nouns are called **declensions**.

In practice, however, the nu sometimes appears when the next word begins with a consonant and sometimes does not appear when the next word begins with a vowel. The movable nu can also appear before a punctuation mark.

For the Curious

In the present active indicative first-person and second-person plural forms, it is easy to see the present stem (λυ-), the connecting vowel (o or ε), and the personal ending (μεν or τε). In the remaining forms it is less obvious. Here is a brief explanation of how these forms are derived. You do *not* need to memorize this—you simply need to memorize the forms as they appear in the above paradigm.

For the first-person singular form, λύω, the original ending was -μι (an ending that we will see later in some very common verbs). The connecting vowel was omicron, as we would expect. But the -μι ending eventually was no longer used for these types of verbs, so without the ending the omicron connecting vowel lengthened to an omega. Such vowel lengthening is common, and we will see it happen in other contexts. When a form does not use an expected morpheme, as in the example of the first-person singular personal ending, this "invisible" ending is sometimes called a **zero** (or null) **morpheme**.[6]

For the second-person singular, λύεις, the original ending was -σι, with an epsilon as the connecting vowel. Greek tries to avoid having a sigma between two vowels (called an **intervocalic sigma**). So, in the original present active indicative form for the second-person singular, λυεσι, the sigma dropped out between the epsilon and the iota. The two remaining vowels formed the diphthong ει. It is not entirely clear why a sigma was then added to the end of the final form.

For the third-person singular, the original ending was -τι, with an original form, λυετι. The tau dropped out between the epsilon connecting vowel and the iota of the personal ending. This explains the diphthong ει of the final form λύει.

Finally, the third-person plural form was originally λυονται. Dentals (such as ν, τ) and sigmas do not really get along, so the ντ dropped out, and the omicron lengthened to the diphthong ου (called **compensatory vowel lengthening**, which we will see in other contexts later on). This explains the final form λύουσι. The diphthong ου likely explains why the sigma does not drop out between these vowels.

You can translate present indicative verbs with either an English simple present, "I release" (as indicated in the paradigm above), or an English continuous

---

6. Black, *Linguistics for Students*, 78–79.

present, "I am releasing." It is important to understand, however, that a Greek present tense-form verb can describe an action that took place in the past, a contemporaneous action (to the time of the speaker or writer), or even a future action. In narrative accounts of historical events, such as parts of the Gospels or Acts, the present tense-form is often used to introduce a new place, event, or person. It can also introduce dialogue, as we noted in the previous chapter.

The third-person singular form is used for a male or female subject, or for a masculine, feminine, or neuter grammatical subject. The *same* form is used for each of these possibilities. The context will make it clear which is intended. For example, Mark 1:44 begins with καὶ λέγει. It is clear from the larger context that Jesus is the one speaking, so we would translate this as "and he says . . ." But John 4:11 begins with λέγει; here we would translate this as "she says" because the context makes it clear that the Samaritan woman is the one speaking.

Remember that finite Greek verbs are inflected to indicate the person and number of the subject of the verb. This means that Greek verbs do not need another word to indicate the subject of the verb, unlike English.[7] In narrative portions of the NT, however, sometimes third-person verbs (both singular and plural) have explicitly stated subjects. This is not grammatically necessary, but it does make clear who the subject is. For example, later in John's account of the Samaritan woman (John 4:17), we read λέγει . . . Ἰησοῦς. We would translate this as "Jesus says," not "he says, Jesus" or "Jesus, he says." Note also that this explicitly stated subject does not have to appear before the verb, as is the case in English.

To indicate the middle voice, Greek uses a *different* set of personal endings. These are the primary *middle* personal endings, which are used with the present, future, and perfect tense-forms (just as the primary *active* personal endings are).

PRIMARY MIDDLE PERSONAL ENDINGS

1 sg	μαι
2 sg	σαι
3 sg	ται
1 pl	μεθα
2 pl	σθε
3 pl	νται

---

7. For example, in English, "says" needs another word to indicate who is speaking, such as "he says" or "she says."

Below is the present middle indicative paradigm for the verb λύω, including possible translations for each form. The connecting vowels and personal endings are set in boldface to help you identify them more easily. The addition of "for myself," "for yourself," and so on in the translations helps to bring out the nuance of the middle voice, which focuses more on the one doing the action than the action itself.

PRESENT MIDDLE INDICATIVE

1 sg	λύ**ομαι**	I release for myself
2 sg	λύ**ῃ**	you (sg) release for yourself
3 sg	λύ**εται**	he/she/it releases for him/her/itself
1 pl	λυ**όμεθα**	we release for ourselves
2 pl	λύ**εσθε**	you (pl) release for yourselves
3 pl	λύ**ονται**	they release for themselves

In the present middle indicative, you can see more clearly how verbs are built in Greek:

present stem	**+ connecting vowel**	**+ personal ending**	**→ inflected form**
λυ	+ ο	+ μαι	→ λύομαι
λυ	+ ε	+ σθε	→ λύεσθε

This is true . . . except for the second-person singular form. If you want to know more about this form, read "For the Curious" below. Otherwise, you can simply memorize this form and move on.

For the Curious

Remember that Greek tries to avoid a sigma caught between two vowels (an **intervocalic sigma**). If we were to add the second-person singular present middle personal ending to the connecting vowel and the tense stem, we'd end up with an intervocalic sigma: λυ + ε + σαι. To get around this, the sigma drops out of the present middle indicative second-person singular form, but that leaves two vowels together that do not form a diphthong, which is another situation that Greek does not like. So, these two (short) vowels (ε and α) combine to form one (long) vowel (η). (We will see this happen again in another context.) An iota will subscript any time that it possibly can, and it can here. Got all that? Here's the process, step-by-step to get from λυ + ε + σαι to λύῃ.

First, the addition of the personal ending σαι to the present verb stem λυ + the connecting vowel ε causes a sigma to be caught between two vowels, so the sigma humbly bows out.

λυ + ε + σαι → λυ + ε + σ̸αι

Next, the ε and the α combine to form the long vowel η, which makes the iota very happy, because now it can subscript under the long vowel η.

λυ + ε + σαι → λυ + ε + σ̸αι → λυ + ε + αι

You don't need to remember this; you simply need to memorize the final form. But it is sometimes helpful to know that even forms that initially look very different are actually playing by their own set of rules!

MORE ON THE MIDDLE VOICE

There are several functions of the middle voice in Koine Greek.[8] The most common use of the middle voice is the **indirect** ("true" or "classical") **middle**, which expresses the idea of acting in one's own interest or for one's own benefit. Consider the difference between these two sentences:

I bought a book for my cousin. (active voice)
I bought a book for myself. (middle voice)

The **direct middle** connotes a reflexive idea, but this is rare in the NT. For example, the active-voice verb ἐνδύω could be translated "I clothe *someone*," whereas the middle-voice verb ἐνδύομαι would be translated "I clothe myself." Keep in mind, though, that Greek has a specific pronoun (ἑαυτοῦ) to indicate reflexivity, which is commonly used. Hence it should *never* be assumed that the middle voice indicates a reflexive idea.

Some verbs have different meanings in the active- and middle-voice forms. For example:

---

8. A few more functions of the middle voice are discussed in chapter 8.

active form	active gloss	middle form	middle gloss
ἄρχω	I rule	ἄρχομαι	I begin
ἅπτω	I light, kindle	ἅπτομαι	I touch
καταλαμβάνω	I seize	καταλαμβάνομαι	I comprehend
πείθω	I persuade	πείθομαι	I obey

There are some verbs that have a *middle*-voice form but do not have an *active*-voice form. This includes many common verbs such as γίνομαι ("I become"), ἔρχομαι ("I come"), πορεύομαι ("I journey, go"), βούλομαι ("I will, wish"), and δέχομαι ("I take, receive"). These verbs are frequently called **deponent** (or **middle deponent**) **verbs** and are often defined as verbs that have "laid aside" their active *form*, even though they are active in *meaning*. More recently, however, some have challenged this concept of deponency.[9] They correctly note that because the essential force of the middle voice is *always* active, it is not entirely clear what has been "laid aside" in these verbs.[10] The situation is not helped when some verbs are classified as **passive deponents** (verbs that have a passive form but are active in meaning). Moreover, a given verb can be "deponent" in one tense-form but not another. For example, ἔρχομαι is "deponent" in the present tense-form, but not in the aorist tense-form, which presents additional challenges for the concept of deponency. Thus, because the concept of deponency is unclear and perhaps even invalid, we will not use this term in this book. Instead we will consider these types of verbs as middle verbs. These verbs are easily recognized in a lexicon because of their -ομαι ending.

Finally, the difference between transitive and intransitive also explains the difference between active- and middle-verb forms for some verbs. For example, παύω (active voice) has a transitive meaning (e.g., "I stop *something/someone*"), but παύομαι (middle voice) has an intransitive meaning (e.g., "I cease"). This form is used in Luke 8:24, where the wind and waves "ceased" at Jesus's command.

LEXICAL FORM AND PARSING

When you look up a verb in a Greek dictionary (often referred to as a *lexicon*), it will usually be listed in the present indicative first-person singular. For many

---

9. E.g., Jonathan T. Pennington, "Deponency in Koine Greek: The Grammatical Question and the Lexicographical Dilemma," *Trinity Journal* 24 (2003): 55–76.

10. For a summary of the debate about deponency, see Dana M. Harris, "The Study of the Greek Language," in *The State of New Testament Studies: A Survey of Recent Research*, ed. Scot McKnight and Nijay K. Gupta (Grand Rapids: Baker Academic, 2019), 120–36; esp. 132–36.

verbs this will be the present *active* indicative form, such as λύω. For verbs without an active form, the present *middle* form will be listed, such as ἔρχομαι.[11] The form that is listed in a lexicon is called (unsurprisingly) the **lexical form**.[12] But most of the time, you will encounter **inflected forms** other than the lexical form, for example, λυόμεθα. This means that you need to be able to identify all the morphological components of the inflected form so that you can determine the lexical form. This process is called **parsing**.

More precisely, to parse a verb is to "unpack," or to identify, all the morphological components of the inflected verb form *in a set order*: the tense-form, voice, mood, person and number, lexical form, and a possible translation of the inflected form. This *possible* translation is also called an **inflected meaning**, although the original context in which the inflected form occurs is always the final determiner for any translation. Parsing enables us to do two things: to understand how a particular word may be functioning in a given context and to locate the word in a lexicon.

Here's how you would parse λυόμεθα.[13]

inflected form	tense-form	voice	mood	person	number	lexical form	inflected meaning
λυόμεθα	pres	mid	ind	1st	pl	λύω	we release for ourselves

Remember that a given Greek word does not "mean" another word in English. Instead, the same Greek word can often be translated by several different English words, depending on the context in which it appears. When you are parsing words in a list, however, there is obviously no context to help you determine which gloss is the most suited for your translation. In this case, you may choose any acceptable gloss for the Greek word assigned to parse. What is important is that you focus on rendering the inflected form accurately into English. In other words, you need to ensure that each of the morphological components of *the inflected form* is clearly reflected in *the inflected meaning*. For example, if a verb is a third-person plural, your English translation needs to reflect this by using the pronoun "they"; if the verb is first-person singular, this needs to be reflected in a translation with "I."

---

11. There is no verb form ἔρχω, which would be the active form for ἔρχομαι.

12. Later we will introduce **principal parts**, which are a minimal set of verb forms from which all other verb forms can be derived. For now, simply note that the **lexical form** is the first principal part of a verb.

13. We use standard abbreviations in these examples, which are listed in the front of the book. See also appendix 17, "Standard Abbreviations and Parsing Order."

HEADS UP! ──────────────────────────────────

Greek likes to recycle various forms or use the same form for different functions. It can do this because context will make it clear which function is intended. In chapter 11, we will learn the forms of the passive voice. We will see that Greek uses the *same form* for the present middle as it does for the present passive. Later we will see that this is also true for the perfect middle and perfect passive. Greek can recycle these forms because the context will make clear whether the verb is middle or passive voice. Don't worry about this now—this is just a head's up so that you won't be surprised later.

REVIEW OF CHAPTER 3

In this chapter we learned how to build a Greek verb. We saw that the present active and middle indicatives are built by taking the present stem and adding primary active or middle endings. A connecting vowel is used to connect these two morphological components. It may be helpful to memorize the primary active and middle endings, although as we have seen, some of these endings change a bit when they are added to the present stem and connecting vowel. For this reason, it is more helpful to memorize the present active and middle indicative paradigms, because these paradigms reflect the forms that you will see in the GNT.

We also discussed some of the more common functions of the middle voice and noted that some verbs have different meanings in the active and middle voices. We also saw that some verbs do not have any active forms, such as ἔρχομαι.

Finally, we introduced the concept of lexical form, which is the form that a Greek word (in this case, Greek verbs) is listed in a lexicon. Since most words in the GNT do not occur in this lexical form, you need to be able to identify the morphological components used to construct the actual form that you are looking at, so that you can determine the lexical form. This process is called parsing.

Study Guide for Chapter 3

1. Be able to identify each of the following components for verb forms:
    present stem
    lexical form
    connecting vowel
    inflected meaning
    primary active personal endings
    primary middle personal endings

2. Be able to explain the following concepts or functions of morphemes:

   movable nu

   parsing

   paradigm

3. Be able to recognize the person and number for each of the primary active and middle personal endings.

4. Be able to parse present active and middle verbs and translate basic Koine sentences as assigned in the workbook.

Vocabulary to Memorize

Here is the vocabulary that you need to memorize for this chapter. Remember that you do not have to memorize all the possible glosses, but you should keep in mind the semantic range for Greek words. Recall that verbs listed with -ομαι endings do not have active forms.

ἀνοίγω	I open (77)
ἀποκρίνομαι	I answer, I reply (231)
ἀσπάζομαι	I greet, I welcome (59)
γίνομαι	I become, I am, I happen, I come into being, I exist (669)
δέχομαι	I receive, I take, I welcome, I accept (56)
διώκω	I pursue, I persecute, I seek after (45)
ἐγείρω	I raise up, I wake; I awaken (pass)[1] (144)
ἔρχομαι	I come, I go (634)
ἔτι	still, yet (93)
εὐαγγελίζω	I announce/bring good news/the gospel, I proclaim, I preach (54)
εὐθύς	immediately, at once, then (59)
ἤδη	now, already (61)
θαυμάζω	I wonder, I marvel, I am amazed (43)
θέλω	I desire, I wish, I will (208)
θεραπεύω	I heal, I restore, I serve (43)
καθίζω	I sit, I cause to sit down (46)
κράζω	I cry out, I call out (56)
νῦν	now; the present (subst)[2] (147)
οὐ (οὐκ, οὐχ)	not, no (1,606)

(cont.)

οὔτε	and not, nor (87)
πάλιν	again, once more (141)
πίπτω	I fall, I perish (90)
πορεύομαι	I journey, I go, I travel (153)
προσεύχομαι	I pray (85)
σπείρω	I sow (52)

[1] Some verbs have different meanings in the middle or passive voice, which is noted in the assigned vocabulary with either (mid) or (pass).

[2] Sometimes adverbs can function as a substantive (subst) and not modify a verb.

Paradigms to Memorize

You need to memorize the following paradigms for this chapter: the present active indicative paradigm of λύω, and the present middle indicative paradigm of λύω. It is essential that you memorize these assigned forms for λύω, because you will build on them in subsequent chapters.

PRESENT ACTIVE INDICATIVE OF λύω

1 sg	λύω
2 sg	λύεις
3 sg	λύει
1 pl	λύομεν
2 pl	λύετε
3 pl	λύουσι(ν)

PRESENT MIDDLE INDICATIVE OF λύω

1 sg	λύομαι
2 sg	λύῃ
3 sg	λύεται
1 pl	λυόμεθα
2 pl	λύεσθε
3 pl	λύονται

chapter **FOUR**

THE GREEK NOUN:
A Case of Form and Function

OBJECTIVES AND OVERVIEW

Chapter 4 introduces the Greek noun and the first and second declension patterns. It introduces the following linguistic concepts, morphemes, and paradigms:

- subject, direct object, and indirect object
- basic functions of the nominative, accusative, dative, and genitive cases
- head noun and genitival modifier
- distinctives of first, second, and third declension noun patterns
- first and second declension paradigms
- grammatical and natural gender
- η-type, α-pure type, and α-impure type first declension noun patterns
- fixed and inflected noun components
- lexical form for nouns and parsing
- neuter plural nouns and singular verbs

BASIC CONCEPTS

Slots, Fillers, Word Order, and Inflection

In chapter 1 we introduced many syntactic and linguistic terms. Perhaps one of the most familiar ones was a **noun**, which designates a person, place, concept, or thing. This is a fundamental phenomenon in language—one that children usually grasp first! It's fun to watch young children learning how to talk as they begin to connect familiar objects with the words that are used to designate them.[1]

---

1. Some approaches to learning Greek start with nouns and then proceed to verbs, based on parallels to how children acquire language. In this book, however, we start with verbs because these are essential for understanding the GNT. As a competent language user of at least one language (perhaps even more!), it makes sense to draw on what you already know about language and to apply that to learning Greek.

Also in chapter 1, we introduced the idea of words (or parts of speech) being able to perform certain functions. We discussed this in terms of "**slots**" (or various functions within a sentence) and "**fillers**" (particular parts of speech or constructions that could fit into those slots). So, for example, if we have the function slot "subject," we could not put a verb in that slot and have a meaningful sentence. Based on the example that we used in chapter 1, consider the following:

(syntactic function)	subject	verb	substantive modifier	direct object	indirect object
"filler"	brings	brings	great	joy	to us.
(part of speech)	verb	verb	adjective	noun	pronoun

Clearly only a noun or a word that functions as a noun (a **substantive**) can be placed into the slot for the *subject* function in a sentence. In the example above, the verb "brings" in the *subject* slot makes no sense. This is also true for the slots that correspond with the *direct object* and *indirect object* functions in a sentence. If we try to put something other than a substantive in these slots, we will not have a meaningful sentence. Also recall from chapter 1 that English usually relies on word order to indicate the function of a substantive in a given sentence. Compare the following two English sentences:

God loves *a cheerful giver.*
A cheerful giver loves **God.**

Clearly the two sentences have very different meanings, but the *spellings* of the English substantives do not indicate their different functions in each of the sentences. Instead their functions are determined by their *word order*, or the order in which they appear in each sentence. In the first sentence, "God" is the subject because it appears first, before the verb, whereas in the second sentence, "a cheerful giver" is the subject of the sentence because it appears before the verb.[2]

Now let's look again at a Greek sentence that we considered in chapter 1. (Words have been set in bold and italicized for clarity in the following discussion.)

---

2. The situation is obviously more complex than this. Sometimes the subject in an English sentence can be placed elsewhere in a sentence—even at the very end of the sentence—but this is usually done for effect and is usually recognized as a "break" from the rules. In general, we will see that Greek also often places a subject at the beginning of a sentence, but it certainly does not *have* to be placed there to indicate that it is functioning as the subject of the clause or sentence. More on this to come.

ὁ θεός	ἀγαπᾷ	ἱλαρὸν	δότην
ἱλαρὸν	δότην	ἀγαπᾷ	ὁ θεός

Even though the Greek words do not appear in the same order, both sentences would be translated as "God loves a cheerful giver." This is because Greek uses *inflections* rather than *word order* to indicate the different function of words in a given sentence. Recall that **inflection** is any change in **form** to indicate a change in **function.** As we will see, for Greek nouns this involves adding a morpheme to a noun stem. So, the ending of θεός (the sigma) tells us that this word ("God") is functioning as the subject, whereas the ending on δότην (the nu) tells us that this word ("giver") is functioning as the direct object of the verb.

We don't really find this type of inflection in English except with personal pronouns (and some other pronouns). Consider the following (or refer to the complete chart in chapter 1):

function	singular	plural
subjective	I	we
objective	me	us
possessive	my	our

Now consider the following sentences:

God loves *us*.
We love **God**.

The different forms of the first-person personal pronouns ("us" and "we") indicate different functions: the subject ("we") versus the object ("us") of the verb. And notice that the word order in the English determines the function of **God** in each sentence. With this in mind, it's time to consider how Greek uses inflections to indicate different functions for Greek substantives.

Functions of Greek Noun Cases

Greek uses different inflections, or endings, to indicate the various functions that a substantive can perform in a given clause or sentence, particularly regarding its relationship to some other word (usually a verb or another substantive). These basic functions are called **cases**, and so these endings are called **case**

endings. By the time of the first century, there were essentially four Greek cases with the following main functions:[3]

case name	basic case function
nominative	indicates the subject of a verb
accusative	indicates the direct object of a verb
dative	indicates the indirect object of a verb
genitive	describes another noun

Let's look at each of these four cases more fully.

The **nominative case** often indicates the subject of a clause or sentence—or what the clause or sentence is "about."[4] Recall that Greek finite verbs are inflected for person and number and do not *need* to have an explicitly stated subject. As we saw, βλέπω is inflected to indicate the subject. This one word may be translated, "I see," and we do not need to add another Greek word to indicate the subject "I." Third-person verbs, however, may have a noun in the nominative case to make the subject explicit. This is particularly true in narrative. For example:

Ἰησοῦς λέγει (cf. John 4:17)
Jesus says

The verb λέγει is complete, indicating both person and number, and it could be translated "he says," "she says," or "it says," depending on the context. The addition of Ἰησοῦς, however, makes explicit that the subject of this sentence is Jesus. Explicitly stated subjects in the nominative case *must* agree in number with the verb with which they are associated. Thus, in the example from John 4:17 the singular form of λέγει agrees with the singular noun Ἰησοῦς.

The nominative is also used to indicate a **predicate nominative** or **predicate adjective** with an **equative verb**.[5] Consider the following sentences:

The students are *believers*.
The students are *faithful*.

---

3. There is a fifth case, the vocative; see "For the Curious" in the main text of this chapter. Sometimes the cases other than the nominative (i.e., accusative, genitive, dative, and vocative) are collectively referred to as **oblique cases**.

4. The term *nominative* itself indicates that this case "names" or "designates" a subject.

5. Refer to the discussion about these types of verbs in chapter 2. Predicate nominatives and adjectives are sometimes called *subject complements* or *predicate complements*, because they "complete" the sentence or the clause.

In the first sentence, *believers* is a noun that functions to make a predication about the students. It is therefore called a **predicate nominative**. In the second sentence, *faithful* is an adjective that functions to makes a predication about the students. It is called a **predicate adjective**. In Greek, both *believers* and *faithful* would be in the nominative case.

The **accusative case** usually indicates the *direct* object of a transitive verb.[6]

The **dative case** can indicate the *indirect* object of a transitive verb. The dative case can also perform functions that English indicates by means of a preposition.[7] For example, it can have a locative function (indicating a location without using a preposition, e.g., "[in] the sea") or an instrumental function (e.g., "[by] a word"). We will discuss these functions in future chapters.

Finally, there is the **genitive case**. This word comes from the Latin word *genus* (think biology!), where this term refers to a classification of a class or kind of species or individuals. This connection is helpful because the primary function of the genitive case is to describe—specifically to describe or modify another substantive.[8] Sometimes this can be a simple description, such as "the Lord of glory," where "glory" further describes "Lord." Sometimes the genitive indicates possession, as in "the kingdom of God," which could also be expressed as "God's kingdom."

It is helpful at this point to introduce two additional concepts associated with the genitive case. The first is a **head noun**, which is the substantive that is being modified by a word in the genitive case, which is called a **genitival modifier**. This second term is helpful for remembering the *function* of the genitive case—it modifies another word. In the preceding examples, "the Lord" and "the kingdom" are head nouns, and "of glory" and "of God" are genitival modifiers. As we will see in future chapters, the head noun can occur in *any* case (nominative, accusative, dative, or genitive), whereas a genitival modifier is always in the genitive case.

Sometimes the English word "of" is a good way of translating the relationship between the head noun and the genitival modifier. In other examples of the genitive, the English word "of" cannot be used; we'll talk more about this later. Genitival modifiers tend to follow the head noun that they modify (τὴν ἀγάπην τοῦ θεοῦ, "the love of God"; John 5:42), but they can (rarely) precede the head noun.

---

6. Recall that a transitive verb is a verb that can "take" a direct object or can "act" upon an object; transitive verbs can also be made into a passive.

7. One of the key functions of this case is to indicate a relationship between nouns, either spatially or temporally, which in English we often indicate by means of prepositions such as "in," "on," "at," etc.

8. You can also think of this in terms of "limiting"; e.g., there are many kingdoms, but the addition of "of God" limits the discussion to only one kingdom. See also Wallace, *Greek Grammar beyond the Basics*, 76.

Declensions, Gender, Number, and Greek Nouns

As we have seen, Greek uses different case endings to indicate different functions of a substantive in a clause or sentence. So far we have discussed four main case functions, so this might suggest that Greek has four different case endings that correspond to each of these case functions. This is partially true, but there is more to it than this. Because nouns can either be singular or plural, there need to be different case endings for singular and plural nouns. Thus, different case endings indicate *both* whether a Greek word is nominative *and* singular or nominative *and* plural, and so on. So case endings must be able to indicate the **number** of a noun, as well as the **function** of the noun. But it is still a bit more complicated than this.

Recall from chapter 1 that we described **declensions** as patterns of inflections that occur with substantives. We looked at an analogy based on how English nouns form their plurals and called nouns that simply add an "s" *first declension nouns*, nouns that add an "es," *second declension nouns*, and nouns that change their stem or spelling, *third declension nouns*.

This is a helpful way to begin to understand Greek noun declensions. In Greek, nouns (and adjectives) are grouped together based on the *pattern* of case endings that they use. This results in three different declensions. **First declension** nouns have a noun stem that ends in an alpha (α) or an eta (η) and use one particular set of case endings. **Second declension** nouns have a stem that ends in an omicron (o) and use a different set of case endings. Finally, **third declension** nouns have stems that end in a consonant and use several different sets of case endings. In this chapter, we will only consider first and second declension nouns. These nouns follow very regular patterns, so if you memorize a few representative nouns and their case-ending patterns, or **paradigms**, then you will be able to recognize any other first or second declension noun that follows this same pattern. Many common Greek nouns in the NT are first and second declension nouns, so by the end of this chapter, you will be able to recognize many more words in the GNT.

These patterns of case endings are further divided according to **grammatical gender** among the three declensions. There is no clear parallel in English for the correlation of certain patterns of case ending with the three genders: masculine, feminine, and neuter. Consequently, it is very important to distinguish between **natural gender** and **grammatical gender**. Natural gender refers to groups of words that correspond to males or females, such as *actor* or *actress*, or *king* or *queen*. Frequently, names of animals also correspond to natural gender, such as a *stallion* or *mare*, or a *bull* or a *cow*. Personal pronouns reflect this natural gender; for example, we use the pronoun *she* to refer to a woman or *he* to refer to a man.

Although we do not think of a neuter gender in English, inanimate objects such as a car, a book, or a laptop are referenced with the pronoun *it*, not normally *he* or *she*.

Greek also has nouns that reflect natural gender, such as ἀνήρ ("man, husband") and γυνή ("woman, wife"). But grammatical gender is a completely separate concept from natural gender—it is a purely *linguistic* category. Thus, there is no inherent masculine aspect to Greek nouns that are masculine, or any feminine traits that can be discerned in Greek nouns that are feminine. A few examples will help to make this clear. Notice the grammatical gender of each of the following Greek nouns:

ἁμαρτία (feminine)	sin
θάνατος (masculine)	death
δύναμις (feminine)	power
ἀγάπη (feminine)	love
ἔλεος (neuter)	mercy
ἁγιασμός (masculine)	holiness

As nice as it might be to think of "love" as a feminine quality, this line of thinking runs into problems with the fact that "sin" also corresponds to a feminine noun in Greek! Similarly, Greek nouns that are neuter that refer to a person do not indicate that that person is somehow impersonal. For example, παιδίον ("little child") and τέκνον ("child") are both grammatically neuter, but this does not mean that a child is considered an "it." Thus, it must be stressed that gender in Greek is a *linguistic* or *grammatical* category. It must also be stressed that the gender of a given noun *does not* change—once a neuter noun, always a neuter noun![9] The importance of this will become apparent later in this chapter. It is also important to memorize the gender of a noun when the noun is assigned as vocabulary. We will talk more about this in the next chapter, but this is why the Greek article is listed with nouns in the assigned vocabulary—to indicate the gender of a given noun.

To summarize: Greek nouns are classified according to their stem ending: first declension nouns have stem endings in alpha or eta (α or η); second declension noun stems end in omicron (o); and third declension noun stems end in consonants. Further divisions within each declension are based on *grammatical*

---

9. A very small number of words in Greek can be either masculine or feminine; e.g., ὁδός. This is very unusual, though.

gender. The majority of first declension nouns are feminine, although there are some masculine first declension nouns. There are no neuter first declension nouns. Second declension nouns are divided between masculine and neuter nouns, although there are a few second declension feminine nouns. Because of this, we often find that first and second declension nouns have certain similarities that make them different from third declension nouns (indicated by the boldface and shading in the table below). We can summarize this distribution of gender among the three noun declensions as follows:

gender	first declension (α or η stems)	second declension (o stems)	third declension (consonant stems)
masculine	minority	**many**	**many**
feminine	**majority**	few	**many**
neuter	none	**many**	**many**

Before we look at first and second declension noun forms, it is important to stress again that the gender of a noun *never* changes. For example, λόγος is a masculine noun, and it will remain a masculine noun until the Lord returns. This also means that λόγος will always be a second declension noun. Thus, gender and declension are *fixed* components of a noun that *do not* change. (The importance of this truth will become clearer as we proceed.) Case endings indicate a noun's function in a given context and are thus determined by the function of a noun in a given clause or phrase. This is why *case endings* change frequently. So it is very important to grasp clearly those noun components that *never* change (gender and declension) and those that *must* change (case endings) according to the context in which a noun occurs.

FIRST AND SECOND DECLENSION PARADIGMS AND TRANSLATIONS

In the first part of this chapter, we discussed basic concepts required for understanding Greek nouns. We also surveyed basic functions of the individual cases. Now we'll focus on the case ending forms used with Greek nouns. We'll learn how to "build" nouns, just as we learned how to build verbs. We will start with second declension nouns because they are very common (there are hundreds of second declension nouns in the GNT!) and because this pattern is very regular (which makes it easier to see the individual morphemes required to build nouns). The majority of second declension nouns are either masculine or neuter, although there are a smaller number of second declension feminine nouns. Then we will learn paradigms for first declension nouns, which are also common and regular. Most of these nouns are feminine, although there are a significant number of first declension masculine nouns. There are no first declension neuter nouns.

Second Declension Paradigms

We will start with a very common second declension noun, λόγος. To build this noun, we take the noun stem and add an ending to indicate the function of the inflected form. For example:

noun stem	case ending	inflected form
λογο-	+ ς	→ λόγος

The noun stem λογο- is *not* an actual word—on no page of the GNT will you encounter the form λογο. It is the stem to which case endings are added. In most forms of second declension nouns, it is easy to see the noun stem and the case ending. In several forms, however, it is harder to see these individual components. For this reason, it is usually easier to memorize the stem ending (in this example, the final omicron of λογο-) together with the case ending rather than the case ending alone. Here is a summary chart of the second declension *masculine* case endings,[10] both with and without the final stem vowel from the noun stem.

	stem ending + case ending	case ending alone
nom sg	ος	ς
gen sg	ου	υ
dat sg	ῳ[1]	ι
acc sg	ον	ν
nom pl	οι	ι
gen pl	ων	ων
dat pl	οις	ις
acc pl	ους	υς

[1] Greek words do not usually end with a short vowel, so the omicron ending lengthens to an omega and the iota subscripts.

10. Very few second declension feminine nouns exist, but they use the same case endings as second declension masculine nouns.

Here is the **paradigm** (or pattern of inflections that a given part of speech follows) of λόγος and possible inflected meanings for each form.[11] The stem ending and the case ending are set in bold. By memorizing this paradigm (exactly!), you can recognize numerous other second declension masculine nouns in the GNT, because they all follow this pattern.[12]

	inflected form	inflected meaning
nom sg	λόγο**ς**	word
gen sg	λόγ**ου**	of (a) word
dat sg	λόγ**ῳ**	to/for/in (a) word
acc sg	λόγο**ν**	word
nom pl	λόγο**ι**	words
gen pl	λόγ**ων**	of words
dat pl	λόγο**ις**	to/for/in words
acc pl	λόγο**υς**	words

Another common noun, τέκνον, will serve as our paradigm for second declension *neuter* nouns. The paradigm for λόγος is included on the right to help you compare the similarities and differences between these two paradigms.

nom sg	τέκν**ον**	child	λόγος
gen sg	τέκνου	of (a) child	λόγου
dat sg	τέκνῳ	to/for/in (a) child	λόγῳ
acc sg	τέκν**ον**	child	λόγον
nom pl	τέκν**α**	children	λόγοι
gen pl	τέκνων	of children	λόγων
dat pl	τέκνοις	to/for/in children	λόγοις
acc pl	τέκν**α**	children	λόγους

---

11. The English indefinite article ("a") has been supplied for clarity in some examples, although the actual Greek word by itself does not indicate this. This will be discussed further in the next chapter.

12. Because second declension feminine nouns use the same case endings as second declension masculine nouns, λόγος functions as the paradigm for both masculine and feminine second declension nouns.

Underlining in this paradigm shows that the same case-ending form is used for the nominative and accusative of second declension *neuter* nouns, whether singular forms (-ov) or plural forms (-α), whereas second declension *masculine* nouns use a different case ending for the nominative and accusative (set in bold), but notice that the accusative singular form (-ov) is the same for both second declension masculine and neuter nouns. Finally, the same case ending is used for genitive singular (-ου) and dative singular (-ῳ) for *both* masculine and neuter nouns. This is also true for the plural genitive (-ων) and dative forms (-οις). (These forms are all italicized.) This is one of the reasons why you must always memorize a noun's gender when you memorize possible glosses for it—the case endings *alone* do not indicate gender, only case function.

It can be confusing to think that the same case ending can indicate multiple functions, so it is helpful to know that context nearly always makes clear what the intended function is. For example, even though neuter nouns use the same form for both the nominative and accusative, the function of the *subject* of a verb is quite different from that of the *direct object* of a verb. We'll talk more about this when we start translating actual verses from the GNT.

Before we look at first declension nouns, let's look at one more very important second declension noun paradigm: the name Ἰησοῦς.

	inflected form	inflected meaning
nom sg	Ἰησοῦς	Jesus
gen sg	Ἰησοῦ	of Jesus
dat sg	Ἰησοῦ	to/by/with/in Jesus
acc sg	Ἰησοῦν	Jesus

There are some forms of this paradigm that may be surprising, such as the diphthong in the nominative and accusative forms or the same form used for both the genitive and dative. This is likely because this is the Greek form of the corresponding Aramaic name. Often words that originated in another language have defective (incomplete) paradigms—some do not decline at all.[13] And, of course, notice that there are no plural forms for Ἰησοῦς.

---

13. Examples of indeclinable nouns include ἡ Ἰερουσαλήμ ("Jerusalem"), τὰ Ἰεροσόλυμα ("Jerusalem"), τὸ πάσχα ("Passover"), and τὸ μάννα ("manna"). If you want to look ahead, you can read more about this in chapter 8.

First Declension Paradigms

Now let's look at paradigms for first declension nouns. As noted, most of these nouns are feminine and have stems ending in an alpha (α) or an eta (η). There are three types of first declension feminine nouns:

η-type, which has an eta (η) throughout the singular forms
α-impure type, which has an alpha (α) in the nominative and accusative
  singular forms, but shifts to an eta (η) in genitive and dative singular forms
α-pure type, which has an alpha (α) throughout singular forms

Here are the paradigms for each of these types of first declension feminine nouns (inflected meanings are only listed for the first paradigm. You can write out the inflected meanings for the other two paradigms on your own as a way of reviewing these inflected meanings.

	η-type	inflected meaning	α-impure type	α-pure type
nom sg	ἀγάπη	love	δόξα	ἡμέρα
gen sg	ἀγάπης	of love	δόξης	ἡμέρας
dat sg	ἀγάπῃ	to/by/with/in love	δόξῃ	ἡμέρᾳ
acc sg	ἀγάπην	love	δόξαν	ἡμέραν
nom pl	ἀγάπαι	loves	δόξαι	ἡμέραι
gen pl	ἀγαπῶν	of loves	δοξῶν	ἡμερῶν
dat pl	ἀγάπαις	to/by/with/in loves	δόξαις	ἡμέραις
acc pl	ἀγάπας	loves	δόξας	ἡμέρας

The rule that determines whether the alpha will shift to an eta is easy to observe and remember. Look at each of the nominative singular forms, which uses the noun stem without any case ending. If the final vowel is an eta as with ἀγάπη, then there will be an eta through all the singular forms (η-type). If the final vowel is an alpha that is preceded by an epsilon, iota, or rho as with ἡμέρα, then there will be an alpha throughout the singular forms (α-pure type). If the final vowel is an alpha that is preceded by any letter *other than* an epsilon, iota, or rho as with δόξα, then the alpha remains in the nominative and accusative singular but shifts to an eta in the genitive and dative singular (α-impure type). We can summarize this as follows:

- If the noun stem ends in η, then all singular forms have an η.
- If the noun stem ends in α, preceded by ε, ι, or ρ, then all singular forms have an α.
- If the noun stem ends in α, *not* preceded by ε, ι, or ρ, then the α in the nominative and accusative singular forms shifts to an η in the genitive and dative singular forms.

This may seem a bit complicated at this point, but knowing these things will help when we learn about adjectives in the next chapter.

Next, notice that for α-pure type first declension feminine nouns, the genitive singular and the accusative plural case endings have the same form (-ας); thus, the genitive singular and the accusative plural of ἡμέρα is ἡμέρας (these forms are boxed in the above paradigm). Context will make it clear which form is intended, because a genitive singular and an accusative plural have very different functions. We will discuss this further in future chapters.

Finally, look carefully at the plural endings for all three paradigms. Yes! They are *exactly* the same for each type of first declension noun. So even though the singular forms may seem a bit complicated, here's the good news—*all* first declension nouns have the *same* plural forms. (These are underlined in the paradigms in this chapter.)

Now we'll look at first declension masculine nouns, which are not as common as first declension feminine nouns. There are two types of first declension masculine nouns. Here is the paradigm for the ης-type, which is more common.[14]

	ης-type	inflected meaning
nom sg	προφήτης	prophet
gen sg	προφήτου	of (a) prophet
dat sg	προφήτῃ	to/by/with/in (a) prophet
acc sg	προφήτην	prophet
nom pl	προφῆται	prophets
gen pl	προφητῶν	of prophets
dat pl	προφήταις	to/by/with/in prophets
acc pl	προφήτας	prophets

14. First declension masculine nouns with an -ης ending usually indicate a class or group of people

This paradigm basically follows the one for ἀγάπη, except the nominative singular is -ης and the genitive singular case ending is -ου (this is the same ending as the one used for second declension masculine and neuter nouns). Again, notice that *all* first declension nouns (masculine and feminine) have the *same* plural endings (underlined in the above paradigm).

So far we have looked at six paradigms that are representative of hundreds of nouns in the GNT. It is very important that you memorize these paradigms exactly. Not only will you be able to recognize many noun forms in the GNT, but you will also be able to recognize many other forms as well because Koine Greek uses (recycles!) these same case endings for forms other than nouns, such as adjectives and participles. We'll look at these other forms in later chapters.

Here is a summary of case endings for first and second declension nouns.[15] The hyphens indicate that no case ending is used for a given case; this is sometimes called a **zero morpheme**.

	with stem vowel			without stem vowel		
	2nd decl masc	1st decl fem	2nd decl neut	2nd decl masc	1st decl fem	2nd decl neut
nom sg	ος	α/η	ον	ς	-	ν
gen sg	ου	ας/ης	ου	υ	ς	υ
dat sg	ῳ	ᾳ/ῃ	ῳ	ι	ι	ι
acc sg	ον	αν/ην	ον	ν	ν	ν
nom pl	οι	αι	α	ι	ι	α
gen pl	ων	ων	ων	ων	ων	ων
dat pl	οις	αις	οις	ις	ις	ις
acc pl	ους	ας	α	υς	ς	α

who perform a certain action; e.g., προφήτης, a prophet; βαπτιστής, one who baptizes; or ἐγράτης, a worker. Another group of less common first declension masculine nouns have -ας in the nominative, -αν in the accusative, -ου in the genitive, and -ᾳ in the dative singular, such as νεανίας, -ου, ὁ, "young man." They have the *same* plural endings as all other first declension nouns.

15. As noted above, it is easier to memorize and recognize the stem vowel with the case ending, so the endings without the stem vowels are listed simply for your reference.

Here are some helpful observations:

- *All* first declension nouns use the *same* set of case endings in the plural forms.
- The *same* ending (-ων) is used for *all* genitive plurals.
- An iota is found in *every* dative form (as a subscript in the singular forms).
- The same form is used for second declension nominative and accusative neuter nouns (-ον in the singular forms and -α in the plural forms).
- Masculine and neuter second declension nouns use the *same* endings in the genitive and dative; this is true for both singular and plural nouns.

The earlier discussion in this chapter suggested that declension and gender are related. In the above chart, notice that one set of endings is used with second declension masculine nouns, another set of endings is used with first declension feminine nouns, and yet another set of endings is used with second declension neuter nouns. This is frequently referred to as a 2-1-2 pattern, which corresponds to this pattern of declensions.

As noted, Greek often recycles morphemes and uses the same morphemes to indicate case functions for other parts of speech, such as the article, adjectives, and participles. Hence the 2-1-2 pattern is seen in other forms. In the next chapter, we will see it with the article and the adjective. There are some remaining case endings that we will have to learn in conjunction with third declension nouns, but for the time being it is very important to memorize these case endings exactly. These endings should become as familiar to you as, say, your name!

It is also important to stress again a few key concepts. Gender and declension are *fixed* components of nouns—they *never* change. The case and number of a noun are *not* fixed components; they are *inflected* components that *must* change according to the context in which the noun occurs. The following summarizes these points.

FIXED COMPONENTS (*NEVER* CHANGE)

Gender	masculine, feminine, neuter
Declension	first, second, third

INFLECTED COMPONENTS (*MUST* CHANGE ACCORDING TO CONTEXT)

Case	nominative, genitive, dative, accusative
Number	singular, plural

GOING DEEPER:
The Vocative Case

There is a fifth case in Greek, the **vocative case**, which is used in direct address. For example, if you were to pray, "Lord, hear me!" the word "Lord" would be in the vocative case, because you are directly addressing the Lord. Greek originally used a separate case to indicate this function of a substantive, but by the time of the NT this form was being replaced by the nominative case in Koine Greek. In fact, the plural forms of the vocative are completely replaced by the nominative plural forms. This is also true for singular neuter nouns; thus, there are no separate forms for plural and neuter vocatives. But in second declension masculine and feminine singular nouns, the vocative ending is an epsilon. For example, the vocative form of κύριος ("lord") is κύριε; for παρθένος ("virgin"), the vocative form is παρθένε. In the first declension, there is no longer a separate vocative form for feminine nouns, but the vocative ending for first declension masculine nouns is an alpha. For example, the vocative form of προφήτης is προφῆτα. In the third declension, which we will learn later, the vocative singular form is normally the same as the nominative singular, with only a few exceptions.

The vocative usually occurs in dialogue. Because this is a very specific context, it is usually clear that the vocative is intended even if it uses the same form as the nominative. Sometimes the vocative is indicated with the addition of "O!" in English. For example, you could translate κύριε as "O Lord!"

Lexical Form and Parsing

When you look up a noun in a lexicon, it will usually be listed in the nominative singular, for example, λόγος or προφήτης. This is the **lexical form** for nouns. The lexical form often also lists the genitive singular ending, as seen in the assigned vocabulary, followed by the article. As noted, the article indicates the noun's gender. The reason for the genitive ending will become clear when we learn third declension nouns in chapter 12.

Similar to our discussion of the lexical form of verbs, you will often encounter forms other than the nominative singular form that is used for the lexical form; for example, προφῆται. So, this means that you need to be able to identify all the morphological components of the **inflected form** so that you can determine the lexical form. Recall that **parsing** "unpacks," or identifies, the morphological components of the inflected form in a set order. For nouns this order is case, number, gender, lexical form, and a possible **inflected meaning** of the inflected form (although the original context in which the inflected form occurs is always the final determiner for any translation). Here's how you would parse προφῆται.[16]

inflected form	case	num	gender	lexical form	inflected meaning
προφῆται	nom	pl	masc	προφήτης, -ης, ὁ	prophets

When parsing an isolated word on a list, there is no surrounding context to indicate how that Greek word might be translated. For example, the word τέκνα could function as either a subject or an object of a verb in a given clause or sentence. As we will see, context will nearly always make it clear which is intended. But when parsing a word in an assignment without any surrounding context, you need to list all *possible* options. This strengthens your ability to recognize all possibilities when you encounter a form in the GNT and then use the context to determine which option is the best fit for that context (and which options are not even viable). Here's how you would parse some nouns with multiple options in the assigned exercises.

inflected form	case	num	gender	lexical form	inflected meaning
τέκνα	nom acc	pl	neut	τέκνον, -ου, τό	children
ἡμέρας	gen acc	sg pl	fem	ἡμέρα, -ας, ἡ	of (a) day/days

Even though you are listing all possibilities in the exercises, it is important to understand that when τέκνα occurs in an actual sentence in the GNT, it can *never* be *both* nominative and accusative at the same time. Similarly, when ἡμέρας occurs in an actual text, it can *never* be *both* genitive singular and accusative plural at the same time. You will soon come to realize that context is one of your best friends.

---

16. You can refer to the front of the book or appendix 17, "Standard Abbreviations and Parsing Order."

Verbs with Neuter Plural Nouns

We have already noted that nouns must agree with verbs. In other words, singular nouns in the nominative case (and hence functioning as the subject) must have singular verbs, and plural nouns in the nominative case must have plural verbs. There are a few exceptions to this. Sometimes neuter plural nouns can have a singular verb, for example, πετεινὰ ἐσθίει ("birds [pl] eat" [sg]). This suggests that the group of birds is perceived as a whole, somewhat similar to the idea of a collective noun in English (e.g., a family or the church).

Translation Tips

You have already learned some basic conjunctions, such as such as ἀλλά, δέ, καί, and οὐτέ. In this chapter, you will learn ὡς. Conjunctions are like glue that holds various parts of a sentence together. With these conjunctions and with some of the verbs that we learned in chapters 2 and 3, we can now translate some simple Greek sentences. Let's look at a few sample translations.

> βλέπει Ἰησοῦν καὶ λέγει . . .
> He sees Jesus and he says . . .

It would also be possible to translate βλέπει as "she sees," depending on the context. Similarly, λέγει could be translated "she says" if the context indicated this. The name Ἰησοῦν is in the accusative because it is the direct object of the verb βλέπει.

Here is another example.

> βλέπουσιν ἔργα, καὶ πιστεύουσιν.
> They see works, and they believe.

You could also translate this sentence as follows:

> They are seeing works, and are believing.

Here is one final example:

> ἔχει ἐξουσίαν ὡς θέλει.
> He has authority as he wills.

This could be translated as follows depending on the context:

She has authority as she wills.

REVIEW OF CHAPTER 4

In this chapter we introduced Greek nouns, including the basic functions of the four main Greek cases: nominative (indicates the subject), accusative (indicates the direct object), dative (indicates the indirect object), and genitive (describes another noun). In conjunction with the nominative, we learned about a predicate nominative or predicate adjective that occurs with an equative verb. In conjunction with the genitive, we learned about a head noun, which is the noun being modified by a noun in the genitive case, which is the genitival modifier. We also learned that Greek uses various morphemes called *case endings* to indicate the function of a noun (or other substantive) in a sentence.

In Greek, nouns (and adjectives) are grouped together based on the *pattern* of case endings that they use, resulting in three declensions: **first declension** nouns have a noun stem that ends in an alpha (α) or an eta (η); **second declension** nouns have a stem that ends in an omicron (ο); and **third declension** nouns have stems that end in a consonant. Related to this is the important distinction between natural gender (male and female) and grammatical gender (masculine, feminine, and neuter). The gender and declension of a given noun are fixed—they never change, even when the function of that noun in a sentence changes; this function is indicated rather by case endings, which must change to indicate different functions.

Then we focused on forms and learned how to build the forms of first and second declension nouns. We learned the case endings that are used with first and second declension nouns. We learned that there are three types of first declension feminine nouns: η-type, which has an eta (η) throughout the singular forms; α-impure type, which has an alpha (α) in the nominative and accusative singular but shifts to an eta (η) in the genitive and dative singular; and α-pure type, which has an alpha (α) throughout the singular forms. Additionally, we learned that *all* first declension nouns use the *same* set of case endings in the plural forms. We learned that the lexical form for nouns is usually the nominative singular, for example, λόγος or προφήτης. The parsing order for nouns is case, number, gender, lexical form, and a possible inflected meaning. Finally, neuter plural nouns can take a singular subject.

Study Guide for Chapter 4

1. Be able to understand each of the following concepts for Greek nouns:

    the concept of slot and filler for understanding noun functions

    the basic function of each of the four Greek noun cases

    the distinction between natural gender and grammatical gender

    the concept of declension and noun stems

    noun case endings

    substantive and modifier

    predicate nominative

    predicate adjective

    genitival modifier

    head noun

    first declension feminine nouns (η-type, α-pure type, α-impure type)

    fixed and inflected components for nouns

    lexical form for nouns

    parsing order for nouns

2. Be able to parse first and second declension nouns and translate basic Koine sentences that also include present active and middle verbs.

Vocabulary to Memorize

Here is the vocabulary for chapter 4. The first entry of the first column is the Greek noun that you need to memorize, followed by the genitive singular case ending. For this chapter only, you can ignore that last Greek word listed. This is the article, which we'll learn about in the next chapter. It indicates the gender of the noun, although you can already determine that by the declension patterns that we have discussed in this chapter. If you are writing out vocabulary cards, however, you should include the article on the card.

ἀγάπη, -ης, ἡ	love (116)
ἄνθρωπος, -ου, ὁ	human being, person, man, humanity (550)
ἄρτος, -ου, ὁ	bread, food (97)
βασιλεία, -ας, ἡ	kingdom, reign (162)
δόξα, -ης, ἡ	glory, brightness, majesty, fame (166)
ἐκκλησία, -ας, ἡ	church, assembly (114)
ἐξουσία, -ας, ἡ	authority, power, ability (102)

ἔργον, -ου, τό	work, deed, action (169)
ἡμέρα, -ας, ἡ	day (389)
θεός, -οῦ, ὁ	God, god (1317)
καρδία, -ας, ἡ	heart, inner self, mind (156)
κύριος, -ου, ὁ	lord, Lord, master, sir (717)
λόγος, -ου, ὁ	word, statement, message, account (330)
μαθητής, -οῦ, ὁ	disciple, learner, follower (261)
ὁδός, -οῦ, ἡ	road, way, conduct (101)
οὐρανός, -οῦ, ὁ	heaven, sky (273)
πρόβατον, -ου, τό	sheep (39)
προφήτης, -ου, ὁ	prophet (144)
τέκνον, -ου, τό	child (99)
τότε	then (160)
υἱός, -οῦ, ὁ	son, descendant (377)
ὑπομονή, -ῆς, ἡ	perseverance, endurance, steadfastness (32)
Χριστός, -οῦ, ὁ	Christ, Anointed One, Messiah (529)
ψυχή, -ῆς, ἡ	life, soul, self, (103)
ὡς	as, like, when (504)

Paradigms to Memorize

The following noun paradigms must be memorized for this chapter: λόγος, -ου, ὁ; τέκνον, -ου, τό; ἡμέρα, -ας, ἡ; δόξα, -ης, ἡ; ἀγάπη, -ης, ἡ; and προφήτης, -ου, ὁ.

PARADIGM OF λόγος, -ου, ὁ

nom sg	λόγος
gen sg	λόγου
dat sg	λόγῳ
acc sg	λόγον
nom pl	λόγοι
gen pl	λόγων
dat pl	λόγοις
acc pl	λόγους

PARADIGM OF τέκνον, -ου, τό

nom sg	τέκνον
gen sg	τέκνου
dat sg	τέκνῳ
acc sg	τέκνον
nom pl	τέκνα
gen pl	τέκνων
dat pl	τέκνοις
acc pl	τέκνα

PARADIGM OF ἡμέρα, -ας, ἡ

nom sg	ἡμέρα
gen sg	ἡμέρας
dat sg	ἡμέρᾳ
acc sg	ἡμέραν
nom pl	ἡμέραι
gen pl	ἡμερῶν
dat pl	ἡμέραις
acc pl	ἡμέρας

PARADIGM OF δόξα, -ης, ἡ

nom sg	δόξα
gen sg	δόξης
dat sg	δόξῃ
acc sg	δόξαν
nom pl	δόξαι
gen pl	δοξῶν
dat pl	δόξαις
acc pl	δόξας

PARADIGM OF ἀγάπη, -ης, ἡ

nom sg	ἀγάπη
gen sg	ἀγάπης
dat sg	ἀγάπῃ
acc sg	ἀγάπην
nom pl	ἀγάπαι
gen pl	ἀγαπῶν
dat pl	ἀγάπαις
acc pl	ἀγάπας

PARADIGM OF προφήτης, -ου, ὁ

nom sg	προφήτης
gen sg	προφήτου
dat sg	προφήτῃ
acc sg	προφήτην
nom pl	προφῆται
gen pl	προφητῶν
dat pl	προφήταις
acc pl	προφήτας

THE ARTICLE AND
THE ADJECTIVE;
THE VERB εἰμί

OBJECTIVES AND OVERVIEW

Chapter 5 introduces the following linguistic concepts, morphemes, and paradigms:

- the article paradigm
- lexical form of the article and parsing
- basic functions of the article
- articular and anarthrous
- first and second declension adjective paradigms
- 2-1-2 and 2-2 declension adjective patterns
- lexical form for adjectives and parsing
- functions of the adjective: substantive, attributive, and predicate
- verbless clause, noun phrase
- first and second attributive positions
- first and second predicate positions
- the paradigm for the present of εἰμί

THE ARTICLE

In Greek there is only one form of the article, whereas English has the *definite* article ("the") and the *indefinite* article ("a/an"). We will first look at the forms of the Greek article, then we will discuss its function. The use of the article in Greek differs quite a bit from English, so we will discuss the function of the Greek article at several points in this book.

The Forms of the Article

It is best to think of the **article** as a type of **adjective** that modifies a **substantive** (any word, including a noun, that functions like a noun). So far we have only looked at noun paradigms, but all substantives in Greek use inflections (case endings) to indicate different case functions. Recall that there are three grammatical genders for Greek nouns: masculine, feminine, and neuter, and that nouns have *fixed* gender. Thus, a given noun has eight possible forms (singular and plural forms for the nominative, genitive, dative, and accusative cases). Any *modifier* of a substantive must agree with the substantive in case, number, and gender. As a substantive modifier, an article must be able to modify a substantive in any case, number, *and* gender. Therefore, there must be twenty-four forms of the article (four cases, singular and plural, three genders) so that it can modify any substantive. Here is the full paradigm for the Greek article.

	2 masculine	1 feminine	2 neuter
nom sg	ὁ	ἡ	τό
gen sg	τοῦ	τῆς	τοῦ
dat sg	τῷ	τῇ	τῷ
acc sg	τόν	τήν	τό
nom pl	οἱ	αἱ	τά
gen pl	τῶν	τῶν	τῶν
dat pl	τοῖς	ταῖς	τοῖς
acc pl	τούς	τάς	τά

Most of these endings should already look familiar. The numbers, 2-1-2, at the top of the paradigm indicate that the masculine forms of the article follow the pattern for masculine second declension nouns, the feminine forms of the article follow the pattern for feminine first declension nouns (following the η-type first declension feminine noun paradigm), and the neuter forms of the article follow the pattern for neuter second declension nouns. Yet there are some important exceptions:

- There is *no* sigma ending on the nominative singular masculine form of the article, which is what you might expect from the masculine second declension paradigm (e.g., λόγος).
- There is *no* nu ending on the nominative and accusative singular neuter forms of the article, which is what you might expect from the neuter second declension paradigm (e.g., τέκνον).

Note also that the masculine and feminine nominative forms (both singular and plural) have **rough breathing marks**; all other forms of the article begin with a tau.

Because Greek recycles morphemes, it is relatively easy to memorize the paradigm for the Greek article. This is another paradigm that you need to know perfectly. You should know this paradigm so well that you do not have to stop to think through which form you see. In fact, you should aim for knowing this paradigm even *better* than your name!

Why is it so important to know this form so well? Unlike other things in life, the Greek article never lies and never lets you down. Because it is a type of adjective, it *must* agree *exactly* with the substantive that it modifies in case, number, and gender. This means that you can always know the case, number, and gender of any word that is modified by an article, even if you aren't able to remember or figure out the parsing of that form itself. In other words, if a substantive is directly modified by the dative plural feminine form of the article, that substantive *must* be dative plural feminine . . . end of discussion. Once you fully grasp the significance of this, you may end up thinking of the Greek article as your new best friend.

Understanding that the Greek article must agree with the substantive that it modifies in case, number, and gender, does *not* mean, however, that the ending of the substantive will be *the exact same ending* of the article. Consider the following examples:

τὸν λόγον	(accusative singular masculine)
ταῖς ἡμέραις	(dative plural feminine)
τὰ τέκνα	(nominative or accusative plural neuter)

In each of the above examples, the case endings of the article are indeed identical with the case ending of the nouns. But now consider the following examples:

ἡ βασιλεία	(nominative singular feminine)
τὸν μαθητήν	(accusative singular masculine)
αἱ ὁδοί	(nominative plural feminine)
τὸ τέκνον	(nominative or accusative singular neuter)
τὴν παρθένον	(accusative singular feminine)
τῆς ἡμέρας	(genitive singular feminine)

In the above examples, the article still never lies, even though the case endings of the articles are *not* identical with the case endings of the nouns. Yet notice that in every example the article agrees exactly in case, number, and gender with the noun that it modifies. This is a significant concept to understand, especially when we learn third declension nouns.

Lexical Form and Parsing

The **lexical form** for the article is ὁ, ἡ, τό, which lists the nominative singular masculine form, the nominative singular feminine form, and the nominative singular neuter form of the article. In the assigned vocabulary for nouns in the last chapter, you saw that the lexical form for nouns lists the nominative singular form, the genitive singular case ending, and the nominative singular form of the article that corresponds to the noun's gender. This is shorthand for the entire noun paradigm. Similarly, the lexical form of the article (ὁ, ἡ, τό) is shorthand for the entire paradigm of the article. We will see something similar with the lexical form of adjectives and other parts of speech that can modify substantives in all three genders.

Here's how you would parse forms of the article. The parentheses in the inflected meaning indicate that the article modifies a substantive with which it agrees in case, number, and gender.

inflected form	case	num	gender	lexical form	inflected meaning
τούς	acc	pl	masc	ὁ, ἡ, τό	the (pl masc subst)
τῷ	dat	sg	masc neut	ὁ, ἡ, τό	to/for the (sg masc subst) *or* to/for the (sg neut subst)
αἱ	nom	pl	fem	ὁ, ἡ, τό	the (pl fem subst)

The Functions of the Article

As noted, English has a definite article and an indefinite article. The function of the definite article in English is often to specify one particular object from a larger set of objects. For example:

I think that **an** apple would be a good snack. (**no** particular apple is specified)
The apple on the counter looks good! (**one** particular apple is specified)

It is easy for beginning Greek students to think that the presence of the Greek article corresponds to the definite article in English and that the absence of the Greek article corresponds to the indefinite article in English, but this is *not true*! The word θεός frequently has the article in the GNT, but when it does not we would not necessarily translate it as "a god."[1] For example, John 1:12 talks about those who have become God's children, using the phrase τέκνα θεοῦ. This could *not* be translated "children of a god," even though θεοῦ is not modified by an article. The overall *context* makes it clear that God (not "a god") is intended in John 1:12. At this point, it is helpful to introduce two important terms: **articular** (or less commonly **arthrous**) means that a given word *is* modified by the article; **anarthrous** means that a given word *is not* modified by the article.

We will talk more about the functions of the Greek article throughout this book. For now it is best to understand that the Greek article often functions quite differently than the definite article in English. Proper names, such as Ἰησοῦς, are often articular, as are abstract nouns, such as love and truth; for example, ἡ ἀγάπη μακροθυμεῖ ("love is patient"; 1 Cor 13:4), but we would never translate these as "the Jesus" or "the love." Moreover, nouns that are clearly definite, such as the Son (referring to Jesus) are often anarthrous in Greek when the *quality* of the noun is being stressed (e.g., ἐν υἱῷ, "in *the* Son"; Heb 1:2). Other times, the context clearly indicates that anarthrous nouns are definite. For example, John 1:1 begins as follows: ἐν ἀρχῇ. We will learn about the preposition ἐν in the next chapter, but this prepositional phrase clearly indicates "in *the* beginning," even though ἀρχῇ is anarthrous, because there is only *one* beginning.

One comment about word order and the Greek article. We have noted that word order is flexible in Greek, especially when compared to English; yet Greek

---

1. There are some very (in)famous issues concerning the anarthrous use of θεός in John 1:1. We will not discuss this specific issue in this book, but later in your Greek studies you'll learn about Colwell's Rule. For now it is important to stress that *almost nothing is proved or disproved by the presence or absence of the article in Greek.*

word order is not completely free. The article *always* precedes the substantive that it modifies (e.g., ἡ ἀγάπη). There may be other modifiers between the article and the substantive, but the article will never follow the substantive that it modifies. The significance of this will be more evident in the discussion of adjectives.

THE ADJECTIVE: SECOND AND FIRST DECLENSION PATTERNS

The most common function of an adjective is to modify a noun or other substantive. Adjectives often add important, but not *syntactically* necessary, information. Consider, for example, the following sentence: "The *beloved* disciple was very close to Jesus." If the adjective *beloved* were removed, the sentence would still be syntactically correct, but it would not communicate nearly as much. Greek is a particularly adjective-rich language. As we will see, in addition to adjectives, Greek also uses participles (e.g., attributive) and phrases (e.g., prepositional) to modify substantives.

The Forms of Adjectives

Recall that the article is a type of adjective that modifies a noun or substantive. Remember also that because an article must be able to modify any substantive (in any case, number, and gender), there must be twenty-four forms of the article. The same is true for adjectives. The Greek article has only one paradigm—the one that we just looked at. The article follows a **2-1-2 declension pattern** (even when it is modifying third declension nouns, which we'll look at later). It's not that simple for adjectives. The adjectives that we are looking at in this chapter also follow a 2-1-2 pattern, but other patterns exist as well.[2] Here is the paradigm for a frequently occurring 2-1-2 pattern adjective, ἀγαθός, often translated "good." The case endings are bolded for clarity.

	2 masculine	1 feminine	2 neuter
nom sg	ἀγαθ**ός**	ἀγαθ**ή**	ἀγαθ**όν**
gen sg	ἀγαθ**οῦ**	ἀγαθ**ῆς**	ἀγαθ**οῦ**
dat sg	ἀγαθ**ῷ**	ἀγαθ**ῇ**	ἀγαθ**ῷ**
acc sg	ἀγαθ**όν**	ἀγαθ**ήν**	ἀγαθ**όν**

---

2. These are sometimes called *three-termination* or *three-ending* adjectives. Later, we will learn 3-1-3 declension pattern adjectives, which follow third and first declension noun endings. We will also learn about *two-termination* or *two-ending* adjectives in this chapter.

	2 masculine	1 feminine	2 neuter
nom pl	ἀγαθοί	ἀγαθαί	ἀγαθά
gen pl	ἀγαθῶν	ἀγαθῶν	ἀγαθῶν
dat pl	ἀγαθοῖς	ἀγαθαῖς	ἀγαθοῖς
acc pl	ἀγαθούς	ἀγαθάς	ἀγαθά

Unlike the article, notice that the endings for the masculine and neuter forms of the 2-1-2 pattern adjective follow exactly the case endings for the masculine and neuter second declension nouns. Notice also that the feminine forms for ἀγαθός have the same endings as η-type first declension feminine nouns throughout the paradigm. This is because the stem of this adjective is ἀγαθ-. Recall from the previous chapter that there are three types of first declension feminine nouns: η-type, α-impure type, and α-pure type, and that α-pure type nouns have an alpha throughout the singular forms because the letter before the alpha ending of the noun stem is preceded by an epsilon, iota, or rho. This same rule can now be applied to adjectives. In the above example, the adjective stem is ἀγαθ-. Because the adjective stem ends in a theta, the feminine forms of this adjective have an eta in *all* the singular endings. But now let's look at another common adjective, ἅγιος, often translated "holy." The stem for this adjective is ἁγι-, so the feminine forms have an alpha in *all* the singular endings. Here is the paradigm for ἅγιος. The case endings are bolded for clarity.

	2 masculine	1 feminine	2 neuter
nom sg	ἅγιος	ἁγία	ἅγιον
gen sg	ἁγίου	ἁγίας	ἁγίου
dat sg	ἁγίῳ	ἁγίᾳ	ἁγίῳ
acc sg	ἅγιον	ἁγίαν	ἅγιον
nom pl	ἅγιοι	ἅγιαι	ἅγια
gen pl	ἁγίων	ἁγίων	ἁγίων
dat pl	ἁγίοις	ἁγίαις	ἁγίοις
acc pl	ἁγίους	ἁγίας	ἅγια

Like the article, when an adjective modifies a substantive, it *must* agree with the substantive in case, number, and gender. Also like the article, this does not necessarily mean that the case ending for an adjective will look identical to the case ending of the substantive that it modifies, although the two will *always* agree in case, number, and gender. Consider the following examples, especially paying attention to the bolded case endings.

τὸν ἀγαθὸν λόγ**ον**	the good word	(accusative singular masculine)
τ**αῖς** ἀγαθ**αῖς** ἡμέρ**αις**	to/for/in the good days	(dative plural feminine)
ἡ ἀγαθ**ὴ** βασιλεί**α**	the good kingdom	(nominative singular feminine)
τὸν ἀγαθὸν μαθητ**ήν**	the good disciple	(accusative singular masculine)
αἱ ἅγιαι ὁδ**οί**	the holy ways	(nominative plural feminine)
τ**ὴν** ἁγί**αν** παρθέν**ον**	the holy virgin	(accusative singular feminine)
τ**ῆς** ἁγί**ας** ἡμέρ**ας**	of the holy day	(genitive singular feminine)
τ**ὰς** ἁγί**ας** ἡμέρ**ας**	the holy days	(accusative plural feminine)

Another common pattern for adjectives is the **2-2 declension pattern**, where one form of the adjective is used to modify masculine and feminine nouns and another form is used for neuter nouns.[3] Here is the paradigm for a common 2-2 pattern adjective, ἁμαρτωλός, often translated "sinful."

	2 masculine/ feminine	2 neuter
nom sg	ἁμαρτωλός	ἁμαρτωλόν
gen sg	ἁμαρτωλοῦ	ἁμαρτωλοῦ
dat sg	ἁμαρτωλῷ	ἁμαρτωλῷ
acc sg	ἁμαρτωλόν	ἁματωλόν
nom pl	ἁμαρτωλοί	ἁμαρτωλά
gen pl	ἁμαρτωλῶν	ἁμαρτωλῶν
dat pl	ἁμαρτωλοῖς	ἁμαρτωλοῖς
acc pl	ἁμαρτωλούς	ἁμαρτωλά

---

3. These are sometimes called *two-termination* or *two-ending* adjectives.

For 2-2 pattern adjectives, the form that follows second declension masculine case endings is used to modify both masculine and feminine nouns; the form that follows second declension neuter case endings is used to modify neuter nouns. Consider the following examples.

ταῖς ἁμαρτωλοῖς ἡμέραις	to/for/in the sinful days	(dative plural feminine)
τὸ ἁμαρτωλὸν ἔργον	the sinful work	(nominative or accusative singular neuter)
αἱ ἁμαρτωλοὶ ὁδοί	the sinful ways	(nominative plural feminine)

It is important to stress that adjectives *must* agree with the substantives that they modify in case, number, and gender, but not necessarily in declension. In other words, if a noun is first declension masculine (e.g., προφήτης), it must be modified by the *masculine* form of an adjective, even if the adjective is a 2-1-2 or 2-2 pattern adjective, which follows *second declension* masculine case endings (e.g., ἀγαθός or ἁμαρτωλός). Or if a noun is second declension *feminine* (e.g., ὁδός), it must be modified by the feminine form of an adjective, even if that adjective form follows first declension feminine endings (e.g., ἁγία) or uses the same endings as those used for second declension masculine adjectives (e.g., ἁμαρτωλός). You might think of an adjective like a shadow—whatever the noun is, the adjective must exactly shadow it in case, number, and gender.

Lexical Form and Parsing

The **lexical form** for 2-1-2 pattern adjectives lists the nominative singular form, followed by the endings that are used for the feminine and neuter forms. Thus, the lexical form for ἀγαθός is ἀγαθός, -ή, -όν. (Sometimes the entire feminine and neuter forms are listed.) Based on the final letter of the adjective stem, you can determine if the feminine forms follow the paradigm for η-type, α-impure type, or α-pure type first declension nouns. For 2-2 pattern adjectives, the lexical form lists the nominative singular form used to modify masculine and feminine nouns, followed by the ending for the neuter form of the adjective. Thus, the lexical form for ἁμαρτωλός is ἁμαρτωλός, -όν.

Here's how you parse adjectives. Remember that when you are parsing isolated words in a list, you must list all possibilities. The inflected meaning is tricky; the adjective could be modifying a substantive with which it agrees in case, number, and gender (as indicated in the inflected meaning of the parsing), or it could actually be functioning as a substantive, as we'll see in the next section.

inflected form	case	num	gender	lexical form	inflected meaning
ἀγαθόν	acc nom *or* acc	sg	masc neut	ἀγαθός, -ή, -όν	good (masc or neut sg entity)
ἁμαρτωλῶν	gen	pl	masc fem neut	ἁμαρτωλός, -όν	of sinful (gen pl entity)

The Functions of Adjectives

Greek adjectives have three basic functions. In the **attributive function**, an adjective *modifies* a substantive (as seen in the examples above); the adjective is functioning *attributively*.[4] In the **substantival function**, an adjective functions as a substantive; it is functioning *substantivally*. These first two functions are close to English; for example, "the holy word" (the adjective "holy" is functioning attributively) or "the good, the bad, and the ugly" (the three adjectives are functioning substantivally). Finally, in the **predicate function**, an adjective functions as a predicate adjective, often without a verb, to *make a predication* about a substantive. When a form of an equative verb (such as εἰμί, which we learn in this chapter) is assumed but not present, this is sometimes called a **verbless clause**. There is no real parallel in English to this third function of the Greek adjective in a verbless clauses, as we'll see in the examples below. Now we'll look at each of these functions in more detail.

The Attributive Function of the Adjective

If the adjective is **articular** (immediately preceded by the article) and there is a substantive in close proximity that agrees with the adjective in case, number, and gender, then it is functioning attributively. Furthermore, Greek uses the order in which the article, an adjective, and a modified substantive appear in a phrase to indicate two types of attributive adjectives. Consider the following examples:

ὁ ἅγιος κύριος	the holy lord	(first attributive position)
ὁ κύριος ὁ ἅγιος	the holy lord	(second attributive position)

Notice that in each example the adjective is articular (as indicated in *italics*). Greek uses two different constructions for the attributive function of the

---

4. Sometimes the terms *adjectival* and *attributive* are used interchangeably, but it is better to think of *adjectival* as the larger term and *attributive*, *substantival*, and *predicate* as the three adjectival functions. Thus, we will refer to the attributive (*not* adjectival) function of the adjective when the adjective is modifying another substantive.

adjective, and each construction has the same translation value—regardless of whether it is first or second position, each of the above Greek adjectival phrases would be translated "the holy lord." These two types of constructions are very common in Greek. Moreover, these constructions are not limited to adjectives and nouns but apply to any word or construction that can modify a substantive. Hence it is helpful to summarize these constructions as follows:[5]

first attributive position: *article*-modifier-substantive
second attributive position: *article*-substantive-*article*-modifier

As we continue, we'll see that an attributive modifier can be an adjective, another substantive, a participle, or a prepositional phrase, and that a substantive can be a noun, a participle, an infinitive, or even an adjective. So, it is important to be able to recognize these first and second attributive positions. It is actually easy to keep these two constructions straight if you simply count the articles (in *italics* above)—*one* article means *first* attributive and *two* articles means *second* attributive.[6] In the second attributive construction the modifier comes *after* the substantive, and the article is *repeated* before the modifier. Later we'll see that this construction is sometimes used when an entire phrase functions as a modifier of a substantive.

The Substantival Function of the Adjective

The substantival function of the adjective is fairly easy to recognize—there is no noun (or other part of speech functioning as a substantive) immediately near the adjective that matches the adjective in case, number, and gender. In other words, the adjective stands alone. For example:

τοῖς ἁγίοις ἐν Χριστῷ   to the holy ones in Christ

Notice that there is no other dative plural substantive around that ἁγίοις could be modifying; hence, it is functioning substantivally. Notice also that the form of ἁγίοις is dative plural and could be masculine or neuter. In this example, however, ἁγίοις refers to believers, because the context is an epistle (the above is modified from Col 1:2). Since ἁγίοις refers to people, the gender is masculine.

---

5. There is also a **third attributive position**: substantive-article-modifier, which is much less common.
6. If you can count to two, you can do a lot of Greek and can keep potentially confusing distinctions straight in your thinking. This simple idea of counting to two can also aid you with a few other grammatical elements introduced later in the book.

In Greek, a masculine substantival adjective often refers to men *and* women (we'll talk about this more in a future chapter).

The gender of a substantival adjective often indicates an implied substantive. For example, a masculine adjective would imply men or people in general, whereas a feminine adjective would most likely refer to women specifically. The neuter plural substantival adjective can often imply "things." Consider the following possible translations for substantival adjectives. (Substantival adjectives are not always articular, although they frequently are.)

ὁ ἀγαθός	the good man
οἱ ἀγαθοί	the good men, the good men and women, the good people
ἡ ἀγαθή	the good woman
ταῖς ἀγαθαῖς	to/for the good women
τὰ ἀγαθά	the good things

The Predicate Function of the Adjective

Remember that Greek uses the word order of the article, an adjective, and a modified substantive to indicate the function of an adjective. Consider the following examples:

ἅγιος ὁ κύριος	the lord *is* holy	(first predicate position)
ὁ κύριος ἅγιος	the lord *is* holy	(second predicate position)

In these examples, the adjective is anarthrous, whereas the modified substantive is articular (indicated in *italics* above). This indicates the predicate function of an adjective. An equative verb (such as εἰμί, which we'll look at next in this chapter) may be present or only assumed, but a verb is required in the English translation. If the verb is assumed but not stated explicitly, then this is a **verbless clause**.

So far, we have looked at examples of adjective constructions that include an article. Ambiguity arises when no article is present. In such cases, context is key! It is helpful to understand that an attributive adjective construction forms a noun **phrase** that is likely functioning as a subject, direct object, or indirect object. As such, it could not stand alone as a complete sentence. A predicate adjective construction, however, is making a predication and functions like a verb **clause**, even if an equative verb is only assumed. The following constructions could either indicate an attributive or a predicate adjective, although the actual context would make clear which was intended.[7]

---

7. The possible translation assumes that κύριος is definite, but "a lord" is also a possible translation.

ἅγιος κύριος	the holy lord
	the lord is holy
κύριος ἅγιος	the holy lord
	the lord is holy

Determining the Function of Adjectives

The only way to determine the function of an adjective is to look carefully at its immediate context. Once you have identified this, three questions will help you determine an adjective's function.

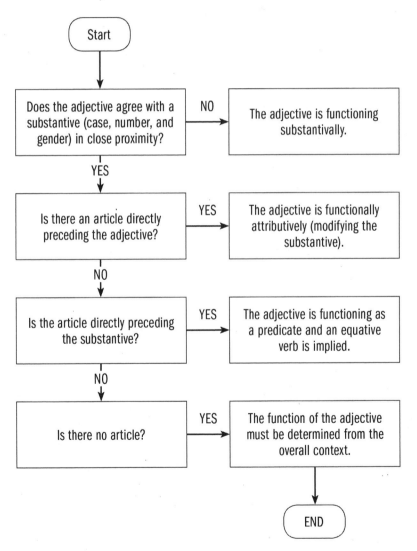

Example One: τῇ ἐσχάτῃ ἡμέρᾳ

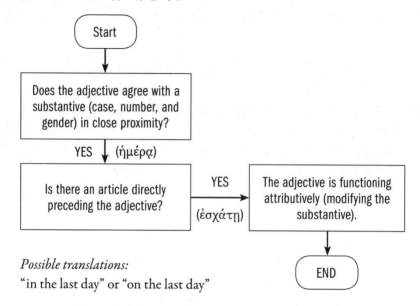

Possible translations:
"in the last day" or "on the last day"

Example Two: αἱ ἡμέραι πονηραί

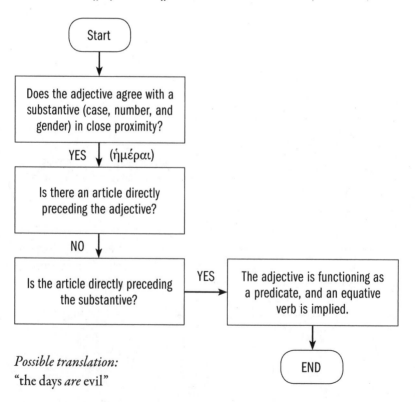

Possible translation:
"the days *are* evil"

Example Three: πιστὸς ὁ θεός

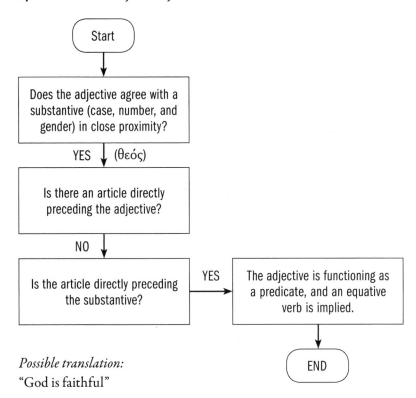

Possible translation:
"God is faithful"

THE VERB εἰμί

In chapter 3, we discussed **equative verbs**, which "link" a subject with some predication about that subject. For example, "God is love"; "love" makes a predication, or a statement, about God. Making predications about subjects is a basic function of language, so it is unsurprising that the most common verb in any language is often an equative verb, such as the English verb "to be." In chapter 3 we also discussed **intransitive verbs**, verbs that cannot take a direct object or be made into a passive. In this chapter, we will learn the Greek equative, intransitive verb εἰμί. There is no voice (active, middle, or passive) with εἰμί, because it is an equative, intransitive verb. Instead, εἰμί indicates a state of being or affairs. The present indicative tense-form for εἰμί is as follows:

1 sg	εἰμί	I am
2 sg	εἶ	you (sg) are
3 sg	ἐστί(ν)	he/she/it is
		(cont.)

1 pl	ἐσμέν	we are
2 pl	ἐστέ	you (pl) are
3 pl	εἰσί(ν)	they are

Recall that Koine Greek has two classes of verbs: omega verbs (such as λύω) and μι verbs. Clearly, εἰμί is a μι verb! As noted previously, μι verbs are older verb forms that occur frequently, as εἰμί does in the GNT. In fact, a form of εἰμί occurs on every page of the GNT! We will see more examples of other common μι verbs in later chapters. Although εἰμί appears to be irregular, it is actually a regular conjugation that uses several different personal endings from those that you memorized for the present active indicative of λύω. To learn how the individual forms for εἰμί were derived, read "For the Curious."

For the Curious

The actual stem for εἰμί is εσ-. This is visible in the third-person singular (ἐστί), first-person plural (ἐσμέν), and second-person plural (ἐστέ). The derivation of the other three forms follows phonological rules, some of which we have observed previously.

εἰμί	εσ + μι → σ drops before μ; compensatory lengthening explains the diphthong ει → εἰμί
εἶ	εσ + σι → intervocalic σ drops out; compensatory lengthening explains the diphthong ει → εἶ
εἰσί	εσ + ντι → ντ (dentals) drop after σ; compensatory lengthening explains the diphthong ει → εἰσί

You don't need to know how the forms of εἰμί were derived, but you *must* memorize the paradigm for εἰμί perfectly—backward, forward, and with accents and breathing marks. That's because there are several other forms that look very close to these forms. Remember that a form of εἰμί occurs on every page of the GNT.

In chapter 4 we noted that one function of the nominative case is as a **predicate nominative** or **predicate adjective** with an equative verb—most frequently εἰμί.[8] Consider the following example from the GNT:

---

8. There are two other Greek verbs that can sometimes function as equative verbs: γίνομαι, which you learned in chapter 3, and ὑπάρχω, which you will learn in chapter 7.

ὁ θεὸς ἀγάπη ἐστίν (1 John 4:16)
God is love.

Notice that both ὁ θεός (the subject) and ἀγάπη (the predicate nominative) are in the nominative case. This is often a clue that you should look for a form of εἰμί—when two substantives in close proximity are both in the nominative case.

HEADS UP!

As noted, εἰμί is classified as a μι verb. Although this type of verb formation eventually gave way to the ω-type of verb formation, several μι verbs are very common in the NT. If you want to look ahead, look through the present indicative forms for μι verbs in chapter 24 and see if you can spot the similarities between the personal endings used for μι verbs and the paradigm for εἰμί presented in this chapter. As we introduce new tense-forms, we will direct your attention to the corresponding μι-verb forms in chapters 24 and 25. You do not need to memorize those forms now, but if you keep peeking ahead, you will find that you already know most of the forms by the time we reach chapters 24 and 25.

REVIEW OF CHAPTER 5

In this chapter we introduced the Greek article, which is a type of adjective, or substantive modifier. Because the article must be able to modify any substantive, there are twenty-four forms in total, which must be memorized exactly. The article agrees with the substantive that it modifies in case, number, and gender; sometimes the *ending* of the article will be the same as the *case ending* of the word that it modifies, but not always. Even so, the article always agrees with the substantive that it modifies. We also learned the lexical form and how to parse forms of the article.

The function of the article in Greek is not simple to grasp. The absence of the article does not mean that the substantive is indefinite, and the article is often present in Greek when it is not in English. We also introduced two important terms: *articular* (modified by an article) and *anarthrous* (not modified by an article).

In this chapter, we also learned the form of first and second declension adjectives, including those that follow a 2-1-2 pattern and those that follow a 2-2 pattern. Like the article, an adjective must agree in case, number, and gender with the substantive that it modifies. The lexical form of the adjective is like shorthand that indicates what the nominative singular endings of the masculine, feminine, and neuter are (or the masculine and neuter endings for 2-2 pattern adjectives). The most common function of the adjective is to modify a substantive attributively. It can also function as a substantive. Finally, the adjective can function to give a predication about a substantive. The attributive and predicate functions are determined by the word order of the adjective, substantive, and article:

ὁ ἅγιος κύριος	the holy lord	(first attributive position)
ὁ κύριος ὁ ἅγιος	the holy lord	(second attributive position)
ἅγιος ὁ κύριος	the lord *is* holy	(first predicate position)
ὁ κύριος ἅγιος	the lord *is* holy	(second predicate position)

When there is no article present, context alone determines if the adjective is functioning attributively or as a predicate.

Finally, we introduced the verb εἰμί, which often is used with a predicate nominative or predicate adjective. The present indicative forms of εἰμί must be memorized exactly.

Study Guide for Chapter 5

1. Be able to understand each of the following concepts:

   articular/arthrous

   anarthrous

   attributive function of the adjective

   substantival function of the adjective

   predicate function of the adjective

   verbless clause

   first attributive position

   second attributive position

   equative verb

   intransitive verb

   predicate nominative

   predicate adjective

2. Be able to parse forms of the article, first and second declension adjectives, and present indicative forms of εἰμί, and translate basic Koine sentences.

Vocabulary to Memorize

Here is the vocabulary for chapter 5. The "(subst)" following the glosses for an adjective indicate a possible translation for the substantival use of that adjective. If you see "(pass)," this means that the given verb has that possible meaning in the passive voice.

ἀγαθός, -ή, -όν	good, useful; possessions (pl; subst)[1] (102)
ἀγαπητός, -ή, -όν	beloved, dear (61)
ἅγιος, -α, -ον	holy, pure, set apart; saints, God's people (subst) (233)
ἀλήθεια, -ας, ἡ	truth, truthfulness (109)
ἁμαρτάνω	I sin, I do wrong (270)
ἁμαρτωλός, -όν	sinful; sinner (subst) (47)
ἀναβλέπω	I look up, I receive sight, I regain sight (25)
δίκαιος, -α, -ον	just, righteous, right, upright (79)
εἰμί	I am, I exist, I live, I am present (2,462)
ἔξω (+gen)	outside (impr prep);[2] outside (adv)[3] (63)
εὐαγγέλιον, -ου, τό	good news, gospel (76)
ἤ	or, either . . . or, than (343)
κακός, -ή, -όν	bad, evil, dangerous (50)
καλός, -ή, -όν	good, beautiful, useful (100)
κωφός, -ή, -όν	deaf, mute, dumb (14)
μᾶλλον	more, rather, much more (81)
νεκρός, -ά, -όν	dead, useless; corpse (subst) (128)
ὁ, ἡ, τό	the (19,867)
πιστός, -ή, -όν	faithful, believing, trustworthy (67)
σημεῖον, -ου, τό	sign, miracle (77)
σοφός, -ή, -όν	wise, skillful, learned (20)
τέλειος, -α, -ον	perfect, complete, mature (19)
τυφλός, -ή, -όν	blind (50)
φαίνω	I shine; I appear (mid; pass) (31)
φόβος, -ου, ὁ	fear, terror, respect, reverence (47)

1 When this adjective is plural and is functioning substantivally, it has this meaning.

2 This preposition is followed by a substantive in the genitive case; it is also an "improper" preposition; you'll learn more about this in the next two chapters. To distinguish between verbs that take an object in the genitive or dative case, the case associated with a preposition is listed immediately after the preposition.

3 Some prepositions can also function adverbially, which is indicated with (adv).

Paradigms to Memorize

The following paradigms must be memorized for this chapter: the article (ὁ, ἡ, τό), the following adjectives: ἀγαθός, -ή, -όν; ἅγιος, -ία, -ιον; ἁμαρτωλός, -όν; and the present indicative of εἰμί. Remember that knowing the article and the paradigm for εἰμί will pay back richly. The adjective paradigms are a good chance to review the case endings for first and second declension nouns, so they shouldn't be too hard to memorize.

PARADIGM OF THE ARTICLE (ὁ, ἡ, τό)

	masc (2)	fem (1)	neut (2)
nom sg	ὁ	ἡ	τό
gen sg	τοῦ	τῆς	τοῦ
dat sg	τῷ	τῇ	τῷ
acc sg	τόν	τήν	τό
nom pl	οἱ	αἱ	τά
gen pl	τῶν	τῶν	τῶν
dat pl	τοῖς	ταῖς	τοῖς
acc pl	τούς	τάς	τά

PARADIGM OF ἀγαθός, -ή, -όν

	masc (2)	fem (1)	neut (2)
nom sg	ἀγαθός	ἀγαθή	ἀγαθόν
gen sg	ἀγαθοῦ	ἀγαθῆς	ἀγαθοῦ
dat sg	ἀγαθῷ	ἀγαθῇ	ἀγαθῷ
acc sg	ἀγαθόν	ἀγαθήν	ἀγαθόν
nom pl	ἀγαθοί	ἀγαθαί	ἀγαθά
gen pl	ἀγαθῶν	ἀγαθῶν	ἀγαθῶν
dat pl	ἀγαθοῖς	ἀγαθαῖς	ἀγαθοῖς
acc pl	ἀγαθούς	ἀγαθάς	ἀγαθά

PARADIGM OF ἅγιος, -ία, -ιον

	masc (2)	fem (1)	neut (2)
nom sg	ἅγιος	ἁγία	ἅγιον
gen sg	ἁγίου	ἁγίας	ἁγίου
dat sg	ἁγίῳ	ἁγίᾳ	ἁγίῳ
acc sg	ἅγιον	ἁγίαν	ἅγιον
nom pl	ἅγιοι	ἅγιαι	ἅγια
gen pl	ἁγίων	ἁγίων	ἁγίων
dat pl	ἁγίοις	ἁγίαις	ἁγίοις
acc pl	ἁγίους	ἁγίας	ἅγια

PARADIGM OF ἁμαρτωλός, -όν

	masc/fem (2)	neut (2)
nom sg	ἁμαρτωλός	ἁμαρτωλόν
gen sg	ἁμαρτωλοῦ	ἁμαρτωλοῦ
dat sg	ἁμαρτωλῷ	ἁμαρτωλῷ
acc sg	ἁμαρτωλόν	ἁμαρτωλόν
nom pl	ἁμαρτωλοί	ἁμαρτωλά
gen pl	ἁμαρτωλῶν	ἁμαρτωλῶν
dat pl	ἁμαρτωλοῖς	ἁμαρτωλοῖς
acc pl	ἁμαρτωλούς	ἁμαρτωλά

PRESENT INDICATIVE OF εἰμί

1 sg	εἰμί
2 sg	εἶ
3 sg	ἐστί(ν)
1 pl	ἐσμέν
2 pl	ἐστέ
3 pl	εἰσί(ν)

chapter SIX

PREPOSITIONS, PERSONAL PRONOUNS, AND BASIC CONJUNCTIONS

OBJECTIVES AND OVERVIEW

Chapter 6 introduces the following linguistic concepts, morphemes, and paradigms:

- preposition and prepositional phrase; object of a preposition
- oblique cases (accusative, dative, genitive)
- pronoun, antecedent
- forms of the first-, second-, and third-person personal pronouns
- functions of the personal pronoun
- adjectival functions of αὐτός
- lexical form for personal pronouns and parsing
- basic coordinating and subordinating conjunctions
- postpositive position

PREPOSITIONS AND PREPOSITIONAL PHRASES

A **preposition** is a word (often very small) that is used with a substantive to show its relationship to another syntactic unit, such as another substantive, a verb, or a clause.[1] For example, to show the relationship between *plate* and *table*, we could say, "the plate is *on* the table." The preposition "on" indicates the spatial relationship between the plate and the table.

---

1. Prepositions are sometimes called *function words* because they show the relationship between a substantive and another syntactic unit.

The word *preposition* indicates its placement in the "pre-position." In other words, a preposition is always placed before another substantive. Additionally, a preposition introduces **a prepositional phrase**. The substantive in this phrase is called *the object of the preposition*. For example:

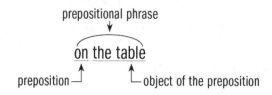

The object of a preposition will always be a substantive (even if it is not a noun), so the entire construction is a prepositional *phrase*, not a *clause*, because it does not contain a finite verb. This is important for determining the boundaries of a prepositional phrase. Once you encounter a finite verb, you know that you have gone "outside" the prepositional phrase. We will discuss this further with some basic Greek sentences below.

There is usually only one substantive that functions as the object of the preposition, although this substantive may have several modifiers.[2] In the prepositional phrase "on the large table," "table" is the object of the preposition, whereas "the" and "large" are modifying the noun "table."

Prepositions can indicate a spatial relationship between two objects, as seen in the example of the plate and the table above. Prepositional phrases can also function adverbially. For example, "Jesus was raised *on the third day*." The prepositional phrase "on the third day" indicates *when* Jesus was raised from the dead. Notice that we could substitute an adverb for this prepositional phrase that would have the same *syntactic* (adverbial) function as the prepositional phrase. For example:

Jesus was raised *on the third day.*   (adverbial prepositional phrase)
Jesus was raised *victoriously.*   (adverb)

In Greek, the meaning of a preposition depends upon the case of its object, which will be in one of the **oblique cases** (accusative, genitive, or dative).[3] In this chapter, we will learn some Greek prepositions that are associated with only one case. In future chapters, we learn prepositions that are associated with two or

---

2. Occasionally there are two substantives joined by a conjunction that form the object of the preposition; e.g., "peace *from* God our Father *and* the Lord Jesus Christ" (Eph 1:2).

3. This is sometimes expressed in terms of a preposition "governing" the case of a substantive.

three cases. But before we do, it is helpful to understand that each of the oblique cases itself has an inherent spatial or temporal orientation. This can be summarized as follows:

case	spatial orientation	temporal orientation
genitive	motion from or from out of	type of time
dative	stationary (no motion)	point in time
accusative	motion toward or into	duration

The spatial orientations can be illustrated as follows:

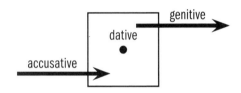

To illustrate these temporal orientations, consider the noun *day*: *day* in the accusative could indicate "throughout the day" (duration) without any accompanying preposition; *day* in the genitive case could indicate "daytime" (type of time) without any accompanying preposition; and *day* in the dative could indicate "on the day" (point in time) without any accompanying preposition. These distinctions were more pronounced in Attic Greek. So, this is an example of how Koine was simplifying by using prepositions to make explicit the nuances implicit in each case. Even so, knowing these basic orientations can help when memorizing prepositions in the assigned vocabulary.

Here are examples from the GNT of several of the prepositions (which are italicized) that are assigned in this chapter.[4]

ἔρχεται *εἰς* τὸν οἶκον	he goes *into* the house (Matt 9:7)
ἐν τῇ ὁδῷ	*on* the way (Matt 5:25)
ἀποστέλλω τὸν ἄγγελόν μου *πρὸ* προσώπου σου	I send my messenger *before* you (Mark 1:2)

---

4. As with previous examples, the actual verbs have sometimes been modified to present tense-forms. Also don't worry if you don't know all the Greek words yet—you will by the end of this book.

Greek prepositions often have a range of possible meanings, so you should never associate only one English word with a given preposition. For example, it is easy to think of εἰς as spatially indicating "into," but in the majority of the occurrences in GNT εἰς indicates *purpose* and is best translated "for." Additionally, sometimes the use of the genitive case or the dative case without a preposition in the Greek requires an English preposition to indicate the case function, such as "of" in a genitival construction or "to" with the dative (e.g., the indirect-object function). This has to do with the inherent meaning of Greek cases, as discussed above, which can only be rendered by using prepositions in English translations. It is also important to understand that when a genitive or dative is the *object* of a preposition, the preposition "governs" the meaning of its object, so English prepositions such as "of" or "to" that can be used to indicate case functions when there is no preposition are set aside when there is a preposition. For example, ἡ ἀγάπη τοῦ θεοῦ could be translated "the love *of* God," even though there is no preposition "of" in the Greek. The preposition "of" is required in English. But the prepositional phrase ἐκ τοῦ θεοῦ would not be translated "from *of* God" (as if "of" is required with the genitive, which it is not), but would be translated simply "from God."

One of the nice things about prepositions is that they are indeclinable, which means that you do not have to memorize an entire paradigm for each one. The form of a preposition does change, however, depending on the spelling of the word that follows it. For example, the preposition ἀπό drops its final vowel before an object that begins with a vowel (called *elision*); for example, ἀπ᾽ αὐτοῦ, *not* ἀπό αὐτοῦ, and ἀφ᾽ ἡμῶν *not* ἀπό ἡμῶν.[5] As a second example, the preposition ἐκ has the form ἐξ before an object that begins with a vowel; for example, ἐξ οἴκου, *not* ἐκ οἴκου.

Prepositional phrases can function either adverbially or adjectivally. The adverbial function of prepositional phrases is very common. Consider the following examples:

πιστεύεις εἰς τὸν υἱὸν τοῦ ἀνθρώπου (John 9:35)
you believe *in the son of man*

ἀποστέλλω τὸν ἄγγελόν μου *πρὸ προσώπου σου* (Mark 1:2)[6]
I send my messenger *before you*

---

5. We have already seen this phonological phenomenon with the negative adverb οὐ, which uses the form οὐκ before verb forms beginning with a vowel that has a smooth breathing mark and the form οὐχ before verb forms beginning with a rough breathing mark.

6. You may have noticed that the word ἄγγελόν has two accents. This is because the accent on the

In the first example, the preposition phrase (*in italics*) limits the verb πιστεύεις; it specifies what is believed. In the second example, the prepositional phrase tells *where* the object of the verb is sent. Notice also the "boundaries" of the prepositional phrase—only of the words in *italics* in the above examples are part of the prepositional phrase.

Prepositional phrases may function adjectivally by further describing a substantive. Consider the following example:

ἄνθρωπος ἐν πνεύματι ἀκαθάρτῳ (Mark 1:23)
a man *with an unclean spirit*

This adjectival function often uses the second attributive position that we saw with adjectives (article-substantive-article-modifier), where the prepositional phrase is understood as filling the "modifier" slot. Notice also that this construction is usually translated as a relative clause in English, because a relative clause also modifies a substantive. For example:

τὸ φῶς τὸ ἐν σοί (Matt 6:23)
the light *that is in you*

Sometimes, when the article is used with a prepositional phrase, the article can be understood as functioning substantivally. The overall context is essential for understanding this function of the article. Consider the following example:

Πέτρος καὶ οἱ σὺν αὐτῷ (Luke 9:32)
Peter and the ones *with him*

In this example, the nominative plural masculine article implies people, which is indicated with the English word "ones." This use of the article and a prepositional phrase is relatively common.

Finally, it is not uncommon for the object of a preposition to be anarthrous. For example, ἐξ οἴκου would be translated "from *the* house" if the context made it clear that a particular house was intended. Recall that John 1:1 begins with ἐν ἀρχῇ and that ἀρχῇ is definite even though it is anarthrous; that is, "in *the*

---

personal pronoun μου has "thrown" its accent back on the noun ἄγγελον. There are several small words in Greek, called *enclitics*, that like to do this, so that they will be pronounced as part of the preceding word. You can read more about this in appendix 1, "Overview of Greek Accents."

beginning." This construction is anarthrous in part due to the fact that ἀρχῇ is the object of the preposition ἐν.

PERSONAL PRONOUNS

A **pronoun** is a word that "stands in the place of" another substantive; it is sometimes called a *grammatical substitute* or *grammatical proxy.*[7] The substantive for which it substitutes is called an **antecedent**. Because a pronoun is a proxy for an antecedent, a pronoun *must* agree with its antecedent in *number* and *gender*— think of the pronoun as the "stunt double" of its antecedent. An antecedent is often a single word, but it can also be a group of words, an entire clause, or even a previously mentioned topic or argument. (We will discuss this broader understanding of an antecedent in future chapters.)

The *case* of the antecedent is determined by its function in the original clause or sentence in which it occurs, but the *case* of the pronoun is determined by its function in the clause or sentence in which it occurs. For example:

The Lord (antecedent) is gracious.	(*subject* of sentence)
We praise *him* (pronoun).	(*direct object* of verb)

The pronoun *him* is masculine singular because it agrees with its antecedent, *the Lord*, which is also masculine singular. *The Lord* is the subject and would be in the nominative case in Greek. Notice, however, that the form of the *pronoun* is not "he" (nominative case) but "him" (accusative case), because the pronoun functions as the direct object of the verb "praise." We will come back to this.

Greek has many different types of pronouns. In this chapter we will focus on personal pronouns, which are the most frequently used Greek pronouns. These pronouns stand in the place of *persons*, in the first and second person, and persons or objects in the third person. The first-person personal pronoun is ἐγώ; the second-person personal pronoun is σύ; and the third-person personal pronoun is αὐτός.

The Forms of the Personal Pronoun

Here are the forms for the first- and second-person personal pronouns. The forms in parentheses indicate the emphatic form of each pronoun, which is often used when the pronoun is the object of a preposition. We will discuss this emphatic use further below. The case endings are set in bold.

---

7. Wallace, *Greek Grammar beyond the Basics*, 316.

FIRST-PERSON PERSONAL PRONOUN (ἐγώ)

nom sg	ἐγώ	I
gen sg	μου (ἐμοῦ)	my
dat sg	μοι (ἐμοί)	to/for/in me
acc sg	με (ἐμέ)	me
nom pl	ἡμεῖς	we
gen pl	ἡμῶν	our
dat pl	ἡμῖν	to/for/in us
acc pl	ἡμᾶς	us

SECOND-PERSON PERSONAL PRONOUN (σύ)

nom sg	σύ	you (sg)
gen sg	σου (σοῦ)	your (sg)
dat sg	σοι (σοί)	to/for/in you (sg)
acc sg	σε (σέ)	you (sg)
nom pl	ὑμεῖς	you (pl)
gen pl	ὑμῶν	your (pl)
dat pl	ὑμῖν	to/for/in you (pl)
acc pl	ὑμᾶς	you (pl)

You need to memorize these forms exactly. Here are some hints that might make this easier. The first-person singular form (ἐγώ) is the Greek word from which we get the English word *ego*; all the other singular forms begin with a mu (μ), which might remind you of the m in *me* and *my*. The plural forms all begin with η, which is a lengthened ε, which has an "ee" sound (in modern Greek!) that rhymes with *we*. The second-person singular forms all start with a sigma (σ), which might remind you of the s in *second*; the plural forms all have an "oo" vowel sound that rhymes with *you*. Notice that the only difference between the first-person nominative *plural* form (ἡμεῖς) and the second-person nominative *plural* form (ὑμεῖς) is the initial vowel; both forms have rough breathing.

The first- and second-person endings are a bit different from ones that you have seen so far, although there are some similarities. For example, all the dative forms have an iota (ι); -ου is the genitive singular ending, and -ων is the genitive plural ending, which is unsurprising, nor is -ας as the accusative plural ending. In any event, you need to memorize these forms exactly.

Here is the chart for the third-person personal pronoun. The case endings are set in bold.

THIRD-PERSON PERSONAL PRONOUN (αὐτός, αὐτή, αὐτό)

	2		1		2	
nom sg	αὐτός	[he][1]	αὐτή	[she]	αὐτό	[it]
gen sg	αὐτοῦ	his	αὐτῆς	her	αὐτοῦ	its
dat sg	αὐτῷ	to/for him	αὐτῇ	to/for her	αὐτῷ	to/for it
acc sg	αὐτόν	him	αὐτήν	her	αὐτό	it

(cont.)

nom pl	αὐτοί	[they]	αὐταί	[they]	αὐτά	[they]
gen pl	αὐτῶν	their	αὐτῶν	their	αὐτῶν	their
dat pl	αὐτοῖς	to/for them	αὐταῖς	to/for them	αὐτοῖς	to/for them
acc pl	αὐτούς	them	αὐτάς	them	αὐτά	them

[1] The nominative inflected meanings are in square brackets because personal pronouns in the nominative case often indicate emphasis and do not function as a grammatical proxy.

Notice that the third-person personal pronoun has masculine, feminine, and neuter forms and follows a **2-1-2 declension pattern**. The masculine forms follow the second declension masculine case endings exactly, and the feminine forms follow the first declension feminine endings for η-type nouns exactly. The neuter forms follow the second declension neuter forms *except* that there is *no* nu in the nominative and accusative singular forms. This parallels the article (τό), but not the second declension noun (τέκνον).

The Functions of the Personal Pronoun
Grammatical Proxies and Possession

In the accusative and dative cases, Greek personal pronouns often function as grammatical proxies, standing in the place of their antecedents. Consider the following examples:[8]

θεραπεύει αὐτούς	he heals *them* (antecedent: the people following Jesus; function of the pronoun: direct object; Matt 12:15)
μυστήριον ὑμῖν λέγω	I tell a mystery *to you* (antecedent: the Corinthian recipients of the epistle; function of the pronoun: indirect object; 1 Cor 15:51)
λέγει αὐτῇ ὁ Ἰησοῦς	Jesus says *to her* (antecedent: Martha; function of pronoun: indirect object; John 11:25)

Emphatic forms of first- and second-person personal pronouns indicate emphasis, or function as the object of a preposition. For example:

ἐμὲ οὐ πάντοτε ἔχετε	you do not always have *me* (Matt 26:11)
εἰς ἐμὲ πιστεύετε	believe in *me* (John 14:1)

8. Some tense-forms have been modified, and some words have been deleted in these GNT examples. Some examples have been adapted from Goetchius, *Language of the New Testament*, 86–89.

Notice also the emphatic position of ἐμέ at the beginning of the first example.

In the genitive case, however, personal pronouns frequently indicate possession, as indicated by the inflected meanings listed in the paradigms above. Consider the following examples:

ἐν τῇ αὐτοῦ παρουσίᾳ	in *his* appearing (1 Thess 2:19)
ὑμῶν ἡ καρδία	*your* hearts (John 14:1)
αὐτοῦ τοὺς ὀφθαλμούς	*his* eyes (John 9:21)
ἡ ψυχή μου	*my* soul (Luke 1:46)

In the second example above, notice that the substantive ἡ καρδία is singular, whereas the use of the plural personal pronoun to indicate possession is plural. This occurs frequently in the GNT.

Emphasis with the Nominative Case

Remember that Greek finite verbs are inflected to indicate person and number—a noun or a pronoun is *not used* to indicate the subject of the verb, as is the case in English. Also recall that third-person verbs *may* have a nominative-case substantive to make the subject explicit, particularly in narrative. This concept has a parallel to personal pronouns. The use of *any* first- and second-personal pronoun in the nominative case indicates *emphasis* and thus is not *required* syntactically. (The third-person pronoun is discussed below.) It is hard to capture this in translation, although the addition of "-self" can help. Consider the following examples:

ἐγώ εἰμι ὁ ἄρτος τῆς ζωῆς	*I myself* am the bread of life (John 6:35)
σὺ εἶ ὁ υἱὸς τοῦ θεοῦ	*you yourself* are the son of God (Luke 4:41)
ὑμεῖς καθαροί ἐστε	*you yourselves* are pure (John 15:3)

In all the above examples, the personal pronoun is not required syntactically; we would have complete clauses in all three examples if the personal pronoun were omitted. Instead, it adds an element of emphasis.

Additional Translation Issues

The pronoun *must* agree with the grammatical gender of its antecedent. Thus, a masculine pronoun is used for a masculine antecedent. Yet this does not mean that this masculine pronoun is always translated as a masculine pronoun in English. Instead, you will need to translate Greek pronouns according to conventional English usage as the following examples illustrate.[9]

---

9. The following examples are from Goetchius, *Language of the New Testament*, 87.

Unless a grain [ὁ κόκκος] of wheat dies *it* [αὐτός] remains a single grain. (John 12:24)

The earth [ἡ γῆ] brought forth *its* [αὐτῆς] fruit. (Jas 5:18)

They were going to call *him* [αὐτό, referring to τὸ παιδίον] Zacharias. (Luke 1:59)

In the example from John 12:24, you would not translate αὐτός as "he" even though the inflected meaning lists "he" for αὐτός. This is because in English we normally use personal pronouns to reflect natural gender, not grammatical gender. So, a grain is an "it," not a "he" in English. The same is true for the example from James 5:18. In the example from Luke 1:59, the neuter pronoun αὐτό refers to the neuter antecedent παιδίον ("young child"). Yet in English we would not refer to a baby with "it," but rather with a masculine or feminine pronoun. Sometimes, however, Greek also does not follow grammatical gender with a neuter noun that refers to a person. For example, αὐτός or αὐτή is sometimes used according to the *natural* gender of παιδίον (e.g., a boy or a girl), when αὐτό would be expected grammatically in Greek.

Adjectival Functions of αὐτός

The most common function of αὐτός is as a pronoun, standing in the place of a previously named substantive. There are, however, two additional functions for αὐτός that are indicated by its word order with relation to an article and substantive in the same case, number, and gender. In both of these functions, αὐτός is functioning as a modifier of a substantive.

When a form of αὐτός, an article, and substantive in the same case, number, and gender occur in the attributive position (either first or second), αὐτός has the meaning of "the same." Consider the following examples:

ὁ αὐτὸς κύριος	the *same* lord (first attributive position; article-modifier-substantive; 1 Cor 12:5)
ὁ κύριος ὁ αὐτός	the *same* lord (second attributive position; article-substantive-article-modifier)

Here is an example from the GNT:

ὁ αὐτὸς θεός	the *same* God (1 Cor 12:6)

When a form of αὐτός, an article, and a substantive in the same case, number, and gender occur in the predicate position (either first or second), αὐτός has the meaning of "-self." This function of αὐτός is usually in the nominative case. Consider the following examples:

αὐτὸς ὁ κύριος	the lord *himself* (first predicate position; modifier-article-substantive)
ὁ κύριος αὐτός	the lord *himself* (second predicate position; article-substantive-modifier)

Here are some examples from the GNT.[10] (Note that sometimes the English word "very" is a possible translation of this use of αὐτός).

αὐτὸς ὁ θεός	God *himself* (Rev 21:3)
τὰ ἔργα αὐτά	the works *themselves* (John 14:11)
αὐτὴ ἡ ὥρα	that *very* hour (Acts 16:18)

Be sure to compare the example from Revelation 21:3 carefully with the previous example from 1 Corinthians 12:6.

Sometimes αὐτός functions substantivally, as the following example illustrates.

οἱ ἁμαρτωλοὶ τὸ αὐτὸ ποιοῦσιν
sinners do *the same thing* (Luke 6:33)

Finally, αὐτός in the nominative case can indicate emphasis, as we already saw with the first- and second-person personal pronouns in the nominative case.[11] For example:

Σίμων αὐτὸς ἐπίστευσεν
Simon himself believed (Acts 8:13)

This differs from the two adjectival functions of αὐτός because the article is not present. Instead αὐτός in the nominative case occurs by itself to indicate emphasis. Here is another example of αὐτός in the nominative case indicating emphasis and αὐτοῦ indicating the possessive function of the personal pronoun.

---

10. These examples are from Goetchius, *Language of the New Testament*, 81.

11. In the following examples from the GNT, the verb tense-forms have not been modified, so some of these forms will not be familiar to you. You should, however, be able to recognize the personal endings.

αὐτὸς σώσει τὸν λαὸν αὐτοῦ
He himself will save his people. (Matt 1:21)

Moreover, a unique function of αὐτός is that this *third-person* personal pronoun in the nominative case can also indicate emphasis for *first-* and *second-person* verbs. Consider the following examples:

αὐτὸς ἄνθρωπός εἰμι
I *myself* am a man (Acts 10:26)

αὐτοί γάρ ἠκούσαμεν
for we *ourselves* heard (Luke 22:71)

ὄψεσθε αὐτοί
you *yourselves* will see (Acts 18:15)

As you can see, αὐτός can have a wide variety of functions. The most common use of αὐτός, however, is as a grammatical proxy in the oblique (accusative, genitive, dative) cases.

Lexical Form and Parsing

The **lexical form** for the first- and second-person pronouns is the nominative singular; specifically, the lexical form for the first-person personal pronoun is ἐγώ, and for the second-person personal pronoun it is σύ. Here is how you would parse first- and second-person personal pronouns—note that there is no gender with these pronouns. To indicate this, "n/a" indicates that this category does "not apply" to first- and second-person personal pronouns.

inflected form	case	num	gender	lexical form	inflected meaning
ὑμῖν	dat	pl	n/a	σύ	to/for you (pl)
μου	gen	sg	n/a	ἐγώ	my
ἡμᾶς	acc	pl	n/a	ἐγώ	us (pl)

The **lexical form** for the third-person personal pronoun is αὐτός, -ή, -ό. This is similar to the lexical form for an adjective in that the nominative singular masculine form is followed by the endings for the feminine and neuter endings. Remember that when you are parsing isolated words in a list, you must list all possibilities. Here's how you would parse forms of αὐτός.

inflected form	case	num	gender	lexical form	inflected meaning
αὐτοῦ	gen	sg	masc neut	αὐτός, -ή, -ό	his its
αὐτάς	acc	pl	fem	αὐτός, -ή, -ό	them

BASIC CONJUNCTIONS

A **conjunction** is a word that connects two or more syntactic units (such as sentences, clauses, phrases, or words). Think of a conjunction as grammatical glue. There are two main types of conjunctions. **Coordinating conjunctions** join two or more *equal* syntactic units, such as a noun and a noun, a verb and a verb, a clause and a clause, etc. **Subordinating conjunctions** introduce subordinate clauses—clauses that are dependent in some way on a main, or independent, clause. Consequently, subordinate clauses cannot stand on their own. Consider the following examples from English:

We love to study Greek *and* Hebrew.	The word *and* is a coordinating conjunction that connects a noun (*Greek*) with another noun (*Hebrew*).
We love to study Greek, *because* we want to understand God's Word.	The word *because* is a subordinating conjunction that connects the subordinate clause (*because we want to understand God's Word*) to the main clause (*We love to study Greek*).

We have already learned several very basic Greek conjunctions: ἀλλά, δέ, καί, οὔτε, and ἤ. These are all coordinating conjunctions, which join equal syntactic units. Consider the following examples:

οὐκ ἐγὼ *ἀλλὰ* ὁ κύριος (1 Cor 7:10)
not I, *but* the Lord

Ἰάκωβος *καὶ* Ἰωσὴφ *καὶ* Σίμων (Matt 13:55)
James *and* Joseph *and* Simon

λαμβάνουσιν τέλη *ἢ* κῆνσον (Matt 17:25)
they receive taxes *or* tribute

Some coordinating conjunctions (such as οὔτε) also have a *correlative* function, such as "either/or" or "neither/nor." For example:

οὔτε θάνατος οὔτε ζωή (Rom 8:38)
neither death *nor* life

In this chapter we introduce three new conjunctions: γάρ, ὅτι, and οὖν. We'll look at each one in turn. The coordinating conjunction γάρ has a *causal* function; it usually gives a reason or an explanation for a previous clause, sentence, or even paragraph. It is often translated "for," "then," or "because." This conjunction is **postpositive**, meaning that it can never appear as the first word in the clause in which it occurs. It is often the second word, but it can sometimes be the third word in a clause. Often, however, it is translated in English as the first word according to conventional English usage. This is a very common conjunction. Here is an example of its use:

ἰδοὺ γὰρ ἡ βασιλεία τοῦ θεοῦ ἐντὸς ὑμῶν ἐστιν (Luke 17:21)
For see the kingdom of God is in your midst.

Next is the important and common subordinating conjunction ὅτι, which always introduces a dependent clause. Moreover, a ὅτι clause is dependent on the verb of the main clause and further explains the main verb in some way. There are three main functions of ὅτι. First, it often introduces a clause that gives a reason for the verbal idea in the main clause and is often translated "because." Here are some examples of this use of ὅτι:

ἐδίωκον οἱ Ἰουδαῖοι τὸν Ἰησοῦν, ὅτι ταῦτα ἐποίει ἐν σαββάτῳ.
    (John 5:16)
    The Jews were persecuting Jesus, *because* he was doing these things on
    the Sabbath.

ὑμεῖς δὲ μαρτυρεῖτε, ὅτι ἀπ᾽ ἀρχῆς μετ᾽ ἐμοῦ ἐστε (John 15:27)
    But you yourselves also bear witness, *because* you are with me from
    the beginning.

The second function of ὅτι is to give the content of a verb of knowing, perceiving, understanding, speaking, etc. This function of a ὅτι clause is parallel to a substantive functioning as the direct object of the verb. You can often test this out by looking at the verb on which the ὅτι clause depends and asking "what?" Consider the following Greek sentence:

λέγω ὅτι σὺ εἶ Πέτρος (Matt 16:18)
I say *that you yourself are Peter*

The ὅτι clause gives the content or the "what?" of the verbal idea expressed by λέγω. Notice that we could rewrite this sentence with a substantive in the accusative case functioning as the direct object of the verb: λέγω τὸν λόγον ("I say the word").

The third function of ὅτι is to introduce discourse, which can either be a direct quotation or indirect discourse.[12] Greek does not use quotation marks, but they are unnecessary because there are many ways to indicate a direct quotation. Perhaps the most common way that a quotation is indicated is by a change of person and/or number. In the following example, notice the shift from third person (αὐτῷ) to second person (σε).[13] This use of ὅτι parallels the use of quotation marks in English.

λέγουσιν αὐτῷ ὅτι πάντες ζητοῦσίν σε (Mark 1:37)
They say to him, *"Everyone is seeking you."*

The final conjunction introduced in this chapter is οὖν, which is an *inferential* coordinating conjunction. This conjunction draws a logical conclusion at the end of an argument. Frequently οὖν begins a new paragraph that draws a conclusion based on the previous paragraph or paragraphs. Οὖν is also postpositive, although it is often translated in English as the first word of the clause. For example:

παρακαλῶ οὖν ὑμᾶς, μιμηταί μου γίνεσθε (1 Cor 4:16)
Therefore, I urge you, be imitators of me.

This exhortation follows a long discussion of the nature of true apostleship and the dangers of factions within the body. So οὖν summarizes that discussion and draws an inference based on it.

REVIEW OF CHAPTER 6

In this chapter we introduced prepositions, which are function words that show the relationship between a substantive and another word or syntactic unit.

---

12. This is sometimes called a *recitative* ὅτι clause or ὅτι *recitativum*.
13. Indirect discourse is also called *reported speech*. We will discuss this further in a later chapter.

This second word is the object of the preposition, and together with the preposition it forms a prepositional phrase. Different prepositions require different cases used for the object, and there is often a correlation between the inherent meaning of each case (both spatial and temporal) and the case required by the preposition. We also saw that Greek prepositions have a range of meanings and that they can change their forms when the word following begins with a vowel. Finally, we saw that prepositional phrases can function adverbially or attributively.

In this chapter, we also introduced personal pronouns, which are used to stand in the place of previously mentioned substantives (antecedents). The pronoun must agree with its antecedent in number and gender, while its case is determined by its function in the clause in which it occurs.

The forms of the first- and second-person personal pronouns parallel some parts of the noun declensions that we have already learned, although there are several new forms. The third-person personal pronoun follows a 2-1-2 pattern with the exception of the nominative and accusative neuter singular forms. The function of the first- and second-person personal pronouns in the oblique cases is to stand in the place of an antecedent or to indicate possession (in the genitive case). The function of the third-person personal pronoun is similar, although when used in conjunction with the article in the attributive position it indicates "the same," and in the predicate position, it indicates "-self." The use of the personal pronoun in the nominative case (without an article) indicates emphasis, since the pronoun is not syntactically required. We also learned the lexical forms and how to parse personal pronouns.

Finally, we introduced the function of coordinating conjunctions (ἀλλά, δέ, καί, οὔτε, ἤ) assigned previously in the vocabulary, and introduced three subordinating conjunctions (γάρ, ὅτι, οὖν) and looked at examples of the function of these conjunctions. We learned that some conjunctions are postpositive, which means that they cannot occur at the beginning of a Greek clause, although they are often translated that way in English due to English grammar.

Study Guide for Chapter 6

1. Be able to understand each of the following concepts introduced in chapter 6:

   function of a preposition
   object of a preposition
   prepositional phrases and how to identify their boundaries
   the basic temporal and spatial orientation of each of the oblique cases
   antecedent

        grammatical proxy

        possessive function of personal pronouns

        emphatic function of personal pronouns

        adjectival functions of αὐτός

        coordinating conjunction

        subordinating conjunction

        postpositive

2. Be able to parse forms of personal pronouns, identify prepositional phrases, identify subordinating and coordinating clauses, and translate basic Koine sentences.

Vocabulary to Memorize

These are the vocabulary words to memorize for chapter 6. Notice that the case associated with each preposition is indicated in a parenthesis. You need to memorize the cases as well as possible glosses for the preposition.

ἄγγελος, -ου, ὁ	angel; messenger (175)
ἀπό (+gen)	from, away from (646)
αὐτός, αὐτή, αὐτό	he, she, it (pron); -self, even, same (adj) (5597)
γάρ	for, since, then (1,041)
δικαιοσύνη, -ης, ἡ	righteousness, justice, uprightness (92)
ἐγώ	I (2,666)
εἰς (+acc)	into, in, toward, for (1,767)
ἐκ (+gen)	from, out of, away from (914)
ἐκλέγομαι	I choose, I select (22)
ἐν (+dat)	in, on, by, among, with (2,752)
ἐνώπιον (+gen)	before, in the presence of (impr prep)[1] (94)
εὐθέως	immediately, at once (36)
καθώς	as, just as, even as (182)
καταβολή, -ῆς, ἡ	foundation, beginning (11)
κόσμος, -ου, ὁ	world, universe, humankind (186)
ὅτι	that, because (1,296)
οὖν	therefore, then, consequently (499)
οὕτως	in this manner, thus, so (208)
πρό (+gen)	before, in front of (47)

(cont.)

προσέρχομαι	(+dat) I come to, I go to, I approach (86)
πρῶτος, -η, -ον	first, earlier (155)
σύ	you (2,907)
σύν (+dat)	with, together with (128)
φωνή, -ῆς, ἡ	sound, voice, noise (139)
ὥρα, -ας, ἡ	hour, occasion, moment, time (106)

[1] Improper prepositions are prepositions that cannot be prefixed to a verb stem; we will learn about them in the next chapter.

Paradigms to Memorize

The following pronoun paradigms must be memorized for this chapter: the person pronouns ἐγώ and σύ; and αὐτός, αὐτή, αὐτό.

FIRST-PERSON PERSONAL PRONOUN (ἐγώ)

nom sg	ἐγώ
gen sg	μου (ἐμοῦ)
dat sg	μοι (ἐμοί)
acc sg	με (ἐμέ)
nom pl	ἡμεῖς
gen pl	ἡμῶν
dat pl	ἡμῖν
acc pl	ἡμᾶς

SECOND-PERSON PERSONAL PRONOUN (σύ)

nom sg	σύ
gen sg	σου (σοῦ)
dat sg	σοι (σοί)
acc sg	σε (σέ)
nom pl	ὑμεῖς
gen pl	ὑμῶν
dat pl	ὑμῖν
acc pl	ὑμᾶς

THIRD-PERSON PERSONAL PRONOUN (αὐτός, αὐτή, αὐτό)

	masc (2)	fem (1)	neut (2)
nom sg	αὐτός	αὐτή	αὐτό
gen sg	αὐτοῦ	αὐτῆς	αὐτοῦ
dat sg	αὐτῷ	αὐτῇ	αὐτῷ
acc sg	αὐτόν	αὐτήν	αὐτό
nom pl	αὐτοί	αὐταί	αὐτά
gen pl	αὐτῶν	αὐτῶν	αὐτῶν
dat pl	αὐτοῖς	αὐταῖς	αὐτοῖς
acc pl	αὐτούς	αὐτάς	αὐτά

chapter SEVEN

THE IMPERFECT ACTIVE AND MIDDLE INDICATIVE; MORE ON PREPOSITIONS

OBJECTIVES AND OVERVIEW

Chapter 7 introduces the following linguistic concepts, morphemes, and paradigms:

- imperfect tense-form
- augment and vocalic augmentation
- secondary active and middle personal endings
- imperfect active and middle indicative paradigms
- function of the imperfect indicative
- lexical form for imperfect indicatives and parsing
- the paradigm for the imperfect of εἰμί
- compound verb forms and their meanings
- proper and improper prepositions

THE IMPERFECT ACTIVE AND MIDDLE INDICATIVE

In chapter 3, we learned how to "build" the present active and middle indicative tense-forms. In this chapter, we will learn how to "build" the imperfect active and middle tense-forms. Before we start building, however, we need to understand some concepts for the imperfect tense-form.

The **imperfect tense-form** is constructed by using the same tense stem as the present tense. This means that the imperfect tense-form has the same imperfective aspect as the present tense-form (ongoing, internal), because the tense stem indicates the verbal aspect. The imperfect tense-form only occurs with indicative-mood verbs and usually occurs in narrative. As noted previously, the imperfect tense-form also uses an **augment**. This is a morpheme that consists of an epsilon that is prefixed to the front of a verb stem. The augment is found only in indicative verbs.

There are three augmented tense-forms—the imperfect, the aorist, and the pluperfect (although the augment is sometimes dropped in the pluperfect tense-form). Recall that these are also called secondary tenses. In chapter 3, we learned the *primary* active and middle personal endings. These endings are used with the unaugmented tense-forms: present, future, and perfect. The augmented tense-forms use *secondary* personal endings.[1]

The Forms of the Imperfect Active and Middle Indicative

The secondary active personal endings are as follows. The primary active endings are listed in gray on the right for comparison.

	secondary active personal endings	primary active personal endings
1 sg	ν	ω
2 sg	ς	εις
3 sg	–	ει
1 pl	μεν	μεν
2 pl	τε	τε
3 pl	ν	ουσι(ν)

Here's how to build the imperfect active indicative with the augment, present tense-stem, and secondary active ending.

augment	present stem	connecting vowel	secondary personal ending	inflected form
ἐ	+ λυ	+ ο	+ ν	→ ἔλυον

Here is the imperfect active indicative paradigm for λύω and inflected meanings for each form. The connecting vowels and personal endings are set in bold. The present active indicative forms are listed in gray on the right for comparison.

---

1. See appendix 13, "Summary of Primary and Secondary Personal Endings for Greek Verbs."

IMPERFECT ACTIVE INDICATIVE

1 sg	ἔλυον	I was releasing	λύω
2 sg	ἔλυες	you were (sg) releasing	λύεις
3 sg	ἔλυε(ν)	he/she/it was releasing	λύει
1 pl	ἐλύομεν	we were releasing	λύομεν
2 pl	ἐλύετε	you (pl) were releasing	λύετε
3 pl	ἔλυον	they were releasing	λύουσι(ν)

Recall that the connecting vowel will be an omicron if the personal ending begins with a mu or nu; otherwise, the connecting vowel is an epsilon. Notice that the personal endings are clearly visible in the imperfect forms, whereas they are not visible in all the corresponding forms of the present active indicative. The first- and second-person plural personal endings (-μεν and -τε) are the same in the present active and imperfect active indicative. Finally, recall that the ν at the end of the third-person singular form is called a **movable nu**.

Look carefully at the above paradigm. The first-person singular is identical to the third-person plural. It can be confusing to learn that the same form can have two different functions. How will you be able to know which form is which? Easily! A first-person singular verb occurs in a specific context—either when the subject is the one speaking or writing. Examples of this in the GNT would include dialogue or parts of an epistle (i.e., when Paul gives biographical information). Third-person plural verbs tend to occur in narratives. Think of it this way: the same form can be used to indicate two different functions precisely because those two functions are different enough to avoid confusion. The good news is that shared forms mean that you have less to memorize!

Now it's time to learn the secondary middle personal endings. As you probably guessed, these forms are used with augmented middle-voice forms, such as the imperfect middle indicative below. (The present middle indicative forms are listed in gray on the right for comparison.) Notice also that the first- and second-person plural personal endings are the same in the present middle and imperfect middle indicative (-μεθα and -σθε).

	secondary middle personal endings	primary middle personal endings
1 sg	μην	μαι
2 sg	σο	σαι
3 sg	το	ται
1 pl	μεθα	μεθα
2 pl	σθε	σθε
3 pl	ντο	νται

Here is the imperfect middle indicative paradigm for the verb λύω, including inflected meanings for each form. The connecting vowels and personal endings are set in bold. The present middle indicative forms are listed in gray on the right for comparison.

IMPERFECT MIDDLE INDICATIVE

1 sg	ἐλυόμην	I was releasing for myself	λύομαι
2 sg	ἐλύου	you (sg) were releasing for yourself	λυῇ
3 sg	ἐλύετο	he/she/it was releasing for him/her/itself	λύεται
1 pl	ἐλυόμεθα	we were releasing for ourselves	λυόμεθα
2 pl	ἐλύεσθε	you (pl) were releasing for yourselves	λύεσθε
3 pl	ἐλύοντο	they were releasing for themselves	λύονται

For the Curious

Remember that Greek tries to avoid a sigma caught between two vowels (an **intervocalic sigma**). To get around this, the sigma drops out of the imperfect middle indicative second-person singular form, but that leaves two vowels together that do not form a diphthong, which is another situation that Greek does not like. So, these two (short) vowels (ε and ο) combine to form one (long) diphthong (ου). This process is called *contraction*. Here are the steps that Greek follows to end up with the final form for ἐλύου.

First, we start with the augmented present tense stem (ε + λυ-) and add the connecting vowel (ε), and then add the personal ending -σο. This causes the sigma caught between two vowels to drop out.

ἐλυ + ε + σο → ἐλυ + ε + ⁄σο

Next, the ε and the ο combine to form the diphthong ου.

ἐλυ + ε + σο → ἐλυ + ε + ⁄σο → ἔλυου

You don't need to remember this; you simply need to memorize the final form.

More about the Augment

In the above examples, prefixing an augment was simply a matter of adding an ε to the front of the present stem. But what if the verb stem begins with a vowel, as in ἐγείρω? Remember that Greek avoids having two vowels together that do not form a diphthong. Recall that the ε + α in the second-person singular present middle indicative form of λύω lengthens to form an η (λυ + ε + σαι → λυ + ε + αι → λυῇ). A similar phonological phenomenon happens with the augment. When the ε prefix combines with ε, the resulting lengthened form is an η. For example, the first-person singular imperfect indicative for ἐγείρω is ἤγειρον. Here is a chart that summarizes these vowel lengthenings.

augment	initial verb stem vowel	resulting vowel	lexical form	augmented form
ε	+ α	→ η	ἄγω	ἦγον
ε	+ ε	→ η	ἐγείρω	ἤγειρον
ε	+ ο	→ ω	ὀφείλω	ὤφειλον
ε	+ αι	→ η	αἰτέω	ᾔτουν
ε	+ οι	→ ῳ	οἰκοδομέω	ᾠκοδόμουν
ε	+ αυ	→ ηυ	αὐξάνω	ηὔξανον
ε	+ ευ	→ ευ[1]	εὑρίσκω	εὕρισκον

[1] Often there is no change, and the diphthong ευ remains in the augmented form.

The Functions of the Imperfect Indicative

You can translate imperfect active indicative verbs with an English continuous past, e.g., "I was releasing." It is important to understand, however, that although an imperfect tense-form often occurs in narrative and thus describes a past action, "past time" is not a semantic (or uncancelable) feature of the tense-form (you can review the segment in chapter 3, "Introduction to Verbal Aspect"). It is better to think that the imperfect is well-suited to describe past continuous or habitual actions, but it is able to function in other ways as well. For example, it can indicate an action that was attempted (but not completed) or that was habitual. It can also indicate an ingressive action (an action that was begun). It can sometimes indicate background, or nonessential, information in a narrative. (This is sometimes described as "remoteness," which can either be spatially, temporally, or logically understood. We will talk about this more in future chapters.)

Lexical Form and Parsing

Recall that the **lexical form** for many verbs is the present active indicative first-person singular, or the present middle first person for other verbs.[2] To find the lexical form for imperfect tense-forms, you need to "reverse engineer" the inflected form by removing the augment and the secondary personal endings so that you can see the present tense stem; for example, λυ-. Once you have done that, you should either be able to recognize the verb or be able to locate it in a lexicon. This process is a bit trickier for verbs whose present stems begin with a vowel. For these verbs, you will need to "undo" the vowel contraction that takes place when the augment is prefixed to the present stem (e.g., ἦγον → ε + α → ἄγω).

One of the nice benefits of memorizing verbs is that you are memorizing the lexical form. This means that once you have identified the present stem, you know what the lexical form is. The importance of this will become more evident when we learn the aorist tense-form in a few chapters.

Here's how you would parse ἔλυον.

inflected form	tense	voice	mood	person	num	lexical form	inflected meaning
ἔλυον	impf	act	ind	1st 3rd	sg pl	λύω	I was releasing they were releasing

Remember that when you are parsing a word in an assignment, without any surrounding context, you need to list all possible options.

---

2. We noted in chapter 3 that you can also think of the lexical form as the first principal part.

The Imperfect of εἰμί

The imperfect indicative tense-form for εἰμί is as follows[3] and must be memorized exactly:

1 sg	ἤμην	I was
2 sg	ἦς	you (sg) were
3 sg	ἦν	he/she/it was
1 pl	ἦμεν	we were
2 pl	ἦτε	you (pl) were
3 pl	ἦσαν	they were

HEADS UP!

As noted previously, εἰμί is classified as a μι verb. If you want to look ahead, you can look through the imperfect indicative forms for μι verbs in chapter 24 and see how many forms you can recognize based on what you have learned in this chapter. You don't need to memorize any of these forms now, but you should be able to recognize the forms of the imperfect indicative.

COMPOUND VERBS AND IMPROPER PREPOSITIONS

Recall that a preposition is a word that is used with a substantive to show its relationship to another syntactic unit. Greek prepositions that can be prefixed to verb stems are called **proper prepositions**. On the other hand, **improper prepositions** *cannot* be prefixed to verb stems. An example of an improper preposition is ἐνώπιον, "before."

The Forms of Compound Verbs

Proper prepositions can be prefixed to a verb stem to form a new verb. For example, there is the verb βάλλω ("I throw," "I cast"); when ἐκ is prefixed to this verb, the resulting verb is ἐκβάλλω ("I cast out"). It is important to understand

---

3. There are two older forms for this paradigm; twice in the GNT the second-person singular occurs as ἦσθα; five times the first-person plural occurs as ἤμεθα. You don't need to memorize these, but don't be surprised if you see these forms!

that this is a new verb, whose lexical form is ἐκβάλλω. This is similar to compound verbs in English, such as "undertake" and "overestimate"; they are different verbs than "take" and "estimate."

Recall that some phonological changes occur when a preposition is followed by a word that begins with a vowel. This same phenomenon occurs with compound verbs, especially with augmented tense-forms (imperfect, aorist, pluperfect). Recall also that an augment is prefixed to the beginning of a *verb* stem. This means that the compounded preposition is prefixed to the *augmented* form of a verb for augmented tense-forms. Consider the following examples:

ἀπέστελλον
ἐξεβάλλετε

The first example is the imperfect active indicative first-person singular *or* third-person plural form of ἀποστέλλω. The augment ε- is prefixed directly to the present tense stem στελλ-, to which is added the connecting vowel plus the secondary personal ending, -ον. The preposition ἀπό is prefixed to the front of this augmented tense stem, but the final omicron of ἀπό drops off (or elides) before the augment, resulting in ἀπ, which is then prefixed to the augmented tense stem εστελλον, resulting in the final form ἀπέστελλον.[4] The second example is the imperfect active indicative second-person plural of ἐκβάλλω. The augment ε- is prefixed directly to the present tense stem βαλλ-, to which is added the connecting vowel plus the secondary personal ending, -ετε. The preposition ἐκ is then prefixed to εβαλλετε, but the kappa changes to a xi before the augment (vowel) ε-, resulting in the final form ἐξεβάλλετε.

The Meaning of Compound Verbs

When a proposition is compounded to a verb stem, there are three possible results in meaning. The first possible result we can call the *sum of the parts*, because the meaning of the preposition and the meaning of the verb are not changed when they are compounded. For example, ἐκ can be translated "out from," and βάλλω can be translated "I throw" or "I cast," so it is unsurprising that ἐκβάλλω can be translated "I cast out." Similarly, it is unsurprising that

---

4. This elision is true of all proper prepositions that end in a vowel except for πέρι and πρό, which do not elide their final vowel.

εἰσπορεύομαι can be translated "I go into" or "I enter," since the meanings of the preposition and the verb are not changed when they are compounded. This meaning of compound verbs is the easiest to understand—but be careful! The only way to know that a compound verb is essentially the sum of its parts is to memorize its glosses. Not every compound verb has this meaning.

In the second possible result, the compounded preposition can intensify the inherent meaning of the verb to which it is compounded. For example, κρίνω can be translated "I judge," but κατακρίνω can be translated "I condemn." The verb ἐσθίω can be translated "I eat," but κατεσθίω can be translated "I devour."

Finally, in the third possible result, compound verbs can have an entirely different meaning from the verb without the compound. For example, γινώσκω can be translated "I know," but ἀναγινώσκω, "I read." Thus you must memorize compound verbs as new vocabulary words and not try to guess their meanings by simply looking at the preposition and the compounded verb.

REVIEW OF CHAPTER 7

In this chapter we introduced another indicative tense-form, the imperfect. We learned how to build this tense form by beginning with the present tense stem, to which an augment (ε-) is prefixed and to which secondary active and middle personal endings are added. Because the imperfect is built from the present tense stem, it has imperfective (ongoing, continuous) aspect. The imperfect often occurs in narratives and provides background information to the main story line. When the augment is prefixed to a verb stem beginning with a vowel, predictable vowel lengthening occurs. The imperfect forms must be "reverse engineered" to identify the lexical form, although the lexical form is often easily recognizable because of the present stem. We also learned the forms of the imperfect indicative of εἰμί.

Finally, in this chapter we discussed the form and function of compound verbs. When a proper preposition is prefixed to an augmented verb stem, the same morphological changes occur as when the preposition precedes a word beginning with a vowel. There are three possible results in meaning when a preposition is compounded with a verb: (1) the meaning of the preposition and verb are retained and simply added together, (2) the meaning of the uncompounded verb is intensified, or (3) the compound verb has a new meaning altogether.

Study Guide for Chapter 7

1. Be able to understand each of the following concepts:

   the morphological components of the imperfect indicative

   the aspect of the imperfect tense-form

   the augment

   vowel lengthening that occurs with an augment and a verb stem that
   begins with a vowel

   secondary active and middle personal endings

   proper and improper prepositions

   compound verbs (both morphological changes and resultant meanings)

2. Be able to parse forms of the imperfect indicative and translate basic Koine
   sentences that incorporate forms and concepts from previous chapters.

Vocabulary to Memorize

These are the vocabulary words to memorize for chapter 7. Remember to
memorize the case associated with assigned prepositions.

ἀπολύω	I release, I set free, I dismiss (66)
γραφή, -ῆς, ἡ	writing, Scripture (50)
δεξιός, -ά, -όν	right (direction); right hand, right side (subst) (54)
ἐκεῖ	there, in that place (105)
ἐμός, -ή, -όν	my, mine (76)
ἐντολή, -ῆς, ἡ	commandment, law (67)
ἐπαγγελία, -ας, ἡ	promise, what is promised (52)
ἕτερος, -α, -ον	other, another, different; neighbor (subst) (98)
ζωή, -ῆς, ἡ	life (135)
ἴδιος, -α, -ον	one's own (114)
ἱερόν, -οῦ, τό	temple (71)
μακάριος, -α, -ον	blessed (50)
μαρτυρία, -ας, ἡ	testimony, witness (37)
μένω	I remain, I stay, I abide, I dwell (118)
νόμος, -ου, ὁ	law, rule, principle (194)
οἰκία, -ας, ἡ	house, home, household, family (93)
ὀπίσω (+gen)	behind, after (impr prep) (35)
παραβολή, -ῆς, ἡ	parable (50)

πονηρός, -ά, -όν	evil, wicked, bad (78)
σός, σή, σόν	your, yours (27)
ὑπάρχω	I am, I exist (60)
ὑποστρέφω	I turn back, I return (35)
φυλάσσω	I guard, I keep, I protect, I observe (31)
χαρά, -ᾶς, ἡ	joy, gladness, delight (59)
χωρίς (+gen)	apart from, without (impr prep) (41)

Paradigms to Memorize

The following paradigms should be memorized for chapter 7: the imperfect active and middle indicative of λύω; imperfect indicative of εἰμί.

IMPERFECT ACTIVE INDICATIVE OF λύω

1 sg	ἔλυον
2 sg	ἔλυες
3 sg	ἔλυε(ν)
1 pl	ἐλύομεν
2 pl	ἐλύετε
3 pl	ἔλυον

IMPERFECT MIDDLE INDICATIVE OF λύω

1 sg	ἐλυόμην
2 sg	ἐλύου
3 sg	ἐλύετο
1 pl	ἐλυόμεθα
2 pl	ἐλύεσθε
3 pl	ἐλύοντο

IMPERFECT INDICATIVE FOR εἰμί

1 sg	ἤμην
2 sg	ἦς
3 sg	ἦν
1 pl	ἦμεν
2 pl	ἦτε
3 pl	ἦσαν

chapter EIGHT

ETCETERAS:
More on Cases and Voice[1]

OBJECTIVES AND OVERVIEW

Chapter 8 develops some previously introduced concepts or forms and presents a few new concepts. The main focus of this chapter, however, is on integrating what you have learned from chapters 1–7. Chapter 8 covers the following linguistic concepts, morphemes, and paradigms:

- more uses of the article
- apposition
- expressing possession
- more functions of oblique cases
- indeclinable nouns
- foreign names
- more functions of the middle voice

MORE ON THE USES OF THE ARTICLE

As we noted in chapter 5, the function of the article in Greek is surprisingly complex. There we noted that the article is really a modifier of substantives—as such, it can perform a wide range of functions. Sometimes it functions almost like a personal pronoun, as in the following example:

ὁ δὲ ὀπίσω μου ἐρχόμενος ἰσχυρότερός μού ἐστιν (Matt 3:11)
but *he* who comes after me is stronger than I

---

1. *Etceteras* are ancillary but important concepts and forms that build on concepts and forms that you have learned in chapters 1–7.

146

Sometimes the article followed by δέ can indicate a change of subject. Matthew 2:3–4 records Herod's distress over the report of Jesus's birth and says that he called together his chief priests and scribes. When the narrative continues in verse 5, the subject has shifted from Herod to this assembled group. Notice the use of the article in this verse.

οἱ δὲ εἶπαν αὐτῷ . . . (Matt 2:5)
but *they* said to him . . .

The article can also function to indicate possession. Consider the following example—in the larger context, it is clear that Paul is exhorting husbands to love their *own* wives!

ἀγαπᾶτε τὰς γυναῖκας (Eph 5:25)
love *your* wives

Sometimes the article can function substantivally. Consider the following examples:

οἱ περὶ αὐτόν (Mark 4:10)
the ones [*people*] around him

οἱ παρὰ τὴν ὁδόν (Mark 4:15)
the ones [*seeds*] beside the road

τὰ ἄνω ζητεῖτε (Col 3:1)
the things above, seek

When the article appears before a prepositional phrase, it often occurs in the context of a second attributive construction, where the prepositional phrase is functioning as a modifier of a substantive. Consider the following examples and note the article-substantive-article-modifier construction. As we have seen before, this type of Greek construction is often best rendered by an English relative clause.

τὸ φῶς τὸ ἐν σοί (Matt 6:23)
the light *that is* in you

τὴν ἀγάπην *τὴν εἰς πάντας τοὺς ἁγίους* (Eph 1:15)[2]
the love *that* [*you have*] for all the saints

As we proceed in this book, we will call attention to other functions of the Greek article.

APPOSITION

Closely related to the function of an attributive adjective is the concept of **apposition**, in which one substantive further explains or defines another substantive. It is important to understand that apposition involves two *substantives*, not an adjective and a substantive. Frequently, an appositive further modifies a proper name. Consider the following:

Ἰωάννης ὁ βαπτίζων	John, the Baptist
Φοίβην τὴν ἀδελφὴν ἡμῶν	Phoebe, our sister
Τιμόθεος ὁ ἀδελφός	Timothy, our brother[3]

In each of these examples, the word that occurs first (Ἰωάννης, Φοίβην, or Τιμόθεος) is further defined or explained by the second noun phrase, the appositive (ὁ βαπτίζων, τὴν ἀδελφὴν ἡμῶν, or ὁ ἀδελφός). Notice that, in Greek, the first noun and the appositive have the *same* case and number, and they refer to the *same* entity. Apposition may occur in any case, although it is common in the nominative case. We will see many more examples of apposition throughout the rest of the book.

EXPRESSING POSSESSION

There are four main ways that Greek expresses possession. We have already seen three of these ways, so this is in part a summary.[4]

First, the personal pronoun in the genitive case (μου, ἡμῶν, σου, ὑμῶν, αὐτοῦ, αὐτῶν) can indicate possession. The personal pronoun usually follows the modified word. For example:

---

2. Some words from the larger context have been supplied for this example.
3. This is another example of the article indicating possession.
4. See Wallace, *Greek Grammar beyond the Basics*, 348.

Ὁ κύριός μου καὶ ὁ θεός μου (John 20:28)
My Lord and *my* God!

Second, possession can be indicated by possessive adjectives (ἐμός, σός, ἡμέτερος, ὑμέτερος), which are generally articular. For example:

ὁ καιρὸς ὁ ἐμός (John 7:6)
my time

Third, the article (ὁ, ἡ, τό) can indicate possession, as we have seen in the above examples involving more uses of the article. Finally, the adjective ἴδιος, -α, -ον ("one's own") can indicate possession, as the following example shows:

εἰς τὰ ἴδια ἦλθεν (John 1:11)
he came to *his own*

MORE ON THE FUNCTIONS OF THE OBLIQUE CASES

In chapter 6 and the discussion of prepositions, we noted that cases (without any accompanying prepositions) may describe time and movement in certain ways. This can be summarized as follows:

- the genitive may indicate the kind of time (Nicodemus came to Jesus at *nighttime*)
- the genitive may indicate motion away from an object or place (Jesus departed *from the crowd*)

- the dative may indicate a point of time (Nicodemus came to Jesus *at midnight*)
- the dative may indicate arrival to a place (Jesus arrived *in Jerusalem*)

- the accusative may indicate the extent or duration of time (Nicodemus and Jesus talked *throughout the night*)
- the accusative may indicate motion toward or entrance into an object or place (Jesus entered *the house*)

Prepositions often make the inherent meaning of the oblique cases clearer. Thus, a preposition may clarify or strengthen the inherent meaning of the case with which it is associated.

INDECLINABLE NOUNS AND FOREIGN NAMES

Every language has certain phonological rules that govern which sounds are "acceptable" in that particular language. For example, Greek words can begin with κτ (as in κτίσις, -εως, ἡ, "creation") whereas there is no English word that begins with the letters "kt." Conversely, English words can end with t, d, l, m, or ph, but Greek words cannot end in a τ, δ, λ, μ, or φ. So the presence of words ending in these letters is an indication of a foreign name or word that has simply been transliterated into Greek.[5] We have already seen several such examples of Hebrew names: Ἀβραάμ, Δαυίδ, and Ἰσραήλ. We also see this with important place names in the GNT, such as Ναζαρέτ and Ἰερουσαλήμ. It is unsurprising that these foreign names are indeclinable in Greek, meaning that they only occur in one form and do not decline to indicate case functions. Instead, their function in a sentence is often indicated by the *case* of the article if they are articular (proving once again the importance of the article). Some names that derive from Hebrew can also have incomplete (or defective) paradigms. We have already seen the declension for Ἰησοῦς (see chapter 4), which uses the same form for the genitive and dative. Similarly, the declension for Μωϋσῆς contains some irregularities.

Some foreign names, however, do follow Greek noun declension patterns (some of these names were slightly altered when they entered Greek). For example, Ἄννα and Μαρία follow first declension patterns for feminine nouns, and Ἰωάννης follows one of the first declension patterns for masculine nouns. Λάζαρος and Μαθθαῖος follow second declension masculine patterns; Σίμων follows the third declension pattern also found in the noun αἰών ("age").

Some of these names have already been assigned as vocabulary, while others are easily recognizable. You do not need to memorize the declensions for these names. You simply need to be aware of the presence of foreign names and to pay close attention to the use of the article, as many of these words have irregular declensions or are indeclinable.

EVEN MORE ON THE MIDDLE VOICE

In the **permissive middle**, the subject allows an action to be done to himself or herself.[6] For example:

---

5. This is similar to the presence of a *loanword*, which is a word from another language that is used or spelled as it is in the original language, even if the spelling is unusual in the target language. An example of a loanword from Old Persian to Turkish (through Italian!) into English is the word *bazaar*.

6. There are a few examples where the permissive middle suggests a passive understanding of the verb (e.g., 1 Cor 6:11). My thanks to graduate student Carson Long for bringing this to my attention.

διὰ τί οὐχὶ μᾶλλον *ἀδικεῖσθε*; (1 Cor 6:7)
Why not rather *let yourselves be wronged*?

A **reciprocal middle** indicates an exchange between members of a plural subject. For example:

σταυροῦσιν αὐτὸν καὶ *διαμερίζονται* τὰ ἱμάτια αὐτοῦ (Mark 15:24)
They crucified him and *divided* his garments *among themselves*.

INTEGRATION OF CHAPTERS 1–7

In this section, we will use the following passage (adapted from various NT verses) as the basis of reviewing concepts and forms that have been presented in chapters 1–7.[1] The important topics that we covered were present and imperfect indicative verbs, first and second declension nouns, prepositions and prepositional phrases, the article and first and second declension pattern adjectives, and personal pronouns.

PART ONE

It is crucial to be able to identify finite verb forms as you study Greek. So, begin by <u>double underlining</u> and parsing each finite verb in the following text. After you have done this on your own, turn the page for the answers.

1. καὶ ἐν ταῖς πρώταις ἡμέραις οἱ μαθηταὶ εὐηγγέλιζον καὶ ἐκήρυσσον τὴν βασιλείαν
2. τοῦ θεοῦ ταῖς ἐκκλησίαις. αὐτὸς δὲ Ἰησοῦς προσέρχεται αὐταῖς καὶ ἐδίδασκεν αὐτάς
3. ἐν παραβολαῖς. ἐν αὐτῷ ζωὴ ἐστίν, καὶ ἡ ζωὴ ἐστίν ἡ ἐπαγγελία ἡ ἀπὸ τῶν οὐρανῶν.
4. τὰ πρῶτα σημεῖα τοῦ θεοῦ αὐτοὶ πιστεύουσιν·
5. αὐτοὶ γὰρ γινώσκομεν ὅτι ὁ Ἰησοῦς ἐστίν ὁ κύριος τοῦ κόσμου.
6. καὶ ἡμεῖς μένομεν ἐν σοι ὅτι σὺ εἶ ὁ ἅγιος τοῦ θεοῦ.
7. καὶ δοξάζομεν τὸν υἱὸν τοῦ θεοῦ.

---

1. You may want to copy the text and mark it on your own as we go through this segment. A copy of this text is also provided in the accompanying workbook.

ANSWERS TO PART ONE

Did you come up with the following on your own?

1. καὶ ἐν ταῖς πρώταις ἡμέραις οἱ μαθηταὶ <u>εὐηγγέλιζον</u> καὶ <u>ἐκήρυσσον</u> τὴν βασιλείαν
2. τοῦ θεοῦ ταῖς ἐκκλησίαις. αὐτὸς δὲ Ἰησοῦς <u>προσέρχεται</u> αὐταῖς καὶ <u>ἐδίδασκεν</u> αὐτάς
3. ἐν παραβολαῖς. ἐν αὐτῷ ζωὴ <u>ἐστίν</u>, καὶ ἡ ζωὴ <u>ἐστίν</u> ἡ ἐπαγγελία ἡ ἀπὸ τῶν οὐρανῶν.
4. τὰ πρῶτα σημεῖα τοῦ θεοῦ αὐτοὶ <u>πιστεύουσιν</u>·
5. αὐτοὶ γὰρ <u>γινώσκομεν</u> ὅτι ὁ Ἰησοῦς <u>ἐστίν</u> ὁ κύριος τοῦ κόσμου.
6. καὶ ἡμεῖς <u>μένομεν</u> ἐν σοι ὅτι σὺ <u>εἶ</u> ὁ ἅγιος τοῦ θεοῦ.
7. καὶ <u>δοξάζομεν</u> τὸν υἱὸν τοῦ θεοῦ.

Parsing

inflected form	tense	voice	mood	person	case	num	gender	lexical form	inflected meaning
εὐηγγέλιζον	impf	act	ind	3rd	n/a	pl	n/a	εὐαγγελίζω	they were proclaiming the gospel
ἐκήρυσσον	impf	act	ind	3rd	n/a	pl	n/a	κηρύσσω	they were preaching
προσέρχεται	pres	mid	ind	3rd	n/a	sg	n/a	προσέρχομαι	he comes to
ἐδίδασκεν	impf	act	ind	3rd	n/a	sg	n/a	διδάσκω	he began to teach
ἐστίν	pres	n/a	ind	3rd	n/a	sg	n/a	εἰμί	it is
πιστεύουσιν	pres	act	ind	3rd	n/a	pl	n/a	πιστεύω	they believe
γινώσκομεν	pres	act	ind	1st	n/a	pl	n/a	γινώσκω	we know
μένομεν	pres	act	ind	1st	n/a	pl	n/a	μένω	we remain
εἶ	pres	n/a	ind	2nd	n/a	sg	n/a	εἰμί	you (sg) are
δοξάζομεν	pres	act	ind	1st	n/a	pl	n/a	δοξάζω	we glorify

Additional Notes:

- The form εὐηγγέλιζον could be first-person singular or third-person plural. The narrative context of this passage indicates that the verb is third-person plural. The imperfect εὐηγγέλιζον could be understood with an ingressive nuance and translated "they began to proclaim the gospel." These same comments apply to ἐκήρυσσον.

- The verb προσέρχεται could also be translated "he came to"; see the discussion at the end of this chapter concerning the final translation.

- The verb ἐδίδασκεν could also be translated "he was teaching." The translation here reflects an ingressive understanding of the imperfect.

- Both προσέρχεται and ἐδίδασκεν have Ἰησοῦς as their subject; hence they are translated with "he" in the parsings.

- Some of the present tense-forms could also have been translated with an English present continuous (e.g., "we are remaining," or "we are glorifying") except for the form of εἰμί.

PART TWO

We will now focus on nouns, adjectives, and pronouns. Hopefully by now you quickly recognize nouns and related forms. If not, it is essential to review the assigned noun, article, adjective, and pronoun paradigms. To help you review these forms and functions, work through the assigned passage given above, following the instructions listed below. Although the questions often ask for only one example, working through *every* example that occurs in the passage will help you the most. Once you have completed your own work, then turn to the next pages for a complete list of these constructions and further discussion of them.

1. Give one example of a direct object and answer the following questions:
   a. How do you know that this substantive is functioning as a direct object?
   b. For which finite verb is this substantive functioning as a direct object?
2. Give at least two examples of a genitival construction.
   a. Which word is the genitival modifier?
   b. Which word is the head noun?
3. Give one example of an indirect object and answer the following questions:
   a. How do you know that this substantive is functioning as an indirect object?
   b. For which finite verb is this substantive functioning as an indirect object?
4. Give one example of a predicate nominative.
   a. What type of verb confirms that this is a predicate nominative?
   b. What is the subject of this verb?
5. Give one example of the emphatic use of a personal pronoun.
   a. How do you know that this pronoun is functioning emphatically?
   b. Is there anything unusual about this particular example?
6. Give one example of a third-person personal pronoun in an oblique case.
   a. What is the antecedent of this pronoun?
   b. How do you know?
7. Give one example of an adjective functioning attributively.
   a. How do you know that this adjective is functioning attributively?
   b. Draw a line from the adjective to the modified substantive and label the adjective ATTR.
8. Give one example of an adjective functioning substantivally.
   a. How do you know that this adjective is functioning substantivally?
   b. Label the adjective SUB.

ANSWERS TO PART TWO

Here is a complete list of all possible answers for questions 1–8. You should check your own work against this and see if you missed anything. If so, then use this as a means of reviewing forms, functions, and concepts that were discussed in chapters 1–7.

1. Here are all examples of direct objects and the answers to the following questions for each:
   a. How do you know that this substantive is functioning as a direct object?
   b. For which finite verb is this substantive functioning as a direct object?

   Lines 1–2: τὴν βασιλείαν τοῦ θεοῦ
   a. The accusative case of βασιλείαν indicates that it is functioning as a direct object.
   b. βασιλείαν is the direct object of ἐκήρυσσον; it is further modified by the article and the genitival modifier τοῦ θεοῦ.

   Line 2: αὐτάς
   a. The accusative case of αὐτάς indicates that it is functioning as a direct object.
   b. αὐτάς is the direct object of ἐδίδασκεν.

   Line 4: τὰ πρῶτα σημεῖα τοῦ θεοῦ
   a. The accusative case of σημεῖα indicates that it is functioning as a direct object.
   b. σημεῖα is the direct object of πιστεύουσιν; it is further modified by the article, the adjective πρῶτα, and the genitival modifier τοῦ θεοῦ.

   Line 7: τὸν υἱὸν τοῦ θεοῦ
   a. The accusative case of υἱόν indicates that it is functioning as a direct object.
   b. υἱόν is the direct object of δοξάζομεν; it is further modified by the article and the genitival modifier τοῦ θεοῦ.

2. Each of the genitival constructions in this passage has been marked below.
   a. Which word is the genitival modifier? This word is labeled *GM*.
   b. Which word is the head noun? An *arrow* is drawn from the GM to this word.

1. Καὶ ἐν ταῖς πρώταις ἡμέραις οἱ μαθηταὶ <u>εὐηγγέλιζον</u> καὶ <u>ἐκήρυσσον</u> τὴν βασιλείαν

   GM ⟋

2. τοῦ θεοῦ ταῖς ἐκκλησίαις. Αὐτὸς δὲ Ἰησοῦς <u>προσέρχεται</u> αὐταῖς καὶ <u>ἐδίδασκεν</u> αὐτάς

3. ἐν παραβολαῖς. Ἐν αὐτῷ ζωὴ <u>ἐστίν</u>, καὶ ἡ ζωὴ <u>ἐστίν</u> ἡ ἐπαγγελία ἡ ἀπὸ τῶν οὐρανῶν.

   ⟋———GM

4. Τὰ πρῶτα σημεῖα τοῦ θεοῦ αὐτοὶ <u>πιστεύουσιν·</u>

   ⟋——————— GM

5. Αὐτοὶ γὰρ <u>γινώσκομεν</u> ὅτι ὁ Ἰησοῦς <u>ἐστίν</u> ὁ κύριος τοῦ κόσμου.

   ⟋——————— GM

6. Καὶ ἡμεῖς <u>μένομεν</u> ἐν σοι ὅτι σὺ <u>εἶ</u> ὁ ἅγιος τοῦ θεοῦ.

   ⟋——————— GM

7. Καὶ <u>δοξάζομεν</u> τὸν υἱὸν τοῦ θεοῦ.

3. There is only one example of an indirect object in this passage: ταῖς ἐκκλησίαις (line 2).
   a. How do you know that this substantive is functioning as an indirect object? We know this because ταῖς ἐκκλησίαις is in the dative case, which often indicates an indirect-object function.
   b. For which finite verb is this substantive functioning as an indirect object? The phrase ταῖς ἐκκλησίαις is the indirect object of ἐκήρυσσον. (Note: The verb προσέρχεται requires a substantive in the dative case, here αὐταῖς, so this is not an indirect object. We will talk about this in a later chapter.)

4. There are three examples of predicate nominatives in this passage. The predicate nominative is underlined; modifiers for the predicate nominative are shaded.

   Line 3: ἡ ζωὴ <u>ἐστίν</u> ἡ <u>ἐπαγγελία</u> ἡ ἀπὸ τῶν οὐρανῶν
   a. What type of verb confirms that this is a predicate nominative? The equative verb ἐστίν confirms that this is a predicate nominative.
   b. What is the subject of this verb? The word ἡ ζωή is the subject of this verb.

Line 5: ὁ Ἰησοῦς ἐστίν ὁ <u>κύριος</u> τοῦ κόσμου

  a. What type of verb confirms that this is a predicate nominative? The equative verb ἐστίν confirms that this is a predicate nominative.

  b. What is the subject of this verb? ὁ Ἰησοῦς is the subject of this verb.

Line 6: σὺ εἶ ὁ <u>ἅγιος</u> τοῦ θεοῦ

  a. What type of verb confirms that this is a predicate nominative? The equative verb εἶ confirms that this is a predicate nominative.

  b. What is the subject of this verb? The "you" of the verb εἶ is the subject of this verb. The pronoun σύ is functioning emphatically.

Note: The adjective is functioning substantivally, so this is still a predicate nominative.

5. There are *five* examples of the emphatic use of a personal pronoun in this passage. They are listed below; each pronoun is underlined.

  Line 2: <u>αὐτὸς</u> δὲ Ἰησοῦς προσέρχεται

  Line 4: <u>αὐτοὶ</u> πιστεύουσιν

  Line 5: <u>αὐτοὶ</u> γὰρ γινώσκομεν

  Line 6: <u>ἡμεῖς</u> μένομεν

  Line 7: <u>σὺ</u> εἶ

  a. How do you know that this pronoun is functioning emphatically?

    For each example, we know that the pronoun is functioning emphatically because it is in the nominative case with a finite verb. The verb form (shaded above) is inflected for person and number, so the pronoun is not indicating the subject but adding emphasis.

    Additionally, the first example, αὐτὸς δὲ Ἰησοῦς προσέρχεται, illustrates the adjectival function of the third-person personal pronoun αὐτός. If this is not clear, you can go back and review this in the segment on personal pronouns in chapter 6.

  b. If you didn't pick the first pronoun in line 5, you might want to look at it now. It could be a bit challenging! What is unusual about this particular example? The pronoun αὐτοί is a *third*-person personal pronoun, but it is functioning emphatically for the *first*-person finite verb γινώσκομεν. Only the third-person personal pronoun can function emphatically with finite verbs that are not third person. In the next example, ἡμεῖς is a first-person personal pronoun that is functioning emphatically with a first-person finite verb, μένομεν. Finally, σύ is a second-person personal pronoun that is functioning emphatically with the second-person finite verb, εἶ. In all these examples, note that the *number* of the personal pronoun agrees with the number of the finite verb.

6. There are *three* examples of a third-person personal pronoun in an oblique case.
   a. What is the antecedent of this pronoun?
   b. How do you know?

   Line 2: αὐταῖς
   a. The antecedent of this pronoun is ταῖς ἐκκλησίαις.
   b. The antecedent for αὐταῖς must be plural feminine; there are no other possibilities in close proximity, except possibly ἡμέραις, but this would not make any sense. Note that οἱ μαθηταί is plural masculine. A pronoun and its antecedent must agree in *number* and *gender*; the *case* of each is determined by its function in its respective clause.

   Line 2: αὐτάς
   a./b. The antecedent of this pronoun is also ταῖς ἐκκλησίαις for the same reasons listed above.

   Line 3: ἐν αὐτῷ
   a. The antecedent of this pronoun is Ἰησοῦς.
   b. How do you know? There is no other singular masculine substantive in close proximity, so Ἰησοῦς is the best option. You might have thought about θεοῦ, but it is not common to skip over a substantive that agrees in number and gender with a pronoun unless there are compelling contextual reasons to do so.

7. Give one example of an adjective functioning attributively.
   a. How do you know that this adjective is functioning attributively?
   b. Draw a line from the adjective to the modified substantive and label the adjective ATTR.

8. Give one example of an adjective functioning substantivally.
   a. How do you know that this adjective is functioning substantivally?
   b. Label the adjective SUB.

Each adjective is underlined below, and its function is labeled above it. The substantive modified by an attributive adjective is indicated by an arrow.

ATTR ⟶

1. Καὶ ἐν ταῖς <u>πρώταις</u> ἡμέραις οἱ μαθηταὶ <u>εὐηγγέλιζον</u> καὶ <u>ἐκήρυσσον</u> τὴν βασιλείαν

GM ⟶

2. τοῦ θεοῦ ταῖς ἐκκλησίαις. Αὐτὸς δὲ Ἰησοῦς <u>προσέρχεται</u> αὐταῖς καὶ <u>ἐδίδασκεν</u> αὐτάς

3. ἐν παραβολαῖς. Ἐν αὐτῷ ζωὴ <u>ἐστίν</u>, καὶ ἡ ζωὴ <u>ἐστίν</u> ἡ ἐπαγγελία ἡ ἀπὸ τῶν οὐρανῶν.

ATTR ⟶   ⟵ GM

4. Τὰ <u>πρῶτα</u> σημεῖα τοῦ θεοῦ αὐτοὶ <u>πιστεύουσιν·</u>

⟵ GM

5. Αὐτοὶ γὰρ <u>γινώσκομεν</u> ὅτι ὁ Ἰησοῦς <u>ἐστίν</u> ὁ κύριος τοῦ κόσμου.

SUB ⟵ GM

6. Καὶ ἡμεῖς <u>μένομεν</u> ἐν σοι ὅτι σὺ <u>εἶ</u> ὁ <u>ἅγιος</u> τοῦ θεοῦ.

⟵ GM

7. Καὶ <u>δοξάζομεν</u> τὸν υἱὸν τοῦ θεοῦ.

PART THREE

Two other important syntactic constructions that we covered were prepositional phrases and dependent clauses. Using this same passage, complete the following. Once you have completed you own work, then turn to the next page for a complete list of these constructions and our further discussion of them. After this discussion, you should write out a translation of this passage.

9. Give one example of a prepositional phrase.
   a. How do you know that you have correctly identified the boundaries of the phrase?
   b. How is the phrase functioning? In other words, what type of information is the prepositional phrase supplying?

10. Identify each subordinate clause.
   a. How do you know that you have correctly identified the boundaries of the clause?
   b. How is the clause functioning with regard to the main clause on which it depends?

ANSWERS TO PART THREE

9. There are *five* examples of prepositional phrases; they are marked in [brackets] below. Further discussion follows the marked text.

1. Καὶ [ἐν ταῖς πρώταις ἡμέραις] οἱ μαθηταὶ εὐηγγέλιζον καὶ ἐκήρυσσον τὴν βασιλείαν

2. τοῦ θεοῦ ταῖς ἐκκλησίαις. Αὐτὸς δὲ Ἰησοῦς προσέρχεται αὐταῖς καὶ ἐδίδασκεν αὐτάς

3. [ἐν παραβολαῖς]. [Ἐν αὐτῷ] ζωὴ ἐστίν, καὶ ἡ ζωὴ ἐστίν ἡ ἐπαγγελία ἡ [ἀπὸ τῶν οὐρανῶν].

4. Τὰ πρῶτα σημεῖα τοῦ θεοῦ αὐτοὶ πιστεύουσιν·

5. Αὐτοὶ γὰρ γινώσκομεν ὅτι ὁ Ἰησοῦς ἐστίν ὁ κύριος τοῦ κόσμου.

6. Καὶ ἡμεῖς μένομεν [ἐν σοι] ὅτι σὺ εἶ ὁ ἅγιος τοῦ θεοῦ.

7. Καὶ δοξάζομεν τὸν υἱὸν τοῦ θεοῦ.

Line 1: [ἐν ταῖς πρώταις ἡμέραις]
   a. How do you know that you have correctly identified the boundaries of the phrase? The substantive following ἡμέραις is in the nominative case, so it could not also be the object of the preposition ἐν, which can only have an object in the dative case.
   b. How is this phrase functioning? This phrase is functioning adverbially, giving temporal information about the verbs εὐηγγέλιζον and ἐκήρυσσον; that is, *when* they proclaimed the good news and preached.

Line 3: [ἐν παραβολαῖς]
   a. How do you know that you have correctly identified the boundaries of the phrase? The word following παραβολαῖς is another preposition. Although it is possible to have one

prepositional phrase embedded within another one, there is no logical link between the two prepositional phrases in this context.

b. How is this phrase functioning? The phrase is functioning adverbially, indicating the means by which the finite verb ἐδίδασκεν is occurring, that is, *how* he was teaching them. He was teaching them *in parables.*

Line 3: [ἐν αὐτῷ]

a. How do you know that you have correctly identified the boundaries of the phrase? The substantive following αὐτῷ is in the nominative case, so it could not also be the object of the preposition ἐν, which can only have an object in the dative case.

b. How is this phrase functioning? The subject of ἐστίν is ζωή. The prepositional phrase is adverbially indicating *where* life is.

Line 3: [ἀπὸ τῶν οὐρανῶν]

a. How do you know that you have correctly identified the boundaries of the phrase? The substantive following οὐρανῶν is in the accusative case, so it could not also be the object of the preposition ἀπό, which can only have an object in the genitive case.

b. How is this phrase functioning? This phrase is functioning adjectivally, modifying the substantive ἐπαγγελία, specifying *which* promise. It is *the promise from heaven*. Notice that this is a second attributive construction (article-substantive-article-modifier), in which the modifier is a prepositional phrase.

Line 6: [ἐν σοί]

a. How do you know that you have correctly identified the boundaries of the phrase? The word following σοί is the conjunction ὅτι, which could not be part of a prepositional phrase because it introduces a dependent clause.

b. How is this phrase functioning? This phrase is functioning adverbially to indicate the location (metaphorically understood) in which the speakers are remaining; they remain *in you.*

10. There are *two* subordinate clauses in this passage; the subordinating conjunction has a gray background, and the dependent clause is in parentheses. Further discussion is below the marked text.

ATTR ⟶

1. Καὶ [ἐν ταῖς πρώταις ἡμέραις] οἱ μαθηταὶ εὐηγγέλιζον καὶ ἐκήρυσσον τὴν βασιλείαν

GM ⟋

2. τοῦ θεοῦ ταῖς ἐκκλησίαις. Αὐτὸς δὲ Ἰησοῦς προσέρχεται αὐταῖς καὶ ἐδίδασκεν αὐτάς

3. [ἐν παραβολαῖς]. [Ἐν αὐτῷ] ζωὴ ἐστίν, καὶ ἡ ζωὴ ἐστίν ἡ ἐπαγγελία ἡ [ἀπὸ τῶν οὐρανῶν].

ATTR ⟶ ⟵ GM

4. Τὰ πρῶτα σημεῖα τοῦ θεοῦ αὐτοὶ πιστεύουσιν·

⟵ GM

5. Αὐτοὶ γὰρ γινώσκομεν (ὅτι ὁ Ἰησοῦς ἐστίν ὁ κύριος τοῦ κόσμου).

SUB ⟵ GM

6. Καὶ ἡμεῖς μένομεν [ἐν σοι] (ὅτι σὺ εἶ ὁ ἅγιος τοῦ θεοῦ).

⟵ GM

7. Καὶ δοξάζομεν τὸν υἱὸν τοῦ θεοῦ.

Line 5: (ὅτι ὁ Ἰησοῦς ἐστίν ὁ κύριος τοῦ κόσμου).
  a. How do you know that you have correctly identified the boundaries of the clause? The ὅτι clause is introduced by the subordinating conjunction ὅτι and ends with κόσμου. You might have thought that the clause introduced by the καί in line 6 could have also been included in the ὅτι clause, but the change from the third-person singular ἐστίν to first-person plural μένομεν argues against this.
  b. How is the clause functioning with regard to the main clause on which it depends? The ὅτι clause is indicating the content of the verb γινώσκομεν.

Line 6: (ὅτι σὺ εἶ ὁ ἅγιος τοῦ θεοῦ)
  a. How do you know that you have correctly identified the boundaries of the clause? The ὅτι clause is introduced by the subordinating

conjunction ὅτι and ends with θεοῦ. You might have thought that the clause introduced by the καί in line 7 could have also been included in the ὅτι clause, but the change from the second person singular εἶ to first person plural δοξάζομεν argues against this.

b. How is the clause functioning with regard to the main clause on which it depends? The ὅτι clause is functioning causally to indicate the reason why the subjects "are remaining" (μένομεν).

PART FOUR

Based on this discussion, write out a translation for this passage. You may check your translation against the one provided on the following page.

POSSIBLE TRANSLATION FOR PART FOUR

1. And in the first days, the disciples were proclaiming the gospel and were preaching the kingdom
2. of God to the churches. Then[2] Jesus himself came[3] to them and he began to teach them
3. in parables. In him is life, and the life is the promise that is from heaven.
4. They themselves are believing the first signs of God;
5. For we ourselves know that Jesus is the Lord of the world.
6. And we ourselves remain in you because you are the holy one of God.
7. And we glorify the Son of God.

---

2. The conjunction δέ often indicates a development in a narrative; it is often translated "and" or "then" in narratives.

3. Recall the discussion of the present tense used in narratives in chapter 3. If you translated this as "and Jesus himself comes," that is fine at this point. But as we will see, the present tense often occurs in narrative and is often rendered with the past tense in English.

REVIEW AND STUDY GUIDE FOR CHAPTERS 1-7

Congratulations! You are halfway through the first semester of beginning Greek! Here are some concepts and forms that you need to know backward, forward, and even upside down by this point in the course.

- the alphabet
- basic diacritical marks (breathing marks, accents, iota subscript, punctuation)
- the article
- present and imperfect active and middle indicative forms
- first and second declension case endings
- the paradigm for the present and imperfect indicative of εἰμί
- vocabulary and paradigms for chapters 1–7

Additionally, essential concepts that you should know include the following:

- parsing, lexical form, and inflected meaning
- clauses and phrases
- verb tense stems, connecting vowels, augment
- primary and secondary personal endings
- finite verbs
- active and middle voices
- basic grasp of verbal aspect
- imperfective and perfective aspects
- substantive and modifier
- natural versus grammatical gender
- noun case functions
- predicate nominative and adjective
- head noun and genitival modifier
- articular, arthrous, anarthrous
- first and second attributive positions for adjectives
- predicate function of the adjective
- object of preposition and prepositional phrases
- basic functions of coordinating and subordinating conjunctions
- compound verbs

Chapter 8 is a time to review and solidify these concepts and forms. The more firmly these concepts and forms are in place, the more fun and satisfying your Greek journey will be! If your professor is giving a midterm exam, it will test you on these basic concepts, forms, functions, parsing, and translation. In addition, you may be asked to mark Greek texts as you have done for the integration text in this chapter and for the assigned exercises in the workbook. Be prepared to discuss the syntactic function of various Greek words or constructions. If you have been keeping up with your assignments and reviewing previous material, you'll do fine!

chapter NINE

RELATIVES, DEMONSTRATIVES, AND MORE PREPOSITIONS

OBJECTIVES AND OVERVIEW

Chapter 9 introduces the following linguistic concepts, morphemes, and paradigms:

- relative pronoun and relative clause
- relative-pronoun paradigms
- functions of relative pronouns
- demonstrative paradigms
- function of demonstratives
- prepositions that take objects in two cases
- prepositions that take objects in three cases

RELATIVE PRONOUNS AND CLAUSES

A **relative pronoun** joins (or *relates*) a dependent clause within a sentence to a substantive elsewhere in the sentence, hence its name *relative* pronoun. Consider the following sentence:

The students who are really blessed are studying Greek.

There is actually one sentence embedded within another sentence in this example.

The students are studying Greek. (main sentence)
The students are really blessed. (embedded sentence)

In both sentences, the subject is "the students," but the second sentence gives more information about these students. It would be cumbersome to have to repeat the subject (indicated in square brackets below) and keep both sentences, so this second sentence can be embedded into the first sentence by means of the relative pronoun "who":

> **The students** <u>who [the students] are really blessed</u> **are studying Greek.**

The main sentence (in **bold**) of the original two sentences has become the main clause (**bold**) of the combined sentence, and the embedded sentence (<u>underlined</u>) of the original two sentences has become the dependent relative clause (<u>underlined</u>). The relative pronoun "who" stands in the place of the repeated subject "the students" (in square brackets). Additionally, "the students" is the **antecedent** of the relative pronoun "who."

For the Curious

Technically, an *antecedent* refers to a substantive for which a pronoun substitutes when that substantive appears before (*ante-*, "before") the pronoun; a pronoun that precedes its referent has a *postcedent*.

Based on these observations, we see that a relative pronoun introduces a relative clause, which is *always* a dependent clause. This dependent clause functions to give more information about a substantive (or a group of substantives) in the main clause. Thus, a relative clause functions as a *modifier* of a substantive. We can verify this by drawing upon the "slot" and "filler" concept and by substituting an adjective in the place of the relative clause. If this substitution makes sense, then we can see that the relative clause and the adjective have the same *syntactic function* in this example.

> **The students** <u>who are really blessed</u> **are studying Greek.**
> **The** <u>good</u> **students are studying Greek.**

English grammar requires that the adjective be placed before the substantive that it modifies, but it is clear that both the underlined relative clause and the underlined adjective are functioning to give more information about the students. After we look at the forms of the Greek relative pronoun, we'll look at some examples of its function in the GNT, which will make clear the function of the relative clause to modify a substantive.

The Forms of the Relative Pronoun

Here is the paradigm for the relative pronoun. Because it must be able to stand in the place of any substantive, there need to be twenty-four forms of the pronoun. This is parallel to what we saw with the forms of the article and adjectives. Like the article, the relative pronoun follows a 2-1-2 pattern, which should look very familiar by now. (If not, then we have a problem!)

	masc (2)	fem (1)	neut (2)	inflected meaning: person	inflected meaning: thing
nom sg	ὅς	ἥ	ὅ	who	that, which
gen sg	οὗ	ἧς	οὗ	whose	whose
dat sg	ᾧ	ᾗ	ᾧ	with/by/in whom	to/by/with/in which
acc sg	ὅν	ἥν	ὅ	whom	that, which
nom pl	οἵ	αἵ	ἅ	who	that, which
gen pl	ὧν	ὧν	ὧν	whose	whose
dat pl	οἷς	αἷς	οἷς	with/by/in whom	to/by/with/in which
acc pl	οὕς	ἅς	ἅ	whom	that, which

The paradigm for the relative pronoun is *very* similar to the article—but be careful! Here are some clues that will help you keep from getting these two paradigms confused. The article has *either* rough breathing (with *no* accent) *or* begins with tau (*with* an accent), whereas the relative pronoun *always* has *both* rough breathing *and* an accent. Carefully compare the following forms:

article	(form)	relative pronoun	(form)
ὁ	(rough breathing and *no accent*)	ὅς	(rough breathing and *accent*)
ἡ	(rough breathing and *no accent*)	ἥ	(rough breathing and *accent*)
οἱ	(rough breathing and *no accent*)	οἵ	(rough breathing and *accent*)
αἱ	(rough breathing and *no accent*)	αἵ	(rough breathing and *accent*)
τό	(*tau* and accent)	ὅ	(*rough breathing* and accent)
τῆς	(*tau* and accent)	ἧς	(*rough breathing* and accent)
τοῖς	(*tau* and accent)	οἷς	(*rough breathing* and accent)
τῶν	(*tau* and accent)	ὧν	(*rough breathing* and accent)

This is another paradigm that you must memorize exactly, including accents and breathing marks. (Now might be a good time to review the forms of the article from chapter 5 so that you can clearly distinguish between these two similar forms.)

The Functions of the Relative Pronoun

As we saw in the examples above, a relative pronoun introduces a relative clause that modifies the antecedent of the relative pronoun. Another way to think of this is that a relative pronoun "relates" the relative clause back to its antecedent. Remember that a pronoun is a proxy, or substitute, for a previously mentioned substantive, so as with other pronouns, a relative pronoun must have the same *number* and *gender* as its antecedent. Also parallel to other pronouns, the *case* of the relative clause is determined by its own syntactic function within the relative clause that it introduces. Consider the following example (the relative clause is in *italics*):

ἐφώνησαν οὖν τὸν ἄνθρωπον . . . ὃς ἦν τυφλός (John 9:24)
Then they called the man . . . *who was blind*

In John 9:24 the relative pronoun is masculine singular because its antecedent, τὸν ἄνθρωπον, is masculine singular.[1] The *case* of the antecedent τὸν ἄνθρωπον is accusative because it is functioning as the *direct object* of the verb ἐφώνησαν. (Don't worry about the form of this verb; we'll look at it in chapter 10; did you remember that οὖν is postpositive?) The *case* of the relative pronoun ὅς is nominative because it is functioning as the *subject* of the relative clause. Remember that a relative clause is an embedded sentence. So we can rewrite this verse as a main sentence and the embedded sentence, and then substitute the antecedent for the relative pronoun:

ἐφώνησαν οὖν τὸν ἄνθρωπον.
Then they called the man.

ὁ ἄνθρωπος ἦν τυφλός.
The man was blind.

---

1. Occasionally the relative pronoun reflects the natural gender of the antecedent. So, we might find a feminine singular relative pronoun used for παιδίον if the child in view is a girl, even though παιδίον is a *neuter* noun. This is sometimes called *attraction*. Relative pronouns can sometimes also be attracted to the case of the antecedent. We'll consider some examples of this in later chapters.

The syntax of the main sentence requires that τὸν ἄνθρωπον be in the accusative case, whereas the syntax of the embedded sentence requires that ὁ ἄνθρωπος be in the nominative case. When the relative pronoun is substituted for its antecedent, it must therefore be in the nominative case. Thus, the case of the antecedent is determined by its function in the clause (i.e., the main sentence) in which it appears, and the case of the relative pronoun is determined by its function in the relative clause (the embedded sentence). Here's another example:

> ἐν τῷ ὀνόματι Ἰησοῦ Χριστοῦ τοῦ Ναζωραίου ὃν ὑμεῖς ἐσταυρώσατε
> (Acts 4:10)
> In the name of Jesus Christ the Nazarene, *whom you crucified*

In this example, the relative pronoun is masculine singular because its antecedent is Ἰησοῦ Χριστοῦ, which is also masculine singular. Ἰησοῦ Χριστοῦ is in the genitive case because it is functioning as the genitival modifier of the substantive ὀνόματι ("name").[2] The relative pronoun, however, is in the accusative case because it is functioning as the direct object of the verb ἐσταυρώσατε ("you crucified"). In this example, the embedded sentence is "you crucified Jesus Christ."

Sometimes the antecedent of a relative clause is not expressed but is implied from the larger context. Consider the following examples:

> καὶ νῦν ὃν ἔχεις οὐκ ἔστιν σου ἀνήρ (John 4:18)
> and now the one *whom you have* is not your husband

> ὃ ἦν ἀπ᾽ ἀρχῆς (1 John 1:1)
> *that which was from the beginning*

In the example from John 4:18, the relative pronoun clearly refers to a man (ὅν), but its antecedent does not explicitly appear in the text. For this reason, we can supply the antecedent as "the one" or even "the man." In the example from 1 John 1:1, the antecedent is the entire testimony about the word of life to which John bears witness, which is outlined in 1 John 1:1–3. This is sometimes called a *neuter of general reference*. We will see more examples of this throughout this book.

---

2. You haven't had this word yet, but the case ending clearly is an iota. Based on what you know, can you guess its case? If you said "dative," you were right!

Relative clauses are common and often important in the GNT. Every time that you see a relative pronoun, you should do the following. **First**, start with the relative pronoun and then determine the boundaries of the relative clause (the "embedded" sentence) that it introduces. In the above example, the relative clauses are italicized. **Second**, identify the antecedent of the relative pronoun by looking *back* (or occasionally looking *forward*) in the text for a substantive that has the same *number* and *gender* as the relative pronoun. **Third**, determine the syntactic function of the antecedent in the main clause (indicated by its case) and of the relative pronoun in the relative clause (indicated by its case in the relative clause). If you follow these steps, you will be able to identify and understand nearly all the relative clauses in the GNT.

DEMONSTRATIVE ADJECTIVES AND PRONOUNS

A **demonstrative** is a word that "points" to an object such as a person or an event; for example, "this man," "those women," "that day," etc. This function of pointing can either indicate something near (proximate) or far (remote), whether spatial or temporal. So, for example:

This book that I'm holding is the one I just read.	(near spatial)
We are studying Greek *this* year.	(near temporal)
That book on the back table is hard to understand.	(far spatial)
In *that* day, we will see the Lord face to face.	(far temporal)

Sometimes a near demonstrative can indicate the proximity (metaphorically understood) of a subject to the author. For example, when the voice from heaven speaks, "This is my beloved Son" (Matt 3:17), we see the closeness of the Son to the Father.[3]

The Forms of Demonstratives

The good news about demonstratives is that they also follow a 2-1-2 pattern, which should be looking very familiar by now. Here is the paradigm for the near demonstrative οὗτος, αὕτη, τοῦτο, "this."

---

3. This is also called *discourse proximity* (Porter, Reed, and O'Donnell, *Fundamentals of New Testament Greek*, 134).

	masc (2)	fem (1)	neut (2)	inflected meaning
nom sg	οὗτος	αὕτη	τοῦτο	this, this one
gen sg	τούτου	ταύτης	τούτου	of this, of this one
dat sg	τούτῳ	ταύτῃ	τούτῳ	to/for/in this
acc sg	τοῦτον	ταύτην	τοῦτο	this, this one
nom pl	οὗτοι	αὗται	ταῦτα	these
gen pl	τούτων	τούτων	τούτων	of these
dat pl	τούτοις	ταύταις	τούτοις	to/for/in these
acc pl	τούτους	ταύτας	ταῦτα	these

There are some helpful similarities between this paradigm and the one for the article. Like the article, rough breathing occurs with the nominative singular and plural forms of the masculine and feminine. For the article, these forms are ὁ, ἡ, οἱ, αἱ; for the near demonstrative, they are οὗτος, αὕτη, οὗτοι, αὗται. All the remaining forms for both the article and the demonstrative begin with a tau. Also, similar to the article paradigm is the omission of the final nu in the nominative and accusative singular neuter (e.g., τό and τοῦτο compared with τέκνον in the second declension neuter noun paradigm).

There may, however, appear to be a confusing shift between the diphthongs αυ and ου in the near demonstrative paradigm. Here's a tip to understand where each of these diphthongs occurs. If the final syllable contains an omicron or omega, then the diphthong in the first syllable will be ου (e.g., τούτου); if the final syllable contains an alpha or eta, then the diphthong in the first syllable will be αυ (e.g., ταύτης). The genitive plural form is the *same* for the masculine, feminine, and neuter (i.e., τούτων). Notice carefully the differences between the personal pronoun αὐτή (smooth breathing, with an accent on the last syllable) and the demonstrative αὕτη (rough breathing, with the accent on the first syllable), as well as the personal pronoun αὐταί (smooth breathing, with the accent on the last syllable) and the demonstrative αὗται (rough breathing, with the accent on the first syllable).

Below is the paradigm for the remote demonstrative ἐκεῖνος, -η, -ο, "that."

This paradigm follows a 2-1-2 declension pattern. The feminine forms follow the η-type pattern because the demonstrative pronoun stem (ἐκειν-) ends with a nu. Unlike the article and the near demonstrative, the same stem (ἐκειν-) appears throughout the entire paradigm. Like the article and the near demonstrative, the neuter nominative and accusative singular forms do not have a nu at the end (e.g., ἐκεῖνο).

	masc (2)	fem (1)	neut (2)	inflected meaning
nom sg	ἐκεῖνος	ἐκείνη	ἐκεῖνο	that, that one
gen sg	ἐκείνου	ἐκείνης	ἐκείνου	of that, of that one
dat sg	ἐκείνῳ	ἐκείνῃ	ἐκείνῳ	to/for/in that
acc sg	ἐκεῖνον	ἐκείνην	ἐκεῖνο	that, that one
nom pl	ἐκεῖνοι	ἐκεῖναι	ἐκεῖνα	those
gen pl	ἐκείνων	ἐκείνων	ἐκείνων	of those
dat pl	ἐκείνοις	ἐκείναις	ἐκείνοις	to/for/in those
acc pl	ἐκείνους	ἐκείνας	ἐκεῖνα	those

The Functions of Demonstratives

Demonstratives have two distinct functions. **Demonstrative adjectives** modify a substantive; **demonstrative pronouns** stand in place of a previously mentioned substantive.[4] Below are some examples from the GNT of demonstrative *adjectives* (italicized). Notice that they occur *only* in predicate position (modifier-article-substantive or article-substantive-modifier), even though they are *modifying* a substantive, not making a predication. This is unlike regular adjectives. You can think of it this way: the demonstrative pronoun is anarthrous, and the modified substantive is articular. The demonstrative adjective can occur before or after the articular noun.

οὗτος ὁ λαός (Mark 7:6)
this people

ὁ λαὸς οὗτος (Matt 15:8)
this people

ὥστε παρακαλεῖτε ἀλλήλους ἐν τοῖς λόγοις *τούτοις* (1 Thess 4:18)
Therefore, encourage one another with *these* words.

τότε νηστεύσουσιν ἐν *ἐκείναις* ταῖς ἡμέραις (Luke 5:35)
Then they will fast in *those* days.

---

4. These functions are summarized in appendix 6, "Guide to Adjective, Pronoun, and Demonstrative Functions."

Demonstrative *pronouns* often point back to a previously mentioned antecedent, although demonstrative pronouns (italicized below) often function almost parallel to the third-person personal pronoun (which is listed in English in brackets in the examples below for comparison).

ἐκεῖνος κλέπτης ἐστίν (John 10:1)
That man [he] is a thief.[5]

περὶ γὰρ ἐμοῦ ἐκεῖνος ἔγραψεν (John 5:46)
For *that one* [he] wrote about me.

Sometimes, the antecedent is not expressed and must be inferred from the context. In the following example, the antecedent of τοῦτο in John 11:7 refers to the events that have just taken place, namely, the days that Jesus waited after hearing of Lazarus's illness:

μετὰ τοῦτο λέγει τοῖς μαθηταῖς . . . (John 11:7)
After *this*, he says to his disciples . . .

Sometimes, demonstrative pronouns can point forward or call attention to something that is about to be discussed. Consider the following example:

οὗτός ἐστιν ὁ υἱός μου ὁ ἀγαπητός (Matt 3:17)
This is my beloved Son.

In the account of Jesus's baptism, the demonstrative pronoun points forward, or calls attention to, the beloved Son, as the Father speaks from heaven.

Finally, there are some idiomatic expressions that occur frequently in the NT involving demonstratives. For example, τοῦτ᾽ ἔστιν can be translated as "that is" or even "namely."

τοῦτ᾽ ἔστιν τοὺς ἀδελφοὺς αὐτῶν (Heb 7:5)
namely, their brothers

---

5. This cannot be translated "he is **that** thief" because ἐκεῖνος can only function adjectivally with *articular* nouns.

The expression ἐν τούτῳ is very common and can be translated "by this," "because of this," "this is how," and so on. Notice the various translations for the following phrase from 1 John 2:5:

ἐν τούτῳ γινώσκομεν ὅτι ἐν αὐτῷ ἐσμεν
By this we may know that we are in him. (ESV)
This is how we know we are in him. (NIV, CSB)

In later chapters, we'll talk more about various English translations of the GNT, but for now it is helpful to see that many expressions in Greek can be idiomatic, meaning that there can be a range of options for translating these expressions into English and that they cannot just be translated "literally."

PREPOSITIONS WITH TWO CASES

Recall that a **preposition** is a word that is used with a substantive to show its relationship to another syntactic unit, such as another substantive, a verb, or a clause. So far we have seen prepositions that have objects in one case. For example, εἰς has an object in the accusative case and ἐν has an object in the dative case. In this section, we are going to look at prepositions that have objects in two cases; in the next section, we'll look at prepositions that can have objects in all three oblique cases. (The conceptual basics about prepositions from chapter 6 applies equally to any preposition, whether it is associated with one, two, or three cases.) Recall that each of the oblique cases has an inherent spatial or temporal orientation, which we can summarize as follows:

case	spatial orientation	temporal orientation
genitive	motion from or out of	type of time
dative	stationary (no motion)	point in time
accusative	motion toward or into	duration

This still holds, although prepositions can also indicate relationships that are not spatially or temporally oriented; instead, they often indicate logical relationships such as purpose, reason, result, and so on. We have already discussed this in connection with εἰς, which often indicates purpose and is often best translated as "for."

Look carefully at the following examples from the GNT. These will help you to see how certain prepositions function when they are associated with two different cases. The function of the preposition with each case must be memorized. Remember that prepositions often drop their final vowel before another word that begins with a smooth-breathing mark. There are other morphological changes that occur before words that begin with a rough-breathing mark. These alternate forms are listed for each preposition. Prepositions in examples are italicized for clarity.

The Preposition διά

With the accusative case, διά indicates reason and can be translated "because of," "on account of."[6]

ἐπίστευσαν *διὰ* τὸν λόγον (John 4:41)
They believed *because of* the word.

With the genitive case, διά can indicate the means by which an action occurs and can be translated "through"; it can also have a spatial sense of "through," or indicate duration and be translated as "during, with, by."

δι' αὐτοῦ (Col 1:16)
through him [i.e., Jesus]

διὰ τῆς Σαμαρείας (John 4:4)
through Samaria

The Preposition κατά

With the accusative case, κατά can be translated "according to," indicating a standard.[7] It can also have a distributive function; for example, κατὰ πόλιν, "from city to city."

κατὰ τὰ στοιχεῖα τοῦ κόσμου (Col 2:8)
according to the elemental principles of the world.

With the genitive, κατά can have an adversarial sense and may be translated "down from," "against."

---

6. The form is δι' before a word beginning with a vowel.
7. The form is κατ' before a vowel with smooth breathing and καθ' before rough breathing.

οὐκ ἔστιν *καθ᾽ ἡμῶν* (Mark 9:40)
He is not *against* us.

The Preposition μετά

With the accusative case, μετά can be translated "after" or "behind."[8]

μετὰ δὲ τὰς ἡμέρας ταύτας (Acts 21:15)
after these days

With the genitive case, μετά can be translated "with" or "among."

ἦν *μετὰ τῶν θηρίων* (Mark 1:13)
He was *with* the wild beasts.

The Preposition περί

With the accusative case, περί can be translated "around," "about," or "near."[9]

ἰδὼν δὲ ὁ Ἰησοῦς ὄχλον *περὶ αὐτόν* . . . (Matt 8:18)
But Jesus, seeing the crown *around* him . . .

With the genitive case, περί can be translated "concerning," "about," or "for."

ἐξετάσατε . . . *περὶ τοῦ παιδίου* (Matt 2:8)
Search out . . . *concerning* the child.

The Preposition ὑπέρ

With the accusative case, ὑπέρ can be translated "above," "over," or "beyond."[10]

αὐτὸν ἔδωκεν κεφαλὴν *ὑπὲρ πάντα* τῇ ἐκκλησίᾳ (Eph 1:22)
He appointed him head *over* all things for the church.

With the genitive case, ὑπέρ can be translated "on behalf of," "for," or "about."

---

8. The form is μετ᾽ before a vowel with smooth breathing and μεθ᾽ before rough breathing.
9. This preposition does not change its form before a noun that begins with a vowel.
10. This preposition does not change its form before a noun that begins with a vowel.

εὔχεσθε ὑπὲρ ἀλλήλων (Jas 5:16)
Pray *for* one another.

The Preposition ὑπό

With the accusative case, ὑπό can be translated "under" or "below."[11]

ὑπὸ τὴν κλίνην (Mark 4:21)
under the bed

With the genitive case, ὑπό most often indicates agency with passive-voice verbs (which we'll look at in chapter 11).

ἐβαπτίζοντο ὑπ᾽ αὐτοῦ (Mark 1:5)
They were being baptized *by* him.

You will notice that the prepositions that are assigned as vocabulary for this chapter and the next have different glosses assigned to each case associated with each preposition. It is best to make a separate vocabulary card (or however you are memorizing vocabulary) for each of the different cases. It is also important to understand that the function of a preposition can sometimes be complex—it is tempting to think that prepositions are "easy" because they are often small words. But it is not uncommon to find that significant theological discussions can center around the meaning of a single preposition! As we continue through this book, we will call attention to some NT verses in which the meaning of a preposition plays a very important role. Finally, it is important to note the following idioms involving prepositions. It is best to treat each of these idioms as a separate vocabulary entry.

διὰ τοῦτο	"therefore"
κατ᾽ ἰδίαν	"privately," "alone"
καθ᾽ ἡμέραν	"daily"
μετὰ τοῦτο	"after this"
μετὰ ταῦτα	"after these things"

---

11. The form is ὑπ᾽ before vowel with smooth breathing and ὑφ᾽ before rough breathing.

PREPOSITIONS WITH THREE CASES

Now we'll consider prepositions that have different functions associated with all three oblique cases.

The Preposition ἐπί

This preposition is very idiomatic, so the following are simply some outlines of how it is used in the GNT.[12] With the accusative case, ἐπί can be translated "on," "to," or "at."

ἔρχεται ἡ ὀργὴ τοῦ θεοῦ ἐπὶ τοὺς υἱοὺς τῆς ἀπειθείας (Eph 5:6)
The wrath of God is coming *on* the son of disobedience.

With the genitive case, ἐπί can be translated "on," "over," or "when."

ἐπὶ Ἀβιαθὰρ ἀρχιερέως (Mark 2:26)
when Abiathar, the high priest

With the dative case, ἐπί can be translated "on," "at," or "in."

ἐκαθέζετο . . . ἐπὶ τῇ πηγῇ (John 4:6)
He sat down *at* the well.

The Preposition παρά

With the accusative case, παρά can be translated "to (the side of)," "at," or "on."[13]

παρὰ τὴν θάλασσαν (Matt 4:18)
by (along the side of) the sea

With the genitive case, παρά can be translated "away from (the side of)."

τὸ πνεῦμα τῆς ἀληθείας . . . παρὰ τοῦ πατρός (John 15:26)
the Spirit of truth *from* the Father

With the dative case, παρά can be translated "at (the side of)," "beside," or "with."

---

12. The form is ἐπ' before a vowel with smooth breathing and ἐφ' before rough breathing.
13. The form is παρ' before a vowel.

παρὰ δὲ θεῷ πάντα δυνατά (Matt 19:26)
But *with* God all things are possible.

REVIEW OF CHAPTER 9

In this chapter, we introduced relative pronouns and relative clauses. A relative clause modifies, or provides more information about, a substantive (its antecedent) by means of an embedded sentence. A relative clause gives additional information about the antecedent, and hence it functions adjectivally. A relative pronoun must agree with this antecedent in number and gender. The case of the relative pronoun is determined by its function in the relative clause; the case of the antecedent is determined by its function in the clause in which it appears. Sometimes an antecedent is not stated directly and must be inferred from the larger context. The form of the relative pronoun (ὅς, ἥ, ὅ) looks similar to the article (ὁ, ἡ, τό), so careful attention must be paid to the differences in the forms. They must be memorized exactly.

We also introduced demonstratives and distinguished between their function as pronouns or adjectives. The forms of the near demonstrative (οὗτος, αὕτη, τοῦτο) follow a 2-1-2 pattern and have some similarities with the form of the article. The forms of the remote demonstrative (ἐκεῖνος, -η, -ο) follow a 2-1-2 pattern and use the same stem.

Finally, we looked at prepositions that take objects in two or three cases. The possible meanings associated with each case for these prepositions must be memorized.

Study Guide for Chapter 9

1. Be able to identify and explain each of the following concepts and forms:

    the functions of a relative pronoun

    the functions of an antecedent and how to recognize it

    the differences between forms of the article and relative pronoun

    determining the boundaries of a relative clause

    the forms and functions of demonstrative adjectives and pronouns

    various meanings associated with prepositions that take more than one case

    various idiomatic expressions involving prepositions

2. Be able to parse forms of the relative pronoun, identify its antecedent, and determine the boundaries of the relative clause, as well as translate basic Koine sentences that incorporate forms and concepts from previous chapters.

3. Be able to parse forms of the near and remote demonstrative.

Vocabulary to Memorize

Here is the assigned vocabulary for chapter 9. We are giving you a bit of a break here. Only prepositions that are used with two cases are assigned in this chapter. We've saved the ones that use three cases for the next chapter.

ἀδελφός, -οῦ, ὁ	brother, fellow believer (343)
ἄξιος, -α, -ον	worthy, proper, fit, deserving (41)
ἀπόστολος, -ου, ὁ	apostle, messenger (80)
γῆ, γῆς, ἡ	earth, land, soil, region (250)
διά (+acc)	because of, on account of (667; all occurrences)[1]
διά (+gen)	through, during, by (667; all occurrences)
διό	therefore, for this reason (53)
ἐκβάλλω	I drive out, I send out, I cast (81)
ἐκεῖνος, -η, -ο	that, those (pl); that person or thing, he, she, it, they (265)
ἐργάζομαι	I work, I do, I bring about (41)
καινός, -ή, -όν	new, unknown (42)
κατασκευάζω	I prepare, I build, I construct (11)
λαός, -οῦ, ὁ	people, nation (142)
μετά (+acc)	after (469; all occurrences)
μετά (+gen)	with, among (469; all occurrences)
μή	not, no (1,042)
ὅς, ἥ, ὅ	who, which, what, that (1,398)
οὐδέ	and not, neither, nor, not even (143)
οὗτος, αὕτη, τοῦτο	this, these (pl); this person or thing; he, she, it, they (subst) (1,387)
ὄχλος, -ου, ὁ	crowd, multitude (175)
παλαιός, -ά, -όν	old, former (19)
παραλαμβάνω	I take, I take along, I receive (49)
παρουσία, -ας, ἡ	coming, presence (24)
σωτηρία, -ας, ἡ	salvation, deliverance (46)
τελώνης, -ου, ὁ	tax collector (21)
ὑπέρ (+acc)	above, beyond, over (150; all occurrences)

ὑπέρ (+gen)	on behalf of, for, about (150; all occurrences)
ὑπό (+acc)	under, below (220; all occurrences)
ὑπό (+gen)	by (agent) (220; all occurrences)

[1] The frequency listed here includes all occurrences of this proposition, regardless of the case of its object.

Paradigms to Memorize

The following paradigms should be memorized for chapter 9: the relative pronoun, the near demonstrative οὗτος, αὕτη, τοῦτο, and the far demonstrative ἐκεῖνος, -η, -ς.

RELATIVE PRONOUNS
(ὅς, ἥ, ὅ)

	masc (2)	fem (1)	neut (2)
nom sg	ὅς	ἥ	ὅ
gen sg	οὗ	ἧς	οὗ
dat sg	ᾧ	ᾗ	ᾧ
acc sg	ὅν	ἥν	ὅ
nom pl	οἵ	αἵ	ἅ
gen pl	ὧν	ὧν	ὧν
dat pl	οἷς	αἷς	οἷς
acc pl	οὕς	ἅς	ἅ

NEAR DEMONSTRATIVE PRONOUN
(οὗτος, αὕτη, τοῦτο)

	masc (2)	fem (1)	neut (2)
nom sg	οὗτος	αὕτη	τοῦτο
gen sg	τούτου	ταύτης	τούτου
dat sg	τούτῳ	ταύτῃ	τούτῳ
acc sg	τοῦτον	ταύτην	τοῦτο
nom pl	οὗτοι	αὗται	ταῦτα
gen pl	τούτων	τούτων	τούτων
dat pl	τούτοις	ταύταις	τούτοις
acc pl	τούτους	ταύτας	ταῦτα

REMOTE DEMONSTRATIVE PRONOUN
(ἐκεῖνος, -η, -ο)

	masc (2)	fem (1)	neut (2)
nom sg	ἐκεῖνος	ἐκείνη	ἐκεῖνο
gen sg	ἐκείνου	ἐκείνης	ἐκείνου
dat sg	ἐκείνῳ	ἐκείνῃ	ἐκείνῳ
acc sg	ἐκεῖνον	ἐκείνην	ἐκεῖνο
nom pl	ἐκεῖνοι	ἐκεῖναι	ἐκεῖνα
gen pl	ἐκείνων	ἐκείνων	ἐκείνων
dat pl	ἐκείνοις	ἐκείναις	ἐκείνοις
acc pl	ἐκείνους	ἐκείνας	ἐκεῖνα

ROOTS, STEMS, AND PRINCIPAL PARTS; THE AORIST ACTIVE AND MIDDLE INDICATIVE

OBJECTIVES AND OVERVIEW

Chapter 10 is another chapter that introduces key concepts that are foundational and that will be developed throughout the rest of the book. Chapter 10 introduces and develops the following linguistic concepts, morphemes, and paradigms:

- verbal root and tense stem
- principal parts
- suppletive verbs
- aorist active and middle tense formative
- first aorist active indicative paradigm
- first aorist liquid active indicative paradigm
- second aorist active indicative paradigm
- first aorist middle indicative paradigm
- second aorist middle indicative paradigm
- changes when a sigma is added to a verb stem
- function of the aorist tense-form
- lexical form for aorist indicatives and parsing

VERBAL ROOTS AND TENSE STEMS

So far, we have learned the active and middle forms of the present and imperfect indicative verbs. We have also seen that the lexical form of Koine verbs is the present indicative first-person singular form. So far so good! In this chapter, you will learn the aorist active and middle indicative forms. Without a few key concepts in place, however, Greek verbs can suddenly seem much harder and very confusing. So, first we are going to review verbal roots and tense stems, and learn about principal parts. If you can grasp these concepts, your continuing journey through the Greek verbal system will be much smoother.

When you are first learning Greek, it is easy to think that the lexical form (nearly always the present indicative) is the *most basic form* of the verb. You may then think that the present tense stem is used to construct the other forms of the verb. This idea can be reinforced when you learn the imperfect indicative, because it uses the same stem as the present indicative. But it is *essential* to grasp that the present stem is just *one* stem in the Greek verbal system. As we begin to learn aorist, future, and perfect forms, it is very important to understand that the present stem is *never* used to construct these other tense-forms, even though it is used in the *imperfect* form. It is better to think that the present and imperfect indicative simply *share* the same tense stem.

Remember the tree metaphor from chapter 2? The **verbal root** is the most basic morpheme of a verb and is the basis of the various **tense stems**, which are used to construct tense-forms. As we have seen, some tense-forms share the same stem, such as the present and imperfect indicative and the perfect and pluperfect indicative. As noted above, at this point in your Greek studies you might think that the verbal root for the verb γινώσκω would be √γινωσκ. (Recall that the verbal root is not an actual Greek word; it is an abstraction used to construct tense stems. This is why the root symbol √ is used.) But then when you see that the aorist active indicative first-person singular form of this verb is ἔγνων, it is very hard to imagine how anyone could ever get from the present stem of γινώσκω to the aorist stem of ἔγνων! And that's because no one ever did! Again, the present tense stem is *never* used to derive the aorist, future, or perfect stems—ever. Instead, the verbal *root* is used to derive each of the tense stems.[1] So let's go back to the tree metaphor and apply it to γινώσκω. The verbal root of this verb is actually √γνω. The various tense stems for γινώσκω that are derived from this one verbal root are now placed on our tree. (Tense stems end with a hyphen because they are not actual Greek words either; they are the stems that are used to derive the rest of the verbal paradigm in a given tense-form). Here's γινώσκω on our leafless tree.

---

1. This is an important concept to grasp. With regular verbs, such as λύω, this seems like a silly point to stress, because all the stems look the same (λυ-) and are identical to the verbal root (√λυ). But this is not the case for many Greek verbs, so some conceptual clarity here will serve you well.

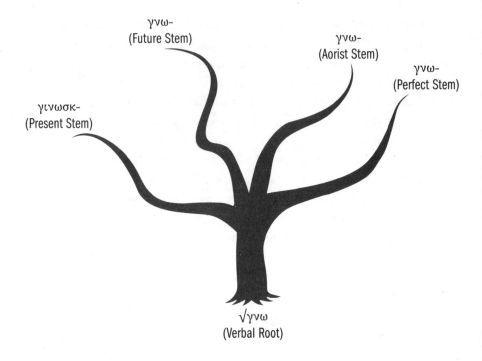

γνω-
(Future Stem)

γνω-
(Aorist Stem)

γνω-
(Perfect Stem)

γινωσκ-
(Present Stem)

√γνω
(Verbal Root)

In this illustration, it is evident that the future, aorist, and perfect tense stems are easily derived from the verbal root—in fact, in this case they are identical. To construct the actual verb forms, various other morphemes, such as the augment, tense formatives (which we'll learn about in this chapter), and personal endings are added. Consider the following:

√γνω → γνώσομαι   (future tense stem plus additional morphemes)

√γνω → ἔγνων   (aorist tense stem plus additional morphemes)

√γνω → ἔγνωκα   (perfect tense stem plus additional morphemes)

It is also evident that something strange and mysterious takes place from the verbal root to the present tense stem, which clearly is not used to form the future, aorist, and perfect tense stems.[2]

√γνω → γινώσκω   (root plus mysterious morphological processes!)

---

2. For more on these mysterious morphological processes, see appendix 10, "More on Verbal Roots."

Another analogy might be helpful here: your hand. The wrist is like the verbal root, the thumb is like the present stem, and the fingers are the other verb stems. This analogy helps to illustrate that the present stem often differs quite a bit from the verbal root and the other tense stems, just as the thumb looks different from the other fingers. It also helps to visualize that the present tense stem is not used to derive the future, aorist, or perfect tense stems, but that all stems derive from the verbal root.

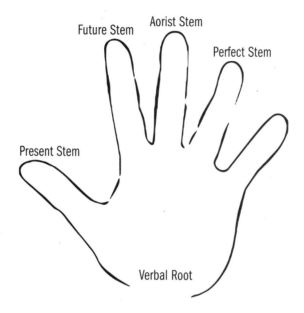

Apart from conceptual clarity, one of the main reasons to grasp this concept is this: you will always know the present stem of a verb because this is evident in the lexical form that you memorize. (This is true for nearly all the verbs that you will learn in this book with only one or two exceptions.) When you see a verb form that does not look exactly like the lexical form, then you know that you do not have a present stem and, hence, you do not have a present form of the verb, which also means that the verb cannot be an imperfect indicative either.

With this concept in place, we can now begin to refine our tree illustration a bit. The aorist actually uses a different tense stem for the passive, which we will learn in chapter 11. (The future passive then "borrows" this aorist passive tense stem, but we'll save that for chapter 19.) Similarly, the perfect often has one tense stem for the active and a different one for the middle (and passive). So, we can refine the tree illustration as follows:

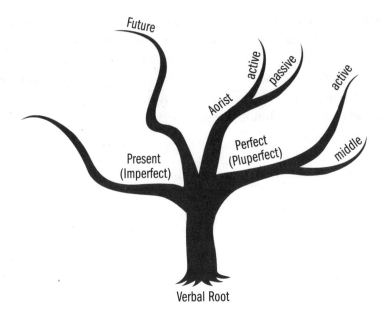

Verbal Root

Principal Parts

The refined tree illustration is a helpful introduction to **principal parts**, which are a shorthand method for recognizing Greek verbs based on the concept of verbal roots and tense stems. Each of the final stems in the tree corresponds to one of the six principal parts for Greek verbs.[3] The Greek verbal system strives for efficiency and uses the fewest possible morphemes in unique combinations to construct the entire verbal system. We have already seen that the same stem is used for present and imperfect tense-forms. This is possible because additional morphemes are added to this stem to distinguish the present tense-form from the imperfect one. For example, the augment is prefixed to the present tense stem to construct the imperfect tense-form of the verb. Similarly, present indicative verbs use primary personal endings, whereas imperfect indicative verbs use secondary personal endings. Although the use of one tense stem to construct more than one tense-form and the "recycling" of morphemes can seem confusing, there is a good system for keeping this all straight—principal parts.

Principal parts are the least number of parts that you need to know to be able to recognize the *entire* paradigm for a given Greek verb. This is good news! Instead of memorizing over a hundred different forms for *every* Greek verb,

---

3. You have already learned the first principal part for all the verbs that you have memorized in the assigned vocabulary, because the first principal part is the same as a verb's lexical form.

you can simply memorize a verb's principal parts and the various morphemes that are used to construct Greek verbs. A verb has six principal parts, which are actual verb forms and are as follows:

1st principal part	present active indicative first singular
2nd principal part	future active indicative first singular
3rd principal part	aorist active indicative first singular
4th principal part	perfect active indicative first singular
5th principal part	perfect middle indicative first singular
6th principal part	aorist passive indicative first singular

From these six parts, the following forms can be derived:

Principal Part		Forms Derived from This Principal Part
1st principal part	→	present active[1] present middle present passive imperfect active imperfect middle imperfect passive
2nd principal part	→	future active future middle
3rd principal part	→	aorist active aorist middle
4th principal part	→	perfect active pluperfect active
5th principal part	→	perfect middle perfect passive pluperfect middle pluperfect passive
6th principal part	→	aorist passive future passive

[1] Remember that we told you to think of the lexical form in terms of the first principal part—now you can see why.

Here's another way to visualize the same information (principal part numbers are in parentheses below):

	active	middle	passive
present	(1)		
imperfect			
future	(2)		(6)
aorist	(3)		
perfect	(4)		(5)
pluperfect			

Like the lexical form of the verb, the principal parts of a verb are listed in the first-person singular form. Here are the principal parts for λύω in the format in which they are usually listed:

λύω, λύσω, ἔλυσα, λέλυκα, λέλυμαι, ἐλύθην

With a regular verb such as λύω, the benefit of principal parts is not evident, because once you know all the morphemes and endings for Greek verbs, you can easily figure out the forms for λύω. But with irregular verbs, principal parts are essential. In fact, principal parts are the *only* way to recognize some Greek verbs. There are some verb paradigms in Greek that use different verbs to form their paradigm. These are called **suppletive verbs**. One such example is the verb ἔρχομαι. The present stem for this verb is ερχ-, but the aorist active indicative first-person singular of this verb is ἦλθον. The unaugmented aorist active tense stem for this verb is ελθ-. There is no morphological slight of hand that could ever get from ερχ- to ελθ-! Instead, these are the tense stems from two different verbs. In fact, *three* different verbs came together to form the paradigm for the verb ἔρχομαι, but we'll save that for later. We have something similar in English with the verb "to go": we have "go" in the present tense, but "went" in the past tense; the present tense form "wenden" is no longer used in English. Thus, two different English verbs merged to form one verb paradigm.[4] The principal parts for ἔρχομαι are as follows:

ἔρχομαι, ἐλεύσομαι, ἦλθον, ἐλήλυθα, –, –

The two dashes indicate that there is no fifth or sixth principal part for this verb. This means that these tense-forms do not occur for this verb in the GNT.[5]

---

4. Some other common suppletive Greek verbs include ἐσθίω, λέγω, οἶδα, ὁράω, and φέρω. Knowing the principal parts for these verbs is essential. They will be assigned along the way in this book.

5. Some of these forms may occur in the larger Koine corpus.

When memorizing principal parts, it is thus important to know both the form of each principal part and when a given principal part does *not* occur.

Beginning with this chapter, you will need to memorize the principal parts of various verbs. We are only assigning principal parts for irregular verbs, many of which occur frequently in the GNT. We will also assign the principal parts of verbs that are representative of other verbs whose paradigms have similar patterns. Knowing the principal parts of these verbs will greatly enhance your ability to recognize verb forms as you read and study the GNT, without having to memorize the entire paradigm of every verb in the GNT.

THE AORIST ACTIVE AND MIDDLE INDICATIVE

So far, we have learned how to "build" the present and imperfect indicatives. Now we will learn how to "build" the aorist active and middle indicative forms. Unlike the imperfect, which was constructed with the same tense stem used for the present indicative, the aorist uses a different tense stem that you have not seen yet. With the aorist, we will also introduce the concept of a **tense formative**, which is used to indicate several tense-forms.[6] Like the imperfect, the aorist has an augment and uses secondary personal endings,[7] but unlike the imperfect, the aorist uses a different tense stem, which means that it has a different verbal aspect, namely, a perfective aspect or external point of view. Remember that verbal aspect is related to the tense stem. We'll discuss this further below.

The Forms of the Aorist Indicative

Aorist tense-forms are divided between first and second aorists.[8] First aorists are also called *weak* (or *regular*) aorists; second aorists are also called *strong* (or *irregular*) aorists. There is no *functional* difference between these two types of aorist, even though they are *morphologically* different. This is somewhat parallel to the different ways that English verbs form past tenses. There are verbs that predictably add "-ed" (such as walk → walked, and listen → listened), and there are verbs that have different types of spelling changes (such as think → thought,

---

6. This is also called a *tense formant* (Goetchius, *Language of the New Testament*, 133).

7. Now might be a good time to review secondary endings and the vowel lengthenings that occur with the augment.

8. Verbs are *either* first *or* second aorist, although there is at least one verb that apparently couldn't decide. There is probably no theological significance that this verb happens to be ἁμαρτάνω ("I sin"); it has the first aorist form ἥμάρτησα ("I sinned") as well as the second aorist form ἥμαρτον ("I sinned").

sing → sang). There is no functional difference between these English past tenses—they all communicate an action in the past. The difference is merely at the formal or morphological level.

First Aorist Tense-Forms

First aorist forms have tense stems that are identical (or nearly identical) to the present tense stem, such as λύω. Because there is little or no difference between the present and aorist tense stems, first aorist tense-forms add the tense formative -σα to the end of the aorist tense stem to indicate the aorist stem.[9] So we "build" a first aorist form as follows:

augment	aorist active tense stem	aorist act/mid tense formative	secondary personal ending[1]	inflected form
ἐ	+ λυ	+ σα	+ ν	→ ἔλυσαν

[1] You can review the secondary personal endings in chapter 7. The first-person singular form for the first aorist active form does not have a nu, but otherwise the endings are consistent throughout the aorist paradigm.

Notice that there is no omicron or epsilon connecting vowel, as is the case with the present and imperfect indicative forms. That's because the alpha of the tense formative -σα provides the same function. Here are the paradigms for the first aorist active and middle indicative of λύω. The tense formative is in bold.

FIRST AORIST ACTIVE INDICATIVE

1 sg	ἔλυσα	I released
2 sg	ἔλυσας	you (sg) released
3 sg	ἔλυσε(ν)[1]	he/she/it released

1 pl	ἐλύσαμεν	we released
2 pl	ἐλύσατε	you (pl) released
3 pl	ἔλυσαν	they were released

[1] Because the first-person singular form in the first aorist active indicative paradigm does not use the personal ending -ν, the vowel of the third-person singular form shifts from α to ε so as to distinguish the two forms.

---

9. Scholars debate as to whether the tense formative is -σα or more likely just -σ. Later when we discuss the future tense, we will note that there are several similarities between the future and aorist tense forms, including the use of the tense formative -σ. For our purposes, however, we will treat -σα as the aorist tense formative in active and middle.

FIRST AORIST MIDDLE INDICATIVE

1 sg	ἐλυσάμην	I released for myself
2 sg	ἐλύσω[1]	you (sg) released for yourself
3 sg	ἐλύσατο	he/she/it released for his/her/itself
1 pl	ἐλυσάμεθα	we released for ourselves
2 pl	ἐλύσασθε	you (pl) released for yourselves
3 pl	ἐλύσαντο	they were released for themselves

[1] Recall the discussion of an intervocalic sigma in chapter 7. The same phenomenon occurs with the second-person singular form of the first aorist middle indicative. Here is the process: ἐ + λύ + σα + σο → ἐ + λύ + σα + ϕο → ἐ + λύ + σα + ο → ἐλύσω (an alpha and an omicron contract to form an omega).

Some things in these paradigms should look familiar, such as the augment and many of the secondary active and middle personal endings. Apart from the omission of the nu on the aorist active indicative first-person singular and the form of the aorist middle indicative second-person singular, there are no real surprises in these paradigms.

With verbs whose aorist tense stem ends in a vowel (often an upsilon), such as λύω, the aorist tense formative is simply suffixed onto the aorist tense stem. But things are not as simple when the aorist tense stem ends in a consonant—the combination of a consonant and a sigma almost always results in some type of spelling change. Recall from chapter 1 that consonants can be divided according to the place in the mouth where the air coming from the lungs is stopped or obstructed. As is usually the case in Greek, morphological (or spelling) changes are the result of phonological (or sound) changes. We won't get more technical than this right now, but it helps to know that *any* time a sigma is combined with a certain type of consonant (such as a labial) the same phonological process results in the same morphological change. The same is true for dental and guttural consonants. Look carefully at the following table.

CHANGES TO STEMS WHEN A SIGMA IS ADDED

Labial	π	β	φ		+	σ	→	ψ
Dental	(ν)τ	δ	θ	ζ	+	σ	→	σ
Guttural	κ	γ	χ		+	σ	→	ξ

These morphological changes occur *whenever* a sigma is added to a stem that ends in one of these consonants.[10] In this chapter, we are considering (first) aorist

---

10. These changes are summarized in appendix 4, "Changes to a Stem When a Sigma, Theta, Tau, or Mu Is Added."

tense stems that end in one of these consonants and the addition of the tense formative -σα. In future chapters, however, we'll see these same exact morphological changes with third declension nouns whose stems end in one of these consonants and case endings that begin with a sigma, and again when the future tense formative (σ) is added to a future tense stem ending in a consonant. So, when you memorize this chart, there will be multiple dividends! Here are some examples of these morphological changes with some common first aorist verbs. The final consonant of the tense stem and the resulting change when this consonant meets a sigma are both set in bold.

present tense-form	first aorist tense-form
βλέπω	ἔβλεψα
γράφω	ἔγραψα
ὑπάρχω	ὑπηρξάμην[1]

[1] Notice that the aorist form of this verb does not have active forms.

First Aorist Liquid Verbs

Certain verbs are sometimes called *liquid* verbs, because they have stems that end in one of the following consonants: λ, ρ, μ, or ν.[11] The aorist forms for liquid verbs can be understood as a subset of first aorists. There is debate as to what happens with the aorist tense formative in liquid verbs. The most likely explanation is that when the sigma of the tense formative -σα is joined to liquid or nasal consonants, the combination is phonologically unstable, so the sigma drops out. The loss of the sigma sometimes causes compensatory vowel lengthening, which we have seen elsewhere. In any event, the key factor in recognizing liquid aorist forms is that they have an alpha (or epsilon in the third-person singular) rather than the omega or epsilon that we would see in an imperfect indicative. Let's consider the paradigm for κρίνω ("I judge"). For comparison, the imperfect active indicative paradigm is listed on the right in gray.

FIRST AORIST LIQUID ACTIVE INDICATIVE			
1 sg	ἔκρινα	I judged	ἔκρινον
2 sg	ἔκρινας	you (sg) judged	ἔκρινες
3 sg	ἔκρινε(ν)	he/she/it judged	ἔκρινε(ν)

---

11. Technically, only λ and ρ are liquid consonants; μ and ν are nasals. They are treated as one group, however, because they follow the same morphological patterns.

1 pl	ἐκρίναμεν	we judged	ἐκρίνομεν
2 pl	ἐκρίνατε	you (pl) judged	ἐκρίνετε
3 pl	ἔκριναν	they judged	ἔκρινον

Look closely at the aorist and imperfect forms. Note that in five of the six forms, there is an alpha (bold) in the aorist indicative that does not occur in the imperfect indicative (note the connecting vowels set in bold). This means that when you see an augmented tense stem and an alpha connecting vowel, then you probably have a (liquid) (first) aorist indicative. Notice also that the form in the third-person singular is the same for the (liquid) (first) aorist and imperfect indicative (ἔκρινε[ν]). How will you be able to tell which is which? As usual, context will nearly always make this clear. Here are some other common liquid first aorists. (Notice the placement of the augment for compound verbs—prefixed directly to the verb stem, to which the compound preposition is then prefixed.)

lexical form	first aorist
αἴρω	ἦρα
ἀποστέλλω	ἀπέστειλα[1]
ἐγείρω	ἤγειρα

[1] The diphthong in ἀπέστειλα is an example of compensatory lengthening.

Second Aorist Tense-Forms

As we have seen, first aorist verbs have aorist stems that are identical (or nearly identical) to their corresponding present stems. Hence the aorist tense formative (-σα) is necessary to indicate the aorist forms of these regular verbs. Second aorist verbs, however, are verbs that have an aorist tense stem that is visibly different from the present tense stem. For example, the present tense stem of λαμβάνω is λαμβαν-, but its aorist tense stem is λαβ-. Because of the visible difference in the tense stems, no tense formative is needed to indicate the aorist form. This means that there is no vowel that can function as a connecting vowel as was the case with the tense formative -σα. As a result, a connecting vowel (ε or ο) is needed. So, let's look at a second aorist active indicative paradigm. Carefully compare the second aorist active paradigm for λαμβάνω with the imperfect active paradigm on the right. (The different stems have been set in bold.)

SECOND AORIST ACTIVE INDICATIVE

1 sg	ἔλαβον	I received	ἐλάμβανον
2 sg	ἔλαβες	you (sg) received	ἐλάμβανες
3 sg	ἔλαβε(ν)	he/she/it received	ἐλάμβανε(ν)
1 pl	ἐλάβομεν	we received	ἐλαμβάνομεν
2 pl	ἐλάβετε	you (pl) received	ἐλαμβάνετε
3 pl	ἔλαβον	they received	ἐλάμβανον

The difference in tense stems is quite obvious with verbs such as λαμβάνω. You can easily tell the imperfect because the tense stem looks like the lexical form (the present tense stem) that you memorized. You probably won't confuse ἐλάμβανον and ἔλαβον. Sometimes, however, the difference is less dramatic. The present tense stem for γίνομαι is γιν-, whereas the aorist tense stem is γεν-. The difference between the two stems is only a vowel, but this is still sufficient for distinguishing between the present and aorist tense stems. Carefully compare the aorist middle paradigm for γίνομαι with the imperfect middle paradigm on the right.

SECOND AORIST MIDDLE INDICATIVE

1 sg	ἐγενόμην	I became	ἐγινόμην
2 sg	ἐγένου	you (sg) became	ἐγίνου
3 sg	ἐγένετο	he/she/it became	ἐγίνετο
1 pl	ἐγενόμεθα	we became	ἐγινόμεθα
2 pl	ἐγένεσθε	you (pl) became	ἐγίνεσθε
3 pl	ἐγένοντο	they became	ἐγίνοντο

Although second aorists use a different tense stem than is used for the present tense-form, it can initially be a bit confusing to recognize the differences between first and second aorists or between imperfects and second aorists. There are some good tips for keeping all these forms straight, which we'll look at toward the end of this chapter in a chart entitled "Sorting Out Aorists and Imperfects."

It should also be noted that some second aorists sometimes have an alpha connecting vowel. For example, an alternate form of εἶπον is εἶπαν, and an alternate form of ἤλθομεν is ἤλθαμεν. These verbs tend to be those with long history in the Greek language (which may be why they can get away with this!). These vowel shifts reflect some of the changes that were taking place between Attic Greek and Koine Greek. This is simply something to note—there is no need to memorize these alternate forms. You will still be able to recognize them.

The Functions of the Aorist

It is very important to stress that there is no *functional* difference between first and second aorists or between liquid or nonliquid aorists. In fact, in parsing we don't even indicate whether an aorist form is first, liquid, or second. Those terms simply refer to the morphology of a given aorist form. First aorists are "regular" verbs with little or no difference between other tense stems (such as the present tense stem), and second aorists are "irregular" verbs with visible differences between tense stems (especially the present tense stem). So, at the functional level an aorist is an aorist is an aorist!

All aorist forms have the same verbal aspect, which is indicated by the tense stem. The aorist tense stem has a perfective aspect, which views an action or event from an external, summary perspective. This is like a photo, whereas the imperfective aspect (indicated by the present stem) gives an internal viewpoint, such as a running video.

The aorist is the most frequent tense form. It is often used in narrative to indicate main events, whereas the imperfect indicative may give background information.[12] We can see some of this distinction in the following English example. (Although these examples involve the English past-tense verbs, it is important to note that the aorist and imperfect do not *semantically* indicate past time.) Recall an example from chapter 1. If I say, "I walked yesterday," that simply indicates what I did but does not give any indication whether it was for five minutes or five hours—it merely states that the action occurred. If I say, "I was walking yesterday," however, there is an expectation that I am going to say something more; for example, "I was walking yesterday when you texted me." In the first example, "I walked yesterday" establishes the action of walking, whereas "I was walking yesterday" gives background information to the action of receiving a text.

The aorist portrays an action as a summary or as undifferentiated; it simply indicates that an action took place, but it does not indicate how long the action

---

12. Because the imperfect occurs less frequently, and because an author usually has a choice between imperfects and aorists (especially in narrative), it is always important to ask why an imperfect is used in cases where an aorist could have been used instead. We will discuss this at later points in the book.

lasted or even if the action was completed. As noted previously, the English word *aorist* comes from the Greek word ἀόριστος, which means "indefinite." Because it indicates an action as a summary, it is well suited to summarize events in narrative, although the aorist does not semantically indicate past action. Indeed, it is possible to have aorists that are present referring (with respect to the author) or even future referring. There is no real equivalent to this in English, which has a time-based verbal system. Some exegetes and commentaries find more significance in the aorist than is warranted. Far from communicating some special nuance (e.g., once-and-for-all or punctiliar), the aorist is best understood as the default tense.[13] This can be difficult to grasp at first, but we will discuss this further as we go along. Here's an example from the GNT that might help, though.

ἐβασίλευσεν ὁ θάνατος ἀπὸ Ἀδὰμ μέχρι Μωϋσέως (Rom 5:14)
Death reigned from Adam until Moses.

In Paul's argument in Romans 5, he is not focusing on how many years there were between Adam and Moses but is simply establishing the fact that death reigned during that time period. It is a summary statement. We will discuss issues such as this more throughout the course.

Lexical Form and Parsing

Finding the lexical form of first aorist tense-forms is relatively simple: you simply "reverse engineer" the inflected form by removing the augment, the aorist tense formative, and the secondary personal endings, at which point you will probably recognize the verb or be able to locate it in a lexicon. It is not as simple with second aorist forms, however. This is one of the main reasons why you must learn principal parts. Even if you remove the augment and the secondary endings from ἐλάβομεν, you still might not recognize that the lexical form is λαμβάνω. With verbs that combine different verb paradigms (**suppletive verbs**) such as ἔρχομαι, it is impossible to "reverse engineer" the aorist form. But, we have principal parts to the rescue!

---

13. *Punctiliar action* is a "point-in-time" action, such as a wave hitting a boat or a stick striking an object. It is sometimes claimed that this is the type of action indicated by an aorist, but this is incorrect. Notice that there is a punctiliar sense inherent in lexemes such as "hit" or "strike." Hence a punctiliar action is indicated by the *lexical* meaning of a given verb or the *context* in which a verb occurs. For example, "breathing" is usually conceived as a durative action, but in the following context it could be considered punctiliar: "He breathed his last breath and died." This issue involves lexical semantics and pragmatics, some of which we have already discussed. So, for now just keep in mind that the aorist all by itself does not indicate "once-and-for-all," "point-in-time," punctiliar action.

Remember that when you are parsing a word in an assignment, without any surrounding context, you need to list all possible options, including masculine, feminine, and neuter subjects for third-person verbs, and all possibilities with shared forms, such as ἔλαβον as either first-person singular or third-person plural. Also keep in mind that indicative verbs in Greek do not semantically indicate time, but when we are parsing Greek verbs it is helpful to render the imperfect with a past continuous English translation and the aorist with an English simple past translation. In actual translations, you may need to alter your initial translation according to the overall context.

Here's how you would parse three pairs of imperfect and aorist verbs:

inflected form	tense	voice	mood	pers	num	lexical form	inflected meaning
ἔλυεν	impf	act	ind	3rd	sg	λύω	he/she/it was releasing
ἔλυσεν	aor	act	ind	3rd	sg	λύω	he/she/it released
ἐλαμβάνετε	impf	act	ind	2nd	pl	λαμβάνω	you (pl) were receiving
ἔλαβον	aor	act	ind	1st sg 3rd pl		λαμβάνω	I received they received
ἤρχετο	impf	mid	ind	3rd	sg	ἔρχομαι	he/she/it was coming/going
ἤλθομεν	aor	act	ind	1st	pl	ἔρχομαι	we came/went

One final comment about ἤλθομεν. Recall that a verb can be lacking an active form in one tense stem but not another. The lexical form for ἤλθομεν is ἔρχομαι, which indicates that this verb does not have an active present tense form, but the third principal part of this verb is ἦλθον, which indicates that this verb does have an active form in the aorist.

HEADS UP!

As noted earlier, there is another class of Greek verbs, μι verbs. It may be helpful to look through the aorist indicative forms for μι verbs in chapter 24 and see how many forms you can recognize based on what you have learned in this chapter. You don't need to memorize any of these forms, but just begin to familiarize yourself with them.

SORTING OUT AORISTS AND IMPERFECTS

When you see an augmented verb form, it can sometimes be difficult to tell whether you have an imperfect, a first (or liquid) aorist, or a second aorist, especially since they all use secondary personal endings. So once you have confirmed that the ε is truly an augment (and not part of the actual tense stem, which is uncommon but does occur with some verbs), then here is a series of questions to ask that will help you sort all of these verb forms out.

After you have identified the presence of the augment, you should confirm that there are secondary personal endings. Then ask yourself whether this tense stem looks like any lexical form that you have memorized. Remember that when you memorize the lexical form of verbs, you are memorizing the verb's present stem, or first principal part. Of course, this presupposes that you have already learned the verb. (We'll talk about identifying verbs that you have never seen before below.) If the tense stem does look like the lexical form of a verb that you recognize, then you should look for a sigma after the tense stem. But be careful! Remember the possible morphological changes that can cause a sigma to go "under cover." (Technically, you are actually looking for the tense formative -σα, but it is easiest just to concentrate on looking for a sigma.) If you find a sigma, then you have a first aorist tense-form. If you don't find a sigma, then you have an imperfect tense form. If the tense stem does not look like the lexical form, then you have a second aorist. This is summarized in the chart below.

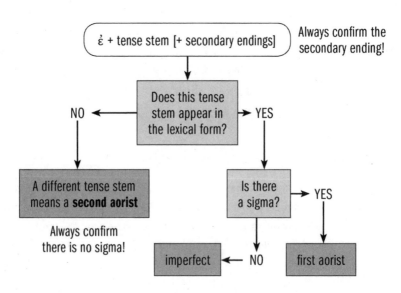

Here's another hint for distinguishing between first and second aorists. Recall that you will either have a **tense formative** (-σα) with first aorists or you will have a different stem (i.e., a stem that does not appear like the lexical form) with second aorists, but you will not have both. So, when you see an augmented verb form, and the tense stem looks familiar, then look for a -σα (or just a sigma), which will confirm that you have a first aorist indicative form. But if you see an augmented verb form with an unfamiliar looking tense stem, then you probably have a second aorist. Think of the aorist tense formative and a stem that is visibly different from a verb's lexical form as being inversely related—if you have one, you cannot have the other. This can be summarized as follows:

ε (aug)	+ —	+	-σα tense formative	+ secondary endings → first aorist
ε (aug)	+ different-looking stem	+	—	+ secondary endings → second aorist

With this in mind, let's look at a few examples.

Example 1: ἔβαλλον

If you remove the augment, does this tense stem appear in the lexical form of a verb that you have memorized?

ἔβαλλον → -βαλλον → βάλλω

Yes! This tense stem appears in βάλλω. Next, do you see a sigma? No! So, this must be an imperfect. It is an imperfect active indicative, first-person singular or third-person plural (these two forms are the same in the imperfect) from βάλλω. Only context will make clear whether this is a first-person singular or third-person plural.

Example 2: ἔλαβον

If you remove the augment, does this tense stem appear in the lexical form of a verb that you have memorized?

ἔλαβον → -λαβον → ???

You might be tempted to think that there is a verb λάβω, but resist this temptation! There is no Greek verb λάβω. If you weren't sure, you could try to look it up in a lexicon, but you wouldn't find it. So, no, this tense stem does not appear in the lexical form of any verb that you have memorized. Moreover, there is no sigma, which rules out a first aorist form. Thus, this form is a second aorist—it is the aorist active indicative, first-person singular or third-person plural of λαμβάνω. Like the imperfect, these two forms are the same in the second aorist. Only the context will tell you whether this aorist form is a first-person singular or third-person plural.

Example 3: ἐπίστευσα

If you remove the augment, does this tense stem appear in the lexical form of a verb that you have memorized?

ἐπίστευσα → -πίστευσα → πιστεύω

Yes! It appears in πίστευω. Next, do you see a sigma after the tense stem? Yes! This is the tense formative -σα, so this must be a first aorist. It is the aorist active indicative first-person singular form of πιστεύω. (There is no overlap between the first-person singular and any other form for first aorists.)

OK, let's try one final example, which is a bit harder.

Example 4: ἔβαλον

If you remove the augment, does this tense stem appears in the lexical form of a verb that you have memorized? Be careful! You might be tempted to think that the tense stem is the same as βάλλω. But one lambda does not equal two lambdas! (If you can count to two, you can understand a lot of Greek!)

ἔβαλον → -βαλον ≠ βάλλω

So, the tense stem βαλ- is not identical to the one in the lexical form βάλλω. This means that this form is a second aorist. It is an aorist active indicative, first-person singular or third-person plural of βάλλω. Like the imperfect, these forms are often the same in the second aorist. Context will tell whether this aorist form is a first-person singular or third-person plural.

One final comment. Much of this discussion presupposes that you will recognize if a tense stem appears in a lexical form. But what if you encounter a verb that you haven't learned yet? In this case, the above procedures will help you determine what to look up in a lexicon. For example, you will know that most likely an ε at the beginning of a verb form is an augment, so you would begin by removing that to see the tense-form. If you see -σα, then you would know that the lexical form should look very close, if not identical, to the tense stem in question. If there is no tense formative, then you would start with what you had and probably find your way from there. Many good lexica list second aorist forms that might not be easy to parse and guide you to the correct lexical form. For example, if you looked up ἔμαθον, you would be directed to μανθάνω, "I learn."

HOW TO SET UP PRINCIPAL-PART CARDS

Recent studies have shown that writing information down (as opposed to viewing it on a screen or typing it in a laptop) increases our ability to recall that information. With this in mind, one way to learn principal parts is to set up a 3 x 5 inch card for each new verb as follows:

SIDE 1

λύω

SIDE 2

1. I release	4. λέλυκα
2. λύσω	5. λέλυμαι
3. ἔλυσα	6. ἐλύθην

The first principal part goes on side 1 of the card. The numbers on side 2 correspond to the verb's principal parts, except for (1), which is a gloss for the verb.

Here's another example (dashes indicate forms that do not occur in a given tense stem):

SIDE 1

ἔρχομαι

SIDE 2

1. I go	4. ἐλήλυθα
2. ἐλεύσομαι	5. –
3. ἦλθον	6. –

REVIEW OF CHAPTER 10

This is another chapter that covers a lot of ground. We won't cover this much conceptual material again for a while, and the next few chapters will reinforce what is covered in this chapter. We began by discussing verbal roots and tense stems. Although some of this discussion may seem technical or even redundant, grasping these concepts will make things much clearer as we journey along. The key concept to grasp is that a verb has one verbal root that is then used to derive the main tense stems (present, future, aorist, and perfect). These tense stems are then used to build the various tense-forms (such as the present/imperfect indicative and the aorist indicative). We also introduced the shorthand system of principal parts, which are six actual verb forms from which you can reconstruct a given verb's entire verbal paradigm. (A system for memorizing principal parts was also suggested.)

Then we introduced the forms of the aorist indicative, beginning with the first aorist, whose verbs have tense stems that are identical (or nearly identical) to present tense stems, so the addition of a tense formative is used to distinguish the aorist tense-form from the imperfect tense-form. Because this tense formative begins with a sigma, certain predictable morphological changes occur when the sigma combines with verb stems that end in consonants. We also looked at liquid verbs, which are a type of first aorist tense-form, and noted that the presence of an alpha where one would expect an omicron or epsilon connecting vowel is how the aorist tense-forms are distinguished from the imperfect ones. Second aorists, however, have stems that are visibly different from the present tense stem, so a tense formative is unnecessary. What is key here is to recognize that the tense stem differs from the present tense stem. We also considered some of the functions of the aorist tense-form, particularly its perfective aspect.

Study Guide for Chapter 10

1. Be able to understand each of the following concepts and forms:
    verbal root
    tense stems
    first aorists and the use of tense formatives
    liquid stems
    second aorists
    principal parts
    morphological changes due to the addition of a sigma
    perfective aspect

the morphological differences between imperfect and aorist indicative forms

2. Be able to parse first and second aorist active and middle indicative forms, as well as translate basic Koine sentences that incorporate forms and concepts from previous chapters.

Vocabulary to Memorize

Here is the assigned vocabulary for chapter 10.

ἄν	particle of contingency or conditionality (166)
ἀναβαίνω	I go up, I ascend, I embark (82)
ἀποκαλύπτω	I reveal, I disclose (26)
ἀποκτείνω	I kill (74)
αὐξάνω	I increase, I grow (23)
διαθήκη, -ης, ἡ	covenant, decree, testament (33)
δοῦλος, -ου, ὁ	slave, servant (124)
εἰ	if, whether (502)
εἴτε	if, whether (65)
ἐπί (+acc)	on, to, against (890; all occurrences)
ἐπί (+dat)	on, at, on the basis of (890; all occurrences)
ἐπί (+gen)	on, over, when (890; all occurrences)
θάνατος, -ου, ὁ	death (120)
θρόνος, -ου, ὁ	throne (62)
καθαρίζω	I purify, I cleanse, I declare clean (31)
κατά (+acc)	according to, during, throughout (473; all occurrences)
κατά (+gen)	down from, against (473; all occurrences)
κρίνω	I judge, I condemn, I decide (114)
ὅτε	when, while, as long as (103)
παρά (+acc)	alongside, by (194; all occurrences)
παρά (+dat)	in the presence of, beside, with (194; all occurrences)
παρά (+gen)	away from, from (194; all occurrences)
πάσχω	I suffer, I endure (42)
πειράζω	I tempt, I attempt, I test (38)
πέραν	beyond, across; the other side (subst) (23)

(cont.)

περί (+acc)	around, near (333; all occurrences)
περί (+gen)	concerning, about, for (333; all occurrences)
περισσεύω	I abound, I exceed, I overflow (39)
πρός (+acc)	to, toward, with (700)
συναγωγή, -ῆς, ἡ	synagogue, assembly, meeting place (56)
τρεῖς, τρία	three (68)

Principal Parts to Memorize

These are the principal parts that you need to memorize for chapter 10. For now, you are only memorizing the first and third parts (the parts that you do not have to memorize now have been grayed out). As we continue, you will be assigned both new verbs and new parts for verbs that you have already been assigned. So you should set up cards or other ways of memorizing these forms that will allow you to easily add new forms to verbs that have already been assigned. By introducing only the parts for verb stems that you know, you will be able to focus on those forms without being distracted or confused by forms that you have not yet learned. The full "Principal Parts Chart" is in appendix 14. You will need to refer to this chart in later chapters to "fill in" the principal parts assigned in this chapter.

1st prin part	2nd prin part	3rd prin part	4th prin part	5th prin part	6th prin part
βλέπω	βλέψω	ἔβλεψα	n/a	n/a	n/a
ἔρχομαι	ἐλεύσομαι	ἦλθον	ἐλήλυθα	n/a	n/a
ἐσθίω	φάγομαι	ἔφαγον	n/a	n/a	n/a
ἔχω	ἕξω	ἔσχον	ἔσχηκα	n/a	n/a
πάσχω	n/a	ἔπαθον	πέπονθα	n/a	n/a

Paradigms to Memorize

In addition to vocabulary and principal parts, the following paradigms should be memorized for chapter 10: aorist active and middle indicative of λύω, aorist active indicative of κρίνω, aorist active indicative of λαμβάνω, and aorist middle of γίνομαι. Knowing these paradigms will enable you to recognize many verb forms in the GNT.

AORIST ACTIVE INDICATIVE OF λύω

1 sg	ἔλυσα
2 sg	ἔλυσας
3 sg	ἔλυσε(ν)
1 pl	ἐλύσαμεν
2 pl	ἐλύσατε
3 pl	ἔλυσαν

AORIST MIDDLE INDICATIVE OF λύω

1 sg	ἐλυσάμην
2 sg	ἐλύσω
3 sg	ἐλύσατο
1 pl	ἐλυσάμεθα
2 pl	ἐλύσασθε
3 pl	ἐλύσαντο

AORIST ACTIVE INDICATIVE OF κρίνω

1 sg	ἔκρινα
2 sg	ἔκρινας
3 sg	ἔκρινε(ν)
1 pl	ἐκρίναμεν
2 pl	ἐκρίνατε
3 pl	ἔκριναν

AORIST ACTIVE INDICATIVE OF λαμβάνω

1 sg	ἔλαβον
2 sg	ἔλαβες
3 sg	ἔλαβε(ν)
1 pl	ἐλάβομεν
2 pl	ἐλάβετε
3 pl	ἔλαβον

AORIST MIDDLE INDICATIVE OF γίνομαι

1 sg	ἐγενόμην
2 sg	ἐγένου
3 sg	ἐγένετο
1 pl	ἐγενόμεθα
2 pl	ἐγένεσθε
3 pl	ἐγένοντο

chapter ELEVEN

PASSIVES AND CONDITIONALS

OBJECTIVES AND OVERVIEW

Chapter 11 introduces the following linguistic concepts, morphemes, and paradigms:

- active and passive voice
- present passive indicative
- imperfect passive indicative
- aorist passive tense formative
- first aorist passive indicative
- second aorist passive indicative
- changes when a theta is added to a verb stem
- agency (ultimate and intermediate) and instrumentality
- conditional clauses
- protasis and apodosis
- function of first-class conditionals
- function of second-class conditionals

PRESENT, IMPERFECT, AND AORIST PASSIVE INDICATIVE VERBS

As we saw in chapter 2, voice indicates how the subject is related to the action of the verb in a clause or sentence. We have already looked at the active and middle voices for the present, imperfect, and aorist indicative tense-forms. In this chapter, we will look at the third and final voice in the Greek verbal system, the passive voice for these same tense-forms. Recall that in the **active voice**, the subject *performs, produces, or experiences the action of the verb*. In the **passive voice**, however, *the subject is acted upon or receives the action of the verb*. Consider the following examples:

We love the Lord.　　　　　　(active voice–the subject performs the action)

We are loved by the Lord.　　(passive voice–the subject receives the action)

We will first consider the passive forms for the present, imperfect, and aorist indicative tense-forms. Then we will look at the functions of the passive and some examples of its use from the GNT. Keep mind that these concepts will also apply to the future, perfect, and pluperfect passive tense-forms when we learn them in later chapters.

The Forms of the Present, Imperfect, and Aorist Passive Indicative

In English, we use an auxiliary verb and a past participle to express the passive, such as in the above example: "are loved."[1] In Greek, however, passive verbs often use different personal endings and may use a tense formative. The good news is that we have already learned these personal endings in chapters 3 and 7, so this is another example of Greek recycling. Here they are again for review.[2]

	primary middle personal endings	secondary middle personal endings
1 sg	μαι	μην
2 sg	σαι	σο
3 sg	ται	το
1 pl	μεθα	μεθα
2 pl	σθε	σθε
3 pl	νται	ντο

The Greek verbal system is efficient. The primary middle endings are used for *both* the present middle indicative and the present passive indicative, and

---

1. The use of English auxiliary verbs can be somewhat confusing. Even though each of the following sentences looks very similar, they have very different functions: "we *are* studious" (equative verb and predicate adjective) and "we *are* loved" (auxiliary verb with past participle). It is essential not to confuse these two functions of the verb "to be" in English in your translations of Greek equative verbs and passive-voice verbs.

2. These endings are sometimes called middle/passive endings or simply passive endings. One unfortunate consequence of calling these endings "middle/passive" is that students often equate the middle voice with the passive, which is clearly not the case. Remember that the middle voice is active but with some additional nuance; the middle voice almost never communicates a passive sense (although see 1 Cor 6:11, where the permissive middle parallels a passive sense).

the secondary middle endings are used for *both* the imperfect middle indicative and the imperfect passive indicative. At first, it may seem overwhelming that the same endings can be used for both middle and passive verbs. (This is not the case for the aorist passive, which we will discuss below.) But context will always make clear whether a verb is middle or passive. The passive voice indicates that the subject *receives* the action, which is quite different from the middle voice, which indicates that the subject *performs* the action with some additional emphasis on the subject. It might be helpful to observe that Greek verbs can share (or recycle) the same forms precisely because the context makes clear which is intended. This is why it is so important to consider the entire context in which a verb occurs rather than trying to translate each verb (or word) in isolation.

Here are the present and imperfect passive indicative paradigms for λύω, including possible translations for each form. These forms should look very familiar to you—you've seen them before. (As before, the connecting vowels and personal endings are in bold.)

PRESENT PASSIVE INDICATIVE

1 sg	λύ**ομαι**	I am being released
2 sg	λυ**ῇ**	you (sg) are being released
3 sg	λύ**εται**	he/she/it is being released
1 pl	λυ**όμεθα**	we are being released
2 pl	λύ**εσθε**	you (pl) are being released
3 pl	λύ**ονται**	they are being released

IMPERFECT PASSIVE INDICATIVE

1 sg	ἐλυ**όμην**	I was being released
2 sg	ἐλύ**ου**	you (sg) were being released
3 sg	ἐλύ**ετο**	he/she/it was being released
1 pl	ἐλυ**όμεθα**	we were being released
2 pl	ἐλύ**εσθε**	you (pl) were being released
3 pl	ἐλύ**οντο**	they were being released

In the previous chapter, you learned the forms of the aorist active and middle indicative. Based on the present and imperfect passive indicative, you might think that the aorist passive would use the same form as the aorist middle, but it does not. It does do a bit of recycling though. It uses secondary *active* endings, but it uses a different tense formative (-θη) to distinguish it from the aorist active indicative. Because the tense formative ends with a vowel, there is no need for a connecting vowel (just as is the case with the tense formative -σα).

Here is how you build a first aorist passive indicative verb.

augment	aorist pass tense stem	aorist pass tense formative	secondary act personal ending[1]	inflected form
ἐ	+ λυ	+ θη	+ ν	→ ἐλύθην

[1] You can review the secondary active personal endings in chapter 7.

Because Greek verbs are efficient, they use a minimal number of morphemes that are combined in unique ways. The good news is that this means less to memorize; the challenge is learning how to identify all the morphemes in a given verb form and thus to be able to parse the form correctly.

Here is the first aorist passive indicative paradigm for λύω, including possible translations for each form.

FIRST AORIST PASSIVE INDICATIVE

1 sg	ἐλύθην	I was released
2 sg	ἐλύθης	you (sg) were released
3 sg	ἐλύθη	he/she/it was released
1 pl	ἐλύθημεν	we were released
2 pl	ἐλύθητε	you (pl) were released
3 pl	ἐλύθησαν	they were released

We have seen that certain morphological changes occur when a sigma is added to a stem that ends in a consonant. Similar morphological changes occur when a theta is added to a stem that ends in a consonant. Thus, for example, the aorist passive of ἄγω is ἤχθην, and the aorist passive of πείθω is ἐπείσθην. These are summarized below.

CHANGES TO STEMS WHEN A THETA IS ADDED

Labial	π	β	φ	ττ	+	θ	→	φθ
Dental	(ν)τ	δ	θ	ζ	+	θ	→	σθ
Guttural	κ	γ	χ		+	θ	→	χθ

For the Curious

As we have seen, morphology (a word's form) is driven by phonology (how sounds are made). The θ is classified as a fricative, meaning that the air flowing from the lungs is obstructed, but it is not stopped completely, as is the case with a labial stop such as π or β. When consonants are placed next to each other, they tend to assimilate, or to become like each other. Like θ, both φ and χ are also fricatives, so a labial stop will assimilate to a labial fricative (φ) before a θ, and a guttural stop will assimilate to a guttural fricative (χ) before a θ. With dentals, θθ (or any other dental combination) would be very hard to pronounce, so dentals assimilate to the sibilant σ before a θ. Even this can be explained further, but we'll stop for now. You can also go back and review the "Consonant Classification" chart in chapter 1, if you're curious. See also appendix 4, "Changes to a Stem When a Sigma, Theta, Tau, or Mu Is Added."

At this point, you might be expecting to see the second aorist passive indicative paradigm. In the second aorist passive, the tense formative shortens to -η. So we would expect to see this with second aorist verbs. But something unusual happens with second aorists in the passive.[3] Many verbs that are second aorist still use the full tense formative -θη. For example, consider βάλλω, which is clearly a second aorist (visibly different stem in the aorist and present). The aorist passive indicative is ἐβλήθην, which uses both a different aorist passive tense stem and uses the tense formative -θη. This provides an extra clue for recognizing the aorist passive. This is also another reason why principal parts are necessary—the sixth principal lists a verb's aorist passive tense stem. For this reason, it is unnecessary to memorize the second aorist passive indicative paradigm.

---

3. Something unusual also seems to happen with some first aorist verbs. Some verbs that are otherwise considered "regular" have *second* aorist passives, such as γράφω (e.g., ἐγράφην). Again, this is why principal parts are so helpful. This is also true for several liquid verbs, e.g., ἀποστέλλω and φαίνω.

The Functions of the Passive

There are two additional concepts that are essential for understanding the passive voice: agency and instrumentality. **Agency** refers to the *person* responsible for a given action, and **instrumentality** refers to an *object* that is used to carry out an action. Agency can be further specified in terms of **ultimate agency** (also called primary or direct agency), which refers to the person who is ultimately responsible for an action; this is often expressed by a passive-voice verbal form followed by ὑπό plus the genitive. Consider the following example:

ἦλθεν Ἰησοῦς . . . καὶ ἐβαπτίσθη εἰς τὸν Ἰορδάνην ὑπὸ Ἰωάννου (Mark 1:9)
Jesus came . . . and was baptized in the Jordan *by* John.

We can also speak of **intermediate agency** (also called secondary agency), which refers to the person who carries out an action for the ultimate agent; this is often expressed by a passive-voice verb followed by διά plus the genitive. Consider the following example:

τὰ πάντα δι᾿ αὐτοῦ καὶ εἰς αὐτὸν ἔκτισται (Col 1:16)
All things have been created *through* him and for him.

Instrumentality (also called *impersonal agency* or *means*) refers to the instrument used to carry out an action; this is most often expressed by a passive-voice verb followed by ἐν plus the dative or sometimes the dative alone. Consider the following examples:

ἐν ἑνὶ πνεύματι ἡμεῖς πάντες εἰς ἓν σῶμα ἐβαπτίσθημεν (1 Cor 12:13)
by one Spirit we were all baptized into one body.

λογιζόμεθα γὰρ δικαιοῦσθαι πίστει ἄνθρωπον (Rom 3:28)
For we maintain a person is justified *by* faith.

Sometimes agency is not explicitly expressed but is implied; this may involve the so-called *divine passive* or *theological passive*. God is the implied agent, even if not stated as such explicitly.

μακάριοι οἱ πενθοῦντες, ὅτι αὐτοὶ παρακληθήσονται (Matt 5:4)
Blessed are those who mourn, for they shall be comforted.

┌─ **HEADS UP!** ───┐

Look through the present, imperfect, and aorist *passive* indicative forms for μι verbs in chapter 24 and see how many forms you can recognize based on what you have learned in this chapter. The present and imperfect passive forms are identical to the present and imperfect middle forms. But look carefully at the aorist passive forms. The aorist passive tense formative is prominent.

└──┘

FIRST- AND SECOND-CLASS CONDITIONALS

Conditional sentences posit a condition (in the form of an "if" clause), and a result stating the outcome if the condition is met (in the form of a "then" clause). For example: "If we pass beginning Greek, then we will proceed to Greek exegesis." In Greek, the "if" clause is called a **protasis**; the "then" clause is called the **apodosis**. The protasis is grammatically dependent; the apodosis is the independent clause.

The Classification of Greek Conditional Sentences

Greek conditionals are classified according to the presence of εἰ or ἐάν in the protasis and the presence or absence of the particle ἄν in the apodosis. In this chapter, we will focus only on conditionals that begin with εἰ. This can be summarized as follows:

type	protasis ("if")	apodosis ("then")
1st class	εἰ + any tense indicative - if negated, uses οὐ	any tense or mood
2nd class	εἰ + impf/aor indicative - if negated, uses μή	ἄν + same indicative tense as protasis

The key to identifying first- and second-class conditionals, therefore, is to identify the εἰ that begins the protasis. Next, look for ἄν in the following clause. If it is there, you have a second-class conditional; if it is not, you have a first-class conditional.[4]

---

4. Again, if you can count to two, then you can do a lot of Greek. For first-class conditionals, you just need *one* particle, εἰ. For second-class conditionals, you need *two* particles, εἰ and ἄν.

The Functions of Greek Conditionals

First- and second-class conditionals are often used rhetorically or to posit a point in a larger argument. In **first-class conditionals**, the protasis presents a condition that is assumed to be true for the sake of the argument, although in fact it may not be true. For example:

> Εἰ ὁ κόσμος ὑμᾶς μισεῖ, γινώσκετε ὅτι ἐμὲ πρῶτον ὑμῶν μεμίσηκεν.
> (John 15:18)
> If the world hates you, [then] know that it hated me first.

In the example from John 15:18, the condition is true. But sometimes a condition is presented as if it were true (even though it is not) to make a point. So, in 1 Corinthians 15:32 Paul challenges false teachers by stating:

> εἰ νεκροὶ οὐκ ἐγείρονται, φάγωμεν καὶ πίωμεν, αὔριον γὰρ ἀποθνῄσκομεν.
> If the dead are not raised, [then] let us eat and drink, for tomorrow we die.

Clearly in this example Paul is presenting a condition that is assumed to be true *only* for the sake of the argument, but in fact it is not true, because in Christ the dead *are* raised. As is so often the case, context is essential for understanding how the conditional is functioning in the overall argument. Consider the earlier part of Paul's argument in 1 Corinthians 15:13:

> εἰ δὲ ἀνάστασις νεκρῶν οὐκ ἔστιν, οὐδὲ Χριστὸς ἐγήγερται.
> But if there is no resurrection of the dead, neither has Christ been raised.

Again, Paul's argument assumes that something is true (that there is no resurrection) and then makes a point if that condition *were* in fact true (that Christ would not be raised either). Paul's point in 1 Corinthians 15 is to expose the Corinthian's faulty thinking and to show why Christ's resurrection is paramount.

In **second-class conditionals**, the protasis presents a condition that is known to be false or clearly understood to be false by the one making the argument. (This is sometimes called a *contrary-to-fact conditional*.) Consider the following examples:

> εἰ γὰρ ἐπιστεύετε Μωϋσεῖ, ἐπιστεύετε ἂν ἐμοί. (John 5:46)
> For if you had believed Moses, you would have believed me.

εἰ γὰρ ἔγνωσαν, οὐκ ἂν τὸν κύριον τῆς δόξης ἐσταύρωσαν. (1 Cor 2:8)
For if they [the rulers of this age] had understood, then they would not have
    crucified the Lord of glory.

In the example from John 5:46, Jesus presents the protasis as if the Jewish
leaders had believed Moses, but in fact it was clear that they had not. The same
logic applies to Paul's argumentation in 1 Corinthians 2:8. In many second-
class conditionals, therefore, the conditional serves to expose some type of false
thinking. For example, the Jewish leaders that Jesus addressed certainly thought
that they believed Moses, but they did not. Similarly, "the rulers of this age" who
crucified Jesus thought that they were crucifying a wrongdoer, but they had no
idea that he was the Lord of glory.

As is the case with first-class conditionals, even though the protasis is
assumed to be false for the sake of the argument, it may in fact be true. Consider
the following:

οὗτος εἰ ἦν προφήτης, ἐγίνωσκεν ἂν τίς . . . ἡ γυνὴ ἥτις ἅπτεται αὐτοῦ
    (Luke 7:39)
If this man was a prophet, then he would have recognized who . . . this
    woman is who is touching him.

Clearly Jesus was (and is!) a prophet, although those who were accusing him
denied it. It is important to keep in mind that first- and second-class conditionals
present a condition to make a rhetorical point. A first-class conditional presents a
condition as if it were true (whether it actually is), and a second-class conditional
presents a condition that is assumed to be false (whether it actually is), for the
sake of a larger argument. The form of the conditional indicates which rhetorical
effect is intended.

REVIEW OF CHAPTER 11

In this chapter we introduced the forms of the present, imperfect, and aorist passive indicative. You have already learned the forms of the present and imperfect
passive indicative because it shares the same form as the present and imperfect
middle indicative. Context is essential for determining whether the middle or
passive voice is intended. For the aorist passive, we introduced the tense formative -θη and discussed the predictable morphological changes that occur when
the theta combines with verb stems that end in consonants. We also saw that the

aorist passive uses secondary *active* personal endings, which offers another clue for recognizing this form. In addition to understanding that the passive voice indicates that the subject is acted upon or receives the action of the verb, we also discussed agency (the person responsible for the action) and instrumentality (the object used to perform the action). Sometimes agency is assumed, often when God is understood to be the agent.

We then presented first- and second-class conditional clauses and the contextual clues that help to identify each construction. Both first- and second-class conditionals are introduced by the particle εἰ. Second-class conditionals also have the particle ἄν in the protasis. Finally, we discussed the rhetorical function of first- and second-class conditional clauses. In first-class conditionals, the protasis is assumed to be true (whether or not it actually is) for the sake of the argument, whereas second-class conditionals present a conditional that is assumed to be false (whether or not it is) for the sake of the argument.

Study Guide for Chapter 11

1. Be able to understand each of the following concepts and forms:
   aorist passives and the use of tense formatives
   the construction of passive indicative tense-forms
   morphological changes due to the addition of a theta
   ultimate and intermediate agency
   instrumentality
   function of first- and second-class conditionals
2. Be able to parse present, imperfect, and aorist passive indicative forms, as well as translate basic Koine sentences that incorporate forms and concepts from previous chapters.

Vocabulary to Memorize

Here is the assigned vocabulary for chapter 11. Notice that ἕως can function as both a conjunction or a preposition.

ἀρχιερεύς, -έως, ὁ	high priest (122)
βασιλεύς, -έως, ὁ	king (115)
διδάσκαλος, -ου, ὁ	teacher (59)
ἕκαστος, -η, -ον	each, every; each one, everyone (subst) (82)
ἐξέρχομαι	I go out, I go away, I come out (218)

(cont.)

ἕως	until, while (conj);[1] +gen: until, as far as (146)
καιρός, -οῦ, ὁ	time, appointed time, season (85)
καλέω	I call, I name, I invite (148)
λογίζομαι	I account, I calculate, I consider (40)
μηδέ	and not, but not, nor, not even (56)
οἶκος, -ου, ὁ	house, home, household, family (114)
ὅλος, -η, -ον	whole, entire, complete; entirely (109)
ὅπου	where, since (82)
ὅσος, -η, -ον	as much as, as many as, how great (110)
ὅστις, ἥτις, ὅτι	who, which, whoever, whichever (153)
ὅταν	when, whenever (123)
πρεσβύτερος, -α, -ον	older; elder (subst) (66)
σάββατον, -ου, τό	Sabbath, week (68)
συνάγω	I gather, I bring together (59)
συνέδριον, -ου, τό	Sanhedrin, council (22)
τέ	and, and so, so (215)
ὑπάγω	I depart, I go away, I go (79)
φίλος, -η, -ον	beloved, loving, friendly; friend (subst) (29)
χαίρω	I rejoice, I am glad (74)
χρόνος, -ου, ὁ	time, period of time (54)

[1] When this word functions as a conjunction, it has this meaning.

Principal Parts to Memorize

These are the principal parts that you need to memorize for chapter 11. In addition to the first and third, you now need to memorize the *sixth* principal part (the parts that you do not have to memorize now have been grayed out). Remember, you should set up cards or other ways of memorizing these forms that will allow you to easily add new forms. You should now add the sixth principal part to the principal parts assigned in chapter 10. You will need to refer to appendix 14 for the full "Principal Parts Chart" in order to add these forms.

1st prin part	2nd prin part	3rd prin part	4th prin part	5th prin part	6th prin part
ἄγω	ἄξω	ἤγαγον	n/a	ἦγμαι	ἤχθην
γίνομαι	γενήσομαι	ἐγενόμην	γέγονα	γεγένημαι	ἐγενήθην
ἐγείρω	ἐγερῶ	ἤγειρα	n/a	ἐγήγερμαι	ἠγέρθην
λαμβάνω	λήμψομαι	ἔλαβον	εἴληφα	εἴλημμαι	ἐλήμφθην
λέγω	ἐρῶ	εἶπον	εἴρηκα	εἴρημαι	ἐρρέθην

Paradigms to Memorize

You will need to memorize the following paradigms for chapter 11: the present, imperfect, and aorist passive indicative of λύω.

PRESENT PASSIVE INDICATIVE OF λύω

1 sg	λύομαι
2 sg	λύῃ
3 sg	λύεται
1 pl	λυόμεθα
2 pl	λύεσθε
3 pl	λύονται

IMPERFECT PASSIVE INDICATIVE OF λύω

1 sg	ἐλυόμην
2 sg	ἐλύου
3 sg	ἐλύετο
1 pl	ἐλυόμεθα
2 pl	ἐλύεσθε
3 pl	ἐλύοντο

AORIST PASSIVE INDICATIVE OF λύω

1 sg	ἐλύθην
2 sg	ἐλύθης
3 sg	ἐλύθη
1 pl	ἐλύθημεν
2 pl	ἐλύθητε
3 pl	ἐλύθησαν

THIRD DECLENSION PARADIGMS: THE REST OF NOUNS AND ADJECTIVES; MORE PRONOUNS (INTERROGATIVE AND INDEFINITE)

OBJECTIVES AND OVERVIEW

Chapter 12 introduces the following linguistic concepts, morphemes, and paradigms:

- third declension case endings
- third declension noun paradigms
- third declension adjective paradigms
- 3-1-3 and 3-3 declension patterns
- interrogative-pronoun paradigm and function
- indefinite-pronoun paradigm and function
- the numeral "one" and related compounds
- questions

THIRD DECLENSION NOUN AND ADJECTIVE PARADIGMS

In chapter 4, we learned the paradigms for first and second declension nouns. Because the noun stems for both first and second declension nouns end in vowels, adding case endings is straightforward. In this chapter, we will present third declension nouns, which have stems that end in consonants. Moreover, third declension nouns use a different set of case endings, some of which begin with a sigma (as was also true for some case endings for first and second declension nouns). We have seen already that the aorist tense formative that begins with a sigma (-σα) causes predictable morphological changes when it is added to a stem that ends in a consonant. These *same* morphological rules apply anytime that a sigma is added to a consonant. Thus, the morphological patterns that are found with third declension nouns are also predictable. Indeed, you have already seen many of them.

All the *concepts* and *functions* that were presented for noun cases in chapter 4 apply here as well. What is different is the *form* of third declension nouns. But the *functions* for a noun in the genitive case do not change whether that noun is first, second, or third declension. Remember, declensions are merely ways of organizing groups of nouns that follow the same morphological patterns.

There are many different types of third declension nouns, but we will only consider several representative ones. Despite the (possibly overwhelming!) diversity of third declension patterns, if you memorize these representative paradigms, you will be able to recognize the vast majority of third declension nouns in the GNT.

Third Declension Case Endings

Here are the case endings used with third declension nouns. Notice that there is much overlap between these endings and the ones used for the first and second declensions. For example, an iota is a reliable clue for the dative,[1] and -ων is a sure clue for genitive plural.

	3rd decl masc/fem	3rd decl neut
nom sg	ς/–	–
gen sg	ος	ος
dat sg	ι	ι
acc sg	α[1]	–
nom pl	ες	α
gen pl	ων	ων
dat pl	σι(ν)	σι(ν)
acc pl	ας	α

[1] Occasionally this ending is a nu (ν). We will discuss this further below.

It is helpful to observe that in the *second* declension there are many similarities between the masculine and neuter (such as sharing the same case endings for

1. Recall that an iota subscripts whenever possible, such as with first and second declension noun stems that end with vowels. This is not the situation with third declension nouns because their stems end in consonants.

the genitive and dative). In the *third* declension, it is the masculine and feminine forms that share case endings (although there is also a lot of overlap with third declension neuter nouns as well).

Third Declension Noun Paradigms

Let's look at a very common type of third declension noun, with three representative paradigms. (A common gloss is provided for each paradigm; for possible translations of each of the cases, refer to the paradigms in chapter 4.)

	σωτήρ, -ῆρος, ὁ savior stem: σωτηρ-	σάρξ, σαρκός, ἡ flesh/body stem: σαρκ-	ἐλπίς, -ίδος, ἡ hope stem: ελπιδ-
nom sg	σωτήρ	σάρξ	ἐλπίς
gen sg	σωτῆρος	σαρκός	ἐλπίδος
dat sg	σωτῆρι	σαρκί	ἐλπίδι
acc sg	σωτῆρα	σάρκα	ἐλπίδα
nom pl	σωτῆρες	σάρκες	ἐλπίδες
gen pl	σωτήρων	σαρκῶν	ἐλπίδων
dat pl	σωτῆρσι(ν)	σαρξί(ν)	ἐλπίσι(ν)
acc pl	σωτῆρας	σάρκας	ἐλπίδας

Until now, you have been memorizing the genitive singular form of a noun together with the article and its lexical form. The reason why will now be evident. Because a sigma occurs in the nominative singular of third declension masculine and feminine nouns, which results in predictable morphological changes, it is difficult to determine the actual noun stem from the lexical form alone. Now consider the following:

noun stem	genitive case ending	inflected form
σαρκ-	+ ος	→ σαρκός

The noun stem is clearly visible in the genitive singular form, once the case ending -ος is removed. Thus, the stem for σάρξ is σαρκ-, and the stem for ἐλπίς is ελπιδ-. The sigma case ending of the nominative singular accounts for the ξ in σάρξ and the ς in ἐλπίς. The noun σωτήρ does not use a case ending in the nominative singular, so the noun stem is σωτηρ. These noun paradigms are representative of many masculine and feminine third declension nouns, so when you memorize these paradigms, you will be able to recognize many other third declension nouns in the GNT. Here is the paradigm for another very common third declension neuter noun pattern.

	πνεῦμα, πνεύματος, τό
	spirit/breath
	stem: πνευματ-
nom sg	πνεῦμα
gen sg	πνεύματος
dat sg	πνεύματι
acc sg	πνεῦμα
nom pl	πνεύματα
gen pl	πνευμάτων
dat pl	πνεύμασι(ν)
acc pl	πνεύματα

The noun stem (seen clearly in the genitive singular) is πνευματ-. All nouns with stems that end in -ματ are neuter third declension nouns, which is good to know, because there are many nouns in the GNT that follow this pattern. Look carefully at the paradigm. Four different forms end with an alpha! We have already seen that the nominative and accusative forms are the same for neuter nouns. And we have also seen an alpha ending for neuter nominative and accusative *plurals*, but an alpha for the neuter nominative and accusative *singular* is new. So here's a tip: when you see the alpha ending, look to see if the -ματ stem is also visible. If so, then you have a plural form. (It helps to note that the plural form also has more letters!) As with second declension neuter nouns, context will make it clear if the form is nominative or accusative. In the singular forms, there is no case ending for the nominative and accusative (parallel to σωτήρ), so you would expect the form to be πνεύματ. But Greek doesn't like to have a tau at the end of a word, so the tau drops off and the final form is πνεῦμα. Finally, when the sigma of the dative plural case ending is added to the -ματ stem, the tau drops off and the form is πνεύμασι(ν).

Here are two other common types of third declension patterns.

	πόλις, -εως, ἡ city stem: πολι/ε-	βασιλεύς, -έως, ὁ king stem: βασιλευ/ε-
nom sg	πόλις	βασιλεύς
gen sg	πόλεως	βασιλέως
dat sg	πόλει	βασιλεῖ
acc sg	πόλιν	βασιλέα
nom pl	πόλεις	βασιλεῖς
gen pl	πόλεων	βασιλέων
dat pl	πόλεσι(ν)	βασιλεῦσι(ν)
acc pl	πόλεις	βασιλεῖς

Although it seems as if these nouns have vowel stems, they are still classified with consonant stems because of the residual effects of two consonants, the digamma (ϝ) and the consonantal iota (ι̯), that eventually dropped out of the Greek alphabet.[2] Notice that the nominative and accusative singular feminine endings retain the iota (e.g., πόλις and πόλιν), but otherwise the stems shifts to an epsilon throughout the rest of the paradigm. These patterns are common, so you need to memorize them. With them, you will be able to recognize many additional nouns in the GNT.

Finally, here are three additional, fairly common patterns for third declension nouns. It would be helpful to memorize these as well, but you don't have to if you are at capacity. The key is being able to *recognize* these patterns when you see them in the GNT.

	ἔθνος, -ους, τό nation stem: εθνο/ε-	πατήρ, πατρός, ὁ father stem: πατ(ε)ρ-	ὕδωρ, ὕδατος, τό water stem: υδατ-
nom sg	ἔθνος	πατήρ	ὕδωρ
gen sg	ἔθνους	πατρός	ὕδατος
dat sg	ἔθνει	πατρί	ὕδατι
acc sg	ἔθνος	πατέρα	ὕδωρ
nom pl	ἔθνη	πατέρες	ὕδατα
gen pl	ἐθνῶν	πατέρων	ὑδάτων
dat pl	ἔθνεσι(ν)	πατράσι(ν)	ὕδασι(ν)
acc pl	ἔθνη	πατέρας	ὕδατα

---

2. If you recall, we talked about these disappearing letters in chapter 1. The curious should consult William D. Mounce, *The Morphology of Biblical Greek* (Grand Rapids: Zondervan, 1994), 202–6.

The Article

At this point, you may be feeling overwhelmed with the number and diversity of third declension noun patterns. So this is probably a good time to remind you about the article—your best (Greek) friend, who *never* lies! You might not have realized what a good friend the article is when you were learning first and second declension nouns, because the article paradigm follows first and second declension patterns. But now you will begin to realize what a valuable friend you have in the article. The article always agrees with the noun that it modifies in case, number, and gender . . . *always*. Consider the following examples:

οἱ σωτῆρες	(nominative plural masculine)
τῶν ἐλπίδων	(genitive plural feminine)
τῷ πνεύματι	(dative singular neuter)
τὸ ἔθνος	(nominative or accusative singular neuter)
τοῦ πατρός	(genitive singular masculine)
τοῖς ὕδασιν	(dative plural neuter)

Note especially τοῦ πατρός. At first glance, you might have thought that this noun was a nominative singular masculine second declension noun, but if the article is τοῦ, then the noun must be genitive singular, either masculine or neuter. This means that you must have a third declension noun. So, you always want to pay attention to the article with articular nouns. Even if you aren't sure about the parsing of the noun, the article will make clear the case, number, and gender of the articular noun.

Third Declension Adjective Patterns

In chapter 5, we introduced adjectives. First and second declension adjectives follow either a 2-1-2 pattern (i.e., second declension masculine case endings for masculine forms, first declension feminine case endings for feminine forms, and second declension neuter case endings for neuter forms) or a 2-2 pattern (i.e., second declension masculine case endings for masculine and feminine forms, and second declension neuter case endings for neuter forms). Something similar happens with third declension adjectives. There are **3-1-3 declension pattern** adjectives (i.e., third declension masculine case endings for masculine forms, first declension feminine case endings for feminine forms, and third declension neuter case endings for neuter forms) or **3-3 declension pattern** adjectives (i.e., third declension masculine case endings for masculine and feminine forms, and third declension neuter case endings for neuter forms). We will see examples of the 3-3 pattern with the pronouns that are introduced later in this chapter and examples of the 3-1-3 pattern with adjectives and the participle forms that are introduced in the next chapter.

INTERROGATIVE AND INDEFINITE PRONOUNS

In this section, we introduce two new pronouns. **Interrogative pronouns** are used to introduce questions by asking "who?," "why?," or "what?" **Indefinite pronouns** are used to introduce a member of a class without further identification, such as "someone" or "anyone," when a statement could apply to any person or object. We will also learn the paradigm for the numeral one.

The Forms of the Interrogative and Indefinite Pronouns

These pronouns follow a 3-3 pattern. The stem of both these pronouns is τιν-. In the nominative singular and dative plural for masculine and feminine forms, the final nu drops before a sigma (as we have seen before).[3] Otherwise, the third declension masculine and feminine case endings are simply added to the stem τιν-. As we have seen before in the second declension, a final nu does not appear in the nominative and accusative singular neuter forms. Here are the paradigms for each pronoun.

	Interrogative Pronoun τίς, τί		Indefinite Pronoun τις, τι	
	masc/fem (3)	**neut (3)**	**masc/fem (3)**	**neut (3)**
nom sg	τίς	τί	τις	τι
gen sg	τίνος	τίνος	τινός	τινός
dat sg	τίνι	τίνι	τινί	τινί
acc sg	τίνα	τί	τινά	τι
nom pl	τίνες	τίνα	τινές	τινά
gen pl	τίνων	τίνων	τινῶν	τινῶν
dat pl	τίσι(ν)	τίσι(ν)	τισί(ν)	τισί(ν)
acc pl	τίνας	τίνα	τινάς	τινά

---

3. Recall that in the present active indicative third-person plural, the ντ of the personal ending drops out before a sigma. See "For the Curious" in the main text of chapter 3.

The forms of these two pronouns are identical except for the accent. Here is an easy way to keep these two pronouns from being confused. For the *interrogative pronoun*, there is *always* an accent on the first syllable—even if there is only one syllable! For the *indefinite pronoun*, there is *no* accent on first syllable, so if there is only one syllable the pronoun does not have an accent.

More on the Functions of Interrogative and Indefinite Pronouns

Interrogative pronouns are used to ask questions; τίς usually asks "who?" and τί asks either "what?" or "why?" Consider the following examples.

τίνα με λέγουσιν οἱ ἄνθρωποι εἶναι; (Mark 8:27)
Who do people say that I am?

ἀλλὰ τί ἐξήλθατε ἰδεῖν; (Matt 11:9)
But what did you come to see?

εἰ ἀπεθάνετε . . . τί ὡς ζῶντες ἐν κόσμῳ δογματίζεσθε; (Col 2:20)
If you died . . . why, as if you are living in the world, do you submit yourself
    to decrees?

Below is an example of an indefinite pronoun. Note that indefinite pronouns are *postpositive*, meaning that they cannot appear as the first word in a sentence or clause. This is another way that you can distinguish the two pronouns.

ἰδού τινες τῶν γραμματέων εἶπαν . . . (Matt 9:3)
Look, some of the scribes said . . .

THE NUMERAL "ONE" AND RELATED COMPOUNDS

The numeral "one," εἷς, μία, ἕν, follows a very common 3-1-3 declension pattern for adjectives.[4] This adjective does not have plural forms, for an obvious reason! Apart from the nominative singular, the stem εν- is visible throughout the paradigm for the masculine and neuter forms. The feminine form follows an α-pure pattern for first declension feminine nouns.

---

4. Numerals are a type of adjective. **Cardinals** indicate numeric values, e.g., one, two, three (or 1, 2, 3); **ordinals** indicate numeric order, e.g., first, second, third (or 1st, 2nd, 3rd).

	masc (3)	fem (1)	neut (3)
nom sg	εἷς	μία	ἕν
gen sg	ἑνός	μιᾶς	ἑνός
dat sg	ἑνί	μιᾷ	ἑνι
acc sg	ἕνα	μίαν	ἕν

For the Curious

In the masculine nominative of εἷς, μία, ἕν, the nu drops before the sigma case ending, and the epsilon lengthens. See Mounce, *Morphology*, 229, for more discussion of this and the derivation of the feminine stem.

There are two related paradigms that are derived from εἷς, μία, ἕν. The first is οὐδείς, οὐδεμία, οὐδέν, which can be translated "no one" or "nothing." This adjective is used with indicative-mood verbs. To form this paradigm, you simply prefix the εἷς, μία, ἕν paradigm with οὐδ-. The related adjective μηδείς, μηδεμία, μηδέν is used with nonindicative-mood verbs, which we will learn in later chapters. To form this paradigm, you simply prefix the εἷς, μία, ἕν paradigm with μηδ-. Here are a few examples of these adjectives (italicized) from the GNT.

ἐξ ὑμῶν *εἷς* διάβολός ἐστιν. (John 6:70)
One from among you is a devil.

οὐκ ἔφαγεν *οὐδὲν* ἐν ταῖς ἡμέραις ἐκείναις. (Luke 4:2)
He did not eat *anything [nothing]* in those days.

QUESTIONS

Originally, Greek was written in all uppercase letters, without word divisions and without punctuation. Most modern editions, however, use punctuation marks, including the symbol ";" to indicate a question. Punctuation, however, is unnecessary. Interrogative words, such as interrogative pronouns (e.g., τίς, τί), can indicate the presence of a question. For example:

τίς ἐστιν ἡ μήτηρ μου; (Matt 12:48)
Who is my mother?

Often context alone is sufficient for determining whether a question or statement is intended. Consider for example Pilate's encounter with Jesus as recorded in Mark 15:2:

σὺ εἶ ὁ βασιλεὺς τῶν Ἰουδαίων

In this context, it is clear that Pilate was not stating that Jesus was the king of the Jews, but rather in his interrogation he was *asking* Jesus this question. Hence most modern critical editions of the GNT punctuate this clause accordingly and translate it as a question: "Are you the king of the Jews?"

There are, however, several ways that Greek can introduce questions when a certain answer is anticipated. A question that has an indicative-mood verb that is negated by μή usually expects a negative reply.[5] (Again, this is to be determined from the overall context.) This may be translated with a negative statement, followed by a *positive* tag question[6] in English, such as "is it?" or "has he?" In both of the following examples, the expected answer is no.

μὴ ἀπώσατο ὁ θεὸς τὸν λαὸν αὐτοῦ; (Rom 11:1)
God has not rejected his people, has he?

μὴ πάντες γλώσσαις λαλοῦσιν; (1 Cor 12:30)
All do not speak in tongues, do they?

Alternatively, a question that has an indicative-mood verb that is negated by οὐ usually expects a positive reply. This may be translated by a *negative* question (e.g., 1 Cor 9:1, see below) or the use of a positive statement followed by a *negative* tag question (e.g., Mark 6:3, see below) in English, such as "isn't it?" or "won't he?" The expected answer for both examples is yes.

Οὐκ εἰμὶ ἐλεύθερος; οὐκ εἰμὶ ἀπόστολος; (1 Cor 9:1)
Am I not free? Am I not an apostle?

οὐχ οὗτός ἐστιν ὁ τέκτων . . .; (Mark 6:3)
This one is the carpenter, isn't he?

---

5. Less frequently, the form μήτι can be used.
6. A *tag question* is a short little question that turns an indicative statement into a question.

Finally, certain adverbs also introduce questions, such as ποῦ.

Ποῦ ἐστιν ὁ πατήρ σου; (John 8:19)
Where is your father?

REVIEW OF CHAPTER 12

In this chapter, we introduced third declension noun and adjective forms. Since these stems end with a consonant, predictable morphological changes occur when the sigma of a case ending combines with the consonant of the noun or adjective stem. The noun stem is not always visible in the nominative singular (lexical form), but it is visible in the genitive singular form, which is why vocabulary is listed with the genitive singular form or ending. Because of the diversity of third declension nouns, a few representative paradigms and the ability to recognize patterns will enable you to recognize many third declension noun forms in the GNT. Once again, the value of knowing the article without hesitation (better than your own name?) is seen since the article never lies when it modifies a noun. So even if you do not recognize a noun form, you will know its case and number (and sometimes gender) from the article that modifies it. We also looked at the concept of 3-1-3 and 3-3 declension-pattern adjectives and learned several key paradigms with these patterns.

We introduced the paradigms for interrogative and indefinite pronouns and considered their functions. Interrogative pronouns introduce questions, and indefinite pronouns introduce a member of a class without further distinction, such as "someone." We then introduced the paradigm for the numeral "one," εἷς, μία, ἕν, and related compound forms. Finally, we discussed how Greek indicates questions.

Study Guide for Chapter 12

1. Be able to understand each of the following concepts and forms:
   various third declension noun and adjective paradigms
   3-1-3 and 3-3 declension-pattern adjectives
   distinguishing between interrogative- and indefinite-pronoun forms
   εἷς, μία, ἕν and related compounds
2. Be able to parse third declension nouns and adjectives, interrogative- and indefinite-pronoun forms, the forms εἷς, μία, ἕν and compounds derived from this adjective, and translate basic Koine sentences that incorporate forms and concepts from previous chapters.

Vocabulary to Memorize

Here is the assigned vocabulary for chapter 12. You can now finally see the true benefit (and necessity) of listing the genitive singular ending with assigned vocabulary. With this ending, you can see the noun stem and will thus be able to recognize other forms of the noun when you encounter them.

αἷμα, -ατος, τό	blood (97)
ἀληθής, -ές	true, honest, truthful, real (26)
ἔθνος, -ους, τό	nation, people; gentiles (pl) (162)
εἷς, μία, ἕν	one, someone (345)
ἐκχέω	I pour out, I shed; I abandon myself (pass) (27)
ἐλπίς, -ίδος, ἡ	hope, expectation, what is hoped for (53)
νύξ, νυκτός, ἡ	night (61)
ὄνομα, -ματος, τό	name, title, category (231)
οὐδείς, οὐδεμία, οὐδέν	no; no one, nothing (subst); in no way (neut acc) (234)
οὖς, ὠτός, τό	ear, hearing (36)
παιδίον, -ου, τό	child, infant (52)
πᾶς, πᾶσα, πᾶν	each, every, all (1,243)
πίστις, -εως, ἡ	faith, trust, faithfulness, belief (243)
πνεῦμα, -ατος, τό	spirit, breath, wind (379)
πόλις, -εως, ἡ	city, town (162)
πολύς, πολλή, πολύ	much (sg), many (pl), large, great (416)
ποτήριον, -ου, τό	cup, drinking vessel (31)
ποῦ	where? to what place? (48)
πούς, ποδός, ὁ	foot (93)
σάρξ, σαρκός, ἡ	flesh, body, human or sinful nature (147)
σῶμα, -ατος, τό	body (142)
τις, τι	someone, something; a certain one, a certain thing; anyone, anything (525)
τίς, τί	who? what? which?; why? (adv) (556)
ὕδωρ, ὕδατος, τό	water (76)
χάρις, -ιτος, ἡ	grace, favor, kindness, gratitude (155)

Principal Parts to Memorize

These are the principal parts that you need to memorize for chapter 12. For now, you are only memorizing the first, third, and sixth parts (the parts that you do not have to memorize now have been grayed out). Remember, you should set up cards or other ways of memorizing these forms that will allow you easily to add new forms. The full "Principal Parts Chart" is in appendix 14.

1st prin part	2nd prin part	3rd prin part	4th prin part	5th prin part	6th prin part
-βαίνω[1]	-βήσομαι	-ἔβην	-βέβηκα	n/a	n/a
διδάσκω	διδάξω	ἐδίδαξα	n/a	n/a	ἐδιδάχθην
εὑρίσκω	εὑρήσω	εὗρον	εὕρηκα	n/a	εὑρέθην
κηρύσσω	n/a	ἐκήρυξα	n/a	n/a	ἐκηρύχθην
σῴζω	σώσω	ἔσωσα	σέσωκα	σέσῳσμαι	ἐσώθην

[1] This verb stem only occurs in compounded forms in the GNT, but it is frequent enough that knowing the principal parts is helpful.

Paradigms to Memorize

The following paradigms need to be memorized for chapter 12: the paradigms for the third declension nouns σωτήρ, σάρξ, and πνεῦμα; the paradigms for the interrogative pronoun τίς, τί and the indefinite pronoun τις, τι; and the paradigm for the numeral εἷς, μία, ἕν. You are not assigned the other paradigms presented in this chapter, but you should work on being able to recognize these forms when you see them in assigned exercises and when reading the GNT. It may be helpful to spend some time saying the paradigms that are not assigned out loud several times as a way of becoming more familiar with them.

THIRD DECLENSION NOUNS

	σωτήρ, -ῆρος, ὁ	σάρξ, σαρκός, ἡ	πνεῦμα, πνεύματος, τό
nom sg	σωτήρ	σάρξ	πνεῦμα
gen sg	σωτῆρος	σαρκός	πνεύματος
dat sg	σωτῆρι	σαρκί	πνεύματι
acc sg	σωτῆρα	σάρκα	πνεῦμα
nom pl	σωτῆρες	σάρκες	πνεύματα
gen pl	σωτήρων	σαρκῶν	πνευμάτων
dat pl	σωτῆρσι(ν)	σαρξί(ν)	πνεύμασι(ν)
acc pl	σωτῆρας	σάρκας	πνεύματα

τίς, τί AND τις, τι

| | τίς, τί (interrogative pronoun) | | τις, τι (indefinite pronoun) | |
	masc/fem (3)	neut (3)	masc/fem (3)	neut (3)
nom sg	τίς	τί	τις	τι
gen sg	τίνος	τίνος	τινός	τινός
dat sg	τίνι	τίνι	τινί	τινί
acc sg	τίνα	τί	τινά	τι
nom pl	τίνες	τίνα	τινές	τινά
gen pl	τίνων	τίνων	τινῶν	τινῶν
dat pl	τίσι(ν)	τίσι(ν)	τισί(ν)	τισί(ν)
acc pl	τίνας	τίνα	τινάς	τινά

εἷς, μία, ἕν

	masc (3)	fem (1)	neut (3)
nom sg	εἷς	μία	ἕν
gen sg	ἑνός	μιᾶς	ἑνός
dat sg	ἑνί	μιᾷ	ἑνί
acc sg	ἕνα	μίαν	ἕν

THE PRESENT PARTICIPLE AND PARTICIPLE BASICS

OBJECTIVES AND OVERVIEW

Chapter 13 introduces the following linguistic concepts, morphemes, and paradigms:

- participle morphemes
- present participle paradigms
- basic participle functions: substantival, attributive, adverbial
- lexical form for present participles and parsing
- the adjective πᾶς

THE PRESENT PARTICIPLE AND BASIC PARTICIPLE FUNCTIONS

A participle is a *verbal adjective*. This means that it has one foot in the verb world and the other foot in the adjective world. As a *verbal* adjective, it shares characteristics with verbs, such as voice and tense stems (which indicate aspect).[1] Verbal characteristics are also reflected in the fact that a participle can have a direct or indirect object and adverbial modifiers, such as adverbs or adverbial prepositional phrases. As a nonfinite verb, participles do not have person (first, second, or third). Additionally, a participle is usually negated with the particle μή. As a verbal *adjective*, it shares characteristics of adjectives, such as case, number, and gender. For this reason, participles use first, second, or third declension case endings.

Participles function either adverbially or adjectivally. When a participle functions adverbially, it modifies a verb and is dependent on that verb (e.g., "*entering* Capernaum, Jesus preached the gospel"). A participle can never be a main (or independent) verb, because it does not have person and number (hence it is not a finite verb). When a participle

---

1. As a nonfinite verb, a participle does not use personal endings; instead, as a verbal adjective it uses case endings. Personal endings are only used with finite verb forms to indicate the person and number of that finite verb.

functions adjectivally, it either modifies a substantive or functions as a substantive, which parallels how adjectives function (e.g., "the *living* water" or "the *believing* [one]").

Participles are constructed from tense stems. The aspect of participles is indicated by the tense stem from which it is constructed, although aspect is less prominent in participles than it is with finite verbs. In this chapter we will learn present participles, which are constructed using the present tense stem (the first principal part) and have imperfective aspect. In later chapters, we'll learn aorist and perfect participles. (There are a handful of future participles that we'll also discuss later.) The imperfect and pluperfect tense stems only occur in the indicative mood, so there are no imperfect or pluperfect participles.

The Forms of the Present Participle

To "build" a present active masculine or neuter participle, we begin with the present tense stem and then add a connecting vowel and the participle morpheme -ντ. (This morpheme is used for both present and aorist active participles.) To the participle morpheme, we add case endings. The present active masculine or neuter participle uses third declension case endings. When you are looking at a particple form and trying to parse it, first identify the participle morpheme -ντ; anything *before* the participle morpheme involves verb morphemes (such as tense stems, connecting vowels, tense formatives, as we'll see in later chapters) and anything *after* the participle morpheme is a case ending. Knowing this makes it easier to "read" a participle form. This can be summarized as follows:

present tense stem	connecting vowel[1]	ptc morpheme	case ending	inflected form
λυ	+ ο	+ ντ	+ ος	→ λύοντος

[1] Recall that the connecting vowel is an omicron before a mu or nu; before anything else, it is an epsilon.

In the genitive singular participle form, you can clearly see the tense stem and participle morpheme. This is similar to third declension nouns in which the noun stem is visible in the genitive singular form; hence if you know the nominative singular ending and the genitive singular ending of masculine and neuter participles, you can derive the rest of the paradigm. When we learn aorist, perfect, and future participles, the genitive singular form will also be the key to seeing the individual components used to construct these participle forms as well.[2]

---

2. All participle endings are summarized in appendix 11, "Participle Ending Summary Chart," if you want to see an overview of all participle forms.

The present active participle follows a 3-1-3 declension pattern, meaning that the masculine and neuter forms use third declension case endings, and feminine forms use first declension case endings.[3] The feminine forms of the present active participle follow the first declension α-impure pattern. It is easiest to consider -ουσα as the combination of the connecting vowel and the participle morpheme. Actually, it is more complicated than this, but this paradigm follows a first declension pattern, so it is easy to memorize. Here is the paradigm for the present active participle of λύω.

	masc (3)	fem (1)	neut (3)
nom sg	λύων	λύουσα	λῦον
gen sg	λύοντος	λυούσης	λύοντος
dat sg	λύοντι	λυούσῃ	λύοντι
acc sg	λύοντα	λύουσαν	λῦον
nom pl	λύοντες	λύουσαι	λύοντα
gen pl	λυόντων	λυουσῶν	λυόντων
dat pl	λύουσι(ν)	λυούσαις	λύουσι(ν)
acc pl	λύοντας	λυούσας	λύοντα

For the Curious

The participle morpheme for feminine participles is actually -εσ, which is an allomorph (a variant form of a morpheme) of -ντ.[4] When the morpheme is added to the connecting vowel o, the vowels contract to ου. Alternatively, some claim that the morpheme is -ντσ.[5] The sigma causes the ντ to drop and causes compensatory lengthening of the o, which results in -ουσ. Either way, these forms are relatively easy to recognize and memorize.

Similar to the noun stem in third declension nouns, the participle morpheme is visible throughout the masculine and neuter paradigms except in the nominative singular and dative plural. The same morphology concerning the addition of a sigma that we discussed with third declension nouns applies to the morphology of participles. Hence, when the dative plural ending used for the masculine and

---

3. *All* feminine participles use first declension case endings, which makes them easy to recognize.
4. See Goetchius, *Language of the New Testament*, 166.
5. E.g., Porter, Reed, and O'Donnell, *Fundamentals of New Testament Greek*, 105–6.

neuter forms is added to the participle morpheme -ντ, the ντ drops off, and there is compensatory lengthening of the connecting vowel o to the diphthong ου, which explains the final form λύουσι(ν).

For the nominative singular masculine form, there is no case ending, so the participle morpheme -ντ is added to the connecting vowel, but a Greek word cannot end in a tau,[6] so the tau drops off, which results in compensatory lengthening of the connecting vowel o to the long vowel ω, hence the form λύων. A similar phenomenon occurs with the nominative singular neuter form, except that the connecting vowel o does not lengthen, and the result of the dropped tau is the circumflex over the upsilon; hence the form λῦον.

The dative plural masculine and neuter forms of the present active participle are identical to the present active indicative third-person plural form (λύουσιν). As we've seen before, it is possible to use the same form for two different functions because the context will (almost always) indicate which function is intended. A *dative participle* simply does not have the same syntactic function as an indicative verb.

Here is the paradigm for the participle of εἰμί, which looks like the paradigm for λύω minus the present stem λυ-, plus breathing marks. Knowing the paradigm for εἰμί means that you will be able to recognize the many participles in the GNT that parallel this paradigm.

	masc (3)	fem (1)	neut (3)
nom sg	ὤν	οὖσα	ὄν
gen sg	ὄντος	οὔσης	ὄντος
dat sg	ὄντι	οὔσῃ	ὄντι
acc sg	ὄντα	οὖσαν	ὄν
nom pl	ὄντες	οὖσαι	ὄντα
gen pl	ὄντων	οὐσῶν	ὄντων
dat pl	οὖσι(ν)	οὔσαις	οὖσι(ν)
acc pl	ὄντας	οὔσας	ὄντα

The participle morpheme -μεν is used with present middle and passive participles, which follow a 2-1-2 pattern. Just as we saw with the present middle and passive indicative, the present middle and passive participle share the same form.

---

6. We have seen this same phenomenon with neuter third declension nouns with stems that end in -ματ; in the nominative and accusative singular forms the tau drops off (e.g., ὄνομα).

The feminine forms follow the η-type pattern for first declension feminine nouns. Here is the paradigm for the present middle and passive participle of λύω.

	masc (2)	fem (1)	neut (2)
nom sg	λυόμενος	λυομένη	λυόμενον
gen sg	λυομένου	λυομένης	λυομένου
dat sg	λυομένῳ	λυομένῃ	λυομένῳ
acc sg	λυόμενον	λυομένην	λυόμενον
nom pl	λυόμενοι	λυόμεναι	λυόμενα
gen pl	λυομένων	λυομένων	λυομένων
dat pl	λυομένοις	λυομέναις	λυομένοις
acc pl	λυομένους	λυομένας	λυόμενα

As we've noted all along, context will make clear whether the participle is middle or passive. Finally, note that if a verb does not have an active form (e.g., occurs only with the middle form) in a given tense stem, the participle that is constructed using that tense stem will also use this middle form. Thus, the present participle of ἔρχομαι is ἐρχόμενος.

HEADS UP!

Here's another chance to explore μι verbs. Look through the present participle forms for μι verbs in chapter 25 and see how many forms you can recognize based on what you have learned in this chapter.

Basic Functions of Participles

Participle functions can be divided into two main categories: adjectival and adverbial. *Adjectival* participles can be further divided into attributive (modifying another substantive) and substantival (functioning as a substantive).[7] *Adverbial* participles modify a verb by indicating the circumstances under which an action or state of affairs occurs.

The key to identifying these functions involves the article. Recall the two terms, **articular** and **anarthrous**. Articular participles are preceded by the article, and anarthrous participles are not preceded by the article. Adjectival

---

7. This parallels adjective functions, which were discussed in chapter 5.

participles are *usually* articular, whereas adverbial participles are *always* anarthrous. We discuss this further below.[8]

Attributive Participles

The attributive function of participles is common. Like adjectives, attributive participles occur in either first or second attributive position. The attributive participle and the substantive that it modifies together comprise a participial *phrase* (participial *clauses* are discussed in conjunction with the adverbial function of participles below). As you can see from the examples below, attributive participles are usually articular. When a participle is functioning attributively, it *must* agree with the substantive it modifies in *case*, *number*, and *gender*. Because different declensions may be involved, however, this does not mean that the endings of the participle and the substantive that it modifies will *look* exactly the same, just as we saw with adjectives and the article. Here are some examples of attributive participles (italicized) in the first attributive position. (Notice also that the first example involves a passive-voice participle.)

ὁ *λεγόμενος* Χριστός (John 4:25)
the one who is called Christ

ὁ *πέμπων* με πατήρ (John 5:37)[9]
the Father *who sends me*

Here are some examples of attributive participles in the second attributive position.

πόθεν οὖν ἔχεις τὸ ὕδωρ τὸ *ζῶν*; (John 4:11)[10]
Where then do you get this *living* water?

ἐκ τῆς ὀργῆς *τῆς ἐρχομένης* (1 Thess 1:10)
from the *coming* wrath

Attributive participles may be translated as a relative clause in English (e.g., John 4:25; 5:37), even though syntactically a participial *phrase* is not the same as a relative *clause*. This once again highlights some of the differences between Greek and English.

---

8. This is also summarized in the "Participle Function Guide" in appendix 12.
9. This is actually an aorist participle in the GNT.
10. You have memorized glosses for ἔχω as "I have, I hold," but neither of these work here. Instead the English verb "get" makes better sense of the Greek.

καὶ ὁ διάβολος ὁ πλανῶν αὐτοὺς ἐβλήθη εἰς τὴν λίμνην τοῦ πυρός
(Rev 20:10)
And the devil, *who deceived them*, was cast into the lake of fire.

Notice in the examples from John 5:37 and Revelation 20:10 that the attributive participle has a direct object. Remember that a participle is a *verbal* adjective, so even though this participle is functioning attributively it still can have a direct object.

Substantival Participles

Parallel to substantival adjectives, substantival participles function as a substantive. Substantival participles are almost always articular. Notice that there is no substantive in close proximity with the same case, number, and gender of the participle, which is a good clue that the participle is functioning substantivally.

Λέγει ὁ μαρτυρῶν ταῦτα . . . (Rev 22:20)
The one who testifies to these things says . . .

The aspectual force of substantival participles is often reduced; hence, a present participle functioning substantivally may not necessarily indicate a nuance of continuous action—a translation such as "the one who continuously believes in me" would be an overtranslation in the following example.[11]

ὁ πιστεύων εἰς ἐμέ (John 12:44)
the one who believes in me

Adverbial Participles

Adverbial participles are *always* anarthrous. They nearly always modify a finite verb and give additional information about the circumstances under which the action (or state) of the finite verb is occurring. An adverbial participle is frequently in the nominative case because it agrees with the subject of the finite verb that it modifies. For this reason, it also has the same *gender* and *number* of the subject of the finite verb. An adverbial participle, together with any adverbial modifiers (such as adverbs) and any direct or indirect objects, comprises a *dependent participial clause*.[12] Consider the following example from Mark 1:39:

---

11. In fact, some substantival participles function almost as titles (e.g., ὁ βαπτίζων in Mark 1:4) and have no aspectual force (i.e., zero aspect).

12. So far, we have seen dependent clauses that are introduced by a conjunction, such as ὅτι; these are

καὶ ἦλθεν *κηρύσσων* εἰς τὰς συναγωγὰς αὐτῶν
And he went into their synagogues *preaching.*[13]

In the larger context, it is clear that the subject of the finite verb ἦλθεν is Jesus. Notice that the participle is masculine singular because it parallels the subject of the finite verb that it modifies, namely, Jesus (masculine singular). Notice also that the participle is in the nominative case for the same reason. As an adverbial participle, κηρύσσων tells us the circumstances under which Jesus entered synagogues, namely, "preaching." In chapter 15, we will further specify the functions of adverbial participles. For now it is sufficient to think of adverbial participles as giving additional information about the circumstances in which the finite verb occurs.

Lexical Form and Parsing

You should be able to recognize the lexical form of present participles easily because *the present tense stem* (or first principal part) is used to construct present participles. When you are parsing a word in an assigned exercise without any surrounding context, it is obviously not possible to know how the participle is functioning. For this chapter and the next one *only*, you will need to give an inflected meaning that reflects a substantival function for the participle. Beginning with chapter 15, you will need to adjust this a bit.

The parsing order for participles is as follows: tense, voice, participle, case, number, gender, lexical form, and inflected meaning.[14] Here's how you would parse some present participles. The addition of "ones" in the inflected meaning indicates a substantival participle.

inflected form	tense	voice	mood	pers	case	num	gender	lexical form	inflected meaning
πιστεύοντες	pres	act	ptc	n/a	nom	pl	masc	πιστεύω	believing ones
σῳζομένοις	pres	mid / pass	ptc	n/a	dat	pl	masc neut masc neut	σῴζω	to/by/with/in saving ones / to/by/with/in ones being saved

sometimes called *conjunctive clauses.* A dependent conjunctive clause and a dependent participial clause both have the same syntactic function (i.e., an adverbial function) of modifying a verb.

13. The translation reflects English grammar; "he went preaching into their synagogues" is awkward in English.

14. See also appendix 17, "Standard Abbreviations and Parsing Order." Strictly speaking, mood does not apply to participles, but for the sake of convenience place the word *participle* in the mood slot for parsing purposes.

THE ADJECTIVE πᾶς

Πᾶς ("all," "every") is an important adjective that is used frequently in the GNT. The stem for the masculine and neuter forms is παντ-. The morphological rules concerning the addition of a sigma to a stem ending in ντ- apply here (see the previous discussion with the present active participle). The morphology of the feminine form is more complicated, so it is easiest to memorize the nominative singular feminine and to note that the rest of the feminine paradigm follows a first declension α-impure pattern. The complete lexical form for this adjective is πᾶς, πᾶσα, πᾶν.

	masc (3)	fem (1)	neut (3)
nom sg	πᾶς	πᾶσα	πᾶν
gen sg	παντός	πάσης	παντός
dat sg	παντί	πάσῃ	παντί
acc sg	πάντα	πᾶσαν	πᾶν
nom pl	πάντες	πᾶσαι	πάντα
gen pl	πάντων	πασῶν	πάντων
dat pl	πᾶσι(ν)	πάσαις	πᾶσι(ν)
acc pl	πάντας	πάσας	πάντα

Πᾶς is often used substantivally in the neuter plural to indicate "all things" or "everything," as the following example illustrates:

πάντα δι᾽ αὐτοῦ ἐγένετο (John 1:3)
All things came into existence through him.

When πᾶς is used attributively to modify an articular substantive, it can occur in the attributive *or* predicate position. Consider the following examples and the English translations of πᾶς:

ὁ γὰρ πᾶς νόμος . . . (Gal 5:14)
For the *whole* law . . .

πᾶς ὁ ὄχλος ἐζήτουν . . . αὐτόν (Luke 6:19)
The *entire* crowd was seeking him.

πᾶς ὁ ποιῶν τὴν ἁμαρτίαν δοῦλός ἐστιν τῆς ἁμαρτίας (John 8:34)
Everyone who practices sin is a slave of sin.

Πᾶς can also modify an anarthrous substantive, in which case it is usually translated "every." Consider the following example:

πᾶν δένδρον ἀγαθὸν καρποὺς καλοὺς ποιεῖ (Matt 7:17)
Every good tree produces good fruit.

REVIEW OF CHAPTER 13

In this chapter we introduced the participle, which is a verbal adjective. As such it shares properties with both verbs and adjectives. Like verbs, it has aspect and voice, can take direct and indirect objects, and can be modified by adverbs. Like adjectives, it uses case endings, which also indicate number and gender. The form of the present participle uses the present stem, the participle morpheme (-ντ) for the masculine and neuter active forms, followed by third declension case endings; the participle morpheme for feminine active participles is -ουσα, followed by first declension case endings. The present middle forms use the participle morpheme -μεν and use second declension case endings for the masculine and neuter and first declension case endings for the feminine. We also introduced the participle for εἰμί. We then outlined the basic functions of participles and how to determine these functions. The attributive- and substantival-participle functions parallel those same functions for adjectives; the adverbial function of a participle parallels other dependent adverbial clauses, which are introduced by conjunctions. Finally, we looked at one very common and important 3-1-3 declension pattern adjective, πᾶς, πᾶσα, πᾶν, and surveyed some of its functions.

Study Guide for Chapter 13

1. Be able to understand each of the following concepts and forms:
   participle morphemes
   articular, arthrous, anarthrous
   substantival participle functions
   attributive participle functions
   adverbial participle functions
2. Be able to parse present participle forms and forms of πᾶς, πᾶσα, πᾶν, as well as translate basic Koine sentences that incorporate forms and concepts from previous chapters.

Vocabulary to Memorize

ἀγοράζω	I buy (30)
ἀπάγω	I lead away; I am misled (pass) (15)
ἀπέρχομαι	I go away, I depart (117)
ἀποθνῇσκω	I die, I am mortal (111)
ἄρα	so, then, consequently, therefore (49)
ἀρχή, -ῆς, ἡ	beginning, origin, authority (55)
γραμματεύς, -έως, ὁ	scribe, clerk, legal expert (63)
δαιμόνιον, -ου, τό	demon, evil spirit (63)
δεῖπνον, -ου, τό	dinner, main meal, banquet (16)
διαμαρτύρομαι	I charge, I testify (15)
ἐγγίζω	I approach, I come near (42)
ἐπαίρω	I lift up; I am opposed (pass) (19)
κἀγώ	and I, but I, I also, I myself (= καὶ ἐγώ) (84)
μέγας, μεγάλη, μέγα	large, great (243)
ὄρος, -ους, τό	mountain, hill (63)
ὀφθαλμός, -οῦ, ὁ	eye, sight (100)
παῖς, παιδός, ὁ, ἡ	servant, slave; child (24)
παραχρῆμα	at once, immediately (18)
παρρησία, -ας, ἡ	openness, confidence, boldness (31)
πίνω	I drink (73)
πωλέω	I sell (22)
τεσσεράκοντα	forty (22)
ὑπολαμβάνω	I take up, I support, I reply, I suppose (5)
φέρω	I carry, I take along, I endure, I produce (66)
ὧδε	here, in this case (61)

Principal Parts to Memorize

These are the principal parts that you need to memorize for chapter 13. For now, you are only memorizing the first, third, and sixth parts (the parts that you do not have to memorize now have been grayed out). Remember, you should set up cards or other ways of memorizing these forms that will allow you to easily add new forms. You can see the full "Principal Parts Chart" in appendix 14.

1st prin part	2nd prin part	3rd prin part	4th prin part	5th prin part	6th prin part
βάλλω	βαλῶ	ἔβαλον	βέβληκα	βέβλημαι	ἐβλήθην
γινώσκω	γνώσομαι	ἔγνων	ἔγνωκα	ἔγνωσμαι	ἐγνώσθην
γράφω	γράψω	ἔγραψα	γέγραφα	γέγραμμαι	ἐγράφην
φέρω	οἴσω	ἤνεγκα/ ἤνεγκον	ἐνήνοχα	n/a	ἠνέχθην

Paradigms to Memorize

The following are the paradigms to be memorized for chapter 13: the present active and middle participles of the λύω paradigm, and the paradigm of the adjective πᾶς, πᾶσα, πᾶν.

PRESENT ACTIVE PARTICIPLE OF λύω

	masc (3)	fem (1)	neut (3)
nom sg	λύων	λύουσα	λῦον
gen sg	λύοντος	λυούσης	λύοντος
dat sg	λύοντι	λυούσῃ	λύοντι
acc sg	λύοντα	λύουσαν	λῦον
nom pl	λύοντες	λύουσαι	λύοντα
gen pl	λυόντων	λυουσῶν	λυόντων
dat pl	λύουσι(ν)	λυούσαις	λύουσι(ν)
acc pl	λύοντας	λυούσας	λύοντα

PRESENT MIDDLE PARTICIPLE OF λύω

	masc (2)	fem (1)	neut (2)
nom sg	λυόμενος	λυομένη	λυόμενον
gen sg	λυομένου	λυομένης	λυομένου
dat sg	λυομένῳ	λυομένῃ	λυομένῳ
acc sg	λυόμενον	λυομένην	λυόμενον
nom pl	λυόμενοι	λυόμεναι	λυόμενα
gen pl	λυομένων	λυομένων	λυομένων
dat pl	λυομένοις	λυομέναις	λυομένοις
acc pl	λυομένους	λυομένας	λυόμενα

πᾶς, πᾶσα, πᾶν

	masc (3)	fem (1)	neut (3)
nom sg	πᾶς	πᾶσα	πᾶν
gen sg	παντός	πάσης	παντός
dat sg	παντί	πάσῃ	παντί
acc sg	πάντα	πᾶσαν	πᾶν
nom pl	πάντες	πᾶσαι	πάντα
gen pl	πάντων	πασῶν	πάντων
dat pl	πᾶσι(ν)	πάσαις	πᾶσι(ν)
acc pl	πάντας	πάσας	πάντα

chapter FOURTEEN

ETCETERAS: *More on Adjectives,*
Verbs, and Adverbs

OBJECTIVES AND OVERVIEW

Chapter 14 develops some previously introduced concepts or forms and presents a few new concepts. The main focus of this chapter, however, is on integrating what you have learned from chapters 9–13.

Chapter 14 covers the following linguistic concepts, morphemes, and paradigms:

- irregular adjectives: μέγας, μεγάλη, μέγα, and πολύς, πολλή, πολύ
- comparatives and superlatives
- verbs that take a direct object in a case other than the accusative
- "passive deponents"
- basic adverb formation
- summary of dependent clauses

IRREGULAR ADJECTIVES

So far we have learned the various patterns that adjectives follow, such as 2-1-2, 2-2, 3-1-3, and 3-3 declension patterns. There are some adjectives that follow these patterns, but which have certain irregularities in their paradigms. Consider the two adjective paradigms found on the opposite page.

Based on what you have seen so far, you would not expect to find a mix between (primarily) second and (some) third declension endings in the masculine and neuter forms for these two adjectives. The feminine form, however, follows the η-type pattern for first declension feminine nouns exactly. In both of the paradigms, the nominative and accusative singular for both the masculine and neuter forms (underlined) play by *third* declension rules and have a *shortened* version of the stem than is used in the rest of the paradigm, namely μεγα- and πολ-. The remaining masculine and neuter forms then play by *second* declension rules, using the *longer* version of the adjective stem, namely μεγαλ- and πολλ-.

μέγας, μεγάλη, μέγα

	masc (3)	fem (1)	neut (3)
nom sg	μέγας	μεγάλη	μέγα
gen sg	μεγάλου	μεγάλης	μεγάλου
dat sg	μεγάλῳ	μεγάλῃ	μεγάλῳ
acc sg	μέγαν	μεγάλην	μέγα
nom pl	μεγάλοι	μεγάλαι	μεγάλα
gen pl	μεγάλων	μεγάλων	μεγάλων
dat pl	μεγάλοις	μεγάλαις	μεγάλοις
acc pl	μεγάλους	μεγάλας	μεγάλα

πολύς, πολλή, πολύ

	masc (3)	fem (1)	neut (3)
nom sg	πολύς	πολλή	πολύ
gen sg	πολλοῦ	πολλῆς	πολλοῦ
dat sg	πολλῷ	πολλῇ	πολλῷ
acc sg	πολύν	πολλήν	πολύ
nom pl	πολλοί	πολλαί	πολλά
gen pl	πολλῶν	πολλῶν	πολλῶν
dat pl	πολλοῖς	πολλαῖς	πολλοῖς
acc pl	πολλούς	πολλάς	πολλά

Sometimes students get forms from πολύς, πολλή, πολύ confused with the noun πόλις. Here are some tips for keeping these two words straight. First, πόλις *never* has two lambdas, so if you can count to two . . . and count two lambdas in a form that begins with πολ-, then you know that it must be from πολύς, πολλή, πολύ. Second, there is *no* upsilon in *any* form of the πόλις paradigm, so if you see a single lambda followed by an upsilon, then you must also have a form of πολύς, πολλή, πολύ.

You do not need to memorize these paradigms, but you should be familiar with how to recognize them, as they occur frequently in the GNT. Πολύς, πολλή, πολύ is very common in the GNT, especially its substantival use. Here are a few examples:

καὶ ἐθεράπευσεν πολλοὺς ... καὶ δαιμόνια πολλὰ ἐξέβαλεν (Mark 1:34)
And he healed *many [people]* ... and he cast out *many* demons.

καὶ ἐξελθὼν εἶδεν πολὺν ὄχλον (Matt 14:14)
And exiting, he saw a *great* crowd.

Mark 1:34 provides a good example of πολύς, πολλή, πολύ functioning both substantivally (πολλούς, with "people" understood from the context in the first part of the verse) and attributively (πολλά, modifying δαιμόνια in the second part of the verse).

COMPARATIVES AND SUPERLATIVES

Some adjectives indicate a **positive** (e.g., ἀγαθός, "good") or **negative** (e.g., κακός, "bad") quality or attribute. A **comparative** shows the degree of that quality between two entities (e.g., "better" or "worse"), and a **superlative** shows the degree of that quality between more than two entities (e.g., "best" or "worst"). An *elative* describes intensification of a quality (e.g., "very good" or "very bad").

In English, comparative adjectives are often formed by adding -er to an adjective, and superlative adjectives are often formed by adding -est. For example:

holy	*adjective*
holier	*comparative*
holiest	*superlative*

In Greek, the ending -τερος, -τερα, -τερον (2-1-2) is often added to an adjective form to indicate a comparative; -τατος, -τατη, -τατον (2-1-2) is often added to an adjective form to indicate a superlative. For example:

μικρός	small	*adjective*
μικρότερος	smaller	*comparative*
μικρότατος	smallest	*superlative*

By the time of the NT, however, positives and negatives were taking over the duties of comparatives and superlatives. Thus, sometimes a positive or negative is used in the GNT when a comparative, or even a superlative, is expected. For example, πρῶτος ("first") and ἔσχατος ("last") are not actually superlative forms, even though they are often used with this meaning in the GNT. (Instead, they are ordinals, if you're curious.)

There are also comparative and superlative adverbs. These are frequently found in the accusative singular neuter form of the comparative or superlative adjective. For example, ἰσχυρότερον is a comparative adverb ("more strongly"), and ἰσχυρότατα is a superlative adverb ("most strongly"), and both forms are derived from the accusative singular neuter form of the adjective ἰσχυρός, -ή, -όν ("strong").

You do not need to memorize any paradigms for comparatives and superlatives, but if you memorize the endings -τερος, -τερα, -τερον (2-1-2) that are added to an adjective form to indicate a comparative, and -τατος, -τατη, -τατον (2-1-2) for the superlative, then you will be able recognize comparative and superlative adjectives and adverbs when you encounter them in the GNT.

VERBS THAT TAKE A DIRECT OBJECT IN A CASE OTHER THAN THE ACCUSATIVE

So far we have seen the direct object of verbs in the accusative case, but there are some verbs that have direct objects in the genitive or dative cases. A good lexicon will specify in which case (or cases) a direct object occurs for a given verb, but here are some helpful guidelines.

Verbs that involve the senses, such as hearing, touching, perceiving, holding, and remembering often have a direct object in the genitive. Some common examples include the following:

ἀκούω	I hear
ἅπτομαι	I touch
γεύομαι	I taste
ἐπιθυμέω	I desire
μνημονεύω	I remember

The following verbs often have a direct object in the dative case. Some of these verbs involve speaking.

ἀκολουθέω	I follow
διακονέω	I serve
δουλεύω	I serve
ἐγγίζω	I draw near
ἐπιτιμάω	I rebuke
μαρτυρέω	I bear witness
πιστυέω	I believe
προσκυνέω	I worship
ὑπακούω	I obey

Not all these verbs have been in the assigned vocabulary yet, but the vocabulary lists in this book indicate the case that a verb takes for its direct object if is it not the accusative case.

"PASSIVE DEPONENTS"

We have already discussed the concept of deponency and the debate surrounding it, but the discussion has thus far only concerned the middle voice. Some verbs, however, have what is sometimes called a "passive deponent," such as ἀπεκρίθην and συνήχθην. It is clear from the context in which these forms occur that a passive sense (e.g., "I was answered" or "I was gathered together") is *not* intended. Moreover, in these contexts there is no occurrence of ὑπό indicating agency, which often occurs with passive verbs. Thus, the aorist passive in these instances indicates an intransitive, active sense of the verb. Consider the following examples:

καὶ ἀπεκρίθη αὐτῷ εἷς ἐκ τοῦ ὄχλου, Διδάσκαλε ... (Mark 9:17)
And one from the crowd answered him, "Teacher ..."

συνήχθησαν οἱ ἀρχιερεῖς καὶ οἱ Φαρισαῖοι πρὸς Πιλᾶτον (Matt 27:62)
The chief priests and the Pharisees gathered before Pilate.

In both examples, clearly neither ἀπεκρίθη nor συνήχθησαν reflect a passive voice. In the first example, the person in the crowd is answering Jesus, not being answered. Similarly, in the second example the chief priests and Pharisees gathered themselves before Pilate; they were not gathered together by some other agent. The reasons for this phenomenon are complex, but fortunately, both ἀποκρίνομαι and συνάγω often occur in the passive with an active meaning. You will become so used to this that you won't think much about it.[1]

BASIC ADVERB FORMATION

In English, adverbs are often formed by adding the suffix -ly to an adjective, as in quick + -ly → quickly, or faithful + -ly → faithfully, and so on. Something similar occurs for adverbs in Greek that end with -ως. Greek adverbs begin with the genitive plural form of a Greek adjective. For example, the genitive plural form of the adjective καλός, -ή, -όν ("good") is καλῶν. If we remove the nu from the genitive plural and add a sigma, we have the adverb καλῶς ("well").

There are other types of adverbs in which the ending often indicates broadly the type of information that the adverb is supplying. Consider the following:[2]

adverb ending	category	examples
-οτε	time	πάντοτε, ποτέ, τότε
-θεν	origin	πόθεν, ὅθεν, ἔμπροσθεν
-ω	location	ἄνω, ἔξω, ὀπίσω
-ου	location	οὗ, ὅπου, ποῦ
-ις	frequency	τρίς, πολλάκις

Again, this isn't something that you need to memorize, but it can be helpful information to refer to as you are working through texts in the GNT.

SUMMARY OF DEPENDENT CLAUSES INTRODUCED SO FAR

The following is a summary of the different types of dependent clauses that we have seen in chapters 1–13. In the following examples, the subordinating conjunction is indicated with a gray background, and the dependent clause is in a parenthesis. Notice also that the dependent clause is aligned under the word that it modifies. Specifically, ὅτι clauses and adverbial participial clauses are aligned under the verb that they modify (underlined), and the relative clause is aligned under its antecedent (underlined). Notice also the parallel syntactic function of the ὅτι clause and the adverbial participial clause.

---

1. For the curious, see Harris, "Study of the Greek Language," 132–36.
2. Adapted from Goetchius, *Language of the New Testament*, 206–7, and Dana and Mantey, *Manual Grammar*, 237.

ὅτι Clauses

ἀλλὰ ὑμεῖς <u>οὐ πιστεύετε</u>,
            (ὅτι οὐκ ἐστὲ ἐκ τῶν προβάτων τῶν ἐμῶν). (John 10:26)

But you yourselves <u>do not believe</u>,
            because you are not from my sheep.

Adverbial Participial Clauses

καὶ <u>περιῆγεν</u> ἐν ὅλῃ τῇ Γαλιλαίᾳ
    διδάσκων ἐν ταῖς συναγωγαῖς αὐτῶν καὶ
    κηρύσσων τὸ εὐαγγέλιον . . . (Matt 4:23)
And <u>he went around</u> the whole of Galilee,
    teaching in their synagogues and
    preaching the gospel . . .

Relative Clauses

Ἰδοὺ ἀποστέλλω <u>τὸν ἄγγελόν μου</u> πρὸ προσώπου σου,
            (ὃς κατασκευάσει τὴν ὁδόν σου). (Mark 1:2)[3]

See! I send <u>my messenger</u> before you,
            who will prepare your way.

It is always important to identify the boundaries of a dependent clause. This often involves identifying the subordinating conjunction and then identifying the boundary of the depdendent clause that the conjunction introduces. Then you need to identify the word(s) that the dependent clause is modifying. For participles, this first involves recognizing that the participle is adverbial, then identifying the boundaries of the participial clause, and finally identifying which finite verb the adverbial participle is modifying. For relative clauses, you begin by identifying the relative pronoun and the boundaries of the relative clause that it introduces. Then identify the substantive that the relative clause modifies. By indenting the dependent clause under either the verb on which it depends or the antecedent, you can begin to "see" the syntax in a text. We will keep developing this in this book.

---

3. The verb κατασκευάσει is a future indicative verb. The future will be introduced in chapter 19.

INTEGRATION OF CHAPTERS 9–13

In this chapter, we will use the following passage (adapted from various NT verses) as the basis of reviewing concepts and forms that have been presented in chapters 9–13. Some of the key concepts that we covered were relative pronouns and clauses, aorist active and middle indicative forms, third declension nouns, the passive-voice forms for the present, imperfect, and aorist indicative, and finally, the present participle. You may want to copy this page to use as you work through the questions. A copy of this text is included in the workbook.

PART ONE

It is crucial to be able to identify finite verb forms. So, let's begin by double underlining and parsing each finite verb. Then, put boxes around and parse each participle. After you have done this on your own, go to the next page for the answers.

Pop-Up Lexicon

ἀναλαμβάνω	I take up, I carry
πατήρ, πατρός, ὁ	father, ancestor
ὁράω	I see, I notice, I perceive

If you do not recognize a verbal form, try looking at the verb's principal parts in appendix 14, "Principal Parts Chart."

Pop-Up Principal Parts

ὁράω, ὄψομαι, εἶδον, ἑώρακα, n/a, ὤφθην

---

1. εἴ τις πιστεύει Ἰησοῦ, ἤρχετο εἰς τὴν βασιλείαν τοῦ θεοῦ.
2. πάντες οἱ πιστεύοντες τῷ ὀνόματι τοῦ υἱοῦ τοῦ ἀνθρώπου οὐ πιστεύουσιν εἰς αὐτὸν
3. ἀλλὰ εἰς τὸν πατέρα τὸν ἀποστέλλοντα αὐτόν.
4. μακάριοι οἱ πιστεύοντες εἰς χριστόν, ὅτι αὐτοὶ τὸν θεὸν ἔβλεπον.
5. μακάριοι οἱ βαπτιζόμενοι ὑπὸ τῶν μαθητῶν τούτων, ὅτι ἐκαθαρίσθησαν τῇ καρδίᾳ αὐτῶν.
6. καὶ ἀληθής ἐστιν ἡ τῶν ἀποστόλων μαρτυρία
7. ὃς ἠγέρθη ἐν σαρκί,
8. διεμαρτυρήθη ἐν πνεύματι,
9. ὤφθη ἀγγέλοις,
10. ἐκηρύχθη ἐν ἔθνεσιν,
11. ἐπιστεύθη ἐν κόσμῳ,
12. ἀνελήμφθη ἐν δόξῃ.

ANSWERS TO PART ONE

Did you come up with the following?

1. εἴ τις <u>πιστεύει</u> Ἰησοῦ, <u>ἤρχετο</u> εἰς τὴν βασιλείαν τοῦ θεοῦ.
2. πάντες οἱ πιστεύοντες τῷ ὀνόματι τοῦ υἱοῦ τοῦ ἀνθρώπου οὐ <u>πιστεύουσιν</u> εἰς αὐτὸν
3. ἀλλὰ εἰς τὸν πατέρα τὸν ἀποστέλλοντα αὐτόν.
4. μακάριοι οἱ πιστεύοντες εἰς χριστόν, ὅτι αὐτοὶ τὸν θεὸν <u>ἐβλέπον</u>.
5. μακάριοι οἱ βαπτιζόμενοι ὑπὸ τῶν μαθητῶν τουτῶν, ὅτι <u>ἐκαθαρίσθησαν</u> τῇ καρδίᾳ αὐτῶν.
6. καὶ ἀληθής <u>ἐστιν</u> ἡ τῶν ἀποστόλων μαρτυρία·
7. ὃς <u>ἠγέρθη</u> ἐν σαρκί,
8. <u>διεμαρτυρήθη</u> ἐν πνεύματι,
9. <u>ὤφθη</u> ἀγγέλοις,
10. <u>ἐκηρύχθη</u> ἐν ἔθνεσιν,
11. <u>ἐπιστεύθη</u> ἐν κόσμῳ,
12. <u>ἀνελήμφθη</u> ἐν δόξῃ.

Parsing

inflected form	tense	voice	mood	person	case	num	gender	lexical form	inflected meaning
πιστεύει	pres	act	ind	3rd	n/a	sg	n/a	πιστεύω	he/she/it believes
ἤρχετο	impf	mid	ind	3rd	n/a	sg	n/a	ἔρχομαι	he/she/it was coming
πιστεύοντες	pres	act	ptc	n/a	nom	pl	masc	πιστεύω	believing ones
πιστεύουσιν	pres	act	ind	3rd	n/a	pl	n/a	πιστεύω	they are believing
ἀποστέλλοντα	pres	act	ptc	n/a	acc	sg	masc	ἀποστέλλω	sending one
πιστεύοντες	pres	act	ptc	n/a	nom	pl	masc	πιστεύω	believing ones
ἐβλέπον	impf	act	ind	3rd	n/a	pl	n/a	βλέπω	they were seeing
βαπτιζόμενοι	pres	pass	ptc	n/a	nom	pl	masc	βαπτίζω	ones being baptized
ἐκαθαρίσθησαν	aor	pass	ind	3rd	n/a	pl	n/a	καθαρίζω	they were cleansed

(cont.)

inflected form	tense	voice	mood	person	case	num	gender	lexical form	inflected meaning
ἐστίν	pres	n/a	ind	3rd	n/a	sg	n/a	εἰμί	it is
ἠγέρθη	aor	pass	ind	3rd	n/a	sg	n/a	ἐγείρω	he was raised
διεμαρτυρήθη	aor	pass	ind	3rd	n/a	sg	n/a	διαμαρτύρομαι	he was declared
ὤφθη	aor	pass	ind	3rd	n/a	sg	n/a	ὁράω	he was seen
ἐκηρύχθη	aor	pass	ind	3rd	n/a	sg	n/a	κηρύσσω	he was proclaimed
ἐπιστεύθη	aor	pass	ind	3rd	n/a	sg	n/a	πιστεύω	he was believed
ἀνελήμφθη	aor	pass	ind	3rd	n/a	sg	n/a	ἀναλαμβάνω	he was taken up

Additional Notes:

- The final six lines of this passage are adapted from 1 Timothy 3:16, which is likely a creedal confession that was recited in the early church.
- Hopefully you recognized that ἤρχετο could not be an aorist form because you remembered that the third principal part for ἔρχομαι is ἦλθον, which means that this could only be an imperfect.
- Even though πιστεύουσιν is the same form as the present active participle dative plural masculine/neuter, this form could only be a present active indicative third-person plural for two reasons. First, notice that the form is negated with οὐ, which would not be true for a participle. Second, notice that the overall context requires a third-person plural verb due to the plural subject.
- The fact that ἀποστέλλοντα is modified by the accusative singular masculine form of the article confirms that this form is accusative singular masculine and not nominative or accusative plural neuter, even though the form is the same for all three possibilities.
- The presence of αὐτοί means that ἐβλέπον could only be third-person plural, even though the first-person singular has the same form. Moreover, this could only be an imperfect form of βλέπω; if it were aorist, the sigma of the aorist tense formative would have combined with the π to form ψ, and there would be an alpha instead of an omicron: ἔβλεψαν.
- Notice how distinctive the -θη tense formative is! It's hard to miss all those aorist passive indicatives.

PART TWO

We will now focus on the passive finite verbs in this passage. You have already identified these forms and parsed them. Now go through the passage and indicate the agent or instrument of the passive finite verb and discuss how you know this. The first occurrence of a passive finite verb is used as an example. Once you have finished, you can check your work against the discussion on the next page. Example:

Line 5: ἐκαθαρίσθησαν – The agent of this passive verb is not expressed directly in this passage. The dative phrase, τῇ καρδίᾳ αὐτῶν, is functioning locatively, to indicate the "location" (or sphere) of the cleansing. This is likely an example of a divine passive, indicating that God is the one who has done the cleansing.

ANSWERS TO PART TWO

Here are the agents or instruments, if any, of each of the passive finite verbs in this passage.

Line 7: ἠγέρθη – In this example, the agent or instrument is not stated. This is likely another example of a divine passive, indicating that God is the one who has taken up Jesus.

Line 8: διεμαρτυρήθη – The agent for this passive verb is indicated by the prepositional phrase ἐν πνεύματι; the Spirit declared solemnly about Jesus.

Line 9: ὤφθη – The agent for this passive finite verb is indicated by the instrumental use of the dative ἀγγέλοις; the angels saw Jesus.

Line 10: ἐκηρύχθη – In this example, the agent or instrument is not stated. The prepositional phrase is functioning locatively to indicate where Jesus is proclaimed, namely, ἐν ἔθνεσιν ("among the nations"). The agent is not specified, but ostensibly it is his followers.

Line 11: ἐπιστεύθη – In this example, the agent or instrument is also not stated. The prepositional phrase is functioning locatively to indicate where Jesus is believed, namely, ἐν κόσμῳ ("in the world"). The agent is not specified, but again, ostensibly it is his followers.

Line 12: ἀνελήμφθη – In this example, the agent or instrument is once again not stated. This is likely another example of a divine passive, indicating that God is the one who has taken up Jesus.

Passive Form without Passive Meaning
Line 1: ἤρχετο – Recall that this verb (ἔρχομαι) does not have an active form in the present, which means that it does not have an active form in the imperfect either. A passive meaning would not be possible because this is an intransitive verb.

PART THREE

Now we'll focus on the participles in this passage. You have already identified these forms and parsed them. Now go through the passage and indicate the function of each participle by labeling the participle SUB, ATTR, or ADV. For ATTR and ADV participles, draw an arrow to the word being modified by the participle. The first participle is used as an example. Once you have finished, you can check your own work against the discussion on the next page.

SUB

Line 7: πιστεύοντες – This participle is functioning substantivally; it is articular, and there is no substantive that is in immediate proximity that is also nominative plural masculine. This substantive participle is further modified by the adjective πάντες.

ANSWERS TO PART THREE

Here is how each participle is functioning in this passage.

Line 3: ἀποστέλλοντα – This participle is functioning attributively to modify πατέρα. It is articular, and it agrees with πατέρα in case, number, and gender. It is part of a second attributive construction: article-substantive-article-modifier.

ATTR
3. ἀλλὰ εἰς τὸν πατέρα τὸν ἀποστέλλοντα αὐτόν.

Line 4: πιστεύοντες – This participle is functioning substantivally; it is articular, and there is no substantive that is in immediate proximity that is also nominative plural masculine. It functions parallel to πιστεύοντες in line 2. Furthermore, the adjective μακάριοι is in the predicate position, so this is a verbless clause, in which the adjective is making a predication about the substantival participle.

SUB
4. μακάριοι οἱ πιστεύοντες εἰς χριστὸν, ὅτι αὐτοὶ τὸν θεὸν ἐβλέπον.

Line 5: βαπτιζόμενοι – This participle is functioning substantivally; it is articular, and there is no substantive that is in immediate proximity that is also nominative plural masculine. It functions parallel to πιστεύοντες in both lines 2 and 4. Again, the adjective μακάριοι is in the predicate position, so this is a verbless clause, in which the adjective is making a predication about the substantival participle. It is also a passive participle; the agent is indicated by the prepositional phrase ὑπὸ τῶν μαθητῶν τουτῶν.

SUB
5. μακάριοι οἱ βαπτιζόμενοι ὑπὸ τῶν μαθητῶν τουτῶν, ὅτι ἐκαθαρίσθησαν τῇ καρδίᾳ αὐτῶν.

PART FOUR

We will now focus on nouns and pronouns, which you should be able to quickly recognize by now. If, however, you are still unsure of these forms, go back and review the assigned noun paradigms.

Use this passage to work through the following instructions. Although the instructions often ask for only one example, working through *every* example that occurs in the passage will help you the most. Once you have completed your work, then turn to the page following the last question for a complete list of these constructions and further discussion of them. Following this discussion, there are two remaining questions covering dependent clauses and prepositional phrases.

1. Give one example of a direct object and answer the following questions:
    a. How do you know that this substantive is functioning as a direct object?
    b. For which finite verb is this substantive functioning as a direct object?
2. Give at least two examples of a genitival construction.
    a. Which word is the genitival modifier?
    b. Which word is the head noun?
3. Give one example of a predicate nominative or a predicate adjective.
    a. What type of verb confirms that this is a predicate nominative?
    b. What is the subject of this verb?
4. Give one example of the emphatic use of a personal pronoun.
    a. How do you know that this pronoun is functioning emphatically?
5. Give one example of a third-person personal pronoun in an oblique case.
    a. What is the antecedent of this pronoun?
    b. How do you know?
6. Give one example of a demonstrative.
    a. Is this demonstrative functioning as an adjective or a pronoun?
    b. How do you know?
7. Give one example of the adjective πᾶς.
    a. Is this form of πᾶς functioning attributively or substantivally?
    b. How do you know?
8. Give one example of an interrogative or indefinite pronoun.
    a. Is this an interrogative or indefinite pronoun?
    b. How do you know?

POSSIBLE ANSWERS FOR PART FOUR

Here is a complete list of all possible answers for questions 1–8. You should check your work against this and see if you missed anything. If so, then use this as a means of reviewing forms, functions, and concepts that were discussed in chapters 1–13.

1. Here are all examples of direct objects and answers to the following questions for each:
   a. How do you know that this substantive is functioning as a direct object?
   b. For which finite verb is this substantive functioning as a direct object?

   Line 1: Ἰησοῦ
   a. This is an example of a verb that takes a direct object in a case other than the accusative case.
   b. Ἰησοῦ is the direct object of πιστεύει, even though it is in the dative case.

   NOTE: Because Ἰησοῦ is in the dative case, this could be understood as a pure dative and translated "believes in Jesus." In chapter 8 we noted that the dative alone could indicate a point in space. Here it is also functioning to indicate a "location," or sphere (in a metaphorical sense). The dative is also functioning in this way in line 2.

   Line 3: αὐτόν
   a. The accusative case of αὐτόν indicates that it is functioning as a direct object.
   b. αὐτόν is the direct object of the participle ἀποστέλλοντα.

   Line 4: θεόν
   a. The accusative case of θεόν indicates that it is functioning as a direct object.
   b. θεόν is the direct object of the verb ἐβλέπον.

2. Each of the genitival constructions in this passage has been marked below. (Lines in which no genitival constructions occur are not included.)
   a. Which word is the genitival modifier? This word is labeled *GM*.
   b. Which word is the head noun? An *arrow* is drawn from the *GM* to this word.

— GM

1. εἴ τις πιστεύει Ἰησοῦ, ἤρχετο εἰς τὴν βασιλείαν τοῦ θεοῦ.

— GM — GM

2. πάντες οἱ πιστεύοντες τῷ ὀνόματι τοῦ υἱοῦ τοῦ ἀνθρώπου οὐ πιστεύουσιν εἰς αὐτὸν

5. μακάριοι οἱ βαπτιζόμενοι ὑπὸ τῶν μαθητῶν, ὅτι ἐκαθαρίσθησαν

— GM

τῇ καρδίᾳ αὐτῶν.

GM —

6. καὶ ἀληθής ἐστιν ἡ τῶν ἀποστόλων μαρτυρία·

3. There are no examples of predicate nominatives in this passage. There are *three* examples of predicate adjectives (underlined) in this passage.
   a. What type of verb confirms that this is a predicate adjective?
   b. What is the subject of this verb?

   Line 4: μακάριοι οἱ πιστεύοντες
   Line 5: μακάριοι οἱ βαπτιζόμενοι
   a. In both examples, the predicate position of the adjective (here: adjective-article-substantive) indicates a verbless clause in which an equative verb is assumed.
   b. οἱ πιστεύοντες is the subject of the assumed equative verb in line 4; οἱ βαπτιζόμενοι is the subject of the assumed equative verb in line 5.

   Line 6: καὶ ἀληθής ἐστιν ἡ τῶν ἀποστόλων μαρτυρία·
   a. The equative verb ἐστίν confirms that this is a predicate adjective.
   b. ἡ τῶν ἀποστόλων μαρτυρία is the subject of this verb.

4. There is *one* example of the emphatic use of a personal pronoun in this passage.

   Line 4: αὐτοὶ τὸν θεὸν ἐβλέπον
   a. We know that the pronoun is functioning emphatically because it is in the nominative case with a finite verb. The verb form is inflected for person and number, so the pronoun is not indicating the subject but rather is adding emphasis.

5. There are *three* examples of a third-person personal pronoun in an oblique case.
   a. What is the antecedent of this pronoun?

b. How do you know?

Line 2: αὐτόν

    a. The antecedent of this pronoun is υἱοῦ.

    b. The pronoun also agrees with ἀνθρώπου in number and gender, but τοῦ υἱοῦ τοῦ ἀνθρώπου is a construction that should be considered as a unit. Hence τοῦ ἀνθρώπου is modifying the antecedent τοῦ υἱοῦ. The antecedent could not be τῷ ὀνόματι because it is neuter, and this pronoun is masculine.

Line 3: αὐτόν

    a. The antecedent of this pronoun is also υἱοῦ, with which it agrees in number and gender.

    b. The comments for αὐτόν in line 2 also apply here as well. Clearly the antecedent could not be πατέρα, because the Father does not send himself.

Line 5: αὐτῶν

    a. The antecedent of this pronoun is οἱ βαπτιζόμενοι.

    b. The pronoun agrees with βαπτιζόμενοι in number and gender. Although the pronoun also agrees with μαθητῶν in number and gender, this would not make sense in the overall context of this passage.

6. There is one example of a demonstrative in this passage.
    a. In line 5, τουτῶν is functioning as an adjective.
    b. τουτῶν agrees with μαθητῶν in case, number, and gender, which indicates that it is functioning attributively.

7. There is one example of the adjective πᾶς in this passage.
    a. In line 2, πάντες is functioning attributively, modifying the substantival participle, οἱ πιστεύοντες.
    b. πάντες agrees with πιστεύοντες in case, number, and gender, which indicates that it is functioning attributively to modify this substantive. Recall that the adjective πᾶς appears in the predicate position when it is functioning attributively.

8. There is one example of an indefinite pronoun in this passage.
    a./b. τις is an indefinite because there is no accent on the first syllable.

PART FIVE

We'll take one more pass through this passage, focusing on dependent clauses and prepositional phrases. Go through the passage and put parentheses around each (dependent clause) and brackets around each [preposition phrase]. For each dependent clause, highlight (here indicated with a gray background) the subordinating conjunction or the relative pronoun and identify what type of clause it is and then indicate how it is functioning. For each prepositional phrase, indicate how you know the boundary of the prepositional phrase. Once you have finished, you can check your own work against the discussion on the next page.

ANSWERS TO PART FIVE

1. (εἴ τις πιστεύει Ἰησοῦ), ἤρχετο [εἰς τὴν βασιλείαν τοῦ θεοῦ].
2. πάντες οἱ πιστεύοντες τῷ ὀνόματι τοῦ υἱοῦ τοῦ ἀνθρώπου οὐ πιστεύουσιν [εἰς αὐτὸν]
3. ἀλλὰ [εἰς τὸν πατέρα τὸν ἀποστέλλοντα αὐτόν].
4. μακάριοι οἱ πιστεύοντες [εἰς χριστόν], (ὅτι αὐτοὶ τὸν θεὸν ἐβλέπον).
5. μακάριοι οἱ βαπτιζόμενοι [ὑπὸ τῶν μαθητῶν τουτῶν], (ὅτι ἐκαθαρίσθησαν τῇ καρδίᾳ αὐτῶν).
6. καὶ ἀληθής ἐστιν ἡ τῶν ἀποστόλων μαρτυρία
7. ὃς ἠγερθῇ [ἐν σαρκί],
8. διεμαρτυρήθη [ἐν πνεύματι],
9. ὤφθη ἀγγέλοις,
10. ἐκηρύχθη [ἐν ἔθνεσιν],
11. ἐπιστεύθη [ἐν κόσμῳ],
12. ἀνελήμφθη [ἐν δόξῃ].

Dependent Clauses

- Line 1: (εἴ τις πιστεύει Ἰησοῦ) is the protasis of a first-class conditional. Review the discussion of conditionals in chapter 11.
- Line 4: (ὅτι αὐτοὶ τὸν θεὸν ἐβλέπον) is functioning causally to indicate how the ones who believe in the Christ are blessed, namely, because they were seeing God. To be more precise, this ὅτι clause could be understood as functioning *epexegetically*, which means that it further explains or defines how the ones who believe in the Christ are blessed. This is a term that you will learn more about in Greek exegesis.
- Line 5: (ὅτι ἐκαθαρίσθησαν τῇ καρδίᾳ αὐτῶν) is also functioning causally to indicate how the ones who have been baptized are blessed, namely, that they have been cleansed in their hearts. This could also be understood more precisely as an epexegetical function of the ὅτι clause.
- Line 7: The use of the relative pronoun here actually introduces a hymn or creedal statement. If you put parentheses around lines 7–12, you were thinking along the right track, but these do not comprise a dependent clause. The antecedent is understood from the larger context to be Jesus.

Prepositional Phrases

- Line 1: [εἰς τὴν βασιλείαν τοῦ θεοῦ] – βασιλείαν is in the accusative case, which indicates that it is the object of the preposition εἰς; θεοῦ is a genitival modifier of the head noun βασιλείαν. The word following, πάντες, is in the nominative case, so it could not be part of the prepositional phrase.

- Line 2: [εἰς αὐτόν] - αὐτόν is in the accusative case, which indicates that it is the object of the preposition εἰς. The word following, ἀλλά, is a conjunction, which is followed by another prepositional phrase, so it could not be part of the first prepositional phrase.

- Line 3: [εἰς τὸν πατέρα τὸν ἀποστέλλοντα αὐτόν] - πατέρα is in the accusative case, which indicates that it is the object of the preposition εἰς; the attributive participle is modifying the substantive πατέρα, and αὐτόν is the direct object of the participle. The word following, μακάριοι, is in the nominative case, so it could not be part of the prepositional phrase. Did you notice that this is a second attributive adjective construction?

- Line 4: [εἰς χριστόν] - χριστόν is in the accusative case, which indicates that it is the object of the preposition εἰς. The word following, ὅτι, is a subordinating conjunction that introduces a dependent clause, which could not be part of the prepositional phrase.

- Line 5: [ὑπὸ τῶν μαθητῶν τουτῶν] – μαθητῶν is in the genitive case, which indicates that it is the object of the preposition ὑπό; both τῶν and τουτῶν modify μαθητῶν. The word following, ὅτι, is a subordinating conjunction that introduces a dependent clause, which could not be part of the prepositional phrase.

- Line 7: [ἐν σαρκί] – σαρκί is in the dative case, which indicates that it is the object of the preposition ἐν. The word that follows, διεμαρτυρήθη, is a finite verb, which could not be part of the prepositional phrase.

- Line 8: [ἐν πνεύματι] – πνεύματι is in the dative case, which indicates that it is the object of the preposition ἐν. The word that follows, ὤφθη, is a finite verb, which could not be part of the prepositional phrase.

- Line 10: [ἐν ἔθνεσιν] – ἔθνεσιν is in the dative case, which indicates that it is the object of the preposition ἐν. The word that follows, ἐπιστεύθη, is a finite verb, which could not be part of the prepositional phrase.

- Line 11: [ἐν κόσμῳ] – κόσμῳ is in the dative case, which indicates that it is the object of the preposition ἐν. The word that follows, ἀνελήμφθη, is a finite verb, which could not be part of the prepositional phrase.

- Line 12: [ἐν δόξῃ] – δόξῃ is in the dative case, which indicates that it is the object of the preposition ἐν. This prepositional phrase concludes the passage—an obvious indication of the end of the phrase.

PART SIX

Finally, write out a final translation for this passage that reflects your work throughout this exercise. You can compare your translation with the one on the next page.

POSSIBLE TRANSLATION FOR PART SIX

1. If anyone believes in Jesus, he or she was coming into the kingdom of God.
2. All who believe in the name of the Son of Man do not believe in him
3. but in the Father who sent him.
4. Blessed are the ones who believe in (the) Christ, because they themselves were seeing God.
5. Blessed are the ones who have been baptized by these disciples, because they were cleansed in their hearts.
6. And the testimony of the apostles is true:
7. The one was raised in the flesh,
8. he was declared by the Spirit,
9. he was seen by angels,
10. he was proclaimed among the nations,
11. he was believed in the world,
12. he was taken up in glory.

Additional Notes:
- Line 1. Because this was modified from the original text, the switch from the present tense-form to the imperfect tense-form seems awkward.
- Lines 4 and 5. You could also translate "the ones" as "those."
- Line 4. The object of a preposition is often anarthrous, even if the substantive is definite, so εἰς χριστόν could be translated with the article in English.
- Lines 4 and 5. An English perfect tense could also be used to translate both the imperfect in line 4 and the aorist in line 5: "They themselves have seen God," and, "They have been cleansed in their hearts."
- Line 7 and 8. Both objects of the prepositional phrases in these lines are definite in meaning even though they are anarthrous grammatically (e.g., "in the flesh" and "in the Spirit").

REVIEW AND STUDY GUIDE FOR CHAPTERS 9-13

Congratulations! You are halfway through the first year of beginning Greek! Here are some concepts and forms that you need to know from chapters 9–13. You should also make sure that concepts and forms from chapter 1–8 are firmly in place.

- relative pronoun forms (and how to distinguish these from forms of the article)
- the function of relative clauses and how to determine the boundaries of relative clauses
- demonstrative adjective and pronoun forms and functions
- the function of prepositions that can have objects in more than one case
- verbal roots and tense stems
- present indicative forms and functions (all voices)
- imperfect indicative forms and functions (all voices)
- aorist indicative forms and functions (all voices)
- morphological changes that result from the addition of a sigma or theta
- first- and second-class conditionals
- third declension noun and adjective patterns
- question formation in Greek
- present participle forms
- basic participle functions (substantival, attributive, adverbial)
- forms and functions of the adjective πᾶς
- vocabulary, paradigms, and principal parts for chapters 9–13

Once again, the more firmly these concepts and forms are in place, the more fun you will have learning Greek and translating from the NT.

chapter FIFTEEN

THE AORIST PARTICIPLE AND ADDITIONAL PARTICIPLE FUNCTIONS

OBJECTIVES AND OVERVIEW

Chapter 15 introduces the following linguistic concepts, morphemes, and paradigms:

- first aorist active, middle, and passive participle paradigms
- second aorist active and middle participle paradigms
- adverbial participle functions: temporal, causal, purpose, instrumental
- genitive absolute participles

THE AORIST PARTICIPLE

In chapter 13, we learned that the participle is a *verbal adjective*, which means that it shares characteristics of verbs, such as voice and aspect (indicated by tense stems). The participle can have an object and an adverbial modifier (or modifiers). The participle also shares characteristics of adjectives, such as case, number, and gender. We also saw that participles function either adverbially or adjectivally (attributively or substantivally). When a participle functions adverbially, it modifies a verb and is dependent on that verb. In this chapter, we will look at additional adverbial participle functions. These functions apply to a participle built from any tense stem (or principal part). But before we explore these functions more, we'll look at the forms of aorist participles.

The Forms of Aorist Participles

As we noted, the aspect of a participle is indicated by the tense stem from which it is constructed. Aorist participles are constructed using aorist tense stems and thus have perfective aspect. Recall that aorist tense-forms are classified as either first or second aorists.

First Aorist Participles

First aorist forms have tense stems that are identical (or nearly identical) to the present tense stem, as for example, λύω. Because there is little or no difference between the present and aorist tense stems, first aorist active and middle forms add the tense formative -σα to the aorist tense stem. This is true both for indicative and nonindicative forms. (Remember that the morphological changes that occur when a sigma is added to a consonantal stem are the same, whether for nouns or verb forms.)

Like present active participles, aorist active masculine or neuter participles also use the participle morpheme (-ντ). Remember that verb components occur before the participle morpheme, whereas case endings are suffixed onto the participle morpheme. We can "build" a first aorist active participle as follows:

aorist tense stem	tense formative	ptc morpheme	case ending	inflected form
λυ	+ σα	+ ντ	+ ος	→ λύσαντος

Notice that there is no augment with aorist participles. Augmented verb forms only occur with indicative verbs. The aorist active participle follows a 3-1-3 declension pattern (i.e., masculine and neuter forms use third declension case endings, and feminine forms use first declension case endings). The feminine forms of the aorist active participle follow the first declension α-impure pattern. As we saw with present participles, it is easiest to consider -σασα as the combination of the connecting vowel and the participle morpheme. Here is the paradigm for the first aorist active participle of λύω.[1]

	masc (3)	fem (1)	neut (3)
nom sg	λύσας	λύσασα	λῦσαν
gen sg	λύσαντος	λυσάσης	λύσαντος
dat sg	λύσαντι	λυσάσῃ	λύσαντι
acc sg	λύσαντα	λύσασαν	λῦσαν
nom pl	λύσαντες	λύσασαι	λύσαντα
gen pl	λυσάντων	λυσασῶν	λυσάντων
dat pl	λύσασι(ν)	λυσάσαις	λύσασι(ν)
acc pl	λύσαντας	λυσάσας	λύσαντα

---

1. These endings are identical to those in the πᾶς, πᾶσα, πᾶν paradigm.

For the Curious

As we saw in chapter 13, for feminine participles the participle morpheme is -εσ, an allomorph of -ντ. When the morpheme is added to the tense formative -σα, the α and ε contract to the long α (although the alpha looks the same for both). Thus, for the aorist active participle nominative singular feminine, the following occurs: λυ + σα + εσ + α → (α + ε → α) → λυ + σ + α + σ + α → λύσασα.[2] Alternatively, Porter, Reed, and O'Donnell claim that the morpheme is -ντσ.[3] The sigma causes the ντ to drop out, which results in -ασ, to which α-impure first declension feminine endings are added.

As we have seen previously, the participle morpheme -ντ is visible through-out the masculine and neuter paradigm except in the nominative singular and dative plural; in the dative plural the sigma of the case ending causes the -ντ to drop out (λύσασι[ν]). This is also true for the nominative singular masculine, where the sigma case ending causes the -ντ to drop out (λύσας). With the nomi-native and accusative singular neuter participle forms, there is no case ending, so the final tau drops off, which results in the circumflex over the upsilon (λῦσαν).

Like the aorist indicative, aorist participles have a separate form for the middle and passive voices. The first aorist middle participle uses both the tense formative -σα and the participle morpheme -μεν. The aorist middle participle follows a 2-1-2 declension pattern, with the feminine forms following the η-type pattern for first declension feminine nouns. Here is the paradigm for the first aorist middle participle of λύω.

	masc (2)	fem (1)	neut (2)
nom sg	λυσάμενος	λυσαμένη	λυσάμενον
gen sg	λυσαμένου	λυσαμένης	λυσαμένου
dat sg	λυσαμένῳ	λυσαμένῃ	λυσαμένῳ
acc sg	λυσάμενον	λυσαμένην	λυσάμενον
nom pl	λυσάμενοι	λυσάμεναι	λυσάμενα
gen pl	λυσαμένων	λυσαμένων	λυσαμένων
dat pl	λυσαμένοις	λυσαμέναις	λυσαμένοις
acc pl	λυσαμένους	λυσαμένας	λυσάμενα

---

2. Goetchius, *Language of the New Testament*, 184.
3. Porter, Reed, and O'Donnell, *Fundamentals of New Testament Greek*, 106.

First aorist passive participles follow a 3-1-3 declension pattern and use the tense formative -θε. (This is actually the same tense formative used for aorist passive indicatives, except that the vowel lengthens in the indicative [-θη], whereas its actual tense formative is -θε.) Here is the paradigm for the aorist passive participle.

	masc (3)	fem (1)	neut (3)
nom sg	λυθείς	λυθεῖσα	λυθέν
gen sg	λυθέντος	λυθείσης	λυθέντος
dat sg	λυθέντι	λυθείσῃ	λυθέντι
acc sg	λυθέντα	λυθεῖσαν	λυθέν
nom pl	λυθέντες	λυθεῖσαι	λυθέντα
gen pl	λυθέντων	λυθεισῶν	λυθέντων
dat pl	λυθεῖσι(ν)	λυθείσαις	λυθεῖσι(ν)
acc pl	λυθέντας	λυθείσας	λυθέντα

For the nominative singular masculine form, the case ending is sigma, which causes the -ντ of the participle morpheme to drop off, which results in the compensatory lengthening of the epsilon to the diphthong ει (λυθείς). This also explains the dative plural masculine and neuter forms (λυθεῖσιν). With the nominative and accusative singular neuter forms, there is no case ending, so the final tau drops off (λυθέν); notice, however, that there is no circumflex over the upsilon as was true with the first aorist active nominative and accusative singular neuter participles forms. The feminine forms follow the first declension α-impure pattern. It is easiest to consider -θεισα as the combination of the tense formative and the participle morpheme.

For the Curious

As noted, the participle morpheme for feminine participles is -εσ, an allomorph of -ντ. When the tense formative -θε is added to this participle morpheme, the sigma drops out and the epsilons contract to the diphthong ει. Thus, for the aorist passive participle nominative singular feminine, the following occurs: λυ + θε + εσ + α → (ε + ε → ει) → λυ + θ + ει + σ + α → λυθεῖσα.[4] Alternatively, Porter, Reed, and O'Donnell claim that the morpheme is -ντσ.[5] The sigma causes the ντ to drop and causes compensatory lengthening of the ε of the tense formative -θε to the diphthong ει, which results in -εισα.

---

4. Goetchius, *Language of the New Testament*, 187.
5. Porter, Reed, and O'Donnell, *Fundamentals of New Testament Greek*, 273.

Second Aorist Participles

Recall that second aorist verbs have an aorist tense stem that is visibly different from the present tense stem, which means that no tense formative is needed to indicate the aorist form. (This stem is used to construct the third principal part, which you have been memorizing.) For second aorist participles, this means that there will be a connecting vowel between the aorist tense stem and the participle morpheme. Here is how we "build" a second aorist active participle:

aorist tense stem	connecting vowel	ptc morpheme	case ending	inflected form
λαβ	+ ο	+ ντ	+ ος	→ λαβόντος

Here is the paradigm for the second aorist active participle of λαμβάνω.

	masc (3)	fem (1)	neut (3)
nom sg	λαβών	λαβοῦσα	λαβόν
gen sg	λαβόντος	λαβούσης	λαβόντος
dat sg	λαβόντι	λαβούσῃ	λαβόντι
acc sg	λαβόντα	λαβοῦσαν	λαβόν
nom pl	λαβόντες	λαβοῦσαι	λαβόντα
gen pl	λαβόντων	λαβουσῶν	λαβόντων
dat pl	λαβοῦσι(ν)	λαβούσαις	λαβοῦσι(ν)
acc pl	λαβόντας	λαβούσας	λαβόντα

If a verb does not have active forms in a given tense stem, the participle that is constructed using that tense stem also does not have active forms. Thus, because γίνομαι does not have active forms in the aorist (as reflected in the third principal part ἐγενόμην), its aorist participle does not have active forms. Here is the second aorist middle participle paradigm of γίνομαι.

	masc (2)	fem (1)	neut (2)
nom sg	γενόμενος	γενομένη	γενόμενον
gen sg	γενομένου	γενομένης	γενομένου
dat sg	γενομένῳ	γενομένῃ	γενομένῳ
acc sg	γενόμενον	γενομένην	γενόμενον

(cont.)

	masc (2)	fem (1)	neut (2)
nom pl	γενόμενοι	γενόμεναι	γενόμενα
gen pl	γενομένων	γενομένων	γενομένων
dat pl	γενομένοις	γενομέναις	γενομένοις
acc pl	γενομένους	γενομένας	γενόμενα

HEADS UP!

All along, we've suggested looking ahead at the forms of μι verbs before we actually get to those chapters. You can look through the aorist participle forms for μι verbs in chapter 25 and see how many forms you can recognize based on what you have learned in this chapter. Look for morphemes that are used in both forms, such as the participle morphemes -ντ and -μεν.

Additional Adverbial Functions of Participles

Participle functions can be divided into two main categories: adjectival and adverbial. The key to identifying these functions involves the article—adjectival participles are *usually* articular, whereas adverbial participles are *always* anarthrous. In this chapter, we will consider some important subcategories of adverbial participles. Adverbial participles usually modify a finite verb, which is also often the main verb, but adverbial participles can occasionally modify another participle or even an infinitive. These functions apply to any participles, whether they are present, aorist, perfect, or future.

Temporal Participles

It is often helpful to think in terms of an adverbial participle answering a specific question regarding the verb that it modifies. So in the case of a temporal participle, this adverbial function answers the question "when?" Consider the following example. (Participles are italicized for clarity.)

παράγων εἶδεν Λευὶν τὸν τοῦ Ἀλφαίου (Mark 2:14)
Passing by, he saw Levi the son of Alphaeus.

In this example, the adverbial participle παράγων agrees in number and gender with the subject of the finite verb that it modifies, εἶδεν, which the larger context indicates is Jesus. This participle tells *when* Jesus saw Levi, namely, as he was walking along. Let's consider another example:

καὶ ἐξελθὼν εἶδεν πολὺν ὄχλον (Matt 14:14)
And *leaving*, he saw a great crowd.

In this example, the adverbial participle ἐξελθὼν agrees in number and gender with the subject of the finite verb that it modifies, εἶδεν, also understood from the larger context to be Jesus. It tells *when* Jesus saw the crowd; namely, after he had left, or come out of, a solitary place (see Matt 14:13). There are several possibilities for translating this temporal participle, but there is a certain sequence here that indicates that the action of seeing came after the action of leaving, so we could translate the verse as follows:

And after he left, he saw a great crowd.
And after leaving, he saw a great crowd.

In general, a *present* temporal participle indicates an action that occurs at the same time (i.e., contemporaneously) as the verb that the participle modifies; this is sometimes indicated with the English words "as" or "when" (e.g., "When he passed by, he saw Levi."). An *aorist* temporal participle *may* indicate an event antecedent to the verb. This can often be rendered with "having" or "after" plus the past participle of a verbal idea, as we saw in the example from Matthew 14:14. Here are some more examples:

νηστεύσας ἡμέρας τεσσεράκοντα καὶ νύκτας τεσσεράκοντα[6] ὕστερον ἐπείνασεν (Matt 4:2)
After having fasted during forty days and forty nights, afterwards he was hungry.

Δικαιωθέντες οὖν ἐκ πίστεως εἰρήνην ἔχομεν πρὸς τὸν θεόν (Rom 5:1)
Therefore, *having been justified* by faith, we have peace with God.

The following offers a good example of an aorist and a present temporal participle in the same verse. Notice how the participial clauses are translated with finite verbs *in English.*

---

6. Remember that the accusative can indicate duration in the context of time; this is indicated by the English word "during."

Ἐγένετο δέ μοι ὑποστρέψαντι εἰς Ἰερουσαλὴμ καὶ προσευχομένου μου ἐν
τῷ ἱερῷ γενέσθαι με ἐν ἐκστάσει (Acts 22:17)
And it happened *after I returned* to Jerusalem, and *while I was praying* in the
temple, I was in a trance.

Causal Participles

The adverbial function of a causal participle answers the question "why?"
Consider the following example.

Εὐχαριστοῦμεν . . . *ἀκούσαντες* τὴν πίστιν ὑμῶν ἐν Χριστῷ Ἰησοῦ καὶ τὴν
ἀγάπην ἣν ἔχετε εἰς πάντας τοὺς ἁγίους (Col 1:3–4)
We give thanks . . . *because we have heard* of your faith in Christ Jesus and
the love that you have for all the saints.

In this example, the participle ἀκούσαντες indicates the reason why Paul
and Timothy give thanks. Yet notice that this overlaps with a temporal understanding of this aorist participle, which could also be translated as "having
heard." This is also true for the example from Romans 5:1, cited earlier. This
reflects that fact that there is a logical overlap between an antecedent event and
a cause and effect relationship. Thus "because we have been justified" and "after
we have been justified" actually overlap in meaning. This overlap is frequent
with aorist participles that could be understood as functioning either temporally
or causally.

Purpose Participles

The adverbial function of purpose participles also answers the question
"why?," but instead of giving a reason *why*, this participle indicates the purpose
for the action of the verb that the participle modifies. Consider these examples:

ἴδωμεν εἰ ἔρχεται Ἡλίας *σώσων* αὐτόν (Matt 27:49)
Let us see if Elijah comes *for the purpose of saving* him.

ἀπέστειλεν αὐτὸν *εὐλογοῦντα* ὑμᾶς (Acts 3:26)
He sent him *for the purpose of blessing* us.

In both examples, the participle indicates the purpose of the finite verb.
In English, however, purpose is often indicated by the infinitive, so the above
examples would more naturally be translated as follows:

ἴδωμεν εἰ ἔρχεται Ἡλίας σώσων αὐτόν (Matt 27:49)
Let us see if Elijah comes *to save* him.

ἀπέστειλεν αὐτὸν εὐλογοῦντα ὑμᾶς (Acts 3:26)
He sent him *to bless* us.

The line between purpose and cause is sometimes difficult to determine, which is why both causal and purpose participles answer the question "why?" Often it is a matter of perspective—once a purpose has been accomplished, it can be understood as the cause or basis of an action. Context usually makes clear whether a participle is functioning to indicate cause or purpose, although it is not uncommon to find commentaries that describe the same participle as either causal or purpose . . . or both!

Instrumental Participles

The adverbial function of an instrumental participle answers the question "how?" It indicates or explains how the action of the verb that is modified occurred. Consider the following example:

ἡμεῖς καταγγέλλομεν *νουθετοῦντες* πάντα ἄνθρωπον καὶ *διδάσκοντες* πάντα ἄνθρωπον (Col 1:28)
We proclaim (him) *by admonishing* everyone and *by teaching* everyone.

In this example, the two participles indicate how Christ (understood from the larger context) is proclaimed, namely, *by admonishing* and *by teaching*. There is also overlap in this verse with a temporal understanding of these participles, so this verse could also be translated, "We proclaim him *while admonishing* . . . and *while teaching* . . ." This might be a good opportunity to compare various English versions of this verse to see how each translates these participles.

Genitive Absolute Participles

A genitive absolute construction is an adverbial participial construction in which the subject of the genitive clause is not *grammatically* related to the rest of the sentence (hence it is *absolute*), but it is *logically*, or *semantically*, related to the sentence, often supplying additional information about the circumstances accompanying the main verb. Consider the following English example:

All things considered, we decided to proceed with the sale.

The subject of the first (dependent) clause is "all things," whereas the subject of the second (main) clause is "we." Clearly these are not the same grammatical subject, but equally clearly these two clauses are logically related—the "things" considered did not hinder the sale.

In Greek, this construction contains three features that help to identify it:

1. a substantive or a pronoun in the genitive case (although occasionally neither of these is present);
2. an anarthrous participle in the genitive case that agrees with the number and gender of the substantive or pronoun in the genitive case (if a substantive or pronoun is present);
3. the entire construction is usually placed at the beginning of the sentence.[7]

In the examples below, the subjects of the genitive absolute and the main clause are italicized (when specified). Notice that they do not refer to the same entity. Notice also that the substantive or the pronoun in the genitive case functions as the "subject" of the participle and is usually translated with a finite verb *in English.*

Καὶ πορευομένων *αὐτῶν* ἐν τῇ ὁδῷ εἶπέν *τις* πρὸς αὐτόν . . . (Luke 9:57)
And while *they* were going on the road, *someone* said to him . . .

Ταῦτα δὲ *αὐτῶν* λαλούντων *αὐτὸς* ἔστη ἐν μέσῳ αὐτῶν καὶ λέγει αὐτοῖς, Εἰρήνη ὑμῖν (Luke 24:36)
But while *they* were speaking these things, *he himself* stood in their midst and was saying to them, "Peace be with you."

In the above examples, the switch in number (from plural to singular) is a confirming clue that the subject of the participle is *not* the same as that of the finite verb. Sometimes, however, the subjects of the genitive absolute participle and the finite verb are the same number (and/or gender) and can be ambiguous apart from the overall context.

ἐκβληθέντος *τοῦ δαιμονίου* ἐλάλησεν *ὁ κωφός* (Matt 9:33)
After *the demon* was cast out, *the mute man* spoke.

---

7. From Wallace, *Greek Grammar beyond the Basics,* 654–55.

The most important concept to keep in mind with genitive absolute participles is that a *genitive*-case participle cannot directly modify a finite verb—only a *nominative*-case participle can do that. Additionally, the relationship between the genitive absolute construction and the finite verb is logical, not syntactical. Notice in the other examples of adverbial participles that the number and gender of the participle agree with the logical subject of the finite verb that it modifies and that the adverbial participle is usually in the nominative case. This is not true for genitive absolute participles. Genitive absolute constructions are common in the GNT, especially in the Epistle to the Hebrews, so it is important to be able to recognize them. A commentary that focuses on the GNT should also alert you to the presence of a genitive absolute.

REVIEW OF CHAPTER 15

In this chapter we introduced the forms of aorist participles. Aorist participles do not have an augment. First aorist forms use the tense formative -σα, and second aorist forms use the tense stem that is used to construct the corresponding indicative forms. Both first and second aorists follow a 3-1-3 declension pattern. Both first and second aorist middle participles use the participle morpheme -μεν and follow a 2-1-2 declension pattern. We also covered adverbial functions of participles and how to determine these functions, including temporal, causal, purpose, and instrumental participles, as well as the genitive absolute construction.

Study Guide for Chapter 15

1. Be able to understand each of the following concepts and forms:
   participle morphemes
   tense formatives
   temporal adverbial participles
   causal adverbial participles
   purpose adverbial participles
   instrumental adverbial participles
   genitive absolute participles
2. Be able to parse aorist participle forms and translate basic Koine sentences that incorporate forms and concepts from previous chapters.

Vocabulary to Memorize

Here is the assigned vocabulary for chapter 15.

αἰών, -ῶνος, ὁ	age, eternity, world (122)
ἀκολουθέω	(+dat) I follow, I accompany (90)
ἁμαρτία, -ας, ἡ	sin (173)
ἀνάστασις, -εως, ἡ	resurrection (42)
ἀνήρ, ἀνδρός, ὁ	man, male, husband (216)
γλῶσσα, -ης, ἡ	tongue, language (50)
γυνή, γυναικός, ἡ	woman, wife (215)
δύναμις, -εως, ἡ	power, ability (119)
εἰρήνη, -ης, ἡ	peace (92)
ἐπιστρέφω	I turn, I turn around, I turn back, I return (36)
ἔρημος, -ον	abandoned, desolate; wilderness (fem subst) (48)
θάλασσα, -ης, ἡ	sea, lake (91)
ἱμάτιον, -ου, τό	clothing, robe (60)
κάθημαι	I sit, I sit down, I live (91)
καταβαίνω	I come down, I go down (81)
μέν	on the one hand, indeed (179)
μέσος, -η, -ον	middle; the middle (subst); in the midst of (impr prep) (58)
μηδείς, μηδεμία, μηδέν	no one, nothing (90)
μνημεῖον, -ου, τό	tomb, grave, monument (40)
ὅπως	how, that, in order that (53)
πρόσωπον, -ου, τό	face, appearance (76)
πῦρ, πυρός, τό	fire (71)
πῶς	how? in what way? (103)
Φίλιππος, -ου, ὁ	Philip (37)
χείρ, χειρός, ἡ	hand, finger (177)

Principal Parts to Memorize

These are the principal parts that you need to memorize for chapter 15. For now, you are only memorizing the first, third, and sixth parts (the parts that you do not have to memorize now have been grayed out). Remember, you should set up cards or other ways of memorizing these forms that will allow you easily to add new forms. The full "Principal Parts Chart" is in appendix 14.

1st prin part	2nd prin part	3rd prin part	4th prin part	5th prin part	6th prin part
ἀκούω	ἀκούσω	ἤκουσα	ἀκήκοα	n/a	ἠκούσθην
ἀποθνῄσκω	ἀποθανοῦμαι	ἀπέθανον	n/a	n/a	n/a
θέλω	θελήσω	ἠθέλησα	n/a	n/a	n/a
πίπτω	πεσοῦμαι	ἔπεσον	πέπτωκα	n/a	n/a

Paradigms to Memorize

The following paradigms should be memorized for chapter 15: the first aorist active, middle, and passive participles of λύω; the second aorist active participle of λαμβάνω; and the second aorist middle participle of γίνομαι.

FIRST AORIST ACTIVE PARTICIPLE OF λύω

	masc (3)	fem (1)	neut (3)
nom sg	λύσας	λύσασα	λῦσαν
gen sg	λύσαντος	λυσάσης	λύσαντος
dat sg	λύσαντι	λυσάσῃ	λύσαντι
acc sg	λύσαντα	λύσασαν	λῦσαν
nom pl	λύσαντες	λύσασαι	λύσαντα
gen pl	λυσάντων	λυσασῶν	λυσάντων
dat pl	λύσασι(ν)	λυσάσαις	λύσασι(ν)
acc pl	λύσαντας	λυσάσας	λύσαντα

FIRST AORIST MIDDLE PARTICIPLE OF λύω

	masc (2)	fem (1)	neut (2)
nom sg	λυσάμενος	λυσαμένη	λυσάμενον
gen sg	λυσαμένου	λυσαμένης	λυσαμένου
dat sg	λυσαμένῳ	λυσαμένῃ	λυσαμένῳ
acc sg	λυσάμενον	λυσαμένην	λυσάμενον
nom pl	λυσάμενοι	λυσάμεναι	λυσάμενα
gen pl	λυσαμένων	λυσαμένων	λυσαμένων
dat pl	λυσαμένοις	λυσαμέναις	λυσαμένοις
acc pl	λυσαμένους	λυσαμένας	λυσάμενα

FIRST AORIST PASSIVE PARTICIPLE OF λύω

	masc (3)	fem (1)	neut (3)
nom sg	λυθείς	λυθεῖσα	λυθέν
gen sg	λυθέντος	λυθείσης	λυθέντος
dat sg	λυθέντι	λυθείσῃ	λυθέντι
acc sg	λυθέντα	λυθεῖσαν	λυθέν
nom pl	λυθέντες	λυθεῖσαι	λυθέντα
gen pl	λυθέντων	λυθεισῶν	λυθέντων
dat pl	λυθεῖσι(ν)	λυθείσαις	λυθεῖσι(ν)
acc pl	λυθέντας	λυθείσας	λυθέντα

SECOND AORIST ACTIVE PARTICIPLE FOR λαμβάνω

	masc (3)	fem (1)	neut (3)
nom sg	λαβών	λαβοῦσα	λαβόν
gen sg	λαβόντος	λαβούσης	λαβόντος
dat sg	λαβόντι	λαβούσῃ	λαβόντι
acc sg	λαβόντα	λαβοῦσαν	λαβόν
nom pl	λαβόντες	λαβοῦσαι	λαβόντα
gen pl	λαβόντων	λαβουσῶν	λαβόντων
dat pl	λαβοῦσι(ν)	λαβούσαις	λαβοῦσι(ν)
acc pl	λαβόντας	λαβούσας	λαβόντα

SECOND AORIST MIDDLE PARTICIPLE FOR γίνομαι

	masc (2)	fem (1)	neut (2)
nom sg	γενόμενος	γενομένη	γενόμενον
gen sg	γενομένου	γενομένης	γενομένου
dat sg	γενομένῳ	γενομένῃ	γενομένῳ
acc sg	γενόμενον	γενομένην	γενόμενον
nom pl	γενόμενοι	γενόμεναι	γενόμενα
gen pl	γενομένων	γενομένων	γενομένων
dat pl	γενομένοις	γενομέναις	γενομένοις
acc pl	γενομένους	γενομένας	γενόμενα

chapter SIXTEEN

THE PERFECT AND PLUPERFECT INDICATIVE

OBJECTIVES AND OVERVIEW

Chapter 16 introduces the following linguistic concepts, morphemes, and paradigms:

- stative aspect; imperfective aspect
- heightened proximity and heightened remoteness
- perfect tense formative
- pluperfect tense formative
- reduplication and vocalic reduplication
- perfect active and middle indicative paradigms
- pluperfect active and middle indicative paradigms
- functions of the perfect tense-form
- functions of the pluperfect tense-form

ROOTS, STEMS, AND ASPECT

In this chapter, we will learn a new tense stem and the two indicative tense-forms that are formed from this stem. Recall that the **verbal root** is the most basic morpheme of a verb and is the basis of the various **tense stems**. Let's go back to the tree illustration that we last saw in chapter 10 and focus on the perfect tense stem. As you can see, there is one tense stem used for the perfect active and a different one used for perfect middle forms. This corresponds to a verb's fourth and fifth principal parts. (Although for many regular verbs, these stems often look identical.) Additionally, the perfect tense stem has some parallels to the present tense stem. First, the perfect middle and passive have the same form, which is also true for the present middle and passive. Second, the pluperfect is built from the perfect tense stem, which parallels the imperfect, which is built from the present tense stem. This means that the perfect and pluperfect share the same aspect, just as the present and imperfect both have imperfective aspect.

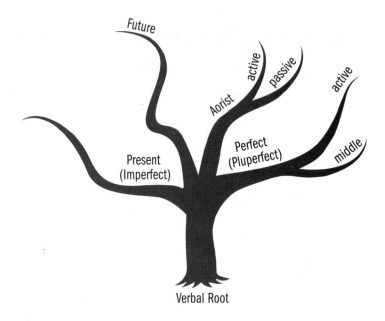

Unlike the imperfective aspect of the present stem, however, there is much discussion concerning the aspect indicated by the perfect tense stem. Some claim that the perfect tense stem indicates **stative aspect**, although it is debated whether this is actually an aspect. Others claim that the perfect tense stem indicates **imperfective aspect**, perhaps indicating **heightened proximity** (or some type of emphasis or summary). The latter is the approach adopted in this book. What is clear is that because the perfect tense is not as common as the present, aorist, future, or imperfect tenses, the use of the perfect tense usually reflects a *deliberate* choice on the part of the writer or speaker. The pluperfect is even less common; there are eighty-six pluperfect forms in the GNT. Thus, the use of the pluperfect also probably indicates a deliberate choice by a writer or speaker. The pluperfect has the same aspect as the perfect (imperfective), but instead of heightened proximity, it likely indicates **heightened remoteness**.[1]

Both the perfect and pluperfect tense stems use reduplication, which is the repetition of the initial consonant of the perfect tense stem. We discuss this below. Scholars debate what this morphology indicates semantically. (This is similar to the debate about what the morphology of the augment indicates semantically.)

---

1. The terms *heightened proximity* and *heightened remoteness* used in this paragraph are from Campbell, *Basics of Verbal Aspect*, 51–52.

Traditional grammars claim that reduplication indicates a completed action, but this is not true for all occurrences of perfect tense-forms. Currently, the semantic meaning of the perfect tense is receiving a significant amount of attention from Greek scholars. It seems best, therefore, to remain open to the semantic function of reduplication until the perfect tense is more fully understood.[2]

Many traditional grammars suggest that the perfect tense indicates a past action with ongoing results, but this can only be understood from the larger context and is not true for every occurrence of the perfect tense-form. Moreover, occurrences exist where the focus of the perfect tense verb is indeed on the resulting state of a past action, even though the past action may not be completed. In these instances, Greek perfects may be translated as English presents. We will discuss the function of the perfect tense more after we look at its forms.

THE FORMS OF THE PERFECT INDICATIVE

So far, we have learned how to "build" the present, imperfect, and aorist indicatives. In this chapter, we will "build" the perfect and pluperfect indicative forms. Like the aorist, the perfect and pluperfect tense forms use a **tense formative**. Unlike any other tense-form that we have seen so far, however, the perfect and pluperfect also use **reduplication**, which is a unique indicator of these tenses.[3] Reduplication is a morphological process wherein a part of a root or stem is repeated. In some languages, reduplication involves the repetition of an entire word, but in Koine Greek reduplication usually involves the doubling of the initial consonant and the insertion of an epsilon. So, we can "build" a perfect active indicative form as follows:

reduplication	perfect active tense stem	perfect tense formative	primary active personal ending	inflected form
λε	+ λυ	+ κα	+ μεν	→ λελύκαμεν

Here is the paradigm for the perfect active indicative of λύω.[4]

---

2. For the curious, see Harris, "Study of the Greek Language," 125–27.

3. We will see another type of reduplication with the present tense stem in μι verbs, but that reduplication will use an iota, whereas the reduplication with the perfect and pluperfect (for both omega and μι verbs) uses an epsilon. So reduplication with an epsilon is an indicator of the perfect or pluperfect for all Koine Greek verbs, whereas reduplication with an iota is an indicator of present or imperfect verb forms for μι verbs.

4. Some grammars distinguish between first and second perfects, analogous to first and second aorists. Thus, for some verbs, such as γράφω, the tense formative -κα is shortened simply to -α. Many such verbs are common, including γέγονα, γέγραφα, εἴληφα, and ἐλήλυθα. We will not distinguish between first and second perfects as we did for first and second aorists, as this distinction is unnecessary. The presence of reduplication is nearly always sufficient for recognizing perfect forms.

1 sg	λέλυκα	I have released
2 sg	λέλυκας	you (sg) have released
3 sg	λέλυκε(ν)	he/she/it has released
1 pl	λελύκαμεν	we have released
2 pl	λελύκατε	you (pl) have released
3 pl	λελύκασι(ν)	they have released

Notice that the third-person singular uses an epsilon and not an alpha; this is parallel to what we saw with the first aorist active indicative paradigm.

Like the present tense, the perfect tense shares the same form in the middle and passive voices. Unlike the perfect active tense form, however, the perfect middle and passive tense forms do not use a tense formative—so the *absence* of both the -κα tense formative as well as a connecting vowel is key to recognizing these forms! Here's how we build a present middle/passive indicative:

reduplication	perfect middle tense stem	primary middle personal ending	inflected form
λε	+ λυ	+ μεθα	→ λελύμεθα

The same form is used for the perfect passive indicative; the glosses below reflect the perfect passive. Here is the paradigm for the perfect middle indicative of λύω.

1 sg	λέλυμαι	I have been released
2 sg	λέλυσαι	you (sg) have been released
3 sg	λέλυται	he/she/it has been released
1 pl	λελύμεθα	we have been released
2 pl	λέλυσθε	you (pl) have been released
3 pl	λέλυνται	they have been released

More on Reduplication

As we have seen, there are predictable morphological changes that occur when some consonants combine. Predictable morphological processes also explain reduplicated forms that do not have a simple doubling of the initial consonant of the verb stem (e.g., λ + ε + λυ-). If a perfect tense stem begins with a fricative,[5] such as

---

5. A *fricative* is a consonant whose sound is made by forcing the air flow from the lungs through a narrowing or constriction, such as through the lips (φ), the alveolar ridge and the tongue (θ), or the back of the throat (χ).

φ, θ, or χ, then the reduplicated consonant is the corresponding voiceless stop,[6] such as π, τ, or κ. For example:

φανερόω	→	πεφανέρωμαι
θεραπεύω	→	τεθεράπευμαι
χωρίζω	→	κεχώρισμαι

Recall from chapter 1 that two consonants (ξ and ψ) are sometimes called **double consonants** and that some consonants form **consonant clusters**, such as γν- and κτ-. With double consonants, consonant clusters, and the sibilant ζ, an epsilon prefixes to the perfect tense stem, and no consonant is reduplicated.[7] For example:

ξηραίνω	→	ἐξήραμμαι
√γνω	→	ἔγνωκα
κτίζω	→	ἔκτισμαι

It is very important to recognize that this prefixed epsilon indicates reduplication; this epsilon must not be confused with the augment.

If a perfect tense stem begins with a vowel, then the initial vowel lengthens; this is called vocalic reduplication. For example:

ἁμαρτάνω	→	ἡμάρτηκα
ἑτοιμάζω	→	ἡτοίμακα

But if the verb stem begins with diphthong, there is often no visible reduplication; for example:

εὑρίσκω	→	εὕρηκα

Because reduplication involves the verb stem, a compounded preposition essentially "steps aside" and prefixes itself to the reduplicated tense stem. (This is similar to the augment, which prefixes itself to the tense stem, not the compounded preposition.)

---

6. *Corresponding* here refers to the place of articulation, such as the lips (labial), etc. The corresponding *voiceless* stop is used because fricatives are also voiceless and because the inserted epsilon is *voiced*. You don't need to remember this, but it does show that these spelling changes are all driven by phonology.

7. Some note that if the second letter of a consonant cluster is λ, ρ, μ, or ν, then only the first letter of the consonant cluster is reduplicated, as with γράφω → γέγραφα. Yet this is not observed consistently. It is best to realize that reduplication is generally easy to recognize, so it is unnecessary to memorize the various patterns of reduplication.

ἀπολύω   →   ἀπολέλυμαι

προσέρχομαι   →   προσελήλυθα

Finally, some verbs evidence so-called Attic reduplication, in which the first syllable of the stem is double. This explains the perfect form of ἀκούω:

ἀκούω   →   ἀκήκοα

You do not need to memorize these patterns, but knowing about them helps to recognize perfect verb forms in the GNT.

More on the Tense Formative (or the Lack Thereof)

If a perfect tense stem ends in τ, δ, θ, or ζ, then this consonant often drops before the -κα tense formative; for example:

ἐλπίζω   →   ἤλπικα

σώζω   →   σέσωκα

As noted, the perfect middle and passive indicative forms do not use the -κα tense formative or a connecting vowel. This means that the primary middle personal endings attach directly to the end of the perfect middle tense stem, which also means that certain predictable morphological changes occur when the final consonant of the verb stem combines with the -μ, -σ, -τ, or -σθ of certain personal endings. (Something even more interesting happens with the third-person plural forms, but we'll save that for the next chapter.)

The good news is that you do not have to memorize these morphological changes, because you will often be able to recognize these perfect forms easily due to the presence of reduplication and the lack of the -κα tense formative. One way to test this out is the look at the "Principal Parts Chart" in appendix 14 and skim over the column for the fourth and fifth principal parts. You should be able to see the similarities in the perfect active and middle forms and that they are relatively easy to recognize. You can also review these changes in appendix 4, "Changes to a Stem When a Sigma, Theta, Tau, or Mu Is Added."

THE FORMS OF THE PLUPERFECT INDICATIVE

Like the imperfect, the pluperfect tense only occurs in the indicative mood. Because it is an augmented tense, it uses secondary personal endings. The augment is often dropped from pluperfect forms, perhaps because reduplication plus the use of secondary personal endings is sufficient to indicate the pluperfect. Like the perfect tense, the pluperfect also uses a tense formative that begins with a kappa, but it does not use an alpha. Instead, the tense formative for the pluperfect active is -κει, which is visible throughout the paradigm and is one of the key indicators of the pluperfect. Like the perfect tense forms, the pluperfect middle and passive share the same form.

The pluperfect paradigms are not ones that you need to *memorize*, but you should be able to *recognize* forms when you encounter them.[8]

PLUPERFECT ACTIVE PARADIGM OF λύω		PLUPERFECT MIDDLE PARADIGM OF λύω	
1 sg	ἐλελύκειν	1 sg	ἐλελύμην
2 sg	ἐλελύκεις	2 sg	ἐλέλυσο
3 sg	ἐλελύκει(ν)	3 sg	ἐλέλυτο
1 pl	ἐλελύκειμεν	1 pl	ἐλελύμεθα
2 pl	ἐλελύκειτε	2 pl	ἐλέλυσθε
3 pl	ἐλελύκεισαν	3 pl	ἐλέλυντο

HEADS UP!

Here's another opportunity to preview μι verbs. You can look through the perfect and pluperfect indicative forms for μι verbs in chapter 24 and see how many forms you can recognize based on what you have learned in this chapter. Notice especially the different types of reduplication.

THE FUNCTIONS OF THE PERFECT AND PLUPERFECT INDICATIVE

As noted above, much scholarly debate surrounds the aspect of the perfect tense stem. We will simply outline here some of the common functions of the perfect tense in the GNT. One common usage is to emphasize the results or present state produced by a past action. This is sometimes called the *resultative* perfect. For example:

καθὼς γέγραπται ὅτι Οὐκ ἔστιν δίκαιος οὐδὲ εἷς (Rom 3:10)
Just as *it is written*, "There is no righteous one, not even one."

---

8. For possible translations of the pluperfect, see appendix 7, "Guide for Translating Greek Finite Verbs."

Closely related is the *consummative* usage of the perfect, which emphasizes the completion of a past action.

κἀγὼ ἑώρακα καὶ μεμαρτύρηκα ὅτι οὗτός ἐστιν ὁ υἱὸς τοῦ θεοῦ
  (John 1:34)
I also have seen and *have borne witness* that this is the son of God.

Often, however, these nuances are not clear, and it seems that the perfect tense form is indicating some type of emphasis or summary:

καὶ ἰδοὺ πεπληρώκατε τὴν Ἰερουσαλὴμ τῆς διδαχῆς ὑμῶν (Acts 5:28)
And look, *you have filled* Jerusalem with your teaching.

τὸν καλὸν ἀγῶνα ἠγώνισμαι, τὸν δρόμον τετέλεκα, τὴν πίστιν τετήρηκα
  (2 Tim 4:7)
I have fought the good fight, *I have finished* the race, *I have kept* the faith.

Some verbs occur in the perfect tense form with a present sense and no apparent heightened proximity, such as οἶδα, ἕστηκα, πέποιθα, and μέμνημαι. The verb οἶδα is unique in that it occurs *only* in the future, perfect, and pluperfect tense forms. Thus, the perfect is usually understood to have a present force, and the pluperfect is understood to correspond to the imperfect tense.

τὰς ἐντολὰς οἶδας (Mark 10:19)
You know the commands.

Sometimes the perfect tense form is used in a context that is clearly past referring. In these cases, the Greek perfect is usually translated with an English simple past. For example:

ὅτι Χριστὸς ἀπέθανον . . . καὶ ὅτι ἐγήγερται . . . (1 Cor 15:3–4)
That Christ died . . . and that *he was raised* . . .

As noted previously, the pluperfect may indicate "heightened remoteness." Recall that in narrative, the imperfect can function to provide background information to the main narrative events. In narrative, the pluperfect appears to indicate even more "remote" background information. For example:

ἦν δὲ ὁ λεγόμενος Βαραββᾶς μετὰ τῶν στασιαστῶν δεδεμένος *οἵτινες ἐν
τῇ στάσει φόνον πεποιήκεισαν.* (Mark 15:7)
And there was one called Barabbas imprisoned with the insurrectionists
who had committed murder in the uprising.

Notice that the comment about Barabbas gives background information to
Jesus's trial, but the pluperfect πεποιήκεισαν gives additional background information to indicate why Barabbas was in prison. (Notice also that the augment
has been dropped from the pluperfect form.)

REVIEW OF CHAPTER 16

In this chapter we introduced the perfect and pluperfect indicative forms. These
forms use the perfect tense stem, which has a stem for the active and a stem for
the middle and passive. Parallel to the present and imperfect indicative, the perfect tense stem is the basis for the pluperfect. We also introduced the morphological process of reduplication, which is one of the clearest indicators of the perfect
tense stem. Although there are many types of reduplication, the resulting forms
are generally easy to recognize. We saw that the perfect active form uses the tense
formative -κα and that the pluperfect uses the tense formative -κει. One of the
most debated topics in Greek studies currently is the aspect and semantics of the
perfect tense-form, which seems to indicate imperfective aspect with heightened
proximity for the perfect tense-form and heightened remoteness for the pluperfect tense-form.

Study Guide for Chapter 16

1. Be able to understand each of the following concepts and forms:
   imperfective aspect
   heightened proximity
   heightened remoteness
   reduplication
2. Be able to parse perfect and pluperfect indicative forms and translate
   basic Koine sentences that incorporate forms and concepts from
   previous chapters.

Vocabulary to Memorize

Here are the assigned vocabulary words for chapter 16.

εἰσέρχομαι	I come in(to), I go in(to), I enter (194)
ἔμπροσθεν (+gen)	before, in front of (impr prep) (48)
ἔσχατος, -η, -ον	last, least (52)
θέλημα, -ματος, τό	will, wish, desire (62)
θηρίον, -ου, τό	beast, animal (46)
ἱερεύς, -έως, ὁ	priest (31)
καρπός, -οῦ, ὁ	fruit, harvest (66)
κεῖμαι	I lie, I am laid, I exist (24)
λίθος, -ου, ὁ	stone (59)
μήτηρ, μητρός, ἡ	mother (83)
μικρός, -ά, -όν	little, small, short (46)
μιμνῄσκομαι	(+gen) I remember, I am reminded (pass) (23)
μόνος, -η, -ον	only, alone (114)
ναός, -οῦ, ὁ	temple (45)
νεφέλη, -ης, ἡ	cloud (25)
οἶδα	I know, I understand (318)
οὗ	where, to which (24)
πατήρ, πατρός, ὁ	father, ancestor (413)
πλοῖον, -ου, τό	boat (68)
σφραγίζω	I seal, I mark (15)
σωτήρ, -ῆρος, ὁ	savior, deliverer, redeemer (24)
τοιοῦτος, -αύτη, -οῦτον	of such a kind, such (57)
τόπος, -ου, ὁ	place, location (94)
τρίτος, -η, -ον	third; third time (adv) (56)
φεύγω	I flee, I escape (29)

Principal Parts to Memorize

These are the principal parts that you need to memorize for chapter 16. Beginning with this chapter, you will also be memorizing the fourth and fifth parts in addition to the first, third, and sixth parts (you do not have to memorize the second principal part for now, so it has been grayed out). Some of the verbs assigned for this chapter have been previously assigned, so you will need to add the fourth and fifth principal parts to these verbs. These parts are listed fully in the "Principal Parts Chart" in appendix 14. Or you can refer to the grayed out sections of previously assigned principal parts.

1st prin part	2nd prin part	3rd prin part	4th prin part	5th prin part	6th prin part
ἔρχομαι	ἐλεύσομαι	ἦλθον	ἐλήλυθα	n/a	n/a
καλέω	καλέσω	ἐκάλεσα	κέκληκα	κέκλημαι	ἐκλήθην
λαμβάνω	λήμψομαι	ἔλαβον	εἴληφα	εἴλημμαι	ἐλήμφθην
n/a	εἰδήσω	n/a	οἶδα (plpf ᾔδειν)	n/a	n/a
πίνω	πίομαι	ἔπιον	πέπωκα	n/a	ἐπόθην

Paradigms to Memorize

The following paradigms should be memorized for chapter 16: the perfect active and middle/passive indicative of λύω.

PERFECT ACTIVE PARADIGM OF λύω

1 sg	λέλυκα
2 sg	λέλυκας
3 sg	λέλυκε(ν)
1 pl	λελύκαμεν
2 pl	λελύκατε
3 pl	λελύκασι(ν)

PERFECT MIDDLE PARADIGM OF λύω

1 sg	λέλυμαι
2 sg	λέλυσαι
3 sg	λέλυται
1 pl	λελύμεθα
2 pl	λέλυσθε
3 pl	λέλυνται

THE PERFECT PARTICIPLE AND MORE PARTICIPLE FUNCTIONS

OBJECTIVES AND OVERVIEW

Chapter 17 introduces the following linguistic concepts, morphemes, and paradigms:

- present participle morphemes
- periphrasis
- perfect active and middle participle paradigms
- relative time and participles

THE PERFECT PARTICIPLE

So far, we have learned the forms of present and aorist participles, which comprise most of the participles in the GNT (and present participles occur more frequently than aorist participles).[1] In this chapter we will learn the forms of perfect participles and more about participle functions, particularly an adverbial function of the participle called **periphrasis**. Like perfect indicatives, perfect participles occur less frequently than either present or aorist participles, which means that they likely reflect a deliberate choice on the part of a writer or speaker.

The Forms of Perfect Participles

Perfect active participles are built using the perfect active tense stem, which is visible in the fourth principal part. As we have seen, the aspect of a participle is indicated by the tense stem from which it is constructed. Thus, the debate surrounding the aspect of the perfect tense stem also applies to perfect participles,

---

1. There is also a handful of future participles, which we will look at briefly in chapter 19.

although aspect is diminished in nonfinite verb forms, such as participles. Like perfect indicatives, perfect participles have reduplication; this is unlike aorist participles, which do not have an augment. Perfect active participles use the participle morpheme -κοτ. Let's look at how to build a perfect active participle.

reduplication	perfect active tense stem	perfect ptc morpheme	case ending	inflected form
λε	+ λυ	+ κοτ	+ ος	→ λελυκότος

The perfect active participle follows a 3-1-3 declension pattern. The feminine forms of the perfect active participle follow the first declension α-pure pattern. It is easiest to consider the morpheme -κυια in the feminine form as the combination of the connecting vowel and the participle morpheme. Here is the paradigm for the perfect active participle for λύω.[2]

	masc (3)	fem (1)	neut (3)
nom sg	λελυκώς	λελυκυῖα	λελυκός
gen sg	λελυκότος	λελυκυίας	λελυκότος
dat sg	λελυκότι	λελυκυίᾳ	λελυκότι
acc sg	λελυκότα	λελυκυῖαν	λελυκός
nom pl	λελυκότες	λελυκυῖαι	λελυκότα
gen pl	λελυκότων	λελυκυιῶν	λελυκότων
dat pl	λελυκόσι(ν)	λελυκυίαις	λελυκόσι(ν)
acc pl	λελυκότας	λελυκυίας	λελυκότα

The participle morpheme -κοτ is visible throughout the masculine and neuter paradigms except in the nominative singular and dative plural; in the dative-plural form the sigma of the case ending causes the tau of the participle morpheme to drop out (λελυκόσι[ν]). This is also true for the nominative singular masculine, and here, additionally, there is compensatory lengthening of the omicron to an omega (λελυκώς). With the nominative and accusative singular neuter participle forms, the case ending is sigma, which causes the tau to drop out, but there is no compensatory lengthening (λελυκός).

---

2. For help with translating perfect participles, see appendix 9, "Guide for Translating Greek Participles."

For the Curious

The perfect participle morpheme is -υσ, which is added to ͺα (recall that the consonantal iota, ͺ, was no longer used when the NT was written). The intervocalic sigma drops out, with the resulting form -υια.[3]

Like the perfect indicative, perfect participles share the same form in the middle and passive voices. These participles follow a 2-1-2 declension pattern, with the feminine forms following the η-type pattern for first declension feminine nouns. Perfect middle and passive participles are built from the perfect middle tense stem, which is evident in the fifth principal part. As with the perfect middle and passive indicative, perfect middle and passive participles do not use a tense formative or connecting vowel. Instead, the participle morpheme is added directly to the perfect middle tense stem. Here is the paradigm for the perfect middle and passive participle of λύω.[4]

	masc (2)	fem (1)	neut (2)
nom sg	λελυμένος	λελυμένη	λελυμένον
gen sg	λελυμένου	λελυμένης	λελυμένου
dat sg	λελυμένῳ	λελυμένῃ	λελυμένῳ
acc sg	λελυμένον	λελυμένην	λελυμένον
nom pl	λελυμένοι	λελυμέναι	λελυμένα
gen pl	λελυμένων	λελυμένων	λελυμένων
dat pl	λελυμένοις	λελυμέναις	λελυμένοις
acc pl	λελυμένους	λελυμένας	λελυμένα

HEADS UP!

Here's your chance to preview even more μι verbs. Look through the perfect participle forms for μι verbs in chapter 25 and see how many forms you can recognize based on what you have learned in this chapter. Note especially the presence (or absence!) of the participle morphemes -κα, -κυια, and -κοτ.

---

3. See William D. Mounce, *Morphology of Biblical Greek*, 151–57.
4. Although we are not considering separate paradigms for second perfect forms, it should be noted that some participles have a modified participle morpheme, namely, -οτ (e.g., γεγονώς, -ότος or ἐληλυθώς, -ότος).

PERIPHRASIS

So far, we have seen that there are three main participle functions: attributive, substantival, and adverbial. We will now look at another type of adverbial participle. **Periphrasis** involves a circumlocution of, or "going around," one form with another (often longer) construction. A periphrastic participle is an adverbial (hence anarthrous) participle that is constructed with a form of εἰμί (or sometimes ὑπάρχω) that results in a construction that functions parallel to a finite verb. This is a common construction in the GNT. In the following examples, the form of εἰμί and the participle are italicized.

> ἐστὲ ἐν αὐτῷ πεπληρωμένοι (Col 2:10)
> In him *you have been made complete.*

An indicative form of εἰμί in a periphrastic construction with a perfect participle parallels the function of a perfect indicative and could easily be replaced with the indicative form. For example, in Colossians 2:10 Paul could have used πεπλήρωσθε instead of the construction ἐστὲ πεπληρωμένοι, and it would have conveyed the same idea. Notice that the corresponding finite verb (πεπλήρωσθε; a perfect passive indicative second-person plural) has the same mood (indicative), person (second), and number (plural) as the form of εἰμί (which is ἐστέ in Col 2:10), and the same tense-form (perfect) and voice (passive) as the periphrastic participle (πεπληρωμένοι).

Periphrasis occurs frequently with present and perfect participles (and only very rarely with aorist participles), but can occur with any form of εἰμί, such as a present, imperfect, or future indicative form of εἰμί, a subjunctive form of εἰμί (which we will learn about in a future chapter), or even a participle of εἰμί. The most common combination in the GNT is an imperfect form of εἰμί and a present participle, as in the example from Matthew 7:29 (see below). No consensus exists regarding the function of periphrastic participles. Some verbs require a periphrastic construction for the third-person plural perfect passive.[5] But in other instances, periphrasis is not required. This could be a matter of an individ-

---

5. Some of the morphological processes that occur with the perfect middle/passive indicative forms when the primary middle endings are added directly to the end of the perfect middle tense stem can result in complex verbal forms. Apparently even Greeks felt that some of these resulting forms were a bit unwieldy and better avoided, particularly those involving the -ντ of the third-person personal ending. Periphrasis was thus the "way around" this problem, with the result that a combination of εἰμί and a perfect participle was preferred over the corresponding indicative form. For more, see Porter, Reed, and O'Donnell, *Fundamentals of New Testament Greek*, 348–51.

ual author's style or perhaps a means of expressing emphasis. In general, however, a periphrastic construction is not exegetically significant.

Periphrastic participles are nearly always in the nominative case and follow the main verb. Here are a few more examples of periphrastic participles from the GNT:

τοῦ εὐαγγελίου . . . ἐστὶν καρποφορούμενον καὶ αὐξανόμενον (Col 1:5–6)
The gospel . . . *is bearing fruit* and *multiplying.*

ἦν γὰρ διδάσκων αὐτούς (Matt 7:29)
For *he was teaching* them.

MORE ABOUT ADVERBIAL TEMPORAL PARTICIPLES

Although there is debate as to whether Koine Greek indicative forms indicate time, there is virtual agreement that time is not a semantic feature of participles (or any other nonindicative form). At times, however, participles may indicate *relative time* with respect to a main verb. We have already seen that a present temporal participle may communicate an event that is contemporaneous to the action of the main verb, and that an aorist temporal participle may communicate an event that is antecedent to the action of the main verb. In a similar way, a perfect temporal participle may communicate an event that is subsequent to the action of the main verb. For example:

ἔρχεται ὁ Ἰησοῦς τῶν θυρῶν κεκλεισμένων καὶ ἔστη εἰς τὸ μέσον
(John 20:26)
Jesus came, *after the doors had been locked*, and stood among them.

REVIEW OF CHAPTER 17

In this chapter we learned the forms of the perfect participle, which uses reduplication and the participle morpheme -κοτ in the active forms, but not the middle ones. Like other participles, the perfect participle uses a 3-1-3 declension pattern for the active forms and a 2-1-2 declension pattern for the middle forms. We also introduced periphrasis, which is a "round about" construction that uses a form of εἰμί and a participle to form a construction that is basically parallel to a corresponding indicative-only form. Finally, we learned about temporal adverbial participles, specifically their "relative time" regarding the main verb on which they depend.

Study Guide for Chapter 17

1. Be able to understand each of the following concepts and forms:
   tense formatives
   participle morphemes
   periphrasis
2. Be able to parse perfect participle forms, recognize periphrastic constructions, and translate basic Koine sentences that incorporate forms and concepts from previous chapters.

Vocabulary to Memorize

ἀκοή, -ης, ἡ	report, hearing (24)
ἀνάγω	I lead up, I bring up; I set sail (mid or pass) (23)
ἀναιρέω	I take away, I do away with, I kill (24)
ἄρτι	now, at once, immediately (36)
ἀσθένεια, -ας, ἡ	weakness, sickness (24)
ἀστήρ, -έρος, ὁ	star (24)
βασιλεύω	I reign, I rule, I become king (21)
γνωρίζω	I make known, I know (25)
δοκιμάζω	I put to the test, I examine, I prove by testing, I approve (22)
δουλεύω	I am a slave, I serve (25)
δῶρον, -ου, τό	gift, offering (19)
εἰσπορεύομαι	I go, I come in, I enter (18)
ἕνεκα, ἕνεκεν (+gen)	because of, on account of (impr prep) (26)
ἐπιθυμία, -ας, ἡ	desire, longing, lust, passion (38)
θεάομαι	I look at, I see, I behold (22)
καθαρός, -ά, -όν	clean, pure (27)
κρίμα, -ατος, τό	judgment, verdict, condemnation (27)
Μαρία, -ας, ἡ	Mary (27)
μήτε	and not, nor (34)
νοῦς, νοός, ὁ	mind, understanding, thought (24)
παραγγέλλω	I give orders, I command, I instruct (32)
ποῖος, -α, -ον	of what kind? which? what? (33)

(cont.)

ποτέ	at some time, once, formerly, ever (29)
προσέχω	I pay attention to, I devote myself to (24)
σταυρός, -οῦ, ὁ	cross (27)

Principal Parts to Memorize

These are the principal parts that you need to memorize for chapter 17. Some of the verbs assigned for this chapter have been previously assigned, so you will need to add the fourth and fifth principal parts to these verbs. The full "Principal Parts Chart" is in appendix 14.

1st prin part	2nd prin part	3rd prin part	4th prin part	5th prin part	6th prin part
γίνομαι	γενήσομαι	ἐγενόμην	γέγονα	γεγένημαι	ἐγενήθην
γράφω	γράψω	ἔγραψα	γέγραφα	γέγραμμαι	ἐγράφην
διδάσκω	διδάξω	ἐδίδαξα	n/a	n/a	ἐδιδάχθην
κηρύσσω	n/a	ἐκήρυξα	n/a	κεκήρυγμαι	ἐκηρύχθην
λέγω	ἐρῶ	εἶπον	εἴρηκα	εἴρημαι	ἐρρέθην
σῴζω	σώσω	ἔσωσα	σέσωκα	σέσῳσμαι	ἐσώθην

Paradigms to Memorize

The following paradigms should be memorized for chapter 17: the perfect active and middle participle of λύω.

PERFECT ACTIVE PARTICIPLE FOR λύω

	masc (3)	fem (1)	neut (3)
nom sg	λελυκώς	λελυκυῖα	λελυκός
gen sg	λελυκότος	λελυκυίας	λελυκότος
dat sg	λελυκότι	λελυκυίᾳ	λελυκότι
acc sg	λελυκότα	λελυκυῖαν	λελυκός
nom pl	λελυκότες	λελυκυῖαι	λελυκότα
gen pl	λελυκότων	λελυκυιῶν	λελυκότων
dat pl	λελυκόσι(ν)	λελυκυίαις	λελυκόσι(ν)
acc pl	λελυκότας	λελυκυίας	λελυκότα

PERFECT MIDDLE PARTICIPLE FOR λύω

	masc (2)	fem (1)	neut (2)
nom sg	λελυμένος	λελυμένη	λελυμένον
gen sg	λελυμένου	λελυμένης	λελυμένου
dat sg	λελυμένῳ	λελυμένῃ	λελυμένῳ
acc sg	λελυμένον	λελυμένην	λελυμένον
nom pl	λελυμένοι	λελυμέναι	λελυμένα
gen pl	λελυμένων	λελυμένων	λελυμένων
dat pl	λελυμένοις	λελυμέναις	λελυμένοις
acc pl	λελυμένους	λελυμένας	λελυμένα

chapter EIGHTEEN

CONTRACT VERBS

OBJECTIVES AND OVERVIEW

Chapter 18 introduces the following linguistic concepts, morphemes, and paradigms:

- vowel-contraction rules
- verb stem ending in α, present and imperfect active and middle indicative paradigms
- verb stem ending in ε, present and imperfect active and middle indicative paradigms
- verb stem ending in o, present and imperfect active and middle indicative paradigms
- stem-vowel lengthening before tense formatives

INITIAL CONCEPTS

So far, we have considered verbs whose stems end in consonants or an upsilon. As we have noted previously, an upsilon—whether alone (e.g., λύω) or as the second vowel of a diphthong (e.g., ἀκούω)—acts more like a consonant in some contexts.[1] For example, an upsilon and a connecting vowel do not contract or lengthen as is true with other vowels. Additionally, a sigma between a stem that ends in an upsilon and a connecting vowel (i.e., an intervocalic sigma) does not drop out as it does with other vowels. In this chapter, we will look at verb stems that end in an alpha, epsilon, or omicron. When connecting vowels (an epsilon or omicron) are added to any of these vowels, they contract according to predictable patterns. Hence, such verbs are called **contract verbs**.

Contract verbs are considered regular verbs because the individual tense stems

---

1. In fact, this "behavior" actually reflects the presence of a consonant, the digamma ϝ, that had dropped out of Greek by the Koine period. You don't need to remember this, but it is helpful to know that there is a reason why an upsilon acts more like a consonant in various contexts.

are identical to the verbal root. Consequently, contract verbs are classified as first aorist and use tense formatives in their aorist forms. They also use tense formatives in the perfect and pluperfect active tense forms. This means that vowel contraction only takes place with the present stem and those forms that are built using the present or imperfect stem (including *all* present tense-forms, such as participles and other nonindicative forms, and all forms of the imperfect indicative). Although vowel contraction does not take place when a tense formative is used (i.e., forms other than present or imperfect tense-forms), contract verbs still want to stand out from other verbs, so they lengthen their final stem vowel before tense formatives, which we discuss below. We begin by looking at the patterns of vowel contractions that occur when the final vowel of a contract-verb stem combines with a connecting vowel. We then look at several representative present and imperfect indicative paradigms of contract verbs, as well as representative present participle examples.

There is no difference in the *semantic* function of contract verbs. Thus, everything that we have discussed about the aspect and functions of the present, imperfect, aorist, perfect, or pluperfect indicative or about the functions of participles applies to contract verbs. Contract verbs only differ from other verbs in their *morphology*.

VOWEL CONTRACTION RULES

Vowel contraction for contract verbs only takes place with forms derived from the present tense stem. Because the connecting vowels used for present tense-forms are epsilon and omicron, vowel contraction for contract verbs involves combinations of an alpha, epsilon, or omicron *and* an epsilon or omicron. The following are basic patterns of vowel contraction for verb stems ending in an alpha, epsilon, or omega and a connecting vowel.[2]

α	+ α	→	α (long)	ε	+ ο/ου	→	ου
α	+ ε/η	→	α (long)	ε	+ ω	→	ω
α	+ ει	→	ᾳ (long)	ο	+ ε/ο	→	ου
α	+ ο/ω	→	ω	ο	+ ου	→	ου
α	+ οι/ου	→	ω	ο	+ η/ω	→	ω
ε	+ α	→	η	ο	+ ει/οι	→	οι
ε	+ ε/ει	→	ει				

---

2. This accounts for the most common vowel contractions; to see all possible vowel contractions, see appendix 16, "Vowel Contractions Tables." Less common forms are compiled from Goetchius, *Language of the New Testament*, 136; Porter, Reed, and O'Donnell, *Fundamentals of New Testament Greek*, 7, 172.

If a stem vowel is followed by a diphthong that begins with the same vowel, the stem vowel drops out—as with the present middle/passive indicative second-person singular forms (see below).

Once you are familiar with these equations, it is relatively easy to memorize the assigned paradigms for contract verbs. These paradigms are representative of all the contract verbs that occur in the GNT. In other words, once you have memorized the paradigms for τιμάω, you will be able to recognize forms of all other alpha contract verbs in the GNT. The same is true for ποιέω and πληρόω. Notice especially the circumflex accent over the long vowel or diphthong that results from the vowel contraction—this is a good clue for recognizing contract-verb forms.

LEXICAL FORM: τιμάω[1]

	final form	uncontracted vowels
1 sg	τιμῶ	(αω)
2 sg	τιμᾷς	(αεις)
3 sg	τιμᾷ	(αει)
1 pl	τιμῶμεν	(αομεν)
2 pl	τιμᾶτε	(αετε)
3 pl	τιμῶσι(ν)	(αουσι)

[1] The lexical form for contract verbs is the uncontracted present active indicative first-person singular form. It is important to note, however, that this form will never appear in the NT; instead the contracted forms occur as τιμῶ, ποιῶ, πληρῶ, etc.

LEXICAL FORM: ποιέω

	final form	uncontracted vowels
1 sg	ποιῶ	(εω)
2 sg	ποιεῖς	(εεις)
3 sg	ποιεῖ	(εει)
1 pl	ποιοῦμεν	(εομεν)
2 pl	ποιεῖτε	(εετε)
3 pl	ποιοῦσι(ν)	(εουσι)

LEXICAL FORM: πληρόω

	final form	uncontracted vowels
1 sg	πληρῶ	(οω)
2 sg	πληροῖς	(οεις)
3 sg	πληροῖ	(οει)
1 pl	πληροῦμεν	(οομεν)
2 pl	πληροῦτε	(οετε)
3 pl	πληροῦσι(ν)	(οουσι)

The vowel-contraction equations occur as expected in the middle/passive forms. For example:

1 sg	τιμῶμαι	ποιοῦμαι	πληροῦμαι
2 sg	τιμᾷ	ποιῇ	πληροῖ
3 sg	τιμᾶται	ποιεῖται	πληροῦται
1 pl[1]	τιμώμεθα	ποιούμεθα	πληρούμεθα
2 pl	τιμᾶσθε	ποιεῖσθε	πληροῦσθε
3 pl	τιμῶνται	ποιοῦνται	πληροῦνται

[1] Notice the switch from the circumflex accent that occurs in all the contracted verb forms that we have seen so far to the acute accent in the present middle indicative first-person plural forms. The circumflex indicates that vowel contraction has occurred, but a circumflex cannot appear on the antepenultimate (the third from the last) syllable, so the accent switches to the acute.

The second-person singular forms, however, require a bit more explanation. You do not need to memorize these derivations—you only need to memorize the final form. Consider the following derivations of the present middle/passive indicative second-person singular forms:

	Step 1	Step 2	Step 3	Step 4	Final Form
τιμα + εσαι	→ τιμα + εαι	→ τιμα + αι	→ τιμα + ι	→ ᾳ	→ τιμᾷ
ποιε + εσαι	→ ποιε + εαι	→ ποι + εαι	→ ποι + ηι	→ ῃ	→ ποιῇ
πληρο + εσαι	→ πληρο + εαι	→ πληρο + ει			→ πληροῖ

For all forms, the intervocalic sigma drops out (step 1), which we have seen all along. For alpha contract-verb forms, after the sigma drops out, the alpha and epsilon contract to a long alpha (step 2), then the second alpha drops out (step 3), and the iota subscripts under the long alpha (step 4). For epsilon contract-verb forms, after the sigma drops out (step 1), the first epsilon drops out or "simplifies" (step 2), then the epsilon and alpha contract to an eta (step 3), and the iota subscripts under the long eta (step 4). For omicron contract-verb forms, after the sigma drops out (step 1), the process is a bit more complicated. The alpha apparently drops out (step 2), leaving the omicron and diphthong to contract to the diphthong οι. Most scholars agree that this is an irregular example of vowel contraction.

Vowel contraction also occurs with imperfect indicative forms for contract verbs, because they are built using the present stem. Here are the imperfect active indicatives and imperfect middle passive indicatives of the assigned paradigms:

1 sg	ἐτίμων	ἐποίουν	ἐπλήρουν
2 sg	ἐτίμας	ἐποίεις	ἐπλήρους
3 sg	ἐτίμα	ἐποίει	ἐπλήρου
1 pl	ἐτιμῶμεν	ἐποιοῦμεν	ἐπληροῦμεν
2 pl	ἐτιμᾶτε	ἐποιεῖτε	ἐπληροῦτε
3 pl	ἐτίμων	ἐποίουν	ἐπλήρουν

1 sg	ἐτιμώμην	ἐποιούμην	ἐπληρούμην
2 sg	ἐτιμῶ	ἐποιοῦ	ἐπληροῦ
3 sg	ἐτιμᾶτο	ἐποιεῖτο	ἐπληροῦτο
1 pl	ἐτιμώμεθα	ἐποιούμεθα	ἐπληρούμεθα
2 pl	ἐτιμᾶσθε	ἐποιεῖσθε	ἐπληροῦσθε
3 pl	ἐτιμῶντο	ἐποιοῦτο	ἐπληροῦντο

In the imperfect forms, all middle/passive second-person singular forms follow regular vowel-contraction rules once the intervocalic sigma drops out.

As noted, vowel contraction only occurs with forms that use the present stem. This means that present participles for contract verbs also have vowel contraction. Here are the nominative singular and genitive singular masculine, feminine, and neuter forms of the present participles of the assigned paradigms. These participles follow a 3-1-3 declension pattern in the present active forms, and a 2-1-2 declension pattern (with the participle morpheme -μεν) in the present middle forms.

nom sg	τιμῶν	τιμῶσα	τιμῶν
gen sg	τιμῶντος	τιμώσης	τιμῶντος

nom sg	ποιῶν	ποιοῦσα	ποιοῦν
gen sg	ποιοῦντος	ποιούσης	ποιοῦντος

nom sg	πληρῶν	πληροῦσα	πληροῦν
gen sg	πληροῦντος	πληρούσης	πληροῦντος

Because contract verbs are "regular" verbs, they use tense formatives in the aorist, perfect, and pluperfect tense-forms, as well as the future tense-form.

We will look at the future in the next chapter. Contract verbs lengthen their final vowel before a tense formative, which makes them relatively easy to recognize. For the examples below, only the first-person singular of the aorist, perfect, and pluperfect indicative forms is listed below, but vowel lengthening before a tense formative occurs with nonindicative verb forms, such as participles and other nonindicative forms that will be learned in future chapters.[3] The lengthened stem vowel is set in bold in the examples below. Notice also that vowel lengthening occurs with the perfect and pluperfect middle and passive forms, even when there is no tense formative. Perhaps vowel lengthening was such an ingrained habit for contract verbs that it was hard to break even without a tense formative, but the lengthened stem vowel before the personal endings for the perfect and pluperfect middle and passive forms is important to note.

VOWEL LENGTHENING BEFORE AORIST TENSE FORMATIVES:

ἐτίμ**η**σα, ἐτιμ**η**σάμην, ἐτιμ**ή**θην

ἐπο**ί**ησα, ἐπο**ι**ησάμην, ἐπο**ι**ήθην

ἐπλ**ή**ρωσα, ἐπλ**η**ρωσάμην, ἐπλ**η**ρώθην

VOWEL LENGTHENING BEFORE PERFECT TENSE FORMATIVES:

τετίμ**η**κα, τετίμ**η**μαι

πεπο**ί**ηκα, πεπο**ί**ημαι

πεπλ**ή**ρωκα, πεπλ**ή**ρωμαι

VOWEL LENGTHENING BEFORE PLUPERFECT TENSE FORMATIVES:

ἐτετιμ**ή**κειν, ἐτετιμ**ή**μην

ἐπεπο**ι**ήκειν, ἐπεπο**ι**ήμην

ἐπεπλ**η**ρώκειν, ἐπεπλ**η**ρώμην

REVIEW OF CHAPTER 18

In this chapter we introduced contract verbs, which are a large class of verbs that have stems ending in the vowels α, ε, or ο. When connecting vowels are joined to these stems ending in a vowel in the present and imperfect tense-forms, the vowels contract following a predictable set of vowel-contraction rules. We also learned that contract verbs lengthen their final stem vowel before tense formatives (i.e., in the aorist, perfect, and pluperfect).

---

3. Not all of the forms listed occur in the GNT, so just focus on identifying the lengthened connecting vowel.

Study Guide for Chapter 18

1. Be able to understand each of the following concepts and forms:

   contract-verb forms when vowel contraction occurs with the present stem

   vowel contraction

   vowel lengthening before a tense formative

2. Be able to parse contract-verb forms and translate basic Koine sentences that incorporate forms and concepts from previous chapters.

Vocabulary to Memorize

Here are the vocabulary words to memorize for chapter 18.

ἀγαπάω	I love (143)
ἀδικέω	I wrong, I do wrong, I mistreat (28)
αἰτέω	I ask, I request, I demand (70)
διακονία, -ας, ἡ	service, office, ministry, help (34)
δικαιόω	I justify, I vindicate, I acquit (39)
ἐμβαίνω	I embark, I get into (16)
ἐπερωτάω	I ask, I ask for (56)
ἐρωτάω	I ask, I request (63)
ζητέω	I seek, I look for, I try to obtain (117)
καυχάομαι	I boast (intrans); I boast about (trans)[1] (37)
κοπιάω	I labor, I become weary, I work hard (23)
λαλέω	I speak, I say (296)
λυπέω	I grieve, I offend; I mourn, I become sad (pass) (26)
μαρτυρέω	(+dat) I bear witness, I testify (76)
ὁράω	I see, I notice, I perceive (454)
παρακαλέω	I exhort, I comfort, I encourage, I urge (109)
περιπατέω	I walk, I conduct my life (95)
πληρόω	I fill, I complete, I fulfill (86)
ποιέω	I do, I make (568)
προσκυνέω	(+dat) I worship, I bow down before (60)
σταυρόω	I crucify (46)
τελειόω	I make complete, I make perfect, I fulfill (23)
τηρέω	I keep, I guard, I obey (70)

| τιμάω | I honor, I value (21) |
| φρονέω | I think, I ponder (26) |

[1] Some verbs can be both transitive and intransitive. Their meaning varies accordingly.

Principal Parts to Memorize

These are the principal parts that you need to memorize for chapter 18. Some of the verbs assigned for this chapter have been previously assigned, so you will need to add the fourth and fifth principal parts to these verbs. The full "Principal Parts Chart" is in appendix 14.

1st prin part	2nd prin part	3rd prin part	4th prin part	5th prin part	6th prin part
ἄγω	ἄξω	ἤγαγον	n/a	ἦγμαι	ἤχθην
ἐγείρω	ἐγερῶ	ἤγειρα	n/a	ἐγήγερμαι	ἠγέρθην
εὑρίσκω	εὑρήσω	εὗρον	εὕρηκα	n/a	εὑρέθην
ποιέω[1]	ποιήσω	ἐποίησα	πεποίηκα	πεποίημαι	ἐποιήθην
ὁράω	ὄψομαι	εἶδον	ἑώρακα	n/a	ὤφθην

[1] This verb is representative of contract verbs with verb stems ending in -ε.

Paradigms to Memorize

The following paradigms should be memorized for chapter 18: the present and imperfect indicatives for τιμάω (paradigmatic for all alpha contract verbs), ποιέω (paradigmatic for all epsilon contract verbs), and πληρόω (paradigmatic for all omicron contract verbs).

A-Type Contract-Verb Paradigms

PRESENT ACTIVE INDICATIVE PARADIGM OF τιμάω

1 sg	τιμῶ
2 sg	τιμᾷς
3 sg	τιμᾷ
1 pl	τιμῶμεν
2 pl	τιμᾶτε
3 pl	τιμῶσι(ν)

PRESENT MIDDLE INDICATIVE PARADIGM OF τιμάω

1 sg	τιμῶμαι
2 sg	τιμᾷ
3 sg	τιμᾶται
1 pl	τιμώμεθα
2 pl	τιμᾶσθε
3 pl	τιμῶνται

IMPERFECT ACTIVE INDICATIVE PARADIGM OF τιμάω

1 sg	ἐτίμων
2 sg	ἐτίμας
3 sg	ἐτίμα
1 pl	ἐτιμῶμεν
2 pl	ἐτιμᾶτε
3 pl	ἐτίμων

IMPERFECT MIDDLE INDICATIVE PARADIGM OF τιμάω

1 sg	ἐτιμώμην
2 sg	ἐτιμῶ
3 sg	ἐτιμᾶτο
1 pl	ἐτιμώμεθα
2 pl	ἐτιμᾶσθε
3 pl	ἐτιμῶντο

E-Type Contract-Verb Paradigms

PRESENT ACTIVE INDICATIVE PARADIGM OF ποιέω

1 sg	ποιῶ
2 sg	ποιεῖς
3 sg	ποιεῖ
1 pl	ποιοῦμεν
2 pl	ποιεῖτε
3 pl	ποιοῦσι(ν)

PRESENT MIDDLE INDICATIVE PARADIGM OF ποιέω

1 sg	ποιοῦμαι
2 sg	ποιῇ
3 sg	ποιεῖται
1 pl	ποιούμεθα
2 pl	ποιεῖσθε
3 pl	ποιοῦνται

IMPERFECT ACTIVE INDICATIVE PARADIGM OF ποιέω

1 sg	ἐποίουν
2 sg	ἐποίεις
3 sg	ἐποίει
1 pl	ἐποιοῦμεν
2 pl	ἐποιεῖτε
3 pl	ἐποίουν

IMPERFECT MIDDLE INDICATIVE PARADIGM OF ποιέω

1 sg	ἐποιούμην
2 sg	ἐποιοῦ
3 sg	ἐποιεῖτο
1 pl	ἐποιούμεθα
2 pl	ἐποιεῖσθε
3 pl	ἐποιοῦντο

O-Type Contract-Verb Paradigms

PRESENT ACTIVE INDICATIVE PARADIGM OF πληρόω

1 sg	πληρῶ
2 sg	πληροῖς
3 sg	πληροῖ
1 pl	πληροῦμεν
2 pl	πληροῦτε
3 pl	πληροῦσι(ν)

PRESENT MIDDLE INDICATIVE PARADIGM OF πληρόω

1 sg	πληροῦμαι
2 sg	πληροῖ
3 sg	πληροῦται
1 pl	πληρούμεθα
2 pl	πληροῦσθε
3 pl	πληροῦνται

IMPERFECT ACTIVE INDICATIVE PARADIGM OF πληρόω

1 sg	ἐπλήρουν
2 sg	ἐπλήρους
3 sg	ἐπλήρου
1 pl	ἐπληροῦμεν
2 pl	ἐπληροῦτε
3 pl	ἐπλήρουν

IMPERFECT MIDDLE INDICATIVE PARADIGM OF πληρόω

1 sg	ἐπληρούμην
2 sg	ἐπληροῦ
3 sg	ἐπληροῦτο
1 pl	ἐπληρούμεθα
2 pl	ἐπληροῦσθε
3 pl	ἐπληροῦντο

THE FUTURE INDICATIVE AND PARTICIPLE

OBJECTIVES AND OVERVIEW

Chapter 19 introduces the following linguistic concepts, morphemes, and paradigms:

- future tense formatives
- future active, middle, and passive indicative paradigms
- liquid future active and middle indicative paradigms
- future forms for contract verbs
- future indicative paradigm of εἰμί
- future forms of suppletive verbs
- future active, middle, and passive participle forms
- function of future indicatives and participles

THE FUTURE INDICATIVE

In this chapter, we will learn the final indicative tense-form, the future tense. We will learn a new stem that is used to build the future active and middle tense-forms, which is evident in a verb's second principal part. Greek does some more "recycling" in the future indicative and uses the aorist passive tense stem to form the future passive tense-forms. So, let's return to the tree illustration for one final time and focus on the future tense stem. As you can see, the branch for the aorist passive now twists around and touches the future stem. (Perhaps you've had an actual tree that does similar twists!)

This illustrates that future passive forms use the aorist passive stem, which is visible in a verb's sixth principal part. Below the tree illustration is the summary chart that indicates which tense-forms are constructed from each principal part (indicated in parentheses) that we introduced in chapter 10. You can review that section of chapter 10 if this is still not clear. In this chapter, we will focus on the second and sixth principal parts.

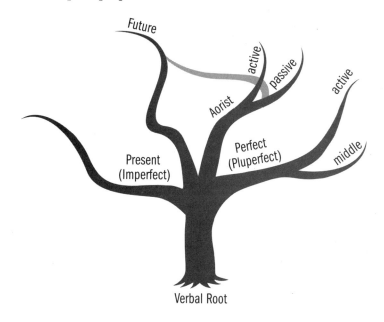

Verbal Root

	active	middle	passive
present		(1)	
imperfect			
future	(2)		(6)
aorist	(3)		
perfect	(4)		(5)
pluperfect			

As with the perfect tense stem, there is much discussion concerning the aspect indicated by the future tense stem. Some claim that the future tense "does not contrast meaningfully with the aorist, present and perfect tense-forms and, to that extent, does not clearly convey verbal aspect." Rather, the future tense indicates "expectation."[1] Others, however, claim that the future tense-form is the *only* place in the Greek verbal system that indicates future *time*, based on the fact that time appears to be an uncancelable feature of every occurrence of the future

---

1. Porter, Reed, and O'Donnell, *Fundamentals of New Testament Greek*, 86.

tense-form in the GNT.[2] At present, it seems best to conclude that the future tense stem indicates future time.

The Forms of the Future Indicative

As far as building a verb goes, future indicative forms are relatively easy. We will start with the future active and middle indicative forms for regular verbs. Like the aorist, the perfect, and the pluperfect tense-forms, the future uses a **tense formative**. For future active and middle forms, this is a sigma. So we can "build" a future active indicative form as follows:

future active tense stem	future active tense formative	connecting vowel	primary active personal ending	inflected form
λυ	+ σ	+ ο	+ μεν	→ λύσομεν

Here is the paradigm for the future active indicative of λύω.

1 sg	λύσω	I will release
2 sg	λύσεις	you (sg) will release
3 sg	λύσει	he/she/it will release
1 pl	λύσομεν	we will release
2 pl	λύσετε	you (pl) will release
3 pl	λύσουσι(ν)	they will release

The future middle indicative is built with essentially the same components, except that it uses primary middle personal endings. Here is the paradigm for the future middle indicative of λύω.

1 sg	λύσομαι	I will release for myself
2 sg	λύσῃ	you (sg) will release for yourself
3 sg	λύσεται	he/she/it will release for him/her/itself
1 pl	λυσόμεθα	we will release for ourselves
2 pl	λύσεσθε	you (pl) will release for yourselves
3 pl	λύσονται	they will release for themselves

The future passive tense formative -θησ is quite distinctive and easy to recognize, especially with regular verbs such as λύω. Here is the paradigm for the future passive indicative of λύω.

---

2. E.g., Campbell, *Basics of Verbal Aspect*, 84–85.

1 sg	λυθήσομαι	I will be released
2 sg	λυθήσῃ	you (sg) will be released
3 sg	λυθήσεται	he/she/it will be released
1 pl	λυθησόμεθα	we will be released
2 pl	λυθήσεσθε	you (pl) will be released
3 pl	λυθήσονται	they will be released

The future passive is built from the sixth principal part. For regular verbs, such as λύω, the aorist passive stem looks the same as all other stems of λύω. But for verbs that have visibly different stems, the future passive often looks quite different from the future active and middle forms. For example, the future active indicative of καλέω is καλέσω, but the future passive indicative is κληθήσομαι.

We have already seen that the addition of a sigma does not occur quietly, morphologically speaking. This is also true with the future tense formative (-σ). The good news is that the same predictable morphological changes that occur when a sigma is added to a consonantal stem for third declension nouns and first aorist indicatives apply with the tense formative -σ in future active and middle tense forms.[3] For example:

βλέπω → βλέψω

συνάγω → συνάξω

There is more good news: the -θησ tense formative in future passive tense-forms is easy to recognize. Consider the following example. The -θησ tense formative stands out clearly.

οὐκ ἐγὼ ἐξουσιασθήσομαι ὑπό τινος (1 Cor 6:12)
I will not be mastered by anything.

Many future passives are either contract verbs (which lengthen the connecting vowel before the -θησ tense formative) or are second future passives, which use the tense formative -ησ. Even with this shortened tense formative, it is still relatively easy to recognize future passive forms; for example:

3. You can review these changes with the chart in appendix 4, "Changes to a Stem When a Sigma, Theta, Tau, or Mu Is Added."

ἀνοιγήσεται ὑμῖν (Matt 7:7)
It will be opened to you.

The Future Forms of Liquid Verbs

Recall that liquid verbs have stems ending in a liquid (λ, ρ) or nasal (μ, ν) and are considered as a group with regard to certain morphological processes. For the future active and middle tense-forms of these verbs, an epsilon is added to the tense formative -σ, since adding a sigma to any of these consonants would result in forms that Greek tended to avoid. Thus, the tense formative is -εσ, which causes the intervocalic sigma to drop out, and the epsilon to contract with the connecting vowel. These vowel contractions reflect the same patterns that we observed with contract verbs (see chapter 18). So, for example, consider the formation of the future active indicative first-person plural for κρίνω:

$$\text{κριν} + \text{εσ} + \text{ο} + \text{μεν} \;\rightarrow\; \text{κριν} + \text{ε}\,\cancel{\sigma} + \text{ο} + \text{μεν} \;\rightarrow\; \text{κριν} + \text{ου} + \text{μεν} \;\rightarrow\; \text{κρινοῦμεν}$$

It is very important to distinguish between present indicative *contract* verbs and future *liquid* verbs, because both forms have vowel contraction that is indicated by a circumflex accent. Here are the paradigms of the liquid future active and middle indicative forms for κρίνω. The *present* paradigm for ποιέω is listed in gray for comparison.

FUTURE ACTIVE INDICATIVE OF κρίνω

1 sg	κρινῶ	I will judge	ποιῶ
2 sg	κρινεῖς	you (sg) will judge	ποιεῖς
3 sg	κρινεῖ	he/she/it will judge	ποιεῖ
1 pl	κρινοῦμεν	we will judge	ποιοῦμεν
2 pl	κρινεῖτε	you (pl) will judge	ποιεῖτε
3 pl	κρινοῦσι(ν)	they will judge	ποιοῦσι(ν)

FUTURE MIDDLE INDICATIVE OF κρίνω

1 sg	κρινοῦμαι	I will judge for myself	ποιοῦμαι
2 sg	κρινῇ	you (sg) will judge for yourself	ποιῇ
3 sg	κρινεῖται	he/she/it will judge for his/her/itself	ποιεῖται
1 pl	κρινούμεθα	we will judge for ourselves	ποιούμεθα
2 pl	κρινεῖσθε	you (pl) will judge for yourselves	ποιεῖσθε
3 pl	κρινοῦνται	they will judge for themselves	ποιοῦνται

Generally speaking, a long vowel or diphthong with a circumflex that is preceded by a liquid consonant (in this instance a nu) indicates a liquid future, but this is not always the case. For example, the *present* active indicative third-person singular of ἀσθενέω is ἀσθενεῖ. Ultimately, determining whether a form is a present contract or a liquid future depends on knowing the lexical form of the verb, which clearly distinguishes these two types of verbs.

The Future Forms of Contract Verbs

As we saw in chapter 18, contract verbs lengthen their stem vowel before tense formatives. We saw that with aorist, perfect, and pluperfect forms of contract verbs, the final alpha or epsilon of a contract verb stem lengthens to an eta, and the final omicron of a contract-verb stem lengthens to an omega. The same is true for the future tense-forms for contract verbs. For example, the future indicative first-person singular for the assigned paradigm verbs from chapter 18 are as follows:[4]

future active	future middle	future passive
τιμήσω	τιμήσομαι	τιμηθήσομαι
ποιήσω	ποιήσομαι	ποιηθήσομαι
πληρώσω	πληρώσομαι	πληρωθήσομαι

The Future of εἰμί

The future indicative paradigm of εἰμί is as follows and must be memorized exactly. As we have seen with other indicative forms of εἰμί, voice does not apply to this equative, intransitive verb.

1 sg	ἔσομαι	I will be
2 sg	ἔσῃ	you (sg) will be
3 sg	ἔσται	he/she/it will be
1 pl	ἐσόμεθα	we will be
2 pl	ἔσεσθε	you (pl) will be
3 pl	ἔσονται	they will be

---

4. Not all of these forms occur in the GNT, so just focus on recognizing the lengthened stem vowel before the tense formative.

Other Future Forms

Finally, there are some verbs whose future forms must be memorized as principal parts. There is no way to derive the future for these forms, because the future tense-form comes from another verb altogether. Recall that these are called suppletive verbs. For example:

ἔρχομαι	→	ἐλεύσομαι
ἐσθίω	→	φάγομαι
λέγω	→	ἐρῶ
οἶδα	→	εἰδήσω
ὁράω	→	ὄψομαι
φέρω	→	οἴσω

There are also several other patterns for future stems, which you can learn more about in the chart in appendix 10, "More on Verbal Roots," if you are curious. None of the patterns needs to be memorized, but it helpful to see the patterns so that you can recognize them in the GNT.

THE FORMS OF FUTURE PARTICIPLES

There are only twelve future participles in the GNT.[5] It is unnecessary to memorize the paradigms, as the forms are easily recognized and are built as follows:[6]

future active tense stem	future active tense formative	connecting vowel	participle morpheme	case ending	inflected form
λυ	+ σ	+ ο	+ ντ	+ ος	→ λύσοντος

future active tense stem	future active tense formative	connecting vowel	participle morpheme	case ending	inflected form
λυ	+ σ	+ ο	+ μεν	+ ου	→ λυσομένου

future active tense stem	future passive tense formative	connecting vowel	participle morpheme	case ending	inflected form
λυ	+ θησ	+ ο	+ μεν	+ ου	→ λυθησομένου

---

5. Actually, there may be thirteen; because accents did not appear in the original NT manuscripts, it is unclear if the form κατακρινῶν in Rom 8:34 should be understood as a future active participle or a present active participle.

6. You can see the full paradigms at the end of this chapter.

The future active participle is the more common form, occurring nine times in the GNT. The future middle participle occurs in Luke 22:49 and 1 Corinthians 15:37; the future passive participle only occurs in Hebrews 3:5.

THE FUNCTIONS OF THE FUTURE INDICATIVE AND PARTICIPLE

In keeping with the likelihood that the future tense-form indicates future time, it is not surprising that one of the main functions of the future tense-form is to indicate an action that has yet to occur. This is sometimes called the **predictive future**. For example:

πολλοὶ *ἐροῦσίν* μοι ἐν ἐκείνῃ τῇ ἡμέρᾳ, Κύριε κύριε . . . (Matt 7:22)
Many *will say* to me on that day, "Lord, Lord . . ."

ὁ δὲ παράκλητος, τὸ πνεῦμα τὸ ἅγιον, ὃ *πέμψει* ὁ πατὴρ ἐν τῷ ὀνόματί μου, ἐκεῖνος ὑμᾶς *διδάξει* πάντα (John 14:26)
But the Paraclete, the Holy Spirit, whom the Father *will send* in my name, that one *will teach* you all things.

καὶ *καλέσεις* τὸ ὄνομα αὐτοῦ Ἰησοῦν (Matt 1:21)
And *you will call* his name Jesus.

Sometimes, especially with OT quotations, the future tense-form indicates a command, or a **volitional** or **imperatival** function. The citation in 1 Peter 1:16 is adapted from Leviticus 19:2.

ἅγιοι *ἔσεσθε*, ὅτι ἐγὼ ἅγιος (1 Pet 1:16)
Be holy, because I am holy.

Many of the future participles in the GNT indicate purpose (and are often translated as purpose infinitives in English); for example:

ἀνέβην *προσκυνήσων* εἰς Ἰερουσαλήμ (Acts 24:11)
I went up to Jerusalem *to worship*.

REVIEW OF CHAPTER 19

In this chapter we introduced the final tense stem, the future (the second principal part). We learned the forms of the future indicative and participle. For most future active and middle verbs, this involves the use of the tense formative -σ, although liquid futures use the modified tense formative -εσ. As we have seen elsewhere, contract verbs lengthen the final vowel of their stem before a tense formative. We learned that the future passive is built from the sixth principal part, which is also used to construct the aorist passive. The function of the future indicative is often predictive or sometimes imperatival, whereas the future participle often indicates purpose.

Study Guide for Chapter 19

1. Be able to understand each of the following concepts and forms:

    tense formative for the future indicative and participle and for liquid verbs

    lengthening of final stem vowel before tense formatives with contract verbs

    predictive function of the future tense stem

    volitional or imperatival function of the future tense stem

2. Be able to parse future tense verb forms and translate basic Koine sentences that incorporate forms and concepts from previous chapters.

Vocabulary to Memorize

γεννάω	I beget, I father, I give birth, I produce (97)
δεύτερος, -α, -ον	second, secondly (43)
ἐπιτιμάω	(+dat) I rebuke, I reprove, I warn, I punish (29)
ζάω	I live, I remain alive (140)
κατακρίνω	I condemn, I pass judgment on (18)
κατοικέω	I live, I dwell, I reside (44)
κρίσις, -εως, ἡ	judgment, condemnation (47)
λοιπός, -ή, -όν	remaining, the rest (subst); finally, henceforth (adv) (55)
μεριμνάω	I worry, I am anxious, I care for (19)
μετανοέω	I repent, I change my mind (34)
ὅμοιος, -α, -ον	like, similar (+dat = to someone, something) (45)
ὁμολογέω	I confess, I admit, I declare (26)
οὐκέτι	no longer (47)
οὐχί	not, no (54)
πάντοτε	always, at all times (41)
πλανάω	I lead astray, I mislead, I deceive; I go astray (mid) (39)

πλούσιος, -α, -ον	rich, wealthy (28)
πτωχός, -ή, -όν	poor, miserable (34)
ῥῆμα, -ατος, τό	word, utterance, saying, matter (68)
στόμα, -ματος, τό	mouth (78)
τελέω	I finish, I complete, I fulfill, I accomplish (28)
τίκτω	I bear, I give birth (18)
φιλέω	I love, I like, I kiss (25)
φοβέω	I scare, I am afraid, I fear (pass) (95)
φῶς, φωτός, τό	light (73)

Principal Parts to Memorize

These are the principal parts that you need to memorize for chapter 19. Beginning with this chapter, you will need to memorize all six parts for each assigned verb. Some of the verbs assigned for this chapter have been previously assigned, so you will now need to add the second principal part to these verbs. The full "Principal Parts Chart" is in appendix 14, or you can refer to the grayed out sections of previously assigned principal parts in earlier chapters.

1st prin part	2nd prin part	3rd prin part	4th prin part	5th prin part	6th prin part
γίνομαι	γενήσομαι	ἐγενόμην	γέγονα	γεγένημαι	ἐγενήθην
ἐγείρω	ἐγερῶ	ἤγειρα	n/a	ἐγήγερμαι	ἠγέρθην
ἔρχομαι	ἐλεύσομαι	ἦλθον	ἐλήλυθα	n/a	n/a
κρίνω[1]	κρινῶ	ἔκρινα	κέκρικα	κέκριμαι	ἐκρίθην
λαμβάνω	λήμψομαι	ἔλαβον	εἴληφα	εἴλημμαι	ἐλήμφθην
λέγω	ἐρῶ	εἶπον	εἴρηκα	εἴρημαι	ἐρρέθην

[1] This verb is representative of liquid verbs.

Paradigms to Memorize

The following paradigms should be memorized for chapter 19: the future active, middle, and passive indicative for λύω; the future indicative for εἰμί; and the future active and middle indicative for κρίνω. We have also listed the future active, middle, and passive participle for λύω for reference, but you do not need to memorize these forms.

FUTURE ACTIVE INDICATIVE OF λύω

1 sg	λύσω
2 sg	λύσεις
3 sg	λύσει
1 pl	λύσομεν
2 pl	λύσετε
3 pl	λύσουσι(ν)

FUTURE MIDDLE INDICATIVE OF λύω

1 sg	λύσομαι
2 sg	λύση
3 sg	λύσεται
1 pl	λυσόμεθα
2 pl	λύσεσθε
3 pl	λύσονται

FUTURE PASSIVE INDICATIVE PARADIGM OF λύω

1 sg	λυθήσομαι
2 sg	λυθήση
3 sg	λυθήσεται
1 pl	λυθησόμεθα
2 pl	λυθήσεσθε
3 pl	λυθήσονται

FUTURE INDICATIVE OF εἰμί

1 sg	ἔσομαι
2 sg	ἔση
3 sg	ἔσται
1 pl	ἐσόμεθα
2 pl	ἔσεσθε
3 pl	ἔσονται

FUTURE ACTIVE INDICATIVE OF κρίνω

1 sg	κρινῶ
2 sg	κρινεῖς
3 sg	κρινεῖ
1 pl	κρινοῦμεν
2 pl	κρινεῖτε
3 pl	κρινοῦσι(ν)

FUTURE MIDDLE INDICATIVE OF κρίνω

1 sg	κρινοῦμαι
2 sg	κρινῇ
3 sg	κρινεῖται
1 pl	κρινούμεθα
2 pl	κρινεῖσθε
3 pl	κρινοῦνται

Paradigms to Recognize but Not Memorize

FUTURE ACTIVE PARTICIPLE OF λύω

	masc (3)	fem (1)	neut (3)
nom sg	λύσων	λύσουσα	λῦσον
gen sg	λύσοντος	λυσούσης	λύσοντος
dat sg	λύσοντι	λυσούσῃ	λύσοντι
acc sg	λύσοντα	λύσουσαν	λῦσον

nom pl	λύσοντες	λύσουσαι	λύσοντα
gen pl	λυσόντων	λυσουσῶν	λυσόντων
dat pl	λύσουσι(ν)	λυσούσαις	λύσουσι(ν)
acc pl	λύσοντας	λυσούσας	λύσοντα

FUTURE MIDDLE PARTICIPLE OF λύω

	masc (2)	fem (1)	neut (2)
nom sg	λυσόμενος	λυσομένη	λυσόμενον
gen sg	λυσομένου	λυσομένης	λυσομένου
dat sg	λυσομένῳ	λυσομένῃ	λυσομένῳ
acc sg	λυσόμενον	λυσομένην	λυσόμενον
nom pl	λυσόμενοι	λυσόμεναι	λυσόμενα
gen pl	λυσομένων	λυσομένων	λυσομένων
dat pl	λυσομένοις	λυσομέναις	λυσομένοις
acc pl	λυσομένους	λυσομένας	λυσόμενα

FUTURE PASSIVE PARTICIPLE OF λύω

	masc (2)	fem (1)	neut (2)
nom sg	λυθησόμενος	λυθησομένη	λυθησόμενον
gen sg	λυθησομένου	λυθησομένης	λυθησομένου
dat sg	λυθησομένῳ	λυθησομένῃ	λυθησομένῳ
acc sg	λυθησόμενον	λυθησομένην	λυθησόμενον
nom pl	λυθησόμενοι	λυθησόμεναι	λυθησόμενα
gen pl	λυθησομένων	λυθησομένων	λυθησομένων
dat pl	λυθησομένοις	λυθησομέναις	λυθησομένοις
acc pl	λυθησομένους	λυθησομένας	λυθησόμενα

chapter TWENTY

ETCETERAS: *Fine-Tuning* εἰμί *and* γίνομαι; More on Conjunctions

OBJECTIVES AND OVERVIEW

Chapter 20 develops some previously introduced concepts or forms and presents a few new concepts. The main focus of this chapter, however, is on integrating what you have learned from chapters 15–19.

Chapter 20 covers the following linguistic concepts, morphemes, and paradigms:

- preparatory use of "there" and "it" and impersonal verbs
- uses of γίνομαι
- correlative conjunctions and καί compounds
- object complements

PREPARATORY USE OF *THERE* AND *IT* WITH εἰμί AND IMPERSONAL VERBS

In English, the pronoun *there* or the personal pronoun *it* can be used as the subject of a sentence with no real referential value or actual antecedent. For example, "there is great joy in obedience" or "it is lawful." This is sometimes referred to as the "preparatory use" of *there* or *it*, because they point forward to the subject that will be discussed.[1] This has parallels in Greek. For example:

μείζων τούτων ἄλλη ἐντολὴ οὐκ ἔστιν (Mark 12:31)
There is no other command greater than this one.

---

1. Cf. Mounce, *Basics of Biblical Greek*, 234.

καλόν ἐστιν ἡμᾶς ὧδε εἶναι (Mark 9:5)
It is good for us to be here.

This usage must be inferred from the overall context. In Greek, this often occurs with impersonal verbs, such as δεῖ ("it is necessary") or ἔξεστιν ("it is lawful"). As we will see in a later chapter, these verbs are often followed by an infinitive.

USES OF γίνομαι

So far, we have mainly been translating γίνομαι as "I become," but this is a very flexible verb with a wide semantic range. It is probably too much to say that γίνομαι can mean practically whatever one would want it to mean, but it is not too much of an exaggeration either! It can often indicate that something happened or appeared, especially the aorist indicative third-person singular ἐγένετο. For example:

καὶ ἐγένετο φωνὴ ἐκ τῆς νεφέλης (Mark 9:7)
And a voice came from the cloud.

The phrases καὶ ἐγένετο or ἐγένετο δέ are quite common in narrative and may reflect a Hebrew idiom. It is possible that this construction, especially in Luke's writings, was intended to reflect the style of the Septuagint. Older English translations often translate these expressions as "it came to pass," but they can more simply be translated as "it happened that," or in some contexts just be left untranslated.

Ἐγένετο δὲ ἐν ταῖς ἡμέραις ἐκείναις ἐξῆλθεν δόγμα παρὰ Καίσαρος
Αὐγούστου . . . (Luke 2:1)
And [it happened that] in those days, a decree went out from Caesar
Augustus . . .

Finally, γίνομαι can function parallel to εἰμί. For example:

μὴ γίνεσθε ὡς οἱ ὑποκριταί (Matt 6:16)
Do not be like the hypocrites.

CORRELATIVE CONJUNCTIONS AND καί COMPOUNDS

Some conjunctions often occur in pairs and indicate the correspondence between two or more units, as for example the English conjunctions, "either . . .

or," "both . . . and," or "not only . . . but also." One of the most common such pairs in Greek is μέν . . . δέ. Both conjunctions (which are sometimes called particles[2]) are *postpositive*, which means that neither will occur as the first word of a clause. This pair can sometimes be rendered "on the one hand . . . on the other hand," although this is often an overtranslation. The pair is often better and simply rendered as "and" or "but"; often the μέν is better left untranslated.

> Ὁ μὲν θερισμὸς πολύς, οἱ δὲ ἐργάται ὀλίγοι (Matt 9:37)
> [On the one hand] the harvest is great, but [on the other hand] the workers are few.

Another correlative is τέ . . . καί, which often can be rendered "both . . . and" or "as well as." For example:

> ὅ τε γὰρ ἁγιάζων καὶ οἱ ἁγιαζόμενοι ἐξ ἑνὸς πάντες (Heb 2:11)
> For both the one who sanctifies and those who are sanctified are all from the same source.

Notice also that τέ is enclitic, meaning that it "throws" its accent back onto the previous word; in Hebrews 2:11 the accent from τέ is thrown back onto the article.

Another common construction is οὐ μόνον . . . ἀλλὰ καί, which can be translated "not only . . . but also." For example:

> οὐ μόνον ἔλυεν τὸ σάββατον, ἀλλὰ καὶ πατέρα ἴδιον ἔλεγεν τὸν θεὸν (John 5:18)
> Not only was he breaking the Sabbath, but he was also saying that God was his own Father.

Another common combination is οἱ μέν . . . ἄλλοι δέ or οἱ δέ, which can be translated as "some . . . but others . . ." For example:

---

2. A *particle* is generally understood to be a small, indeclinable word, such as μέν, δέ, τέ, ἄν, etc. This is a rather ambiguous term and often functions as a catch-all category, into which some grammars lump conjunctions, prepositions, negative adverbs, etc. As far as possible, we try to identify words by their precise part of speech.

οἱ μὲν ἔλεγον ὅτι Ἀγαθός ἐστιν, ἄλλοι [δὲ] ἔλεγον, Οὔ, ἀλλὰ πλανᾷ τὸν ὄχλον (John 7:12)
Some were saying, "He is a good man," but others were saying, "No, [but] he deceives the crowd."

οἱ μὲν ἦσαν σὺν τοῖς Ἰουδαίοις, οἱ δὲ σὺν τοῖς ἀποστόλοις (Acts 14:4)
Some were with the Jews, but others, with the apostles.

Finally, the conjunction καί can combine with a word that begins with a vowel to form a new compound. This is called *crasis*. In the examples below, notice that the smooth breathing mark is retained in these forms.

κἀγώ	from καὶ ἐγώ	and I
κἀκεῖ	from καὶ ἐκεῖ	and there
κἀκεῖθεν	from καὶ ἐκεῖθεν	and from there
κἀκεῖνος	from καὶ ἐκεῖνος	and that one, and he
κἄν	from καὶ ἐάν or ἄν	and if

OBJECT COMPLEMENTS

Some verbs can take two accusative-case objects. Often the first accusative is the direct object of the verb, and the second accusative completes or makes a predication about the action involving the first accusative. This second substantive is called an **object complement**, which is a noun, pronoun, or adjective in the accusative case that is a predicate that describes or designates the direct object of a verb. This is also sometimes referred to as a *double accusative*. The action may involve designating a person something or making an object something else. For example, in the sentence "he called the twelve," "the twelve" is the direct object of the verb "called." Now, consider the sentence "he called the twelve apostles." The noun "apostles" designates *what* the twelve are called.

Not all verbs can have an object complement. This usage frequently occurs with verbs involving teaching, anointing, inquiring, and asking, but such verbs may also occur with only one object. The following verbs often have object complements: καλέω, διδάσκω, αἰτέω, ἐρωτάω, ποιέω, ἐνδύω, ἐκδύω, ὀνομάζω. Consider the following examples (the object complement is italicized):

οὐκέτι λέγω ὑμᾶς δούλους (John 15:15)
No longer do I call you *slaves*.

οὐκ ἐπαισχύνεται ἀδελφοὺς αὐτοὺς καλεῖν (Hebrews 2:11)
He is not ashamed to call them *brothers and sisters*.

Sometimes the object complement further specifies an action performed when the first accusative concerns a person or group. For example:

ἐδίδασκεν αὐτοὺς ἐν παραβολαῖς *πολλά* (Mark 4:2)
He taught them *many things* in parables.

ἐκεῖνος ὑμᾶς διδάξει *πάντα* (John 14:26)
He will teach you *all things*.

In passive constructions, the object of the verb occurs in the nominative, as does the object complement. Consider the following:

Ὁ οἶκός μου *οἶκος προσευχῆς* κληθήσεται (Matt 21:13)
My house will be called *a house of prayer*.

If this clause were to be rewritten as an active construction, we would have the following:[3]

καλέσουσιν τὸν οἶκόν μου *οἶκον προσευχῆς*.
They will call my house *a house of prayer*.

γίνομαι, γινώσκω, γεννάω—HOW TO KEEP THEM STRAIGHT

There are several verb forms that students often have trouble keeping straight: γίνομαι, γινώσκω, and γεννάω. Here are some hints to help:

- The consonant cluster γν only occurs with γινώσκω, so whenever you see a gamma followed immediately by a nu, it can *only* be a form of γινώσκω.
- The stem γεν- *only* occurs with γίνομαι, so anytime you see γεν- with only *one* nu it must be from γίνομαι.
- Any form of γεννάω always has *two* nus, so anytime that you see γενν- it must be from γεννάω. (This is another example of the importance of being able to count to at least two for learning Greek!)

---

3. Goetchius, *Language of the New Testament*, 145.

PRINCIPAL PARTS TO MEMORIZE

Although we take a break from vocabulary and paradigms in these integration chapters, the march for prinicipal parts must go on! These are the principal parts that you need to memorize for chapter 20. Some of the verbs assigned for this chapter have been previously assigned, so you will now need to ensure that all principal parts are included for previously assigned verbs. The full "Principal Parts Chart" is in appendix 14.

1st prin part	2nd prin part	3rd prin part	4th prin part	5th prin part	6th prin part
ἄγω	ἄξω	ἤγαγον	n/a	ἦγμαι	ἤχθην
διδάσκω	διδάξω	ἐδίδαξα	n/a	n/a	ἐδιδάχθην
εὑρίσκω	εὑρήσω	εὗρον	εὕρηκα	n/a	εὑρέθην
κηρύσσω	n/a	ἐκήρυξα	n/a	κεκήρυγμαι	ἐκηρύχθην
λύω	λύσω	ἔλυσα	λέλυκα	λέλυμαι	ἐλυθην
ποιέω[1]	ποιήσω	ἐποίησα	πεποίηκα	πεποίημαι	ἐποιήθην

[1] This verb is representative of contract verbs with stems ending in -ε.

INTEGRATION OF CHAPTERS 15–19

In this chapter, we will use the following passage (adapted from various NT verses) as the basis of reviewing concepts and forms that have been presented in chapters 15–19. Some of the key concepts that we covered were the aorist-participle, adverbial-participle functions, the perfect and pluperfect indicative, perfect participles, periphrasis, contract verbs, and the future indicative and participle. You may want to make a copy of this text and mark it on your own as we go through this segment.

PART ONE

As we have stressed all along, it is crucial to be able to identify finite verb forms. So, let's begin by double underlining and parsing each finite verb. Then identify nonfinite verbs forms by putting boxes around them. You should also parse these forms. After you have done this on your own, turn to the following page.

Pop-Up Lexicon

βαπτιστής, -οῦ, ὁ	Baptist (of John)
Ἠλίας, -ου, ὁ	Elijah
Καισάρεια, -ας, ἡ	Caesarea
λῃστής, -οῦ, ὁ	robber
προσευχή, -ῆς, ἡ	prayer, place of prayer
Φίλιππος, -ου, ὁ	Philip

Hint: If you don't recognize a verb form, be sure to consult appendix 14, "Principal Parts Chart."

1. καὶ ἐξῆλθεν ὁ Ἰησοῦς καὶ οἱ μαθηταὶ αὐτοῦ εἰς τὰς κώμας Καισαρείας τῆς Φιλίππου·

2. καὶ ἐν τῇ ὁδῷ ἐπηρώτα τοὺς μαθητὰς αὐτοῦ λέγων αὐτοῖς·

3. τί περὶ ἐμοῦ λέγουσιν οἱ ἄνθρωποι;

4. οἱ δὲ εἶπαν αὐτῷ·

5. τινες λέγουσιν ὅτι σὺ εἶ Ἰωάννης ὁ βαπτιστής, καὶ τινες Ἠλίας,

6. τινες δὲ ὅτι εἷς τῶν προφητῶν.

7. καὶ αὐτὸς ἐπηρώτα αὐτούς, ὑμεῖς δὲ τί περὶ ἐμοῦ λέγετε;

8. ἀποκριθεὶς ὁ Πέτρος λέγει αὐτῷ· σὺ εἶ ὁ χριστός.

9. τότε ἐδίδασκεν τοὺς μαθητὰς αὐτοῦ καὶ ἔλεγεν αὐτοῖς ὅτι

10. ὁ υἱὸς τοῦ ἀνθρώπου ἀπεκτάνθη ἐν χειρὶν ἀνθρώπων,

11. καὶ ἀποκτανθεὶς μετὰ τρεῖς ἡμέρας ἐγερθήσεται.

12. καὶ ἔρχονται εἰς Ἱεροσόλυμα. καὶ εἰσελθὼν εἰς τὸ ἱερὸν ἐξέβαλεν τοὺς πωλοῦντας

13. καὶ τοὺς ἀγοράζοντας ἐν τῷ ἱερῷ. καὶ ἐδίδασκεν καὶ ἔλεγεν αὐτοῖς,

14. οὐ γέγραπται ὅτι ὁ οἶκός μου οἶκος προσευχῆς κληθήσεται πᾶσιν τοῖς ἔθνεσιν;

15. ὑμεῖς δὲ πεποιήκατε αὐτὸν οἶκον λῃστῶν.

16. καὶ ἤκουσαν οἱ ἀρχιερεῖς καὶ οἱ γραμματεῖς καὶ ἐζήτουν πῶς αὐτὸν ἀποκτενοῦσιν·

17. ἐφοβοῦντο γὰρ αὐτόν, πᾶς γὰρ ὁ ὄχλος ἐθαυμάζοντο ἐπὶ τῇ διδαχῇ αὐτοῦ.

ANSWERS TO PART ONE

Did you come up with the following?

1. καὶ <u>ἐξῆλθεν</u> ὁ Ἰησοῦς καὶ οἱ μαθηταὶ αὐτοῦ εἰς τὰς κώμας Καισαρείας τῆς Φιλίππου·
2. καὶ ἐν τῇ ὁδῷ <u>ἐπηρώτα</u> τοὺς μαθητὰς αὐτοῦ $\boxed{\text{λέγων}}$ αὐτοῖς·
3. τί περὶ ἐμοῦ <u>λέγουσιν</u> οἱ ἄνθρωποι;
4. οἱ δὲ <u>εἶπαν</u> αὐτῷ·
5. τινες <u>λέγουσιν</u> ὅτι σὺ <u>εἶ</u> Ἰωάννης ὁ βαπτιστής, καὶ τινες Ἡλίας,
6. τινες δὲ ὅτι εἷς τῶν προφητῶν.
7. καὶ αὐτὸς <u>ἐπηρώτα</u> αὐτούς, ὑμεῖς δὲ τί περὶ ἐμοῦ <u>λέγετε</u>;
8. $\boxed{\text{ἀποκριθεὶς}}$ ὁ Πέτρος <u>λέγει</u> αὐτῷ· σὺ <u>εἶ</u> ὁ χριστός.
9. τότε <u>ἐδίδασκεν</u> τοὺς μαθητὰς αὐτοῦ καὶ <u>ἔλεγεν</u> αὐτοῖς ὅτι
10. ὁ υἱὸς τοῦ ἀνθρώπου <u>ἀπεκτάνθη</u> ἐν χειρὶν ἀνθρώπων,
11. καὶ $\boxed{\text{ἀποκτανθεὶς}}$ μετὰ τρεῖς ἡμέρας <u>ἐγερθήσεται</u>.
12. καὶ <u>ἔρχονται</u> εἰς Ἱεροσόλυμα. καὶ $\boxed{\text{εἰσελθὼν}}$ εἰς τὸ ἱερὸν <u>ἐξέβαλεν</u> τοὺς $\boxed{\text{πωλοῦντας}}$
13. καὶ τοὺς $\boxed{\text{ἀγοράζοντας}}$ ἐν τῷ ἱερῷ. καὶ <u>ἐδίδασκεν</u> καὶ <u>ἔλεγεν</u> αὐτοῖς,
14. οὐ <u>γέγραπται</u> ὅτι ὁ οἶκός μου οἶκος προσευχῆς <u>κληθήσεται</u> πᾶσιν τοῖς ἔθνεσιν;
15. ὑμεῖς δὲ <u>πεποιήκατε</u> αὐτὸν οἶκον λῃστῶν.
16. καὶ <u>ἤκουσαν</u> οἱ ἀρχιερεῖς καὶ οἱ γραμματεῖς καὶ <u>ἐζήτουν</u> πῶς αὐτὸν <u>ἀποκτενοῦσιν</u>·
17. <u>ἐφοβοῦντο</u> γὰρ αὐτόν, πᾶς γὰρ ὁ ὄχλος <u>ἐθαυμάζοντο</u> ἐπὶ τῇ διδαχῇ αὐτοῦ.

Parsing

inflected form	tense	voice	mood	person	case	num	gender	lexical form	inflected meaning
ἐξῆλθεν	aor	act	ind	3rd	n/a	sg	n/a	ἐξέρχομαι	he came
ἐπηρώτα	impf	act	ind	3rd	n/a	sg	n/a	ἐπερωτάω	he was asking
λέγων	pres	act	ptc	n/a	nom	sg	masc	λέγω	saying
λέγουσιν	pres	act	ind	3rd	n/a	pl	n/a	λέγω	they are saying
εἶπαν	aor	act	ind	3rd	n/a	pl	n/a	λέγω	they said

inflected form	tense	voice	mood	person	case	num	gender	lexical form	inflected meaning
εἶ	pres	n/a	ind	2nd	n/a	sg	n/a	εἰμί	you (sg) are
λέγετε	pres	act	ind	2nd	n/a	pl	n/a	λέγω	you (pl) say
ἀποκριθείς	aor	pass	ptc	n/a	nom	sg	masc	ἀποκρίνομαι	answering
λέγει	pres	act	ind	3rd	n/a	sg	n/a	λέγω	he says
ἐδίδασκεν	impf	act	ind	3rd	n/a	sg	n/a	διδάσκω	he was teaching
ἔλεγεν	impf	act	ind	3rd	n/a	sg	n/a	λέγω	he was saying
ἀπεκτάνθη	aor	pass	ind	3rd	n/a	sg	n/a	ἀποκτείνω	he was killed
ἀποκτανθείς	aor	pass	ptc	n/a	nom	sg	masc	ἀποκτείνω	after being killed
ἐγερθήσεται	fut	pass	ind	3rd	n/a	sg	n/a	ἐγείρω	he will be raised
ἔρχονται	pres	mid	ind	3rd	n/a	pl	n/a	ἔρχομαι	they come
εἰσελθών	aor	act	ptc	n/a	nom	sg	masc	εἰσέρχομαι	after entering
ἐξέβαλεν	aor	act	ind	3rd	n/a	sg	n/a	ἐκβάλλω	he cast out
πωλοῦντας	pres	act	ptc	n/a	acc	pl	masc	πωλέω	selling ones
ἀγοράζοντας	pres	act	ptc	n/a	acc	pl	masc	ἀγοράζω	buying ones
γέγραπται	pf	pass	ind	3rd	n/a	sg	n/a	γράφω	it has been written
κληθήσεται	fut	pass	ind	3rd	n/a	sg	n/a	καλέω	it will be called
πεποιήκατε	pf	act	ind	2nd	n/a	pl	n/a	ποιέω	you (pl) have made
ἤκουσαν	aor	act	ind	3rd	n/a	pl	n/a	ἀκούω	they heard
ἐζήτουν	impf	act	ind	3rd	n/a	pl	n/a	ζητέω	they were seeking
ἀποκτενοῦσιν	fut	act	ind	3rd	n/a	pl	n/a	ἀποκτείνω	they will kill
ἐφοβοῦντο	impf	mid	ind	3rd	n/a	pl	n/a	φοβέομαι	they were fearing
ἐθαυμάζοντο	impf	mid	ind	3rd	n/a	pl	n/a	θαυμάζω	they were amazed

Additional Notes:

- As you probably guessed, we have modified this text from several NT passages: Mark 8:27–30; 9:31–32; 11:15–18. Now would be a good time to read these passages in your GNT. There are still some grammatical concepts and forms that you need to learn, but it will be encouraging to see how much Greek you have grasped at this point!

- The form ἐπηρώτα may have been challenging. Hopefully you recognized that ἐπ was the elided form of the preposition ἐπί, which has been compounded to the verb ἐρωτάω. That means that η must be an augment, which means that the form is either an imperfect or aorist indicative. Remember that contract verbs are regular and that they lengthen their contract vowel before tense formatives. So, if this were an aorist, then there would be a sigma, and the form would look like this: ἐπηρώτησα. So this means that the form must be an imperfect. The person and number should be readily recognizable.

- The close proximity of ἀπεκτάνθη (line 10) and ἀποκτανθείς (line 11) in the text offers a good chance to review passive forms. Notice that ἀπεκτάνθη has an augment after the prefixed preposition, but ἀποκτανθείς does not. This is an essential clue that ἀποκτανθείς is not an indicative form. Although both forms are built from the same principal part, nonindicative forms do not have an augment. The -θη is a clear indicator that ἀπεκτάνθη is an aorist passive indicative; similarly, the -θε indicates that ἀποκτανθείς is an aorist passive participle.

- The -θησ tense formative is very distinctive—it's hard to miss all those future passive indicatives.

- Remember, if you can count to two, then you can do a lot of Greek. The one lambda in ἐξέβαλεν clearly distinguishes this aorist form from an imperfect (which would have two lambdas).

- Remember that contract verbs lengthen the final vowel of their stem before a tense formative, as it evident in πεποιήκατε.

- The form ἀποκτενοῦσιν is a good chance to review essentials about the future. There is no augment, because the future is a primary (or unaugmented) tense stem. There is a lengthened connecting vowel, which indicates here that this is a liquid future form.

PART TWO

Now we'll focus on the participles in this passage. You have already identified these forms and parsed them. Now go through the passage and indicate the function of each participle by labeling the participle SUB, ATTR, or ADV For ATTR and ADV participles, draw an arrow to the word being modified by the participle. The first participle is used as an example. Once you have finished, you can check your own work against the discussion on the following page.

> Line 2: λέγων – This participle is functioning adverbially; notice that it is anarthrous and that there is no substantive that is in immediate proximity that is also nominative singular masculine. As an adverbial participle, it modifies the finite verb ἐπηρώτα and agrees with it in number (singular).
>
>   ADV
>
>   2. καὶ ἐν τῇ ὁδῷ ἐπηρώτα τοὺς μαθητὰς αὐτοῦ λέγων αὐτοῖς·

ANSWERS TO PART TWO

Here is how the rest of the participles are functioning in this passage.

Line 8: ἀποκριθείς – This participle is functioning adverbially; notice that it is anarthrous. As an adverbial participle, it modifies the finite verb λέγει and agrees with it in number (singular).

ADV ⟶
8. ἀποκριθεὶς ὁ Πέτρος λέγει αὐτῷ· σὺ εἶ ὁ χριστός.

Line 11: ἀποκτανθείς – This participle is functioning adverbially; notice that it is anarthrous and that there is no substantive that is in immediate proximity that is also nominative singular masculine. As an adverbial participle, it modifies the finite verb ἐγερθήσεται and agrees with it in number (singular).

ADV ⟶
11. καὶ ἀποκτανθεὶς μετὰ τρεῖς ἡμέρας ἐγερθήσεται.

Line 12: εἰσελθών – This participle is functioning adverbially; notice that it is anarthrous and that there is no substantive that is in immediate proximity that is also nominative singular masculine. As adverbial participle, it modifies the finite verb ἐξέβαλεν, and agrees with it in number (singular).

ADV ⟶
12. Καὶ ἔρχονται εἰς Ἱεροσόλυμα. Καὶ εἰσελθὼν εἰς τὸ ἱερὸν ἐξέβαλεν
SUB
τοὺς πωλοῦντας

Line 12: πωλοῦντας – This participle is functioning substantivally; notice that it is articular and that there is no substantive that is in immediate proximity that is also accusative plural masculine.

Line 13: ἀγοράζοντας – This participle is also functioning substantivally; notice that it is articular and that there is no substantive that is in immediate proximity that is also accusative plural masculine. It functions parallel to πωλοῦντας.

SUB

13. καὶ τοὺς ἀγοράζοντας ἐν τῷ ἱερῷ. καὶ ἐδίδασκεν καὶ ἔλεγεν
αὐτοῖς,

Here is the complete passage with participles marked.

1. Καὶ ἐξῆλθεν ὁ Ἰησοῦς καὶ οἱ μαθηταὶ αὐτοῦ εἰς τὰς κώμας Καισαρείας
τῆς Φιλίππου·

ADV

2. καὶ ἐν τῇ ὁδῷ ἐπηρώτα τοὺς μαθητὰς αὐτοῦ λέγων αὐτοῖς·
3. τί περὶ ἐμοῦ λέγουσιν οἱ ἄνθρωποι;
4. οἱ δὲ εἶπαν αὐτῷ·
5. τινες λέγουσιν ὅτι σὺ εἶ Ἰωάννης ὁ βαπτιστής, καὶ τινες Ἠλίας,
6. τινες δὲ ὅτι εἷς τῶν προφητῶν.
7. καὶ αὐτὸς ἐπηρώτα αὐτούς, ὑμεῖς δὲ τί περὶ ἐμοῦ λέγετε;

ADV

8. ἀποκριθεὶς ὁ Πέτρος λέγει αὐτῷ· σὺ εἶ ὁ χριστός.
9. Τότε ἐδίδασκεν τοὺς μαθητὰς αὐτοῦ καὶ ἔλεγεν αὐτοῖς ὅτι
10. ὁ υἱὸς τοῦ ἀνθρώπου ἀπεκτάνθη ἐν χειρὶν ἀνθρώπων,

ADV

11. καὶ ἀποκτανθεὶς μετὰ τρεῖς ἡμέρας ἐγερθήσεται.

ADV

12. Καὶ ἔρχονται εἰς Ἱεροσόλυμα. Καὶ εἰσελθὼν εἰς τὸ ἱερὸν ἐξέβαλεν

SUB

τοὺς πωλοῦντας

SUB

13. καὶ τοὺς ἀγοράζοντας ἐν τῷ ἱερῷ. καὶ ἐδίδασκεν καὶ ἔλεγεν αὐτοῖς,
14. οὐ γέγραπται ὅτι ὁ οἶκός μου οἶκος προσευχῆς κληθήσεται πᾶσιν τοῖς
ἔθνεσιν;
15. ὑμεῖς δὲ πεποιήκατε αὐτὸν οἶκον λῃστῶν.
16. Καὶ ἤκουσαν οἱ ἀρχιερεῖς καὶ οἱ γραμματεῖς καὶ ἐζήτουν πῶς αὐτὸν
ἀποκτενοῦσιν ·
17. ἐφοβοῦντο γὰρ αὐτόν, πᾶς γὰρ ὁ ὄχλος ἐθαυμάζοντο ἐπὶ τῇ διδαχῇ
αὐτοῦ.

PART THREE

We will now focus on nouns and pronouns. You should be able to quickly recognize these forms. Use this passage to work through the following instructions. Although the instructions often ask for only one example, working through *every* example that occurs in the passage will help you the most. Once you have completed you work, turn to the following pages for a complete list of these constructions and further discussion of them. Following this discussion there are two remaining questions covering dependent clauses and prepositional phrases.

1. Give one example each of a direct object and an indirect object; then answer the following questions:
   a. How do you know that this substantive is functioning as a direct or indirect object?
   b. For which finite verb is this substantive functioning as a direct or indirect object?

2. Give at least two examples of a genitival construction.
   a. Which word is the genitival modifier?
   b. Which word is the head noun?

3. Give one example of a predicate nominative or a predicate adjective.
   a. What type of verb confirms that this is a predicate?
   b. What is the subject of this verb?

4. Give one example of the emphatic use of a personal pronoun.
   a. How do you know that this pronoun is functioning emphatically?

5. Give one example of a third-person personal pronoun in an oblique case.
   a. What is the antecedent of this pronoun?
   b. How do you know?

6. Give one example of a demonstrative.
   a. Is this demonstrative functioning as an adjective or a pronoun?
   b. How do you know?

7. Give one example of the adjective πᾶς.
    a. Is this form of πᾶς functioning attributively or substantivally?
    b. How do you know?

8. Give one example of an interrogative or indefinite pronoun.
    a. Is this an interrogative or indefinite pronoun?
    b. How do you know?

9. Give one example of apposition.
    a. Which words comprise this construction?
    b. How do you know?

10. Give one example of an object complement.
    a. Which words comprise this construction?
    b. Which word is the object, and which is the complement?

ANSWERS TO PART THREE

Here is a complete list of all possible answers for questions 1–10. You should check your work against this and see if you missed anything. If so, then use this as a means of reviewing forms, functions, and concepts that have been discussed so far.

1. Here are all examples of direct and indirect objects and answers to the following questions for each:
   a. How do you know that this substantive is functioning as a direct or indirect object?
   b. For which finite verb is this substantive functioning as a direct or indirect object?

   Line 2: μαθητάς
   a. The accusative case of μαθητάς indicates that it is functioning as a direct object.
   b. μαθητάς is the direct object of ἐπηρώτα.

   Line 2: αὐτοῖς
   a. The dative case of αὐτοῖς indicates that it is functioning as the indirect object of λέγων; a direct object is implied (e.g., "words").
   b. αὐτοῖς is the indirect object of λέγων.

   Line 3: τί
   a. The accusative case of τί indicates that it is functioning as a direct object.
   b. τί is the direct object of λέγουσιν.

   Line 4: αὐτῷ
   a. The dative case of αὐτῷ indicates that it is functioning as the indirect object of εἶπαν; a direct object is implied (e.g., "words").
   b. αὐτῷ is the indirect object of εἶπαν.

   Line 7: αὐτούς
   a. The accusative case of αὐτούς indicates that it is functioning as a direct object.
   b. αὐτούς is the direct object of ἐπηρώτα.

Line 7: τί
    a. The accusative case of τί indicates that it is functioning as a direct object.
    b. τί is the direct object of λέγετε.

Line 8: αὐτῷ
    a. The dative case of αὐτῷ indicates that it is functioning as the indirect object of λέγει; a direct object is implied (e.g., "words").
    b. αὐτῷ is the indirect object of λέγει.

Line 9: μαθητάς
    a. The accusative case of μαθητάς indicates that it is functioning as a direct object.
    b. μαθητάς is the direct object of ἐδίδασκεν.

Line 9: αὐτοῖς
    a. The dative case of αὐτοῖς indicates that it is functioning as the indirect object of ἔλεγεν; a direct object is implied (e.g., "words").
    b. αὐτοῖς is the indirect object of ἔλεγεν.

Line 12: πωλοῦντας
    a. The accusative case of πωλοῦντας indicates that it is functioning as a direct object.
    b. πωλοῦντας is the direct object ἐξέβαλεν.

Line 13: ἀγοράζοντας
    a. The accusative case of ἀγοράζοντας indicates that it is functioning as a direct object.
    b. ἀγοράζοντας is the direct object of ἐξέβαλεν.

Line 13: αὐτοῖς
    a. The dative case of αὐτοῖς indicates that it is functioning as the indirect object of ἔλεγεν; a direct object is implied (e.g., "words").
    b. αὐτοῖς is the indirect object of ἔλεγεν.

Line 15: αὐτόν

  a. The accusative case of αὐτόν indicates that it is functioning as a direct object.

  b. αὐτόν is the direct object of πεποιήκατε.

Line 16: αὐτόν

  a. The accusative case of αὐτόν indicates that it is functioning as a direct object.

  b. αὐτόν is the direct object of ἀποκτενοῦσιν.

Line 17: αὐτόν

  a. The accusative case of αὐτόν indicates that it is functioning as a direct object.

  b. αὐτόν is the direct object of ἐφοβοῦντο.

2. Each of the genitival constructions in this passage has been marked below. (Lines in which no genitival constructions occur are not included.)

  a. Which word is the genitival modifier? This word is labeled *GM*.

  b. Which word is the head noun? An *arrow* is drawn from the GM to this word.

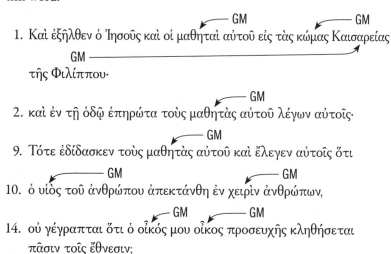

3. Here are all examples of predicate nominatives and answers to the following questions for each. There are no examples of predicate adjectives.
   a. What type of verb confirms that this is a predicate?
   b. What is the subject of this verb?

   Line 5: τινες λέγουσιν ὅτι σὺ εἶ Ἰωάννης ὁ βαπτιστής
   a. The equative verb εἶ confirms that Ἰωάννης ὁ βαπτιστής is a predicate nominative.
   b. The subject of this verb is reflected in the inflected form εἶ. The pronoun σύ is functioning emphatically. Ἰωάννης ὁ βαπτιστής is the predicate nominative.

   Line 5: τινες Ἡλίας
   a. This clause is elliptical and parallels the first clause in line 5. Thus, the equative verb εἶ is implied and confirms that this is a predicate nominative. The full sentence would be σὺ εἶ Ἡλίας.
   b. The subject of this verb is implied in the assumed form εἶ. Ἡλίας is the predicate nominative.

   Line 6: τινες δὲ ὅτι εἷς τῶν προφητῶν.
   a. This clause is also elliptical and also parallels the first clause in line 5. Thus, the equative verb εἶ is implied and confirms that this is a predicate nominative.
   b. The subject of this verb is implied in the assumed form εἶ; εἷς is the predicate nominative.

   Line 8: σὺ εἶ ὁ χριστός.
   a. The equative verb εἶ confirms that ὁ χριστός is a predicate nominative.
   b. The subject of this verb is reflected in the inflected form εἶ; ὁ χριστός is the predicate nominative. The pronoun σύ is functioning emphatically.

4. There are *seven* examples of the emphatic use of a *personal pronoun* (highlighted in *italics* below) in this passage.

   Line 5: τινες λέγουσιν ὅτι σὺ εἶ Ἰωάννης ὁ βαπτιστής

Line 5: τινες Ἠλίας (σύ implied by ellipsis and parallelism)

Line 6: τινες δὲ ὅτι εἷς τῶν προφητῶν. (σύ implied by ellipsis and parallelism)

Line 7 (two examples): καὶ *αὐτὸς* ἐπηρώτα αὐτούς, *ὑμεῖς* δὲ τί περὶ ἐμοῦ λέγετε;

Line 8: ἀποκριθεὶς ὁ Πέτρος λέγει αὐτῷ· *σὺ* εἶ ὁ χριστός.

Line 15: *ὑμεῖς* δὲ πεποιήκατε αὐτὸν οἶκον λῃστῶν.

> a. We know that each of these pronouns is functioning emphatically because it is in the nominative case with a finite verb. The verb form is inflected for person and number, so the pronoun is not indicating the subject; rather, it is adding emphasis.

5. There are thirteen examples of a third-person personal pronoun in an oblique case.
   a. What is the antecedent of this pronoun?
   b. How do you know?

   Line 1: αὐτοῦ
   > a. The antecedent of this pronoun is ὁ Ἰησοῦς.
   > b. The pronoun agrees with ὁ Ἰησοῦς in number and gender.

   Line 2: αὐτοῦ
   > a. The antecedent of this pronoun is also ὁ Ἰησοῦς.
   > b. The pronoun agrees with ὁ Ἰησοῦς in number and gender.

   Line 2: αὐτοῖς
   > a. The antecedent of this pronoun is οἱ μαθηταί.
   > b. The pronoun agrees with οἱ μαθηταί in number and gender.

   Line 4: αὐτῷ
   > a. The antecedent of this pronoun is also ὁ Ἰησοῦς; even though this is a new sentence, and ὁ Ἰησοῦς is not explicitly stated, it is clear from the context that the antecedent is ὁ Ἰησοῦς.
   > b. The pronoun agrees with ὁ Ἰησοῦς in number and gender.

Line 7: αὐτούς
  a. The antecedent of this pronoun is οἱ μαθηταί.
  b. The pronoun agrees with οἱ μαθηταί in number and gender.

Line 8: αὐτῷ
  a. The antecedent of this pronoun is ὁ Ἰησοῦς.
  b. The pronoun agrees with ὁ Ἰησοῦς in number and gender.

Line 9: αὐτοῦ
  a. The antecedent of this pronoun is ὁ Ἰησοῦς.
  b. The pronoun agrees with ὁ Ἰησοῦς in number and gender.

Line 9: αὐτοῖς
  a. The antecedent of this pronoun is οἱ μαθηταί.
  b. The pronoun agrees with οἱ μαθηταί in number and gender.

Line 13: αὐτοῖς
  a. The antecedent of this pronoun is τοὺς πωλοῦντας and τοὺς γοράζοντας.
  b. The pronoun is masculine plural, which means that there are several options for the antecedent. In the overall context of this passage, the antecedent could be οἱ μαθηταί, especially in light of the verb ἐδίδασκεν. But the content of what Jesus is saying makes it more likely that the antecedent of αὐτοῖς is τοὺς πωλοῦντας and τοὺς ἀγοράζοντας, which are also the nearest substantives that are masculine plural. As we have seen before, it is essential pay careful attention to the overall context for determining the antecedent of a pronoun.

Line 15: αὐτόν
  a. The antecedent of this pronoun is ὁ οἶκος.
  b. The pronoun agrees with ὁ οἶκος in number and gender.

Line 16: αὐτόν
  a. The antecedent of this pronoun is ὁ Ἰησοῦς.
  b. The pronoun agrees with ὁ Ἰησοῦς in number and gender.

Line 17: αὐτόν
  a. The antecedent of this pronoun is ὁ Ἰησοῦς.

  b. The pronoun agrees with ὁ Ἰησοῦς in number and gender.

Line 17: αὐτοῦ
  a. The antecedent of this pronoun is ὁ Ἰησοῦς.
  b. The pronoun agrees with ὁ Ἰησοῦς in number and gender.

6. There are *no* examples of a demonstrative in this passage.

7. There are *two* examples of the adjective πᾶς in this passage.
  a. In line 14, πᾶσιν is functioning attributively, modifying the substantive ἔθνεσιν.
  b. πᾶσιν agrees with ἔθνεσιν in case, number, and gender, which indicates that it is functioning attributively to modify this substantive. Recall that the adjective πᾶς appears in the predicate position when it is functioning attributively.

  a. In line 17, πᾶς is functioning attributively, modifying the substantive ὄχλος.
  b. πᾶς agrees with ὄχλος in case, number, and gender, which indicates that it is functioning attributively to modify this substantive.

8. There are *two* examples of an interrogative pronoun and *three* examples of an indefinite pronoun in this passage.

Line 3: τί περὶ ἐμοῦ λέγουσιν οἱ ἄνθρωποι;

Line 7: καὶ αὐτὸς ἐπηρώτα αὐτούς, ὑμεῖς δὲ τί περὶ ἐμοῦ λέγετε;

a.–b. In both lines, τί is an interrogative pronoun because there is an accent on the first syllable.

Line 5 (two examples): τινες λέγουσιν ὅτι σὺ εἶ Ἰωάννης ὁ βαπτιστής, καὶ τινες Ἡλίας,

Line 6: τινες δὲ ὅτι εἷς τῶν προφητῶν.

a.–b. In both lines, τινες is an indefinite pronoun because there is no accent on the first syllable.

9. There is *one* example of apposition in line 5.
    a. The words Ἰωάννης ὁ βαπτιστής comprise this construction.
    b. How do you know? Apposition involves one substantive that further explains or defines another substantive, which is frequently a proper name. Both substantives have the same case and number and refer to the *same* entity.

10. There is *one* clear example of an object complement and *one* less obvious example.
    a. In line 15, the words in *italics* comprise this construction.

    ὑμεῖς δὲ πεποιήκατε αὐτὸν *οἶκον λῃστῶν*.

    b. The object of πεποιήκατε is αὐτόν (referring back to ὁ οἶκός μου in line 14); the complement is οἶκον λῃστῶν.

    a. In line 14, the passive construction also contains an object complement, although both the object and complement are in the nominative case due to the passive verb γέγραπται.
    b. The subject of κληθήσεται is ὁ οἶκός μου; the complement is οἶκος προσευχῆς.

PART FOUR

We'll take one more pass through this passage, focusing on dependent clauses and prepositional phrases. Go through the passage and put parentheses around each (dependent clause) and brackets around each [prepositional phrase]. For each dependent clause, highlight the subordinating conjunction or the relative pronoun and identify what type of clause it is and then indicate how it is functioning. For each prepositional phrase, indicate how you know the boundary of the prepositional phrase. Once you have finished, you can check your own work against the discussion on the next page.

ANSWERS TO PART FOUR

Did you come up with the following?

1. καὶ <u>ἐξῆλθεν</u> ὁ Ἰησοῦς καὶ οἱ μαθηταὶ αὐτοῦ [εἰς τὰς κώμας Καισαρείας τῆς Φιλίππου]·
2. καὶ [ἐν τῇ ὁδῷ] <u>ἐπηρώτα</u> τοὺς μαθητὰς αὐτοῦ |λέγων| αὐτοῖς·
3. τί [περὶ ἐμοῦ] <u>λέγουσιν</u> οἱ ἄνθρωποι;
5. τινες <u>λέγουσιν</u> (ὅτι σὺ εἶ Ἰωάννης ὁ βαπτιστής), καὶ τινες (Ἡλίας),
6. τινες δὲ (ὅτι εἷς τῶν προφητῶν).
7. καὶ αὐτὸς <u>ἐπηρώτα</u> αὐτούς, ὑμεῖς δὲ τί [περὶ ἐμοῦ] <u>λέγετε</u>;
9. τότε <u>ἐδίδασκεν</u> τοὺς μαθητὰς αὐτοῦ καὶ <u>ἔλεγεν</u> αὐτοῖς (ὅτι
10. ὁ υἱὸς τοῦ ἀνθρώπου <u>ἀπεκτάνθη</u> [ἐν χειρὶν ἀνθρώπων],
11. καὶ |ἀποκτανθεὶς| [μετὰ τρεῖς ἡμέρας] <u>ἐγερθήσεται</u>).
12. καὶ <u>ἔρχονται</u> [εἰς Ἱεροσόλυμα]. καὶ |εἰσελθὼν| [εἰς τὸ ἱερὸν] <u>ἐξέβαλεν</u> τοὺς |πωλοῦντας|
13. καὶ τοὺς |ἀγοράζοντας| [ἐν τῷ ἱερῷ]. καὶ <u>ἐδίδασκεν</u> καὶ <u>ἔλεγεν</u> αὐτοῖς,
14. οὐ <u>γέγραπται</u> (ὅτι ὁ οἶκός μου οἶκος προσευχῆς <u>κληθήσεται</u> πᾶσιν τοῖς ἔθνεσιν;)
16. καὶ <u>ἤκουσαν</u> οἱ ἀρχιερεῖς καὶ οἱ γραμματεῖς καὶ <u>ἐζήτουν</u> (πῶς αὐτὸν <u>ἀποκτενοῦσιν</u>)
17. <u>ἐφοβοῦντο</u> γὰρ αὐτόν, πᾶς γὰρ ὁ ὄχλος <u>ἐθαυμάζοντο</u> [ἐπὶ τῇ διδαχῇ αὐτοῦ].

Dependent Clauses
- Line 5 – (ὅτι σὺ εἶ Ἰωάννης ὁ βαπτιστής) is functioning to indicate the direct speech, or quote, introduced by the verb λέγουσιν.
- Line 5 – (Ἡλίας) functions parallel to the previous clause with λέγουσιν ὅτι σὺ εἶ understood from the previous clause. If you missed this one, don't worry—it certainly wouldn't be obvious at this point in your Greek studies.
- Line 6 – (ὅτι εἷς τῶν προφητῶν) is also functioning to indicate the content of direct speech, or quote, introduced by the implied verb λέγουσιν.
- Lines 9–11 – (ὅτι ὁ υἱὸς τοῦ ἀνθρώπου <u>ἀπεκτάνθη</u> [ἐν χειρὶν ἀνθρώπων], καὶ |ἀποκτανθεὶς| [μετὰ τρεῖς ἡμέρας] <u>ἐγερθήσεται</u>) is also functioning to indicate the content of the verb ἔλεγεν. This is an example of reported, or indirect speech.
- Line 14 – (ὅτι ὁ οἶκός μου οἶκος προσευχῆς <u>κληθήσεται</u> πᾶσιν τοῖς ἔθνεσιν) is functioning to indicate the content of direct speech, or the quote, introduced by the verb γέγραπται.

- Line 16 – (πῶς αὐτὸν ἀποκτενοῦσιν) – The interrogative adverb πῶς is functioning to introduce the dependent subjunctive clause αὐτὸν ἀποκτενοῦσιν.

Prepositional Phrases

- Line 1 – [εἰς τὰς κώμας Καισαρείας τῆς Φιλίππου] – κώμας is in the accusative case, which indicates that it is the object of the preposition εἰς; Καισαρείας is a genitival modifier of the head noun κώμας; τῆς Φιλίππου is a genitival modifier of the head noun Καισαρείας. Notice that the same word (i.e., Καισαρείας) can be both a genitival modifier and a head noun, at the same time! The punctuation and syntax indicate that Φιλίππου is the end of the prepositional phrase.
- Line 2 – [ἐν τῇ ὁδῷ] – ὁδῷ is in the dative case, which indicates that it is the object of the preposition ἐν. The word following is a verb, so it could not be part of the prepositional phrase.
- Line 3 – [περὶ ἐμοῦ] – ἐμοῦ is in the genitive case, which indicates that it is the object of the preposition περί. The word following is a verb, so it could not be part of the prepositional phrase.
- Line 7 – [περὶ ἐμοῦ] – ἐμοῦ is in the genitive case, which indicates that it is the object of the preposition περί. The word following is a verb, so it could not be part of the prepositional phrase.
- Line 10 – [ἐν χειρὶν ἀνθρώπων] – χειρίν is in the dative case, which indicates that it is the object of the preposition ἐν; ἀνθρώπων is a genitival modifier of the head noun χειρίν. The word following, καί, is followed by a verb, so it could not be part of the prepositional phrase.
- Line 11 – [μετὰ τρεῖς ἡμέρας] – ἡμέρας is in the genitive case, which indicates that it is the object of the preposition μετά; τρεῖς modifies ἡμέρας. The word following is a verb, so it could not be part of the prepositional phrase.
- Line 12 – [εἰς Ἱεροσόλυμα] – Ἱεροσόλυμα is in the accusative case, which indicates that it is the object of the preposition εἰς. The word following, καί, is followed by a verb, so it could not be part of the prepositional phrase.
- Line 12 – [εἰς τὸ ἱερὸν] – ἱερόν is in the accusative case, which indicates that it is the object of the preposition εἰς. The word that follows is a finite verb, which could not be part of the prepositional phrase.
- Line 13 – [ἐν τῷ ἱερῷ] – ἱερῷ is in the dative case, which indicates that it is the object of the preposition ἐν. The word following, καί, is followed by a verb, so it could not be part of the prepositional phrase.
- Line 17 – [ἐπὶ τῇ διδαχῇ αὐτοῦ] – διδαχῇ is in the dative case, which indicates that it is the object of the preposition ἐπί. This is the end of the passage, so it is also the end of the prepositional phrase!

PART FIVE

Finally, write out a final translation for this passage that reflects your work throughout this exercise. You can compare your translation with the one on the next page.

POSSIBLE TRANSLATION FOR PART FIVE

1. And Jesus left with his disciples to the village of Caesarea Philippi.
2. And on the way he began to question his disciples, saying to them,
3. "What do people say about me?"
4. And they said to him,
5. "Some say that *you* are John the Baptist, and some [say that you are] Elijah
6. and some [say] that [you are] one of the prophets."
7. And *he* asked them, "But what do you yourselves say about me?"
8. Peter answered and said to him, "*You* are the Christ."
9. Then he began to teach his disciples and he was saying to them,
10. "The son of man will be killed by the hands of men,
11. and after being killed, he will be raised after three days."
12. And they came to Jerusalem. And after entering the temple, he threw out those who buy
13. and sell in the temple. And he began to teach, and he was saying to them,
14. "Isn't it written, 'My house will be called a house of prayer for all nations?'
15. But *you* have made it a house of robbers."
16. And the chief priests and scribes heard [it], and they began to seek how they might kill him,
17. for they feared him, because the entire crowd was marveling at his teaching.

Additional Notes:

- Line 1 – The singular verb ἐξῆλθεν agrees with ὁ Ἰησοῦς even though οἱ μαθηταί is also part of the subject. In English, a compound subject usually requires a *plural* verb, but not so in Greek. The translation "with his disciples" is one way to render this in English. You could also have translated it as follows: "Jesus and his disciples left . . ." Moreover, although ἐξῆλθεν ("he left," "he departed") and the preposition εἰς ("to," "into") sound awkward in English, the verb indicates that Jesus left one location, and the preposition indicates that he entered another location.
- Line 2 – The translation reflects an ingressive understanding of ἐπήρωτα.
- Line 5 – The emphatic pronoun σύ is probably best left untranslated. In writing, the emphasis can sometimes be captured with italics.
- Lines 5 and 6 – The ellipses in these lines could be frustrating, but this type of ellipsis occurs frequently in the GNT.
- Line 7 – The emphatic use of the personal pronoun αὐτός is sometimes best left untranslated, as in this example. The emphatic use of the personal

pronoun ὑμεῖς could be indicated by intonation (if spoken) or by italics (if written): "But what do *you* say about me?"

- Line 8 – The combination of ἀποκριθείς and λέγει is very common in the GNT. English requires a conjunction (i.e., "and") between the two verb forms.

- Lines 9, 13 – Notice the ingressive force of ἐδίδασκεν.

- Line 10 – The verb ἀπεκτάνθη is aorist, but the context indicates that it is not past referring and is probably future referring instead. Although this passage has been modified from the GNT, there are examples of future-referring aorist indicatives in the GNT (e.g., Mark 11:24), so this is good practice. The prepositional phrase ἐν χειρὶν ἀνθρώπων could also be translated "at the hands of men"; ἀνθρώπων could also be rendered "people."

- Line 12 – The narrative context indicates that ἔρχονται is past referring.

- Line 16 – Notice the ingressive understanding of ἐζήτουν.

- Line 17 – The singular subject (ὄχλος) is a collective noun, which explains the plural verb (ἐθαυμάζοντο)—notice the ingressive understanding of this verb in the translation.

REVIEW AND STUDY GUIDE FOR CHAPTERS 15-19

Congratulations! You are halfway through the second semester of beginning Greek!

Here are some forms that you need to know by this point in the book:

- first and second aorist participle forms
- perfect and pluperfect indicative forms
- perfect participle forms
- contract verb forms
- future indicative forms
- future participle forms
- future forms of liquid verbs
- future forms of contract verbs
- the future forms of εἰμί
- vocabulary, paradigms, and principal parts for chapters 15–19

Additionally, essential concepts that you should know include the following:

- participle morphemes and tense formatives
- basic adverbial functions of participles: temporal, causal, purpose, instrumental, genitive absolute
- verbal roots and tense stems
- reduplication
- the aspect of the perfect and pluperfect tense-forms
- functions of the perfect and pluperfect indicative: resultative, consummative
- periphrasis
- vowel contraction rules
- functions of the future indicative: predictive, volitional/imperatival

Chapter 20 is a time to review and solidify these concepts and forms. The more firmly these concepts and forms are in place, the more fun and satisfying will be your Greek journey.

THE SUBJUNCTIVE:
Forms and Functions

OBJECTIVES AND OVERVIEW

Chapter 21 introduces the following linguistic concepts, morphemes, and paradigms:

- lengthened connecting vowel
- present active and middle subjunctive paradigms
- aorist subjunctive tense formative
- aorist active, middle, and passive subjunctive paradigms
- aorist subjunctive paradigms for contract verbs
- subjunctive paradigm of εἰμί
- main-clause functions of the subjunctive: hortatory, deliberative, prohibition, emphatic negation
- adverbial subordinate-clause functions of the subjunctive: purpose, negative purpose
- substantival subordinate-clause functions of the subjunctive: subject, predicate, content
- indefinite relative clauses
- indefinite temporal or spatial clauses
- third-class conditionals

As we have seen, finite verbs are inflected to indicate person and number. So far, we have only looked at one finite mood, the indicative. Recall that mood indicates how the speaker chooses to portray the actuality or potentiality of an event. Mood has to do with the manner in which a statement is made and not necessarily the truth of a statement. The indicative mood makes an assertion or statement. The subjunctive mood, our focus for this chapter, is the mood of probability or potentiality. It indicates an action that is uncertain but probable; it may also express futurity.

The indicative mood is by far the most common mood in the GNT, but the subjunctive is the most common oblique (nonindicative) mood. Some functions of the subjunctive overlap with the imperative and optative—indeed, the subjunctive was "taking over" some optative functions by the Koine period.

Debates about whether tense stems semantically indicate time only concern the indicative mood. The tense stems of all nonindicative moods and verbal forms, such as the participle and infinitive, only indicate aspect. There is consensus on this point in all major grammars. Outside of the indicative, the primary opposition is between the present tense stem and the aorist tense stem, although the perfect tense stem sometimes occurs as well, as we saw with participles.[1] Nearly all subjunctives in the GNT, however, are present or aorist.[2] The aorist subjunctive (perfective aspect) may be understood as the default, whereas the present subjunctive reflects a deliberate choice to indicate imperfective (continuous) aspect.

THE FORMS OF THE SUBJUNCTIVE

Subjunctive forms are relatively easy to memorize because many morphemes that we have already seen are used to form the subjunctive. The present and aorist tense stems, visible in a verb's principal parts, are used the build the subjunctive. Additionally, *all* subjunctive forms use *primary* active or middle personal endings, including aorist subjunctives. Recall that there is no augment outside of the indicative. Thus, there is no augment used for aorist subjunctives. The essential sign of the subjunctive, therefore, is the connecting vowel, which is a lengthened form of the connecting vowel used in the indicative. Specifically, an omicron lengthens to an omega, and an epsilon lengthens to an eta.[3]

To build present subjunctive forms, we begin with the present tense stem, use a lengthened connecting vowel, and add a primary personal ending. For example:

present tense stem	lengthened connecting vowel	primary active personal ending	inflected form
λυ	+ ω	+ μεν	→ λύωμεν

---

1. Please refer to appendix 18, "Verbal Aspect and the Distribution of Tense-Forms, Verbal Moods, and Nonfinite Verb Forms."

2. The handful of perfect active subjunctives in the GNT all involve the verb οἶδα. The perfect passive subjunctive is extremely rare and is expressed by means of **periphrasis** involving a perfect participle and the subjunctive of εἰμί (e.g., John 3:27).

3. There is some debate as to whether there is one set of connecting vowels (e.g., o and ε) that has been lengthened (e.g., Mounce, *Basics of Biblical Greek*, 355) or whether the ω and η represent a different set of connecting vowels, or "stem formatives" (e.g., Goetchius, *Language of the New Testament*, 265). In the end, all that matters is that you recognize the long vowels as indicating the subjunctive mood.

Here are the paradigms for the present active and middle subjunctive of λύω. The corresponding forms of the present indicative are listed in gray for comparison. Also listed are possible inflected meanings, although it is important to realize that there is a range of possible translations for the Greek subjunctive, as the examples from the GNT below will show. Consequently, when you are parsing Greek subjunctives, "would," "should," "might," or "could," are acceptable.

PRESENT ACTIVE SUBJUNCTIVE PARADIGM OF λύω

1 sg	λύω	I would release	λύω
2 sg	λύῃς	you (sg) would release	λύεις
3 sg	λύῃ	he/she/it would release	λύει
1 pl	λύωμεν	we would release	λύομεν
2 pl	λύητε	you (pl) would release	λύετε
3 pl	λύωσι(ν)	they would release	λύουσι(ν)

PRESENT MIDDLE SUBJUNCTIVE PARADIGM OF λύω

1 sg	λύωμαι	I would release for myself	λύομαι
2 sg	λύῃ	you (sg) would release for yourself	λύῃ
3 sg	λύηται	he/she/it would release for himself/herself/itself	λύεται
1 pl	λυώμεθα	we would release for ourselves	λυόμεθα
2 pl	λύησθε	you (pl) would release yourselves	λύεσθε
3 pl	λύωνται	they would release for themselves	λύονται

In the present active subjunctive paradigm, some forms overlap with indicative forms. Specifically, the present active subjunctive first-person singular has the same form as a present active indicative first-person singular (λύω). Notice also that there are five possibilities for the form λύῃ: present active subjunctive third-person singular, present middle or passive subjunctive second-person singular, or present middle or passive indicative second-person singular. Before you begin to feel too overwhelmed by all these possibilities, keep in mind that context will nearly always indicate which form is intended. As we will see below, there are several clear contextual clues that occur with subjunctive forms that nearly always distinguish them from indicative forms. Also remember that the context in which a second-person and third-person verb occur is quite different.

To build first aorist subjunctive forms, we begin with the aorist tense stem, use a tense formative, use a lengthened connecting vowel, and add a *primary* personal ending. For example:

aorist tense stem	tense formative	lengthened connecting vowel	primary active personal ending	inflected form
λυ	+ σ	+ ω	+ μεν	→ λύσωμεν

As you are looking at these forms, you may think they look like future indicative forms, so it is very important to remember that there is *no* future subjunctive. For most of the first aorist subjunctive forms, the presence of the lengthened connecting vowel clearly distinguishes this form from a future indicative form, although contextual clues will also help to identify the form as an aorist subjunctive.

Here are the paradigms for the first aorist active and middle subjunctive of λύω. The corresponding forms of the future indicative are listed in gray for comparison.

FIRST AORIST ACTIVE SUBJUNCTIVE PARADIGM OF λύω

1 sg	λύσω	I would release	λύσω
2 sg	λύσῃς	you (sg) would release	λύσεις
3 sg	λύσῃ	he/she/it would release	λύσει
1 pl	λύσωμεν	we would release	λύσομεν
2 pl	λύσητε	you (pl) would release	λύσετε
3 pl	λύσωσι(ν)	they would release	λύσουσι(ν)

FIRST AORIST MIDDLE SUBJUNCTIVE PARADIGM OF λύω

1 sg	λύσωμαι	I would release for myself	λύσομαι
2 sg	λύσῃ	you (sg) would release for yourself	λύσῃ
3 sg	λύσηται	he/she/it would release for himself/herself/itself	λύσεται
1 pl	λυσώμεθα	we would release for ourselves	λυσόμεθα
2 pl	λύσησθε	you (pl) would release yourselves	λύσεσθε
3 pl	λύσωνται	they would release for themselves	λύσονται

In the first aorist active subjunctive paradigm, the first-person singular could be confused with a future active indicative first-person singular because the forms are identical (λύσω). Additionally, there are three possibilities for the form λύσῃ: aorist active subjunctive third-person singular, aorist middle subjunctive second-person singular, or future middle indicative second-person singular. As we noted regarding the overlap of forms for the present subjunctive paradigm, context will indicate which form is intended. And remember, there is no future subjunctive in Greek.

There is no overlap with the forms of the aorist passive subjunctive and other paradigms. Here is the paradigm for the first aorist passive subjunctive of λύω.

FIRST AORIST PASSIVE SUBJUNCTIVE PARADIGM OF λύω

1 sg	λυθῶ	I would be released
2 sg	λυθῇς	you (sg) would be released
3 sg	λυθῇ	he/she/it would be released
1 pl	λυθῶμεν	we would be released
2 pl	λυθῆτε	you (pl) be released
3 pl	λυθῶσι(ν)	they would be released

For second aorist subjunctive forms, the aorist stem is sufficient for identifying the form as an aorist, and no tense formative is necessary. Thus, to build second aorist subjunctive forms, we begin with the aorist tense stem, use a lengthened connecting vowel, and add a *primary* personal ending. For example:

aorist tense stem	lengthened connecting vowel	primary active personal ending	inflected form
λαβ	+ ω	+ μεν	→ λάβωμεν

Here is the paradigm for the second aorist subjunctive in all three voices.

SECOND AORIST SUBJUNCTIVE

	active	middle	passive
1 sg	λάβω	γένωμαι	φανῶ
2 sg	λάβῃς	γένῃ	φανῇς
3 sg	λάβῃ	γένηται	φανῇ
1 pl	λάβωμεν	γενώμεθα	φανῶμεν
2 pl	λάβητε	γένησθε	φανῆτε
3 pl	λάβωσι(ν)	γένωνται	φανῶσι(ν)

You don't need to memorize these forms if you focus on memorizing principal parts, identifying the lengthened connecting vowel, and remembering that the augment is not used in nonindicative forms. With all these clues, you should be able to recognize these forms without memorizing them.

The subjunctive forms for contract verbs follow the patterns of vowel contraction discussed in chapter 18 for the present subjunctive paradigm. Because some of the vowel-contraction patterns result in lengthened vowels, there is overlap between present subjunctive and present indicative forms for contract verbs. Consider the following paradigms in which corresponding indicative forms are listed in gray. Again, context will indicate which form is intended. For the aorist subjunctive, the final vowel of the verb stem lengthens before the tense formative, but because there is no augment with the subjunctive and the indicative uses secondary personal endings, there is no overlap in aorist forms (e.g., the aorist active indicative of ποιέω is ἐποίησα, but the aorist active subjective is ποιήσω).

PRESENT ACTIVE SUBJUNCTIVE FORMS (CONTRACT VERBS)

1 sg	τιμῶ	τιμῶ	ποιῶ	ποιῶ	πληρῶ	πληρῶ
2 sg	τιμᾷς	τιμᾷς	ποιῇς	ποιεῖς	πληροῖς	πληροῖς
3 sg	τιμᾷ	τιμᾷ	ποιῇ	ποιεῖ	πληροῖ	πληροῖ
1 pl	τιμῶμεν	τιμῶμεν	ποιῶμεν	ποιοῦμεν	πληρῶμεν	πληροῦμεν
2 pl	τιμᾶτε	τιμᾶτε	ποιῆτε	ποιεῖτε	πληρῶτε	πληροῦτε
3 pl	τιμῶσι(ν)	τιμῶσι(ν)	ποιῶσι(ν)	ποιοῦσι(ν)	πληρῶσι(ν)	πληροῦσι(ν)

PRESENT MIDDLE SUBJUNCTIVE FORMS (CONTRACT VERBS)

1 sg	τιμῶμαι	τιμῶμαι	ποιῶμαι	ποιοῦμαι	πληρῶμαι	πληροῦμαι
2 sg	τιμᾷ	τιμᾷ	ποιῇ	ποιῇ	πληροῖ	πληροῖ
3 sg	τιμᾶται	τιμᾶται	ποιῆται	ποιεῖται	πληρῶται	πληροῦται
1 pl	τιμώμεθα	τιμώμεθα	ποιώμεθα	ποιούμεθα	πληώμεθα	πληρούμεθα
2 pl	τιμᾶσθε	τιμᾶσθε	ποιῆσθε	ποιεῖσθε·	πληρῶσθε	πληροῦσθε
3 pl	τιμῶνται	τιμῶνται	ποιῶνται	ποιοῦνται	πληρῶνται	πληροῦνται

Finally, here is the paradigm for the subjunctive for εἰμί.

1 sg	ὦ	I would be
2 sg	ἦς	you (sg) would be
3 sg	ἦ	he/she/it would be
1 pl	ὦμεν	we would be
2 pl	ἦτε	you (pl) would be
3 pl	ὦσι(ν)	they would be

HEADS UP!

You can look through the subjunctive forms for μι verbs in chapter 24 and see how many forms you can recognize based on what you have learned in this chapter. Look for the lengthened connecting vowel and the use of primary personal endings.

THE FUNCTIONS OF THE SUBJUNCTIVE

Subjunctives are finite verbs, which means that they can occur as the main verb in an independent clause or as a subordinate verb in a dependent clause. This differs from participles, which are not finite verbs and can only occur in dependent clauses when they are functioning adverbially. The subjunctive in Greek has a wide range of functions. We will distinguish between subjunctive functions in main clauses and dependent clauses.

Main-Clause Functions

There are four ways that a subjunctive can occur as a main (or independent) verb in a main clause. First, it can function as a **hortatory** subjunctive, which is functionally equivalent to a command or an exhortation. This always occurs in the first person, and nearly always in the plural.[4] Although this type of subjunctive only occurs with the first person, it is important to understand that not all first-person subjunctives are hortatory subjunctives. Despite the fact that hortatory subjunctives are usually translated with "let us," which could be understood as a suggestion in English, the hortatory subjunctive is an appeal to volition just as an imperative is. In fact, when we discuss imperatives in the next chapter, you will

---

4. One of the rare examples of the first-person singular is found in Matt 7:4 (//Luke 6:42): Ἄφες ἐκβάλω τὸ κάρφος ἐκ τοῦ ὀφθαλμοῦ σου, "Let me cast out the speck in your eye."

see that the imperative does not occur in the first person. So, you can think of the hortatory subjunctive as "completing" the paradigm for the imperative. We'll talk about this more in the next chapter. Consider the following example:

καὶ εἶπεν πρὸς αὐτούς, *Διέλθωμεν* εἰς τὸ πέραν τῆς λίμνης (Luke 8:22)
And he said to them, "*Let us go* to the other side of the lake."

If you keep reading in this narrative account, it is quite evident that the disciples understood this subjunctive to be a command, because they all got into the boat! This use of the subjunctive is common in the GNT. Here are some other examples:

τρέχωμεν τὸν προκείμενον ἡμῖν ἀγῶνα (Heb 12:1)
Let us run the race set before us.

ἀγαπητοί, *ἀπαγῶμεν* ἀλλήλους (1 John 4:7)
Beloved, *let us love* one another.

Deliberative subjunctives are not as common as hortatory subjunctives. As with hortatory subjunctives, however, deliberative subjunctives appear in independent clauses. As the term suggests, this use of the subjunctive poses a question for deliberation. This may be a real question that deliberates some actual situation. For example:

τί *φάγωμεν*; (Matt 6:31)
What *shall we eat*?

Alternatively, a deliberative subjunctive may pose a rhetorical question. For example:

τί ... *δοῖ* ἄνθρωπος ἀντάλλαγμα τῆς ψυχῆς αὐτοῦ; (Mark 8:37)[5]
What *might* a person *give* in exchange for his soul?

Aorist subjunctives can function to indicate a **prohibition**, or a negated command. This use of the subjunctive does not occur with present subjunctives

---

5. If you have been looking at μι verbs with the "Heads Up!" pointers, you might have guessed that this was an aorist subjunctive of δίδωμι. If not, don't worry—you'll have time to get to know δίδωμι better later.

and occurs commonly with the second person, and only rarely with the third person.[6] There is debate as to whether this use of the subjunctive indicates a general prohibition or the command not to even begin an action. We will discuss this further in conjunction with the imperative in the next chapter.

μὴ οὖν *μεριμνήσητε* εἰς τὴν αὔριον (Matt 6:34)
Therefore, *do not worry* about tomorrow.

μὴ *σφραγίσῃς* τοὺς λόγους τῆς προφητείας τοῦ βιβλίου τούτου
(Rev 22:10)
Do not seal up the words of the prophecy of this book.

Finally, subjunctives can function to indicate **emphatic negation** or denial. This use of the subjunctive also only occurs with the aorist tense-form. The use of οὐ μή plus the aorist subjunctive (or less commonly the future indicative) is the strongest form of negation in Koine.[7] You might think of emphatic negation as turning up the volume as high as it will go! There are various ways to capture this in English, as you can see from the following example. (This might be a good time to compare various English translations of this verse to see how this Greek idiom is rendered.)

ὃς ἂν μὴ *δέξηται* τὴν βασιλείαν τοῦ θεοῦ ὡς παιδίον, *οὐ μὴ εἰσέλθῃ* εἰς
αὐτήν (Mark 10:15)
Whoever does not receive the kingdom of God as a little child *will certainly
never* enter into it.

Subordinate-Clause Functions—Adverbial

Most of the subjunctives in the GNT occur in dependent clauses that are introduced with particular subordinating conjunctions. These contextual clues are often reliable clues as to the presence of a subjunctive. One of the most common uses of the subjunctive is as a dependent verb in a ἵνα clause indicating purpose. (This clause is sometimes called a *purpose clause* or a *telic clause*.) This usage is so common that you should look for a subjunctive when you see ἵνα. Consider the following examples (the ἵνα clause is italicized):

---

6. The aorist subjunctive functioning as a prohibition is used in place of negated aorist imperatives, as we will discuss in the next chapter.

7. This is an example of the overlap in function between the aorist subjunctive and the future indicative (previously only overlapping forms were mentioned).

οὗτος ἦλθεν εἰς μαρτυρίαν ἵνα μαρτυρήσῃ περὶ τοῦ φωτός (John 1:7)
This one came as a witness *so that he might witness concerning the light.*

ταῦτα λαλῶ ἐν τῷ κόσμῳ ἵνα ἔχωσιν τὴν χαρὰν τὴν ἐμὴν πεπληρωμένην
ἐν αὐτοῖς (John 17:13)
I say these things in the world *in order that they might have my joy fulfilled
in them.*

ταῦτα γράφω ὑμῖν ἵνα μὴ ἁμάρτητε (1 John 2:1)
I write these things to you *in order that you might not sin.*

Less commonly, the subordinating conjunction ὅπως can also introduce a
purpose clause with a dependent subjunctive.

ἀπαγγείλατέ μοι, ὅπως κἀγὼ . . . προσκυνήσω αὐτῷ (Matt 2:8)
Report to me *so that I also . . . might worship him.*

When μή is used in a ἵνα or ὅπως clause (e.g., ἵνα μή or ὅπως μή), it indicates
a negative purpose, so that the consequence of the dependent clause might not
happen; this usage can be rendered with "lest" in English. For example:

γρηγορεῖτε καὶ προσεύχεσθε, ἵνα μὴ εἰσέλθητε εἰς πειρασμόν (Matt 26:41)
Watch and pray, *lest you fall into temptation.*

This could also be translated as follows: "Watch and pray *so that* you do not
fall into temptation."
The subjunctive is often used after verbs of fearing or warning and is introduced by μή or one of its compounds, such as μήποτε. This negative purpose is
also sometimes rendered with the English word "lest." For example:

φοβηθῶμεν οὖν, μήποτε . . . δοκῇ τις ἐξ ὑμῶν ὑστερηκέναι (Heb 4:1)
Therefore, let us fear *lest . . . any one of you might seem to have fallen short.*

Finally, sometimes ἵνα plus the subjunctive may indicate result.

τίς ἥμαρτεν, οὗτος ἢ οἱ γονεῖς αὐτοῦ, ἵνα τυφλὸς γεννηθῇ; (John 9:2)
Who sinned, this man or his parents *that [with the result that] he was
born blind?*

Subordinate-Clause Functions—Substantival

Less frequently, a ἵνα clause can function substantivally, as the subject or predicate of a finite verb. Consider the following example:

λέγει αὐτοῖς ὁ Ἰησοῦς, Ἐμὸν βρῶμά ἐστιν *ἵνα ποιήσω τὸ θέλημα τοῦ πέμψαντός με* (John 4:34)
Jesus says to them, "My food is *that I do the will of the one who sent me.*"

Notice here that the ἵνα clause is functioning as a predicate nominative. To test this out, you could substitute a substantive for the clause to see if it makes sense, such as ὁ ἄρτος (i.e., "my food is *bread*"); in this way, you can see that this substantive and the ἵνα clause have the same syntactic function, namely, as a predicate nominative.

A ἵνα clause may also indicate the content of a finite verb. In the example below from Luke 4:3, the ἵνα clause indicates the content of the verb εἰπέ (i.e., what Jesus should say).

εἰ υἱὸς εἶ τοῦ θεοῦ, εἰπὲ τῷ λίθῳ τούτῳ *ἵνα γένηται ἄρτος.* (Luke 4:3)
"If you are the son of God, say to this stone that *it should become bread.*"

Finally, a ἵνα clause may function epexegetically or appositionally to further explain something. In the following example, the ἵνα clause indicates *how* the Father is glorified.

ἐν τούτῳ ἐδοξάσθη ὁ πατήρ μου, *ἵνα καρπὸν πολὺν φέρητε καὶ γένησθε ἐμοὶ μαθηταί* (John 15:8)
By this my Father is glorified, *that you bear much fruit and be my disciples.*

Indefinite Relative Clauses

Subjunctives often occur in indefinite relative clauses when the antecedent is either unknown or not intended to be specified, often because it indicates a generic class rather than a specific individual. Let's return to an example that we have already considered.

ὃς ἂν μὴ δέξηται τὴν βασιλείαν τοῦ θεοῦ ὡς παιδίον, οὐ μὴ εἰσέλθῃ εἰς αὐτήν (Mark 10:15)
Whoever does not receive the kingdom of God as a little child will certainly never enter into it.

The use of ὅς ἄν or ὃ ἄν is common; somewhat less common are ὅς ἐάν and ὃ ἐάν. The indefinite relative pronoun, ὅστις, ἥτις, ὅτι, can also be followed by the subjunctive, although this usage was beginning to be replaced by the indicative by the time of the GNT.

Indefinite Temporal or Spatial Clauses

Similar to the use of the subjunctive with indefinite relative clauses is its use with adverbs, often used in combination with the particle ἄν, to indicate indefinite temporal or spatial clauses. These same adverbs can sometimes be used with the indicative if the actual time or place is known, as is indicated in some of the following examples. Consider the following examples. In the first, ὅταν occurs with the subjunctive, whereas in the second, ὅτε occurs with the indicative. (The temporal particle ὅταν is formed from ὅτε and ἄν.)

σὺ δὲ ὅταν προσεύχῃ, εἴσελθε εἰς τὸ ταμεῖόν σου ... (Matt 6:6)
But you [yourself], *whenever you pray*, enter into your storeroom ...

καὶ ὅτε ἐγγίζουσιν εἰς Ἱεροσόλυμα ... ἀποστέλλει δύο τῶν μαθητῶν αὐτοῦ (Mark 11:1)[8]
And *when they were coming near to Jerusalem* ... he sent two of his disciples.

Similarly, ἕως ἄν is usually followed by the subjunctive, whereas ἕως is followed by the indicative. Other indefinite temporal and spatial clauses are introduced by ὅπου ἄν, ἄχρις οὗ, μέχρις οὗ, and other related adverbs and particles.

Third-Class Conditional Clauses

We have already discussed the use of the particle εἰ to introduce the protasis of first- and second-class conditional clauses. The conjunction ἐάν (formed from εἰ and ἄν) is used to introduce the protasis of a *third*-class conditional, although as some of the above examples indicate, this is not the only function for ἐάν.

Third-class conditionals are quite common. Whereas first- and second-class conditionals present the protasis in a certain way for the sake of the argument, a third-class conditional presents a simple condition, that, if met, has a specified result—there are no "rhetorical" assumptions intended. Third-class conditionals are sometimes further classified as *future probable* (or *future more probable*) or

---

8. Notice the use of the present tense-form in narration—the so-called "historical present." English requires a past-tense verb here.

present general.[9] A certain element of futurity is inherent in many conditionals, but a future-probable conditional presents a condition that, if met, will lead to a future outcome. An example of this in English would be, "If we finish our courses, then we will graduate." Here is an example from the GNT (notice that the apodosis comes first and the protasis follows in this example):

ταῦτά σοι πάντα δώσω, ἐὰν πεσὼν προσκυνήσῃς μοι (Matt 4:9)
I will give all these things to you, *if you fall down and worship me.*

A present-general condition presents a general truth, such as, "If it rains, the ground gets wet"—there is no inherent futurity to the statement. For example:

ἐὰν εἴπωμεν ὅτι ἁμαρτίαν οὐκ ἔχομεν, ἑαυτοὺς πλανῶμεν καὶ ἡ ἀλήθεια
    οὐκ ἔστιν ἐν ἡμῖν. (1 John 1:8)
If we say that we have no sin, [then] we deceive ourselves and the truth is
    not in us.

It should be clear from these examples that the Greek subjunctive has a wide range of meanings and functions. As you work through the above examples, you might consider comparing various English versions to see how the subjunctive is rendered. You are likely to find many variations in these translations!

REVIEW OF CHAPTER 21

In this chapter we learned the subjunctive mood, the mood of probability or potentiality. We saw that the subjunctive occurs in only the present or aorist tense stem. The present subjunctive uses the present tense stem and a lengthened connecting vowel. First aorists use the aorist tense stem, plus the tense formative -σ and a lengthened connecting vowel. Second aorists also use the aorist tense stem but no tense formative, since their tense stem is visibly different from the present stem. There is no augment used for aorist subjunctives. Both present and aorist subjunctives use primary endings.

The subjunctive has a wide range of functions in Greek. It occurs in main clauses as a hortatory (paralleling a command), a deliberative, a prohibition, or to indicate emphatic denial. In subordinate clauses, the most common function

---

9. Wallace designates a *future-more-probable* condition as a third-class conditional, and a *present-general* condition as a fifth-class conditional (*Greek Grammar beyond the Basics*, 696–99), although most grammars combine both types of conditions into third-class conditionals.

of the subjunctive clause is to indicate purpose when introduced by ἵνα. The use of the particle ἐάν indicates a third-class conditional, which indicates a general condition. Subjunctives also occur in clauses that function substantivally and in indefinite relative, temporal, or spatial clauses.

Study Guide for Chapter 21

1. Be able to understand each of the following concepts and forms:

    the concept of verbal mood

    present subjunctive forms

    aorist subjunctive forms

    contract-verb subjunctive forms

    subjunctive mood functions: main-clause functions (hortatory, deliberative, prohibition, emphatic negation or denial) and subordinate-clause functions (adverbial [purpose], substantival)

    indefinite relative clauses

    indefinite temporal and spatial clauses

    third-class conditional clauses

2. Be able to parse subjunctive verb forms and translate basic Koine sentences that incorporate forms and concepts from previous chapters.

Vocabulary to Memorize

Here is the vocabulary for chapter 21.

δέω	I bind, I tie (43)
διέρχομαι	I go through, I cross over, I come (43)
ἐάν	if, when (351)
ἐγγύς	near, close to (31)
ἐκεῖθεν	from there (37)
ἐκπορεύομαι	I go out, I come out (33)
ἐπιγινώσκω	I know, I understand, I recognize, I learn, I know well (44)
εὐλογέω	I bless, I praise, I speak well of (42)
θεωρέω	I look at, I see, I observe (58)
ἵνα	in order that, that, so that (663)
καλῶς	well, commendably, rightly (37)
κεφαλή, -ῆς, ἡ	head (75)
κλαίω	I weep, I cry; I mourn (40)

κρατέω	(+gen) I seize, I grasp, I hold, I hold fast (47)
μέρος, -ους, τό	part, piece, party, region (42)
νίπτω	I wash (17)
προσευχή, -ῆς, ἡ	prayer, place of prayer (36)
προσφέρω	I offer, I present, I bring to (47)
σπέρμα, -ατος, τό	seed, descendants (43)
τιμή, -ῆς, ἡ	honor, price, value, respect (41)
τολμάω	I dare, I am bold, I am courageous (16)
ὑψόω	I exalt, I lift up (20)
φανερόω	I reveal, I make known (49)
χρεία, -ας, ἡ	need, necessity, lack (49)
ὥσπερ	as, just as, even as (36)

Principal Parts to Memorize

These are the principal parts that you need to memorize for chapter 21. Some of the verbs assigned for this chapter have been previously assigned, so you will now need to ensure that all principal parts are included for previously assigned verbs. The full "Principal Parts Chart" is in appendix 14.

1st prin part	2nd prin part	3rd prin part	4th prin part	5th prin part	6th prin part
ἀποθνῄσκω	ἀποθανοῦμαι	ἀπέθανον	n/a	n/a	n/a
βλέπω	βλέψω	ἔβλεψα	n/a	n/a	n/a
ἐσθίω	φάγομαι	ἔφαγον	n/a	n/a	n/a
ἔχω	ἕξω	ἔσχον	ἔσχηκα	n/a	n/a
καλέω	καλέσω	ἐκάλεσα	κέκληκα	κέκλημαι	ἐκλήθην
σῴζω	σώσω	ἔσωσα	σέσωκα	σέσῳσμαι	ἐσώθην

Paradigms to Memorize

The following paradigms should be memorized for chapter 21: the present active and middle subjunctive for λύω; the subjunctive for εἰμί; the aorist active, middle, and passive subjunctive for λύω.

PRESENT ACTIVE SUBJUNCTIVE PARADIGM OF λύω

1 sg	λύω
2 sg	λύῃς
3 sg	λύῃ
1 pl	λύωμεν
2 pl	λύητε
3 pl	λύωσι(ν)

PRESENT MIDDLE SUBJUNCTIVE PARADIGM OF λύω

1 sg	λύωμαι
2 sg	λύῃ
3 sg	λύηται
1 pl	λυώμεθα
2 pl	λύησθε
3 pl	λύωνται

SUBJUNCTIVE PARADIGM OF εἰμί

1 sg	ὦ
2 sg	ᾖς
3 sg	ᾖ
1 pl	ὦμεν
2 pl	ἦτε
3 pl	ὦσι(ν)

AORIST ACTIVE SUBJUNCTIVE PARADIGM OF λύω

1 sg	λύσω
2 sg	λύσῃς
3 sg	λύσῃ
1 pl	λύσωμεν
2 pl	λύσητε
3 pl	λύσωσι(ν)

AORIST MIDDLE SUBJUNCTIVE PARADIGM OF λύω

1 sg	λύσωμαι
2 sg	λύσῃ
3 sg	λύσηται
1 pl	λυσώμεθα
2 pl	λύσησθε
3 pl	λύσωνται

AORIST PASSIVE SUBJUNCTIVE PARADIGM OF λύω

1 sg	λυθῶ
2 sg	λυθῇς
3 sg	λυθῇ
1 pl	λυθῶμεν
2 pl	λυθῆτε
3 pl	λυθῶσι(ν)

chapter **TWENTY-TWO**

THE IMPERATIVE: *Forms and Functions;*
More Pronouns

OBJECTIVES AND OVERVIEW

Chapter 22 introduces the following linguistic concepts, morphemes, and paradigms:

- imperative personal endings
- present active and middle imperative paradigms
- aorist active, middle, and passive imperative paradigms
- forms of imperatives for contract verbs
- imperative paradigm of εἰμί
- functions of the imperative: command, prohibition
- translation of third-person imperatives
- first-, second-, and third-person reflexive-pronoun paradigms
- reciprocal-pronoun paradigm

THE IMPERATIVE: FORMS AND FUNCTIONS

So far, we have looked at two finite moods, the indicative and the subjunctive. In this chapter we learn a third finite mood, the imperative. The indicative mood makes an assertion or statement. The subjunctive mood is the mood of probability or potentiality. The imperative mood is used to communicate a command. It is the mood of intention and involves volition; it is the attempt to direct someone's actions. As with the subjunctive mood, the primary opposition in the imperative mood is between the present tense stem and the aorist tense stem.[1] Imperatives only occur in direct discourse and never in the parts

---

1. The perfect imperative is very rare and only unambiguously occurs twice in the GNT: πεφίμωσο in Mark 4:39 and ἔρρωσθε in Acts 15:29. There are two other possible occurrences, ἴστε in Eph 5:5 and in Jas 1:19; this rare plural form of οἶδα is ambiguous because it could also be an indicative. See also appendix 18, "Verbal Aspect and the Distribution of Tense-Forms, Verbal Moods, and Nonfinite Verb Forms."

of narrative that record events that took place (they do, of course, occur in the recorded speeches within those narratives). Moreover, imperatives only occur in main clauses.

The Forms of the Imperative

Imperative *forms* only occur in the second and third person. As we noted previously, there is a *functional* overlap between the subjunctive and the imperative, which is summarized as follows:

	Command
1st person	hortatory subjunctive
2nd person	imperative
3rd person	imperative

The present and aorist tense stems are used to build the imperative. Additionally, there are different sets of endings that are used with the imperative, which need to be memorized. These distinctive endings are the biggest formal clue for recognizing the imperative. Like the subjunctive, there is no augment used for aorist imperatives.

To build present imperative forms, we begin with the present tense stem, use a connecting vowel, and add an imperative ending. For example:

present tense stem	connecting vowel	imperative ending	inflected form
λυ	+ ε	+ τωσαν	→ λυέτωσαν

The second-person singular imperative endings are irregular and must be memorized as follows:

-ε	present active and second aorist active
-ου	present middle and passive; second aorist middle
-ον	first aorist active
-αι	first aorist middle
-τι	aorist passive

The remaining endings, however, are regular and occur as follows:

	active and aorist passive	middle
2 sg	various	various
3 sg	-τω	-σθω
2 pl	-τε	-σθε
3 pl	-τωσαν	-σθωσαν

Here are the paradigms for the present imperative and possible inflected meanings. Although the present imperative indicates imperfective aspect, this is not usually rendered in translation as it would be with the present or imperfect indicative. If necessary, the addition of "keep on" or "continuously" can communicate the imperfective aspect. In most cases, however, such translations feel overtranslated and are unhelpful.

PRESENT ACTIVE IMPERATIVE PARADIGM OF λύω

2 sg	λῦε	(you [sg]) release!
3 sg	λυέτω	let him/her/it release!
2 pl	λύετε	(you [pl]) release!
3 pl	λυέτωσαν	let them release!

PRESENT MIDDLE IMPERATIVE PARADIGM OF λύω[1]

2 sg	λύου	(you [sg]) release for yourself! (you [sg]) be released!
3 sg	λυέσθω	let him/her/it release for -self! let him/her/it be released!
2 pl	λύεσθε	(you [pl]) release for yourselves! (you [pl]) be released!
3 pl	λυέσθωσαν	let them release for themselves! let them be released!

[1] The same form is used for both the present middle and passive imperative. A possible translation for the middle voice is listed first, followed by a possible translation for the passive voice. Context will indicate which is intended.

Notice that the second-person plural imperative forms are identical to the corresponding second-person plural indicative forms (i.e., λύετε and λύεσθε). As usual, context will clarify which is intended, although there are some intances where the intended meaning is debated.

The first aorist active and middle imperatives use the tense formative -σα, and the first aorist passive imperative uses the tense formative -θη. To build a first aorist active imperative form, we begin with the aorist tense stem, use a tense formative, and add an imperative ending. For example:

aorist tense stem	tense formative	imperative ending	inflected form
λυ	+ σα	+ τωσαν	→ λυσάτωσαν

Here are the paradigms for the first aorist imperative of λύω. The inflected meanings are the same as the corresponding present imperative forms.

	active	middle	passive
2 sg	λῦσον	λῦσαι	λύθητι
3 sg	λυσάτω	λυσάσθω	λυθήτω
2 pl	λύσατε	λύσασθε	λύθητε
3 pl	λυσάτωσαν	λυσάσθωσαν	λυθήτωσαν

Unlike the present imperative, there is no overlap between the second-person plural imperative and the second-person plural indicative because the aorist imperative has no augment.

Second aorist imperatives are built with the aorist stem, which is visible in the third principal part for second aorist active and middle imperatives and the sixth principal part for second aorist passive imperatives. Here are some second aorist paradigms.

SECOND AORIST IMPERATIVE FORMS

	active	middle	passive[1]
2 sg	λάβε	γενοῦ	ἐπιστράφητι
3 sg	λαβέτω	γενέσθω	ἐπιστραφήτω
2 pl	λάβετε	γένεσθε	ἐπιστράφητε
3 pl	λαβέτωσαν	γενέσθωσαν	ἐπιστραφήτωσαν

[1] The passive forms are from Decker, *Reading Koine Greek*, 485.

The same vowel contraction rules that applied to forms of contract verbs that are built from the present stem apply to the present imperative forms of contract verbs. The aorist forms have a lengthened stem vowel before the tense formative (either -σα or -θη). The forms of the aorist active, middle, and passive for ποιέω only are listed, as the remaining forms are not hard to derive.

Here are the forms of the imperative for contract verbs.

PRESENT

	active	middle	active	middle	active	middle
2nd sg	τίμα	τιμῶ	ποίει	ποιοῦ	πλήρου	πληροῦ
3rd sg	τιμάτω	τιμάσθω	ποιείτω	ποιείσθω	πληρούτω	πληρούσθω
2nd pl	τιμᾶτε	τιμᾶσθε	ποιεῖτε	ποιεῖσθε	πληροῦτε	πληροῦσθε
3rd pl	τιμάτωσαν	τιμάσθωσαν	ποιείτωσαν	ποιείθωσαν	πληρούτωσαν	πληρούσθωσαν

AORIST

	active	middle	passive
2nd sg	ποίησον	ποίησαι	ποιήθητι
3rd sg	ποιησάτω	ποιησάσθω	ποιηθήτω
2nd pl	ποιήσατε	ποιήσασθε	ποιήθητε
3rd pl	ποιησάτωσαν	ποιησάσθωσαν	ποιηθήτωσαν

Finally, the paradigm for εἰμί must also be memorized. The inflected meanings are also included.

2 sg	ἴσθι	(you [sg]) be!
3 sg	ἔστω	let him/her/it be!
2 pl	ἔστε	(you [pl]) be!
3 pl	ἔστωσαν	let them be!

HEADS UP!

If you've been previewing μι verbs, look through the imperative forms for μι verbs in chapter 24 and see how many forms you can recognize based on what you have learned in this chapter. Look especially for the distinctive personal endings used for the imperative.

The Functions of the Imperative

There are two main functions of the imperative: to command or prohibit an action. In the second person, this parallels the English imperative. The Greek third-person imperative, however, has no direct equivalent in English. Consequently, third-person imperatives need to be translated with the word "let" plus a pronoun (e.g., "let them") or a pronoun and the word "must" (e.g., "they must"). If a noun is specified, the pronoun is not used.

Commands

The most common use of the imperative is to indicate a command. Present imperatives may command an action as an ongoing process. For example:

λέγει αὐτῷ, Ἀκολούθει μοι (Mark 2:14)
He said to him, "*Follow* me!"

εἰ δέ τις ὑμῶν λείπεται σοφίας, αἰτείτω παρὰ . . . θεοῦ (Jas 1:5)
But if any of you lacks wisdom, *let that one ask* God.

Aorist imperatives sometimes command an action as a whole, or they may involve a summary command. For example, notice the function of the aorist imperative in 1 Peter 2:17 to indicate a summary, which is then followed by three present imperatives that give specific examples of the aorist imperative:

πάντας τιμήσατε, τὴν ἀδελφότητα ἀγαπᾶτε, τὸν θεὸν φοβεῖσθε, τὸν βασιλέα τιμᾶτε (1 Pet 2:17)
Honor all, *love* the brothers and sisters, *fear* God, *honor* the king.

As the example from 1 Peter indicates, aorist and present commands can be better understood by comparing their uses in close proximity in the same passage. Finally, aorist imperatives are often used in prayers. For example:

ἐλθέτω ἡ βασιλεία σου· γενηθήτω τὸ θέλημά σου, ὡς ἐν οὐρανῷ καὶ ἐπὶ γῆς (Matt 6:10)
Let your kingdom *come*; *let* your will *be done*, just as in heaven, also on earth.

Prohibitions

Prohibitions are used to forbid an action and use the negative particle μή (or cognates). We have already seen that some functional overlap exists between the subjunctive and the imperative.[2] In the second-person prohibitions, Greek sometimes uses a present imperative, but an *aorist subjunctive* (*not* an aorist impera-

---

2. There is some overlap with the negated future indicative, which can also indicate a prohibition, but

tive) is much more common. (Recall from the last chapter that οὐ μή plus aorist *subjunctive* indicates strong denial.) This is summarized as follows:

PROHIBITION FUNCTION AND TENSE-FORMS

1st person	hortatory present subjunctive	hortatory aorist subjunctive
2nd person	present imperative	aorist subjunctive
3rd person	present imperative	aorist imperative

A present imperative forbids a habitual action, or in some cases commands the cessation of an ongoing action.[3] The assumption of an ongoing action, however, must be understood from the larger context. Moreover, some examples are ambiguous. Consider the following:

μὴ πλανᾶσθε· οὔτε πόρνοι οὔτε εἰδωλολάτραι οὔτε μοιχοὶ ... βασιλείαν θεοῦ κληρονομήσουσιν (1 Cor 6:9–10)
Do not be deceived, neither fornicators nor idolaters nor adulterers ...
   will inherit the kingdom of God.

Given the state of the Corinthian church, it is likely that a nuance of "stop being deceived" is intended here, although most major English translations have "do not be deceived." This would be an important point to track down in standard commentaries.

As indicated above, Greek uses an aorist subjunctive instead of an aorist imperative for second-person prohibitions. For example:

Μὴ ἅψῃ μηδὲ γεύσῃ μηδὲ θίγῃς (Col 2:21)
Do not handle, do not taste, do not touch!

Third-person prohibitions, however, use present and aorist *imperatives*.

ὁ ἐπὶ τοῦ δώματος μὴ καταβάτω ἆραι τὰ ἐκ τῆς οἰκίας αὐτοῦ, καὶ ὁ ἐν τῷ ἀγρῷ μὴ ἐπιστρεψάτω ὀπίσω ἆραι τὸ ἱμάτιον αὐτου (Matt 24:17–18)
The one on the housetop *must not go down* to take things out of his house,
   and the one in the field *must not turn* back to take his coat.

---

this form is nearly always found in OT citations (e.g., Matt 19:18), or passages that are influenced by these citations (see Wallace, *Greek Grammar beyond the Basics*, 569).

3. This was a common assumption of older Greek grammars, but more recent research has not confirmed the claim that present prohibitions necessarily concern an action that has already begun. The implications of this are important—there is a great deal of difference between saying "stop lying" and "do not lie." If the cessation of an action that has already begun is intended, it must be inferred from the overall context.

Translation of Third-Person Imperatives

Generally, the translation of second-person imperatives poses no real challenge, as the function of the Greek imperative closely parallels the function of the English imperative. As noted, the third-person imperative is not as clear-cut. The words "let him/her/it . . ." or "let them . . ." are often used with Greek third-person imperatives. It is also possible to use the words "he/she/it must . . ." or "they must . . ." Unfortunately, these translations can sound like suggestions in English, so it is important to understand that the third-person imperative is a command, or if negated, a prohibition—it is not merely a suggestion! Finally, sometimes an exclamation point is used when translating imperatives.

REFLEXIVE AND RECIPROCAL PRONOUNS

Reflexive Pronouns

A reflexive pronoun refers back to the subject of the clause to indicate that the subject is performing the action upon itself; hence, it never occurs in the nominative case. Reflexive pronouns always occur in the predicate position. Here are some examples of reflexive pronouns in the GNT.

> ἐγώ ἁγιάζω ἐμαυτόν (John 17:19)
> I [myself] consecrate *myself.*

> ἑαυτοὺς πλανῶμεν (1 John 1:8)
> We deceive *ourselves.*

> ἄλλους ἔσωσεν, σωσάτω ἑαυτόν (Luke 23:35)
> He saved others, let him save *himself.*

Notice that the *first-person* reflexive pronoun uses the prefix ἐμ-; the rest of the form follows the paradigm of αὐτός, αὐτή, αὐτό, but notice also that this form only occurs in the singular. It indicates "myself."

The *second-person* reflexive pronoun uses the prefix σε-; the rest of the form follows the paradigm of αὐτός, αὐτή, αὐτό, but notice that this form only occurs in the singular. It indicates "yourself."

The third-person reflexive pronoun uses the prefix ἑ-; the rest of the form follows the paradigm of αὐτός, αὐτή, αὐτό. This form occurs in both the singular ("itself") and the plural ("themselves"). The plural forms are also used for the first-person ("ourselves") and second-person ("yourselves") reflexive pronouns.

FIRST-PERSON REFLEXIVE PRONOUN

	masc (2)	fem (1)
nom sg	-	-
gen sg	ἐμαυτοῦ	ἐμαυτῆς
dat sg	ἐμαυτῷ	ἐμαυτῇ
acc sg	ἐμαυτόν	ἐμαυτήν

SECOND-PERSON REFLEXIVE PRONOUN

	masc (2)	fem (1)
nom sg	-	-
gen sg	σεαυτοῦ	σεαυτῆς
dat sg	σεαυτῷ	σεαυτῇ
acc sg	σεαυτόν	σεαυτήν

THIRD-PERSON REFLEXIVE PRONOUN

	masc (2)	fem (1)	neut (2)
nom sg	-	-	-
gen sg	ἑαυτοῦ	ἑαυτῆς	ἑαυτοῦ
dat sg	ἑαυτῷ	ἑαυτῇ	ἑαυτῷ
acc sg	ἑαυτόν	ἑαυτήν	ἑαυτό
nom pl	-	-	-
gen pl	ἑαυτῶν	ἑαυτῶν	ἑαυτῶν
dat pl	ἑαυτοῖς	ἑαυταῖς	ἑαυτοῖς
acc pl	ἑαυτούς	ἑαυτάς	ἑαυτά

Personal pronouns can sometimes be used to indicate a reflexive idea. For example:

ἄρατε τὸν ζυγόν μου ἐφ᾽ ὑμᾶς (Matt 11:29)
Take my yoke upon yourselves.

The Reciprocal Pronoun

This pronoun is derived from the adjective ἄλλος and can be translated "one another" or "each other." The action of the verb is either performed by members of a group acting upon each other or mutually applies within the group. This form does not occur in the nominative or singular. Here is the full paradigm.

RECIPROCAL PRONOUN

	masc (2)	fem (1)	neut (2)
nom pl	-	-	-
gen pl	ἀλλήλων	ἀλλήλων	ἀλλήλων
dat pl	ἀλλήλοις	ἀλλήλαις	ἀλλήλοις
acc pl	ἀλλήλους	ἀλλήλας	ἀλλήλα

Here is an example of the reciprocal pronoun in the GNT.

κοινωνίαν ἔχομεν μετ᾽ ἀλλήλων (1 John 1:7)
We have fellowship with *one another*.

A reciprocal idea may also be indicated by the reflexive pronoun or the phrase εἰς τὸν ἕνα. For example:

κρίματα ἔχετε μεθ᾽ ἑαυτῶν (1 Cor 6:7)
You have lawsuits against *one another*.

οἰκοδομεῖτε εἰς τὸν ἕνα (1 Thess 5:11)
Build *one another* up.

REVIEW OF CHAPTER 22

In this chapter we learned the imperative mood and saw how, together with the first-person subjunctive, it completes the function of command for all persons and numbers. We learned the distinctive endings for the present and aorist personal endings for the imperative, the only two tense-forms in which the imperative occurs. We also considered the function of the imperative, which is to command, either positively or negatively (a prohibition). We considered some of the difficulties of rendering third-person imperatives into English. In this chapter, we also learned the form and function of reflexive and reciprocal pronouns.

Study Guide for Chapter 22

1. Be able to understand each of the following concepts and forms:
   present imperative forms
   aorist imperative forms
   forms of the imperative for contract verbs
   imperative mood functions: commands, prohibitions
   translating third-person imperatives
   reflexive-pronoun forms
   reciprocal-pronoun forms
2. Be able to parse imperative verb forms and translate basic Koine sentences that incorporate forms and concepts from previous chapters.

Vocabulary to Memorize

These are the vocabulary words that you need to memorize for chapter 22.

ἀλλήλων	one another, each other (100)
ἄλλος, -η, -ο	other, another (155)
ἄνεμος, -ου, ὁ	wind (31)
ἀπαγγέλλω	I announce, I proclaim, I report, I tell (45)
ἅπτω	(+gen) I kindle, ignite; I touch, I take hold (mid) (39)
ἄχρι (+gen)	until, as far as; until (conj) (49)
βιβλίον, -ου, τό	book, scroll, document (34)
ἑαυτοῦ, -ῆς, -οῦ	(of) himself, herself, itself; themselves (pl) (319)
ἐλπίζω	I hope, I expect (31)
ἐμαυτοῦ, -ῆς	(of) myself (37)
ἐνδύω	I clothe, I dress; I put on, I wear (mid) (27)
ἐπιζητέω	I search, I wish for, I seek after (13)
ἑτοιμάζω	I prepare, I make ready (40)
ἔτος, -ους, τό	year (49)
εὐχαριστέω	I give thanks, I am thankful (38)
θλῖψις, -εως, ἡ	tribulation, oppression, trouble (45)
καταισχύνω	I humiliate, I put to shame; I am disappointed (pass) (13)
μισέω	I hate, I disdain (40)
ὁμοιόω	(+dat) I make like, I compare; I resemble (pass) (15)
πράσσω	I do, I accomplish, I practice (39)
σεαυτοῦ, -ῆς	(of) yourself (43)
ταράσσω	I trouble, I disturb, I upset (17)
ὑπακούω	(+dat) I obey (21)
φυλακή, -ῆς, ἡ	watch, guard, prison, watch (47)
φωνέω	I call, I summon, I invite (43)

Principal Parts to Memorize

These are the principal parts that you need to memorize for chapter 22. Some of the verbs assigned for this chapter have been previously assigned, so you will now need to ensure that all principal parts are included for previously assigned verbs. The full "Principal Parts Chart" is in appendix 14.

1st prin part	2nd prin part	3rd prin part	4th prin part	5th prin part	6th prin part
-βαίνω	-βήσομαι	-ἔβην	-βέβηκα	n/a	n/a
βάλλω	βαλῶ	ἔβαλον	βέβληκα	βέβλημαι	ἐβλήθην
γινώσκω	γνώσομαι	ἔγνων	ἔγνωκα	ἔγνωσμαι	ἐγνώσθην
ὁράω	ὄψομαι	εἶδον	ἑώρακα	n/a	ὤφθην
φέρω	οἴσω	ἤνεγκα	ἐνήνοχα	n/a	ἠνέχθην

Paradigms to Memorize

The following paradigms should be memorized for chapter 22: the present active and middle imperative for λύω; the imperative for εἰμί; the aorist active, middle, and passive imperative for λύω; the aorist active imperative for λαμβάνω; the aorist middle imperative for γίνομαι; reflexive pronoun forms (first, second, third person); reciprocal pronoun.

PRESENT ACTIVE IMPERATIVE PARADIGM OF λύω

1 sg	-
2 sg	λῦε
3 sg	λυέτω
1 pl	-
2 pl	λύετε
3 pl	λυέτωσαν

PRESENT MIDDLE IMPERATIVE PARADIGM OF λύω

1 sg	-
2 sg	λύου
3 sg	λυέσθω
1 pl	-
2 pl	λύεσθε
3 pl	λυέσθωσαν

IMPERATIVE PARADIGM OF εἰμί

1 sg	-
2 sg	ἴσθι
3 sg	ἔστω
1 pl	-
2 pl	ἔστε
3 pl	ἔστωσαν

FIRST AORIST ACTIVE IMPERATIVE PARADIGM OF λύω

1 sg	-
2 sg	λῦσον
3 sg	λυσάτω
1 pl	-
2 pl	λύσατε
3 pl	λυσάτωσαν

FIRST AORIST MIDDLE IMPERATIVE PARADIGM OF λύω

1 sg	-
2 sg	λῦσαι
3 sg	λυσάσθω
1 pl	-
2 pl	λύσασθε
3 pl	λυσάσθωσαν

FIRST AORIST PASSIVE IMPERATIVE PARADIGM OF λύω

1 sg	-
2 sg	λύθητι
3 sg	λυθήτω
1 pl	-
2 pl	λύθητε
3 pl	λυθήτωσαν

SECOND AORIST ACTIVE IMPERATIVE PARADIGM OF λαμβάνω

1 sg	-
2 sg	λάβε
3 sg	λαβέτω
1 pl	-
2 pl	λάβετε
3 pl	λαβέτωσαν

SECOND AORIST MIDDLE IMPERATIVE PARADIGM OF γίνομαι

1 sg	-
2 sg	γενοῦ
3 sg	γενέσθω
1 pl	-
2 pl	γένεσθε
3 pl	γενέσθωσαν

FIRST-PERSON REFLEXIVE PRONOUN

	masc (2)	fem (1)
nom sg	-	-
gen sg	ἐμαυτοῦ	ἐμαυτῆς
dat sg	ἐμαυτῷ	ἐμαυτῇ
acc sg	ἐμαυτόν	ἐμαυτήν

SECOND-PERSON REFLEXIVE PRONOUN

	masc (2)	fem (1)
nom sg	-	-
gen sg	σεαυτοῦ	σεαυτῆς
dat sg	σεαυτῷ	σεαυτῇ
acc sg	σεαυτόν	σεαυτήν

THIRD-PERSON REFLEXIVE PRONOUN

	masc (2)	fem (1)	neut (2)
nom sg	-	-	-
gen sg	ἑαυτοῦ	ἑαυτῆς	ἑαυτοῦ
dat sg	ἑαυτῷ	ἑαυτῇ	ἑαυτῷ
acc sg	ἑαυτόν	ἑαυτήν	ἑαυτό
nom pl	-	-	-
gen pl	ἑαυτῶν	ἑαυτῶν	ἑαυτῶν
dat pl	ἑαυτοῖς	ἑαυταῖς	ἑαυτοῖς
acc pl	ἑαυτούς	ἑαυτάς	ἑαυτά

RECIPROCAL PRONOUN

	masc (2)	fem (1)	neut (2)
nom pl	-	-	-
gen pl	ἀλλήλων	ἀλλήλων	ἀλλήλων
dat pl	ἀλλήλοις	ἀλλήλαις	ἀλλήλοις
acc pl	ἀλλήλους	ἀλλήλας	ἄλληλα

chapter **TWENTY-THREE**

THE INFINITIVE: *Forms and Functions*

OBJECTIVES AND OVERVIEW

Chapter 23 introduces the following linguistic concepts, morphemes, and paradigms:

- present, aorist, future, and perfect active, middle, and passive infinitive paradigms
- infinitive of εἰμί
- infinitive forms for contract verbs
- adverbial functions of infinitives: purpose, result, causal, temporal
- complementary infinitives
- "subject" of an infinitive
- substantival infinitives

The Greek infinitive is a verbal noun. The infinitive expresses a verbal idea as an abstract concept, which is generally rendered in English as "to *verbal idea*"; for example, "to love" or "to study."[1] Like *verbs*, infinitives have aspect (indicated by tense stems) and voice, but no person and mood. Thus, infinitives are not finite verbs—as the term *infinitive* would suggest. An infinitive can also have a direct object and adverbial modifiers, such as a prepositional phrase or an adverb. Infinitives are normally negated by μή. Like *nouns*, infinitives may function as a subject or an object; they may also be modified by an adjective or the neuter singular article. (The neuter underscores the use of the infinitive to express a verbal action as an abstract concept.) Anarthrous infinitives, however, are more common than articular infinitives.

Infinitives may be built from the present, aorist, future, or perfect tense stems, which indicate the aspect of the infinitive. Future infinitives are relatively rare. The aorist infinitive, however, may be understood as the "default" aspect,

---

1. The use of "to" as a verbal auxiliary here should not be confused with the preposition "to."

which is used unless there are reasons to use the present (less frequent) or the perfect infinitive (even less frequent). Thus, the choice of a present or perfect infinitive often represents a deliberate choice by an author or speaker. It is often difficult to render aspectual differences of Greek infinitives in English, but adding "continuously" to present infinitives is sometimes possible, although often this can be awkward or unnecessary.

THE FORMS OF THE INFINITIVE

The forms of the infinitive are relatively easy to memorize because they do not decline (as is true with participle forms). This means that there are comparatively few forms to memorize. Here are the infinitive paradigms.[2] The infinitive of εἰμί is εἶναι.

	pres (λύω)	1st aor (λύω)	2nd aor (various)	fut (λύω)	pf (λύω)
act	λύειν	λῦσαι	λαβεῖν	λύσειν	λελυκέναι
mid	λύεσθαι	λύσασθαι	λαβέσθαι	λύσεσθαι	λελύσθαι
pass	λύεσθαι	λυθῆναι	γραφῆναι	λυθήσεσθαι	λελύσθαι

Notice that the connecting vowel ε is used in the present middle and passive forms, the second aorist middle form, and the future middle and passive forms because the infinitive ending for these forms do not end in a mu or nu. Notice also that the second aorist forms are built on the unaugmented aorist tense stems, which can be determined from the third (active) and sixth (passive) principal parts. The use of tense formatives follows the patterns that we have seen so far (with the predictable morphological changes already noted). These tense formatives can be summarized as follows:

-σα is used with the first aorist active and middle forms
-θη is used with the first aorist passive form
-σ is used with the future active and middle forms
-θησ is used with the future passive form
-κ is used with the perfect active form
- no tense formative (or connecting vowel) is used with the perfect middle and passive forms

---

2. A guide for translating Greek infinitives is found in appendix 8.

All infinitive morphemes, except the present active and second aorist active, end in αι. As was true with the participle, subjunctive, and imperative, there is no augment with the aorist infinitive. But like the participle, subjunctive, and imperative, reduplication occurs with perfect infinitives. Vowel-contraction rules explain the infinitive forms for contract verbs, which follow regular vowel-contraction rules in the present infinitive forms, except that the ending for the present active infinitive with contract verbs is -εν, not -ειν.[3] Here are the forms for the three contract verbs that you memorized in chapter 18. You do not need to memorize these forms, but you should be able to recognize them when you see them in the GNT.

	pres	1st aor		pres	1st aor		pres	1st aor
act	τιμᾶν	τιμῆσαι	*act*	ποιεῖν	ποιῆσαι	*act*	πληροῦν	πληρῶσαι
mid	τιμᾶσθαι		*mid*	ποιεῖσθαι		*mid*	πληροῦσθαι	

> **HEADS UP!**
>
> We are almost there, but if you want to look ahead, look through the infinitive forms for μι verbs in chapter 25 and see how many forms you can recognize based on what you have learned in this chapter.

THE FUNCTIONS OF THE INFINITIVE

Infinitives can either function adverbially or substantivally. The adverbial function is more common. Additionally, several adverbial constructions involving an articular Greek infinitive as the object of a preposition have no direct parallel in English. Rendering these constructions in English can sometimes be challenging, which is often indicated by the wide range of translations among English versions for such constructions. These idiomatic constructions must be memorized, as any attempt to translate these constructions word-for-word will not make sense. These constructions are discussed according to their function (e.g., purpose, result, temporal) so that parallel functions of the infinitive that use different syntax can be seen more clearly. In these examples, notice that although the *case* of

---

3. Actually, the infinitive ending is always -εν, but with the connecting vowel ε this contracts to -ειν. With contract verbs, however, the connecting vowel is not used.

the article changes as required by the preposition, the *form* of the infinitive does not change because it is indeclinable. Also notice that this prepositional *phrase* is best rendered in English as a subordinate *clause*.

Adverbial Infinitives—Purpose

Perhaps the most common use of the adverbial infinitive is to indicate **purpose**. This can be done in one of three ways. First, an anarthrous Greek infinitive that occurs by itself to modify a main verb nearly always indicates purpose. This is common:

ἤλθομεν *προσκυνῆσαι* αὐτῷ. (Matt 2:2)
We came *to worship* him.

Second, an articular (specifically, the genitive singular neuter τοῦ) infinitive that modifies a main verb also indicates purpose. This is also common. For example:

ἐξῆλθεν ὁ σπείρων *τοῦ σπεῖραι* (Luke 8:5)
The sower went out *to sow*.

Third, there are two articular infinitive constructions that also indicate purpose: εἰς or πρός followed by τό plus an infinitive indicate purpose (or less commonly result). The accusative article is required by both εἰς and πρός. Both constructions are often translated "in order that." For example:

οἱ δὲ ἀρχιερεῖς καὶ ὅλον τὸ συνέδριον ἐζήτουν κατὰ τοῦ Ἰησοῦ μαρτυρίαν
εἰς τὸ θανατῶσαι αὐτόν (Mark 14:55)
But the chief priests and the whole Sanhedrin were seeking testimony against Jesus *in order to kill him.*

προσέχετε [δὲ] τὴν δικαιοσύνην ὑμῶν μὴ ποιεῖν ἔμπροσθεν τῶν ἀνθρώπων
πρὸς τὸ θεαθῆναι αὐτοῖς (Matt 6:1)
Be careful not to do your [works of] righteousness before people *in order to be seen by them.*

Adverbial Infinitives—Result

Another common adverbial function of infinitives is to indicate *result*. This is most commonly indicated by a dependent ὥστε clause with an infinitive.

If this infinitive is articular, the accusative singular neuter τό is used. Often this is rendered in English as a dependent clause beginning with "so that" or "with the result that" and an English finite verb. For example:

ἔπλησαν ἀμφότερα τὰ πλοῖα ὥστε βυθίζεσθαι αὐτά (Luke 5:7)
[The waves] filled both boats *with the result that they began to sink.*

Adverbial Infinitives—Causal

Adverbial infinitives can also indicate *reason*, or causality, by means of the preposition διά followed by the accusative neuter article τό, followed by an infinitive. Recall that διά in the accusative case indicates cause. This construction is often translated "because." For example:

ὅτε ἀνέτειλεν ὁ ἥλιος ἐκαυματίσθη καὶ διὰ τὸ μὴ ἔχειν ῥίζαν ἐξηράνθη
  (Mark 4:6)
When the sun rose it was scorched and *because it had no root* it was
  withered up.

Adverbial Infinitives—Temporal

Adverbial infinitives can also have a *temporal* function. This function involves an articular infinitive as the object of a preposition. Notice that each of these constructions is usually translated as a subordinate clause in English. *Antecedent time* relative to the main verb is indicated by πρό τοῦ plus an infinitive (or less commonly πρίν τό plus an infinitive). These constructions are usually translated "before." For example:

οἶδεν γὰρ ὁ πατὴρ ὑμῶν ὧν χρείαν ἔχετε πρὸ τοῦ ὑμᾶς αἰτῆσαι αὐτόν
  (Matt 6:8)
For your Father knows what you have need of *before you ask him.*

Contemporaneous time relative to the main verb is indicated by ἐν τῷ plus an infinitive. This construction can be translated "while," "as," or "when." For example:

καὶ ἐν τῷ σπείρειν αὐτὸν ἃ μὲν ἔπεσεν παρὰ τὴν ὁδόν (Matt 13:4)
And *as he sowed* some [seeds] fell by the road.

Subsequent time relative to the main verb may be indicated by μετὰ τό plus an infinitive. Recall that μετά in the accusative case can be translated as "after" or "behind," so this construction follows logically from this use of μετά. Not surprisingly, this construction is often translated "after." For example:

μετὰ δὲ τὸ ἐγερθῆναί με προάξω ὑμᾶς εἰς τὴν Γαλιλαίαν (Matt 26:32)
But *after I have been raised*, I will go ahead of you to Galilee.

Complementary Infinitives

An infinitive can function to complete the meaning of a finite verb, such as δεῖ or ἔξεστιν. Each of these verbs is incomplete by themselves. If we see δεῖ, we are left asking, "It is necessary to do *what*?" The use of the infinitive to complete the meaning of a finite verb is is often called a **complementary infinitive**. The focus is on the verbal action or state of the infinitive; for example, "it is necessary to *believe*." Complementary infinitives are always anarthrous. Other verbs that are frequently followed by a complementary infinitive include the following: ἄρχομαι, βούλομαι, δοκεῖ, δύναμαι, ἐπιτρέπω, ζητέω, θέλω, μέλλω, and ὀφείλω. The use of ἄρχομαι and δύναμαι with complementary infinitives is very common. For example:

οὐ δύνασθε θεῷ δουλεύειν καὶ μαμωνᾷ (Matt 6:24)
You are not able to serve God and money.

The "Subject" of an Infinitive

Strictly speaking, because the infinitive is not a finite verb, it cannot have a grammatical subject. Often, however, there is an implied "subject" of the infinitive, which is frequently the same as the subject of the main verb. For example, in Matthew 2:2, the magi say: ἤλθομεν προσκυνῆσαι αὐτῷ ("we came to worship him"). It is clear here that the subject of the main finite verb and the infinitive is the same, namely, the magi. Sometimes, however, the "subject" of the infinitive is different from the main verb, which is indicated by an accusative-case noun or pronoun.[4] For example:

οὐ θέλω δὲ ὑμᾶς ἀγνοεῖν (Rom 1:13)
I do not want *you* to be ignorant.

Here the subject of the main verb θέλω is Paul, but the "subject" of the infinitive ἀγνοεῖν is ὑμᾶς, the epistle's recipients.

---

4. Technically, this is an accusative of general reference or an accusative of respect, but at this point it is perhaps easier to consider this accusative as functioning as the subject of the infinitive.

Substantival Infinitives

An infinitive may also function as a substantive, either as the subject or as the direct object of a finite verb. An example of an infinitive functioning as a subject occurs in Philippians 1:21:

ἐμοὶ γὰρ τὸ ζῆν Χριστὸς καὶ τὸ ἀποθανεῖν κέρδος
For me *to live* is Christ and *to die* is gain.

An example of an infinitive functioning as a direct object occurs in 1 Corinthians 14:39:

ζηλοῦτε τὸ προφητεύειν
Desire *to prophesy.*

Summary of Infinitive Functions

The functions of the infinitive may be summarized as follows:[5]

ANARTHROUS INFINITIVES

Form	Function
simple infinitive	purpose, result, complementary, subject, direct object (rare), indirect discourse, apposition, epexegesis
πρίν (ἤ) + infinitive	subsequent time
ὡς + infinitive	purpose, result
ὥστε + infinitive	result, purpose (rare)

ARTICULAR INFINITIVES

Form	Function
nom articular (no prep)	subject or appositive
acc articular (no prep)	object or appositive
gen articular (no prep)	purpose, result, contemporaneous time (rare), cause (rare), epexegesis, apposition
διὰ τό + infinitive	cause
εἰς τό + infinitive	purpose, result, epexegesis (rare)

---

5. This chart is summarized from Wallace, *Greek Grammar beyond the Basics*, 609–11.

ἐν τῷ + infinitive	contemporaneous time, means
μετὰ τό + infinitive	antecedent time
πρὸς τό + infinitive	purpose, result

Parsing

As the preceding discussion has shown, rendering Greek infinitives into English is not always straightforward. For the purposes of parsing, however, you should give an inflected meaning as a simple infinitive.[6] For example, the inflected meaning for ἔχειν would be "to have."

REVIEW OF CHAPTER 23

In this chapter we learned about the Greek infinitive, which is a verbal noun. Because the infinitive does not decline (and thus does not use case endings), the forms are relatively simple. Once the distinctive tense-form and voice endings are learned, the infinitive is easy to recognize.

The function of the infinitive is a bit more complicated, although many adverbial infinitives function to indicate purpose or result. Other adverbial infinitives indicate causality or have a temporal function. We also learned about complementary infinitives, which are used to complete the meaning of a finite verb. For many infinitives, the implied subject is the same as that of the finite verb upon which the infinitive depends. When the implied subject is different, a substantive in the accusative can indicate the "subject" of an infinitive. Finally, we saw that infinitives can also function substantivally, as either a subject or direct object of a finite verb.

Study Guide for Chapter 23

1. Be able to understand each of the following concepts and forms:
   present infinitive forms
   aorist infinitive forms
   perfect infinitive forms
   infinitive functions: articular infinitives as the object of a preposition;
      adverbial infinitives (purpose, result, reason, temporal,
      complementary); substantival infinitives

---

6. Moreover, strictly speaking, mood does not apply to infinitives, but for the sake of convenience place the word *infinitive* in the mood slot for parsing purposes. See appendix 17, "Standard Abbreviations and Parsing Order," for more information.

2. Be able to parse infinitive verb forms and translate basic Koine sentences that incorporate forms and concepts from previous chapters.

Vocabulary to Memorize

Here are the vocabulary words that you need to memorize for chapter 23.

ἀναγινώσκω	I read, I read aloud (32)
ἀντί (+gen)	in place of, on behalf of, for, because of (22)
ἄρχω	I rule; I begin (mid) (86)
βούλομαι	I wish, I desire, I intend (37)
γνῶσις, -εως, ἡ	knowledge, esoteric knowledge (29)
δεῖ	it is necessary, one must (impers) (101)
δύναμαι	I am able, I can (210)
ἔξεστι(ν)	it is lawful, it is permitted, it is proper (impers) (31)
ἐχθρός, -ά, -όν	hostile, hating; enemy (subst) (32)
θύρα, -ας, ἡ	door, gate, entrance (39)
μέλλω	I am about to, I intend (109)
μυστήροιν, -ου, τό	secret, mystery (28)
οἰκοδομέω	I build, I build up (40)
ὀλίγος, -η, -ον	little, small; few (pl) (40)
ὀφείλω	I owe, I ought, I am obligated (35)
παραγίνομαι	I come, I appear, I arrive, I stand by (37)
πάσχα, τό	Passover, Passover meal, Passover lamb (29)
περιτέμνω	I circumcise (17)
περιτομή, -ῆς, ἡ	circumcision, those who are circumcised (36)
πρίν (+gen)	before (13)
προσκαλέομαι	I summon, I invite, I call (29)
στρέφω	I turn, I return; I turn around (21)
τέλος, -ους, τό	end, goal; tax (40)
ὑποτάσσω	I subject, I subordinate; I obey (pass) (38)
χωρίζω	I divide, I separate; I go away (pass) (13)

Principal Parts to Memorize

These are the principal parts that you need to memorize for chapter 23. Some of the verbs assigned for this chapter have been previously assigned, so you will now need to ensure that all principal parts are included for previously assigned verbs. The full "Principal Parts Chart" is in appendix 14.

1st prin part	2nd prin part	3rd prin part	4th prin part	5th prin part	6th prin part
γράφω	γράψω	ἔγραψα	γέγραφα	γέγραμμαι	ἐγράφην
δέω	n/a	ἔδησα	δέδεκα	δέδεμαι	ἐδέθην
n/a	εἰδήσω	n/a	οἶδα (plpf ᾔδειν)	n/a	n/a
πάσχω	n/a	ἔπαθον	πέπονθα	n/a	n/a
πίπτω	πεσοῦμαι	ἔπεσον	πέπτωκα	n/a	N/A

Paradigms to Memorize

The following paradigms should be memorized for chapter 23: the present active and middle infinitive for λύω; the infinitive for εἰμί; the aorist active, middle, and passive infinitive for λύω; and the aorist active and middle infinitive for λαμβάνω.

INFINITIVE PARADIGM

	pres (of λύω)	1st aor (of λύω)	2nd aor
act.	λύειν	λῦσαι	λαβεῖν
mid	λύεσθαι	λύσασθαι	λαβέσθαι
pass	λύεσθαι	λυθῆναι	γραφῆναι

Infinitive of εἰμί: εἶναι

chapter TWENTY-FOUR

μι VERBS: *Finite Forms*

OBJECTIVES AND OVERVIEW

Chapter 24 introduces the following linguistic concepts, morphemes, and paradigms:

- distinctive morphology of μι verbs: reduplication in the present stem, stem-vowel lengthening, (some) new personal endings
- present, imperfect, and perfect active and middle indicative paradigms for μι verbs
- future and aorist active, middle, and passive indicative paradigms for μι verbs
- present and aorist active and middle subjunctive paradigms for μι verbs
- present and aorist active and middle imperative paradigms for μι verbs

So far, nearly all the verb forms that we learned have a lexical form that ends in an omega, or -ομαι if the omega verb does not have an active form in the present stem.[1] An important exception to this is εἰμί, which we have been learning along the way. In this chapter, we will learn a different class of verbs that are collectively referred to as μι verbs, of which εἰμί is one example. This is simply a different pattern for verb conjugations, much the same as there are different declensions for nouns. Just as there is no *semantic* difference between a nominative singular noun regardless of whether it is a first, second, or third declension noun, the same is true for μι verbs—there is no *semantic* difference between a present active indicative verb, regardless of whether it is an omega verb or a μι verb. Hence the focus of this chapter will be on the *forms* of μι verbs because their semantic function is exactly the same as omega verbs. Since μι verbs are very common in the GNT, we have been directing you to this chapter and chapter 25 throughout the book. Hopefully by now, these verb forms are beginning to look familiar.

---

1. After so many "Heads Up!" warnings, you are probably glad to get to this chapter and the next! But if you have been looking ahead to these two chapters, all these new forms will feel much less overwhelming.

DISTINCTIVES OF μι VERBS

Omega verbs are sometimes called *thematic* verbs because they use a connecting vowel (ο or ε) between the tense stem and the personal endings. By contrast, μι verbs are sometimes called *athematic* verbs because *they do not use a connecting vowel*. Instead, their stems end in a vowel to which the personal ending is directly added. Because there is no connecting vowel, vowel contraction rules do not apply.

One of the most distinctive features of μι verbs is the *reduplication of the initial letter of the present tense* stem with an iota. This reduplication is seen in *all* forms (finite and nonfinite) that are built from the present stem, including the imperfect indicative. The morphological rules for reduplication that apply to the perfect tense stem also apply to reduplication with μι verbs. So an initial consonant will reduplicate, unless it is a fricative (e.g., φ), which reduplicates to its corresponding voiceless stop (e.g., π), and so on.[2] The vowel that is inserted between the reduplicated letter, however, is an iota, not an epsilon. This reduplication for three examples of μι verbs looks like the following:

root	→ reduplication
√στα	→ ἱστη
√θε	→ τιθη
√δο	→ διδω

Moreover, μι verbs can be further classified according to their root vowel. The lexical form of the verbal root √στα is ἵστημι ("I stand" or "I set"). Once you are familiar with one example of a μι verb that has a root ending in an alpha, such as ἵστημι (notice the η in this form—it is a lengthened α), you will be able to recognize other μι verbs with roots ending with an alpha. Similarly, once you are familiar with a μι verb that has a root ending in an epsilon, such as √θε, whose lexical form is τίθημι ("I place" or "I appoint"), you will be able to recognize other μι verbs with roots ending with an epsilon (notice the η in this form—it is a lengthened ε). Finally, once you are familiar with a μι verb that has a root ending in an omicron, such as √δο, whose lexical form is δίδωμι ("I give"; notice the ω in this form—it is a lengthened ο), you will be able to recognize other verbs with roots ending an omicron. Apart from εἰμί, three of the most common μι verbs in the GNT are δίδωμι, ἵστημι, and τίθημι. These are the paradigms that we will be learning in this chapter and the next.

---

2. Similarly, a θ reduplicates to a τ, and consonant clusters use vocalic reduplication, etc. You can refer to chapter 16 to review this.

As suggested above, the final vowel of the root is often not visible in the various tense stems, because another distinctive of μι verbs is that the *stem vowel frequently lengthens*, as follows:

α /ε   → η
ο   → ω

This vowel lengthening occurs throughout most of the paradigm. In the present indicative, however, only the active singular forms have lengthened stem vowels; in the imperfect active singular forms, stem-vowel lengthening takes the form of a diphthong for roots that end in an omicron, as you will see in the paradigms below. Keep in mind that you will almost always be able to recognize μι verbs, even if you don't remember all these specific morphological distinctives discussed here.

In addition to reduplication and vowel lengthening, there are *three new personal endings* that appear in the present active indicative. All other personal endings are the same as the ones that we have seen so far (you have already seen the first-person singular ending in εἰμί).

-μι	first-person singular
-σι(ν)	third-person singular
-ασι(ν)	third-person plural

Once you have a good grasp of the distinctive characteristics of μι verbs and have memorized the assigned vocabulary, you will be able to recognize most μι-verb forms as they occur in exercises and, more importantly, in the GNT. Because of the distinctive elements in the present, imperfect, and aorist paradigms, those need to be memorized. It is unnecessary, however, to memorize the remaining paradigms, as you should be able to recognize the forms based on what you know already from omega verbs. As we go through the finite-verb paradigms for μι verbs, we will call attention to the distinctive characteristics of these verbs and paradigms that you will need to memorize.

Indicative Forms

With this in mind, let's look at finite forms for μι verbs. For most examples, we will use the common μι verb, δίδωμι. Since not all forms of a given paradigm for δίδωμι occur in the GNT, in some cases we will substitute ἵστημι for some paradigms. Do not get overwhelmed with this parade of paradigms. The goal is to recognize (which you will be able to do) and not to memorize every paradigm. We begin with the present indicative paradigms. Like omega verbs, the present middle and present passive use the same form.

PRESENT INDICATIVE FORMS FOR μι VERBS

	active	middle
1 sg	δίδωμι	δίδομαι
2 sg	δίδως	δίδοσαι
3 sg	δίδωσι(ν)	δίδοται
1 pl	δίδομεν	διδόμεθα
2 pl	δίδοτε	δίδοσθε
3 pl	διδόασι(ν)	δίδονται

As you can see, there is reduplication throughout the paradigm, and the stem vowel lengthens to an omega in the active singular forms (δίδωμι, δίδως, and δίδωσιν); otherwise, the omicron stem ending is visible (δο-). Notice also the three new personal endings (in bold): -μι, -σι(ν), and -ασι(ν). Finally, notice that in the present middle indicative second-person singular the intervocalic sigma does not drop out, even though the ending -σαι is added directly to the present stem διδο-.

Now let's look at the imperfect indicative paradigm for δίδωμι. Notice the reduplication throughout the paradigm and the stem vowel lengthening to the diphthong ου in the active singular forms (ἐδίδουν, ἐδίδους, and ἐδίδου); elsewhere the omicron is visible. Notice also that in the present middle indicative second-person singular the intervocalic sigma does not drop out.

IMPERFECT INDICATIVE FORMS FOR μι VERBS

	active	middle
1 sg	ἐδίδουν	ἐδιδόμην
2 sg	ἐδίδους	ἐδίδοσο
3 sg	ἐδίδου	ἐδίδοτο
1 pl	ἐδίδομεν	ἐδιδόμεθα
2 pl	ἐδίδοτε	ἐδίδοσθε
3 pl	ἐδίδοσαν	ἐδίδοντο

The future indicative forms for μι verbs are straightforward. The verb stem is not reduplicated, and the stem vowel lengthens in all forms.[3]

FUTURE ACTIVE INDICATIVE FORMS FOR μι VERBS

	active
1 sg	δώσω
2 sg	δώσεις
3 sg	δώσει
1 pl	δώσομεν
2 pl	δώσετε
3 pl	δώσουσι(ν)

Another distinctive for μι verbs is that the first aorist tense formative is usually *kappa* rather than a sigma. Consider the paradigms for the first aorist active indicative for δίδωμι. Notice that there is no reduplication, which indicates that this augmented form could not be an imperfect. Also notice that the omicron of the tense stem lengthens throughout the paradigm.

FIRST AORIST ACTIVE INDICATIVE OF δίδωμι

1 sg	ἔδωκα
2 sg	ἔδωκας
3 sg	ἔδωκε(ν)
1 pl	ἐδώκαμεν
2 pl	ἐδώκατε
3 pl	ἔδωκαν

In the aorist middle indicative, however, no tense formative is used. Notice also that the omicron of the tense stem does not lengthen.

FIRST AORIST MIDDLE INDICATIVE OF δίδωμι

1 sg	ἐδόμην
2 sg	ἔδου
3 sg	ἔδοτο

---

3. Only the future active forms are presented here—you can view the middle and passive forms at the end of this chapter (see "Paradigms to Recognize but not Memorize").

1 pl	ἐδόμεθα
2 pl	ἔδοσθε
3 pl	ἔδοντο

In the aorist passive indicative, the tense formative -θη makes these forms easy to recognize. (The paradigm for ἵστημι is used here, since not all forms of the aorist passive of δίδωμι occur in the GNT.)

FIRST AORIST PASSIVE INDICATIVE OF ἵστημι

1 sg	ἐστάθην
2 sg	ἐστάθης
3 sg	ἐστάθη
1 pl	ἐστάθημεν
2 pl	ἐστάθητε
3 pl	ἐστάθησαν

Sometimes μι verbs can have *both* first and second aorist tense forms, such as ἔδωκα and ἔδων. For most μι verbs, there is no semantic difference between these forms, as we have already seen with variant forms of εἰμί. With ἵστημι, however, the first aorist (e.g., ἔστησα) is often transitive (e.g., "I caused to stand"), whereas the second aorist (e.g., ἔστην) is intransitive (e.g., "I stood"). This is noted in the vocabulary assigned for this chapter and the next. Additionally, the present, imperfect, and future active tense-forms of ἵστημι are also transitive, whereas the future middle and passive, and the aorist passive tense-forms are intransitive.[4] A good lexicon will always indicate these differences.

Finally, the perfect active indicative forms of verbs use reduplication with an *epsilon* (as we have already seen) and the -κα tense formative (as we have also already seen).

PERFECT ACTIVE INDICATIVE OF δίδωμι

1 sg	δέδωκα
2 sg	δέδωκας
3 sg	δέδωκε(ν)

(cont.)

---

4. As with many elements of Koine Greek, this distinction is disputed by some scholars. It should not be surprising, therefore, to see a range of translations reflected in English versions for the forms of ἵστημι.

1 pl	δεδώκαμεν
2 pl	δεδώκατε
3 pl	δέδωκαν

Based on what you have learned so far for omega verbs, you should be able to recognize the remaining indicative forms (e.g., the future middle and passive, and the perfect middle) for μι verbs. You can go over the paradigms listed at the end of this chapter to verify this ("Paradigms to Recognize but Not Memorize").

Subjunctive Forms

The same endings that you learned previously for the subjunctive are also used for μι verbs, although they have a lengthened stem vowel rather than the lengthened connecting vowel used with omega verbs. Notice the reduplication with an iota in the present subjunctive forms.

PRESENT SUBJUNCTIVE OF δίδωμι

	active	middle
1 sg	διδῶ	διδῶμαι
2 sg	διδῷς	διδῷ
3 sg	διδῷ	διδῶται
1 pl	διδῶμεν	διδώμεθα
2 pl	διδῶτε	διδῶσθε
3 pl	διδῶσι(ν)	διδῶνται

Aorist subjunctive forms can sometimes be difficult to recognize because all that is "visible" of the verb stem is an initial consonant, for example, the δ of δῶ! This extremely short form, however, is also a clue that you have an aorist subjunctive form of a μι verb. Even so, it is necessary to memorize these forms.

SECOND AORIST SUBJUNCTIVE OF δίδωμι

	active	middle	passive
1 sg	δῶ	δῶμαι	δοθῶ
2 sg	δῷς	δῷ	δοθῇς
3 sg	δῷ	δῶται	δοθῇ

1 pl	δῶμεν	δώμεθα	δοθῶμεν
2 pl	δῶτε	δῶσθε	δοθῆτε
3 pl	δῶσι(ν)	δῶνται	δοθῶσι(ν)

Imperative Forms

The same endings that you learned previously for the imperative omega verbs are also used for μι verbs. Like omega verbs, the second-person singular forms must be memorized. Here are the present tense forms:

PRESENT IMPERATIVE OF δίδωμι

	active	middle
2 sg	δίδου	δίδοσο
3 sg	διδότω	διδόσθω
2 pl	δίδοτε	δίδοσθε
3 pl	διδότωσαν	διδόσθωσαν

Finally, here are the aorist imperative forms:

AORIST IMPERATIVE OF δίδωμι

	active	middle[1]
2 sg	δός	δοῦ
3 sg	δότω	δόσθω
2 pl	δότε	δόσθε
3 pl	δότωσαν	δόσθωσαν

[1] There are no aorist passive subjunctive forms of δίδωμι in the GNT.

EXAMPLES OF FINITE μι VERBS IN THE GNT

As noted, μι verbs are frequent in the GNT. Here some examples of finite forms of δίδωμι, beginning with the indicative and then some imperative and subjunctives. As you look through these examples, try to parse each occurrence of δίδωμι, referring to the paradigms listed above as necessary. The original text of some of these references has been shortened (considerably in some cases), so this would be a great time to look up each reference in your GNT and see how much more of the larger context that you can now sight read. The assigned exercises also include examples of ἵστημι, τίθημι, and other μι verbs from the assigned vocabulary.

αἰτεῖτε καὶ *δοθήσεται* ὑμῖν (Matt 7:7)
Ask and *it will be given* to you.

ὅσοι δὲ ἔλαβον αὐτόν, *ἔδωκεν* αὐτοῖς ἐξουσίαν τέκνα θεοῦ γενέσθαι
(John 1:12)
But as many as received him, *he gave* to them authority to become children of God.

οὕτως γὰρ ἠγάπησεν ὁ θεὸς τὸν κόσμον, ὥστε τὸν υἱὸν τὸν μονογενῆ
ἔδωκεν (John 3:16)
For in this way God loved the world, namely,[5] *he gave* his unique Son.

ἄλλα δὲ ἔπεσεν ἐπὶ τὴν γῆν τὴν καλὴν καὶ *ἐδίδου* καρπόν (Matt 13:8)
But some [seeds] fell on the good soil (earth) and *was bearing [giving]* fruit.

Look carefully at the following verses from John's Gospel (John 4:14–15). Can you identify the two indicative forms of δίδωμι and the one imperative form? They are italicized, which should help!

ὃς δ᾽ ἂν πίῃ ἐκ τοῦ ὕδατος οὗ ἐγὼ *δώσω* αὐτῷ, οὐ μὴ διψήσει εἰς τὸν αἰῶνα, ἀλλὰ τὸ ὕδωρ ὃ *δώσω* αὐτῷ γενήσεται ἐν αὐτῷ πηγὴ ὕδατος ἁλλομένου εἰς ζωὴν αἰώνιον. λέγει πρὸς αὐτὸν ἡ γυνή, Κύριε, *δός* μοι τοῦτο τὸ ὕδωρ.

"But whoever drinks from the water that *I* myself *will give* to him will never ever thirst, but the water that *I will give* to him will become in him a spring of water welling up to eternal life." The woman said to him, "Sir, *give* me this water!"

Here are some more examples to work through.

---

5. The ὥστε clause here is functioning epexegetically to explain how God loved the world.

εἰρήνην τὴν ἐμὴν *δίδωμι* ὑμῖν· οὐ καθὼς ὁ κόσμος *δίδωσιν* ἐγὼ *δίδωμι* ὑμῖν.
(John 14:27)
My peace *I give* to you; not as the world *gives* do I myself give to you.

κἀγὼ τὴν δόξαν ἣν *δέδωκάς* μοι *δέδωκα* αὐτοῖς (John 17:22)[6]
And the glory that *you have given* to me *I* myself *have given* to them.

γίνου πιστὸς ἄχρι θανάτου, καὶ *δώσω* σοι τὸν στέφανον τῆς ζωῆς
(Rev 2:10)
Be faithful until death, and *I will give* you the crown of life.

ἑκάστῳ δὲ *δίδοται* ἡ φανέρωσις τοῦ πνεύματος (1 Cor 12:7)
But to each one *is given* a manifestation of the Spirit.

καθὼς *ἔδωκας* αὐτῷ ἐξουσίαν πάσης σαρκός, ἵνα πᾶν ὃ *δέδωκας* αὐτῷ
δώσῃ αὐτοῖς ζωὴν αἰώνιον (John 17:2)
Just as *you gave* to him authority over all flesh, in order that everything that
you have given to him *he might give* eternal life to them.

τὸν ἄρτον ἡμῶν τὸν ἐπιούσιον *δὸς* ἡμῖν σήμερον (Matt 6:11)
Give our daily bread to us today.

φοβήθητε τὸν θεὸν καὶ *δότε* αὐτῷ δόξαν (Rev 14:7)
Fear God and *give* him glory!

REVIEW OF CHAPTER 24

In this chapter we learned the finite forms and functions of μι verbs. Perhaps the most distinctive elements of μι verbs are the reduplication of the present stem with an iota, the absence of the connecting vowel, and the use of three new personal endings in the present active indicative. Despite the fact that this chapter presented a virtual parade of paradigms, most forms should be recognizable based on your previous learning and memorization. The examples from the GNT show just how common μι verbs are.

---

6. The form κἀγώ is the combination of καί and ἐγώ, which explains the addition of "myself" to the translation.

Study Guide for Chapter 24

1. Be able to understand each of the following concepts and forms:

    distinctives of μι verbs

    - do not use a connecting vowel
    - reduplication of the present tense
    - stem vowel frequently lengthens
    - three new personal endings

    μι-verb indicative forms

    μι-verb subjunctive forms

    μι-verb imperative forms

2. Be able to parse finite μι-verb forms and translate basic Koine sentences that incorporate forms and concepts from previous chapters.

Vocabulary to Memorize

The following vocabulary needs to be memorized for chapter 24.

ἀναλαμβάνω	I take up, I carry (13)
ἀνίστημι	I raise, I bring to life (trans); I stand up, I rise (intrans) (108)
ἀποδίδωμι	I repay, I give away, I pay; I sell (mid) (48)
ἀπόλλυμι	I destroy, I lose; I die, I perish (mid) (90)
ἄρχων, -οντος, ὁ	ruler, prince, official (37)
ἀφίημι	I let go, I forgive, I permit, I divorce (143)
δίδωμι	I give, I grant, I put, I entrust (415)
δοκέω	I think, I suppose, I seem (62)
ἐλεέω	I have mercy, I am merciful; I am shown mercy (pass) (29)
ἐπιβάλλω	I throw over, I lay (hands) on, I put on (18)
ἐπιτίθημι	I lay on, I put upon; I give, I attack (mid) (39)
θυσία, -ας, ἡ	sacrifice, offering (28)
θυσιαστήριον, -ου, τό	altar (23)
ἵστημι	I set, I make stand; I stand (intrans) (155)
μέλος, -ους, τό	member, body part, limb (34)
μερίζω	I divide (14)
μήποτε	lest, that . . . not, perhaps, never (25)
ὁμοίως	likewise, similarly, in the same way (30)

παραδίδωμι	I hand over, I betray, I entrust (119)
παρίστημι	I present, I place beside, I am present (41)
πειρασμός, -οῦ, ὁ	trial, test, process of testing (21)
συνίημι	I understand, I comprehend (26)
συνίστημι	I demonstrate, I recommend (16)
τίθημι	I place, I put, I appoint (100)
ὡσεί	like, as, about (21)

Principal Parts to Memorize

These are the principal parts that you need to memorize for chapter 24.

1st prin part	2nd prin part	3rd prin part	4th prin part	5th prin part	6th prin part
δίδωμι	δώσω	ἔδωκα	δέδωκα	δέδομαι	ἐδόθην
δύναμαι	δυνήσομαι	n/a	n/a	n/a	ἠδυνήθην
ἵστημι	στήσω	ἔστησα	ἔστηκα	n/a	ἐστάθην
τίθημι	θήσω	ἔθηκα	τέθεικα	τέθειμαι	ἐτέθην

Paradigms to Memorize

The following paradigms should be memorized for chapter 24: all assigned forms for δίδωμι and all assigned forms of ἵστημι; rather than rote memorization, however, you should focus on recognizing patterns and endings. Following these paradigms are additional paradigms that you do not have to memorize, but you should be able to recognize.

PRESENT ACTIVE INDICATIVE PARADIGM OF δίδωμι

1 sg	δίδωμι
2 sg	δίδως
3 sg	δίδωσι(ν)
1 pl	δίδομεν
2 pl	δίδοτε
3 pl	διδόασι(ν)

PRESENT MIDDLE INDICATIVE PARADIGM OF δίδωμι

1 sg	δίδομαι
2 sg	δίδοσαι
3 sg	δίδοται
1 pl	διδόμεθα
2 pl	δίδοσθε
3 pl	δίδονται

IMPERFECT ACTIVE INDICATIVE PARADIGM OF δίδωμι

1 sg	ἐδίδουν
2 sg	ἐδίδους
3 sg	ἐδίδου
1 pl	ἐδίδομεν
2 pl	ἐδίδοτε
3 pl	ἐδίδοσαν

IMPERFECT MIDDLE INDICATIVE PARADIGM OF δίδωμι

1 sg	ἐδιδόμην
2 sg	ἐδίδοσο
3 sg	ἐδίδοτο
1 pl	ἐδιδόμεθα
2 pl	ἐδίδοσθε
3 pl	ἐδίδοντο

FUTURE ACTIVE INDICATIVE PARADIGM OF δίδωμι

1 sg	δώσω
2 sg	δώσεις
3 sg	δώσει
1 pl	δώσομεν
2 pl	δώσετε
3 pl	δώσουσι(ν)

AORIST ACTIVE INDICATIVE PARADIGM OF δίδωμι

1 sg	ἔδωκα
2 sg	ἔδωκας
3 sg	ἔδωκε(ν)
1 pl	ἐδώκαμεν
2 pl	ἐδώκατε
3 pl	ἔδωκαν

AORIST MIDDLE INDICATIVE PARADIGM OF δίδωμι

1 sg	ἐδόμην
2 sg	ἔδου
3 sg	ἔδοτο
1 pl	ἐδόμεθα
2 pl	ἔδοσθε
3 pl	ἔδοντο

AORIST PASSIVE INDICATIVE PARADIGM OF δίδωμι[1]

1 sg	ἐδόθην
2 sg	-
3 sg	ἐδόθη
1 pl	-
2 pl	ἐδόθητε
3 pl	-

[1] A dash indicates that this form does not occur in the GNT.

PRESENT ACTIVE SUBJUNCTIVE PARADIGM OF δίδωμι

1 sg	διδῶ
2 sg	διδῷς
3 sg	διδῷ
1 pl	διδῶμεν
2 pl	διδῶτε
3 pl	διδῶσι(ν)

AORIST ACTIVE SUBJUNCTIVE PARADIGM OF δίδωμι

1 sg	δῶ
2 sg	δῷς
3 sg	δῷ
1 pl	δῶμεν
2 pl	δῶτε
3 pl	δῶσι(ν)

PRESENT ACTIVE IMPERATIVE PARADIGM OF δίδωμι

1 sg	-
2 sg	δίδου
3 sg	διδότω
1 pl	-
2 pl	δίδοτε
3 pl	διδότωσαν

AORIST ACTIVE IMPERATIVE PARADIGM OF δίδωμι

1 sg	-
2 sg	δός
3 sg	δότω
1 pl	-
2 pl	δότε
3 pl	δότωσαν

PRESENT ACTIVE INDICATIVE PARADIGM OF ἵστημι

1 sg	ἵστημι
2 sg	ἵστης
3 sg	ἵστησι(ν)
1 pl	ἵσταμεν
2 pl	ἵστατε
3 pl	ἱστᾶσι(ν)

PRESENT MIDDLE INDICATIVE PARADIGM OF ἵστημι

1 sg	ἵσταμαι
2 sg	ἵστασαι
3 sg	ἵσταται
1 pl	ἱστάμεθα
2 pl	ἵστασθε
3 pl	ἵστανται

IMPERFECT ACTIVE INDICATIVE PARADIGM OF ἵστημι

1 sg	ἵστην
2 sg	ἵστης
3 sg	ἵστη
1 pl	ἵσταμεν
2 pl	ἵστατε
3 pl	ἵστασαν

IMPERFECT MIDDLE INDICATIVE PARADIGM OF ἵστημι

1 sg	ἱστάμην
2 sg	ἵστασο
3 sg	ἵστατο
1 pl	ἱστάμεθα
2 pl	ἵστασθε
3 pl	ἵσταντο

AORIST ACTIVE INDICATIVE PARADIGM OF ἵστημι (FIRST AORIST)[1]

1 sg	ἔστησα
2 sg	ἔστησας
3 sg	ἔστησε(ν)
1 pl	ἐστήσαμεν
2 pl	ἐστήσατε
3 pl	ἔστησαν

AORIST ACTIVE INDICATIVE PARADIGM OF ἵστημι (SECOND AORIST)

1 sg	ἔστην
2 sg	ἔστης
3 sg	ἔστη
1 pl	ἔστημεν
2 pl	ἔστητε
3 pl	ἔστησαν

[1] This verb has both first and second aorist active forms. For this reason, both paradigms are presented.

AORIST PASSIVE INDICATIVE PARADIGM OF ἵστημι

1 sg	ἐστάθην
2 sg	ἐστάθης
3 sg	ἐστάθη
1 pl	ἐστάθημεν
2 pl	ἐστάθητε
3 pl	ἐστάθησαν

PRESENT ACTIVE SUBJUNCTIVE PARADIGM OF ἵστημι

1 sg	ἱστῶ
2 sg	ἱστῇς
3 sg	ἱστῇ
1 pl	ἱστῶμεν
2 pl	ἱστῆτε
3 pl	ἱστῶσι(ν)

AORIST ACTIVE SUBJUNCTIVE PARADIGM OF ἵστημι (FIRST AORIST)

1 sg	στήσω
2 sg	στήσῃς
3 sg	στήσῃ
1 pl	στήσωμεν
2 pl	στήσητε
3 pl	στήσωσι(ν)

AORIST ACTIVE SUBJUNCTIVE PARADIGM OF ἵστημι (SECOND AORIST)

1 sg	στῶ
2 sg	στῇς
3 sg	στῇ
1 pl	στῶμεν
2 pl	στῆτε
3 pl	στῶσι(ν)

PRESENT ACTIVE IMPERATIVE PARADIGM OF ἵστημι

1 sg	-
2 sg	ἵστη
3 sg	ἱστάτω
1 pl	-
2 pl	ἵστατε
3 pl	ἱστάτωσαν

AORIST ACTIVE IMPERATIVE PARADIGM OF ἵστημι (FIRST AORIST)

1 sg	-
2 sg	στῆσον
3 sg	στησάτω
1 pl	-
2 pl	στήσατε
3 pl	στησάτωσαν

AORIST ACTIVE IMPERATIVE PARADIGM OF ἵστημι (SECOND AORIST)

1 sg	-
2 sg	στῆθι
3 sg	στήτω
1 pl	-
2 pl	στῆτε
3 pl	στήτωσαν

Paradigms to Recognize but Not Memorize

FUTURE MIDDLE INDICATIVE PARADIGM OF δίδωμι

1 sg	δώσομαι
2 sg	δώσῃ
3 sg	δώσεται
1 pl	δωσόμεθα
2 pl	δώσεσθε
3 pl	δώσονται

FUTURE PASSIVE INDICATIVE PARADIGM OF δίδωμι

1 sg	δοθήσομαι
2 sg	δοθήσῃ
3 sg	δοθήσεται
1 pl	δοθήσομεθα
2 pl	δοθήσεσθε
3 pl	δοθήσονται

PERFECT ACTIVE INDICATIVE PARADIGM OF δίδωμι

1 sg	δέδωκα
2 sg	δέδωκας
3 sg	δέδωκεν
1 pl	δεδώκαμεν
2 pl	δεδώκατε
3 pl	δέδωκαν

PERFECT MIDDLE INDICATIVE PARADIGM OF δίδωμι

1 sg	δέδομαι
2 sg	δέδοσαι
3 sg	δέδοται
1 pl	δεδόμεθα
2 pl	δέδοσθε
3 pl	δέδονται

PLUPERFECT ACTIVE INDICATIVE PARADIGM OF δίδωμι

1 sg	ἐδεδώκειν
2 sg	-
3 sg	ἐδέδωκει
1 pl	-
2 pl	-
3 pl	ἐδεδώκεισαν

PRESENT MIDDLE SUBJUNCTIVE PARADIGM OF δίδωμι

1 sg	διδῶμαι
2 sg	διδῷ
3 sg	διδῷται
1 pl	διδώμεθα
2 pl	διδῶσθε
3 pl	διδῶνται

AORIST MIDDLE SUBJUNCTIVE PARADIGM OF δίδωμι

1 sg	δῶμαι
2 sg	δῷ
3 sg	δῶται
1 pl	δώμεθα
2 pl	δῶσθε
3 pl	δῶνται

PRESENT MIDDLE IMPERATIVE PARADIGM OF δίδωμι

1 sg	-
2 sg	δίδοσο
3 sg	διδόσθω
1 pl	-
2 pl	δίδοσθε
3 pl	διδόσθων

AORIST MIDDLE IMPERATIVE PARADIGM OF δίδωμι

1 sg	-
2 sg	δοῦ
3 sg	δόσθω
1 pl	-
2 pl	δόσθε
3 pl	δόσθωσαν

PERFECT ACTIVE INDICATIVE PARADIGM OF ἵστημι

1 sg	ἕστηκα
2 sg	ἕστηκας
3 sg	ἕστηκε(ν)
1 pl	ἑστήκαμεν
2 pl	ἑστήκατε
3 pl	ἑστήκασιν

PLUPERFECT ACTIVE INDICATIVE PARADIGM OF ἵστημι

1 sg	εἱστήκειν
2 sg	εἱστήκεις
3 sg	εἱστήκει(ν)
1 pl	εἱστήκειμεν
2 pl	-
3 pl	εἱστήκεισαν

PRESENT MIDDLE SUBJUNCTIVE PARADIGM OF ἵστημι

1 sg	ἱστῶμαι
2 sg	ἱστῇ
3 sg	ἱστῆται
1 pl	ἱστώμεθα
2 pl	ἱστῆσθε
3 pl	ἱστῶνται

AORIST PASSIVE SUBJUNCTIVE PARADIGM OF ἵστημι

1 sg	σταθῶ
2 sg	σταθῇς
3 sg	σταθῇ
1 pl	σταθῶμεν
2 pl	σταθῆτε
3 pl	σταθῶσι(ν)

PRESENT MIDDLE IMPERATIVE PARADIGM OF ἵστημι

1 sg	-
2 sg	ἵστασο
3 sg	ἱστάσθω
1 pl	-
2 pl	ἵστασθε
3 pl	ἱστάσθωσαν

chapter TWENTY-FIVE

μι VERBS: *Nonfinite Forms*

OBJECTIVES AND OVERVIEW

Chapter 25 introduces the following linguistic concepts, morphemes, and paradigms:

- infinitive paradigms for μι verbs
- present and aorist active and middle participle paradigms for μι verbs

THE FORMS OF NONFINITE μι VERBS

In this chapter, we will look at the nonfinite forms—participles and infinitives—of μι verbs. The distinctives of μι verbs that we discussed in the last chapter apply to nonfinite forms as well, namely, reduplication of the present tense stem with an iota, the lack of a connecting vowel, and the frequent lengthening of the verb's stem vowel. For this reason, the paradigms for nonfinite μι verbs are generally easy to recognize. Here is the paradigm for the infinitive for δίδωμι:

	present	aorist
active	διδόναι	δοῦναι
middle	δίδοσθαι	δόσθαι
passive	δίδοσθαι	δοθῆναι

Next is the paradigm for the present active participle for δίδωμι. Like omega verbs, this paradigm follows a 3-1-3 declension pattern, and uses the -ντ participle morpheme. This means that there is compensatory lengthening in the nominative singular masculine and dative plural masculine and neuter forms when the participle morpheme drops off: either all of it (e.g., -ντ in the masculine nominative singular [διδούς] and the masculine and neuter dative plural forms [διδοῦσι(ν)]), or just part of it (e.g., the tau in the nominative and accusative neuter singular forms [διδόν]). Notice also the reduplication throughout the paradigm:

	masculine	feminine	neuter
nom sg	διδούς	διδοῦσα	διδόν
gen sg	διδόντος	διδούσης	διδόντος
dat sg	διδόντι	διδούσῃ	διδόντι
acc sg	διδόντα	διδοῦσαν	διδόν
nom pl	διδόντες	διδοῦσαι	διδόντα
gen pl	διδόντων	διδουσῶν	διδόντων
dat pl	διδοῦσι(ν)	διδούσαις	διδοῦσι(ν)
acc pl	διδόντας	διδούσας	διδόντα

Here is the paradigm for the present middle participle of δίδωμι, which follows a 2-1-2 declension pattern:

nom sg	διδόμενος	διδομένη	διδόμενον
gen sg	διδομένου	διδομένης	διδομένου
dat sg	διδομένῳ	διδομένῃ	διδομένῳ
acc sg	διδόμενον	διδομένην	διδόμενον
nom pl	διδόμενοι	διδόμεναι	διδόμενα
gen pl	διδομένων	διδομένων	διδομένων
dat pl	διδομένοις	διδομέναις	διδομένοις
acc pl	διδομένους	διδομένας	διδόμενα

The present participle forms of μι verbs are generally easy to recognize, in part due to the distinctive iota reduplication of the present stem. The aorist forms, however, can be hard to recognize because very little of the stem is visible, as we already saw in the subjunctive forms. For this reason, these paradigms need to be memorized. Here is the aorist active participle of δίδωμι, which follows a 3-1-3 declension pattern.

	masculine	feminine	neuter
nom sg	δούς	δοῦσα	δόν
gen sg	δόντος	δούσης	δόντος
dat sg	δόντι	δούσῃ	δόντι
acc sg	δόντα	δοῦσαν	δόν

nom pl	δόντες	δοῦσαι	δόντα
gen pl	δόντων	δουσῶν	δόντων
dat pl	δοῦσι(ν)	δούσαις	δοῦσι(ν)
acc pl	δόντας	δούσας	δόντα

Here is the paradigm of the aorist middle participle of δίδωμι, which follows a 2-1-2 declension pattern.

nom sg	δόμενος	δομένη	δόμενον
gen sg	δομένου	δομένης	δομένου
dat sg	δομένῳ	δομένῃ	δομένῳ
acc sg	δόμενον	δομένην	δόμενον
nom pl	δόμενοι	δόμεναι	δόμενα
gen pl	δομένων	δομένων	δομένων
dat pl	δομένοις	δομέναις	δομένοις
acc pl	δομένους	δομένας	δόμενα

Based on what you have learned so far for omega verbs, you should be able to recognize the perfect participle forms for μι verbs since they have reduplication and use the perfect active participle morpheme for the active forms. These forms are listed after the assigned paradigms at the end of this chapter. Several examples of perfect participles occur in the examples below.

EXAMPLES OF NONFINITE μι VERBS IN THE GNT

As we saw in the previous chapter, μι verbs are frequent in the GNT. Below are some examples of nonfinite forms of δίδωμι. As with the previous chapter, as you look through these examples, try to parse each occurrence of δίδωμι, referring to the paradigms listed above as necessary. Keep looking up each reference in your GNT to see the larger context for each example given below. The assigned exercises also include examples of ἵστημι, τίθημι, and other μι verbs from the assigned vocabulary.

μακάριόν ἐστιν μᾶλλον *διδόναι* ἢ λαμβάνειν (Acts 20:35)
It is more blessed *to give* than to receive.

ἡ δὲ ἐλπὶς οὐ καταισχύνει, ὅτι ἡ ἀγάπη τοῦ θεοῦ ἐκκέχυται ἐν ταῖς
  καρδίαις ἡμῶν διὰ πνεύματος ἁγίου *τοῦ δοθέντος* ἡμῖν. (Rom 5:5)
And hope does not disappoint, because the love of God has been poured out
in our hearts through the Holy Spirit *who was given* to us.

τῷ δὲ θεῷ χάρις *τῷ διδόντι* ἡμῖν τὸ νῖκος διὰ τοῦ κυρίου ἡμῶν Ἰησοῦ
  Χριστοῦ. (1 Cor 15:57)
And to God, grace to *the one who has given* us victory through our Lord
Jesus Christ.

χάρις ὑμῖν καὶ εἰρήνη ἀπὸ θεοῦ πατρὸς ἡμῶν καὶ κυρίου Ἰησοῦ Χριστοῦ
  τοῦ δόντος ἑαυτὸν ὑπὲρ τῶν ἁμαρτιῶν ἡμῶν (Gal 1:3–4)
Grace and peace to you from God our Father and the Lord Jesus Christ *the
one who gave* himself for our sins.

αὐτὸς δὲ ὁ κύριος ἡμῶν Ἰησοῦς Χριστὸς καὶ [ὁ] θεὸς ὁ πατὴρ ἡμῶν ὁ
  ἀγαπήσας ἡμᾶς καὶ *δοὺς* παράκλησιν αἰωνίαν καὶ ἐλπίδα ἀγαθὴν . . .
  (2 Thess 2:16)
And [may] our Lord Jesus Christ himself and God our Father, who loved us
and *gave* [us] eternal encouragement and good hope . . .

ὁ δοὺς ἑαυτὸν ἀντίλυτρον ὑπὲρ πάντων (1 Tim 2:6)
the one who gave himself as a ransom for all people.

σὺ δέ, παιδίον, προφήτης ὑψίστου κληθήσῃ· προπορεύσῃ γὰρ ἐνώπιον
  κυρίου ἑτοιμάσαι ὁδοὺς αὐτοῦ, *τοῦ δοῦναι* γνῶσιν σωτηρίας τῷ λαῷ
  αὐτοῦ (Luke 1:76–77)
And you, child, will be called a prophet of the Most High; for you will go
before the Lord to prepare his way, *to give* the knowledge of salvation to
his people.

REVIEW OF CHAPTER 25

In this chapter we learned the nonfinite forms and functions of μι verbs. Like
the indicative forms, the most distinctive elements of nonfinite μι-verb forms are
the reduplication of the present stem with an iota and the absence of the connecting vowel. Like the finite forms, most nonfinite forms of μι verbs should be
recognizable based on your previous learning and memorization.

Study Guide for Chapter 25

1. Review the following concepts from chapter 24:

    distinctives of μι verbs

    - do not use a connecting vowel
    - reduplication of the present tense
    - stem vowel frequently lengthens

2. Be able to recognize each of the following forms:

    participle forms for μι verbs

    subjunctive forms

    imperative forms

3. Be able to parse finite and nonfinite μι-verb forms and translate basic Koine sentences that incorporate forms and concepts from previous chapters.

Vocabulary to Memorize

The following vocabulary words need to be memorized for chapter 25.

ἅπας, -ασα, -αν	all, whole; everybody, everything (pl) (34)
ἀρνέομαι	I deny, I refuse, I disown (33)
ἀσθενέω	I am weak, I am powerless, I am sick (33)
γενεά, -ᾶς, ἡ	generation, family, race, age (43)
δείκνυμι	I show, I point out, I explain, I prove (33)
διακονέω	I wait on, I serve, I care for, I serve as a deacon (37)
διάκονος, -ου, ὁ, ἡ	servant, deacon/deaconess, helper (29)
διαμερίζω	I divide, I separate, I distribute, I share (11)
ἔλεος, -ους, τό	mercy, compassion (27)
ἡγεμών, -όνος, ὁ	leader, governor (20)
ἥλιος, -ου, ὁ	sun (32)
θερίζω	I reap, I harvest (21)
ἵππος, -ου, ὁ	horse (17)
λῃστής, οῦ, ὁ	robber (15)
μάρτυς, -υρος, ὁ	witness, martyr (35)
μισθός, -οῦ, ὁ	wages, reward, punishment (29)
παρατίθημι	I set before; I entrust (19)
πλῆθος, -ους, τό	large amount, crowd, multitude (31)

(cont.)

σκότος, -ους, τό	darkness (31)
σοφία, -ας, ἡ	wisdom (51)
συνείδησις, -εως, ἡ	conscience, consciousness (30)
τύπος, -ου, ὁ	mark, image, pattern, type, model, example (15)
φημί	I say, I affirm (66)
φυλή, -ῆς, ἡ	tribe, nation, people (31)
ὥστε	so that, with the result that, therefore (83)

Principal Parts to Memorize

These are the principal parts that you need to memorize for chapter 25. Some of the verbs assigned for this chapter have been previously assigned, so you will now need to ensure that all principal parts are included for previously assigned verbs. The full "Principal Parts Chart" is in appendix 14.

1st prin part	2nd prin part	3rd prin part	4th prin part	5th prin part	6th prin part
ἀκούω	ἀκούσω	ἤκουσα	ἀκήκοα	n/a	ἠκούσθην
δέω	n/a	ἔδησα	δέδεκα	δέδεμαι	ἐδέθην
δύναμαι	δυνήσομαι	n/a	n/a	n/a	ἠδυνήθην
θέλω	θελήσω	ἠθέλησα	n/a	n/a	n/a
πίνω	πίομαι	ἔπιον	πέπωκα	n/a	ἐπόθην

Paradigms to Memorize

The following paradigms should be memorized for chapter 25: all assigned aorist forms for δίδωμι and ἵστημι; rather than rote memorization, you should focus on recognizing patterns and endings. The nominative and genitive forms of the present participle should also be memorized, although the forms are easily recognized. The full present paradigms and additional forms are listed after these paradigms for reference.

PRESENT ACTIVE PARTICIPLE OF δίδωμι

nom sg	διδούς	διδοῦσα	διδόν
gen sg	διδόντος	διδούσης	διδόντος

PRESENT MIDDLE PARTICIPLE OF δίδωμι

nom sg	διδόμενος	διδομένη	διδόμενον
gen sg	διδομένου	διδομένης	διδομένου

AORIST ACTIVE PARTICIPLE OF δίδωμι

nom sg	δούς	δοῦσα	δόν
gen sg	δόντος	δούσης	δόντος
dat sg	δόντι	δούσῃ	δόντι
acc sg	δόντα	δοῦσαν	δόν
nom pl	δόντες	δοῦσαι	δόντα
gen pl	δόντων	δουσῶν	δόντων
dat pl	δοῦσι(ν)	δούσαις	δυῦσι(ν)
acc pl	δόντας	δούσας	δόντα

AORIST MIDDLE PARTICIPLE OF δίδωμι

nom sg	δόμενος	δομένη	δόμενον
gen sg	δομένου	δομένης	δομένου
dat sg	δομένῳ	δομένῃ	δομένῳ
acc sg	δόμενον	δομένην	δόμενον
nom pl	δόμενοι	δόμεναι	δόμενα
gen pl	δομένων	δομένων	δομένων
dat pl	δομένοις	δομέναις	δομένοις
acc pl	δομένους	δομένας	δόμενα

INFINITIVE PARADIGM OF δίδωμι

	present	**aorist**
active	διδόναι	δοῦναι
middle	δίδοσθαι	δόσθαι
passive	δίδοσθαι	δοθῆναι

PRESENT ACTIVE PARTICIPLE OF ἵστημι

nom sg	ἱστάς	ἱστᾶσα	ἱστάν
gen sg	ἱστάντος	ἱστάσης	ἱστάντος

PRESENT MIDDLE PARTICIPLE OF ἵστημι

nom sg	ἱστάμενος	ἱσταμένη	ἱστάμενον
gen sg	ἱσταμένου	ἱσταμένης	ἱσταμένου

AORIST ACTIVE PARTICIPLE OF ἵστημι (FIRST AORIST)

nom sg	στήτας	στήσασα	στῆσαν
gen sg	στήσαντος	στησάσης	στήσαντος
dat sg	στήσαντι	στησάῃ	στήσαντι
acc sg	στήσαντα	στήσασαν	στῆσαν
nom pl	στήσαντες	στήσασαι	στήσαντα
gen pl	στησάντων	στησασῶν	στησάντων
dat pl	στήσασι(ν)	στησάσαις	στήσασι(ν)
acc pl	στήσαντας	στησάσας	στήσαντα

AORIST ACTIVE PARTICIPLE OF ἵστημι (SECOND AORIST)

nom sg	στάς	στᾶσα	στάν
gen sg	στάντος	στάσης	στάντος
dat sg	στάντι	στάσῃ	στάντι
acc sg	στάντα	στᾶσαν	στάν
nom pl	στάντες	στᾶσαι	στάντα
gen pl	στάντων	στασῶν	στάντων
dat pl	στάσι(ν)	στάσαις	στάσι(ν)
acc pl	στάντας	στάσας	στάντα

INFINITIVE PARADIGM OF ἵστημι

	present	aorist
active	ἱστάναι	στῆναι
middle	ἵστασθαι	στήσασθαι
passive	ἵστασθαι	σταθῆναι

Paradigms to Recognize but Not Memorize

PRESENT ACTIVE PARTICIPLE OF δίδωμι

nom sg	διδούς	διδοῦσα	διδόν
gen sg	διδόντος	διδούσης	διδόντος
dat sg	διδόντι	διδούσῃ	διδόντι
acc sg	διδόντα	διδοῦσαν	διδόν
nom pl	διδόντες	διδοῦσαι	διδόντα
gen pl	διδόντων	διδουσῶν	διδόντων
dat pl	διδοῦσι(ν)	διδούσαις	διδοῦσι(ν)
acc pl	διδόντας	διδούσας	διδόντα

PRESENT MIDDLE/PASSIVE PARTICIPLE OF δίδωμι

nom sg	διδόμενος	διδομένη	διδόμενον
gen sg	διδομένου	διδομένης	διδομένου
dat sg	διδομένῳ	διδομένῃ	διδομένῳ
acc sg	διδόμενον	διδομένην	διδόμενον
nom pl	διδόμενοι	διδόμεναι	διδόμενα
gen pl	διδομένων	διδομένων	διδομένων
dat pl	διδομένοις	διδομέναις	διδομένοις
acc pl	διδομένους	διδομένας	διδόμενα

PRESENT ACTIVE PARTICIPLE OF ἵστημι

nom sg	ἱστάς	ἱστᾶσα	ἱστάν
gen sg	ἱστάντος	ἱστάσης	ἱστάντος
dat sg	ἱστάντι	ἱστάσῃ	ἱστάντι
acc sg	ἱστάντα	ἱστᾶσαν	ἱστάν
nom pl	ἱστάντες	ἱστᾶσαι	ἱστάντα
gen pl	ἱστάντων	ἱστασῶν	ἱστάντων
dat pl	ἱστᾶσι(ν)	ἱστάσαις	ἱστᾶσι(ν)
acc pl	ἱστάντας	ἱστάσας	ἱστάντα

PRESENT MIDDLE/PASSIVE PARTICIPLE OF ἵστημι

nom sg	ἱστάμενος	ἱσταμένη	ἱστάμενον
gen sg	ἱσταμένου	ἱσταμένης	ἱσταμένου
dat sg	ἱσταμένῳ	ἱσταμένῃ	ἱσταμένῳ
acc sg	ἱστάμενον	ἱσταμένην	ἱστάμενον
nom pl	ἱστάμενοι	ἱστάμεναι	ἱστάμενα
gen pl	ἱσταμένων	ἱσταμένων	ἱσταμένων
dat pl	ἱσταμένοις	ἱσταμέναις	ἱσταμένοις
acc pl	ἱσταμένους	ἱσταμένας	ἱστάμενα

PERFECT ACTIVE PARTICIPLE OF ἵστημι (FIRST)

nom sg	ἑστηκώς	ἑστηκυῖα	ἑστηκός
gen sg	ἑστηκότος	ἑστηκυίας	ἑστηκότος
dat sg	ἑστηκότι	ἑστηκυίᾳ	ἑστηκότι
acc sg	ἑστηκότα	ἑστηκυῖαν	ἑστηκός
nom pl	ἑστηκότες	ἑστηκυῖαι	ἑστηκότα
gen pl	ἑστηκότων	ἑστηκυιῶν	ἑστηκότων
dat pl	ἑστηκόσι(ν)	ἑστηκυίαις	ἑστηκόσι(ν)
acc pl	ἑστηκότας	ἑστηκυίας	ἑστηκότα

PERFECT ACTIVE PARTICIPLE OF ἵστημι (SECOND)

nom sg	ἑστώς	ἑστῶσα	ἑστός
gen sg	ἑστῶτος	ἑστώσης	ἑστῶτος
dat sg	ἑστῶτι	ἑστώσῃ	ἑστῶτι
acc sg	ἑστῶτα	ἑστῶσαν	ἑστός
nom pl	ἑστῶτες	ἑστῶσαι	ἑστῶτα
gen pl	ἑστώτων	ἑστωσῶν	ἑστώτων
dat pl	ἑστῶσι(ν)	ἑστώσαις	ἑστῶσι(ν)
acc pl	ἑστῶτας	ἑστώσας	ἑστῶτα

THE OPTATIVE: *Forms and Functions*

OBJECTIVES AND OVERVIEW

Chapter 26 introduces the following linguistic concepts, morphemes, and paradigms:

- optative tense formative
- present and first aorist active and middle optative paradigms
- second aorist middle optative paradigm
- optative paradigm of εἰμί
- functions of the optative

In this chapter, we learn the final verbal mood for Koine Greek—the optative. The optative is sometimes called the mood of "wishful thinking." It can be used to indicate the mere possibility of an action. This finite mood is not very common in the GNT and was being replaced by the subjunctive; eventually it disappeared from Greek altogether. It occurs about sixty-eight times in the GNT, mainly in Luke-Acts and Paul, often in the exclamation μὴ γένοιτο! ("May it never be!" or "God forbid!"). As this example shows, if the optative is negated, μή, not οὐ, is used. Although the optative is infrequent, it does occur in some important contexts in the GNT. We will begin by looking at optative forms, then consider some of the primary functions of the optative.

THE FORMS OF THE OPTATIVE

So far, we have seen that each mood has certain morphological characteristics that help to distinguish it from other moods. For example, the indicative alone uses an augment and secondary personal endings, the subjunctive uses a lengthened connecting vowel, and the imperative uses different sets of personal endings. Perhaps the most distinctive formal feature of the optative is the suffixed iota.[1] In the present and second aorist optative forms, the connecting vowel omicron is used with the resulting diphthong οι. In the first aorist active and middle optative forms, the tense formative -σα is used with the resulting form -σαι. The tense formative -θε is used with the first aorist passive optative, plus the suffix -ιη, with the resulting form -θειη. Only present and aorist optatives occur in the GNT. Although the optative is infrequent in the GNT, it is important to be able to *recognize* it.

The present active and middle optatives use nearly all the primary personal endings used with omega verbs, except for a certain "hybrid" tendency in the first-person singular, which uses the ending -μι. Notice also the different ending for the second-person singular in the middle voice (for the present and aorist optative), which is an omicron. As we have seen all along, the present middle and passive share the same form. Here are the paradigms for the present active and middle optative of λύω.

PRESENT ACTIVE AND MIDDLE OPTATIVE OF λύω

	active		middle	
1 sg	λύοιμι	I might release	λυοίμην	I might release for myself
2 sg	λύοις	you (sg) might release	λύοιο	you (sg) might release for yourself
3 sg	λύοι	he/she/it might release	λύοιτο	he/she/it might release for himself/herself/itself
1 pl	λύοιμεν	we might release	λυοίμεθα	we might release for ourselves
2 pl	λύοιτε	you (pl) might release	λύοισθε	you (pl) might release for yourselves
3 pl	λύοιεν	they might release	λύοιντο	they might release for themselves

As we have seen, the augment is not used with nonindicative aorist forms, which is why it does not occur with the aorist optative. Moreover, aorist optative forms use primary personal endings (parallel to the subjunctive). For first aorist forms, the tense formatives -σα (with active and middle forms) and -θε (with passive forms) are used. These tense formatives, together with the iota suffix, make these forms fairly easy to recognize. Below are the paradigms for the first aorist

---

1. This iota is sometimes called a connecting vowel. Since the optative also uses the connecting vowel omicron, it seems best to avoid the terminology of connecting vowel for the optative's distinctive use of the iota. Additionally, some grammars call this a *mood formative*, which is a more helpful way for some to consider this suffix.

optative of λύω. The same inflected meanings for the present active and middle optative (listed above) could also be used for the aorist active and middle optative, although context is the final determiner for any translation. The inflected meaning for the aorist passive optative (listed below) could also be used for a present passive optative.

FIRST AORIST OPTATIVE OF λύω

	active	middle	passive	
1 sg	λύσαιμι	λυσαίμην	λυθείην	I might be released
2 sg	λύσαις	λύσαιο	λυθείης	you (sg) might be released
3 sg	λύσαι[1]	λύσαιτο	λυθείη	he/she/it might be released
1 pl	λύσαιμεν	λυσαίμεθα	λυθείημεν	we might be released
2 pl	λύσαιτε	λύσαισθε	λυθείητε	you (pl) might be released
3 pl	λύσαιεν	λύσαιντο	λυθείησαν	they might be released

[1] You might think that this form looks familiar, and you're right . . . almost! The aorist active infinitive has the same letters, but it is accented with a circumflex: λῦσαι.

The second aorist optative does not use tense formatives and instead uses the aorist tense stem (visible in the verb's third principal part), the connecting vowel omicron, and the iota suffix. Second aorist active optatives occur infrequently in the GNT, hence only the second aorist middle optative is listed; here is the paradigm of γίνομαι.

SECOND AORIST MIDDLE OPTATIVE OF γίνομαι

	middle	
1 sg	γενοίμην	I might become
2 sg	γένοιο	you (sg) might become
3 sg	γένοιτο	he/she/it might become
1 pl	γενοίμεθα	we might become
2 pl	γένοισθε	you (pl) might become
3 pl	γένοιντο	they might become

Finally, the optative εἴη accounts for many of the occurrences of the optative in the GNT. Here is the optative paradigm of εἰμί.

OPTATIVE OF εἰμί

1 sg	εἴην	I might be
2 sg	εἴης	you (sg) might be
3 sg	εἴη	he/she/it might be
1 pl	εἴημεν	we might be
2 pl	εἴητε	you (pl) might be
3 pl	εἴησαν	they might be

Contract verbs occur infrequently as optatives in the GNT, and μι verbs are only present in the following forms: the aorist active of δίδωμι (third singular, δῴη); and the aorist middle of ὀνίνημι ("I help, profit, benefit"; first singular, ὀναίμην). For this reason, these paradigms are not listed.

THE FUNCTIONS OF THE OPTATIVE

The most common use of the optative is in an independent clause to express a wish or a prayer. For example:

> ἰδοὺ ἡ δούλη κυρίου· *γένοιτό* μοι κατὰ τὸ ῥῆμά σου (Luke 1:38)
> See [I am] the servant of the Lord; *may it be done* to me according to
>   your word.

Perhaps the most well-known example of this use of the optative occurs with the expression μὴ γένοιτο in Paul. Consider the following:

> νόμον οὖν καταργοῦμεν διὰ τῆς πίστεως; *μὴ γένοιτο* (Rom 3:31)
> Therefore, do we nullify the law through faith? *May it never be*!

The optative is also used in fourth-class conditionals, although no complete example of this construction occurs in the GNT.[2] If the optative occurs in the apodosis, it functions independently to indicate what would happen if a certain condition were met—notice the use of ἄν in the apodosis, which occurs before the protasis in the following example:

---

2. The full construction would have εἰ plus the optative in the protasis and ἄν plus the optative in the apodosis.

Πῶς γὰρ ἂν δυναίμην ἐὰν μή τις ὁδηγήσει με; (Acts 8:31)
For how *would I be able* unless someone guides me?

If the optative occurs in the protasis, it functions dependently to indicate a condition that is considered to be unlikely. In the following example, the protasis is introduced with εἰ:

ἔσπευδεν γὰρ εἰ δυνατὸν *εἴη* αὐτῷ τὴν ἡμέραν τῆς πεντηκοστῆς γενέσθαι εἰς Ἱεροσόλυμα (Acts 20:16)
For he was eager, if *it would be* possible for him, to be in Jerusalem on the day of Pentecost.

Finally, the optative can occur as a dependent clause after verbs of speaking to indicate indirect discourse. For example:

Ἐπηρώτων δὲ αὐτὸν οἱ μαθηταὶ αὐτοῦ τίς αὕτη *εἴη* ἡ παραβολή (Luke 8:9)
And his disciples were asking him what this parable *might be*.

If this had been recorded as direct discourse, the disciples' question would have been as follows:

τίς αὕτη ἐστὶν ἡ παραβολή;
What is this parable?

REVIEW OF CHAPTER 26

In this chapter we learned the optative, the fourth and final verbal mood in Koine Greek. The forms of the optative are recognizable by the distinctive use of -οι in the present tense forms, the use of -σαι in the aorist active and middle forms, and the use of -θειη in the aorist passive forms. Also distinctive is the use of the ending -μι in the first-person singular. We surveyed the functions of the optative, which often express a wish or a prayer. We also looked at the (incomplete) examples of fourth-class conditionals with optatives in the GNT.

Study Guide for Chapter 26

1. Review the following concepts from chapter 26:
   the function of the optative to express a wish
   the function of the optative in conditional clauses

the negation used with the optative

2. Be able to recognize each of the following forms:

present forms of the optative

aorist forms of the optative

the optative of εἰμί

3. Be able to parse optative forms and translate basic Koine sentences that incorporate forms and concepts from previous chapters.

Vocabulary to Memorize

The following are the assigned vocabulary words for chapter 26.

αἰώνιος, -ον	eternal (71)
ἀσθενής, -ές	weak, sick, powerless (26)
διάβολος, -ον	slanderous; the devil (subst) (37)
διαλογισμός, -οῦ, ὁ	thought, opinion, doubt (14)
διδαχή, -ῆς, ἡ	teaching, instruction (30)
ἐκλεκτός, -ή, -όν	elect, chosen, select (22)
ἐλεύθερος, -α, -ον	free, independent; free person (23)
ἑορτή, -ῆς, ἡ	festival, feast (25)
ἐπεί	because, since, when (26)
ἰσχυρός, -ά, -όν	strong, mighty, powerful (29)
ἰσχύω	I am strong, I am able, I am powerful (28)
καθίστημι	I bring, I appoint, I ordain (21)
καταργέω	I abolish, I nullify, I make ineffective (27)
μηκέτι	no longer (22)
νέος, -α, -ον	new, recent, young (23)
ξένος, -η, -ον	foreign, strange; stranger, foreigner (subst) (14)
ὀργή, -ῆς, ἡ	anger, wrath (36)
οὔπω	not yet (26)
πόσος, -η, -ον	how great (?) how much (?) how many (?) (27)
πότε	when? (19)
σήμερον	today (41)
σκανδαλίζω	I cause to sin, I anger, I take offense at (pass) (29)
τοσοῦτος, -αύτη, -οῦτον	so great, so large, so many, so much (20)
χήρα, -ας, ἡ	widow (26)
χώρα, -ας, ἡ	land, region, field (28)

Principal Parts to Memorize

There are no new principal parts assigned for this chapter. Instead you should review all principal parts beginning with ἄγω through ἐσθίω. Another section will be assigned for review in the next chapter.

Paradigms to Memorize

The following paradigms should be memorized for chapter 26: all assigned forms of the present and aorist optative for λύω; forms of the optative of εἰμί; forms of the aorist middle optative of γίνομαι. Instead of rote memorization, focus on identifying the distinctive elements in the optative and identifying the tense stems, connecting vowels, tense formatives, and personal endings that you already know.

PRESENT ACTIVE OPTATIVE PARADIGM OF λύω

1 sg	λύοιμι
2 sg	λύοις
3 sg	λύοι
1 pl	λύοιμεν
2 pl	λύοιτε
3 pl	λύοιεν

PRESENT MIDDLE OPTATIVE PARADIGM OF λύω

1 sg	λυοίμην
2 sg	λύοιο
3 sg	λύοιτο
1 pl	λυοίμεθα
2 pl	λύοισθε
3 pl	λύοιντο

FIRST AORIST ACTIVE OPTATIVE PARADIGM OF λύω

1 sg	λύσαιμι
2 sg	λύσαις
3 sg	λύσαι
1 pl	λύσαιμεν
2 pl	λύσαιτε
3 pl	λύσαιεν

FIRST AORIST MIDDLE OPTATIVE PARADIGM OF λύω

1 sg	λυσαίμην
2 sg	λύσαιο
3 sg	λύσαιτο
1 pl	λυσαίμεθα
2 pl	λύσαισθε
3 pl	λύσαιντο

FIRST AORIST PASSIVE OPTATIVE PARADIGM OF λύω

1 sg	λυθείην
2 sg	λυθείης
3 sg	λυθείη
1 pl	λυθείημεν
2 pl	λυθείητε
3 pl	λυθείησαν

SECOND AORIST ACTIVE OPTATIVE PARADIGM OF λαμβάνω

1 sg	λάβοιμι
2 sg	λάβοις
3 sg	λάβοι
1 pl	λάβοιμεν
2 pl	λάβοιτε
3 pl	λάβοιεν

SECOND AORIST MIDDLE OPTATIVE PARADIGM OF γίνομαι

1 sg	γενοίμην
2 sg	γένοιο
3 sg	γένοιτο
1 pl	γενοίμεθα
2 pl	γένοισθε
3 pl	γένοιντο

OPTATIVE PARADIGM OF εἰμί

1 sg	εἴην
2 sg	εἴης
3 sg	εἴη
1 pl	εἴημεν
2 pl	εἴητε
3 pl	εἴησαν

OUTLINING NEW TESTAMENT
PASSAGES: *Structural and Narrative Outlines*

OBJECTIVES AND OVERVIEW

Chapter 27 introduces the following concepts:

- structural outlining for didactic passages
- narrative outlining for narrative passages

By now, if you have been using the accompanying workbook, you have had much practice marking the syntactic elements and units of the Greek texts, which has been the focus of these assigned exercises. As much fun as this may be, clearly the end goal is not simply to be able to highlight certain parts of speech or mark texts with certain symbols! The ultimate goal of this exercise is to learn how to "see" the syntax of a given passage and to determine the intrinsic structure of a passage. This structure is part of the overall discourse and is one of the means by which language communicates meaning. For any given text, there is really only one given structure. Even though some secondary elements in a text may be understood differently, the overall structure is determined by such elements as main and subordinate clauses, prepositional phrases, and so on. Again, by now these elements should be very familiar to you.

Determining the structure of the text is one of the key skills required for faithfully exegeting and expositing the text, whether preaching, teaching, leading Bible studies, or any other venue. Sometimes people think that focusing on the text's structure will inhibit their creativity when it comes to proclaiming the text, but the opposite is really the case. Here is an analogy that might help. Nearly all great jazz musicians have spent a great deal of time learning how to play their chosen instruments really well. For many this has included hours spent practicing scales or learning the fundamentals of music. This certainly doesn't mean that every jazz musician sounds exactly the same or that jazz music is predictable. Instead, when a musician knows how music works and understands the basic structure of a given composition, then he or she is free to express that composition in an endless number of ways. Analogously, a biblical text has a certain structure that is determined by the syntax used in that text, like a musical composition. This basic structure is understood by identifying the basic syntactic units and how they function, which is what you have been doing in the required exercises. Once the structure is understood, however, there are any number of ways that the text can be faithfully exposited. Knowing the basic structure of a given biblical text actually gives the Spirit-led freedom to proclaim the same text in a variety of ways depending on the context and needs of the audience. So knowing a text's structure actually leads to more freedom to exposit the text—the opposite of what is sometimes claimed.

Before we talk about finding a text's structure, we need to talk a bit about *genre*, which refers to the type of writing or discourse. Biblical books are usually classified as one of the following genres: narrative, prophecy, poetry, wisdom, epistle, and apocalyptic. (This is genre understood at the macro level.) Within any given biblical book, however, there may be a combination of these types of writings, such as the narrative portions in Galatians. (This is genre understood at the micro level.)

Most of the books of the NT are either narratives or epistles. The Gospels and Acts are classified as narrative, although some epistles and parts of Revelation also contain narrative. Epistles can be understood as didactic, which means that they are intended to instruct. This doesn't mean that we don't learn from narrative, but narrative often *describes* events rather than directly *prescribes* what believers should do, whereas epistles often tell believers directly what they should believe or how they should behave. There are twenty-one epistles in the NT.[1] There are also didactic passages in the Gospels (such as the Sermon on the Mount), Acts (such as the speeches), or Revelation (such as the messages to the seven churches). When outlining a passage, it is important first to determine the genre of the passage that you are considering. A *structural outline* will help determine the structure of a didactic (which is sometimes called *discourse*) passage, whereas a *narrative outline* is necessary for analyzing a narrative passage. (We will not discuss poetry here, but that genre requires yet a different approach to determine its structure.)

STRUCTURAL OUTLINES

The following steps will help you identify and visualize the structure of a didactic passage, whether from an epistle or a didactic passage from the Gospels, Acts, or Revelation.

---

1. To be precise, Revelation is best understood as an epistle, although it is usually identified as apocalyptic.

First, identify the boundaries of the entire passage by ensuring that complete sentences, which often include several verses, are being considered. This must be determined from the Greek text. Often English translations do not reflect the syntax of the Greek and divide a Greek sentence into multiple English sentences. Additionally, verse divisions frequently divide one sentence into multiple verses, so versification should not be considered when determining the boundaries of a passage. (The text, not the versification, is inspired!) Thus, it is important to ensure that you are considering complete Greek sentences when outlining a given passage. You should also ensure that your passage reflects the natural beginning and end of a given paragraph in the GNT. This is not always easy to determine, but you want to ensure that you are not arbitrarily cutting a paragraph in half or leaving off a final sentence, and so on. You can consult commentaries that focus on the Greek text to help determine the natural boundaries of a given passage.

In many respects, didactic passages are driven by verbs, so the **next** step in outlining a passage is to identify all finite verb forms, nonfinite verb forms, and verbal modifiers. This should come fairly naturally after marking texts for the assigned exercises. Then proceed through the following instructions, where "V" stands for verb and the number is keyed to the examples that follow. Hence the discussion of "V1" is then illustrated and labeled with "V1" in the following examples. When you are doing your own outlines, you do not need to number lines with V1, V2, etc. These are simply used here to link the discussion below with the examples that follow. After our initial focus on verbs, we will consider substantives, which will be dicussed in terms of "S1," "S2," and so on.

Verbs and Verb Modifiers (V)

V1. Identify the main finite verb. This will be one of the finite verbs that you have already marked. Not all finite verbs are main verbs, but a main verb must be a finite verb. Remember that a finite verb is an indicative, imperative, subjunctive, or optative. Since main verbs are the anchors of a sentence, they should be placed all the way to the left of the page. (See the examples below labeled V1.)

Most sentences will have only one main verb. If, however, you find two finite verbs in a single sentence, look for a *coordinating* conjunction (such as καί) that links two finite verbs; both finite verbs would be considered to be the main verbs in this case, because such a conjunction coordinates rather than subordinates. Both verbs should go to the left of the page (see the following example from 1 Pet 1:10). It is essential, however, that you verify that a main verb is not actually part of a dependent clause; that is, that the verb is not preceded by ὅτι, ἵνα, etc.

V2. Identify dependent clauses that begin with subordinating conjunctions, such as ὅτι, ἵνα, etc. Indent these clauses under the verb that they modify, which may be a finite main verb, a finite dependent verb, or, somewhat less commonly, a participle or infinitive. It is essential to grasp that a finite verb that is part of a dependent clause can *never* be taken out of the dependent clause in which it appears and be put all the way to the left. *The entire dependent clause is one unit.* A dependent verb is forever a part of the dependent clause in which it appears, even if it wished it weren't! This is perhaps the hardest concept for students to grasp, but it is an absolutely essential one. So, you might think of this in the following way: once a finite verb is placed into a dependent clause, it is joined to that clause with a type of super glue than can *never* be dissolved! Now you can understand why you were asked to put parentheses around dependent clauses— they form *one* syntactic unit.

V3. Identify and align adverbial participles. Remember that substantival participles nearly always have an article and that attributive participles always directly modify a substantive (sharing the same case, number, and gender). Also remember that adverbial participles are *never* articular. Adverbial participles do not function independently, and thus they always modify another verb form. Indent an adverbial participle under the verb that it is modifying. Once you have aligned the participle, you may note in the margin its specific function (i.e., causal, purpose, temporal, result, concessive, etc.). (See the examples below.)

V4. Identify and align adverbial infinitives. If an infinitive is adverbial, indent it under the finite verb that it is modifying. It is best, however, to keep complementary infinitives together with their finite verb. Remember: articular infinitives can also function substantivally (as a subject or direct object); substantival infinitives are discussed in the next section of these instructions.

V5. Indent adverbs under the verbs they modify. Remember that prepositional phrases often function adverbially. These should also be indented under the verb that they modify. Negative adverbs are an exception; they should be kept on the same line as the verb they modify. (See the example from Col 1:9 below.)

Substantives, Pronouns, and Their Modifiers (S)

S1. Keep expressed subjects with third-person verbs on the same line and in the same word order (if possible) with their finite verbs. For all Greek verbs, finite verb forms are inflected to indicate the person and number. But third-person verbs may have an explicitly expressed subject. Also, personal pronouns can be used emphatically; such pronouns should also be kept on the same line and in the same word order with the finite verbs with which they are linked.

S2. Keep direct objects on the same line and in the same word order (if possible) with their verbs, unless the direct object is lengthy. If there is a list of direct objects, line them up in a parallel column list; καί may either follow an item or be placed on a separate line. (See the examples below.)

S3. Indent substantival modifiers (unless there is only one) directly under the substantive they modify. Substantival modifiers can be adjectives, participles, other substantives, prepositional phrases, etc. For second-attributive constructions, it can be helpful to align the modifier under the substantive it modifies. (See the example from Col 1:3–5 below.)

S4. Keep genitival modifiers together on the same line with their head noun. If the genitival modifier is long, however, you can indent it under its head noun.

S5. Identify relative clauses and indent the clause (beginning with the relative pronoun) under the antecedent of the relative pronoun. Keep a finite verb that is part of a dependent relative clause *inside* the dependent clause; it should *never* be put all the way to the left—remember the super glue! The relative clause introduces a dependent clause, so this is parallel to the treatment of dependent clauses that are introduced with a subordinating conjunction.

S6. Appositives can either be aligned one under the other or kept on the same line.

Other Connectors within or between Sentences or Paragraphs and Conditionals (C)

C1. Other Connectors. Some conjunctions, such as γάρ, show the relationship between entire sentences. In this case, you may indent the conjunction above the sentence and try to show its logical connection with what precedes it, perhaps using an arrow. Other conjunctions that also show the relationship between sentences or paragraphs should be indented, on a separate line, to highlight their function. Again, arrows may help to indicate the function of these conjunctions. Remember that subordinating conjunctions that introduce dependent clauses should be indented under the verb that they are modifying.

C2. Conditionals. The protasis of a conditional (as the dependent clause) should be indented, but the apodosis (the independent clause) should be placed to the left. If you have a series of conditionals, try to align the protases and apodoses in such a way that the logic of the argumentation is best preserved.

Examples of Structural Outlines

As you will see in the following examples, outlines are part science and part art. It is generally good to preserve the original word order, as this is often important in exegesis. Thus you can use arrows to indicate the function of a syntactic unit if it is not indented under the word that it modifies, which you can see with the adverb πάντοτε that modifies the following participle (not the finite verb that it follows) in the second example from Colossians 1:3–5.

Example: Colossians 1:9

1:9	Διὰ τοῦτο	V5
	οὐ παυόμεθα	V1/V5
	προσευχόμενοι καὶ	V3
	αἰτούμενοι,	V3
	. . . ὑπὲρ ὑμῶν	V5
	ἵνα πληρωθῆτε τὴν ἐπίγνωσιν τοῦ θελήματος αὐτοῦ	V2/S2/S4

Example: Colossians 1:3–5

1:3	Εὐχαριστοῦμεν	V1
	τῷ θεῷ πατρὶ τοῦ κυρίου ἡμῶν Ἰησοῦ Χριστοῦ	S2
	↓ πάντοτε	V5
	προσευχόμενοι . . .	V3 (means)
	περὶ ὑμῶν	V5
1:4	ἀκούσαντες τὴν πίστιν ὑμῶν ἐν Χριστῷ Ἰησοῦ	V3 (causal)/S2
	καὶ	S2
	τὴν ἀγάπην	S2
	ἣν ἔχετε	S5
	εἰς πάντας τοὺς ἁγίους	V5
1:5	διὰ τὴν ἐλπίδα	V5
	τὴν ἀποκειμένην ὑμῖν	S3
	ἐν τοῖς οὐρανοῖς	V5

Example: 1 Peter 1:10–11

1:10	περὶ ἧς σωτηρίας	V5
	ἐξεζήτησαν	V1
	καὶ	V1
	ἐξηραύνησαν προφῆται	V1/S1
	↑ οἱ . . .προφητεύσαντες	S3
	περὶ τῆς εἰς ὑμᾶς χάριτος	V5
1:11	ἐραυνῶντες εἰς τίνα ἢ	V3 (means)
	ποῖον καιρὸν	S3

NARRATIVE OUTLINES

The steps outlined above are not helpful for outlining narrative passages, which are generally driven by a series of statements about what happened or what was said. By contrast, didactic passages often rely on dependent clauses to give reasons or explanations. In narrative, aorist verbs are frequently used to indicate the main actions, imperfect verbs may indicate background information, and present verbs can be used to introduce dialogue. For clarity, all finite verbs are double underlined. In narrative, it is helpful to identify the characters and actions. These can be labeled as indicated in the example from Luke 2 below. When possible, it can be helpful to label dependent verbs per the steps outlined for didactic passages.

Example: Luke 2:1–7

Introduction to the Event

1	Ἐγένετο δὲ ἐν ταῖς ἡμέραις ἐκείναις	when
	ἐξῆλθεν δόγμα παρὰ Καίσαρος Αὐγούστου	event/character
	ἀπογράφεσθαι πᾶσαν τὴν οἰκουμένην.	V4 (purpose)
2	(αὕτη ἀπογραφὴ πρώτη ἐγένετο ἡγεμονεύοντος τῆς Συρίας Κυρηνίου.	
		historical background)
3	καὶ ἐπορεύοντο πάντες ἀπογράφεσθαι, ἕκαστος εἰς τὴν ἑαυτοῦ πόλιν.	

Main Characters and Main Event

4	Ἀνέβη δὲ καὶ Ἰωσὴφ	main character
	ἀπὸ τῆς Γαλιλαίας	
	ἐκ πόλεως Ναζαρὲθ	
	εἰς τὴν Ἰουδαίαν	
	εἰς πόλιν Δαυὶδ	
	ἥτις καλεῖται Βηθλέεμ,	
	↓ διὰ τὸ εἶναι αὐτὸν ἐξ οἴκου καὶ πατριᾶς Δαυίδ,	V4 (causal)
5	ἀπογράψασθαι σὺν Μαριὰμ τῇ ἐμνηστευμένῃ αὐτῷ, οὔσῃ ἐγκύῳ.	
		main character/V4 (purpose)
6	Ἐγένετο δὲ	introduction to event
	↓ ἐν τῷ εἶναι αὐτοὺς ἐκεῖ	V4 (temporal)
	ἐπλήσθησαν αἱ ἡμέραι τοῦ τεκεῖν αὐτήν,	event
7	καὶ ἔτεκεν τὸν υἱὸν αὐτῆς τὸν πρωτότοκον,	key event
	καὶ ἐσπαργάνωσεν αὐτὸν	event
	καὶ ἀνέκλινεν αὐτὸν ἐν φάτνῃ,	event
	διότι οὐκ ἦν αὐτοῖς τόπος ἐν τῷ καταλύματι.	V4 (causal)

As you can see, this type of outline is very different from the one used for didactic passages. The goal of a narrative outline is to follow the events, people, places, and dialogue in a narrative passage. This will help you to "tell the story" of the narrative more clearly when you are preaching or teaching through such a passage.

OUTLINING NEW TESTAMENT PASSAGES: STRUCTURAL OUTLINE PRACTICE

Now it's time to put structural outlining to practice with a text from the GNT. This is one Greek sentence. Begin by double underlining the finite verbs.

Διὸ ἀναζωσάμενοι τὰς ὀσφύας τῆς διανοίας ὑμῶν νήφοντες τελείως
<u>ἐλπίσατε</u> ἐπὶ τὴν φερομένην ὑμῖν χάριν ἐν ἀποκαλύψει Ἰησοῦ
Χριστοῦ

There is only one finite verb in this sentence, so this finite verb must also be the main verb. So, place this verb to the left. Recall that the letters and numbers on the right are keyed to the instructions given earlier in this chapter.

Διὸ ἀναζωσάμενοι τὰς ὀσφύας τῆς διανοίας ὑμῶν νήφοντες τελείως
<u>ἐλπίσατε</u>   V1
ἐπὶ τὴν φερομένην ὑμῖν χάριν ἐν ἀποκαλύψει Ἰησοῦ Χριστοῦ

Now, look for any dependent clauses that are introduced with a subordinating conjunction (V2). In this example, there aren't any, so move to the next step.

Identify all adverbial participles (V3). Begin by drawing a box around *all* participles. In this example, there are three participles; the first two are adverbial, but the third one is in the first attributive position.

Διὸ ⌈ἀναζωσάμενοι⌉ τὰς ὀσφύας τῆς διανοίας ὑμῶν ⌈νήφοντες⌉ τελείως
<u>ἐλπίσατε</u>   V1
ἐπὶ τὴν ⌈φερομένην⌉ ὑμῖν χάριν ἐν ἀποκαλύψει Ἰησοῦ Χριστοῦ

Now indent the adverbial participles to indicate their subordinate function to the verb they modify (in this case, the main verb). Notice that these two adverbial participles precede the verb that they modify, so they are indented *above* this verb.

Διὸ

ἀναζωσάμενοι τὰς ὀσφύας τῆς διανοίας ὑμῶν		V3
νήφοντες τελείως		V3
ἐλπίσατε		V1
ἐπὶ τὴν φερομένην ὑμῖν χάριν ἐν ἀποκαλύψει Ἰησοῦ Χριστοῦ.		

There are no adverbial infinitives (V4) in this example, so you should next identify any adverbs (V5) and indent them with respect to the verb forms that they modify. Prepositional phrases that are functioning adverbially should also be indented with respect to the verb form that they modify. In this example, there are two examples of this. First, the prepositional phrase ἐπὶ τὴν φερομένην ὑμῖν χάριν is modifying the main verb ἐλπίσατε. Second, the prepositional phrase ἐν ἀποκαλύψει Ἰησοῦ Χριστοῦ is modifying the attributive participle φερομένην. Remember that participles are verbal adjectives, so even when they are functioning attributively (or substantivally) they can still have adverbial modifiers. So this is how you would indent these two prepositional phrases.

Διὸ

ἀναζωσάμενοι τὰς ὀσφύας τῆς διανοίας ὑμῶν	V3
νήφοντες	V3
τελείως	V5
ἐλπίσατε	V1
ἐπὶ τὴν φερομένην ὑμῖν χάριν	V5
ἐν ἀποκαλύψει Ἰησοῦ Χριστοῦ	V5

Now it's time to focus on substantives. The main verb is not a third-person form, and there is no expressed subject for it, nor is there an emphatic pronoun (S1). There is also no direct object for this verb (S2). Notice that the direct object of the first adverbial participle stays on the same line with the participle; together this comprises a *dependent participial clause*.

Now look for substantival modifiers (S3). Remember that it is usually best to keep a genitival modifier with its head noun (S4). In this example, that only leaves χάριν, which is modified by the attributive participle φερομένην. You could "pull" the attributive participle out of the original word order and indent it with respect to χάριν, or you could just leave the collocation as it is in the original word order. (You can indicate that you have modified the original word order with ellipsis, as is demonstrated below.) In this example, there is little difference, but in other examples indenting substantival modifiers can be more helpful. This is the "art" aspect of structural outlines.

Διὸ

$\boxed{\text{ἀναζωσάμενοι}}$ τὰς ὀσφύας τῆς διανοίας ὑμῶν	V3
$\boxed{\text{νήφοντες}}$	V3
τελείως	V5
<u>ἐλπίσατε</u>	V1
ἐπὶ τὴν . . . χάριν	V5
$\boxed{\text{φερομένην}}$ ὑμῖν	V5
ἐν ἀποκαλύψει Ἰησοῦ Χριστοῦ	V5

Finally, let's consider the conjunction διό. It's an inferential conjunction that draws a conclusion from a previous sentence or passage. The sentence that we have been considering is 1 Peter 1:13, so διό is referring back to 1 Peter 1:3–12, which outlines believers' glorious salvation and eternal inheritance. Διό indicates that setting one's hope fully on the grace that will be finally revealed when Jesus returns is the *inference*, or *conclusion*, to be drawn from an understanding of this salvation and eternal inheritance. Because διό links two passages, it is centered all by itself above the rest of 1 Peter 1:13. The arrow indicates that διό is referring back to the previous passage.

Διὸ ↑

$\boxed{\text{ἀναζωσάμενοι}}$ τὰς ὀσφύας τῆς διανοίας ὑμῶν	V3
$\boxed{\text{νήφοντες}}$	V3
τελείως	V5
<u>ἐλπίσατε</u>	V1
ἐπὶ τὴν . . . χάριν	V5
$\boxed{\text{φερομένην}}$ ὑμῖν	V5
ἐν ἀποκαλύψει Ἰησοῦ Χριστοῦ	V5

At this point, you can now see the structure of this sentence very clearly, and you can begin to see how this sentence fits into the context of 1 Peter. The main exhortation here is to "set one's hope." Before Peter elaborates on this, however, there are two preliminary actions that must take place, as indicated by the two adverbial participles that precede the main verb. First, believers need to "gird up the loins" of their minds. This imagery probably refers to the exodus, when the Hebrews were commanded to be ready to leave at any time by binding up their long robes. This is metaphorically describing the need to be ready and possibly to rid ourselves of obstacles or distractions that keep us from setting our hope on Jesus. Second, believers are urged to be clear minded or sober. This metaphorically indicates that believers should not allow anxiety or fear (which the audience of 1 Peter was likely experiencing due to persecution) or other distracting mind-sets, such as worry or bitterness, to keep us from setting our hope on Jesus. Notice how these two dependent participial clauses could easily be developed into key points in a sermon. In some respects, they are the prerequisites for setting our hope on Jesus; alternatively, they could be understood as obstacles that keep us from hoping in Jesus.

Following the main verb, Peter then specifies the object upon which we are to set our hope, namely, grace. This grace is then further explained as the grace that is coming to us at the revelation of Jesus Christ. This draws upon apocalyptic imagery and suggests that even though we experience the Lord's grace partially now, we should set our complete and final hope on the full revelation of that grace when Jesus returns.

Notice that the syntactic structure of this passage is fixed, meaning that the identification of the main verb, the adverbial participles, the attributive participle, and the prepositional phrases are not debated. Additionally, these are fixed syntactic units whose functions are determined by the sentence in which they occur. But notice also that from this foundational structure numerous sermons could be preached in any number of ways. Thus, the structure of the passage does not limit the creative leading of the Spirit; instead, this structure opens numerous possible ways that this passage could be faithfully exposited.

REVIEW OF CHAPTER 27

In this chapter we learned how to make structural and narrative outlines for NT Greek passages. The outlines are part science and part art, but they are very helpful for moving from the syntax of the Greek text to exposition of that text. Although the structure of a given text is fairly fixed—a dependent clause is always a dependent clause—the multiple ways in which a given passage could be taught or preached is "limited" only by the needs of a given congregation and the infinite creativity and wisdom of the Holy Spirit. May this new tool of outlining inspire your desire to bring the Word of God to those to whom you minister!

Study Guide for Chapter 27

In anticipation for the end of the course (and possibly a final exam), you should do the following:

1. Review concepts in chapters 24–26.
2. Review forms in chapters 24–26.

Vocabulary to Memorize

Here are the assigned vocabulary words for chapter 27.

ἁγιάζω	I set apart, I make holy, I consecrate (28)
ἀγρός, -οῦ, ὁ	field, country(side) (36)
ἀκάθαρτος, -ον	impure, unclean (32)
ἀνα (+acc)	upward; each (13)
ἀργύριον, -ου, τό	silver, money (20)
αὔριον	tomorrow, soon (14)
ἄφεσις, -εως, ἡ	forgiveness, release, pardon (17)
βαστάζω	I carry, I bear, I endure (27)
δένδρον, -ου, τό	tree (25)
διότι	because, therefore, for (23)
δυνατός, -ή, -όν	powerful, strong, able, possible (32)
εἰκών, -όνος, ἡ	image, likeness (23)
θυγάτηρ, -τρός, ἡ	daughter, female descendant (28)
ἱκανός, -ή, -όν	sufficient, able, fit (39)
κληρονομέω	I inherit, I receive a share of (18)
κοινωνία, -ας, ἡ	fellowship, participation (19)
κριτής, -οῦ, ὁ	judge (19)
κτίσις, -εως, ἡ	creation, creature (19)
κώμη, -ης, ἡ	village, small town (27)
λίμνη, -ης, ἡ	lake (11)
μανθάνω	I learn, I find out (25)
μάχαιρα, -ης, ἡ	sword (29)
νικάω	I conquer, I overcome (28)
οἶνος, -ου, ὁ	wine, vineyard (34)
παρέρχομαι	I go, I pass by, I pass away, I neglect (29)

Principal Parts to Review

There are no new principal parts assigned for this chapter. Instead you should review all principal parts beginning with εὑρίσκω through φέρω.

Paradigms to Review

There are no new paradigms assigned for this chapter. Instead you should keep on reviewing the paradigms that you have learned so far.

chapter TWENTY-EIGHT

ETCETERAS: *Expressing Purpose and Conditionality; More on Conjunctions and Clauses*

OBJECTIVES AND OVERVIEW

Chapter 28 develops some previously introduced concepts or forms and presents a few new concepts. The main focus of this chapter, however, is on integrating what you have learned from chapters 21–27.

Chapter 28 covers the following linguistic concepts, morphemes, and paradigms:

- expressing purpose
- expressing conditionality
- coordinating and subordinating conjunctions
- temporal clauses
- indirect discourse
- additional functions for ἵνα

EXPRESSING PURPOSE

So far, we have seen several ways in which purpose can be expressed in Koine Greek, so the goal of this section is to summarize these various ways of expressing purpose. Perhaps the most frequent way to express purpose is with ἵνα, or sometimes ὅπως, followed by the subjunctive. For example:

ταῦτα λαλῶ ἐν τῷ κόσμῳ ἵνα ἔχωσιν τὴν χαρὰν τὴν ἐμήν (John 17:13)
I say these things while in the world *in order that they might have my joy.*

καὶ ἐλθὼν κατῴκησεν εἰς πόλιν λεγομένην Ναζαρέτ· ὅπως πληρωθῇ
τὸ ῥηθὲν διὰ τῶν προφητῶν ὅτι Ναζωραῖος κληθήσεται
(Matt 2:23)

And going, he settled in a city called Nazareth, *so that the word spoken through the prophets might be fulfilled*: "He will be called a Nazarene."

We have also seen that the infinitive is used in several constructions to indicate purpose. An anarthrous infinitive that occurs by itself to modify a main verb nearly always indicates purpose. For example:

ἦλθον . . . τελῶναι βαπτισθῆναι (Luke 3:12)
Tax collectors came *to be baptized.*

An articular (with τοῦ) infinitive that modifies a main verb also indicates purpose. For example:

μετέβη ἐκεῖθεν τοῦ διδάσκειν καὶ κηρύσσειν ἐν ταῖς πόλεσιν αὐτῶν (Matt 11:1)
He went on from there *to teach and preach* in their cities.

Finally, recall that an articular infinitive preceded by either εἰς or πρός also indicates purpose.

μὴ οὖν βασιλευέτω ἡ ἁμαρτία ἐν τῷ θνητῷ ὑμῶν σώματι εἰς τὸ ὑπακούειν ταῖς ἐπιθυμίαις αὐτοῦ (Rom 6:12)
Therefore, do not let sin reign in your mortal body *so that you obey its sinful desires.*

ἐνδύσασθε τὴν πανοπλίαν τοῦ θεοῦ πρὸς τὸ δύνασθαι ὑμᾶς στῆναι πρὸς τὰς μεθοδείας τοῦ διαβόλου (Eph 6:11)
Put on the full armor of God *so that you might be able to stand* against the schemes of the devil.

An infinitive with ὥστε can also sometimes indicate purpose. For example:

ἔδωκεν αὐτοῖς ἐξουσίαν πνευμάτων ἀκαθάρτων ὥστε ἐκβάλλειν αὐτὰ καὶ θεραπεύειν πᾶσαν νόσον καὶ πᾶσαν μαλακίαν (Matt 10:1)
He gave them authority over unclean spirits *to cast* them out *and to heal* every disease and every sickness.

We have also seen that adverbial participles can also indicate purpose, which is usually expressed in English with an infinitive. For example:

τοῦτο δὲ ἔλεγεν *πειράζων* αὐτόν (John 6:6)
He said this *to test* him.

EXPRESSING CONDITIONALITY

Koine Greek contains both explicit conditional clauses and implicit expressions of conditionality. Explicit conditionality is expressed with a protasis and apodosis. The three types of explicit conditionality in the GNT can be summarized as follows:[1]

type	protasis ("if")	apodosis ("then")	function
first class	εἰ + any indicative tense - if negated, uses οὐ	any tense or mood	rhetorical; condition true for sake of argument
second class	εἰ + impf/aor indicative - if negated, uses μή	ἄν + same indicative tense as protasis	rhetorical; condition false for sake of argument
third class	ἐάν + subjunctive - if negated, uses μή	any tense or mood	simple condition

You can easily remember these constructions as follows. If you see εἰ, you either have a first- or second-class conditional. If you only see εἰ (one particle), then you have a first-class conditional; if you see both εἰ and ἄν (two particles), then you have a second-class conditional. If you see ἐάν (three letters), then you have a third-class conditional. (Here is where being able to count to three can also be helpful for learning Greek!)

Implicit conditionality does not use these formal constructions and instead must be inferred from the context. For example, consider the following adverbial participle:

καιρῷ γὰρ ἰδίῳ θερίσομεν *μὴ ἐκλυόμενοι* (Gal 6:9)
For at the proper time, we will reap *if we do not give up.*

Or consider this imperative:

---

1. Because there are no complete examples of fourth-class conditionals in the GNT, they are not included in this chart.

δεῦτε πρός με πάντες οἱ κοπιῶντες καὶ πεφορτισμένοι, κἀγὼ ἀναπαύσω ὑμᾶς. (Matt 11:28)

[If you] Come to me, all who are weary and burdened, and [then] I myself will give you rest.

Finally, consider this example containing an indefinite relative clause:

ὅστις σε ἀγγαρεύσει μίλιον ἕν, ὕπαγε μετ᾽ αὐτοῦ δύο. (Matt 5:41)

Whoever [if anyone] forces you to go one mile, [then] go with him two miles.

Implicit conditional clauses are often similar in meaning to third-class conditionals.

COORDINATING AND SUBORDINATING CONJUNCTIONS

We have learned many conjunctions in this course. Here is a convenient summary of those conjunctions that coordinate two or more equal syntactic units and those conjunctions that introduce a subordinate (dependent) clause. A common gloss (or two) is supplied for reference, but remember that conjuctions often have a range of functions, and hence, translations.

coordinating conjunctions	possible gloss(es)
ἀλλά	but
ἄρα	so, then
γάρ	for
δέ	but, and
ἤ	or
καί	and
μήδε	and not, but not
μήτε	and not
οὐδε	and not, but not
οὖν	therefore
οὔτε	and not
τε	and

Subordinating conjunctions can be divided between those that are nearly always followed by verbs in the indicative mood and those that are nearly always followed by verbs in the subjunctive mood. Possible glosses are listed for reference.

subordinating conjunctions followed by the indicative	possible gloss(es)	subordinating conjunctions followed by the subjunctive	possible gloss(es)
διότι	because	ἐάν	if
εἰ	if	ἵνα	so that
ἐπεί	since	ὅπως	in order that
ἕως	until		
καθώς	as, just as		
ὅτι	that, because		
ὡς	as, like		
ὥσπερ	as, just as		
ὥστε	so that, therefore		

TEMPORAL CLAUSES

A temporal clause is a dependent clause that indicates when the action of the main clause occurred. So far, we have seen temporality indicated by adverbial temporal participles. For example:

παράγων παρὰ τὴν θάλασσαν τῆς Γαλιλαίας εἶδεν Σίμωνα καὶ Ἀνδρέαν
   (Mark 1:16)
While he was passing beside the Sea of Galilee, he saw Simon and Andrew.

We have also seen examples of the articular infinitive expressing temporality.

πρό τοῦ δὲ ἐλθεῖν τὴν πίστιν ὑπὸ νόμον ἐφρουρούμεθα (Gal 3:23)
But before faith came we were held captive by the law.

ἐν τῷ εὐλογεῖν αὐτὸν αὐτοὺς διέστη ἀπ᾽ αὐτῶν καὶ ἀνεφέρετο εἰς τὸν
   οὐρανόν. (Luke 24:51)
While he was blessing them, he departed from them and ascended into
   heaven.

μετὰ δὲ τὸ ἐγερθῆναί με προάξω ὑμᾶς εἰς τὴν Γαλιλαίον (Matt 26:32)
And after I am raised, I will go before you into Galilee.

There are several subordinating conjunctions that also function to introduce temporal clauses. Possible glosses are supplied for reference.

ὅτε	when
ὁπότε	when
ὡς	when, since, while
ἕως	until, while

There are also several other constructions that frequently introduce temporal clauses.

ἄχρι οὗ	until
ἐν ᾧ	while
ἀφ' οὗ	since
πρίν	until, before
πρίν ἤ	until, before

INDIRECT DISCOURSE

So far, we have seen that ὅτι is a subordinating conjunction that introduces a dependent clause, which indicates the reason or cause of the main verb. We have also seen that another common function of ὅτι is to indicate the content of verbs of speaking, knowing, perceiving, thinking, etc. Finally, we have seen that ὅτι can also introduce a direct quotation. (See chapter 6 for review.) The conjunction ὅτι can also introduce indirect discourse (also called *indirect speech* or *reported speech*). Consider the following examples:

She said that the man was ill.
She said that the man had been ill.

If each of these sentences were rewritten as direct discourse, we would have the following:

She said, "The man is ill."
She said, "The man has been ill."

Notice that in English, indirect discourse puts the tense of the verb used in the direct discourse (i.e., "is" and "has been) into a past tense when it becomes indirect discourse (i.e., "was" and "had been"). This is not the same in Greek, which uses the tense-form in indirect discourse that would have been used if the original statement had been direct discourse. Consider the following examples. In both examples, standard English would require that the reported speech be shifted to a past tense (i.e. "he was ill" or "Jesus was coming").

ἤκουσεν ὅτι ἀσθενεῖ (John 11:6)
He heard that he is ill.

ἤκουσεν ὅτι Ἰησοῦς ἔρχεται (John 11:20)
She heard that Jesus is coming.

Indirect discourse can also be indicated with the infinitive. Consider the following example:

καὶ ἔρχονται Σαδδουκαῖοι πρὸς αὐτόν, οἵτινες λέγουσιν *ἀνάστασιν μὴ εἶναι*
    (Mark 12:18)
And the Sadducees, who say *that there is no resurrection*, came to him.

An infinitive may also indicate an indirect command; for example:

καὶ εὐθὺς ἠνάγκασεν τοὺς μαθητὰς αὐτοῦ *ἐμβῆναι* εἰς τὸ πλοῖον (Mark 6:45)
And immediately he urged his disciples *to get into* the boat.

Finally, indirect questions are often introduced by interrogative pronouns, such as τίς, τί, ποῦ, and πῶς. For example:

ἐπυνθάνετο παρ᾽ αὐτῶν *ποῦ* ὁ Χριστὸς γεννᾶται (Matt 2:4)
He inquired of them *where* the Christ was to be born.

This could be restated as follows: "He inquired of them, 'Where is the Christ to be born?'"

ADDITIONAL FUNCTIONS OF ἵνα

One of the most frequent uses of the conjunction ἵνα is to introduce a dependent clause with a subjunctive to indicate purpose. But ἵνα can also introduce a dependent clause that indicates the result of the main verb. For example:

> τοῦτο δὲ ὅλον γέγονεν *ἵνα πληρωθῇ τὸ ῥηθὲν ὑπὸ κυρίου* (Matt 1:22)
> All this happened *so that what was spoken by the Lord might be fulfilled.*

The conjunction ἵνα can also introduce a dependent clause that further explains the main clause or expresses the content of the main verb. For example:

> αὕτη δέ ἐστιν ἡ αἰώνιος ζωὴ *ἵνα γινώσκωσιν σὲ τὸν μόνον ἀληθινὸν θεόν* (John 17:3)
> And this is eternal life, *that they might know you, the only true God.*

> οὐ παυόμεθα ὑπὲρ ὑμῶν προσευχόμενοι καὶ αἰτούμενοι, *ἵνα πληρωθῆτε τὴν ἐπίγνωσιν τοῦ θελήματος αὐτοῦ* (Col 1:9)
> We do not cease asking in prayer for you, *that you might be filled with the knowledge of his will.*

In the example from Colossians 1:9, notice that the two adverbial participles, προσευχόμενοι and αἰτούμενοι, complete the main verb παυόμεθα; this complementary function of the participle is parallel to a complementary infinitive. Additionally, these two adverbial participles express ideas that are so closely related that they may be translated as one idea, namely, "asking in prayer." The expression of a single idea by two closely related words is called **hendiadys**.

INTEGRATION OF CHAPTERS 21–27

We will use the following passage as the basis of reviewing concepts and forms that have been presented in chapters 21–27. Some of the key concepts that we covered were the subjunctive, the imperative, reflexive and reciprocal pronouns, the infinitive, μι verbs, the optative, and structural and narrative outlines.

In anticipation of your future Greek studies, the Pop-Up Lexicon is no longer available. Instead, all of the words in this passage that have not yet been assigned as vocabulary are listed in the lexicon. This will give you good practice for looking up inflected words in a lexicon. Think of this as taking the training wheels off because you are now ready to ride your bike all by yourself!

PART ONE

As we have stressed, it is crucial to be able to identify finite verb forms. So, let's begin by <u>double underlining</u> and parsing each finite verb. Then identify non-finite verb forms by putting boxes around them. You should also parse these forms. After you have done this on your own, you can turn to the next page to check your work.

Here is the text:

1. δικαιωθέντες οὖν ἐκ πίστεως εἰρήνην ἔχομεν πρὸς τὸν θεὸν διὰ τοῦ κυρίου ἡμῶν

2. Ἰησοῦ Χριστοῦ, δι' οὗ καὶ τὴν προσαγωγὴν ἐσχήκαμεν τῇ πίστει[1] εἰς τὴν χάριν ταύτην

3. ἐν ᾗ ἑστήκαμεν καὶ καυχώμεθα ἐπ' ἐλπίδι τῆς δόξης τοῦ θεοῦ. οὐ μόνον δέ,

4. ἀλλὰ καὶ καυχώμεθα ἐν ταῖς θλίψεσιν, εἰδότες ὅτι ἡ θλῖψις ὑπομονὴν κατεργάζεται,

5. ἡ δὲ ὑπομονὴ δοκιμήν, ἡ δὲ δοκιμὴ ἐλπίδα. ἡ δὲ ἐλπὶς οὐ καταισχύνει,

6. ὅτι ἡ ἀγάπη τοῦ θεοῦ ἐκκέχυται ἐν ταῖς καρδίαις ἡμῶν διὰ πνεύματος ἁγίου τοῦ δοθέντος ἡμῖν.

7. ἔτι γὰρ Χριστὸς ὄντων ἡμῶν ἀσθενῶν ἔτι κατὰ καιρὸν ὑπὲρ ἀσεβῶν ἀπέθανεν.

8. μόλις γὰρ ὑπὲρ δικαίου τις ἀποθανεῖται· ὑπὲρ γὰρ τοῦ ἀγαθοῦ τάχα τις

9. καὶ τολμᾷ ἀποθανεῖν· συνίστησιν δὲ τὴν ἑαυτοῦ ἀγάπην εἰς ἡμᾶς ὁ θεός,

10. ὅτι ἔτι ἁμαρτωλῶν ὄντων ἡμῶν Χριστὸς ὑπὲρ ἡμῶν ἀπέθανεν.

11. πολλῷ οὖν μᾶλλον δικαιωθέντες νῦν ἐν τῷ αἵματι αὐτοῦ σωθησόμεθα δι' αὐτοῦ

12. ἀπὸ τῆς ὀργῆς. εἰ γὰρ ἐχθροὶ ὄντες κατηλλάγημεν τῷ θεῷ

13. διὰ τοῦ θανάτου τοῦ υἱοῦ αὐτοῦ, πολλῷ μᾶλλον καταλλαγέντες σωθησόμεθα

14. ἐν τῇ ζωῇ αὐτοῦ· οὐ μόνον δέ, ἀλλὰ καὶ καυχώμενοι ἐν τῷ θεῷ

15. διὰ τοῦ κυρίου ἡμῶν Ἰησοῦ Χριστοῦ δι' οὗ νῦν τὴν καταλλαγὴν ἐλάβομεν.

---

1. The Nestle-Aland 28th edition of the Greek New Testament has square brackets around τῇ πίστει to indicate a textual conjecture. You will learn more about this in your exegesis classes. We have included these words in this text without the brackets so as to avoid any confusion with marking the text for syntax.

ANSWERS TO PART ONE

Did you come up with the following?

1. δικαιωθέντες οὖν ἐκ πίστεως εἰρήνην ἔχομεν πρὸς τὸν θεὸν διὰ τοῦ κυρίου ἡμῶν

2. Ἰησοῦ Χριστοῦ, δι᾽ οὗ καὶ τὴν προσαγωγὴν ἐσχήκαμεν τῇ πίστει εἰς τὴν χάριν ταύτην

3. ἐν ᾗ ἑστήκαμεν καὶ καυχώμεθα ἐπ᾽ ἐλπίδι τῆς δόξης τοῦ θεοῦ. οὐ μόνον δέ,

4. ἀλλὰ καὶ καυχώμεθα ἐν ταῖς θλίψεσιν, εἰδότες ὅτι ἡ θλῖψις ὑπομονὴν κατεργάζεται,

5. ἡ δὲ ὑπομονὴ δοκιμήν, ἡ δὲ δοκιμὴ ἐλπίδα. ἡ δὲ ἐλπὶς οὐ καταισχύνει,

6. ὅτι ἡ ἀγάπη τοῦ θεοῦ ἐκκέχυται ἐν ταῖς καρδίαις ἡμῶν διὰ πνεύματος ἁγίου τοῦ δοθέντος ἡμῖν.

7. ἔτι γὰρ Χριστὸς ὄντων ἡμῶν ἀσθενῶν ἔτι κατὰ καιρὸν ὑπὲρ ἀσεβῶν ἀπέθανεν.

8. μόλις γὰρ ὑπὲρ δικαίου τις ἀποθανεῖται· ὑπὲρ γὰρ τοῦ ἀγαθοῦ τάχα τις

9. καὶ τολμᾷ ἀποθανεῖν· συνίστησιν δὲ τὴν ἑαυτοῦ ἀγάπην εἰς ἡμᾶς ὁ θεός,

10. ὅτι ἔτι ἁμαρτωλῶν ὄντων ἡμῶν Χριστὸς ὑπὲρ ἡμῶν ἀπέθανεν.

11. πολλῷ οὖν μᾶλλον δικαιωθέντες νῦν ἐν τῷ αἵματι αὐτοῦ σωθησόμεθα δι᾽ αὐτοῦ

12. ἀπὸ τῆς ὀργῆς. εἰ γὰρ ἐχθροὶ ὄντες κατηλλάγημεν τῷ θεῷ

13. διὰ τοῦ θανάτου τοῦ υἱοῦ αὐτοῦ, πολλῷ μᾶλλον καταλλαγέντες σωθησόμεθα

14. ἐν τῇ ζωῇ αὐτοῦ· οὐ μόνον δέ, ἀλλὰ καὶ καυχώμενοι ἐν τῷ θεῷ

15. διὰ τοῦ κυρίου ἡμῶν Ἰησοῦ Χριστοῦ δι᾽ οὗ νῦν τὴν καταλλαγὴν ἐλάβομεν.

Parsing

inflected form	tense	voice	mood	person	case	num	gen	lexical form	inflected meaning
δικαιωθέντες	aor	pass	ptc	n/a	nom	pl	masc	δικαιόω	having been justified
ἔχομεν	pres	act	ind	1st	n/a	pl	n/a	ἔχω	we have
ἐσχήκαμεν	pf	act	ind	1st	n/a	pl	n/a	ἔχω	we have had
ἑστήκαμεν	pf	act	ind	1st	n/a	pl	n/a	ἵστημι	we stand
καυχώμεθα	pres	mid	ind	1st	n/a	pl	n/a	καυχάομαι	we boast
εἰδότες	pf	act	ptc	n/a	nom	pl	masc	οἶδα	knowing
κατεργάζεται	pres	mid	ind	3rd	n/a	sg	n/a	κατεργάζομαι	it produces
καταισχύνει	pres	act	ind	3rd	n/a	sg	n/a	καταισχύνω	it disappoints
ἐκκέχυται	pf	pass	ind	3rd	n/a	sg	n/a	ἐκχέω	it has been poured out
δοθέντος	aor	pass	ptc	n/a	gen	sg	neut	δίδωμι	who has been given
ὄντων	pres	n/a	ptc	n/a	gen	pl	masc	εἰμί	being
ἀπέθανεν	aor	act	ind	3rd	n/a	sg	n/a	ἀποθήνσκω	he died
ἀποθανεῖται	fut	mid	ind	3rd	n/a	sg	n/a	ἀποθήνσκω	he will die for himself
τολμᾷ	pres	act	subj	3rd	n/a	sg	n/a	τολμάω	he might dare
ἀποθανεῖν	aor	act	inf	n/a	n/a	n/a	n/a	ἀποθήνσκω	to die
συνίστησιν	pres	act	ind	3rd	nom	sg	n/a	συνίστημι	he demonstrates
ὄντων	pres	n/a	ptc	n/a	gen	pl	masc	εἰμί	being
ἀπέθανεν	aor	act	ind	3rd	n/a	sg	n/a	ἀποθήνσκω	he died
δικαιωθέντες	aor	pass	ptc	n/a	nom	pl	masc	δικαιόω	having been justified
σωθησόμεθα	fut	pass	ind	1st	n/a	pl	n/a	σῴζω	we will be saved
ὄντες	pres	n/a	ptc	n/a	nom	pl	masc	εἰμί	being
κατηλλάγημεν	aor	pass	ind	1st	n/a	pl	n/a	καταλλάσσω	we were reconciled
καταλλαγέντες	aor	pass	ptc	n/a	nom	pl	masc	καταλλάσσω	having been reconciled
σωθησόμεθα	fut	pass	ind	1st	n/a	pl	n/a	σῴζω	we will be saved
καυχώμενοι	pres	mid	ptc	n/a	nom	pl	masc	καυχάομαι	boasting
ἐλάβομεν	aor	act	ind	1st	n/a	pl	n/a	λαμβάνω	we received

Additional Notes:

- As you may have guessed, this text is Romans 5:1–11.
- By now, you should be able to parse all these forms. You may have had trouble with εἰδότες. Recall that the verb οἶδα only occurs in the perfect and pluperfect tense-forms. Students sometimes confuse this verb with forms of ὁράω, specifically the forms built on the third principal part (aorist active indicative), εἶδον. Notice carefully, however, that the perfect participle morpheme (-οτ) is clearly visible in εἰδότες. Compare this form with the fourth principal part for ὁράω, which is ἑώρακα, the perfect active indicative. This is yet more evidence of the benefit of knowing principal parts.

PART TWO

Now we'll focus on the participles and infinitives in this passage. You have already identified these forms and parsed them. Now go through the passage and indicate the function of each participle or each infinitive by marking the text as you have done in the assigned exercises. The first participle is used as an example. Once you have finished, you can check your own work against the discussion on the following page.

Line 1: δικαιωθέντες – This participle is functioning adverbially; notice that it is anarthrous and that there is no substantive that is in immediate proximity that is also nominative plural masculine. As an adverbial participle, it modifies the finite verb ἔχομεν and agrees with it in number (plural), which is indicated by the arrow.

ADV ——————————————→
1. Δικαιωθέντες οὖν ἐκ πίστεως εἰρήνην ἔχομεν πρὸς τὸν θεὸν διὰ τοῦ κυρίου ἡμῶν

ANSWERS TO PART TWO

Here is how the rest of the participles and infinitives are functioning in this passage. Relevant arrows are added on the Greek text that follows.

Line 4: εἰδότες – This participle is functioning adverbially; notice that it is anarthrous and that there is no substantive that is in immediate proximity that is also nominative plural masculine. As an adverbial participle, it modifies the finite verb καυχώμεθα and agrees with it in number (plural).

Line 6: δοθέντος – This participle is functioning attributively; notice that it is articular and that it is in the same case and number as πνεύματος ἁγίου. So far you have seen many examples of first and second attributive position modifiers, but this is an example of the less common third attributive position (substantive-article-modifier).

Line 7: ὄντων – The syntax in this sentence is a bit challenging. This participle is part of a genitive absolute construction; notice that the participle is genitive plural and the main verb ἀπέθανεν is singular, so this participle could not be syntactically modifying ἀπέθανεν. Also, notice that the subject of ἀπέθανεν is explicitly indicated, namely, Χριστός.

Line 9: ἀποθανεῖν – This is a complementary infinitive that "completes" the meaning of the main verb τολμᾷ. The subject of the verb is the indefinite pronoun τις. So, this could be translated as "someone might dare to die."

Line 10: ὄντων – This participle is also part of a genitive absolute construction, which is also part of a dependent ὅτι clause. Just as we saw with this same participle in line 7, notice that the participle is genitive plural, and the main verb of the ὅτι clause, ἀπέθανεν, is singular, so this participle could not be syntactically modifying ἀπέθανεν. Also, notice that the subject of ἀπέθανεν is explicitly indicated, namely, Χριστός.

Line 11: δικαιωθέντες – This participle is functioning adverbially; notice that it is anarthrous and that there is no substantive that is in immediate proximity that is also nominative plural masculine. As an adverbial participle, it modifies the finite verb σωθησόμεθα and agrees with it in number (plural).

Line 12: ὄντες – This participle is functioning adverbially, but notice that it agrees with ἐχθροί in case and number. Together ἐχθροὶ ὄντες forms a dependent participial clause, in which ἐχθροί is a predicate adjective. The clause is temporally modifying κατηλλάγημεν, which is part of a protasis: εἰ γὰρ ἐχθροὶ ὄντες κατηλλάγημεν. This could be translated as follows: "for if, while being enemies, we were reconciled . . ."

Line 13: καταλλαγέντες – This participle is functioning adverbially; notice that it is anarthrous and that there is no substantive that is in immediate proximity that is also nominative plural masculine. As an adverbial participle, it modifies the finite verb σωθησόμεθα, and agrees with it in number (plural).

Line 14: καυχώμενοι – This participle is functioning adverbially; notice that it is anarthrous and that there is no substantive that is in immediate proximity that is also nominative plural masculine. As an adverbial participle, it modifies the finite verb ἐλάβομεν and agrees with it in number (plural).

1. ADV ⟶
   Δικαιωθέντες οὖν ἐκ πίστεως εἰρήνην ἔχομεν πρὸς τὸν θεὸν διὰ τοῦ κυρίου ἡμῶν

4. ⟵ ADV
   ἀλλὰ καὶ καυχώμεθα ἐν ταῖς θλίψεσιν, εἰδότες ὅτι ἡ θλῖψις ὑπομονὴν κατεργάζεται,

6. ὅτι ἡ ἀγάπη τοῦ θεοῦ ἐκκέχυται ἐν ταῖς καρδίαις ἡμῶν διὰ πνεύματος
   ATTR ⟶
   ἁγίου τοῦ δοθέντος

7. ἡμῖν, ἔτι γὰρ Χριστὸς ὄντων ἡμῶν ἀσθενῶν ἔτι κατὰ καιρὸν ὑπὲρ ἀσεβῶν
   ἀπέθανεν. ⟵ ADV; GA

9. ADV; comp. inf
   καὶ τολμᾷ ἀποθανεῖν· συνίστησιν δὲ τὴν ἑαυτοῦ ἀγάπην εἰς ἡμᾶς ὁ θεός,

10. ADV; GA ⟶
    ὅτι ἔτι ἁμαρτωλῶν ὄντων ἡμῶν Χριστὸς ὑπὲρ ἡμῶν ἀπέθανεν.

11. ADV ⟶
    πολλῷ οὖν μᾶλλον δικαιωθέντες νῦν ἐν τῷ αἵματι αὐτοῦ σωθησόμεθα
    δι' αὐτοῦ

ADV ⟶

12. ἀπὸ τῆς ὀργῆς. εἰ γὰρ ἐχθροὶ ὄντες κατηλλάγημεν τῷ θεῷ

ADV ⟶

13. διὰ τοῦ θανάτου τοῦ υἱοῦ αὐτοῦ, πολλῷ μᾶλλον καταλλαγέντες σωθησόμεθα

ADV ⟶

14. ἐν τῇ ζωῇ αὐτοῦ· οὐ μόνον δέ, ἀλλὰ καὶ καυχώμενοι ἐν τῷ θεῷ

15. διὰ τοῦ κυρίου ἡμῶν Ἰησοῦ Χριστοῦ δι' οὗ νῦν τὴν καταλλαγὴν ἐλάβομεν.

PART THREE

We will now focus on substantives, adjectives, and pronouns. By now, you should be able to quickly recognize these forms, so we will not focus on every example of a noun or pronoun in this text. Instead, answer the following questions based on this text. Once you have completed your work, turn to the next page for a complete list of these constructions and further discussion of them. Following this discussion there are two remaining questions covering dependent clauses and prepositional phrases.

1. What is the antecedent for οὗ in line 2? What confirms this syntactically?
2. What is the antecedent for ᾗ in line 3? What confirms this syntactically?
3. How is ἁγίου functioning in line 6?
4. How are ἀσθενῶν and ἀσεβῶν functioning in line 7?
5. How are δικαίου and ἀγαθοῦ functioning in line 8?

ANSWERS TO PART THREE

Here are the answers for questions 1–5. You should check your work against this and see if you missed anything. If so, then use this as a means of reviewing forms, functions, and concepts that have been discussed so far.

1. What is the antecedent for οὗ in line 2? What confirms this syntactically?

   The antecedent is Ἰησοῦ Χριστοῦ, which is masculine singular. The relative pronoun οὗ is also masculine singular—recall that an antecedent must have the same gender and number of the pronoun that stands in the antecedent's place. Moreover, Ἰησοῦ Χριστοῦ is the first masculine singular substantive that precedes the relative pronoun οὗ; generally, the antecedent of a pronoun is the closest preceeding substantive that agrees in gender and number with the pronoun. In this example, the relative pronoun and the antecedent are both in the genitive case because of the preposition διά. It is important to stress that a pronoun and its antecedent *must* agree in gender and number, but that the *case* of each is determined by the context in which each occurs.

2. What is the antecedent for ᾗ in line 3? What confirms this syntactically?

   The antecedent is χάριν, which is feminine singular; this agrees with the relative pronoun ᾗ, which is also feminine singular. Additionally, χάριν is the first feminine singular substantive that precedes the relative pronoun ᾗ. In this example, notice that the relative pronoun ᾗ is in the dative case because it is the object of the preposition ἐν. The antecedent χάριν, however, is in the accusative case because it is the object of the preposition εἰς.

3. How is ἁγίου functioning in line 6?

   The adjective ἁγίου is functioning attributively to modify the substantive πνεύματος. Although this adjective often functions substantivally, in this example there is a substantive (πνεύματος) in close proximity with which the adjective agrees in case, number, and gender, so ἁγίου is clearly modifying πνεύματος. It is essential to understand that an adjective *must* agree with the substantive that it modifies in case, number, *and* gender. A pronoun, however, *must* agree with its antecedent in *gender* and *number*—if it also agrees in case, that is coincidental!

4. How are ἀσθενῶν and ἀσεβῶν functioning in line 7?

Both ἀσθενῶν and ἀσεβῶν are adjectives. Ἀσθενῶν is part of the genitive absolute construction, ὄντων ἡμῶν ἀσθενῶν. You may have thought that ἔτι γὰρ Χριστός was part of the genitive absolute construction. But recall that the conjunction γάρ is postpositive, so it is not part of the genitive absolute construction. The substantive Χριστός is in the nominative case and is the explicitly expressed subject of ἀπέθανεν, so it cannot be part of the genitive absolute construction either. The adverb ἔτι functions temporally to indicate when the genitive absolute construction applies and is also not part of the construction. Thus syntactically, the genitive absolute construction is ὄντων ἡμῶν ἀσθενῶν, in which ἀσθενῶν is functioning as the predicate adjective of the participle ὄντων. A possible translation for this clause might be "while we were weak."

The prepositional phrase ὑπὲρ ἀσεβῶν is preceded by the prepositional phrase κατὰ καιρόν and is followed by the finite verb ἀπέθανεν, which confirms the boundaries of ὑπὲρ ἀσεβῶν as a prepositional phrase. Because there is no substantive around that ἀσεβῶν could be modifying, it must be functioning substantivally. It could be translated as "the ungodly ones."

5. How are δικαίου and ἀγαθοῦ functioning in line 8?

The adjective δικαίου is part of the prepositional phrase ὑπὲρ δικαίου, which is preceded by the conjunction γάρ, which cannot be part of the prepositional phrase. This phrase is followed by the indefinite pronoun τις, which is in the nominative case and thus could not be part of the prepositional phrase. This confirms the boundaries of ὑπὲρ δικαίου as a prepositional phrase. Because there is no substantive around that δικαίου could be modifying, it must be functioning substantivally. It could be translated as "the righteous one."

The adjective ἀγαθοῦ is part of the prepositional phrase ὑπὲρ . . . τοῦ ἀγαθοῦ, which is preceded by the finite verb ἀποθανεῖται, which cannot be part of the prepositional phrase. The conjunction γάρ, which is postpositive, also cannot be part of the prepositional phrase. The phrase is followed by the adverb τάχα, which also cannot be a part of the prepositional phrase. This confirms that the boundaries of this prepositional phrase are ὑπὲρ . . . τοῦ ἀγαθοῦ. Because there is no substantive around that ἀγαθοῦ could be modifying, it must be functioning substantivally. Together with the article, it could be translated as "the good one."

PART FOUR

We'll take one more pass through this passage, focusing on dependent clauses and prepositional phrases. Go through the passage and put parentheses around each (dependent clause) and brackets around each [preposition phrase]. For each dependent clause, highlight the subordinating conjunction or the relative pronoun, and identify what type of clause it is and then indicate how it is functioning. For each prepositional phrase, indicate how you know the boundary of the prepositional phrase. Once you have finished, you can check your own work against the discussion on the next page.

ANSWERS TO PART FOUR

Did you come up with the following?

1. δικαιωθέντες οὖν [ἐκ πίστεως] εἰρήνην ἔχομεν [πρὸς τὸν θεὸν] [διὰ τοῦ κυρίου ἡμῶν

2. Ἰησοῦ Χριστοῦ], ([δι᾽ οὗ] καὶ τὴν προσαγωγὴν ἐσχήκαμεν τῇ πίστει [εἰς τὴν χάριν ταύτην]

3. [ἐν ᾗ] ἑστήκαμεν καὶ καυχώμεθα [ἐπ᾽ ἐλπίδι τῆς δόξης τοῦ θεοῦ]). οὐ μόνον δέ,

4. ἀλλὰ καὶ καυχώμεθα [ἐν ταῖς θλίψεσιν], εἰδότες (ὅτι ἡ θλῖψις ὑπομονὴν κατεργάζεται,

5. ἡ δὲ ὑπομονὴ δοκιμήν, ἡ δὲ δοκιμὴ ἐλπίδα). ἡ δὲ ἐλπὶς οὐ καταισχύνει,

6. (ὅτι ἡ ἀγάπη τοῦ θεοῦ ἐκκέχυται [ἐν ταῖς καρδίαις ἡμῶν] [διὰ πνεύματος ἁγίου τοῦ δοθέντος

7. ἡμῖν]), ἔτι γὰρ Χριστὸς ὄντων ἡμῶν ἀσθενῶν ἔτι [κατὰ καιρὸν] [ὑπὲρ ἀσεβῶν] ἀπέθανεν.

8. μόλις γὰρ [ὑπὲρ δικαίου] τις ἀποθανεῖται· [ὑπὲρ γὰρ τοῦ ἀγαθοῦ] τάχα τις

9. καὶ τολμᾷ ἀποθανεῖν· συνίστησιν δὲ τὴν ἑαυτοῦ ἀγάπην [εἰς ἡμᾶς] ὁ θεός,

10. (ὅτι ἔτι ἁμαρτωλῶν ὄντων ἡμῶν Χριστὸς [ὑπὲρ ἡμῶν] ἀπέθανεν).

11. πολλῷ οὖν μᾶλλον δικαιωθέντες νῦν [ἐν τῷ αἵματι αὐτοῦ] σωθησόμεθα [δι᾽ αὐτοῦ]

12. [ἀπὸ τῆς ὀργῆς]. (εἰ γὰρ ἐχθροὶ ὄντες κατηλλάγημεν τῷ θεῷ

13. [διὰ τοῦ θανάτου τοῦ υἱοῦ αὐτοῦ]), πολλῷ μᾶλλον καταλλαγέντες σωθησόμεθα

14. [ἐν τῇ ζωῇ αὐτοῦ]· οὐ μόνον δέ, ἀλλὰ καὶ καυχώμενοι [ἐν τῷ θεῷ]

15. [διὰ τοῦ κυρίου ἡμῶν Ἰησοῦ Χριστοῦ] (δι᾽ οὗ νῦν τὴν καταλλαγὴν ἐλάβομεν).

Dependent Clauses

- Lines 4–5 – (ὅτι ἡ θλῖψις ὑπομονὴν κατεργάζεται, ἡ δὲ ὑπομονὴ δοκιμήν, ἡ δὲ δοκιμὴ ἐλπίδα) is functioning to indicate the content of the participle εἰδότες. Notice also the use of ellipses in this dependent clause. The verb κατεργάζεται is implied in both ἡ δὲ ὑπομονὴ δοκιμήν and ἡ δὲ δοκιμὴ ἐλπίδα.

- Lines 6–7 – (ὅτι ἡ ἀγάπη τοῦ θεοῦ ἐκκέχυται [ἐν ταῖς καρδίαις ἡμῶν] [διὰ πνεύματος ἁγίου τοῦ δοθέντος ἡμῖν]) is functioning causally, to indicate the reason why hope does not disappoint—ἡ δὲ ἐλπὶς οὐ καταισχύνει.

- Line 10 – (ὅτι ἔτι ἁμαρτωλῶν ὄντων ἡμῶν Χριστὸς [ὑπὲρ ἡμῶν] ἀπέθανεν) is functioning to explain further how God demonstrated his love for us— συνίστησιν δὲ τὴν ἑαυτοῦ ἀγάπην [εἰς ἡμᾶς] ὁ θεός; namely, God demonstrated it while we were still sinners.
- Lines 12–13 – (εἰ γὰρ ἐχθροὶ ὄντες κατηλλάγημεν τῷ θεῷ [διὰ τοῦ θανάτου τοῦ υἱοῦ αὐτοῦ]) is functioning as the protasis of a first-class conditional construction. Recall that this construction presents a condition that is true for the sake of the argument—you can see how to translate the entire clause in the final possible translation below.

At this point, you should have been able to identify all the prepositional phrases correctly. If you had any problems, review the comments given for questions 1–5 above.

PART FIVE

As the final part of this exercise, write out a final translation for this passage that reflects your work throughout this exercise. You can compare your translation with the one on the next page.

POSSIBLE TRANSLATION FOR PART FIVE

1. Therefore, having been justified from faith, we have peace with God through our Lord

2. Jesus Christ, through whom also we have access by faith into this grace

3. in which we stand, and we boast in the hope of the glory of God. And not only [this],

4. but we also boast in our tribulations, knowing that tribulation produces endurance,

5. and endurance, character, and character, hope. And hope does not disappoint,

6. because the love of God has been poured out in our hearts through the Holy Spirit who was given

7. to us. For while we were still weak, at the proper time, Christ died for the ungodly.

8. For someone would rarely die for the righteous; for perhaps for a good person someone

9. might dare to die; but God demonstrates his love for us

10. that while we were yet sinners, Christ died for us.

11. Therefore, having now been justified by his blood, how much more will we be saved through him

12. from his [God's] wrath. For if, while being enemies, we were reconciled to God,

13. through the death of his Son, how much more, being reconciled, will we be saved

14. by his life? And not only [this], but also we boast [boasting] in God

15. through our Lord Jesus Christ, through whom now we have received reconciliation.

Well done! You have now translated an entire passage—unmodified!—from the GNT. Be encouraged!

REVIEW AND STUDY GUIDE FOR CHAPTERS 21–27

Congratulations! You are nearing the finish line for your first year of beginning Greek! At this point, you should continue reviewing all assigned vocabulary, paradigms, and principal parts. In addition, here are some items to focus on for this final section of the book:

- present and aorist subjunctive forms
- the forms of the indefinite relative pronoun
- present and aorist imperative forms
- the forms of reflexive and reciprocal pronouns
- present, aorist, and perfect infinitive forms
- the distinctives of μι-verb forms (e.g., reduplication in the present stem, first-person singular endings in the present indicative, absence of connecting vowel)
- recognition of finite and nonfinite μι-verb forms
- present and aorist optative forms
- vocabulary, paradigms, and principal parts for chapters 21–27

Additionally, essential concepts that you should know include the following:

- the concept of verbal mood
- basic functions of subjunctives in both independent and dependent clauses
- indefinite relative clauses
- third-class conditionals
- imperative functions
- translating third-person imperatives
- infinitive functions, both adverbial and substantival
- the translation of preposition constructions with infinitives
- functions of the optative
- basics of outlining both epistles and narratives

Chapter 28 is a time to review and solidify these concepts and forms and all the concepts and forms that you have learned in this book. The more firmly these concepts and forms are in place, the more fun and satisfying will be your Greek journey!

APPENDICES

appendix ONE

OVERVIEW OF GREEK ACCENTS

The autographs of the NT did not include accents. Modern editions, however, include them—probably for the same reasons for which they were eventually added—namely, so that non-native Greek speakers could read Greek. There are three accents in modern editions of the GNT that you will encounter: acute ('), grave (`), and circumflex (ˆ or ˜ or ˄).[1] When accents and breathing marks occur on the same vowel, they are combined as follows: ῎, ῞, ῍, ῝, ῟, or ῁.

A syllable contains one vowel or diphthong. Accents can occur on one of three syllables:

the **ultima** syllable—the last syllable of a word → ἀδελφός

the **penult** syllable—the second-to-last syllable of a word → λαμβάνω

the **antepenult** syllable ("before the penult")—the third to last syllable of a word → παρακαλέσητε

An acute accent may appear on any one of these syllables, but a circumflex may only appear on the penult or antepenult. A grave accent may only occur on the ultima and only occurs on words when they are followed by another word without any intervening punctuation. In this case, an acute accent will shift to a grave accent. For example: εἰ ἀδελφός, but ἀδελφὸς εἰ. The exception to this is that the interrogative pronoun, τίς, τί, does not shift to a grave accent.

Accents only appear on vowels, including diphthongs. (With diphthongs, the accent is placed on the second vowel.) The following vowels are always considered long: η, ῃ, ω, ῳ, ᾳ. The following vowels are always considered short: ε, ο. The following vowels may be short or long, depending on the context: α, ι, υ. Although diphthongs are usually considered to be long, a final αι or οι is

---

1. These forms of the circumflex reflect various fonts that are used to print Greek.

considered as a short syllable if there is no consonant following the diphthong— for example, αι in φωναί is short, but αι in φωναῖς is long.

The antepenult can only have an acute accent and can only be accented if the ultima is short. If the ultima is short and the penult is long and is accented, then a circumflex accent is used. If the ultima is short and is accented, then an acute accent is used. If the ultima is long, and the penult is long and is accented, then an acute accent is used. If the ultima is long and is accented, then a circumflex accent is used. Got that?

The preceding discussion can be summarized in the following chart.

	antepenult	penult	ultima
acute - may appear on a long or short syllable	**yes** if the ultima is short	**yes**	**yes** unless another word follows without intervening punctuation, then the acute changes to grave
circumflex - may only appear on a long syllable	**no**	**yes** if the ultima is short	**yes**
grave - may appear on a long or short syllable	**no**	**no**	**yes**

Accents also "force" some words, especially small words such as some prepositions, some conjunctions, and some pronouns, to be pronounced together with the word that precedes them. Such words are called *enclitics* (from ἐγκλίνω, "I lean on"). Common enclitics include με, μου, μοι, σε, σου, σοι, the indefinite pronoun τις, τι, the adverbs πού, πόθεν, ποτέ, πώς, the conjunction τέ, and the particle γέ. The personal pronouns are commonly listed without an accent, since they usually appear that way in the GNT. The present indicative forms of εἰμί and φημί (except the second-person singular) are also enclitics. If an enclitic follows a word that is accented on the ultima, then the accent of the enclitic is absorbed into this accent; for example: οἱ ἀδελφοί μου (Mark 3:34). If an enclitic follows a word that is accented on the antepenult, then the accent of the enclitic is "thrown" onto the ultima of the preceding word; for example, ὁ ἰσχυρότερός μου (Mark 1:7). Finally, if an enclitic follows a word that is accented on the penult, then the accent of the enclitic is retained; for example, ἄλλοι εἰσίν (Mark 4:18).

Some small words throw their accents forward and are called **proclitics** (from προκλίνω, "I lean forward"). Proclitics include the following forms of the article, ὁ, ἡ, οἱ, αἱ, and prepositions such as εἰς, ἐκ, and ἐν, the conjunctions εἰ and ὡς, and the negative adverb οὐ. If, however, an enclitic precedes a proclitic, the enclitic retains its accent; for example, εἴ τις θέλει (Mark 9:35).

NOUN ACCENTS

The accents on nouns need to be memorized with the lexical form of the noun. Noun accents typically stay on the syllable accented in the lexical form, unless the accent is "forced" to change for the following reasons. (This is sometimes discussed in terms of the noun's accent being "persistent" or "retentive.") The oblique cases and the nominative plural usually have the same accent as the lexical form unless the final syllable forces a change. Thus, for example, λόγος retains the acute accent on the penult throughout the declension. If the ultima is short (short vowel or final αι or οι) and the penult is long, and the penult is to be accented, it must have a circumflex. For example, δοῦλος, not δούλος, because ου is long and ο is short. But if the ultima becomes long due to the presence of a long vowel or diphthong (generally in the genitive or dative cases), then the antepenult cannot be accented. Thus, if a noun has an acute accent on the antepenult in its lexical form, the accent must move to the penult. For example:

ἄγγελος → ἀγγέλου (the diphthong ου is long)

If a noun has a circumflex on the penult in its lexical form and the ultima becomes long, then the accent changes to an acute, but it does not move from that syllable. For example:

δοῦλος → δούλῳ (ῳ is a long vowel)

VERB ACCENTS

Verb accents are generally easier than noun accents because they are recessive, which means that the accent is placed as far to the left as the rules of accentuation allow.

- If the ultima is short, then the verb's accent will recede to the antepenult and must be an acute accent; for example, λείπετε or παρακαλέσητε.
- If the ultima is long, then the verb's accent will recede to the penult and must also be an acute accent; for example, παιδεύεις, not παίδευεις, because ει is long.

Because of these two rules, most verb accents are acute, and on the penult and ultima.

Finally, a verb accent cannot precede an augment or reduplication; for example, ἀπῆγον. The accent here could not "jump" over the augment and go on the initial alpha; the accent must be a circumflex because the final syllable is short and η is long.

The preceding covers the basics of accentuation in the GNT. The following books and grammars contain helpful, more detailed discussions. The short guide by John Lee is especially helpful.

Carson, D. A. *Greek Accents: A Student's Manual.* Grand Rapids: Baker Academic, 1985.

Goetchius, Eugene Van Ness. *The Language of the New Testament.* New York: Scribner, 1965. (See pages 317–28.)

Lee, John A. L. *Basics of Greek Accents: Eight Lessons with Exercises.* Grand Rapids: Zondervan, 2018.

Porter, Stanley E., Jeffrey T. Reed, and Matthew Brook O'Donnell. *Fundamentals of New Testament Greek.* Grand Rapids: Eerdmans, 2010. (See pages 11–14.)

Voelz, James W. *Fundamental Greek Grammar.* 3rd ed. St. Louis: Concordia, 2007. (See pages 8–11, 22–23.)

appendix TWO

THE GREEK ALPHABET AND DIACRITICAL MARKS

THE ALPHABET

Name	Lowercase	Uppercase	Transliteration	Pronunciation Guide
alpha	α	A	a	a as in father
beta	β	B	b	b
gamma	γ	Γ	g	g as in got (not as in gene)
delta	δ	Δ	d	d
epsilon	ε	E	e	e as in bet (short)
zeta	ζ	Z	z	z as in adds/daze
eta	η	H	ē	e as in day (long)
theta	θ	Θ	th	th as in this
iota	ι	I	i	i as in machine
kappa	κ	K	k	k
lambda	λ	Λ	l	l
mu	μ	M	m	m
nu	ν	N	n	n
xi	ξ	Ξ	x	x as in ax (not as is exact)
omicron	ο	O	o	o as in dot (short)
pi	π	Π	p	p
rho	ρ	P	r	r
sigma	σ/ς	Σ	s	s as in sing (not as in rose)
tau	τ	T	t	t
upsilon	υ	Y	u/y	u as in universe
phi	φ	Φ	ph	ph as in phone
chi	χ	X	ch	ch as in loch, Bach
psi	ψ	Ψ	ps	ps as in drops
omega	ω	Ω	ō	o as in obey (long)

DIPHTHONGS

Diphthong	Pronunciation	Greek Example
αι	as in <u>ai</u>sle	καί
ει	as in w<u>ei</u>ght	λύει
οι	as in b<u>oi</u>l	οἶδα
αυ	as in <u>ow</u>l	αὐτός
ου	as in s<u>ou</u>p	οὖν
υι	as in s<u>ui</u>te, q<u>uee</u>n	υἱός
ευ, ηυ	as in f<u>eu</u>d	πιστεύω

IOTA SUBSCRIPT

ᾳ	pronounced the same as α
ῃ	pronounced the same as η
ῳ	pronounced the same as ω

GAMMA COMBINATIONS

Combination	Transliteration	Pronunciation
γγ	ng	ng as in fi<u>ng</u>er
γκ	nk	nk as in thi<u>nk</u>
γξ	nx	nx as in ly<u>nx</u>
γχ	nch	nch as in thi<u>nk</u>[1]

[1] The sound here is difficult for many English speakers to pronounce. If you have ever been to Scotland, the sound is closer to *Loch*. It is a deeper guttural sound than *k*.

BREATHING MARKS

SMOOTH BREATHING MARKS

	Lowercase	Uppercase	Transliteration	Gloss
initial vowel	ἐν	Ἐν	en	"in"
initial diphthong	εἰς	Εἰς	eis	"into"

ROUGH BREATHING MARKS

	Lowercase	Uppercase	Transliteration	Gloss
initial vowel	ἑν	Ἐν	hen	"one"
initial diphthong	εἱς	Εἱς	heis	"one"
initial upsilon	ὕδωρ	Ὕδωρ	huios	"son"
initial rho	ῥημα	Ῥημα	rhēma	"word"

PUNCTUATION

Character	English Form	Greek Function
θεός,	comma	comma
θεός.	period	period
θεός·	dot above line	semicolon or colon
θεός;	semicolon	question mark

DIACRITICAL MARKS

elision (')
diaeresis (¨)
crasis (')

ACCENTS

acute (´)
grave (`)
circumflex (ˆ or ˜ or ^)

DETERMINING THE FUNCTION OF ADJECTIVES

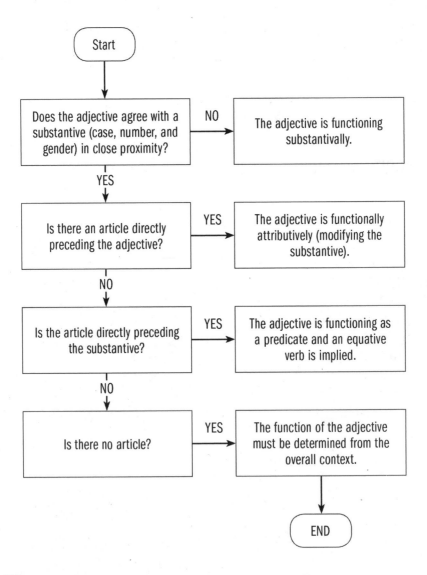

Start

Does the adjective agree with a substantive (case, number, and gender) in close proximity?

NO → The adjective is functioning substantivally.

YES

Is there an article directly preceding the adjective?

YES → The adjective is functionally attributively (modifying the substantive).

NO

Is the article directly preceding the substantive?

YES → The adjective is functioning as a predicate and an equative verb is implied.

NO

Is there no article?

YES → The function of the adjective must be determined from the overall context.

END

appendix FOUR

CHANGES TO A STEM WHEN A SIGMA, THETA, TAU, OR MU IS ADDED

Here is a summary of the morphological changes that involve the addition of a *sigma*. These changes are most frequently seen with third declension nouns, as well as with future and aorist tense formatives.

Labial	π	β	φ		+	σ	→	ψ
Dental	(ν)τ	δ	θ	ζ	+	σ	→	σ
Guttural	κ	γ	χ		+	σ	→	ξ

Here is a summary of the morphological changes that involve the addition of a *theta*. This change is most frequently seen with the future and aorist passive tense formatives.

Labial	π	β	φ	πτ	+	θ	→	φθ
Dental	(ν)τ	δ	θ	ζ	+	θ	→	σθ
Guttural	κ	γ	χ		+	θ	→	χθ

Here is a summary of the morphological changes that involve the addition of a *tau*. This change is most frequently seen in perfect passive tense forms.

Labial	π	β	φ	πτ	+	τ	→	πτ
Dental	(ν)τ	δ	θ	ζ	+	τ	→	στ
Guttural	κ	γ	χ		+	τ	→	κτ

Finally, here is the summary of the morphological changes that involve the addition of a *mu*, which is most often seen in perfect passive forms.

Labial	π	β	φ	ττ	+	μ	→	μμ
Dental	(ν)τ	δ	θ	ζ	+	μ	→	σμ
Guttural	κ	γ	χ		+	μ	→	γμ

Other liquids typically do not cause any morphological changes; that is, the following combinations occur: λθ, ρθ, νθ, λμ, ρμ, νμ, λτ, ρτ, ντ, λκ, ρκ, and νκ. These generally occur in the following contexts: (1) combinations ending in a theta with future and aorist passives; (2) combinations ending with a mu in perfect passive forms; (3) combinations ending with a tau in perfect passive forms; and (4) combinations ending with a kappa in perfect active forms.

These summaries are best understood as examples of assimilation—the resulting sound involves two consonants that are phonologically close. For example, a theta is a fricative; hence when a labial combines with a theta, it "assimilates" to the labial fricative φ, which results in the final form φθ. This is because it is easier to pronounce two similar sounds together than two dissimilar sounds. Consider, for example, the way that the English word "input" is actually pronounced. If you listen carefully, many speakers will say "*im*put" even though the word is spelled "*in*put." This represents an assimilation from the nasal "n" to the labial "m" before the labial "p." Other final forms summarized can be explained similarly.

appendix FIVE

CONSONANT CLASSIFICATION

A little bit of *phonology* (how sounds are made) goes a long way to understanding *morphology* (how forms are spelled) in Koine Greek. Consonants are classified based on the place where the airflow from the lungs is constricted and the manner of constriction involved; this is the *place of articulation*.

- **labials** (or **labial consonants**) involve a complete or partial restriction of the airflow with the lips
- **dentals** (or **dental consonants**) involve a complete or partial restriction of the airflow just behind the upper front teeth (at a part of the mouth called the *alveolar ridge*)
- **gutturals** (or **guttural consonants**) involve a complete or partial restriction of the airflow in the throat

Consonant sounds are further classified based on how the airflow from the lungs is constricted, or the *manner of articulation*.

- **stops** (or *plosives*) involve a complete stop of the airflow from the lungs
- **fricatives** (or **fricative consonants**) involve a partial constriction of the airflow from the lungs and are further subdivided into two categories:
  - **sibilants** involve an "s" sound
  - **aspirates** involve an "h" sound
- **nasals** are formed when the air flows through the nasal passage
- **liquids** are formed with a partial constriction of the airflow involving the tongue; the actual place of articulation varies greatly, which is one of the reasons why there is such variation in "l" and "r" sounds in various languages

Finally, consonants can be further divided between those sounds that involve the vibration of the vocal cords (*voiced*) and those that do not (*voiceless*).
This can be summarized as follows:

CONSONANT CLASSIFICATION

	Labials	Dentals	Gutturals
	Stops		
voiceless	π	τ	κ
voiced	β	δ	γ
	Sibilants		
voiceless	ψ	σ	ξ
voiced		ζ	
	Fricatives		
voiceless	φ	θ	χ
	Nasals		
voiced	μ	ν	
	Liquids		
voiced		λ, ρ	

It is unnecessary to memorize these classifications. But it is helpful to know them because morphology (reflected in spelling changes) in Greek is determined by phonology (the sounds, or pronunciation, of words), such as when consonants combine with a sigma or a theta. These additions cause predictable spelling changes (morphology) based on the types of sounds that are possible in Greek (phonology).

GUIDE TO ADJECTIVE, PRONOUN, AND DEMONSTRATIVE FUNCTIONS

The following chart summarizes the function of various pronouns based on attributive or predicate position. The function of adjectives is provided for comparison.

FORMS

Position	Adjectives Function	αὐτός (Personal Pronoun) Function	οὗτος/ἐκεῖνος (Demonstratives) Function
predicate	makes a predication	adjectival ("-self")	adjective (modifies a substantive)
attributive	modifies a substantive	adjectival ("same")	does not occur
*(substantival)**	substantive (functions as substantive)	substantive (functions as substantive)	pronoun (no substantive modified)

*Technically, there is no "substantival" position, but it is included here for the sake of completeness.

Also keep in mind the following:

- A **pronoun** *always* has the same gender and number of its antecedent; its case is determined by its function in the clause in which it occurs.
- An **adjective** that is functioning attributively always has the same gender, number, *and case* of the substantive that it modifies.

Personal pronouns can be used:

- as *pronouns* (standing in the place of a previously mentioned entity); or
- to show *emphasis* (in the nominative case); they are not grammatically essential because the verb all by itself indicates the subject; or
- to show *possession*, in the genitive case (modifying a noun; e.g., ὁ κύριός μου, "my Lord").[1]

Relative pronouns are not found in either predicate or attribute position; they *always* function as pronouns, referring back to an antecedent (thus matching it in gender and number) or referring to an antecedent that must be inferred from the overall context. Their case is determined by their function in the relative clause in which they occur.

---

1. The pronoun μου is enclitic; this means that it has thrown its accent back to the noun. See appendix 1, "Overview of Greek Accents."

appendix SEVEN

GUIDE FOR TRANSLATING GREEK
FINITE VERBS *(based on the verb λύω)*

Please note that these translations are simply guides to how a given verb form might be rendered in English. Context is the final determiner of any actual translation.

INDICATIVE VERBS

		Active	Middle	Passive
Present		I release, am releasing	I am releasing for myself	I am released, am being released
		you (sg) release, are releasing	you (sg) are releasing for yourself	you (sg) are released, are being released
		he/she/it releases, is releasing	he/she/it is releasing for himself (etc.)	he/she/it is released, is being released
		we release, are releasing	we are releasing for ourselves	we are released, are being released
		you (pl) release, are releasing	you (pl) are releasing for yourselves	you (pl) are released, are being released
		they release, are releasing	they are releasing for themselves	they are released, are being released
Imperfect		I was releasing	I was releasing for myself	I was being released
		you (sg) were releasing	you (sg) were releasing for yourself	you (sg) were being released
		he/she/it was releasing	he/she/it was releasing for himself (etc.)	he/she/it was being released
		we were releasing	we were releasing for ourselves	we were being released
		you (pl) were releasing	you (pl) were releasing for yourselves	you (pl) were being released
		they were releasing	they were releasing for themselves	they were being released

(cont.)

	Active	Middle	Passive
Future	I will release	I will release for myself	I will be released
	you (sg) will release	you (sg) will release for yourself	you (sg) will be released
	he/she/it will release	he/she/it will release for himself (etc.)	he/she/it will be released
	we will release	we will release for ourselves	we will be released
	you (pl) will release	you (pl) will release for yourselves	you (pl) will be released
	they will release	they will release for themselves	they will be released
Aorist	I released	I released for myself	I was released
	you (sg) released	you (sg) released for yourself	you (sg) were released
	he/she/it released	he/she/it released for himself (etc.)	he/she/it was released
	we released	we released for ourselves	we were released
	you (pl) released	you (pl) released for yourselves	you (pl) were released
	they released	they released for themselves	they were released
Perfect	I have released	I have released for myself	I have been released
	you (sg) have released	you (sg) have released for yourself	you (sg) have been released
	he/she/it has released	he/she/it has released for himself (etc.)	he/she/it has been released
	we have released	we have released for ourselves	we have been released
	you (pl) have released	you (pl) have released for yourselves	you (pl) have been released
	they have released	they have released for themselves	they have been released
Pluperfect	I had released	I had released for myself	I had been released
	you (sg) had released	you (sg) had released for yourself	you (sg) had been released
	he/she/it had released	he/she/it had released for himself (etc.)	he/she/it had been released
	we had released	we had released for ourselves	we had been released
	you (pl) had released	you (pl) had released for yourselves	you (pl) had been released
	they had released	they had released for themselves	they had been released

SUBJUNCTIVE VERBS

	Active	Middle	Passive
Present	I would release	I would release for myself	I would be released
	you (sg) would release	you (sg) would release for yourself	you (sg) would be released
	he/she/it would release	he/she/it would release for himself (etc.)	he/she/it would be released
	we would release	we would release for ourselves	we would be released
	you (pl) would release	you (pl) would release for yourselves	you (pl) would be released
	they would release	they would release for themselves	they would be released
Aorist	I would release	I would release for myself	I would be released
	you (sg) would release	you (sg) would release for yourself	you (sg) would be released
	he/she/it would release	he/she/it would release for himself (etc.)	he/she/it would be released
	we would release	we would release for ourselves	we would be released
	you (pl) would release	you (pl) would release for yourselves	you (pl) would be released
	they would release	they would release for themselves	they would be released

IMPERATIVE VERBS[1]

	Active	Middle	Passive
Present	release (sg)!	release for yourself!	be released (sg)!
	let him/her/it release!	let him/her/it release for himself (etc.)!	let him/her/it be released!
	release (pl)!	release for yourselves!	be released (pl)!
	let them release!	let them release for themselves!	let them be released!
Aorist	release (sg)!	release for yourself!	be released (sg)!
	let him/her/it release!	let him/her/it release for himself (etc.)!	let him/her/it be released!
	release (pl)!	release for yourselves!	be released (pl)!
	let them release!	let them release for themselves!	let them be released!

---

1. The imperative does not have first-person forms.

OPTATIVE VERBS

		Active	Middle	Passive
Present		I might release	I might release for myself	I might be released
		you (sg) might release	you (sg) might release for yourself	you (sg) might be released
		he/she/it might release	he/she/it might release for himself (etc.)	he/she/it might be released
		we might release	we might release for ourselves	we might be released
		you (pl) might release	you (pl) might release for yourselves	you (pl) might be released
		they might release	they might release for themselves	they might be released
Aorist		I might release	I might release for myself	I might be released
		you (sg) might release	you (sg) might release for yourself	you (sg) might be released
		he/she/it might release	he/she/it might release for himself (etc.)	he/she/it might be released
		we might release	we might release for ourselves	we might be released
		you (pl) might release	you (pl) might release for yourselves	you (pl) might be released
		they might release	they might release for themselves	they might be released

Charts created by Chi-ying Wang.

appendix EIGHT

GUIDE FOR TRANSLATING GREEK INFINITIVES

Please note that these translations are simply guides to how a given verb form might be rendered in English. Context is the final determiner of any actual translation.

	ACT	MID	PASS
PRES	to release (continuously)	to release (continuously) for oneself	to be released (continuously)
FUT	to (be about to) release	to (be about to) release for oneself	to (be about to) be released
AOR	to release	to release for oneself	to be released
PERF	to have released	to have released for oneself	to have been released

Chart created by Chi-ying Wang.

GUIDE FOR TRANSLATING GREEK PARTICIPLES

Please note that these translations are simply guides to how a given verb form might be rendered in English. Context is the final determiner of any actual translation.

PARTICIPLES—PRESENT ACTIVE

			Masculine	Feminine	Neuter
Adverbial (Temporal)	sg	nom	while he releases, while releasing	while she releases, while releasing	while it releases, while releasing
		gen			
		dat			
		acc			
	pl	nom	while they release, while releasing	while they release, while releasing	while they release, while releasing
		gen			
		dat			
		acc			
Attributive[1]	sg	nom	. . . [subst] who releases	. . . [subst] who releases	. . . [subst] that releases
		gen	. . . of [subst] who releases	. . . of [subst] who releases	. . . of [subst] that releases
		dat	. . . to/by/with/in [subst] who releases	. . . to/by/with/in [subst] who releases	. . . to/by/with/in [subst] that releases
		acc	. . . [subst] who releases	. . . [subst] who releases	. . . [subst] that releases
	pl	nom	. . . [subst] who release	. . . [subst] who release	. . . [subst] that release
		gen	. . . of [subst] who release	. . . of [subst] who release	. . . of [subst] that release
		dat	. . . to/by/with/in [subst] who release	. . . to/by/with/in [subst] who release	. . . to/by/with/in [subst] that release
		acc	. . . [subst] who release	. . . [subst] who release	. . . [subst] that release

			Masculine	Feminine	Neuter
Substantival	sg	nom	he who releases	she who releases	that which releases
		gen	of him who releases	of her who releases	of that which releases
		dat	to/by/with/in him who releases	to/by/with/in her who releases	to/by/with/in that which releases
		acc	him who releases	her who releases	that which releases
	pl	nom	they who release	they who release	those that release
		gen	of them who release	of them who release	of those that release
		dat	to/by/with/in them who release	to/by/with/in them who release	to/by/with/in those that release
		acc	them who release	them who release	those that release

[1]In context, these could all be translated simply as "releasing"; e.g., "the Word that releases" or "the releasing Word." Context and English convention will determine the best translation. This is true for all the attributive participles in this appendix.

PARTICIPLES—PRESENT MIDDLE

			Masculine	Feminine	Neuter
Adverbial (Temporal)	sg	nom	while he releases for himself	while she releases for herself	while it releases for itself
		gen			
		dat			
		acc			
	pl	nom	while they release for themselves	while they release for themselves	while they release for themselves
		gen			
		dat			
		acc			
Attributive	sg	nom	... [subst] who releases for himself	... [subst] who releases for herself	... [subst] that releases for itself
		gen	... of [subst] who releases for himself	... of [subst] who releases for herself	... of [subst] that releases for itself
		dat	... to/by/with/in [subst] who releases for himself	... to/by/with/in [subst] who releases for herself	... to/by/with/in [subst] that releases for itself
		acc	... [subst] who releases for himself	... [subst] who releases for herself	... [subst] that releases for itself
	pl	nom	... [subst] who release for themselves	... [subst] who release for themselves	... [subst] that release for themselves
		gen	... of [subst] who release for themselves	... of [subst] who release for themselves	... of [subst] that release for themselves

(cont.)

			Masculine	Feminine	Neuter
Attributive	pl	dat	. . . to/by/with/in [subst] who release for themselves	. . . to/by/with/in [subst] who release for themselves	. . . to/by/with/in [subst] that release for themselves
		acc	. . . [subst] who release for themselves	. . . [subst] who release for themselves	. . . [subst] that release for themselves
Substantival	sg	nom	he who releases for himself	she who releases for herself	that which releases for itself
		gen	of him who releases for himself	of her who releases for herself	of that which releases of itself
		dat	to/by/with/in him who releases for himself	to/by/with/in her who releases for herself	to/by/with/in that which releases for itself
		acc	him who releases for himself	her who releases for herself	that which releases for itself
	pl	nom	they who release for themselves	they who release for themselves	those that release for themselves
		gen	of them who release for themselves	of them who release for themselves	of those that release for themselves
		dat	to/by/with/in them who release for themselves	to/by/with/in them who release for themselves	to/by/with/in those that release for themselves
		acc	them who release for themselves	them who release for themselves	those which release for themselves

PARTICIPLES—PRESENT PASSIVE

			Masculine	Feminine	Neuter
Adverbial (Temporal)	sg	nom	while he is released, while being released	while she is released, while being released	while it is released, while being released
		gen			
		dat			
		acc			
	pl	nom	while they are released, while being released	while they are released, while being released	while they are released, while being released
		gen			
		dat			
		acc			
Attributive	sg	nom	. . . [subst] who is released	. . . [subst] who is released	. . . [subst] that is released
		gen	. . . of [subst] who is released	. . . of [subst] who is released	. . . of [subst] that is released

			Masculine	Feminine	Neuter
Attributive	sg	dat	. . . to/by/with/in [subst] who is released	. . . to/by/with/in [subst] who is released	. . . to/by/with/in [subst] that is released
		acc	. . . [subst] who is released	. . . [subst] who is released	. . . [subst] that is released
Attributive	pl	nom	. . . [subst] who are released	. . . [subst] who are released	. . . [subst] that are released
		gen	. . . of [subst] who are released	. . . of [subst] who are released	. . . of [subst] that are released
		dat	. . . to/by/with/ in [subst] who are released	. . . to/by/with/ in [subst] who are released	. . . to/by/with/ in [subst] that are released
		acc	. . . [subst] who are released	. . . [subst] who are released	. . . [subst] that are released
Substantival	sg	nom	he who is released	she who is released	that which is released
		gen	of him who is released	of her who is released	of that which is released
		dat	to/by/with/in him who is released	to/by/with/in her who is released	to/by/with/in that which is released
		acc	him who is released	her who is released	that which is released
	pl	nom	they who are released	they who are released	those that are released
		gen	of them who are released	of them who are released	of those that are released
		dat	to/by/with/in them who are released	to/by/with/in them who are released	to/by/with/in those that are released
		acc	them who are released	them who are released	those that are released

Charts created by Chi-ying Wang and Dana M. Harris.

appendix TEN

MORE ON VERBAL ROOTS

The **verbal root** is the most basic morpheme of a verb and is the basis of the various **tense stems**. With "regular" verbs, the individual tense stems do not differ from the verbal root, or they differ very little, as is the case with liquid verbs. This is why tense formatives are used with regular verbs—because their tense stems do not change, there must be some additional indicator of various tense stems. "Irregular" verbs, however, often display significant variation in the tense stems from their verbal roots, especially in the present stem. This variation can appear to defy explanation in some instances, but there are in fact patterns that occur to enable us to classify these variations.

Several patterns are explainable because of the presence of a consonantal iota, which no longer appeared in the alphabet during the Koine period yet still had an impact on the formation of the following verb patterns. The principal parts of representative verbs are listed so that you can see these patterns (dashes indicate principal parts that do not occur in Koine Greek).

Verbs whose roots have a single lambda that doubles in the present stem, such as:
  ἀποστελλω, ἀποστελῶ, ἀπέστειλα, ἀπέσταλκα, ἀπέσταλμαι, ἀπεστάλην
  βάλλω, βαλῶ, ἔβαλον, βέβληκα, βεβλημαι, ἐβλήθην

Verbs whose roots do not have an iota but whose present stem does, such as:
  αἴρω, ἀρῶ, ἦρα, ἦρκα, ἦρμαι, ἤρθην
  φαίνω, φανῶ/φανήσομαι, ἔφηνα/ἔφανα, πέφαγκα, πέφασμαι, ἐφάνθην/ ἐφάνην

Verbs whose roots end in a dental[1] but whose present stem ends in -ιζω, such as:
  βαπτίζω, βαπτίσω, ἐβάπτισα, -, βεβάπτισμαι, ἐβαπτίσθην
  δοξάζω, δοξάσω, ἐδόξασα, δεδόξακα, δεδόξασμαι, ἐδοξάσθην

---

1. The root of βαπτίζω is √βαπτιδ, and the root of δοξάζω is √δοξαδ.

Verbs whose roots end in a guttural[2] but whose present stem ends in -σσ, such as:
ταράσσω, ταράξω, ἐτάραξα, -, τετάραγμαι, ἐταράχθην
κηρύσσω, κηρύξω, ἐκήρυξα, κεκήρυχα, κεκήρυγμαι, ἐκηρύχθην

Several verbs add a consonant, such as a nu, or a combination of consonants, such as πτ or σκ, to the verbal root in the present tense stem. Vowel changes (sometimes significant) may occur as the result of these changes. Here are some examples of these patterns:

πίνω, πίομαι, ἔπιον, πέπωκα, -, ἐπόθην	(adds ν)
πίπτω, πεσοῦμαι, ἔπεσον, πέπτωκα, -, -	(adds πτ)
γινώσκω, γνώσομαι, ἔγνων, ἔγνωκα, ἔγνωσμαι, ἐγνώσθην	(adds σκ)
εὑρίσκω, εὑρήσω, εὗρον, εὕρηκα, -, εὑρέθην	(adds σκ)
ἀποθνήσκω, ἀποθανοῦμαι, ἀπέθανον, -, -, -	(adds σκ)

Finally, some verb uses multiple verbal roots to form different tense stems (suppletion). Memorizing the principal parts for the following verbs is essential:

ἔρχομαι, ἐλεύσομαι, ἦλθον, ἐλήλυθα, -, -
ἐσθίω, φάγομαι, ἔφαγον, -, -, -
λέγω, ἐρῶ, εἶπον, εἴρηκα, εἴρημαι, ἐρρέθην
ὁράω, ὄψομαι, εἶδον, ἑώρακα, -, ὤφθην
φέρω, οἴσω, ἤνεγκα/ἤνεγκον, ἐνήνοχα, ἐνήνεγμαι, ἠνέχθην

For further reading, see William D. Mounce, *The Morphology of Biblical Greek* (Grand Rapids: Zondervan, 1994), esp. 43–45; 73–75.

---

2. The root of ταράσσω is √ταραχ, and the root of κηρύσσω is √κηρυγ.

appendix ELEVEN

PARTICIPLE ENDING SUMMARY CHART

BASIC 3-1-3 PARTICIPLE MORPHEMES

	masc	fem	neut
active	ντ	ουσα	ντ
active	κοτ	κυια	κοτ

PARTICIPLE FORMS THAT FOLLOW A 3-1-3 PATTERN:
- present active *and* second aorist active participle
- first aorist active participle
- first aorist passive participle
- second aorist passive participle
- first perfect active participle

BASIC 2-1-2 PARTICIPLE MORPHEMES

	masc	fem	neut
mid *(mid/pass)*	μεν	μεν	μεν

PARTICIPLE FORMS THAT FOLLOW A 2-1-2 PATTERN
- present middle/passive *and* second aorist middle participle
- first aorist middle participle
- first perfect middle/passive participle

SUMMARY OF ALL PARTICIPLE FORMS

PRESENT ACTIVE *AND* SECOND AORIST ACTIVE PARTICIPLE

	masc	fem	neut
nom sg form	ων	ουσα	ον
gen sg form	οντος	ουσης	οντος

PRESENT MIDDLE/PASSIVE *AND* SECOND AORIST MIDDLE PARTICIPLE

	masc	fem	neut
nom sg form	ομενος	ομενη	ομενον
gen sg form	ομενου	ομενης	ομενου

FIRST AORIST ACTIVE PARTICIPLE

	masc	fem	neut
nom sg form	σας	σασα	σαν
gen sg form	σαντος	σασης	σαντος

FIRST AORIST MIDDLE PARTICIPLE

	masc	fem	neut
nom sg form	σαμενος	σαμενη	σαμενος
gen sg form	σαμενου	σαμενης	σαμενου

FIRST AORIST PASSIVE PARTICIPLE

	masc	fem	neut
nom sg form	θεις	θεισα	θεν
gen sg form	θεντος	θεισης	θεντος

SECOND AORIST PASSIVE PARTICIPLE

	masc	fem	neut
nom sg form	εις	εισα	εν
gen sg form	εντος	εισης	εντος

FIRST PERFECT ACTIVE PARTICIPLE

	masc	fem	neut
nom sg form	κως	κυια	κος
gen sg form	κοτος	κυιας	κοτος

FIRST PERFECT MIDDLE/PASSIVE PARTICIPLE

	masc	fem	neut
nom sg form	μενος	μενη	μενον
gen sg form	μενου	μενης	μενου

PARTICIPLE FUNCTION GUIDE

Participles can function in one of three ways: adverbial, attributive, and substantival. The attributive and substantival functions are subsets of the adjectival function, so we can chart participle functions as follows:

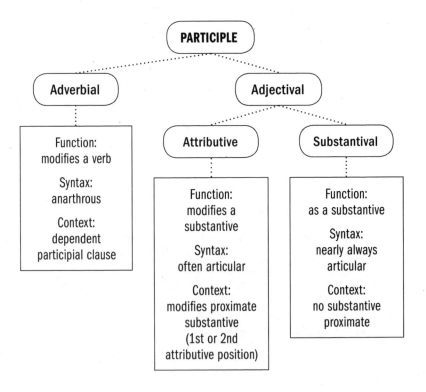

To determine a participle's function, we can follow a series of steps:

1. Step 1 → Determine the Participle Function
   Ask: Is the participle articular?
   A. Yes (two possibilities)
      Ask: Is there a substantive in immediate proximity that agrees with the case, number, and gender of the participle (i.e., that is directly modified by the participle)?

      1. Yes → Then the participle is functioning attributively.
         first attributive position
         ὁ **ζῶν** πατήρ
         the *living* Father
         second attributive position
         ὁ λαὸς ὁ **καθήμενος** ἐν σκότει φῶς εἶδεν μέγα
         The people *living* in darkness saw a great light.

      2. No → Then the participle is functioning substantivally.
         ὁ δὲ **ἀγαπῶν** με ἀγαπηθήσεται ὑπὸ τοῦ πατρός μου
         But *the one who loves* me will be loved by my Father.

   B. No (three possibilities)
      1. The participle is attributively modifying an anarthrous noun.
         [φέροντες] πρὸς αὐτὸν παραλυτικὸν **αἰρόμενον** ὑπὸ τεσσάρων
         [bringing] to him a paralytic *being held up* by four people
      2. The participle is functioning as an anarthrous substantive (rare).
         ἦν γὰρ διδάσκων αὐτοὺς ὡς ἐξουσίαν **ἔχων**
         For he was teaching them as *one having* authority.
      3. The participle is functioning adverbially → proceed to Step Two.

2. Step Two → Determine the Adverbial Function of a Participle

   A. Identify the entire sentence in which the participle occurs.
      ἀσπασάμενοι τοὺς ἀδελφοὺς ἐμείναμεν ἡμέραν μίαν παρ' αὐτοῖς
      After greeting the brothers and sisters, we remained one day with them.

   B. Identify the participial clause.
      ἀσπασάμενοι τοὺς ἀδελφοὺς ἐμείναμεν ἡμέραν μίαν παρ'αὐτοῖς
      After greeting the brothers and sisters, we remained one day with them.

C. Identify the logical subject of the participle by determining the substantive with which the participle agrees in case, number, or gender *or* the subject implied by the main verb.

Example 1:
> ἀσπασάμενοι τοὺς ἀδελφοὺς ἐμείναμεν ἡμέραν μίαν παρ᾽αὐτοῖς
> *After greeting the brothers and sisters*, we remained one day with them.

The main verb is first-person plural (ἐμείναμεν), so the adverbial participle must also be plural (ἀσπασάμενοι).

Example 2:
> εὐθὺς κράξας ὁ πατὴρ τοῦ παιδίου ἔλεγεν, Πιστεύω.
> *Immediately crying out*, the father of the child was saying, "I believe!"

The subject is nominative singular masculine (ὁ πατήρ), so the adverbial participle must also be nominative singular masculine (κράξας).

D. Determine the type of adverbial function indicated by the participle.
1. Is the participle describing something about the time of the main verb?
   → It is a *temporal* adverbial participle, and may be translated using "when," "while," or "after."
2. Is the participle giving the reason for the main verb?
   → It is a *causal* adverbial participle, and may be translated using "because" or "for this reason."
3. Is the participle indicating the purpose of the main verb?
   → It is a *purpose* adverbial participle, and may be translated using "in order that," "so that," or "for."
4. Is the participle indicating the means by which the main verb occurred?
   → It is an *instrumental* adverbial participle, and may be translated using "by," "with," or "in."
5. Is the participle indicating the manner in which the main verb occurred?
   → It is a *manner* adverbial participle, and may be translated using "-ing."

    6. Is the participle indicating something that is true despite the main verb?

        → It is a *concessive* adverbial participle, and may be translated using "even though" or "although."

    7. Is the participle indicating a condition upon which the main verb depends?

        → It is a *conditional* adverbial participle, and may be translated using "if."

3. Genitive Absolute Participles

    Definition: a noun or pronoun plus an anarthrous genitive participle that is *grammatically* unrelated to the main clause, and that usually occurs before the main clause. The subject of the genitive absolute is not the same as the subject of the main clause and is expressed in the genitive case. Thus the genitive absolute is not *grammatically* related to the main clause (hence, it is "absolute"), but it *is logically* or semantically related to the sentence.

    Example:

        ἐκβληθέντος τοῦ δαιμονίου ἐλάλησεν ὁ κωφός (Matt 9:33)

        After the demon was cast out, the mute man began to speak.

SUMMARY OF PRIMARY AND SECONDARY PERSONAL ENDINGS FOR GREEK VERBS

Primary Active Personal Endings

1 sg	ω
2 sg	εις
3 sg	ει
1 pl	μεν
2 pl	τε
3 pl	ουσι(ν)

Primary Middle Personal Endings

1 sg	μαι
2 sg	σαι
3 sg	ται
1 pl	μεθα
2 pl	σθε
3 pl	νται

Secondary Active Personal Endings

1 sg	ν
2 sg	ς
3 sg	–
1 pl	μεν
2 pl	τε
3 pl	ν

Secondary Middle Personal Endings

1 sg	μην
2 sg	σο
3 sg	το
1 pl	μεθα
2 pl	σθε
3 pl	ντο

appendix FOURTEEN

PRINCIPAL PARTS CHART

(1) Pres Act	(2) Fut Act	(3) Aor Act	(4) Perf Act	(5) Perf Mid	(6) Aor Pass
ἄγω	ἄξω	ἤγαγον	n/a	ἦγμαι	ἤχθην
ἀκούω	ἀκούσω	ἤκουσα	ἀκήκοα	n/a	ἠκούσθην
ἀποθνήσκω	ἀποθανοῦμαι	ἀπέθανον	n/a	n/a	n/a
βάλλω	βαλῶ	ἔβαλον	βέβληκα	βέβλημαι	ἐβλήθην
-βαίνω[1]	-βήσομαι	-έβην	-βέβηκα	n/a	n/a
βλέπω	βλέψω	ἔβλεψα	n/a	n/a	n/a
γίνομαι	γενήσομαι	ἐγενόμην	γέγονα	γεγένημαι	ἐγενήθην
γινώσκω	γνώσομαι	ἔγνων	ἔγνωκα	ἔγνωσμαι	ἐγνώσθην
γράφω	γράψω	ἔγραψα	γέγραφα	γέγραμμαι	ἐγράφην
δέω[2]	n/a	ἔδησα	δέδεκα	δέδεμαι	ἐδέθην
διδάσκω	διδάξω	ἐδίδαξα	n/a	n/a	ἐδιδάχθην
δίδωμι	δώσω	ἔδωκα	δέδωκα	δέδομαι	ἐδόθην
δύναμαι	δυνήσομαι	n/a	n/a	n/a	ἠδυνήθην
ἐγείρω	ἐγερῶ	ἤγειρα	n/a	ἐγήγερμαι	ἠγέρθην
ἔρχομαι	ἐλεύσομαι	ἦλθον	ἐλήλυθα	n/a	n/a
ἐσθίω	φάγομαι	ἔφαγον	n/a	n/a	n/a
εὑρίσκω	εὑρήσω	εὗρον	εὕρηκα	n/a	εὑρέθην
ἔχω	ἔξω	ἔσχον	ἔσχηκα	n/a	n/a
θέλω	θελήσω	ἠθέλησα	n/a	n/a	n/a
ἵστημι	στήσω	ἔστησα	ἔστηκα	n/a	ἐστάθην
καλέω	καλέσω	ἐκάλεσα	κέκληκα	κέκλημαι	ἐκλήθην
κηρύσσω	n/a	ἐκήρυξα	n/a	n/a	ἐκηρύχθην
κρίνω[3]	κρινῶ	ἔκρινα	κέκρικα	κέκριμαι	ἐκρίθην

(cont.)

(1) Pres Act	(2) Fut Act	(3) Aor Act	(4) Perf Act	(5) Perf Mid	(6) Aor Pass
λαμβάνω	λήμψομαι	ἔλαβον	εἴληφα	εἴλημμαι	ἐλήμφθην
λέγω	ἐρῶ	εἶπον	εἴρηκα	εἴρημαι	ἐρρέθην
λύω	λύσω	ἔλυσα	λέλυκα	λέλυμαι	ἐλύθην
n/a	εἰδήσω	n/a	οἶδα (plpf ᾔδειν)	n/a	n/a
ὁράω	ὄψομαι	εἶδον	ἑώρακα	n/a	ὤφθην
πάσχω	n/a	ἔπαθον	πέπονθα	n/a	n/a
πίνω	πίομαι	ἔπιον	πέπωκα	n/a	ἐπόθην
πίπτω	πεσοῦμαι	ἔπεσον	πέπτωκα	n/a	n/a
ποιέω[4]	ποιήσω	ἐποίησα	πεποίηκα	πεποίημαι	ἐποιήθην
σῴζω	σώσω	ἔσωσα	σέσωκα	σέσῳσμαι	ἐσώθην
τίθημι	θήσω	ἔθηκα	τέθεικα	τέθειμαι	ἐτέθην
φέρω	οἴσω	ἤνεγκα	ἐνήνοχα	n/a	ἠνέχθην

[1] This verb only occurs in compound forms in the GNT, which is indicated by the hyphen before the form.

[2] This verb is listed because the third to sixth principal parts are similar to those of δίδωμι, so knowing these principal parts will help you to avoid confusion with forms of δίδωμι.

[3] This verb is representative of liquid verbs.

[4] This verb is representative of contract verbs.

appendix FIFTEEN

SUMMARY OF THIRD DECLENSION NOUN STEM PATTERNS

In addition to the assigned paradigms for third declension endings, there are several other types of third declension nouns, including several that are irregular. The following chart gives an overview of almost all third declension noun patterns, including ones that you have memorized and others that you do not need to memorize. The goal is to have a general sense of the variety of third declension noun patterns so that you can recognize them in the GNT or refer to this chart when you are unsure. The noun stem is evident in the genitive singular form. The lexical form indicates the result of the sigma added to the noun stem.[1]

	Lexical Form	Genitive Singular	Gloss
Labial Stems (β, π, φ)			
Examples:	ἡ λαῖλαψ	λαίλαπος	storm
	ὁ Ἄραψ	Ἄραβος	Arab
Dental Stems (δ, τ, θ)			
Examples:	ἡ χάρις	χάριτος	grace
	ἡ ἐλπίς	ἐλπίδος	hope
	ἡ ὄρνις	ὄρνιθος	hen
Subgroup - ματ stem			
Example:	τὸ ὄνομα	ὀνόματος	name

---

1. This chart is summarized and adapted from Goetchius, *Language of the New Testament*, 115–63. See also William Mounce, *Morphology of Biblical Greek*, 190–216.

	Lexical Form	Genitive Singular	Gloss
Subgroup - ντ stem			
Examples:	ὁ ὀδούς	ὀδόντος	tooth
	ὁ ἄρχων	ἄρχοντος	ruler
Subgroup - neuter τ stem			
Examples:	τὸ φῶς	φωτός	light
	τὸ τέρας	τέρατος	wonder
	τὸ ὕδωρ	ὕδατος	water
Velar Stems (κ, γ, χ)			
Examples:	ἡ σάρξ	σάρκος	flesh
	ἡ γυνή	γυναικός (irreg.)	woman
	ἡ σάλπιγξ	σάλπιγγος	trumpet
	ἡ θρίξ	τριχός	hair
"Liquid" Stems (ν, ρ)			
Examples:	ὁ αἰών	αἰῶνος	age
	ὁ ἡγεμών	ἡγεμόνος	leader
	ὁ κύων	κυνός (irreg.)	dog
	ὁ σωτήρ	σωτῆρος	savior
	ὁ ῥήτωρ	ῥήτορος	orator
	ὁ ἀνήρ	ἀνδρός	man
	ἡ θυγάτηρ	θυγατρός	daughter
	ὁ πατήρ	πατρός	father
	ἡ μητήρ	μητρός	mother
Consonantal Iota Stem			
Examples:	ὁ ἰχθύς	ἰχθύος	fish
	ὁ βασιλεύς	βασιλέως	king
	ὁ νοῦς	νοός	mind
	ἡ πίστις	πίστεως	faith
	ἡ πόλις	πόλεως	city
Neuter stems ending in -ος			
Examples:	τὸ γένος	γένους	kind
	τὸ ἔθνος	ἔθνους	nation

appendix SIXTEEN

VOWEL CONTRACTION TABLES

There are several different approaches to understanding vowel contraction in Koine. One approach is to see how vowels contract according to which vowel occurs in a stem. The following are basic patterns of vowel contraction for verb stems ending in an alpha, epsilon, or omega and connecting vowel.[1]

α	+	α	→	α (long)
α	+	ε/η	→	α (long)
α	+	η	→	ᾳ (long)
α	+	ει	→	ᾳ (long)
α	+	o/ω	→	ω
α	+	οι/ου	→	ω
ε	+	α	→	η
ε	+	ε/ει	→	ει
ε	+	η	→	η (long)
ε	+	o/ου	→	ου
ε	+	ω	→	ω
o	+	ε/ο	→	ου
o	+	ου	→	ου
o	+	η/ω	→	ω
o	+	ει/οι	→	οι
o	+	η	→	οι

Alternatively, one can begin with the contracted form and determine which vowel combinations result in that form.[2] For example:

---

1. Adapted from Goetchius, *Language of the New Testament*, 136–38.
2. Summarized from Mounce, *Basics of Biblical Greek*, 141–42; see also 146–47.

Final Form	Possible Combinations
α	αα, αε, αη
ᾳ	αει
ει	εε, εει
η	εα
ῃ	εαι
οι	ο + ει/οι
ου	εο, οε, οο, οου, εου
ω	αο, αω, εω, οη, οω, or α + diphthong

appendix SEVENTEEN

STANDARD ABBREVIATIONS AND PARSING ORDER

As you develop your parsing skills, it is important also to develop consistency in the abbreviations that you use as you list the components of the word that you are parsing. Unfortunately, the letters "i" and "p" can indicate many elements of a Greek verb, so you need to be a bit more precise. The following are standard abbreviations used in parsing Greek verbs and substantives. You may find different abbreviations in various resources, but the abbreviations used here would be understood by anyone who knows Greek.

tense	voice	mood	person	number
pres	act	ind	1st	sg
impf	mid	subj	2nd	pl
fut	pass	impv	3rd	
aor		opt		
pf		inf		
plpf		ptc		

case	number	gender
nom	sg	masc
gen	pl	fem
dat		neut
acc		

In addition to standard abbreviations, it is also important to list the components of a word in a consistent order. The following are the conventional parsing orders that are followed in this book, although you may find variations in other resources.

substantives (nouns, adjectives, pronouns): case, number, gender, lexical form, inflected meaning

verbs: tense, voice, mood, person, number, lexical form, inflected meaning

participles: tense, voice, participle, case, number, gender, lexical form, inflected meaning

infinitives: tense, voice, infinitive, lexical form, inflected meaning

Finally, here are standard abbreviations used for parts of speech.

adj	adjective
adv	adverb
art	article
conj	conjunction
inf	infinitive
noun	noun
prtl	particle
prep	preposition
pron	pronoun
ptc	participle
vb	finite verb

VERBAL ASPECT AND THE DISTRIBUTION OF TENSE-FORMS, VERBAL MOODS, AND NONFINITE VERB FORMS

Although the number of verbal tense-forms, moods, and aspects in the Koine Greek used in the New Testament can appear a bit daunting, the primary contrast (or opposition) is between imperfective and perfective aspect, or between the present and aorist tense-forms.[1] This becomes clearer when the distribution of verb forms as they occur in the six tense-forms, four verbal moods, and two nonfinite verb forms is depicted graphically. In the following chart, an X indicates the presence of a tense-form in a verbal mood or nonfinite verb form; infrequent occurrences are indicated as "few."

As you can see, both the present and aorist tense-forms occur in all verbal moods and nonfinite verb forms. As discussed in chapters 2 and 16, the aspect of the perfect tense-form is debated. Even so, it is clear that the perfect tense stem does not occur in every verbal mood, and only infrequently in nonfinite verb forms. Also as discussed in chapters 2 and 19, the verbal aspect of the future tense stem is debated. Yet, it is clear that the future tense-form is much less frequent than the present, perfect, or aorist tense-forms. So, the following chart shows how a "choice" between imperfective aspect (by means of the present tense-form) and perfective aspect (by means of the aorist tense-form) is possible in every verbal mood and nonfinite verb form.

---

1. Some forms that do not occur in the GNT do occur in the larger Koine corpus, such as the future optative.

VERBAL MOODS AND NONFINITE VERB FORMS

	Mood				Nonfinite Verb Forms	
	indicative	*imperative*	*subjunctive*	*optative*	*infinitive*	*participle*
Imperfective aspect						
present tense-form	X	X	X	X	X	X
imperfective tense-form	X					
future tense-form	X				few	few
perfect tense-form	X	few	few		X	X
pluperfect tense-form	X					
Perfective aspect						
aorist tense-form	X	X	X	X	X	X

GLOSSARY OF KEY TERMS

2-1-2 declension pattern – an inflected substantive or modifier that follows second declension endings for masculine forms, first declension endings for feminine forms, and second declension endings for neuter forms (ch. 5).

2-2 declension pattern – an inflected substantive or modifier that follows second declension endings for masculine and feminine forms, and second declension endings for neuter forms; also referred to as two-ending modifiers (ch. 5).

3-1-3 declension pattern – an inflected substantive or modifier that follows third declension endings for masculine forms, first declension endings for feminine forms, and third declension endings for neuter forms (ch. 12).

3-3 declension pattern – an inflected substantive or modifier that follows third declension endings for masculine and feminine forms, and second declension endings for neuter forms; also referred to as two-ending modifiers (ch. 12).

– A –

abstract noun – names a quality, state, or action, such a "love" or "justice" (ch. 1).

accent – accents originally indicated pitch, but now indicate which syllable should be stressed, or emphasized; Koine Greek has three accents: acute (´), grave (`), and circumflex (ˆ or ˉ or ^) (ch. 1).

accusative case – indicates the direct object of a transitive verb (ch. 4).

active voice – the subject performs, produces, or experiences the action of the verb; the active voice may also indicate that the subject exists in a "state" (ch. 2).

adjectival function of αὐτός – an articular form of αὐτός, with a noun in the same case, number, and gender in the predicate position (either first or second) with the meaning "-self" (ch. 6).

adjective – a word used to modify a noun or pronoun (chs. 1, 5).

adverb – a word used to modify a verb, adjective, or adverb (chs. 1, 14).

agency – the person responsible for a given action (chs. 2, 11); see also **ultimate agency** and **intermediate agency**.

agreement – the form that certain words must have according to grammar; for example, the use of singular nouns with singular verbs or modifiers that match the substantive they modify in case, number, and gender (chs. 2, 6).

Aktionsart – a German term associated with "kind of action"; (ostensibly) involves how an action *objectively* occurs (ch. 2).

α-impure type noun – a first declension feminine noun that shifts to an eta in the genitive and dative singular (ch. 4).

α-pure type noun – a first declension feminine noun that has alpha throughout the singular forms (ch. 4).

anarthrous – indicates that a word is not preceded by the article (ch. 5).

antecedent – the substantive for which a pronoun substitutes (chs. 6, 9).

antepenult – the third-to-last syllable of a word (app. 1).

aorist tense-form – the word *aorist* indicates "undefined" action; it is the default tense-form in narrative and does not indicate the duration of an action—simply that it occurred. The tense-form uses the aorist active tense stem (third principal part) for active and middle forms and the aorist passive tense stem (sixth principal part) for passive forms; it indicates perfective aspect (chs. 2, 10, 11).

apodosis – the "then" clause of a conditional construction (ch. 11).

apposition – a construction in which one substantive further explains or defines another substantive (frequently a proper name); the two (or more) substantives are in the same case, number, and gender (ch. 8).

arthrous – indicates that a word is preceded by the article (less common than the synonymous term *articular*) (ch. 5).

article – a type of adjective that modifies a substantive to refer to a specific item (e.g., *the* child) or class (e.g., *the* priests) (chs. 5, 8).

articular – indicates that a word is preceded by the article (ch. 5).

aspect – involves how a speaker or writer chooses (sometimes subconsciously) to portray an action or event; the *subjective* viewpoint of the speaker or writer; also called **verbal aspect** (ch. 3).

aspirate consonant – a **fricative consonant** with an "h" sound; namely, θ, χ, and φ (ch. 1); also called an *aspirate*.

attributive function – the function of a modifier (such as an adjective or participle) to modify a substantive; sometimes called *attribution* (ch. 5).

augment – a morpheme (ε-) prefixed to the imperfect, aorist, and pluperfect indicative verb forms (chs. 2, 7, 11, 16).

– B –

breathing mark – a diacritical mark used to indicate whether smooth or rough breathing is intended at the beginning of a word that begins with a vowel, diphthong, or rho (ch. 1).

– C –

cardinal – a word used to indicate numeric values; for example, one, two, three (ch. 12).

case – the relationship of a substantive or pronoun in a given clause or phrase, such as subject, object, or indirect object (ch. 4).

case ending – a suffix that indicates the function of a substantive in a given clause or phrase, such as subject, object, or indirect object (chs. 1, 4).

clause – a construction that contains (or assumes) a subject-verb combination, including a finite verb, an adverbial infinitive, or an adverbial participle; clauses may be either **main** or **dependent** (ch. 1).

cognate – a word (such as a noun or verb) that is related to another word (such as a verb or noun) derived from the same lexical root (ch. 2).

collective noun – names a group of persons or objects considered as one entity, such as *crowd* or *flock* (ch. 1).

command – a direct order for another person to do some action (chs. 2, 22).

comparative – indicates the degree of quality between two entities (e.g., "better" or "worse") (ch. 14).

compensatory vowel lengthening – when a letter (often with an **intervocalic sigma**) drops out between two vowels, the vowels often combine, or lengthen, into one long vowel or diphthong (ch. 2).

complementary infinitive – an anarthrous infinitive that completes the meaning of a finite verb, such as δεῖ or ἔξεστιν; other verbs that are frequently followed by a complementary infinitive include ἄρχομαι, βούλομαι, δοκεῖ, δύναμαι, ἐπιτρέπω, ζητέω, θέλω, μέλλω, ὀφείλω (ch. 23).

complex sentence – a sentence that contains a main clause and one or more **subordinate clauses** (ch. 1).

compound sentence – two or more simple sentences joined together to form one sentence (ch. 1).

conjugation – a pattern of inflection that occurs with verb forms (ch. 1).

conjunction – a word used to connect two or more syntactic units, such as sentences, clauses, phrases, or words (chs. 1, 6).

connecting vowel – a vowel that occurs between a verb stem and a personal ending (ch. 2).

consonant – a symbol used to indicate a sound in which the airflow from the lungs is at least partly restricted; a consonant can be combined with a vowel to form a syllable, although a vowel may form a syllable all by itself (ch. 1).

consonant cluster – a combination of consonants that can occur together in a given language, such as στ, τρ, and σκ in Greek (ch. 1).

construction – a combination of words in a fixed pattern, such as a phrase or clause (ch. 1).

continuous aspect – indicates an action that is portrayed as ongoing; the action or event is portrayed from within the event, from an internal point of view (ch. 2).

contract verb – a verb whose stem ends in an alpha, epsilon, or omicron (ch. 18).

coordinating conjunction – a conjunction that joins two or more *equal* syntactic units, such as a noun and a noun, a verb and a verb, or a clause and a clause (ch. 6).

copulative verb – a verb that "links" a subject with some predication about that subject; the verb by itself is incomplete and must be "completed" with a verb complement, such as a predicate nominative, adjective, or pronoun; also called an **equative** or **linking verb** (chs. 2, 5).

correlative conjunction – a pair of conjunctions that indicates a correspondence between two or more units, such as μὲν . . . δέ (ch. 20).

crasis– a process of vowel contraction when a word ends in a vowel and the next word begins with a vowel (Greek avoids two vowels together that do not form a diphthong); the symbol (') indicates a "contraction" of two words in which a vowel (or vowels) has been dropped; for example, κἀγώ, which is formed from καί and ἐγώ (ch. 1).

– D –

dative case – indicates the indirect object of a transitive verb or performs functions parallel to prepositions (ch. 4).

declension – a pattern of inflection that occurs with the **case endings** used for substantives; there are three declensions in Koine Greek based on noun stem endings; **first declension** noun stems end in an alpha (α) or an eta (η); **second declension** noun stems end in an omicron (o); **third declension** noun stems end in consonants (chs. 1, 4).

definition – an analytical description of the meaning of a word; see **gloss** (ch. 1).

deliberative subjunctive – the use of the subjunctive that appears in independent clauses and poses a question (real or rhetorical) for deliberation (ch. 21).

demonstrative – a word that "points" to an object such as a person or an event; either near (proximate) or far (remote), whether spatial or temporal (ch. 9).

demonstrative adjective – modifies a substantive; see also **demonstrative** (ch. 9).

demonstrative pronoun – stands in place of a previously mentioned substantive; see also **demonstrative** (ch. 9).

dental consonant – a consonant (δ and τ) pronounced by stopping the airflow just behind the upper front teeth (the alveolar ridge); also called a *dental* (ch. 1).

dependent clause – a clause that depends on another word or construction in a sentence and cannot stand alone; contains (or assumes) a subject and a verb but does not communicate a complete thought; also called a **subordinate clause** (chs. 1, 14); subordinate clauses are introduced by a **subordinating conjunction** (ch. 28), an adverbial participle (chs. 13, 15), or a relative pronoun (ch. 9).

deponent (or middle deponent) verbs – the concept that some verbs have "laid aside" their active form even though they are active in meaning; this concept, however, is challenged because the essential force of the middle voice is active (ch. 3).

diacritical mark – a symbol, such as an accent, used to indicate a morphological process or a different pronunciation for a vowel that differs from its usual pronunciation (ch. 1).

diaeresis (¨) – a symbol indicating that two vowels that would normally form a diphthong should be pronounced separately, such as Μωϋσῆς (ch. 1).

diphthong – a combination of two vowels to form one sound that differs from the sound of either of the original two vowels; from the Greek word, δίφθογγος, which means "with two sounds" (ch. 1).

direct middle – connotes a reflexive idea (ch. 2).

direct object – a noun (or noun clause) that indicates the person or entity that is the recipient of the action of a **transitive verb** (chs. 1, 4).

double consonant – the combination of a σ with another consonant to form a new consonant; specifically, σ + χ = ξ, and σ + π = ψ (ch. 1).

– E –

elision (᾿) – a symbol indicating the omission of a final short vowel in a word, usually when the next word begins with a vowel, such as δι᾿ αὐτοῦ (ch. 1).

emphatic negation – the use of οὐ μή plus the aorist subjunctive to indicate the strongest level of negation in Koine Greek (ch. 21).

enclitic – a small (usually one-syllable) word that "throws" its accent back onto the previous word so that it is pronounced as part of this preceding word, such as μου (ch. 20 ; app. 1).

equative verb – a verb that "links" a subject with some predication about that subject; the verb by itself is incomplete and must be "completed" with a verb complement, such as a predicate nominative, adjective, or pronoun; also called a **copulative** or **linking verb** (chs. 2, 5).

η-type noun – a first declension feminine noun that has eta throughout the singular (ch. 4).

– F –

filler – a linguistic concept that indicates particular words or constructions that can fit into **slots**, which indicate various syntactic functions within a sentence (chs. 1, 4).

finite verb – a verb form that is inflected with person and number (ch. 2).

first attributive position – the order in which the article, a modifier (e.g., an adjective), and a modified substantive occur so as to attribute some quality to the substantive: article-modifier-substantive (ch. 5).

first-class conditional – conditional that asserts that the protasis is true for the sake of the argument; the protasis presents a condition that is assumed to be true for the sake of the argument, although in fact it may not be true (ch. 11).

first declension – nouns that have stems that ends in an alpha (α) or an eta (η) and use one set of case endings (ch. 4).

first person – the subject is the one who is speaking or writing; see also **verbal person** (ch. 2).

first predicate position – the order in which the article, a modifier (e.g., an adjective), and a modified substantive occur so as to make a predication: modifier-article-substantive (ch. 5).

fixed components – components that never change for a given noun, such as gender and declension (ch. 4).

form – the way that a word looks, either as it appears in a lexicon or as a result of an inflection (ch. 1).

fricative consonant – a consonant pronounced with minimal constriction of the airflow from the lungs; also called a *continuant* or *fricative* (ch. 1).

function – what a word or unit of words does in a given syntactic context (ch. 1).

future tense-form – indicates "expectation"; uses the future tense stem (second principal part) for active and middle forms and the aorist passive tense stem (sixth principal part) for passive forms; occurs in the indicative mood (with primary personal endings) and a limited number of participles and infinitives (ch. 2, 19).

– G –

gamma combination – a gamma followed by a guttural, such as γ, κ, ξ, or χ, resulting in a nasal sound, such as the "ang" sound in ἄγγελος (sometimes called a *gamma nasal*) (ch. 1).

gender – **natural gender** refers to an innate gender property of a noun, such as *king* or *queen*; **grammatical gender** refers to classifications of Greek substantives, often based on their stems or the patterns of case endings that they follow (ch. 4).

genitival modifier – a substantive in the genitive case that modifies another substantive, called a **head noun** (ch. 4).

genitive absolute – a noun or pronoun in the genitive case plus an anarthrous genitive participle that occurs before the main clause that is not grammatically related to the sentence in which it occurs, although it is logically related (ch. 15).

genitive case – describes another substantive; may indicate possession (ch. 4).

gloss – one possible way that a given word could be translated from one language to another; also called a *translation equivalent* (ch. 1).

grammar – the conventional understanding of how words should be used in a language; *grammar* focuses on how words or units of words are used, or the overall system of rules for a language; see also **syntax** (ch. 1).

grammatical gender – refers to classifications of Greek substantives, often based on their stems or the patterns of case endings that they follow (ch. 4).

guttural consonant – a consonant that is pronounced by stopping the airflow in the throat; γ and κ are gutturals; also called a *guttural*. (ch. 1).

– H –

head noun – a substantive that is modified by another substantive in the genitive case, called a **genitival modifier** (ch. 4).

heightened proximity – an aspectual approach to Greek verbs wherein the perfect tense-form presents an action from a "closer" (either temporal or spatial) point of view (chs. 3, 16).

heightened remoteness – an aspectual approach to Greek verbs wherein the pluperfect tense-form presents an action from a "more remote" (either temporal or spatial) point of view (ch. 16).

hendiadys – the expression of a single idea by two closely related words (often two adverbial participles) (ch. 28).

hortatory subjunctive – the use of the subjunctive that appears in independent clauses and is functionally the equivalent of a command or an exhortation (ch. 21).

– I –

imperatival – relating to an appeal to or use of one's will; in Koine Greek the future indicative, hortatory subjunctive, and imperative can all have an imperatival function; the imperatival function of a verb is also referred to as a *volitional function* or a *command* (chs. 19, 21, 22).

imperative mood – the mood of intention, involving volition (chs. 2, 22).

imperfect tense-form – indicates imperfective aspect; only occurs in the indicative mood; uses an augmented present tense stem (first principal part) and secondary personal endings (chs. 2, 7).

imperfective aspect – indicates that an action is ongoing, continuous, or progressing; the action is viewed internally, from "inside" the event, watching the action unfold (ch. 2).

impersonal verb – a verb that only occurs in the third person (usually singular), but not in the first or second person, such as δεῖ (chs. 2, 20).

improper diphthong – a combination of a long vowel and an iota; called *improper* because there is no effect on the pronunciation when the iota subscripts under the long vowel; also called an **iota subscript** (ch. 1).

improper preposition – a preposition that cannot be prefixed to a verb stem, such as ἐνώπιον (ch. 7).

indefinite pronoun – a pronoun that indicates a member of a class without further identification, such as "someone," "anyone" (ch. 12).

independent clause – a clause that is not dependent on another word or construction in a sentence; an independent clause *must* contain (or assume) a subject and a verb, and communicate a complete thought; also called a **main clause** (ch. 1).

indicative mood – makes an assertion or statement (ch. 2).

indirect middle – expresses the idea of acting in one's own interest or for one's own benefit; sometimes called a *true* or *classical* middle (ch. 2).

indirect object – a noun (or noun clause) that indicates the person or entity that is affected by the action of a **transitive verb** but is not the direct recipient of the action of a transitive verb (chs. 1, 4).

infinitive – a type of **nonfinite verb** that indicates the verbal action or idea without limiting it to a particular person or number; a verbal noun (chs. 2, 23).

infix – a morpheme that is inserted within a word stem to create a new form that has a different function or meaning than the original word stem (ch. 1).

inflected component – a component that changes according to the context of the phrase, clause, or sentence, such as case and number for substantives or tense-forms or number for verbs (ch. 4).

inflected form – a form in which a word appears when it has been inflected for its function in a given context (chs. 3, 4).

inflected meaning – a possible translation of an inflected form; the original context in which the inflected form occurs is determinative for any translation (chs. 3, 4).

inflection – any change in form to indicate a change in function, such as case endings for substantives and tense formatives and personal endings for verbs (ch. 1).

instrumentality – refers to the instrument used to carry out an action; also called *impersonal agency* or *means* (ch. 11).

intermediate agency – refers to the person who carries out an action for the ultimate agent; also called *secondary agency* (chs. 2, 11).

interrogative pronoun – a pronoun used to introduce a question (either explicit or implicit) by asking "who?" "why?" or "what?" (ch. 12).

intervocalic sigma – a sigma that occurs between two vowels, which often drops out and causes **compensatory vowel lengthening** (chs. 3, 7).

intransitive verb – a verb that indicates an action that only affects the subject, such as "the world exists" or "you go"; intransitive verbs cannot take a direct object or be made into a passive (chs. 2, 5).

iota subscript – produced when an iota combines with a long vowel; the iota subscripts under the long vowel; there are three possible iota subscripts in Greek: ᾳ, ῃ, ῳ; also called an **improper diphthong** (ch. 1).

– L –

labial consonant – a consonant that is pronounced by stopping the airflow with the lips; in Greek, π and β are labials; also called a *labial* (ch. 1).

lexeme – the minimal linguistic unit that has a lexical (word) meaning or semantic interpretation (ch. 1).

lexical form – the form in which a word appears in a lexicon or dictionary; for nouns, pronouns, and adjectives, the lexical form for Greek is the nominative singular (ch. 4); for verbs, the lexical form for Greek is nearly always the present indicative, or the verb's first principal part (chs. 1, 3, 4).

lexical morpheme – a morpheme that changes the meaning of the word to which it is added (ch. 1).

lexical root – indicates the most basic lexical meaning of a concept; often the same root is used to construct both verb and noun forms (ch. 3).

lexical semantics – refers to the range of meanings that a word can have (ch. 2).

linking verb – a verb that "links" a subject with some predication about that subject; the verb by itself is incomplete and must be "completed" with a verb complement, such as a predicate nominative, adjective, or pronoun; also called a **copulative** or **equative verb** (chs. 2, 5).

liquid consonant – a consonant with a distinctive airflow (such as on either side of the tongue) from the lungs; the pronunciation of these consonants vary significantly across languages; in Greek, λ and ρ are liquid consonants; also called a *liquid* (ch. 1).

– M –

main clause – a clause that is not dependent on another other word or construction in a sentence; a main clause *must* contain (or assume) a subject and a verb, and communicate a complete thought; also called an **independent clause** (ch. 1).

μι verb – an older pattern of verb formation that uses different personal endings in some parts of its conjugation (chs. 3, 24, 25).

middle deponent (or deponent) verbs – the concept that some verbs have "laid aside" their active form even though they are active in meaning; this concept, however, is challenged because the essential force of the middle voice is active (ch. 3).

middle voice – the subject performs or experiences the action expressed by the verb in such a way that emphasizes the subject's participation; the active voice stresses *the action*, whereas the middle voice stresses *the actor* (ch. 2).

modifier – any form that is functioning to modify another word; an adjective is a common type of modifier (ch. 1).

mood – indicates how the speaker chooses to portray the actuality or potentiality of an event (ch. 2); the **indicative mood** makes an assertion or statement (ch. 2); the **imperative mood** is the mood of intention, involving volition (chs. 2, 22); the **subjunctive mood** is the mood of probability or potentiality; it indicates an action that is uncertain but probable (chs. 2, 21); the **optative mood** is the mood of possibility or (strong) contingency (chs. 2, 26).

morpheme – the smallest language element that has meaning; morphemes are the components (or building blocks) of words (ch. 1).

morphology – the study of **morphemes** and how they are used to form words (ch. 1).

movable nu – a nu that often appears at the end of a word that ends with a vowel when the next word begins with a vowel (chs. 3, 7, 10).

– N –

nasal consonant – a consonant pronounced when the airflow from the lungs flows through the nasal passage; in Greek, μ and ν are nasal consonants; also called a *nasal* (ch. 1).

natural gender – refers to words that correspond to actual gender, such *king* or *queen* (ch. 4).

negative – an adjective that indicates a quality or attribute (e.g., "bad"); see also **comparative** and **superlative** (ch. 14).

neutral morpheme – a morpheme that does not change the meaning of the word to which it is added (ch. 3).

nominative case – indicates the subject of a verb in a clause or sentence (ch. 4).

nonfinite verb – a verb form that is not inflected for person and number (ch. 2); there are two types of nonfinite verbs in Greek: the **infinitive** (a verbal noun) and the **participle** (a verbal adjective) (chs. 2, 13, 15, 17, 23).

noun – name of a person, place, concept, or thing (chs. 1, 4).

noun stem – the most basic form of a noun; stems often reflect a linguistic abstraction and do not represent an actual word (e.g., λογο-) (ch. 4).

number – the distinction between singular or plural for a substantive or verb (chs. 3, 4).

– O –

object complement – a noun, pronoun, or adjective in the accusative case that is a predicate that describes or designates the direct object of a verb (ch. 20).

object of the preposition – a substantive (articular or anarthrous) immediately following a preposition in a prepositional phrase (chs. 1, 6).

oblique cases – any case other than the nominative: the accusative, genitive, dative, and vocative cases (chs. 4, 6, 8).

oblique moods – any mood other than the indicative: the subjunctive, imperative, and optative moods; sometimes nonfinite verbal forms (infinitives and participles) are also included (ch. 2).

omega-class verb – a verb that ends with an omega (ω) or -μαι in the lexical form; for example, λύω (ch. 2).

optative mood – the mood of possibility or (strong) contingency (chs. 2, 26).

ordinal – a word that indicates numeric order; for example, first, second, third (ch. 12).

– P –

paradigm – a pattern of inflections that a given part of speech follows (ch. 3).

parsing – the process of identifying all the morphological components of inflected forms in a set order (ch. 3).

participle – a **nonfinite verb** form that is not inflected for person and number (a verbal adjective) (ch. 2, 13, 15, 17).

parts of speech – basic classification of words into their grammatical functions: the main parts of speech in Greek include the following: article, noun, pronoun, adjective, verb, participle, infinitive, adverb, conjunction, and preposition (ch. 1).

passive deponent verbs – the concept that a verb in the passive has "laid aside" its active form even though it is active in meaning; this concept, however, is challenged because the essential force of the middle voice is active (ch. 2).

passive voice – the subject is acted upon or receives the action of the verb (ch. 2, 11).

penult – the second-to-last syllable of a word (app. 1).

perfect tense-form – may indicate some type of emphasis or summary, such as the resulting state of this past action; uses the perfect active tense stem (fourth principal part) for active and middle forms and the perfect passive tense stem (fifth principal part) for passive forms (chs. 2, 16).

perfective aspect – indicates merely that an action occurred with no indication of its duration; portrays an action in summary; the action is viewed externally (ch. 2).

periphrasis – involves a circumlocution or "going around" one form with another (often longer) construction; a periphrastic participle is an adverbial (anarthrous) participle that is used with a form of εἰμί (or sometimes ὑπάρχω) to form a construction that functions parallel to a finite verb (ch. 17).

permissive middle – the subject allows an action to be done to himself or herself (chs. 3, 8).

person – indicates the relationship between the subject and the verb (ch. 2).

personal ending – a suffix used to indicate the person and number (ch. 3).

personal pronoun – a pronoun that stands in the place of *persons*; the first-person personal pronoun is ἐγώ; the second-person personal pronoun is σύ; and the third-person personal pronoun is αὐτός (ch. 6).

phrase – a construction that does not contain (or assume) a subject-verb combination, does not contain a finite verb, and does not express a complete thought, such as a prepositional phrase (ch. 1).

pluperfect tense-form – uses the augmented perfect tense stem; communicates the same aspect as the perfect (chs. 2, 16).

positive – an adjective that indicates a quality or attribute (e.g., "good"); see also **comparative** and **superlative** (ch. 14).

postpositive – a word that never appears as the first word in the clause in which it occurs (ch. 6).

pragmatics – refers to the context-specific functions of a verbal tense stem (ch. 2).

predicate – the statement or assertion being made about a grammatical subject; normally the predicate comprises a verb and often an object or adverbial modifier, such as an adverb (ch. 1).

predicate adjective – a modifier that "completes" an **equative verb** to make a predication about the subject; for example, "he [subject] is faithful [predicate adjective]"; also called a *subject complement* or *predicate complement* (chs. 2, 4, 5).

predicate function – the function of a modifier (such as an adjective) to make a predication about a substantive, often without a corresponding form of εἰμί; such clauses lacking a finite verb are sometimes called a verbless clause; see also **first predicate position** and **second predicate position** (ch. 5).

predicate nominative – a substantive that "completes" an **equative verb** to make a predication about the subject; for example, "he [subject] is the Christ [predicate nominative]"; also called a *subject complement* or *predicate complement* (chs. 2, 4, 5)

predicate pronoun – a pronoun that "completes" an **equative verb** to make a predication about the subject; for example, "he [subject] is mine [predicate pronoun]"; also called a *subject complement* or *predicate complement* (chs. 4, 5).

predictive future – the use of the function of the future-tense form to indicate an action that has yet to occur (ch. 19).

prefix – a morpheme that is attached to the beginning of a word stem to create a new form that has a different function than the original word stem (ch. 1).

preposition – a word used to show the spatial, temporal, or logical relationship between one word and another; often this indicates the relationship of a substantive to another syntactic unit, such as a substantive, a verb, or a clause (chs. 1, 6).

prepositional phrase – a phrase that comprises a preposition and a substantive (articular or anarthrous) that is the **object of the preposition** (chs. 1, 6).

present tense-form – indicates imperfective aspect; uses the present-tense stem (first principal part); finite present-tense verb forms use primary personal endings (ch. 2).

primary (active or middle) personal endings – used with finite verb forms built from primary tense stems (present, future, and perfect), which include unaugmented indicative tense forms (ch. 2).

primary tenses – unaugmented tenses; the present, future, and perfect tenses (ch. 2, 3).

principal parts – a minimal set of verb forms from which all other verb forms can be derived (chs. 2, 10).

proclitic – a small (usually one-syllable) word that "throws" its accent forward onto the next word so that it is pronounced as part of this subsequent word, such as ὁ (app. 1).

prohibition – a negated **command** (chs. 2, 22).

pronoun – a word used in the place of a noun; sometimes called a *grammatical proxy* (chs. 1, 6).

proper diphthong – a combination of two vowels to form one sound that differs from the sound of either of the original two vowels; from the Greek word, δίφθογγος, which means "with two sounds" (ch. 1).

proper noun – names a particular person, place, or object, such as "Jesus" or "Galilee" (ch. 1).

proper preposition – a preposition that can be prefixed to a verb stem, such as ἐκ (ch. 7).

protasis – the "if" clause of a conditional statement (ch. 11).

punctuation – symbols used to indicate the end of a clause or sentence, or a question; Koine Greek uses four punctuation symbols: a comma, a period, a semicolon (·), and a question mark (;) (ch. 1).

– R –

reciprocal middle – indicates an exchange between members of a plural subject (ch. 8).

reciprocal pronoun – a pronoun that can be translated "one another" or "each other"; the action of the verb is either performed by members of a group acting upon each other, or the action mutually applies within the group; does not occur in the nominative or singular (ch. 22).

reduplication – a morphological process that includes part of a root or stem being repeated (chs. 16, 17, 24, 25).

reflexive pronoun – a pronoun that refers back to the subject of the sentence or clause to indicate that the subject is performing the action upon itself; hence, it never occurs in the nominative case and is always in the predicate position (ch. 22).

relative pronoun – joins a dependent clause within a sentence to a substantive elsewhere in sentence (ch. 9).

root – indicates the most basic lexical meaning and form of a concept; often the same root is used to construct both verb and noun forms (ch. 2).

rough breathing mark – a diacritical mark (ʽ) used to indicate that a word beginning with a vowel is pronounced with an initial "h" sound (called aspiration) (ch. 1).

– S –

second attributive position – the order in which the article, a modifier (e.g., an adjective), and a modified substantive occur so as to attribute some quality to the substantive: article-substantive-article-modifier (ch. 5).

second-class conditional – a conditional in which the protasis presents a condition that is assumed to be true for the sake of the argument, even though it may be known to be false or clearly understood to be false by the one making the argument (ch. 11).

second declension – nouns with a stem that ends in an omicron (o) that use a particular set of case endings (ch. 4).

second predicate position – the order in which the article, a modifier (e.g., an adjective), and a modified substantive occur so as to make a predication: article-substantive-modifier (ch. 5).

second person – the subject is being addressed or written about; see also **verbal person** (ch. 2).

secondary personal endings – used with finite verb forms built from secondary tense stems (imperfect, aorist, and pluperfect), which include augmented indicative tense-forms (ch. 7).

semantic range – the range of possible **glosses** that could be used to translate a particular word from one language into another (ch. 1).

semantics – the meaning of a word or construction in its immediate context; more precisely called *lexical semantics*, which considers the meaning of words and relationships between words (ch. 1).

sentence – a group of words that expresses a complete thought or that is complete by itself; a combination of word constructions, which are governed by rules of syntax (ch. 1).

sibilant consonant – a fricative that involve an "s" sound; σ, ζ, ξ, and ψ are sibilant consonants; also called a *sibilant* (ch. 1).

simple sentence – a sentence that contains only a subject and predicate (ch. 1).

slot – a linguistic concept that indicates various syntactic functions within a sentence that can only be performed by specific **fillers** (words or constructions) (chs. 1, 4).

smooth breathing mark – a diacritical mark (᾿) used to indicate that a word beginning with a vowel is not pronounced with an initial "h" sound (called aspiration) (ch. 1).

stative aspect – presents an existing state of affairs or being; some scholars claim that the perfect tense-form and the pluperfect tense-form indicate this aspect (chs. 2, 16).

stem – the most basic form of verbal root in a given tense-form (e.g., the present tense stem) or the most basic form of a noun; stems often reflect a linguistic abstraction and do not represent an actual word (e.g., λογο-) (chs. 2, 4).

stop – a consonant that involves a complete stop of the airflow from the lungs when it is pronounced; also called a *mute* or *plosive* (ch. 1).

subject – names the entity about which some assertion (predication) is being made (ch. 1).

subjunctive mood – the mood of probability or potentiality; it indicates an action that is uncertain but probable (chs. 2, 21).

subordinate clause – a clause that depends on another word or construction in a sentence and cannot stand alone; contains (or assumes) a subject and a verb, but does not communicate a complete thought; also called a **dependent clause** (chs. 1, 14); subordinate clauses are introduced by a **subordinating conjunction** (ch. 28), an adverbial participle (chs. 13, 15), or a **relative pronoun** (ch. 9).

subordinating conjunctions – introduce subordinate clauses, which are dependent in some way upon a main, or independent, clause (chs. 6, 28).

substantival function – an adjective, participle, or infinitive (or other syntactic unit) that functions as a substantive (ch. 5).

substantive – any form that is functioning like a noun or is a noun (chs. 1, 4).

suffix – morphemes that are attached to the end of a word stem to create a new form that has a different function than the original word stem (ch. 1).

superlative – indicates the degree of quality between more than two entities (e.g., "best" or "worst") (ch. 14).

suppletive verbs – a verb whose principal parts are derived from two more different verbs, such as ἔρχομαι (ch. 10).

syllabification – the rules by which a language divides words into individual syllables (ch. 1).

syntax – the rules that govern how words form constructions and syntactic units (ch. 1).

– T –

tense – in a time-based verbal system, such as English, tense refers to time (ch. 2).

tense stem – the most basic morpheme of a given **verbal root** in a given tense-form (chs. 2, 3, 10).

tense formative – a morpheme that is used to indicate a particular tense-form for "regular" verbs; the aorist tense-form uses -σα; the perfect and pluperfect tense-forms uses -κα; the future tense-form uses -σ (chs. 10, 16).

third attributive position – the order in which the article, a modifier (e.g., an adjective), and a modified substantive occur so as to attribute some quality to the substantive: substantive-article-modifier (ch. 5).

third-class conditional – a conditional that makes no assertion or assumption about the truth or falseness of the protasis; often divided into *future (more) probable* and *present general* (ch. 21).

third declension – nouns that have stems that end in consonants and use several different sets of case endings (ch. 4).

third person – the subject is being spoken or written about; see also **verbal person** (ch. 2).

transitive verb – the action of a verb performed by the subject that affects the object or indirect object in some way—the action is "transferred" on to an object or indirect object; transitive verbs are not complete without an object and can be made into a passive (ch. 2).

two-termination or **two-ending adjective** – a common pattern for adjectives, where one form of the adjective is used to modify masculine and feminine nouns and another form is used for neuter nouns; also called the **2-2 declension pattern** (ch. 5).

– U –

ultimate – the last syllable of a word (app. 1).

ultimate agency – refers to the person who is ultimately responsible for an action; also called *primary* or *direct agency* (chs. 2, 11).

– V –

verb – a word used to describe an action or state of being (think, run, exist) (ch. 1).

verbal aspect – involves how a speaker or writer chooses (sometimes subconsciously) to portray an action or event; the *subjective* viewpoint of the speaker or writer; also called **aspect** (ch. 2).

verbal number – refers to the number of subjects in a clause; in Koine Greek this is either singular (one subject) or plural (more than one subject); singular subjects usually use singular verbs, and plural subjects usually use plural verbs (although neuter subjects sometimes "break" these rules) (chs. 2, 4).

verbal person – indicates the relationship between the subject and the verb (ch. 3).

verbal root – indicates the specific action or state of being; morphologically, the root is the basis from which all of the verb's forms are derived (chs. 2, 10).

verbal stem – the most basic form of a verbal root in a given tense-form (e.g., present tense stem) (ch. 2).

verbless clause – see **predicate function** (ch. 5).

vocative case – used in direct address (ch. 4).

voice – indicates how the subject is related to the action of the verb in a clause or sentence (ch. 3).

volition, volitional – relating to an appeal to or use of one's will; in Koine Greek the future indicative, hortatory subjunctive, and imperative can all have a volitional function; the volitional function of a verb is also referred to as an *imperatival function* or a *command* (chs. 19, 21, 22).

vowel – a letter representing a sound that is formed in a distinctive way; Greek has seven vowels: α, ε, η, ι, ο, υ, and ω; η and ω are always long vowels; ε and ο are always short vowels; α, ι, and υ can be either short or long, depending on where they occur in a given word (ch. 1).

vowel contraction – when vowels occur next to each other that do not form a diphthong, as when a verb stem that ends in a vowel is joined to a personal ending that begins with a vowel, the two vowels often combine, or "contract," following set patterns (ch. 18).

– W –

word – formed with combinations of stems and morphemes (ch. 1).

word order – refers to set patterns in which words occur in a language; in English, word order generally determines subject and object; changes in word order may indicate emphasis (ch. 1).

– Z –

zero morpheme – the absence of a morpheme, such as a case ending or tense formative, that has lexical meaning (chs. 2, 4).

LEXICON

The following lexicon lists words that occur in the textbook and workbook. The range of possible English glosses is fairly limited for most words. Students are also encouraged to check a standard lexicon, such as Frederick W. Danker, Walter Bauer, William F. Arndt, and F. Wilbur Gingrich, eds., *A Greek-English Lexicon of the New Testament and Other Early Christian Literature*, 3rd ed. (Chicago: University of Chicago Press, 2000).

KEY:

[ ]	Numbers in square brackets indicate the chapter in which a vocabulary word is assigned. Words without indicated chapters occur in Pop-Up Lexica or footnotes.
( )	Numbers in parentheses indicate a word's frequency in the GNT.
(+acc), (+gen), and/or (+dat) following a preposition	indicates the case of the object of the preposition and possible translations associated with that case.
(adv)	indicates an adverbial meaning associated with an adjective.
"all occurrences"	indicates the total number of occurrences of a preposition that takes an object in more than one case.
(conj)	indicates a conjunctive meaning associated with a preposition.
(+gen) or (+dat) with verbs	indicates that the object of the verb occurs in a case other than the accusative.
(intrans) and (trans)	indicate different meanings when a verb is functioning intransitively or transitively.
(mid)	indicates a different meaning of a verb in the middle voice.
(pass)	indicates a different meaning of a verb in the passive voice.
(subst)	indicates a possible translation for an adjective that is functioning as a substantive.

A	
Ἀβραάμ, ὁ [1]	Abraham (73)
ἀγαθός, -ή, -όν [5]	good, useful; possessions (pl; subst) (102)
ἀγαπάω [18]	I love (143)
ἀγάπη, -ης, ἡ [4]	love (116)
ἀγαπητός, -ή, -όν [5]	beloved, dear (61)
ἄγγελος, -ου, ὁ [6]	angel; messenger (175)
ἁγιάζω [27]	I set apart, I make holy, I consecrate (28)
ἅγιος, -α, -ον [5]	holy, pure, set apart; saints, God's people (subst) (233)
ἀγοράζω [13]	I buy (30)
ἀγρός, -οῦ, ὁ [27]	field, country(side) (36)
ἄγω [2]	I lead, I bring, I go, I arrest (67)
ἀδελφός, -οῦ, ὁ [9]	brother, fellow believer (343)
ἀδικέω [18]	I wrong, I do wrong, I mistreat (28)
ἀδικία, -ας, ἡ	unrighteousness, injustice, evil (25)
αἷμα, -ατος, τό [12]	blood (97)
αἴρω [2]	I take, I take up, I take away, I remove (101)
αἰτέω [18]	I ask, I request, I demand (70)
αἰών, -ῶνος, ὁ [15]	age, eternity, world (122)
αἰώνιος, -ον [26]	eternal (71)
ἀκάθαρτος, -ον [27]	impure, unclean (32)
ἀκοή, -ῆς, ἡ [17]	report, hearing (24)
ἀκολουθέω [15]	(+dat) I follow, I accompany (90)
ἀκούω [2]	I hear, I listen to, I obey, I understand (428)
ἀλήθεια, -ας, ἡ [5]	truth, truthfulness (109)
ἀληθής, -ές [12]	true, honest, truthful, real (26)
ἀληθῶς	truly (18)
ἀλλά [2]	but, yet (638)
ἀλλήλων [22]	one another, each other (100)
ἄλλος, -η, -ο [22]	other, another (155)
ἁμαρτάνω [5]	I sin, I do wrong (270)
ἁμαρτία, -ας, ἡ [15]	sin (173)
ἁμαρτωλός, -όν [5]	sinful; sinner (subst) (47)
ἀμέμπτως	blamelessly (2)
ἀμήν [1]	amen, truly (129)

ἄν [10]	particle of contingency or conditional particle (166)
ἀνά (+acc) [27]	upward; each (13)
ἀναβαίνω [10]	I go up, I ascend, I embark (82)
ἀναβλέπω [5]	I look up, I receive sight, I regain sight (25)
ἀναγινώσκω [23]	I read, I read aloud (32)
ἀνάγω [17]	I lead up, I bring up; I set sail (mid or pass) (23)
ἀναζώννυμι	I bind up (1)
ἀναιρέω [17]	I take away, I do away with, I kill (24)
ἀναλαμβάνω [24]	I take up, I carry (13)
ἀνάστασις, -εως, ἡ [15]	resurrection (42)
ἀνατίθημι	I lay before, I declare (2)
ἄνεμος, -ου, ὁ [22]	wind (31)
ἀνήρ, ἀνδρός, ὁ [15]	man, male, husband (216)
ἄνθρωπος, -ου, ὁ [4]	human being, person, man, humanity (550)
ἀνίστημι [24]	I raise, I bring to life (trans);, I stand up, I rise (intrans) (108)
ἀνοίγω [3]	I open (77)
ἀντί (+gen) [23]	in place of, on behalf of, for, because of (22)
ἄξιος, -α, -ον [9]	worthy, proper, fit, deserving (41)
ἀπαγγέλλω [22]	I announce, I proclaim, I report, I tell (45)
ἀπάγω [13]	I lead away; I am misled (pass) (15)
ἅπας, -ασα, -αν [25]	all, whole; everybody, everything (pl) (34)
ἀπέρχομαι [13]	I go away, I depart (117)
ἀπιστέω	I refuse to believe, I am unfaithful (8)
ἀπιστία, -ας, ἡ	unfaithfulness, unbelief (11)
ἀπό (+gen) [6]	from, away from (646)
ἀποδίδωμι [24]	I repay, I give away, I pay; I sell (mid) (48)
ἀποθνήσκω [13]	I die, I am mortal (111)
ἀποκαλύπτω [10]	I reveal, I disclose (26)
ἀποκάλυψις, -εως, ἡ	revelation (18)
ἀποκρίνομαι [3]	I answer, I reply (231)
ἀποκτείνω [10]	I kill (74)
ἀπόλλυμι [24]	I destroy, I lose; I die, I perish (mid) (90)
ἀπολύω [7]	I release, I set free, I dismiss (66)
ἀποστέλλω [2]	I send, I send out, send away (132)
ἀπόστολος, -ου, ὁ [9]	apostle, messenger (80)

ἅπτω [22]	(+gen) I kindle, I ignite; I touch, I take hold (39)
ἄρα [13]	so, then, consequently, therefore (49)
ἀργύριον, -ου, τό [27]	silver, money (20)
ἀρνέομαι [25]	I deny, I refuse, I disown (33)
ἄρτι [17]	now, at once, immediately (36)
ἄρτος, -ου, ὁ [4]	bread, food (97)
ἀρχή, -ῆς, ἡ [13]	beginning, origin, authority (55)
ἀρχιερεύς, -έως, ὁ [11]	high priest (122)
ἄρχω [23]	I rule; I begin (mid) (86)
ἄρχων, -οντος, ὁ [24]	ruler, prince, official (37)
ἀσεβής, -ές	ungodly (9)
ἀσθένεια, -ας, ἡ [17]	weakness, sickness (24)
ἀσθενέω [25]	I am weak, I am powerless, I am sick (33)
ἀσθενής, -ές [26]	weak, sick, powerless (26)
ἀσπάζομαι [3]	I greet, I welcome (59)
ἀστήρ, -έρος, ὁ [17]	star (24)
αὐξάνω [10]	I increase, I grow (23)
αὔριον [27]	tomorrow, soon (14)
αὐτός, αὐτή, αὐτό [6]	he, she, it (pron); -self, even, same (adj) (5,597)
ἄφεσις, -εως, ἡ [27]	forgiveness, release, pardon (17)
ἀφίημι [24]	I let go, I forgive, I permit, I divorce (143)
ἀφίστημι	I mislead, I go away, I fall away, I keep away (14)
ἄχρι [22] (+gen)	until, as far as; until (conj) (49)

B

βάλλω [2]	I throw, I put (122)
βαπτίζω [2]	I baptize (77)
βαπτιστής, -οῦ, ὁ	Baptist (of John) (12)
βασιλεία, -ας, ἡ [4]	kingdom, reign (162)
βασιλεύς, -έως, ὁ [11]	king (115)
βασιλεύω [17]	I reign, I rule, I become king (21)
βαστάζω [27]	I carry, I bear, I endure (27)
βιβλίον, -ου, τό [22]	book, scroll, document (34)
βλέπω [2]	I see, I look at (133)
βούλομαι [23]	I wish, I desire, I intend (37)

Γ	
Γαλιλαία, -ας, ἡ [1]	Galilee (61)
γάρ [6]	for, since, then (1,041)
γενεά, -ᾶς, ἡ [25]	generation, family, race, age (43)
γεννάω [19]	I beget, I father, I give birth, I produce (97)
γῆ, γῆς, ἡ [9]	earth, land, soil, region (250)
γίνομαι [3]	I become, I am, I happen, I come into being, I exist (669)
γινώσκω [2]	I know, I learn, I understand (222)
γλῶσσα, -ης, ἡ [15]	tongue, language (50)
γνωρίζω [17]	I make known, I know (25)
γνῶσις, -εως, ἡ [23]	knowledge, esoteric knowledge (29)
γραμματεύς, -έως, ὁ [13]	scribe, clerk, legal expert (63)
γραφή, -ῆς, ἡ [7]	writing, Scripture (50)
γράφω [2]	I write (191)
γυνή, γυναικός, ἡ [15]	woman, wife (215)

Δ	
δαιμόνιον, -ου, τό [13]	demon, evil spirit (63)
Δαυίδ, ὁ [1]	David (59)
δέ [2]	but, now, and, on the other hand (2,792)
δεῖ [23]	it is necessary, one must (impers) (101)
δείκνυμι [25]	I show, I point out, I explain, I prove (33)
δεῖπνον, -ου, τό [13]	dinner, main meal, banquet (16)
δέκα [1]	ten (25)
δένδρον, -ου, τό [27]	tree (25)
δεξιός, -ά, -όν [7]	right (direction); right hand, right side (subst) (54)
δεύτερος, -α, -ον [19]	second, secondly (43)
δέχομαι [3]	I receive, I take, I welcome, I accept (56)
δέω [21]	I bind, I tie (43)
διά (+acc) [9]	because of, on account of (667; all occurrences)
διά (+gen) [9]	through, during, by (667; all occurrences)
διάβολος, -ον [26]	slanderous; the devil (subst) (37)
διαθήκη, -ης, ἡ [10]	covenant, decree, testament (33)
διακονέω [25]	I wait on, I serve, I care for, I serve as a deacon (37)

διακονία, -ας, ἡ [18]	service, office, ministry, help (34)
διάκονος, -ου, ὁ, ἡ [25]	servant, deacon/deaconess, helper (29)
διαλλάσσομαι	I become reconciled (1)
διαλογισμός, -οῦ, ὁ [26]	thought, opinion, doubt (14)
διαμαρτύρομαι [13]	I charge, I testify (15)
διαμερίζω [25]	I divide, I separate, I distribute, I share (11)
διάνοια, -ας, ἡ	mind, understanding (12)
διδάσκαλος, -ου, ὁ [11]	teacher (59)
διδάσκω [2]	I teach (97)
διδαχή, -ῆς, ἡ [26]	teaching, instruction (30)
δίδωμι [24]	I give, I grant, I put, I entrust (415)
διέρχομαι [21]	I go through, I cross over, I come (43)
δίκαιος, -α, -ον [5]	just, righteous, right, upright (79)
δικαιοσύνη, -ης, ἡ [6]	righteousness, justice, uprightness (92)
δικαιόω [18]	I justify, I vindicate, I acquit (39)
διό [9]	therefore, for this reason (53)
διότι [27]	because, therefore, for (23)
διώκω [3]	I pursue, I persecute, I seek after (45)
δοκέω [24]	I think, I suppose, I seem (62)
δοκιμάζω [17]	I put to the test, I examine, I prove by testing, I approve (22)
δοκιμή, -ῆς, ἡ	value, character, evidence (7)
δόξα, -ης, ἡ [4]	glory, brightness, majesty, fame (166)
δοξάζω [2]	I glorify, I praise, I honor (61)
δουλεύω [17]	I am a slave, I serve (25)
δούλη, -ης, ἡ	female slave (3)
δοῦλος, -ου, ὁ [10]	slave, servant (124)
δύναμαι [23]	I am able, I can (210)
δύναμις, -εως, ἡ [15]	power, ability (119)
δυνατός, -ή, -όν [27]	powerful, strong, able, possible (32)
δύνω	I set (of the sun) (2)
δύο [1]	two (135)
δώδεκα [1]	twelve (75)
δῶρον, -ου, τό [17]	gift, offering (19)

E

ἐάν [21]	if, when (351)
ἑαυτοῦ, -ῆς, -οῦ [22]	(of) himself, herself, itself; themselves (pl) (319)
ἐγγίζω [13]	I approach, I come near (42)
ἐγγύς [21]	near, close to (31)
ἐγείρω [3]	I raise up, I wake; I awaken (pass) (144)
ἐγώ [6]	I (2666)
ἔθνος, -ους, τό [12]	nation, people; gentiles (pl) (162)
εἰ [10]	if, whether (502)
εἰκών, -όνος, ἡ [27]	image, likeness (23)
εἰμί [5]	I am, I exist, I live, I am present (2,462)
εἰρήνη, -ης, ἡ [15]	peace (92)
εἰς (+acc) [6]	into, in, toward, for (1,767)
εἷς, μία, ἕν [12]	one, someone (345)
εἰσέρχομαι [16]	I come in(to), I go in(to), I enter (194)
εἰσπορεύομαι [17]	I go, I come in, I enter (18)
εἰσφέρω	I bring in, I lead in (8)
εἴτε [10]	if, whether (65)
ἐκ (+gen) [6]	from, out of, away from (914)
ἕκαστος, -η, -ον [11]	each, every; each one, everyone (subst) (82)
ἐκβάλλω [9]	I drive out, I send out, I cast (81)
ἐκεῖ [7]	there, in that place (105)
ἐκεῖθεν [21]	from there (37)
ἐκεῖνος, -η, -ο [9]	that, those (pl); that person or thing, he, she, it, they (265)
ἐκκλησία, -ας, ἡ [4]	church, assembly (114)
ἐκλέγομαι [6]	I choose, I select (22)
ἐκλεκτός, -ή, -όν [26]	elect, chosen, select (22)
ἐκπορεύομαι [21]	I go out, I come out (33)
ἐκχέω [12]	I pour out, I shed; I abandon myself (pass) (27)
ἐλεέω [24]	I have mercy, I am merciful; I am shown mercy (pass) (29)
ἔλεος, -ους, τό [25]	mercy, compassion (27)
ἐλεύθερος, -α, -ον [26]	free, independent; free person (23)
ἐλπίζω [22]	I hope, I expect (31)

ἐλπίς, -ίδος, ἡ [12]	hope, expectation, what is hoped for (53)
ἐμαυτοῦ, -ῆς [22]	(of) myself (37)
ἐμβαίνω [18]	I embark, I get into (16)
ἐμός, -ή, -όν [7]	my, mine (76)
ἔμπροσθεν (+gen) [16]	before, in front of (impr prep) (48)
ἐμφανίζω	I make known, I reveal (10)
ἐν (+dat) [6]	in, on, by, among, with (2,752)
ἐνδύω [22]	I clothe, I dress; I put on, I wear (mid) (27)
ἕνεκα, ἕνεκεν (+gen) [17]	because of, on account of (impr prep) (26)
ἐντέλλομαι	I command, I order (15)
ἐντολή, -ῆς, ἡ [7]	commandment, law (67)
ἐνώπιον (+gen) [6]	before, in the presence of (impr prep) (94)
ἐξέρχομαι [11]	I go out, I go away, I come out (218)
ἔξεστι(ν) [23]	it is lawful, it is permitted, it is proper (impers) (31)
ἐξουσία, -ας, ἡ [4]	authority, power, ability (102)
ἔξω (+gen) [5]	outside (impr prep); outside (adv) (63)
ἑορτή, -ῆς, ἡ [26]	festival, feast (25)
ἐπαγγελία, -ας, ἡ [7]	promise, what is promised (52)
ἐπαίρω [13]	I lift up; I am opposed (pass) (19)
ἐπεί [26]	because, since, when (26)
ἐπερωτάω [18]	I ask, I ask for (56)
ἐπί (+acc) [10]	on, to, against (890; all occurrences)
ἐπί (+dat) [10]	on, at, on the basis of (890; all occurrences)
ἐπί (+gen) [10]	on, over, when (890; all occurrences)
ἐπιβάλλω [24]	I throw over, I lay (hands) on, I put on (18)
ἐπιγινώσκω [21]	I know, I understand, I recognize, I learn, I know well (44)
ἐπιζητέω [22]	I search, I wish for, I seek after (13)
ἐπιθυμία, -ας, ἡ [17]	desire, longing, lust, passion (38)
ἐπιστρέφω [15]	I turn, I turn around, I turn back, I return (36)
ἐπιτίθημι [24]	I lay on, I put upon; I give, I attack (mid) (39)
ἐπιτιμάω [19]	(+dat) I rebuke, I reprove, I warn, I punish (29)
ἑπτά [1]	seven (88)
ἐργάζομαι [9]	I work, I do, I bring about (41)

ἔργον, -ου, τό [4]	work, deed, action (169)
ἔρημος, -ον [15]	abandoned, desolate; wilderness (fem subst) (48)
ἔρχομαι [3]	I come, I go (634)
ἐρωτάω [18]	I ask, I request (63)
ἐσθίω [2]	I eat (158)
ἔσχατος, -η, -ον [16]	last, least (52)
ἕτερος, -α, -ον [7]	other, another, different; neighbor (subst) (98)
ἔτι [3]	still, yet (93)
ἑτοιμάζω [22]	I prepare, I make ready (40)
ἔτος, -ους, τό [22]	year (49)
εὐαγγελίζω [3]	I announce/bring good news/the gospel, I proclaim, I preach (54)
εὐαγγέλιον, -ου, τό [5]	good news, gospel (76)
εὐθέως [6]	immediately, at once (36)
εὐθύς [3]	immediately, at once, then (59)
εὐλογέω [21]	I bless, I praise, I speak well of (42)
εὑρίσκω [2]	I find, I discover (176)
εὐχαριστέω [22]	I give thanks, I am thankful (38)
ἐχθρός, -ά, -όν [23]	hostile, hating; enemy (subst) (32)
ἔχω [2]	I have, I hold (708)
ἕως [11]	until, while (conj); (+gen) until, as far as (146)

Z	
ζάω [19]	I live, I remain alive (140)
ζητέω [18]	I seek, I look for, I try to obtain (117)
ζωή, -ῆς, ἡ [7]	life (135)

H	
ἤ [5]	or, either . . . or, than (343)
ἡγεμών, -όνος, ὁ [25]	leader, governor (20)
ἤδη [3]	now, already (61)
Ἠλίας, -ου, ὁ	Elijah (29)
ἥλιος, -ου, ὁ [25]	sun (32)
ἡμέρα, -ας, ἡ [4]	day (389)

Θ	
θάλασσα, -ης, ἡ [15]	sea, lake (91)
θάνατος, -ου, ὁ [10]	death (120)
θανατόω	I kill, I put to death (11)
θαυμάζω [3]	I wonder, I marvel, I am amazed (43)
θεάομαι [17]	I look at, I see, I behold (22)
θέλημα, -ματος, τό [16]	will, wish, desire (62)
θέλω [3]	I desire, I wish, I will (208)
θεός, -οῦ, ὁ [4]	God, god (1,317)
θεραπεύω [3]	I heal, I restore, I serve (43)
θερίζω [25]	I reap, I harvest (21)
θεωρέω [21]	I look at, I see, I observe (58)
θηρίον, -ου, τό [16]	beast, animal (46)
θλίψις, -εως, ἡ [22]	tribulation, oppression, trouble (45)
θρόνος, -ου, ὁ [10]	throne (62)
θυγάτηρ, -τρός, ἡ [27]	daughter, female descendant (28)
θύρα, -ας, ἡ [23]	door, gate, entrance (39)
θυσία, -ας, ἡ [24]	sacrifice, offering (28)
θυσιαστήριον, -ου, τό [24]	altar (23)

I	
ἴδιος, -α, -ον [7]	one's own (114)
ἰδού [1]	look! see! (200)
ἱερεύς, -έως, ὁ [16]	priest (31)
ἱερόν, -οῦ, τό [7]	temple (71)
Ἱεροσόλυμα, ἡ or τά [1]	Jerusalem (62)
Ἱερουσαλήμ, ἡ [1]	Jerusalem (77)
Ἰησοῦς, -οῦ, ὁ [1]	Jesus; Joshua (917)
ἱκανός, -ή, -όν [27]	sufficient, able, fit (39)
ἱμάτιον, -ου, τό [15]	clothing, robe (60)
ἵνα [21]	in order that, that, so that (663)
Ἰουδαῖος, -α, -ον [1]	Jewish; a Jew (195)
ἵππος, -ου, ὁ [25]	horse (17)

Ἰσραήλ, ὁ [1]	Israel (68)
ἵστημι [24]	I set, I make stand (trans); I stand (intrans) (155)
ἰσχυρός, -ά, -όν [26]	strong, mighty, powerful (29)
ἰσχύω [26]	I am strong, I am able, I am powerful (28)
Ἰωάννης, -ου, ὁ [1]	John (135)

K

κἀγώ [13]	and I, but I, I also, I myself (= καὶ ἐγώ) (84)
καθαρίζω [10]	I purify, I cleanse, I declare clean (31)
καθαρός, -ά, -όν [17]	clean, pure (27)
κάθημαι [15]	I sit, I sit down, I live (91)
καθίζω [3]	I sit, I cause to sit down (46)
καθίστημι [26]	I bring, I appoint, I ordain (21)
καθώς [6]	as, just as, even as (182)
καί [2]	and, even, also (9,161)
καινός, -η, -ον [9]	new, unknown (42)
καιρός, -οῦ, ὁ [11]	time, appointed time, season (85)
Καισάρεια, -ας, ἡ	Caesarea (17)
κἀκεῖ	and there (10)
κακός, -ή, -όν [5]	bad, evil, dangerous (50)
καλέω [11]	I call, I name, I invite (148)
καλός, -ή, -όν [5]	good, beautiful, useful (100)
καλῶς [21]	well, commendably, rightly (37)
καρδία, -ας, ἡ [4]	heart, inner self, mind (156)
καρπός, -οῦ, ὁ [16]	fruit, harvest (66)
κατά (+acc) [10]	according to, during, throughout (473; all occurrences)
κατά (+gen) [10]	down from, against (473; all occurrences)
καταβαίνω [15]	I come down, I go down (81)
καταβολή, -ῆς, ἡ [6]	foundation, beginning (11)
καταισχύνω [22]	I humilitate, I put to shame; I am disappointed (pass) (13)
κατακρίνω [19]	I condemn, I pass judgment on (18)
καταλλαγή, -ης, ἡ	reconciliation (4)
καταλλάσσω	I reconcile (6)
καταργέω [26]	I abolish, I nullify, I make ineffective (27)
κατασκευάζω [9]	I prepare, I build, I construct (11)

κατεργάζομαι	I do, I achieve, I accomplish, I produce (22)
κατοικέω [19]	I live, I dwell, I reside (44)
καυχάομαι [18]	I boast (intrans), I boast about (trans) (37)
κεῖμαι [16]	I lie, I am laid, I exist (24)
κεφαλή, -ῆς, ἡ [21]	head (75)
κηρύσσω [2]	I proclaim, I preach (61)
κλαίω [21]	I weep, I cry; I mourn (40)
κλείς, κλειδός, ἡ	key (6)
κληρονομέω [27]	I inherit, I receive a share of (18)
κοινωνία, -ας, ἡ [27]	fellowship, participation (19)
κοπιάω [18]	I labor, I become weary, I work hard (23)
κόσμος, -ου, ὁ [6]	world, universe, humankind (186)
κράζω [3]	I cry out, I call out (56)
κρατέω [21]	(+gen) I seize, I grasp, I hold, I hold fast (47)
κρίμα, -ατος, τό [17]	judgment, verdict, condemnation (27)
κρίνω [10]	I judge, I condemn, I decide (114)
κρίσις, -εως, ἡ [19]	judgment, condemnation (47)
κριτής, -οῦ, ὁ [27]	judge (19)
κτίσις, -εως, ἡ [27]	creation, creature (19)
κυριεύω	I rule over, I reign (7)
κύριος, -ου, ὁ [4]	lord, Lord, master, sir (717)
κώμη, -ης, ἡ [27]	village, small town (27)
κωφός, -ή, -όν [5]	deaf, mute, dumb (14)

Λ	
λαλέω [18]	I speak, I say (296)
λαλιά, -ᾶς, ἡ	utterance, speaking (3)
λαμβάνω [2]	I take, I receive, I obtain (258)
λαός, -οῦ, ὁ [9]	people, nation (142)
λέγω [2]	I say, I speak, I tell (2354)
λῃστής, οῦ, ὁ [25]	robber (15)
λίθος, -ου, ὁ [16]	stone (59)
λίμνη, -ης, ἡ [27]	lake (11)
λόγιον, ου, τό	word, message, oracle (4)

λογίζομαι [11]	I account, I calculate, I consider (40)
λόγος, -ου, ὁ [4]	word, statement, message, account (330)
λοιπός, -ή, -όν [19]	remaining; the rest (subst); finally, henceforth (adv) (55)
λυπέω [18]	I grieve, I offend; I mourn, I become sad (pass) (26)
λύω [2]	I untie, I release, I destroy (42)

M	
Μαγδαληνή, -ῆς, ἡ	a female inhabitant of Magdala; Magdalene (12)
μαθητεύω	I make disciples (4)
μαθητής, -οῦ, ὁ [4]	disciple, learner, follower (261)
μακάριος, -α, -ον [7]	blessed (50)
μᾶλλον [5]	more, rather, much more (81)
μανθάνω [27]	I learn, I find out (25)
Μαρία, -ας, ἡ [17]	Mary (27)
Μαριάμ, ἡ	Mary (27)
μαρτυρέω [18]	(+dat) I bear witness, I testify (76)
μαρτυρία, -ας, ἡ [7]	testimony, witness (37)
μάρτυς, -υρος, ὁ [25]	witness, martyr (35)
μάχαιρα, -ης, ἡ [27]	sword (29)
μέγας, μεγάλη, μέγα [13]	large, great (243)
μείζων, -ον	greater, greatest
μέλλω [23]	I am about to, I intend (109)
μέλος, -ους, τό [24]	member, body part, limb (34)
μέν [15]	on the one hand, indeed (179)
μένω [7]	I remain, I stay, I abide, I dwell (118)
μερίζω [24]	I divide (14)
μεριμνάω [19]	I worry, I am anxious, I care for (19)
μέρος, -ους, τό [21]	part, piece, party, region (42)
μέσος, -η, -ον [15]	middle; the middle (subst); in the midst of (impr prep) (58)
Μεσσίας, -ας, ὁ	Messiah (2)
μετά (+acc) [9]	after (469; all occurrences)
μετά (+gen) [9]	with, among (469; all occurrences)
μετανοέω [19]	I repent, I change my mind (34)
μετεωρίζομαι	I worry, I am upset (1)
μή [9]	not (1042)

μηδέ [11]	and not, but not, nor, not even (56)
μηδείς, μηδεμία, μηδέν [15]	no one, nothing (90)
μηκέτι [26]	no longer (22)
μήποτε [24]	lest, that . . . not, perhaps, never (25)
μήτε [17]	and not, nor (34)
μήτηρ, μητρός, ἡ [16]	mother (83)
μικρός, -ά, -όν [16]	little, small, short (46)
μιμνήσκομαι [16]	(+gen) I remember, I am reminded (pass) (23)
μισέω [22]	I hate, I disdain (40)
μισθός, -οῦ, ὁ [25]	wages, reward, punishment (29)
μνημεῖον, -ου, τό [15]	tomb, grave, monument (40)
μόλις	rarely (6)
μονογενής, -ές	unique, only (9)
μόνος, -η, -ον [16]	only, alone (114)
μυστήροιν, -ου, τό [23]	secret, mystery (28)
μωρία, -ας, ἡ	foolishness (5)
Μωϋσῆς, -έως, ὁ [1]	Moses (80)

N	
Ναζαρά, Ναζαρέθ, Ναζαρέτ	Nazareth (12; all occurrences of all three forms)
ναός, -οῦ, ὁ [16]	temple (45)
νεκρός, -ά, -όν [5]	dead, useless; corpse (subst) (128)
νέος, -α, -ον [26]	new, recent, young (23)
νεφέλη, -ης, ἡ [16]	cloud (25)
νήφω	I am sober, I am self-controlled (6)
νικάω [27]	I conquer, I overcome (28)
νίπτω [21]	I wash (17)
νόμος, -ου, ὁ [7]	law, rule, principle (194)
νόσος, -ου, ἡ	disease, illness (11)
νοῦς, νοός, ὁ [17]	mind, understanding, thought (24)
νῦν [3]	now; the present (subst) (147)
νύξ, νυκτός, ἡ [12]	night (61)

Ξ	
ξένος, -η, -ον [26]	foreign, strange; stranger, foreigner (subst) (14)

O	
ὁ, ἡ, τό [5]	the (19,867)
ὁδός, -οῦ, ἡ [4]	road, way, conduct (101)
οἶδα [16]	I know, I understand (318)
οἰκία, -ας, ἡ [7]	house, home, household, family (93)
οἰκοδομέω [23]	I build, I build up (40)
οἶκος, -ου, ὁ [11]	house, home, household, family (114)
οἶνος, -ου, ὁ [27]	wine, vineyard (34)
ὀλίγος, -η, -ον [23]	little, small; few (pl) (40)
ὅλος, -η, -ον [11]	whole, entire, complete; entirely (109)
ὅμοιος, -α, -ον [19]	like, similar (+dat = to someone, something) (45)
ὁμοιόω [22]	(+dat) I make like, I compare; I resemble (pass) (15)
ὁμοίως [24]	likewise, similarly, in the same way (30)
ὁμολογέω [19]	I confess, I admit, I declare (26)
ὄνομα, -ματος, τό [12]	name, title, category (231)
ὀπίσω (+gen) [7]	behind, after (impr prep) (35)
ὅπλον, ου, τό	instrument, tool, weapon (6)
ὅπου [11]	where, since (82)
ὅπως [15]	how, that, in order that (53)
ὁράω [18]	I see, I notice, I perceive (454)
ὀργή, -ῆς, ἡ [26]	anger, wrath (36)
ὄρος, -ους, τό [13]	mountain, hill (63)
ὅς, ἥ, ὅ [9]	who, which, what, that (1,398)
ὅσος, -η, -ον [11]	as much as, as many as, how great (110)
ὅστις, ἥτις, ὅτι [11]	who, which, whoever, whichever (153)
ὀσφῦς, -ύος, ἡ	waist, loins (8)
ὅταν [11]	when, whenever (123)
ὅτε [10]	when, while, as long as (103)
ὅτι [6]	that, because (1,296)
οὗ [16]	where, to which (24)
οὐ (οὐκ, οὐχ) [3]	not, no (1,606)
οὐδέ [9]	and not, neither, nor, not even (143)
οὐδείς, οὐδεμία, οὐδέν [12]	no; no one, nothing (subst); in no way (neut acc) (234)
οὐκέτι [19]	no longer (47)
οὖν [6]	therefore, then, consequently (499)

οὔπω [26]	not yet (26)
οὐρανός, -οῦ, ὁ [4]	heaven, sky (273)
οὖς, ὠτός, τό [12]	ear, hearing (36)
οὔτε [3]	and not, nor (87)
οὗτος, αὕτη, τοῦτο [9]	this, these (pl); this person or thing; he, she, it, they (subst) (1,387)
οὕτως [6]	in this manner, thus, so (208)
οὐχί [19]	not, no (54)
ὀφείλω [23]	I owe, I ought, I am obligated (35)
ὀφθαλμός, -οῦ, ὁ [13]	eye, sight (100)
ὄχλος, -ου, ὁ [9]	crowd, multitude (175)

Π

παιδίον, -ου, τό [12]	child, infant (52)
παῖς, παιδός, ὁ, ἡ [13]	servant, slave; child (24)
παλαιός, -ά, -όν [9]	old, former (19)
πάλιν [3]	again, once more (141)
πάντοτε [19]	always, at all times (41)
παρά (+acc) [10]	alongside, by (194; all occurrences)
παρά (+dat) [10]	in the presence of, beside, with (194; all occurrences)
παρά (+gen) [10]	away from, from (194; all occurrences)
παραβολή, -ῆς, ἡ [7]	parable (50)
παραγγέλλω [17]	I give orders, I command, I instruct (32)
παραγίνομαι [23]	I come, I appear, I arrive, I stand by (37)
παραδίδωμι [24]	I hand over, I betray, I entrust (119)
παρακαλέω [18]	I exhort, I comfort, I encourage, I urge (109)
παραλαμβάνω [9]	I take, I take along, I receive (49)
παραλυτικός, -ή, -όν	lame; lame person, paralytic (subst) (10)
παρατίθημι [25]	I set before; I entrust (19)
παραχρῆμα [13]	at once, immediately (18)
παρέρχομαι [27]	I go, I pass by, I pass away, I neglect (29)
παρθένος, -ου, ἡ	virgin (15)
παρίστημι [24]	I present, I place beside, I am present (41)
παρουσία, -ας, ἡ [9]	coming, presence (24)
παρρησία, -ας, ἡ [13]	openness, confidence, boldness (31)

παρρησιάζομαι	I speak freely, I have courage (9)
πᾶς, πᾶσα, πᾶν [12]	each, every, all (1,243)
πάσχα, τό [23]	Passover, Passover meal, Passover lamb (29)
πάσχω [10]	I suffer, I endure (42)
πατήρ, πατρός, ὁ [16]	father, ancestor (413)
Παῦλος, -ου, ὁ [1]	Paul (158)
πείθω [2]	I persuade; I trust (pf) (52)
πειράζω [10]	I tempt, I attempt, I test (38)
πειρασμός, -οῦ, ὁ [24]	trial, test, process of testing (21)
πέμπω [2]	I send (79)
πέντε [1]	five (38)
πέραν [10]	beyond, across; the other side (subst) (23)
περί (+acc) [10]	around, near (333; all occurrences)
περί (+gen) [10]	concerning, about, for (333; all occurrences)
περιάγω	I lead around, I take about, I go around (6)
περιπατέω [18]	I walk, I conduct my life (95)
περισσεύω [10]	I abound, I exceed, I overflow (39)
περιτέμνω [23]	I circumcise (17)
περιτομή, -ῆς, ἡ [23]	circumcision, those who are circumcised (36)
Πέτρος, -ου, ὁ [1]	Peter (156)
Πιλᾶτος, -ου, ὁ [1]	Pilate (55)
πίνω [13]	I drink (73)
πίπτω [3]	I fall, I perish (90)
πιστεύω [2]	(+dat) I believe, I have faith; with εἰς +acc = I believe in (241)
πίστις, -εως, ἡ [12]	faith, trust, faithfulness, belief (243)
πιστός, -ή, -όν [5]	faithful, believing, trustworthy (67)
πλανάω [19]	I lead astray, I mislead, I deceive; I go astray (mid) (39)
πλῆθος, -ους, τό [25]	large amount, crowd, multitude (31)
πληρόω [18]	I fill, I complete, I fulfill (86)
πλοῖον, -ου, τό [16]	boat (68)
πλούσιος, -α, -ον [19]	rich, wealthy (28)
πλουτέω	I am rich, I become rich, I am generous (12)
πνεῦμα, -ατος, τό [12]	spirit, breath, wind (379)
ποιέω [18]	I do, I make (568)

ποῖος, -α, -ον [17]	of what kind? which? what? (33)
πόλις, -εως, ἡ [12]	city, town (162)
πολύς, πολλή, πολύ [12]	much (sg), many (pl), large, great (416)
πονηρός, -ά, -όν [7]	evil, wicked, bad (78)
πορεύομαι [3]	I journey, I go, I travel (153)
πόσος, -η, -ον [26]	how great (?) how much (?) how many (?) (27)
ποτέ [17]	at some time, once, formerly, ever (29)
πότε [26]	when? (19)
ποτήριον, -ου, τό [12]	cup, drinking vessel (31)
ποῦ [12]	where? to what place? (48)
πούς, ποδός, ὁ [12]	foot (93)
πράσσω [22]	I do, I accomplish, I practice (39)
πρεσβύτερος, -α, -ον [11]	older; elder (66)
πρίν (+gen) [23]	before (13)
πρό (+gen) [6]	before, in front of (47)
πρόβατον, -ου, τό [4]	sheep (39)
πρός (+acc) [10]	to, toward, with (700)
προσαγωγή, -ῆς, ἡ	access, right to speak (3)
προσέρχομαι [6]	(+dat) I come to, I go to, I approach (86)
προσευχή, -ῆς, ἡ [21]	prayer, place of prayer (36)
προσεύχομαι [3]	I pray (85)
προσέχω [17]	I pay attention to, I devote myself to (24)
προσκαλέομαι [23]	I summon, I invite, I call (29)
προσκυνέω [18]	(+dat) I worship, I bow down before (60)
προσφέρω [21]	I offer, I present, I bring to (47)
πρόσωπον, -ου, τό [15]	face, appearance (76)
προφήτης, -ου, ὁ [4]	prophet (144)
πρωΐ	early morning, early (12)
πρῶτος, -η, -ον [6]	first, earlier (155)
πτωχεία, -ας, ἡ	poverty (3)
πτωχεύω	I am poor, I become poor (1)
πτωχός, -ή, -όν [19]	poor, miserable (34)
πῦρ, πυρός, τό [15]	fire (71)
πωλέω [13]	I sell (22)
πῶς [15]	how? in what way? (103)

	P
ῥῆμα, -ατος, τό [19]	word, utterance, saying, matter (68)
Ῥώμη, -ης, ἡ	Rome (8)

	Σ
σάββατον, -ου, τό [11]	Sabbath, week (68)
Σαμάρεια, -ας, ἡ	Samaria (11)
Σαμαρίτης, -ου, ὁ	Samaritan (9)
σάρξ, σαρκός, ἡ [12]	flesh, body, human or sinful nature (147)
Σατανᾶς, -ᾶ, ὁ [1]	Satan, the adversary (36)
σεαυτοῦ, -ῆς [22]	(of) yourself (43)
σημεῖον, -ου, τό [5]	sign, miracle (77)
σήμερον [26]	today (41)
Σίμων, -ωνος, ὁ [1]	Simon (75)
Σινᾶ	Sinai (4)
σκανδαλίζω [26]	I cause to sin, I anger; I take offense at (pass) (29)
σκότος, -ους, τό [25]	darkness (31)
σός, σή, σόν [7]	your, yours (27)
σοφία, -ας, ἡ [25]	wisdom (51)
σοφός, -ή, -όν [5]	wise, skillful, learned (20)
σπείρω [3]	I sow (52)
σπέρμα, -ατος, τό [21]	seed, descendants (43)
σταυρός, -οῦ, ὁ [17]	cross (27)
σταυρόω [18]	I crucify (46)
στόμα, -ματος, τό [19]	mouth (78)
στρέφω [23]	I turn, I return; I turn around (21)
σύ [6]	you (2,907)
συζάω	I live with, I live together (3)
σύν (+dat) [6]	with, together with (128)
συνάγω [11]	I gather, I bring together (59)
συναγωγή, -ῆς, ἡ [10]	synagogue, assembly, meeting place (56)
συναντάω	I meet, I happen (6)
συνέδριον, -ου, τό [11]	Sanhedrin, council (22)
συνείδησις, -εως, ἡ [25]	conscience, consciousness (30)
συνίημι [24]	I understand, I comprehend (26)

συνίστημι [24]	I demonstrate, I recommend (16)
συντέλεια, -ας, ἡ	end, completion (6)
συστρέφω	I gather up, I gather, I come together (2)
σφραγίζω [16]	I seal, I mark (15)
σῴζω [2]	I save, I rescue, I deliver (106)
σῶμα, -ατος, τό [12]	body (142)
σωτήρ, -ῆρος, ὁ [16]	savior, deliverer, redeemer (24)
σωτηρία, -ας, ἡ [9]	salvation, deliverance (46)

T	
ταράσσω [22]	I trouble, I disturb, I upset (17)
τάχα	perhaps (2)
τέ [11]	and, and so, so (215)
τέκνον, -ου, τό [4]	child (99)
τέλειος, -α, -ον [5]	perfect, complete, mature (19)
τελειόω [18]	I make complete, I make perfect, I fulfill (23)
τελέω [19]	I finish, I complete, I fulfill, I accomplish (28)
τέλος, -ους, τό [23]	end, goal; tax (40)
τελώνης, -ου, ὁ [9]	tax collector (21)
τέσσαρες [1]	four (41)
τεσσεράκοντα [13]	forty (22)
τηρέω [18]	I keep, I guard, I obey (70)
τίθημι [24]	I place, I put, I appoint (100)
τίκτω [19]	I bear, I give birth (18)
τιμάω [18]	I honor, I value (21)
τιμή, -ῆς, ἡ [21]	honor, price, value, respect (41)
τις, τι [12]	someone, something; a certain one, a certain thing; anyone, anything (525)
τίς, τί [12]	who? what? which?; why? (adv) (556)
τοιοῦτος, -αύτη, -οῦτον [16]	of such a kind, such (57)
τολμάω [21]	I dare, I am bold, I am courageous (16)
τόπος, -ου, ὁ [16]	place, location (94)
τοσοῦτος, -αύτη, -οῦτον [26]	so great, so large, so many, so much (20)
τότε [4]	then (160)

τρεῖς, τρία [10]	three (68)
τρίς [1]	three times (12)
τρίτος, -η, -ον [16]	third; third time (adv) (56)
τύπος, -ου, ὁ [25]	mark, image, pattern, type, model, example (15)
τυφλός, -ή, -όν [5]	blind (50)

Υ

ὕδωρ, ὕδατος, τό [12]	water (76)
υἱός, -οῦ, ὁ [4]	son, descendant (377)
ὑπάγω [11]	I depart, I go away, I go (79)
ὑπακούω [22]	(+dat) I obey (21)
ὑπάρχω [7]	I am, I exist (60)
ὑπέρ (+acc) [9]	above, beyond, over (150; all occurrences)
ὑπέρ (+gen) [9]	on behalf of, for, about (150; all occurrences)
ὑπό (+acc) [9]	under, below (220; all occurrences)
ὑπό (+gen) [9]	by (agent) (220; all occurrences)
ὑπολαμβάνω [13]	I take up, I support, I reply, I suppose (5)
ὑπομονή, -ῆς, ἡ [4]	perseverance, endurance, steadfastness (32)
ὑποστρέφω [7]	I turn back, I return (35)
ὑποτάσσω [23]	I subject, I subordinate; I obey (pass) (38)
ὑψόω [21]	I exalt, I lift up (20)

Φ

φαίνω [5]	I shine; I appear (mid; pass) (31)
φανερόω [21]	I reveal, I make known (49)
Φαρισαῖος, -ου, ὁ [1]	Pharisee (98)
φέρω [13]	I carry, I take along, I endure, I produce (66)
φεύγω [16]	I flee, I escape (29)
φημί [25]	I say, I affirm (66)
φιλέω [19]	I love, I like, I kiss (25)
Φίλιππος, -ου, ὁ [15]	Philip (37)
φίλος, -η, -ον [11]	beloved, loving, friendly; friend (subst) (29)
φοβέω [19]	I scare; I am afraid, I fear (pass) (95)
φόβος, -ου, ὁ [5]	fear, terror, respect, reverence (47)
φρίσσω	I shudder (from fear), I am extremely afraid (1)

φρονέω [18]	I think, I ponder (26)
φυλακή, -ῆς, ἡ [22]	guard, prison, watch (47)
φυλάσσω [7]	I guard, I keep, I protect, I observe (31)
φυλή, -ῆς, ἡ [25]	tribe, nation, people (31)
φωνέω [22]	I call, I summon, I invite (43)
φωνή, -ῆς, ἡ [6]	sound, voice, noise (139)
φῶς, φωτός, τό [19]	light (73)

X

χαίρω [11]	I rejoice, I am glad (74)
χαρά, -ᾶς, ἡ [7]	joy, gladness, delight (59)
χάρις, -ιτος, ἡ [12]	grace, favor, kindness, gratitude (155)
χείρ, χειρός, ἡ [15]	hand, finger (177)
χήρα, -ας, ἡ [26]	widow (26)
χρεία, -ας, ἡ [21]	need, necessity, lack (49)
χρῄζω	I need, I have need of (5)
Χριστός, -οῦ, ὁ [4]	Christ, Anointed One, Messiah (529)
χρόνος, -ου, ὁ [11]	time, period of time (54)
χώρα, -ας, ἡ [26]	land, region, field (28)
χωρίζω [23]	I divide, I separate; I go away (pass) (13)
χωρίς (+gen) [7]	apart from, without (impr prep) (41)

Ψ

ψυχή, -ῆς, ἡ [4]	life, soul, self (103)

Ω

ὧδε [13]	here, in this case (61)
ὥρα, -ας, ἡ [6]	hour, occasion, moment, time (106)
ὡς [4]	as, like, when (504)
ὡσεί [24]	like, as, about (21)
ὥσπερ [21]	as, just as, even as (36)
ὥστε [25]	so that, with the result that, therefore (83)

SCRIPTURE INDEX

Note: References preceded by "cf." have been modified from the GNT. Usually this involves a change in tense-form.

SUBJECT INDEX